A Treatise

on

Limnology

Wooden boss in the roof of Selby Abbey, Yorkshire, England, presumably from the first half of the fourteenth century, depicting a heterophyllous aquatic species of *Ranunculus* with laminar floating leaves and very finely divided submersed leaves. From a photograph by C. J. P. Cave, by permission of the Cambridge University Press.

A Treatise

on

Limnology

VOLUME III

LIMNOLOGICAL BOTANY

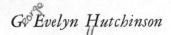

G. Evelyn Hutchinson

DEPARTMENT OF BIOLOGY
YALE UNIVERSITY

A WILEY-INTERSCIENCE PUBLICATION

JOHN WILEY & SONS

New York · London · Sydney · Toronto

Other volumes in A TREATISE ON LIMNOLOGY

A TREATISE ON LIMNOLOGY, Volume I, *Geography, Physics, and Chemistry*

A TREATISE ON LIMNOLOGY, Volume II, *Introduction to Lake Biology and the Limnoplankton*

Copyright © 1975 by John Wiley & Sons, Inc.

Library of Congress Cataloging in Publication Data:

Hutchinson, George Evelyn, 1903-
 A treatise on limnology.
 Includes bibliographies.
 CONTENTS:—v.1. Geography, physics, and chemistry —v. 2. Introduction to lake biology and the limno-plankton.—v. 3. Limnological botany.
 1. Limnology.

QH98.H82   574.92′9   57-8888
ISBN 0-471-42574-5

Printed in the United States of America

10 9 8 7 6 5 4 3 2 1

IN MEMORIAM

R. L. L.   *T. F. G.*

R. H. MacA.

THE WATER CROWVOOT.

O' SMALL-FEÄC'D flow'r that now dost bloom
To stud wi' white the shallow Frome,
An' leäve the clote to spread his flow'r
On darksome pools o' stwoneless Stour,
When sof'ly-rizèn aïrs do cool
The water in the sheenèn pool,
The beds o' snow-white buds do gleam
So feäir upon the sky-blue stream,
As whitest clouds, a-hangèn high
Avore the blueness o' the sky;
An' there, at hand, the thin-heäir'd cows,
In aïry sheädes o' withy boughs,
Or up bezide the mossy raïls,
Do stan' an' zwing their heavy taïls,
The while the ripplèn stream do flow
Below the dousty bridge's bow;
An' quiv'rèn water-gleams do mock
The weäves, upon the sheäded rock;
An' up athirt the copèn stwone
The laïtren bwoy do leän alwone,
A-watchèn, wi' a stedvast look,
The vallèn waters in the brook,
The while the zand o' time do run
An' leäve his errand still undone.
An' oh! as long's thy buds would gleam
Above the softly-slidèn stream,
While sparklèn zummer-brooks do run
Below the lofty-climèn zun,
I only wish that thou could'st stay
Vor noo man's harm, an' all men's jaÿ.
But no, the waterman 'ull weäde
Thy water wi' his deadly bleäde,
To slaÿ thee even in thy bloom,
Fair small-feäced flower o' the Frome.

William Barnes
Poems of Rural Life in the Dorset Dialect
2nd collection, London 1866

Preface

The enormous increase in the price of books and the obvious foolish-
ness of allowing a large amount of manuscript to become out of date
lying in a cupboard have prompted the publication of the rest of *A Treatise
on Limnology* in several volumes smaller than their predecessors.

This volume deals exclusively with botanical matters, covering the conventional ecology of the higher plants and benthic algae, with as much
ancillary material as is needed to make the ecological presentation compre-
hensible. As indicated in Volume II, the treatment of productivity is deferred
until it can be considered in terms of the whole biota of a lake. As far as
possible most attention has been given to subjects not treated in length in
other recent works such as Gessner's *Hydrobotanik* and Sculthorpe's *The
Biology of Aquatic Vascular Plants*.

The ecologist is continually having to look at aspects of nature with
which he is unfamiliar and perforce must be an amateur for much of his
working time. I was brought up in a family which contained no professional
botanists, but in which Bentham and Hooker's *Handbook of the British
Flora* was second only to the Bible as an essential household book. This
was, I think, true of many academic families in England 60–70 years ago.
I have even heard of a man who knew nothing whatever about plants
reading the book for the pleasure that the poetic formality of taxonomic
diagnoses gave him, a point of view that would have delighted Marianne

Moore and might well be considered by scholars in the humanities. The metallic green of a musk beetle on the leaf of a *Sagittaria* and reports of memories of the spread of *Elodea* through the waterways of Britain were part of my childhood. Professionals may carp at omissions, misconstructions, or even downright errors in these pages. Perhaps ultimately they may forgive them for the sake of the overall vision that only the amateur, or the ecologist, blithely sets out to experience.

Some of the plants that are discussed in this volume, transplanted far from their homes, often into waters that have undergone what is politely called cultural eutrophication or that, being newly impounded, have no well-developed native flora, have become noxious weeds on an unprecedented scale. These are considered in their due place, but I have tried throughout the book primarily to emphasize the great intellectual interest of the aquatic flora, hoping that, though some of it may be extremely tiresome, most of it is beautiful and fascinating. I would, therefore, like to express my gratitude to Mr. Geoffrey Grigson's *The Englishman's Flora* for calling my attention to the poem of William Barnes, printed on the verso of the dedication, which expresses this point of view and also conceals, behind its unfamiliar language, a quite interesting botanical observation, as is noted later in the book.

I am, as I was when writing the prefaces to the two previous volumes, deeply grateful to the many people who have helped me. The list includes a number who have been mentioned before, to whom I would add among my Yale colleagues, past or present, Dr. Daniel D. Botkin, Dr. Arthur W. Galton, Dr. Peter A. Jordan, Dr. Luigi Provasoli, Dr. John Reeder, Dr. James E. Rodman, and Dr. Bruce B. Stowe. I am much indebted to those who have generously given me access to their unpublished work in order that it could be mentioned in the book. I would particularly remember my former colleague Dr. Ursula M. Cowgill, now of the University of Pittsburgh, whose help will be patently apparent to anyone using Chapter 30, and Dr. Nancy Slack of Russell Sage College, who allowed me to incorporate in Chapter 27 some of the very important results of her studies made with Dr. Dale H. Vitt of the University of Alberta, on the ecology of littoral species of *Sphagnum*. Dr. Karen Arms of Cornell University, Dr. Walter V. Brown of the University of Texas, Dr. Claude E. Boyd of Auburn University, Dr. Gunnar Lohammar of Uppsala, Dr. Aubrey W. Naylor of Duke University, Dr. Sigurd Olsen of the University of Washington, Seattle, Dr. Raymond A. Paynter of the Museum of Comparative Zoology, Harvard University, D. Vernon W. Proctor of the Texas Technological College, Lubbock, Dr. R. A. Stanley of the Tennessee Valley Authority, Muscle Shoals, Alabama, Mr. Gairdner Stout of the American Museum of Natural History, and Professor T. G. Tutin of the University of Leicester have kindly provided information on specific points. Dr. Alan Covich has been most helpful in the treatment of the Charophyceae in Chapter 27. An unforgettable week spent with Professor John Harper, Professor Paul W. Richards, Dr. T. B. Reynoldson, and Dr. Christine Wood at the University College of North Wales, Bangor, has left a beneficial and indelible, but not easy characterized, impression on the manuscript.

The whole manuscript has been read by Dr. Robert G. Wetzel of the W. K. Kellogg Biological Station, Michigan State University, and by Dr. Daniel A. Livingstone of Duke University and his students Jennifer Angyal, Marilyn Loveless, and John Melack. They have made a number of most useful comments and saved me from numerous minor errors. I am very grateful to all of them.

The intellectual stimulation and companionship of my last two graduate students, Dr. Karen Glaus Porter of the University of Michigan and Dr. Maxine Watson of the University of Utah, and with them Dr. Frances S. Chew, of Tufts University, are also acknowledged with deep appreciation.

I am indebted to Dr. B. R. Allanson of Grahamstown University, South Africa, and the *Journal of Freshwater Biology* for the photographs of Figure 159; to Dr. K. Armitage, the University of Kansas, for the very beautiful photograph reproduced in Figure 86; to Professor D. H. N. Spence, The University, St. Andrews, for the photographs of Figure 143; to Dr. K. Subramanyan and the Council of Scientific and Industrial Research, New Dehli, for permission to use the admirable line drawings of Indian plants in Figures 34, 37, and 49; to Messrs. Collins, London, for permission to use the drawings of Figure 90; to the Director, The Museum of Palaeontology, University of Michigan for permission to use the photographs of Figure 85; and to the Royal Commission on Historic Monuments (England) and the Cambridge University Press for the frontspiece and permission to use it. Many of the drawings of plants are based on material in the Herbarium of the Peabody Museum, Yale University; the other illustrations are modified from sources acknowledged in the legends.

The resources of the Kline Science Library at Yale have made the volume possible, and I am deeply indebted to Mr. John Harrison and all his staff for the extraordinary collection that they have built up and made so easily available.

In spite of all the help that I received, three works of great importance did not become available before the book went to press. These are E. C. S. Little, Ed., *Handbook of Utilization of Aquatic Plants. A Compilation of the World's Publications*, Rome, FAO, Crop Protection Branch, Plant Production and Protection Division, PL:CP/20, 1968; H. I. Aston, *Aquatic Plants of Australia*, Melbourne University Press, 1973; D. S. Correll and H. B. Correll, *Aquatic and Wetland Plants of Southwestern United States*, Stanford University Press, 2 vols., 1975.

The typing of the manuscript was mostly done by Mrs. Emily Derow and Mrs. Beverly Dooling; to them as to Mrs. Alice Pickett I am most grateful. My debt to Mrs. Mary Poulson is hard to express; I can only hope that long association has taught her how much her help is appreciated.

My wife has stood behind me in all my endeavors; it is quite impossible to thank her adequately.

G. EVELYN HUTCHINSON

New Haven, Connecticut
July 1975

Contents

CHAPTER 27

The Lower Rooted Vegetation

The two groups to be considered in this chapter, the Charophyceae and the Bryophyta, are obviously more primitive than the tracheophytes that make up the greater part of the rhizobenthos. Though often abundant and ecologically important, they seem to be at a competitive disadvantage in shallow, moderately productive habitats, in which angiosperms are usually far more conspicuous. They are in fact often best developed at low light intensities in deep water, the Charophyceae frequently in hard and the Bryophyta often in soft water. It is quite likely that these plants were of even greater significance than they are today in the practically unknown lakes of the late Paleozoic or early Mesozoic, before aquatic angiosperms had evolved into successful competitors in the environments most favored by water plants. During the late Jurassic a very specialized charophycean flora, apparently growing in lakes, is known to have existed.

CHAROPHYCEAE

The Charophyceae[1] are a class of green algae, consisting of a single order, the Charales, and a single living family, the Characeae. All the

---

[1] This usage follows the classification of Vol. II, p. 10. Most students of the group elevate it to a division or phylum, the Charophyta. This however, obscures its manifest relationship to the Chlorophyta unless the Protista be abandoned as a classificatory unit, and a new clade recognized containing the Chlorophyta, Charophyta, Bryophyta, and Tracheophyta. The most recent works, however, suggest the Chlorophyta to be diphyletic, so that only part of the group belongs with the Characeae and higher plants (Pickett-Heaps and Marchant 1972; Frederick, Gruber, and Tolbert 1973).

members of the group are macroscopic upright green plants, developing from a primary protonema and rooted by unicellular rhizoids. In these characters they have about the same degree of organization as mosses, though there is no evidence of any close phylogenetic relationship between the two groups.

The plants may be quite large. *Nitella translucens* (*D* of Fig. 2) is recorded as 1.25 m tall in the Étang de Royan, between Cervières and les Salles, Forez, France, by Corillion (1957). The same author indicates that *Chara hispida* may also be more than 1 m tall, and have forms in which the thickness of the stem is as great as 6 mm. In contrast to these plants some of the forms included in or related to *Nitella gracilis* subsp. *gracilis*, such as *Nitella confervacea* (*N. gracilis* subsp. *gracilis* var. *confervacea* f. *confervacea*),[2] may be only 3 cm high and 0.3 mm thick (Wood, in Wood and Imahori 1965). The main axis consists of a series of elongate unicellular internodes alternating with short multicellular nodes from which spring lateral branches organized in the same general way as the main axis. In the genus *Chara*, except in the subgenus *Charopsis*, which includes the important species *Ch. braunii* and *Ch. corallina*, the long internodal cells are covered with parallel threadlike cells derived alternately from the upper and lower nodes at the two ends of the cell. These filaments lie obliquely, on spiral trajectories, and form the cortex. As well as most species of *Chara*, *Lychnothamnus fascicularis* is also corticate, but this is not true of other members of its genus. In one or two taxa, included in or related to the collective species *Chara vulgaris*, the cortex is greatly reduced. Corillion (1957) gives evidence that in *Ch. denudata* (*Ch. vulgaris* var. *denudata* f. *denudata*), the reduced cortex is genetically determined, since its reduction persisted in culture. Unfavorable conditions did, however, reduce the cortication of *Ch. vulgaris*.

In many lakes the Charophyceae cover considerable areas of the bottom and consequently they are of considerable limnological importance, particularly in view of the number of animals that they may harbor. The great size, up to 15 cm long in *Nitella translucens*, of the very accessible internodal cells has made the ecorticate species of *Chara* as well as the members of *Nitella* and *Nitellopsis obtusa* (*J* of Fig. 1), favorite material for research on cell physiology.

Taxonomic considerations. The group consists of a single living family, the Characeae, and at least five fossil families, the oldest species being represented by oospores from the lower Devonian. The history of the class is well reviewed by Peck (1953). By the end of the Jurassic when the

---

[2] The nomenclatural conventions used here are given in the next section.

Purbeck beds of the south of England were laid down, large shallow lakes existed, the floors of which were carpeted with Charophyceae, just as may occur in hard-water lakes today. Some of these late Jurassic plants were, however, specialized and quite peculiar; they throw no light on the origin of the group (Harris 1939).

The living family, the Characeae, is divided into two tribes, the Chareae (Fig. 1) and the Nitelleae (*A–F* of Fig. 2). These two tribes are technically distinguished by the oogonium of the Chareae having an apical crown or *coronula* formed of a single circle of five moderately large cells (*E* of Fig. 1), whereas the Nitelleae have a coronula of two superimposed circles of five very small cells (*F* of Fig. 2). The coronula of the Nitelleae is unfortunately shed from the mature oogonium and no trace remains of the structure in the easily fossilized oospore of either tribe (*F* of Fig. 1). The Chareae contain four recent genera (Daily 1967), *Chara, Lamprothamnium, Lychnothamnus,* and *Nitellopsis,* and in the Nitelleae there are only *Nitella* and *Tolypella.* The number of valid species is a matter of fairly vigorous, if intermittent, debate among the limited number of students of the group. In their standard monograph Wood and Imahori (1965) have reduced the number of species of *Chara* from over 100 to 19 and of *Nitella* from about 180 to 49. The other genera remain quite small.

Wood does recognize a great deal of intraspecific variation, some of which is certainly genetic. An extraordinary example illustrating this is provided by a specimen (*G* of Fig. 2) of what is now termed *Lamprothamnium longifolium,* figured by Proctor, Carl de Donterberg, Hotchkiss, and Imahori (1967) from a pond on Scharbauer Ranch, Andrews County, Texas; one-half of their plant would formerly have been referred to *Chara buckellii* and the other half to *Nitellopsis bulbillifera.* Some sort of mosaic, due to abnormal meiosis or somatic mutation, must be involved. At least this specimen provides a warning not to expect the taxonomy of the Characeae to be an easy study.

Wood's nomenclatural system recognizes in a few cases subspecies, in almost all cases several varieties, and below them a great number of forms. Though these forms are to a large extent equivalent to the species of the older generation of taxonomic students of the group, Wood clearly feels uncomfortable about their recognition. There is, however, some evidence that certain forms are clearly distinguished ecologically and physiologically (Forsberg 1963) from nominotypical specimens of the species to which Wood refers them. For this reason the ecologist must recognize their existence and refer to them in the neatest possible way. Wood's system involves quadrinominal, or occasionally quinquinominal, nomenclature which is far too clumsy to use in everyday ecological practice. Sensing this, Wood has provided a series of microspecific names coordinate with

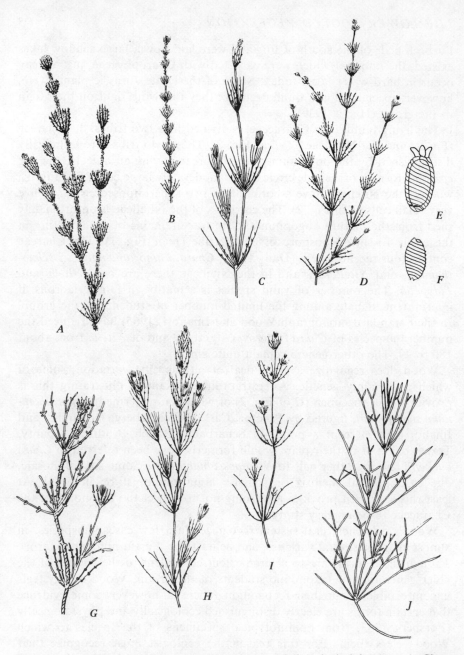

FIGURE 1. Typical members of the tribe Chareae of limnological interest. *A, Chara hispida; B, Ch. aspera; C, Ch. globularis; D, Ch. contraria; E*, intact oogonium of same showing three of the five cells of the coronula; *F*, the same as ordinarily fossilized; *G, Ch. tomentosa; H, Ch. rudis; I, Ch. denudata; J, Nitellopsis obtusa* (from British specimens, Groves and Bullock-Webster).

FIGURE 2. Typical members of the tribe Nitelleae of limnological interest and one anomalous member of the Chareae. *A, Nitella flexilis; B, N. opaca* male; *C, N. opaca* female; *D, N. translucens; E, Tolypella nidifica; F,* oogonium of same showing coronula of two tiers of small cells; *G, Lamprothamnium longifolium,* segregant or somatic mutation combining two supposedly very distinct taxa (*A–E,* Groves and Bullock-Webster; *G,* Proctor et al.).

his forms. In general, though not quite always, the form name is validly used as the microspecific name. The microspecific names are used here as if they referred to species. Except when what Wood regards as the correct name is a nominotypical form name, also used for a microspecies,[3] his full correct name is given in parentheses or as a note when the microspecific name is first employed. As throughout the rest of this treatise, authors' names are given only in the Index of Genera and Species of Organisms, in which all of Wood's full names are given after the microspecific names used in the text.

Proctor's (1972) more recent work strongly suggests that many of the comprehensive species of Wood's scheme are composed of numerous biological species exhibiting considerable sexual isolation. How far these biological species coincide with Wood's microspecies, only further work will show.

Life history.   Certain aspects of the life history of the Charophyceae of ecological interest are conveniently treated before the more limnological aspects of the group are considered.

Germination of Oospores.   The conditions for the germination of oospores are not completely understood and may vary from species to species.   In the species of *temperate latitudes* the mature oospore undergoes an apparently necessary diapause in cold water (Proctor 1960; Forsberg 1965b). In experimental studies germination takes place when the temperature is raised. In one frequently tested sample of oospores of *Chara pedunculata* (sub *aculeolata*)[4] Forsberg found that maintenance at 4°C for 5 months was needed to produce germination, though other collections required but 2. In most cases 1–3 months appears optimal. Forsberg believed that exposure to light was almost essential, whereas Proctor did not find light to be important. Forsberg observed that if oospores were suspended throughout deaerated agar in a tube, germination of the temperate species on which he worked (*Ch. aspera,*[5] *Ch. globularis, Ch. hispida,* and *Ch. vulgaris*) took place only well away from the air–agar interface, suggesting that a very low O_2 tension, or a redox potential below 0.4 V, was needed for the process to occur. This however was not observed in the two more tropical species *Ch. zeylanica* and *Ch. sejuncta* (*Ch. zeylanica* var. *sejuncta* f. *sejuncta*) studied. Proctor germinated oospores in a mixture of water and mud, which may have had a lower redox potential than pure oxygenated water.

---

[3] Parvispecies or even minimispecies reduced to minispecies would actually have been stylistically preferable to the hybrid microspecies.

[4] Wood (in Wood and Imahori 1965, p. 36) says that *C. aculeolata* auctt. is *C. hispida* var. *hispida* f. *polyacantha.*

[5] *Chara globularis* var. *aspera* f. *aspera.*

It is evident from the work of both authors that inhibition by, or competition with, other algae in unsterilized cultures seriously reduces the chance of an oospore becoming a viable plant.

Proctor (1962) found that the oospores retained their viability when passed through the alimentary tracts of ducks. There are clearly unanalyzed limitations imposed by the environment on different species, because Proctor states that he had had very little success in germinating the oospores of *Lamprothamnium longifolium* under any conditions. He had nine successes when they had passed through ducks and only two from any other material of the species that he studied. It is not impossible that passage through a duck facilitates germination in this species (c.f. 223, 224). Imahori (1954) had some comparable experiences.

Development. The zygote nucleus, which is diploid, divides twice in the germination of the oospore, one division evidently being meiotic. Three of the four resulting nuclei disintegrate while the fourth survives and, dividing into two, produces cells from which a *protonema*, which becomes green, and a *rhizoid* that remains colorless are produced. The protonema cell divides in two and from its lower cell a rhizoid node and the first stem node are produced with a greatly elongate internodal cell between them. The main axis of the plant is formed from a lateral branch of the first stem node, the protonema growing on beyond it. Accessory protonemata frequently grow out from the rhizoid node or from the base of the primary rhizoid, and develop plants in the same way as does the primary protonema (Fig. 3). The full details of the cell lineages are summarized from the older literature by Fritsch (1935). The formation of successive multicellular nodes and unicellular internodes now continues along the main axis. The primary lateral branches and the cortical threads arise by tangential divisions of the nodal cells. The branches develop nodes and internodes and from the former secondary branches are produced; the process can occur several times. At maturation, sexual structures appear on the secondary or higher-order branchlets, usually in the upper part of the plant. The oocyte is enclosed in five cells which grow round it in a spiral pattern to form the *oogonium;* from the apices of these five cells, which are probably homologous with a whorl of branchlets, the cells of the coronula are cut off. The walls of the oogonium become thickened and persistent. The *antheridium* is formed of four, or more usually eight, cells which make a spheroidal structure within which the male gametes are produced from threadlike antheridial filaments. Wood (Wood and Imahori 1965) suggests that the wall of the antheridium is, like that of the oogonium, a whorl of branchlets. In monoecious species the oogonium and antheridium are closely associated. The antheridia are yellow, orange, or red, whereas the oogonia vary from golden brown to the more usual black. The reproductive structures, though only about 1 mm in length, are frequently conspicuous owing to

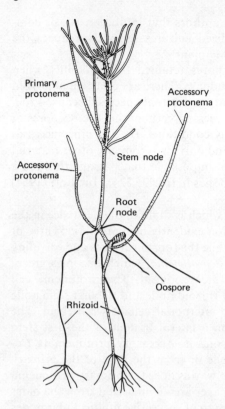

FIGURE 3. A young plant of *Chara canescens* growing from a primary protonema, derived for an oospore; secondary protonemata are present (after Fitsch from DeBary).

Primary protonema

Accessory protonema

Stem node

Accessory protonema

Root node

Oospore

Rhizoid

their coloration. *Protandry* is common, but according to Corillion (1957) *protogyny* can also occur in the group.

Phenology. Migula (1909) states that many species are perennials, some producing oospores in the spring, but most not until the summer and autumn. The majority of the systematic accounts give no significant phenological details about individual species. Flössner (1964) writing particularly of the Stechlin See, points out that the Charophyceae of lakes in temperate regions may persist as green plants well below the ice throughout the winter, when most or all of the other rooted vegetation has died down, thus providing a winter habitat for weed-dwelling animals such as Cladocera. This record probably refers specifically to *Ch. aspera* and *Ch. filiformis* (*Ch. vulgaris* var. *kirghisorum* f. *filiformis*).

The most important phenological summaries have been given by Imahori (1954) for Japan and by Corillion (1957) for northwestern France.

Imahori (1954) found *Chara braunii* and *globularis* to persist throughout the year; *Chara fibrosa* (sub *gymnopitys*), *Ch. zeylanica* and *Ch. corallina*, all three species of low temperate and tropical latitudes, were absent in winter, the last-named not appearing till May. *Ch. globularis* started sexual reproduction in May, the others in June (*Ch. braunii*), July (*Ch. fibrosa*), August (*Ch. zeylanica*), or even September (*Ch. corallina*). Of the 11 of his taxa of *Nitella* now currently recognized, Imahori found only *N. furcata* to be clearly evident through the year. The peculiar *Tolypella*-like *Nitella imahorii* is apparently not found at the height of summer and reproduces sexually both in spring (February–April) and autumn (October–November). *Nitella hyalina* is not recorded in February and March, the other eight taxa are absent in January, and five of them also in December. *N. leptodactyla* (*N. pseudoflabellata* subsp. *pseudoflabellata* var. *leptodactyla* f. *leptodactyla*) and *N. erecta* (*N. furcata* subsp. *orientalis* var. *orientalis* f. *erecta*) are strictly summer and autumn forms, appearing in May, reproducing in August and September, and disappearing in November. *N. rigida* behaves similarily, though appearing a couple of weeks earlier and lasting a little longer. As in Europe, *Nitella flexilis*, though not perennial in Japan, starts its reproductive activity in May.

Corillion, working mainly in northwestern France, found *Nitella capillaris* (*N. syncarpa* var. *capitata*) begins its vegetative development in the middle of November, and starts producing sexual structures in the second half of March. Fructification lasts until the end of June, after which it is implied that the species disappears. The various taxa of *Tolypella* recognized by Corillion start vegetative growth in January and sexual reproduction in late March or April, except *T. prolifera* (*T. intricata* var. *intricata* f. *prolifera*) in which development of the gametangia begins in late May. None of the members of *Tolypella* are recorded after June. *Nitella opaca*[6] appears very late in January with the sexual stages occurring at the end of April until the end of July, whereas *N. syncarpa* with a like vegetative phase continues as a sexual plant until September. *Lamprothamnium papillosum* behaved like these vernal species of *Nitella*. The other species of the latter genus seem to follow one of two disparate patterns. *Nitella flexilis*, *N. translucens*, and *N. mucronata* are found throughout the year with the sexual phase lasting from May to October. The other species are definitely summer plants, *N. gracilis* appearing very late in March, and

---

[6] Wood (in Wood and Imahori 1965) does not distinguish *N. flexilis* and *N. opaca* even as forms, regarding them as monoecious and dioecious genotypes of an otherwise uniform taxon. Since they are ordinarily separated in Europe and elsewhere and are said to show biological differences, the names are retained; to synonymize them might discard information that could conceivably be ecologically useful. Unfortunately, Wood found the type of *opaca* to be monoecious, so the name is not valid for the form or microspecies to which it is usually applied. It is retained here provisionally following previous usage.

N. confervacea and *N. hyalina* in May, all three reproducing sexually from June until the autumn and then disappearing. Corillion found, however, that the supposed annual *N. hyalina* could be kept in aquariums at low temperatures throughout the winter.

In the genus *Chara*, many of the species that Corillion studied, namely, *Ch. braunii, Ch. vulgaris* (*Ch. vulgaris* var. *vulgaris* f. *vulgaris*), *Ch. contraria* (*Ch. vulgaris* var. *vulgaris* f. *contraria*), *Ch. hispida, Ch. aspera*,and *Ch. fragifera* (*Ch. globularis* var. *globularis* f. *fragifera*), were recorded throughout the year, sexual reproduction beginning in early April in *Ch. vulgaris Ch. contraria* and very late in that month or early in May in the other forms. *Nitellopsis obtusa* appears to behave as do these last-mentioned taxa. *Chara galioides* (*Ch. globularis* var. *aspera* f. *galioides*) seems to have disappeared during the autumn and appeared again in January, whereas *Ch. canescens* was absent during December, January, and February and reproduced from June into the early winter, like *Nitella confervacea.* These results suggest that in nature more species of *Chara* than of *Nitella* are likely to be perennial. It is not entirely clear, however, how far the data that indicate strong seasonality refer to events that occur strictly in a liquid medium. Any species primarily occurring in shallow astatic waters may suffer from desiccation of such an habitat in summer, and in a eustatic locality freezing might destroy marginal species in winter.

In Lawrence Lake, Barry County, Michigan, *Chara* in general appears to grow slowly in marginal waters after the lake has frozen, and massive beds of the lower nodes of *Ch. globularis* and *vulgaris* persist under moderately thick ice (Wetzel, personal communication).

There is some detailed information in Corillion's work about individual taxa. *Ch. contraria*, which is perennial, evidently as a complete plant, in the deeper water of lakes, survives marginally only by the persistence of the inferior nodes, the top of the stem dying in winter; it is said, however, to resist cold better than *Ch. vulgaris.*

Ch. hispida, which may persist into December as complete vegetative plants in northwestern France, survives the most rigorous part of winter as stem bases consisting of the lower nodes and internodes. *Ch. baltica* (*Ch. hispida* var. *baltica* f. *baltica*) ordinarily survives throughout the winter in the coastal regions of France but tides over very severe winters by means of its bulbils.

Chara canescens is a summer form in northwestern France but the bases of the stems survive the winter in the Mediterranean region. Both *Ch. globularis* and *Ch. fragifera* are said to persist throughout the winter, at least in the less cold parts of Europe. Wood (in Wood and Imahoi 1965) noted that the apices of *Ch. globularis* may become dormant in winter and that when growth starts in the spring it is very rapid, of the order of 1.5 cm day^{-1}.

Ch. aspera hibernates as bulbils; in France the vegetative stage appears in May, in the Iberian Peninsula in March and April, and in Africa and Asia in February. *Ch. virgata* (*Ch. globularis* var. *virgata* f. *virgata*) and no doubt *Ch. fragifera* in some localities likewise may pass the winter in Europe as bulbils.

Tolypella glomerata may, according to Corillion, persist in a vegetative condition under ice.

It is probable that the records of Corillion are somewhat biased in favor of shallow-water populations and that in deeper water, well away from ice, the survival of grown vegetative plants is rather greater than would be assumed from Corillion's data.

There are doubtless scattered records, in papers devoted to other aspects of the Charophyceae, of the mode of overwintering of individual species. Thus Karling (1924), working in New York, found *Chara globularis* (sub *fragilis*) to persist in a green and healthy state in a frozen pond so long as the plant was below the ice. Andrews and Hasler (1943) imply that *Chara* sp., probably *Ch. crispa* (*Ch. vulgaris* var. *vulgaris* f. *crispa*), disappeared in winter from a very shallow bar in University Bay, Lake Mendota, Wisconsin, presumably as the result of freezing, but persisted, though with a loss of green color, and perhaps in the dormant state recorded by Wood in *Ch. globularis*, on the bottom on either side of the bar (cf. Lind and Cottam 1969).

In the North Island of New Zealand, Starling, Chapman, and Brown (1974b) found *Nitella hookeri* to grow in nature at 10°C, but they could not maintain growth in the laboratory at that temperature.

Pal (1932) has given some phenological information about the Charophyceae of Burma. In the lakes around Rangoon such plants are rare or absent until late in, or after, the monsoon. Pal believes that a general rise in pH late in the season is significant in determining the incidence of the plants. They seem most abundant from October to January, at which time they start to disappear. This disappearance in some cases is due to evaporative lowering of the water level but is also attributed to the water becoming too hot.

Much more systematic study of the phenology of the Charophyceae is obviously needed in view of the probable importance of these plants as substrata for many aquatic animals.

Light and the induction of sexuality. Karling (1924) has found in *Chara globularis* that the incidence of sexual reproduction is due to increasing photoperiod, and that it can easily be induced by prolonged illumination even in quite cold water. At low temperatures the development of the antheridia and oogonia, once initiated, is very slow. Field observations by Hodgetts (1921) on *Nitella flexilis* had already emphasized the importance of light. It is interesting that Corillion (1957) observed that the species found at considerable depths in lakes, apparently over 10 m, are sexually sterile in deep water, depending on asexual reproduction for the maintenance of their populations. This is specifically recorded of *Chara contraria* and of *Nitella flexilis*. Presumably at such depths the period during which the irradiance lies above some critical level never reaches the required day length for sexual structures to develop. It would be interesting to learn if additional illumination could induce gametangia experimentally in such plants.

Parthenogenesis. In the somewhat halophilic *Chara canescens*, dioecious populations, consisting of both male and female plants, occur (Corillion 1957) in the Old World only in Italy, Greece, the Balkans, and Asia Minor, eastward to the Caspian, and at about the same latitudes, in China. Further north in Europe nothing but parthenogenetic female plants occur. Wood (in Wood and Imahori 1965) says that the species is monoecious in Rhode Island, but that the antheridia may be imperfectly formed and perhaps nonfunctional. Monoecious populations occur on the Pacific coast of North America, but for the most part the species is dioecious in the New World; there seems to be no critical information about the distribution of male plants.

Corillion (1957) records that in France the typically dioecious *Nitellopsis obtusa* frequently has male plants with nonfunctional antheridia. However, he gives no evidence of the occurrence of parthenogenesis.

Asexual reproduction. It is probable that asexual reproduction plays a considerable part in maintaining the populations of the Charophyceae. It is quite likely that many such populations consist of a quite limited number of clones, as Wood (Wood and Imahori 1965, pp. 6, 547) suggests.

Initially several plants may develop from the protonemata produced by the germinating and developing oospore. Later secondary protonemata may arise from stem nodes, or long ecorticate branches may grow out of such nodes and from these branches new plants also develop. These types of asexual reproduction may well depend on the abolition of apical dominance when plants are fragmented or otherwise injured. There seems to be little information about the occurrence of such processes in nature (cf. Fritsche 1935).

Many species form bulbils, usually on their rhizoids, and from such structures new plants may be produced. Bulbils are ordinarily formed from the same type of cell as those from which secondary rhizoids are produced. They may be simple or irregularly tuberculate or compound masses (*C* of Fig. 4), 1–3 mm in diameter, or in *Nitellopsis obtusa*, regular star-shaped structures (*D* of Fig. 4). In *Chara*, bulbils (Wood, in Wood and Imahori 1965) are well-known in *Ch. globularis* sens. lat. (i.e. the microspecies *Ch. fragifera*, *Ch. virgata*, *Ch. macounii*, *Ch. aspera*, *Ch. curta*,

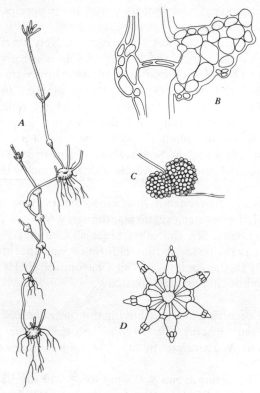

FIGURE 4. *A*, Bulbils on lower nodes of stem in *Chara baltica; B*, the same in section showing relation to node; *C*, compound bulbil of *Ch. fragifera* (×6); *D*, stellate bulbil of *Nitellopsis obtusa* (*A, B*, Giesenhagen; *C*, Imahori; *D*, Groves and Bullock-Webster).

Ch. globularis); other members of this collection of taxa may lack the structures. Bulbils are also recorded, though less commonly, in *Ch. vulgaris* and *Ch. pistianensis* (*Ch. vulgaris* var. *vulgaris* f. *pistianensis*), as well as in the North American *Ch. robbinsii* (*Ch. fibrosa* var. *hydropitys* f. *robbinsii*). Large irregular bulbils (*A, B* of Fig. 4), formed from the lower nodes occur in *Ch. baltica* (*Ch. hispida* var. *hispida* f. *baltica*). Bulbils formed from the lower axial nodes, and having the shape of minute strawberries, are known in the Indian *Ch. pashanii* (*Ch. socotrensis* f. *pashanii*), so their existence does not depend on a temperate habitat. In *Lamprothamnium* they occur in the better-known forms (*L. papulosum, L. pouzolsii, L. macropogon*) of the collective species *L. papulosum* and in *L. longifolium*. In *Nitella, N. trans-lucens* certainly produces composite bulbils (Groves and Bullock-Webster 1920; Corillion 1957; Wood and Imahori 1965), but Corillion suspects they are often overlooked and indicates that other species of the genus may bear bulbils in culture.

Many species of ducks are apt to feed extensively on Charophyceae and some evidently can collect the bulbils of *Chara* selectively. MacAtee (1915) found over 1100 of such bodies in the alimentary tract of a golden eye, *Aythya affinis*, and over 1500 in that of a pintail, *Anas acuta*.

Chemical ecology. The Characeae are almost all aquatic; a single terrestrial member of the group, *Nitella terrestris*, is placed on their excluded list by Wood and Imahori as of uncertain nature. It is a minute plant growing in damp soil in South India (Iyengar 1958); it is clearly described as terrestrial and seems to be a *Nitella*, but with some rather peculiar characters.

Salinity tolerance. Apart from this problematic plant the Characeae are predominantly freshwater organisms, though a few are very successful inhabitants of the Baltic Sea and other brackish localities.

Stroede (1931, 1933) believed that chlorinity was the most important chemical variable in the ecology of the Charophyceae. He distinguished three groups of species in northern Germany.

1. Halophobic occurring in water having not more than 32 mg Cl liter^{-1}: *Chara filiformis* (sub *jubata*), *Ch. virgata* (sub *delicatula*), *Nitella opaca*, *N. mucronata*, and *N. syncarpa*. In other regions most species of *Nitella* belong here.

2. Euryhaline, occurring from $\leq$ 35 mg to $\geq$ 740 mg Cl liter^{-1}. *Chara vulgaris*, *Ch. globularis*, *Ch. hispida*, *Ch. intermedia* (*Ch hispida* var. *major* f. *intermedia*), *Ch. rudis* (*Ch. hispida* var. *major* f. *rudis*), *Ch. aspera*, *Ch. tomentosa* (sub *Ch. ceratophylla*), *Ch. contraria*, *Nitellopsis obtusa* (sub *Tolypellopsis stelligera*), and *Nitella flexilis*. To these may be added *Ch. braunii*, *Ch. corallina*, and *Ch. zeylanica*, species common in low latitudes (Imahori 1954). In Japan, moreover, *Nitella shinii* (*N. furcata* subsp. *orientalis* var. *australis* f. *shinii*) and *N. axilliformis* (N. *translucens* subsp. *translucens* var. *leptoclada* f. *axilliformis*) go to 1630 mg Cl liter^{-1} and two more taxa of *Chara* and six of *Nitella* are found up to 359 mg liter^{-1}. Furthermore *Nitellopsis obtusa* probably belongs here (MacRobbie and Dainty 1958).

Though *Nitella hyalina* was regarded as halophobic by Corillion, it often occurs in brackish water (Imahori 1954; Wood, in Wood and Imahori 1965) and in Japan is recorded from a locality described as polyhaline.

3. Halophilic, occurring only in water containing $\geq$ 2500 mg Cl liter^{-1}: *Chara canescens* (sub *crinita*), *Ch. baltica* (*Ch. hispida* var. *baltica* f. *baltica*), *Ch. horrida* (*Ch hispida* var. *baltica* f. *fastigata*) and *Tolypella nidifica*.

Olsen (1944) indicates that *Lamprothamnium papulosum* occurs in water containing between 8000 and 26,000 Cl liter^{-1}. Corillion would doubtless include *Ch. galioides* here.

The categories are rough, though useful in the present state of our knowledge. Each species is of course likely to have its characteristic range, with *Chara* obviously tending to be a little more euryhaline than *Nitella*.

Lamprothamnium longifolium in North America is said by Proctor, Carl de Donterberg, Hotchkiss, and Imahori (1967) to be found usually in alkaline and slightly brackish water, and it seems probable that the other species of this genus and of *Tolypella* are most likely to occur in somewhat mineralized waters (cf. localities in Wood and Imahori 1965).

Alkalinity and pH. The distribution of the large number of purely freshwater species of Characeae is clearly to some extent determined by chemical factors. There has, however, been divergence of opinion (Iversen 1929; Stroede 1933) about the influence of hydrogen ion and calcium concentration. Olsen (1944), who summarized the earlier work, found, partly following Stroede, that most species of *Chara* live habitually above pH 6, whereas *N. flexilis* could occur at pH 5 and *N. opaca* at 5.2. The slightly more acidic range for *Nitella* than for *Chara* implied by these and other (Zaneveld 1940; Wood 1952) observations on most species of the two genera is not quite general, for the very eurytopic *Ch. globularis* (sub *fragilis*) is recorded from pH 5.0 to 9.6. Both genera also have several more stenionic circumneutral species.

Imahori (1954) gives ranges and means of pH in the habitats of 42 taxa of *Nitella*, regarded as at least microspecifically distinct by Wood, and for eight taxa of *Chara*, from Japan. The overall range for *Nitella* is from 4.6 to 8.0, with a mean at 6.74 and a mode for the individual mean values at 6.3. The much more limited number of taxa of *Chara* give a range from 5.8 to 8.8 with a mean of 7.30 and no clearly defined mode. It is possible that the rather less striking difference between the two genera is due to a general underrepresentation of hard waters containing rich *Chara* florules in the Japanese localities studied. Among Imahori's records of the tolerances of taxa of *Nitella*, those for *N. pulchella* (*N. dualis* var. *pulchella* f. *pulchella*, in part sub *N. dimorpha*) indicate a range from pH 4.6 to 6.8, suggesting a strikingly acidophilic species. *N. furcata* (s. str.), ranging from pH 5.6 to 8.6 in Imahori's table, though not in his text, is second only to *Ch. globularis* as a euryionic charophycean, if the records from more alkaline waters are reliable. Imahori's data are strongly weighted in favor of numerous microspecies of the collective species *N. pseudo-*

flabellata which, together with those, other than the nominotypical form, of *N. furcata*, appear to be circumneutral taxa with, at least in the collective species *N. pseudoflabellata*, a slight tendency to occur in waters on the acidic side of neutrality, as would become a typical member of the genus.

All these results are in general confirmed by Corillion (1957), working on the Charophyceae of northwestern France. All 10 of his taxa of *Nitella* are recorded as living on occasion in water as acidic as pH 6.6 *N. translucens* may be found at pH 5.5, and *N. flexilis*, *N. gracilis*, and *N. capillaris* at 6.0; none of these four species occurred in water more alkaline than pH 7.1. Corillion noted six circumneutral species of *Nitella*, with which may be associated three species of *Chara*, all usually living between pH 6.5 and 7.5–8.0. *Chara fragifera*, occurring from pH 6.5 to 7.3, is clearly the member of the genus most characteristic of fairly soft neutral waters. *Chara globularis* has elsewhere a much greater range than that given by Corillion, and is the one really euryionic member of the Charophyceae known. All other eight taxa of *Chara* that he studied, as well as those of *Tolypella*, with *Lamprothamnium papulosum* and *Nitellopsis obtusa*, never occurred below pH 7.0, mostly extended to 8.5, and elsewhere, occurred in even more alkaline water. Though there is doubtless a continuous transition, without greater discontinuities than might be expected in passing from one species to another, when the whole set of taxa are ordered according to pH preferenda it is convenient to recognize the following rough grouping.

1. An acidic water group (pH 5.5–6.0 to 7.1): *Nitella translucens*, *N. gracilis*, *N. flexilis*, and in Japan, *N. pulchella*.

2. A circumneutral group (pH 6.5 to 8.0): *N. confervacea*, *N. tenuissima*, *N. opaca*, *N. hyalina*, *N. syncarpa*, *N. mucronata*, and the members of the collective species *N. pseudoflabellata*; *Chara fragifera* and, with slightly more alkaline preferenda, *Ch. braunii* and *Ch. zeylanica*; the euryionic *Ch. globularis* may be formally placed in this category, as may *Nitella furcata* (s. str.), though some of its allied microspecies seem to be slightly acidophilic.

3. An alkaline water group (pH 7.0 to $\geq$ 8.0): *Tolypella intricata*, *T. glomerata*,[7] *T. nidifica*, *Ch. vulgaris*, *Ch. hispida*, *Ch. pedunculata*, *Ch. canescens*, *Ch. connivens* (*Ch.globularis* var. *globularis* f. *connivens*), *Ch. aspera*, *Ch. galioides*, and *Lamprothamnium papulosum*.

On comparison of Corillion's characterization with that of Olsen, the only real inconsistency appears to involve *Nitella capillaris*, not entered

---

[7] Corillion also records *T. hispanica* here; Wood (Wood and Imahori 1965) does not separate it microspecifically from *T. glomerata*.

above, which would be put in the acidic water category by Corillion but with the species of circumneutral waters by Olsen. Most uncharacterized species of *Nitella* presumably belong in the first two categories, and most of those of *Chara* in the third.

Nitella translucens, *N. flexilis*, and *N. opaca* are all known from water with much lower calcium concentrations, below about 9 mg Ca liter^{-1}, than support any of the Danish species of *Chara*, the euryionic *Ch. globularis* not occurring below about 14 mg Ca liter^{-1}. Stroede (1933) believed that *Nitella opaca* required less than 6 mg Ca liter^{-1} but that the other members of *Nitella* that he studied needed more, *N. syncarpa* a minimum of 11–19 mg Ca liter^{-1}, *N. flexilis* 29 mg Ca liter^{-1}, and *N. mucronata* 45 mg Ca liter^{-1}. These values are based on occurrences in nature and may not give the real minimum values, as is clearly the case with *N. flexilis*. He believed that *Nitellopsis obtusa*, the very euryionic *Ch. globularis*, the related *Ch. virgata*, *Ch. filiformis*, and *Ch. hispida* all needed a minimum concentration between 11 and 19 mg Ca liter^{-1}, whereas *Ch. aspera*, *Ch. vulgaris*, *Ch. contraria*, *Ch. tomentosa*, *Ch. intermedia*, and *Ch. rudis* had higher minimum requirements, more than 29 mg Ca liter^{-1}. Corillion concluded that of 10 species studied all but the euryionic *Ch. globularis* and *Ch. braunii* needed 25 mg Ca liter^{-1}, and most twice this amount. Anderson (1958) found *Ch. zeylanica* grew well if more than 20 mg Ca liter^{-1} is present; the optimum concentration seems to have been 40–50 mg Ca liter.$^{-1}$

The highest calcium content recorded for the habitat of a species of *Nitella* is 130 mg Ca liter^{-1} for the euryhaline *N. hyalina*; all species of *Chara* so far studied can live in more calcareous waters than this. The general relations are roughly what might be expected from pH requirements, species of *Chara* tending to have a higher calcium requirement than those of *Nitella*.

There may be complications introduced by differences in the reaction of the rhizoids and the green parts of the plant to the calcium contents of their respective environments. Corillion records *Nitella translucens*, *N. mucronata*, *Chara contraria*, and *Ch. aspera* growing together in a French locality on a sediment containing no detectable calcium, though the water was slightly calcareous. The first of these species is definitely in the acidophilic group, but the last is ordinarily somewhat calcicole. This matter might well prove interesting physiologically.

Uptake of HCO$_3^-$ by Charophyceae. Many water plants living in hard waters are able to take up HCO$_3^-$ ions as such, which are then dehydroxylated within the cell so that the resulting CO$_2$ can be used in photosynthesis. The process is discussed in much greater detail in later chapters (see pp. 148–153). In the Charophyceae such uptake was suspected by Dahm (1926). It has been critically established by Smith (1968), who measured the uptake of labeled carbon, added as sodium bicarbonate, by various Charophyceae at pH 6.5 when the added carbon is almost entirely as CO_2, and at pH 9.1–9.2, when it is almost entirely as HCO_3^- with a little CO_3^{2-}. The results are given in Table 1.

TABLE *1*.   *Rate of uptake of carbon as CO_2 (pH 6.5) or as HCO_3^- (pH 9.1–9.2) by various Charophyceae. From data of Smith (1968).*

Species	Source	Rate of Uptake (pmol $cm^{-2}sec^{-1}$)	
		pH 6.5	pH 9.1–9.2
Nitella translucens	Dunkeld, Perth, Scotland	33.5	1.5
	Laboratory culture, Cambridge	31.5	8.1
Tolypella intricata	Cambridge, England	41.5	5.7
Chara australis	Laboratory culture, Norwich	39.7	6.4
Nitellopsis obtusa	Laboratory culture, Cambridge	32.5	9.0

All the material is likely to have been ultimately derived from plants living in hard water except the strain of *N. translucens* from Scotland, the original habitat of which was doubtless a soft slightly acidic water, apparently of pH 6.3.

Though no plant can fix HCO_3^- as fast as it can CO_2, all but the Scottish *N. translucens* can fix HCO_3^- fast enough for it to be an important source of CO_2 in photosynthesis. In the experiments the amount of HCO_3^- in the alkaline medium seems to have been twice the amount of CO_2 in the acidic medium. In many hard waters the amount of HCO_3^- is likely to be very many times greater than any probable amount of free CO_2 that would be present in ordinary soft waters. The capacity to use HCO_3^- is therefore advantageous to any water plant living in even moderately hard water. The Scottish *N. translucens*, however, fixed HCO_3^- at a rate lower than its respiratory output and would not be able to compensate for this loss of carbon photosynthetically. It is reasonable to suppose that most species of *Chara* and the *Tolypella* populations of calcareous waters regularly use HCO_3^-, but that in many species of *Nitella* the faculty is likely to be absent, or present only in strains adapted to hard water, as in the case mentioned here.

Calcium carbonate deposition on Charophyceae. In most species of *Chara* living, as is usually the case, in hard waters, in *Nitellopsis obtusa*, sometimes in *Lamprothamnium papulosum*, and occasionally in *Nitella*, there is considerable precipitation of calcium carbonate on the plant.

The absence of such an incrustation may be merely due to growth in circumneutral or slightly acidic water, as for instance in *Chara fragifera*, which Corillion (1957) says lacks a calcium carbonate deposite, but which is limited to the sandy margins of relatively soft circumneutral waters. The data given by Corillion and by Wood (in Wood and Imahori 1965) also suggest that some (*Ch. baltica, Ch. horrida, Ch. galioides, Ch. connivens*) but not all (*Ch. canescens*) species living in brackish water develop little or no deposit.

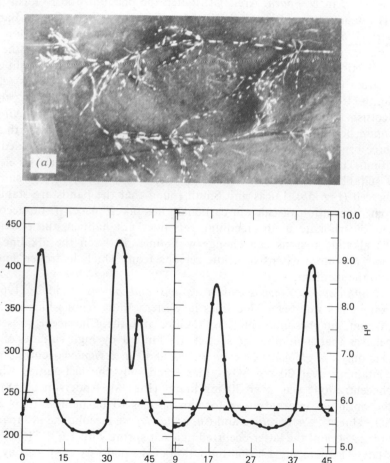

(b)

FIGURE 5.   (*A*) Banded deposit (Arens) of calcium carbonate on *Nitella flexilis;* (*B*) disposition of regions (Lucas and Smith) of varying pH along internodal cell of *Chara australis,* in darkness (▲) or after 2-hr illumination (●).

It is probable that the presence of a carbonate deposit depends fundamentally on the use of HCO_3^- as a carbon source in photosynthesis:

$$HCO_3^- \longrightarrow CO_2 + OH^-$$

$$Ca^{2+} + OH^- + HCO_3^- \longrightarrow CaCO_3 + H_2O$$

In some ecorticate (Corillion 1957) species the deposit forms regular bands, as Arens (1939) observed in *Nitella flexilis* (Fig. 5a) and Corillion has noted in *N. opaca*. Arens attributed the phenomenon to local rises in pH attendant on photosynthesis. More recent work by Spear, Barr, and Barr (1969) on *Nitella clavata* and by Lucas and Smith (1973) on *Chara australis* (*Ch. corallina* var. *nobilis* f. *nobilis*), has shown that the zonal production of calcium carbonate deposits takes place, as one might expect, in areas through which HCO_3^- is being absorbed and OH ions released. Smith (1968) noted in his work on the rate of uptake of HCO_3^- that the Scottish strain of *Nitella translucens* deposited no lime, but *Nitellopsis obtusa* became covered all over with a calcareous precipitate; the other three organisms studied showed a greater or less degree of banded deposition. The position of alkaline areas can be mapped with a glass electrode if suitable precautions are taken to prevent mixing along the surface of the cell (Fig. 5b). Lucas and Smith found that the bands are stable once some deposition of calcium carbonate has taken place. If, on account of low bicarbonate in the medium, this does not happen, the positions of the alkaline regions can change with time. Between the alkaline bands there are more extensive acidic regions from which hydrogen ions pass into the medium.

Limitation by other common cations and anions. Vaidya (1966) has examined a number of localities in western India from which he records calcium, magnesium, chloride, sulfate, and the Characeae present. He believes that a number of species are limited by high sulfate; of his 18 taxa only *Ch. globularis*, *Ch. contraria*, and *Ch. zeylanica* occurred in water containing over 20 mg SO_4^{2-} liter^{-1} and only the last-named when the concentration[8] was over 30 mg liter^{-1} (Fig. 6). Anderson (1958) found the optimum concentration for this species to be no less than 225 mg SO_4^{2-} liter^{-1}. *Ch. corallina* and *Ch. zeylanica* are mesohaline in Japan (Imahori 1954) and the latter occurred in a salt spring with 1.6 % Cl in Vaidya's study. The data suggest that limitation of the majority of species by sulfate is possible, but there are far too few analyses of waters in western India not containing Characeae to make profitable comparisons.

---

[8] Given as "sulphates mg/l," presumably SO_4^{2-}.

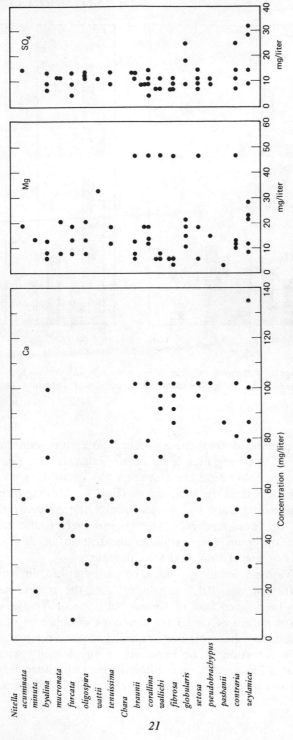

FIGURE 6. Range of concentrations of calcium, magnesium, and sulfate in waters inhabited by Indian Characeae (data from Vaidya).

21

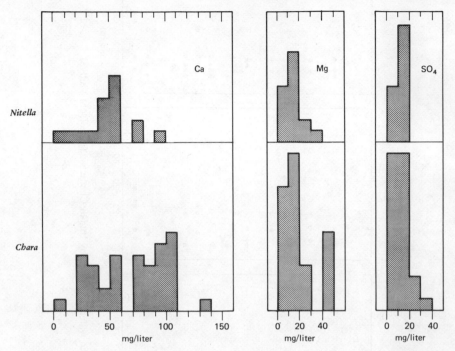

FIGURE 7. Histograms showing number of occurrences of all *Nitella* spp. and all *Chara* spp. in Indian waters of varying concentrations of calcium, magnesium, and sulfate (data from Vaidya).

Anderson concluded that the optimum potassium concentration for *Ch. zeylanica* is 38–60 mg liter^{-1}. As far as Vaidya's data go, *Chara* spp. in west India probably tend, as elsewhere, to occur in somewhat more calcium-rich waters than do *Nitella* spp. (Fig. 7). A comparable relationship with magnesium may well be secondary, the concentration varying with that of calcium. Anderson (1958), however, found that for *Ch. zeylanica*, the optimum magnesium concentration of 40–75 mg liter^{-1} was as high as or higher than that for calcium.

In one of Vaidya's localities, Harnai Pond, Baroda, in which the calcium concentration was 101.7 mg liter^{-1} and the magnesium 46.6 mg liter^{-1}, no less than seven taxa of *Chara*, but none of *Nitella*, were found. The exhuberant nature of the characean flora of this and of some other calcareous lakes may be explained, as will become apparent, by the low phosphate concentration to be expected in any locality where most of the phosphate is likely to be precipitated as an apatite. Vaidya says that the concentration of phosphate was low in all his localities, but he gives no figures.

Minor elements in the nutrition of the Characeae. Buljan (1949) and Anderson (1958) both found boron and iron to be required for normal growth. Buljan believed the same to be true of zinc and manganese for *Ch. globularis* (sub. *fragilis*), but Anderson got little effect by omitting these elements in the culture medium of *Ch. zeylanica*. Anderson, however, did claim[9] that molybdenum, chromium, nickel, and perhaps cobalt were needed by the last-named species, but copper and vanadium were apparently without effect.

Limitation by phosphorus. Anderson (1958) working with *Chara zeylanica* and Forsberg (1964a, 1965c) with this species as well as with *Ch. globularis* and *Ch. contraria* (*C. vulgaris* var. *vulgaris* f. *contraria*) made the interesting discovery that small excesses of phosphorus in the medium inhibit the growth of plants. The inhibition appears to be greater in weak light with short day length, than in strong prolonged illumination. The exact position of the optimum probably varies with the species, but according to Forsberg is ordinarily between 5 and 20 mg m^{-3} of phosphorus. Anderson obtained much higher values, but perhaps did not explore the low optimum range properly, or as Forsberg thinks, the quantitative accuracy of his work was vitiated by the presence of bacteria; in some experiments calcium phosphates may have been precipitated. It is noteworthy that above the optimum the inhibition may at first be marked and then increase very slowly with increasing phosphorus. Thus for *Ch. globularis* (Forsberg 1965c) there was a 27% inhibition between the optimum at 10 mg m^{-3} and 100 mg m^{-3} but only a further 9% in going from that concentration to 1000 mg m^{-3}. Thus though the plants were reduced to about two-thirds of the maximum size, they were obviously not destroyed by the high phosphate. It is likely, however, that in nature a reduction of the kind observed would be distinctly disadvantageous if the plants were involved in competition.

The inhibition by phosphorus is believed by Forsberg to underlie the scarcity of charophytes in very eutrophic localities. In the case of Lake Tåkern, which formerly possessed a rich benthic charophyte flora, appreciated by vast numbers of waterfowl, the water level dropped in a catastrophic dry period from 1932 to 1934 (Forsberg 1964b). This resulted in the death of a great *Chara* meadow which had covered most of the bottom of the lake and which consisted mainly of *C. globularis* in the eastern and *Ch. aspera* in the western part of the basin of the lake. When the lake refilled it appeared to have gained so much phosphorus from the exposed

---

[9] See the legend of his Table 26 and the summary; but on p. 87 the statements are confusing: "rhizoidal formation...was poor in solutions containing nickel, chromium and molybdenum...Plants growing in molybdenum deficient solutions were so weak that the lowermost nodes on two plants collapsed at touch."

mud that the concentration (41–60 mg total P m^{-3}, Lohammar 1938) surpassed that (5–20 mg total P m^{-3}) permitting optimum development of the Characeae. A population of *Myriophyllum* developed with some *Chara*; the former flourished for a time while the *Chara* declined, but later so did the *Myriophyllum* (Fig. 8). This was probably due to suspension of sediment in the water interfering with photosynthesis and to poor conditions over the winter in so shallow a lake. Subsequently *Ranunculus peltatus* colonized extensive areas of the bottom (Lohammar 1965). A dam has now been built to raise the lake level enough to prevent drying. *Chara tomentosa*, not known previously in L. Tåkern, has invaded the lake and the migrating waterfowl again visit it in numbers; up to 1000 swans have on occasion been observed there (Forsberg, verbal communications 1971).

Starling, Chapman, and Brown (1974a) found that *Nitella hookeri* grew best when the phosphorus concentration was about 20 mg P $liter^{-1}$. Very high concentrations of 60–80 mg $liter^{-1}$ were markedly inhibitory. There is a little evidence that the difference between these results and those of other investigators is due to the plants used by Starling, Chapman, and Brown having accumulated some arsenic from arsenite in their native habitat, prior to being brought into the laboratory.

It is reasonable to suppose that the sensitivity to phosphorus is a major factor in determining the distribution of Characeae in lakes. In general they are most abundant in either oligotrophic lakes, usually with fairly clear and not too acidic water, in which *Nitella* may be expected, or in shallow hard-water lakes in which the water is rich in calcium bicarbonate and from which calcium carbonate is easily precipitated in photosynthesis; here several species of *Chara*, with *Nitellopsis* or *Nitella*, are often found. In the former type of lake the external supply of phosphorus is generally limited, while in the latter the phosphorus, which may be abundant in drainage basin, is so easily precipitated as apatite as to be largely out of circulation. Characteristic calcareous *Chara* lakes used to be found in the province of Skåne, on Gotland and Öland, and in other parts of southern Sweden; these have been largely drained (Lohammar 1965). Their vegetation consisted almost entirely of *Chara* spp., blue-green algae, and a girdle of *Cladium mariscus*. Golubić has described Lake Vrana on the island of Cherso (Cres) as a remarkable *Chara* lake, in which *Chara pedunculata* (*Ch. hispida* var. *hispida* f. *polyacantha*) occurs down to 19–21 m, *C. globularis* (sub *fragilis*) occupies the zone from 21 to 26 m, and *Nitella opaca* may in some years occur from 26 to 38–40 m. Less striking examples of *Chara* lakes are perhaps provided by some of the shallow lakes of Kashmir (Mukerji 1934), and more certainly by Laguna Chichancanab in the southern part of the state of Yucatan, Mexico (Covich 1970).

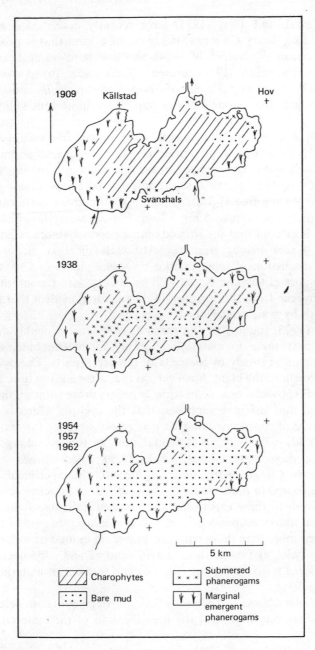

FIGURE 8.   Decline in the *Chara* meadow in Lake Tåkern after the dry period of 1932–1934 (compiled by Forsberg from various sources; symbols slightly modified).

Rich, Wetzel, and Thuy (1971) have recently described a marl lake, Lawrence Lake, Barry County, Michigan, of a kind that is probably the North American equivalent of those shallow hard-water Scandinavian lakes which Naumann (1932) termed *alkalitrophic*. In Lawrence Lake, however, submersed populations of *Scirpus subterminalis* constituted the dominant vegetation, though *Chara* spp. were important subdominants (see p. 42).

Effect of substances in the sediments. It has been observed, particularly by Stroede (1933) but less quantitatively by other investigators, that the mud in which some Charophyceae are rooted may contain very large amounts of free H_2S, in one case, apparently involving *Chara globularis*, as much as 443 mg free H_2S liter^{-1}. Though the green parts can tolerate for 2 or more weeks, up to 5 mg 1 liter^{-1} in the water in which they are growing, it is evident that the rhizoids must be vastly more resistant.

Uptake of nutrients by rhizoids. Although there is much evidence, given in a discussion of ionic uptake by water plants in Chapter 30, of active transport of Cl^- and K^+ as well as HCO_3^- into the internodal cells of Charophyceae from the surrounding water, it is evident that this is not the sole path by which nutrients are absorbed.

Bierberg (1908) found that the rhizoids of *Chara*, probably *vulgaris* or *globularis*, may take up materials, notably methylene blue, which are absorbed far more slowly by the cells of the green parts. The dye is translocated throughout the plant, however, so that after a given time specimens with rhizoids showed a blue coloration, whereas those without, in the same solution, did not. Beirberg supposed that the cyclosis which is a characteristic feature of charophycean cells was responsible for the transport, by instituting eddy diffusivity, as it would now be termed, along the stem.

Following these observations, Vouk (1929), using *Nitella mucronata*, *Chara vulgaris*, *Ch. globularis*, and *Ch. braunii*, did experiments in which plants were rooted in mud, or hung above it, either intact or with the rhizoids removed. In these experiments the rooted individuals showed more growth than those suspended and, of the latter, the individuals with rhizoids grew more than those without. Plants set in mud or soil, moreover, grew about twice as fast as those set in sand. These experiments clearly imply uptake of nutrients by the rhizoids and transfer of material to other parts of the plant.

Chemical composition. Analyses of varying degrees of completeness have been published, but in general the identification of the material has been inadequate.

The data of Riemer and Toth, for four samples of *Chara* sp. from New Jersey, are probably the most reliable that are available and are given in Table 2. Data obtained by Schuette and Alder (1929b) from *Chara* sp.

TABLE 2. *Percentage elementary composition (range and mean) of* Chara *based on material from four localities in New Jersey (Riemer and Toth 1968). The means in parentheses for iron and manganese omit the sample very high in the latter element. Note that* $n \times 10^{-4}\% = n$ *ppm*

Element	Range (%)	Mean
Na	0.02– 0.10	0.04
K	0.40– 3.50	1.39
Mg	0.71– 1.00	0.79
Ca	1.75–30.00	19.5
Mn	0.01– 6.50	1.62 (0.02)
Fe	0.16– 2.40	0.94 (0.45)
Cl	0.34– 1.84	1.00
S	0.26– 0.50	0.39
P	0.10– 0.41	0.29
N	0.93– 2.69	1.71
Cu	14×10^{-4} to 33×10^{-4}	25×10^{-4}
Zn	25×10^{-4} to 125×10^{-4}	68×10^{-4}

growing in Green Lake, Wisconsin, may be compared with those of the New Jersey investigations, but there are some uncertainties in the presentation of the Green Lake figures.

The high calcium contents of two specimens, which would correspond to 62.5% and 75% $CaCO_3$ if all the calcium were present as carbonate, are presumably due to the photosynthetic precipitation of a calcareous incrustation. Part of the variability of the other elements is due to different degrees of dilution by calcium carbonate. Even allowing for this, potassium varies greatly. If all the calcium was supposed to be present as carbonate and the potassium was calculated on a limefree basis, three samples contained 1.45–1.60%, low values when compared with other water plants, and the fourth, which was very poor in calcium, contained 3.66%. Schuette and Alder (1929b) found the very low figure of 0.48% K in *Chara* sp. from Green Lake, whereas their sodium content of 0.26% is much greater than those of Riemer and Toth.

The magnesium content is high in all specimens; the sample poorest in calcium contained 0.75% Mg, exceeded among the 37 angiosperms analyzed by Riemer and Toth only by one specimen of *Ceratophyllum demersum*. It is uncertain how much magnesium in the two more calcareous plants should be assigned to magnesian calcite in the incrustation. All the values, however, lie between 0.71 and 1.00% and probably imply a magnesium content about as great as that of *C. demersum* in New Jersey (0.72–1.09%) and greater than that of other water plants. In line with this, Schuette and Alder (1929b) found 0.71% Mg in their *Chara* sp. from Green Lake, Wisconsin.

Riemer and Toth's two specimens with very high calcium contents also contain considerable amounts of zinc, namely, 95 and 125 ppm, the other two specimens having only 25 and 28.5 ppm. Presumably zinc was precipitated along with calcium in forming the calcareous incrustation on the plant. Copper exhibits no such enrichment.

Manganese and iron seem to be extremely variable; the specimen containing the least calcium contained the greatest quantities of these two elements. The amount of manganese that may be present, namely, 6.5% in the specimen of *Chara* sp. poorest in calcium, is considerably greater than the amount found by Riemer and Toth in any other plant. The amount of iron in this sample, namely, 2.4%, is also high, but is exceeded by several other plants in the series analyzed. In the other samples the uncorrected manganese is low, between 0.01 and 0.04%, or on a limefree basis about 0.04–0.05%. The iron is rather higher, 0.16–0.95%, or on a limefree basis 0.32–2.55%. The single sample poor in calcium but very rich in manganese came from a water low in calcium and magnesium but high in manganese. The pH of this water is given as 8.2, but the anions appear greatly in excess of the cations even without bicarbonate. There is clearly something wrong in the water analysis; moreover, one can hardly avoid a suspicion that the plant in question was not of the same species as the other samples analyzed, and might indeed have belonged to the genus *Nitella*.

Analyses referred to *Chara* sp. and *Nitella* sp. from Lake Seminole, an artificial impoundment of the Chattahoochee River on the boundaries of Alabama, Georgia, and Florida, have been published by Lawrence (1971). These analyses are somewhat puzzling because the ash contents recorded are so much greater than any reasonable summation of the oxides of the 15 nonvolatile elements studied. Perhaps large amounts of silica and some alumina, not determined by Lawrence, were trapped by the plants. Lawrence found 8.89% Ca in *Chara* and 3.63% in *Nitella*. His potassium contents of 0.405 and 0.309%, respectively, are the lowest for any of the water plants that he analyzed.

Lawrence records extremely high figures for copper, zinc, and chromium in *Chara* sp., namely, 725 ppm Cu, 468 ppm Zn, and 252 ppm Cr dry; the quantities in *Nitella* sp. are much lower, namely, 165 ppm Cu, 70 ppm Zn, and 40 ppm Cr. The cadmium content of *Chara* sp. namely, 11.5 ppm, or 2.46% of the zinc content, relative to the latter element is lower than in the analyses of angiosperms from the same region (see p. 336). The strontium contents recorded by Lawrence are 21.8 ppm dry for *Chara* sp. and

10.7 ppm for *Nitella* sp., corresponding to Sr:Ca ratios of 0.245×10^{-3} and 0.295×10^{-3}, values that are lower than those obtained for the other rooted plants analyzed in his investigation.

A number of analyses of the sodium, potassium, and chloride contents of the fluid of the cell vacuoles of various species of Charophyceae have been collected together by MacRobbie (1970) in an excellent review of the transport of ions into and out of such cells. These analyses are summarized in Table 18 of Chapter 30.

It is evident that further work is needed on the chemical composition of the Characeae, but it would yield really significant results only if carefully done on fully and correctly identified material.

Odor of Charophyceae.   At least since the time of Bauhin, who gave the names *Equisetum olidum* (Bauhin 1596) and *Equisetum foetidum sub aqua repens* (Bauhin 1620, 1623) to a species of *Chara*, probably *Ch. vulgaris*, it has been known that some Charophyceae have a strong odor; this characteristic has in fact given rise to popular names, such as skunkweed in North America. The specific epithet *foetidum* Braun, though later than *vulgaris* Linnaeus, has also been very widely used. In spite of this rather obvious property of some of the commonest members of the group, which must be well-known to everyone who has had the experience of pond collecting in hardwater districts, at least in the North Temperate zone, there appear to be almost no chemical studies of the odoriferous principles of the Charophyceae. Amonkar (1969) alone gives some information about the infrared and ultraviolet spectra of a material obtained by methanol extraction and subsequent purification from *Chara globularis* and *Ch. elegans* (*Ch. zeylanica* var. *zeylanica* f. *elegans*). He concluded that he had derived the same compound from both species and that it was characterized by the presence of terminal methylene groups and by a sulfoxide group. He believed the substance to be related to that producing the odor of crushed garlic. This latter material (Stoll and Seebeck 1951; Richmond 1973) is mainly allicin or allyl thiosulfinate, derived enzymatically on crushing from alliin or allyl cysteine sulfoxide. In a later paper on the effect of garlic oil on mosquito larvae, Amonkar and Banerji (1971) concluded that the fairly active larvicidal properties of garlic oil actually are due to the related diallyl disulfide or trisulfide. The structures of the significant compounds are given in Figure 9. It seems quite likely that some such compounds are produced by members of the genus *Chara*, if not by other Charophyceae.

Effects of Charophyceae on mosquitos.   Caballero (1919, 1922a, b), working in Catalonia, concluded that mosquito larvae did not co-occur in nature with several species of *Chara* and that *Ch. vulgaris*, *Ch. globularis*, and *Ch. intermedia* produced a material poisonous to the larvae. *Culex* and *Anopheles* larvae appeared more susceptible than those of *Aedes*. Other

Alliin   Allicin   Diallyl disulfide
FIGURE 9.   Biologically active materials in garlic oil.

workers in Spain (Pardo 1923; Maynar 1923), Morocco (Alluaud 1923), Italy (Federici 1928), Mexico (Vasconcelos 1923), and the United States (Matheson 1930) obtained confirmatory evidence of the action of *Ch. vulgaris*, *Ch. hispida*, and a few other species against mosquito larvae. A considerable number of other investigators, amongst whom Fisher (1923), Barber (1924), Buxton (1924), McGregor (1924), Twinn (1931) and recently Margalit and Lipkin (personal communication) may be mentioned, failed to detect any clear evidence of the effect. Blow (1924, 1927) noted the mutual exclusion of mosquito larvae and Charophyceae, but concluded that there was no causal relation, the occurrences depending on some other factor favoring one and inimical to the other group of organisms. He found that a supposed glucoside derived from *Ch. zeylanica* had no larvicidal properties. Part of the apparent mutual exclusion may be due to mosquito larvae generally occuring in slightly less alkaline waters (Senior-White 1925) than support really massive growths of *Chara*.

Pal (1932) in his first experiments concluded that larvae disappeared when cultured with *Nitella oligospira* (*N. furcata* subsp. *mucronata* var. *mucronata* f. *oligospira*), but later found that they were being eaten by a greenish cryptically colored dragonfly nymph that lurked hidden in the plant.

Matheson and Hinman (1928) observed no larvae living in pools in which *Ch. vulgaris* was common. They later (Matheson and Himnan 1930) observed like effects due to *Ch. virgata* and *Ch. contraria*. Very striking inhibition of egg laying on water surfaces above *Ch. vulgaris* was also observed (Matheson and Hinman 1929). Though at first inclined to attribute the larvicidal effects to a rise in pH incident on photosynthesis, they later concluded that minute bubbles produced in photosynthesis became entangled in the mouth brushes and body hairs as well as being taken up in feeding, thus filling the gut. All such contamination is mechanically injurious to the larvae. The larvicidal effect, which was not observed in the dark, could be imitated by blowing a very fine stream of bubbles through a vessel containing larvae (Matheson and Hinman (1931).

Several investigators have further illuminated the problem a little. Stroede (1931) found eggs and young, but not mature, larvae to be injured by the presence of *Ch. globularis*. Other workers tend to pay little or no attention to the age of their test organisms.

Buhôt (1927) in Queensland did some experiments that initially appear rather crude and uncritical, concluding that the presence of *Nitella phauloteles* (*N. furcata* subsp. *orientalis* var. *phauloteles*) in water inhibited adult female mosquitos from laying eggs on the water surface. He believed this was due to an oil film derived from the plant. Hamlyn-Harris (1928, 1932), however, found this species of *Nitella* associated with three species of mosquito larvae in nature. Buhôt's observations are of some interest, however, as Ophel (1948), working more critically, found that the oviposition of *Culex quinquefasciatus* was inhibited on water surfaces above *Ch. globularis*, but hundreds of egg rafts were deposited over *Nitella* sp. and on the water of a vegetationless control aquarium. Larvae added to the three aquariums showed no differential mortality in the presence of *Ch. globularis*. As has been indicated above, Matheson and Hinman (1928) observed a similar effect due to *Ch. vulgaris*.

In what seem to be the most critical experiments so far conducted, Imahori (1954) studied the fate of larvae of *Aedes albopictus* in the presence of three species of *Chara* and three of *Nitella*. Each plant was set in a glass jar filled to a depth of 17 cm with well water and with a cup of sterilized soil on the bottom. The survival of the larvae is given in Table 3.

These results are rather surprising, suggesting a far greater larvicidal effect from species of *Nitella*, notably *N. flexilis*, whereas *Ch. globularis* was evidently not toxic. The effect of minute gas bubbles is not clearly ruled out in the experiments.

TABLE 3. *Survivorship of* Aedes *larvae in water in which various Charophyceae are growing*

Species of Charophyceae	Initial no. of *Aedes* larvae	Number after 30 hr	Number after 60 hr	Number after 120 hr
Chara globularis	10	10	10	9
Ch. corallina	10	8	6	2
Ch. zeylanica	10	9	5	4
Nitella flexilis	10	0	0	0
N. rigida	10	2	0	0
N. mucronata	10	4	1	1
Control, no plants	10	10	9	8

Independent studies with *Aedes togoi*, *Anopheles sinensis*, and *Culex tritaeniorhynchus* showed that blood-fed females would oviposit on the surface of the water in any of the jars except that containing *Nitella flexilis*. In none of the experiments in which egg laying is inhibited is it likely that minute bubbles were involved in producing the observed effects.

In summary, it would appear that some of the positive effects that have been observed are undoubtedly real, in spite of their great irregularities of occurrence. It seems likely that different samples of the same species of plant differ in their capacity to produce larvicidal substances if indeed they exist, that the effect depends on the age and species of mosquito larvae studied, and that the apparently well-established inhibition of laying by females on the water surface below which certain Charophyceae are growing is a phenomenon to some extent independent of the supposed toxicity of the plants to larvae.

Obviously a great deal more study is needed. Though the cultivation of Charophyceae may not prove to be a practical method of mosquito control, the ecological interest of the matter is considerable. It is hard to see what advantage to the plant is conferred by elimination of mosquito larvae. If the effects observed are due to bubbles produced in photosynthesis no adaptation is in fact likely to be involved. However, if the insecticidal properties are adaptive, they may be directed against some insects other than mosquitos. All insects are clearly not discouraged; beetles of the family Haliplidae, for instance, are freely found in *Chara* (E. J. Pearce in litt.), *Haliplus obliquus* being a characteristic denizen of the plant in England.

The Charophyceae, moreover, are important biotopes for other arthropods, including a great variety of Cladocera. The biota of *Chara* or *Nitella* beds in lakes may well be determined by elimination of some species, permitting a striking abundance of other kinds of animals.

How far some of the observed effects are due to the liberation of materials related to allicin or to diallyl sulfides is uncertain, though Amonkar's results clearly suggest this possibility. It is to be noted that he obtained quite unrelated materials from *Cladophora glomerata* and *Schizothrix friesii*, which appeared still more larvicidal.

Vertical distribution in lakes. In lakes in which very few species of Charophyceae occur, the one or two species present are often found growing in deeper water than are the angiosperms. However, whenever a rich charophycean flora is present, a fairly complicated zonation develops, as Wood (1950) and Corillion (1957) have emphasized. Some examples of this zonation, from the papers of these two authors, are given in Figs. 10–14, and another quite complicated pattern is evident in Fig. 17.

Marked zonation is apparent in all these cases, though the zones may extend all round the perimeter of the lake, but vary with factors other

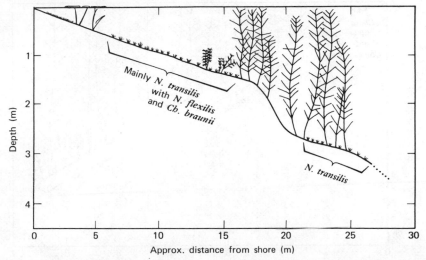

FIGURE 10.   Zonation of Charophyceae and other vegetation in Weeks Pond, Falmouth, Mass., August 1947. The shoremost zone of the littoral supported *Gratiola aurea*, with *Nymphaea* just lakeward; there was then a *Nitelletum*, mainly of *N. transilis* with occasional *N. megacarpa*, and in slightly deeper water *N. flexilis* and *Chara braunii*. At the edge of the littoral shelf *Potamogeton* became dominant but *N. transilis* appeared again in deeper water (Wood, modified).

than depth, such as exposure. There may be areas without Charophyceae, or indeed any vegetation between zones (0.3–1.0 m in Fig. 11). When angiosperms are present a definite layering may be developed, smaller Charophyceae growing between the larger *Potamogeton* or other flowering plants (Fig. 11). Sometimes the same arrangement is shown by a large and small species of *Nitella* (*A* of Fig. 14). In the very simple type of distribution in which a single species of *Nitella*, such as *N. opaca* or *N. flexilis* in the English Lake District, is found below a zone of, say, narrow-leaved *Potamogeton*, we may suspect that the *Nitella* is a shade plant that is unable to compete with angiosperms except at low light intensities. Even this simple explanation is found to need qualification. A somewhat comparable interpretation of the presence of small Charophyceae forming a miniature understory below large plants that might limit themselves by self-shading is reasonable. In most of the complicated cases, no obvious intuitive interpretation immediately comes to mind. It is reasonable to suppose that the nature of the substration, the light intensity, and water movements are the most likely physical variables determining the zonation of Charophyceae, just as they are of great importance to angiosperms. Such little information on the action of these three variables is considered before some of the resulting patterns are discussed in greater detail.

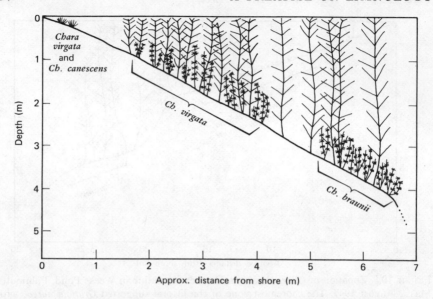

FIGURE 11.   Zonation of Charophyceae and other vegetation in Salt Pond, Falmouth, Mass., July 1947. In the shallowest water a tuft-like form of *Chara virgata* co-occurs with *Ch. canescens*. The former species as an elongate form occurs in rather deeper water accompanying *Potamogeton* sp.; there is a bare sandy zone separating the two morphologically different populations of *Ch. virgata*. In deeper water there is *Ch. braunii*, with some *Potamogeton*. Note the discontinuities between the three charophycean populations.

Nature of substratum.   Most species grow in silt or mud, but there is a small though characteristic group of species which tend to occur in shallow water on sandy bottoms, or on sand covered with a very thin layer of finer material. *Chara aspera* is the chief species of the sandy shores of hard-water lakes in Europe and North America, and *Ch. fragifera* is found in comparable situations in the western part of Europe, usually growing on quartz sand in circumneutral or very slightly acidic water.

Both species can on rare occasions occur in the same body of water and exhibit some zonation (*C* of Fig. 14). They have well-developed rhizoids bearing bulbils, which probably serve not only as reproductive bodies, but also as anchors occupying spaces between the sand grains (Corillion 1957), thus adapting the plants to rather more movement of water than would be expected over finer sediments. Neither *Ch. aspera* nor *Ch. fragifera* are truly rheophile species, however. It is not unlikely that other vicariant taxa, perhaps other microspecies of the collective species *Ch. globularis* to which *Ch. aspera* and *Ch. fragifera* belong, can be found living in similar circumstances in other parts of the world.

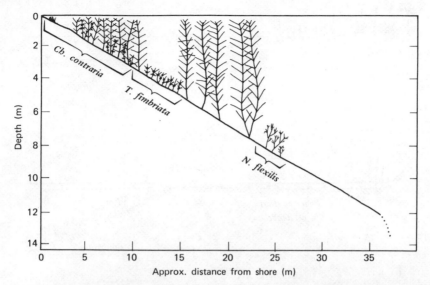

FIGURE 12. Zonation of Charophyceae and other vegetation in Keuka Lake, Keuka, New York, August 1946. Nearest the shore there is a tuftlike form of *Chara contraria;* a taller form growing with *Potamogeton* occurs in somewhat deeper water separated from the tuftlike form by a narrow bare sandy zone. Lower there are *Tolypella fimbriata*, *Potamogeton* without Charophyceae, and at the lower limit of macrophytes, *Nitella flexilis* (Wood, modified).

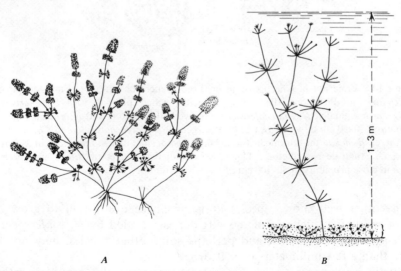

FIGURE 13. *A, Nitella confervacea*, whole plant (natural size, Migula); *B*, schematic drawing of the c-occurrence of *N. confervacea* in loose mud as an understory in a stand of *N. translucens* (Corillion).

35

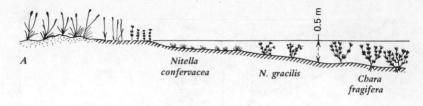

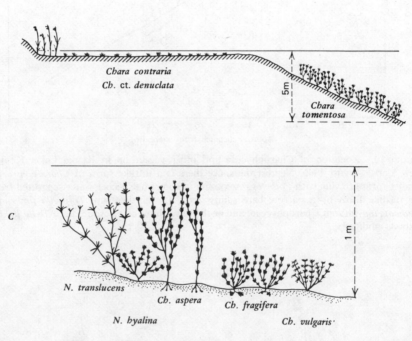

FIGURE 14. Zonation of Charophyceae in three French localities. *A*, Etang de Pas-du-Houx, forest of Paimpont, Ille et Vilaine, acidic water (pH 6.5) with *Eleocharis* and *Sphagnum* marginally, *Nitella confervacea* is very shallow water, and *N. gracilis* and *Ch. fragifera* in 30–50 cm of water. *B*, Lac du Bourget, Jura; *Parvocharacetum* of *Ch. contraria* and *Ch.* cf. *denudata* on littoral shelf and *Magnocharacetum* of *Ch. tomentosa* in 2–5 m of water. *C*, Etang de Neuvillette, Jublains, Mayenne; two species of *Nitella* and three of *Chara* in close proximity in 80–100 cm of water (Corillion).

The other well-known species of Charophyceae all seem to grow on silt or mud; the thickness of the soft deposit needed by *N. confervaceae*, *N. tenuissima*, *N. gracilis*, and perhaps some other species, may not be more than a few millimeters over bedrock.

Nitella confervacea (A of Fig. 13) characteristically grows in rather than on mud, if the latter is a few centimeters thick. Migula (1900, p. 188) says of it "sich mehr in den Schlamm verkriecht und fast mehr mit der Hand gefühlt als mit den Augen gesucht werden muss." It is presumably very shade-tolerant and may actually be inhibited by bright light. In one locality described by Corillion (1957), Etang du Pas-du-Houx, forest of Paimpont, Ille-et-Vilaine, a slightly acidic body of water at pH 6.5 with *Eleocharis* and *Spagnum* at the margin, *N. confervacea* grew in 10–15 cm of water (*A* of Fig. 14), beyond it *N. gracilis* in 15–30 cm, and in still deeper water *Ch. fragifera* to over 1 m, on mud-covered sand. It may occur (*B* of Fig. 13) as an understory below the very tall *N. translucens* in deeper water, but again is more or less covered with mud.

Little is known of the substrate preferences of the other species. Pearsall (1917, 1920, 1921) believed that in the English lakes *Nitella opaca* and *Nitella flexilis*, which Wood regards as belonging to the same microspecies, are regulated in their distribution not only by being potentially shade plants, but also in tolerating rather more rapid silting than some possible competitors such as *Isoetes lacustris*, though not as much as can *Juncus bulbosus* f. *fluitans*. This can give rise to characteristic patterns in the vicinity of islands or the inlets or streams (see Fig. 128).

Light intensity. A great many species are obviously capable of living at quite low light intensities. Corillion (1957), on the basis of distribution in the field, attributes such a capacity to six taxa of *Nitella*, *N. confervacea*, *N. tenuissima*, *N. flexilis*, *N. mucronata*, *N. syncarpa*, and *N. opaca*.

The special habitat of the first-named has already been noted. The other five are all known to descend at least to 10 m according to Corillion, and indeed often deeper in really clear lakes. *N. opaca* is recorded from 40 m in Lake Vättern (Stålberg 1939).

In the genus *Chara*, *Ch. vulgaris*, *Ch. strigosa* (*Ch. globularis* var. *aspera* f. *strigosa*), *Ch. hispida*, *Ch. contraria*, *Ch. tomentosa*, *Ch. globularis*, *Ch. pedunculata*, and *Ch. virgata*, perhaps properly *Ch. globularis* var. *virgata* f. *barbata*, are all known at depths of 10 m or more, sometimes very much more.

None of these plants is confined to low light intensities in nature, though in hard waters the members of the genus *Chara* are usually covered with a deposit of calcium carbonate, which, like the mud enveloping *Nitella confervacea*, is likely to act as an effective screen against solar radiation. For such plants, living in shallow water obviously does not necessarily mean living in a bright light.

In very shallow water the occurrence of Charophyceae may be limited by the shade of a continuous cover of floating-leaved vegetation. Hodgetts (1921) noticed this in Hawkesley Hall Pond, King's Norton, England, where *Nitella flexilis* was common only where the cover provided by leaves of *Potamogeton natans* was interrupted locally. Pal (1932) found similarily that in a small pond in Burma, *Ch. wallichii* (*Ch. corallina* var. *wallichii*) could grow only when the pond was not covered by *Nymphaea* leaves.

Starling, Chapman, and Brown (1974b) found the descent of *Nitella hookeri* in the lakes of the North Island of New Zealand usually limited by the 3% isophote; if the plant goes lower it becomes elongate.

When they are growing in really transparent water the Characeae extend downward well below the limit of the flowering plants. The greatest well-established depth at which any member of the group is recorded is 65.5 m, in Lake Tahoe (Frantz and Cordone 1967), where *Chara virgata* (sub *Ch. delicatula* var. *barbara*), perhaps as a recognizable f. *barbata*, occurred. At this depth the incident radiation is rather more than 2% of that reaching the surface of the lake; elsewhere such a radiation flux, though at much less great depths, supports not only other species of Charophyceae but also some angiosperms (Pearsall, 1917, 1918a, 1920, 1921). Frantz and Cordone found, moreover, a depauperate form of an indeterminable ecorticate species as deep as 164 m, but it is possible that this record does not refer to plants growing in situ. Though there can be little doubt that the lower limit of vertical distribution of the group depends on light penetration, as is obvious

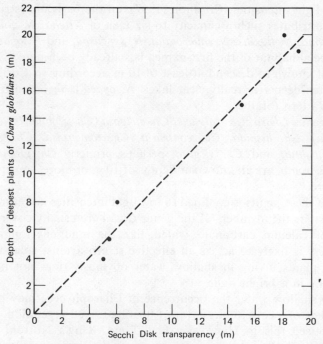

FIGURE 15.   Depth of deepest occurrence of *Chara globularis* as a function of Secchi disk transparencies of Japanese lakes (data of Imahori).

from Imahori's data on *Ch. globularis* in Japanese lakes (Fig. 15), it is clear that this does not explain why *Chara* and *Nitella* can extend into much deeper water in transparent lakes than can the angiosperms growing characteristically in the less deep part of the lower infralittoral zone of the same lakes (see pp. 422, 423).

Golubić (1961) found that in Lake Vrana during a 20-hr period, respiration balanced photosynthesis for *Ch. globularis* at 42 m, and for the less deep water *Ch. pedunculata* at 35 m. Evidently the species occurring in deeper water is photosynthetically more efficient at low light intensities than is the one living on shallower bottoms. Presumably many of the specific differences in vertical distribution within the group could be explained along these lines. There are, however, cases in which other factors must be involved.

Water movements. Corillion (1957) regards *Nitella flexilis*, *N. syncarpa*, and *Chara globularis* as the commonest species in running waters in north-western France. All are known to occur in deep waters in lakes and are not conspicuous littoral forms, but some of the latter such as *Chara aspera* and *Ch. contraria* are rare or absent in streams (Olsen 1944; Corillion 1957). It is probable, however, that water movements are of some importance in regulating the distribution of Charophyceae in lakes.

Olsen (1944) indicates the depth distributions of the species occurring in Fureso and Nors Sø in Denmark, as set out in Table 4. It is obvious that in the two lakes *C. aspera* is a shallow-water form, but *Nitellopsis obtusa*, and *Ch. denudata* in Fureso, tend to occur in deeper water than do the other species. In Nors Sø the last-named species is, however, intermediate in its depth range, whereas *Ch. rudis*, a plant of considerable depth range in Fureso, is limited to the top 2 of Nors Sø. Since the ordering of the other species is much the same in the two lakes, we can hardly suppose that the limitation of *Ch. rudis* to the top 2 m of Nors Sø is dependent solely on restricted light penetration, though the data provide no real indication of what is happening.

When the abundance of each species, expressed as a percentage of the whole characean population, is plotted against depth (Fig. 16) for the three commonest species in Nors Sø, the deep-water *Nitellopsis obtusa* is seen to have a clear maximum at 5.5 m and the shallow-water *Ch. aspera* at 1.5 m. The distribution of *Ch. contraria*, however, is bimodal, with one maximum above and the other below the main range of *Ch. aspera*, suggesting that the latter species excludes *Ch. contraria* in the central but not in the peripheral parts of an otherwise suitable habitat. It is possible that the upper limit of occurrence is often dependent on the capacity or a species to withstand wave action or other littoral water movements. This may be regulating the outcome of competition between *Ch. contraria* and *Ch.*

TABLE 4. Depth distributions of Characeae in two Danish lakes

Species	Depth (m) Fureső	Depth (m) Nors Sø
Chara aspera	0–3	0–4
Ch. contraria	0–7	0–5
Ch. tomentosa	0–7	0–5
Ch. globularis[a]	1.5–7	0–6
Ch, rudis[b]	1–7	0–2
Ch. denudata[c]	1.5–8	2–4
Nitellopsis obtusa	1.5–8	1–7

[a] sub fragilis.
[b] Ch. hispida var. major f. rudis.
[c] Ch. vulgaris var. denudata f. denudata.

aspera. Moreover Olsen thinks that the decrease with decreasing depth of the deep-water Nitellopsis obtusa is determined in this way.

Some distribution patterns in other European lakes. Sauer (1937) has considered the depth distribution of the Characeae of the lakes of Holstein in northern Germany. Using the phytosociological concepts of Braun-Blanquet (1928; 1932) he distinguishes two associations of these plants, the Parvocharacetum primarily found in quite shallow water along exposed shores, and the Magnocharacetum of taller plants growing in deeper water, ordinarily along less exposed shores. The occurrence of the taller plants at greater depths is certainly due to their growing at lower light intensities and is considered in the next section.

Both associations have several variants. The three loosely distinguished variants of the Parvocharacetum are (a) Chara vulgaris (sub foetida f. subinermis) with Potamogeton perfoliatus in 5–100 cm of water, forming cushions, usually on sand but also on peaty bottoms; (b) Chara aspera, Ch. vulgaris (sub foetida), and Ch. globularis (sub fragilis) in 50–100 cm of water, usually on sand but also on gyttja; if cushions are formed these are looser and muddier than the turflike ones of the previous variant; (c) Ch. tomentosa (sub ceratophylla), Ch. contraria, and Nitella opaca in deeper water from 2 to 5 m, on somewhat organic bottoms, and transitional to the Magnocharacetum. In the latter Chara intermedia and Nitella flexilis occur from about 1 down to 6 m, while Nitellopsis obtusa (sub Tolypellopsis stelligera) is found from 4.5 to 8 m. Utricularia neglecta may be associated with the last-named species in some lakes. Before 1890,

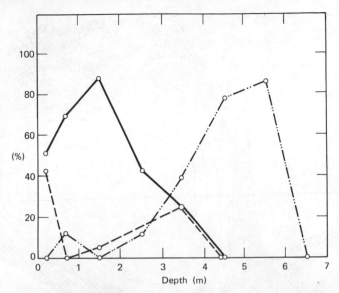

FIGURE 16. Proportion of *Chara aspera* (solid line), *Ch. contraria* (broken line), and *Nitellopsis obtusa* (broken and double dotted line) in the total characean flora of Nors Sø at different depths (Olsen).

N. obtusa occurred in the Grosser Plöner See to a depth of 30 m; the greatest depth, namely, 8 m, recorded for this species in Holstein in Sauer's study of 1934–1935 was in the Schluensee, the most transparent of the lakes that he studied.

Comparable distributions occur further to the east in Germany. Jeschke (1963) studying the smaller lakes of the Nature Reserve on the eastern shore of the Müritz See, south of Waren, found *Chara aspera* growing on exposed shores with sandy bottoms from 0.8 to 1.25 m, and below this, associated with *Ch. tomentosa* which becomes more abundant in deeper water, forming a fairly uniform carpet from 2.4 to 4.0 m; it then gave place to *Nitellopsis obtusa* which at 5 m alone was present. Jeschke (1963) indicates that in eutrophic lakes *Chara filiformis* may occur at the shore but goes deeper than *Ch. aspera*. He also notes that there may be an association of *Nitella flexilis* with *Vaucheria dichotoma* below the *Nitellopsis*.

Krausch (1964) describes like associations in the Grosser Stechlinsee nearby. *Chara aspera* again occurred in 0.2–1.3 m of water on exposed shores with sandy bottoms. *Ch. filiformis* was recorded from 1.2 to 5 m. *Nitellopsis obtusa* was important on calcareous mud between 4 and 10 m; below it on black mud *Nitella flexilis* and some *Chara hedwigii* were

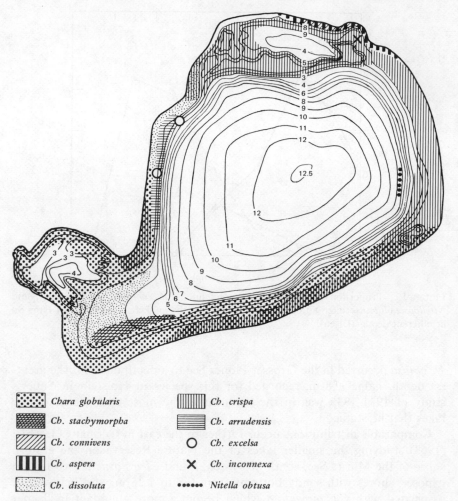

FIGURE 17. Distribution of Characeae in Lawrence Lake, Barry Co., Michigan (Rich, Wetzel, and Thuy).

associated with *Vaucheria dichotoma*. Krausch, like Sauer, used the phytosociological methods of the Zurich–Montpellier school to describe his observations, to which it will be necessary to return when discussing the phytosociological approach to lacustrine vegetation (see p. 489).

Distribution of Charophyceae in a Michigan Marl Lake. Rich, Wetzel, and Thuy (1971) found *Chara* occurring locally to depths of about 6 m in Lawrence Lake, Barry County, Michigan, but the genus was abundant only in the top 3 m (Fig. 17). On the exposed eastern shore *Chara crispa* was the most important species, whereas *Ch. globularis* was found mainly on the less disturbed southern and western shores of the lake. *Ch. dissoluta* (*Ch. vulgaris* var. *imperfecta* f. *dissoluta*) occurred in very shallow water, shoreward from *Ch. arrudensis* (*Ch. vulgaris* var. *imperfecta* f. *arrudensis*) on the western side of the lake, but was also conspicuous on estuarine deposits down to 3 m. *Ch. aspera*, found along the north shore, is here, as elsewhere, a shallow-water species. Four other taxa of *Chara*, with much more limited distributions, were also found. The greater development of the genus on the shallow parts of the lake bottom is probably due to release from competition with *Scirpus subterminalis* which is more easily broken by wave action than are the species of *Chara*, unless the latter have become very encrusted with calcium carbonate. *Nitella* was represented only by *N. obtusa* (*N. flexilis* var. *flexilis* f. *obtusa*) which appeared in a very limited area between 7 and 8 m in July and disappeared in October. Rich, Wetzel, and Thuy suspect the plant to be limited by CO_2, all other Charophyceae in the lake being doubtless able to use HCO_3^-. The appearance of *Nitella* in stratified water in which the pH had fallen from 8.3 to 8.1 supports this view. The mud in which the plant was growing may have supplied more CO_2 to the immediate neighborhood of the green parts than this small fall in pH indicated.

Relation of Growth Form to Light. An interesting relationship has been discovered by Forsberg (1963, 1965a) among the different species of *Chara*. In general in the epilimnion of a lake the height of the plant increases with depth (Corillion 1957) and it can be shown experimentally that this is due to decreasing light intensity, as would be expected and as is observed with other plants (see pp. 165, 195). When the mean height of the plant is plotted against the relative light penetration to any given depth in nature, a concave curve is obtained. However, for different species the slope and position of this curve differ considerably. This is shown in Fig. 18, where the actual points and best fitting lines are shown for *Ch. globularis* and *Ch. aspera*, and the best fitting lines for three other species all growing in the lakes of Sweden. There seems to be no relationship between the extent of the response to declining light and the depth range of the responding plants. *Ch. hispida* (sub *aculeolata*), at least in northern Europe, is a species of the upper infralittoral; Olsen records its depth range as 0–1 m and Stroede (1931) regards it as one of the characteristic species of shallow waters. *Ch. tomentosa* and *Ch. contraria* are both known in fairly deep water, down to 7 m in Furesø and to depths of over 8 m in other parts of Europe (Stroede 1931). *Ch. globularis* is likewise found in water 7 m deep in Furesø, but generally appears to be a less deep-water form than either *Ch. tomentosa* or *Ch. contraria*. The least responsive species, *Ch. aspera*, appears in general to be a shallow-water species often found near lake

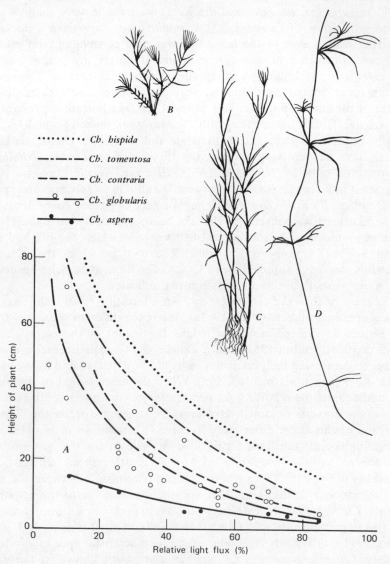

FIGURE 18. *A*, Relationship of plant height to relative light intensity, as percentage, at any depth, of flux at surface, for *Ch. aspera* and *Ch. globularis* (actual points and lines fitted by eye) and for three other species (lines fitted by eye). *B*, *Ch. globularis* in 0.2 m, Metsjön, Uppland, Sweden; *C*, in same lake in 0.5 m; *D*, part of a plant of same species in Svartsjön, Ostergötland, Sweden in 2.5 m (modified from Forsberg).

margins on sandy bottoms, extending to 3 m in Furesø; Stroede (1931) gives its ordinary range as 0.5–4 m, though it has been found in much deeper water. It will be seen that the curves for the species extending into the deeper water (*Ch. tomentosa*, *Ch. contraria*, and *Ch. globularis*) lie between those for the two shallow-water species, *Ch. hispida* and *Ch. aspera*.

Stability of Charophycean Associations. In some newly formed ponds the Charophyceae appear as pioneer vegetation, later to be displaced by angiosperms. Wood (1950) gives an account of a small pool about 6 × 2 m with a depth of 45 cm, at Woods Hole. It was formed during the winter of 1945–1946; it was invaded by *Chara virgata* and *Ch. braunii* which formed extensive populations with a little *Najas flexilis* in the late summer of 1946. In 1947 the areas covered by all three species expanded. *Ch. braunii* disappeared in 1948, however, and the area of *Ch. virgata* was markedly reduced, though *N. flexilis* greatly increased while *Potamogeton* sp. and macroscopic benthic algae became apparent. The process of succession continued so that early in 1949 only a little *Ch. virgata* remained, and this disappeared later in the year. *Najas flexilis* continued as the dominant plant, while *Potamogeton* sp. and the benthic algae increased somewhat.

A dramatic instance of a comparable process of succession evidently took place in Back Bay and North Bay, Virginia. There coastal bodies of water had suffered from the removal of locks and the artificial widening of channels, so that they had lost their macroscopic flora and had been deserted by waterfowl. When locks were reinstated, on the advice of the Boyce Thompson Institute (Crocker 1948) initial colonization by *Chara* and *Nitella* took place, stabilizing the sediments and increasing the transparency of the water. Later the Charophyceae were replaced by angiosperms.

Though both Wood and Corillion regard this kind of transitory Charophycean association as usual, cases are known where associations have persisted for decades. Wood records *Ch. canescens* and *Ch. aspera* as having existed for 59 and 56 years, respectively, in a locality at Watch Hill, Rhode Island; Corillion (1957) noted the same two species as having persisted from 1857 at least to 1946 in localities in S. Finistère, France. In Put-in-Bay, Lake Erie, *Ch. braunii* and *Ch. contraria* have been known for 49 and 51 years, respectively (Wood 1950). Since it is evident that in deep water near the limit of vegetation Charophyceae may do better than angiosperms, persistence under some conditions would be expected. Little information is available about these cases where the species have continued to be found for half a century or more. It would be most interesting to know if in any of them the plants were growing in quite shallow water. Localities such as Lake Tåkern in the old condition (see p. 25) doubtless provided striking cases of the chemical environment determining the indefinite persistence of associations dominated by *Chara*.

BRYOPHYTA

Numerous mosses and liverworts have been recorded as living in water, and though many of these plants belong to the stream flora, several liverworts and a not inconsiderable number of mosses are of some ecological importance in lakes. In the third class of bryophytes, the Anthocerotae, *Anthoceros laevis* has a more or less submerged f. *aquatica*, recorded (Watson 1920) in bog springs and the sides of streams in Somerset, England. Like many other aquatic forms of otherwise terrestrial bryophytes, it appears to be sexually sterile. Three species of *Aspiromitus* (*A. asper*, *A. glandulosa*, and *A. squamulosa*) are known as true aquatics in more than 40 cm of water in springs and streams in Indonesia (Ruttner 1955; Schiffner 1955), but none of the Anthocerotae are yet recorded growing perennially submerged in lakes. Schuster (1953) implies that *Anthoceros macounii* can be eulittoral in Minnesota.

Aquatic Hepaticae. A good many of the more hygrophilous liverworts are recorded as living on occasion underwater, and not infrequently the submersed forms are morphologically distinguishable, presumably as ecophenes. Many such aquatic occurrences are on rocks in streams, but in a number of cases clear evidence exists of liverworts of terrestrial affinities occurring fully submersed in lakes. Thus Fuchsig (1924) records no less than eight species, namely, *Marchantia aquatica* (sub *polymorpha*), *Pellia endiviaefolia*, *Jungermannia tristis*, *Lophozia incisa*, *Lophocolea cuspidata*, *L. bidentata*, *Cephalozia bicuspidata*, and *C. lammersiana* in the upper infralittoral, less than 2 m deep, of the Lunzer Untersee. Most of these, when they occur underwater, show some morphological differentiation from the typical forms of damp but subaerial habitats, the aquatic forms usually being larger, laxer, and sexually sterile. In the case of *Cephalozia bicuspidata*, the var. *aquatica* may have stems 30 cm long, whereas the most extreme terrestrial form of the species in only a few millimeters in length (Schiffner, 1931). It is probable that where the aquatic form is more elongate than the terrestrial forms of the same plant, low light intensity is primarily involved.

Marchantia aquatica, living in fresh water, is now believed to be specifically distinct (Burgeff 1943; Grochowska 1971) from the widespread terrestrial *M. polymorpha*. When growing underwater *M. aquatica* has longer narrower thallus lobes (*A* of Fig. 19) and a less prostrate habit than *M. polymorpha*; it is also less brownish green in color. It can be grown (f. *riparia*) terrestrially (*B* of Fig. 19), when it still has somewhat narrower

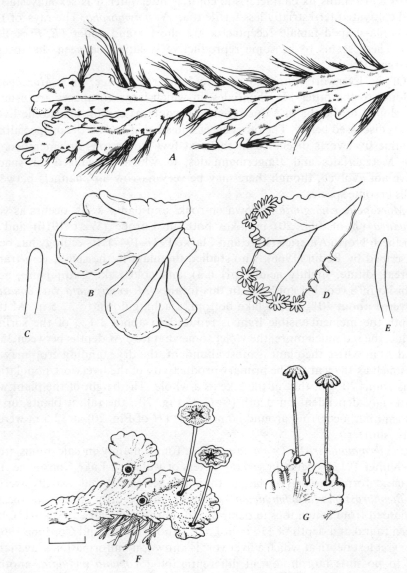

FIGURE 19.　Aquatic and related terrestrial taxa of *Marchantia*. *A*, *M. aquatica* living in water, Poland; *B*, *M. aquatica* cultivated terrestrially; *C*, ray of female receptacle of same; *D*, *M. polymorpha* cultivated like *B; E*, ray of female receptacle of same; *F*, *M. polymorpha* male, Poland; *G*, *M. polymorpha* female, Poland (*A, F, G*, natural size, Grochowska; *B, D*, natural size, Burgeff; *C, E*, × about 7, Burgeff).

lobes and retains its characteristic color. Underwater it is sexually sterile, and cultivated terrestrially less fertile than *N. polymorpha*. The rays of the umbrella-shaped female receptacles are shorter and wider (*E, F* of Fig. 19). There seems to be some reproductive isolation between the species (Burgeff 1943).

Of the liverworts known from the Lunzer Untersee, only *Marchantia* belongs to the order Marchantiales, in which large air spaces are usually developed in the thallus; this order also contains certain pleustonic liverworts discussed below. The other species just listed and all the unspecialized benthic liverworts discussed in the next few paragraphs are members of the Metzgeriales and Jungermanniales, in which specialized air spaces have not evolved, though there may be very narrow air channels between cells in some species.

Marsupella emarginata, known on rocks and damp walls, occurs as var. *aquatica* (*B* of Fig. 20) in lakes both in Europe (West 1910) and in northern North America (Frye and Clarke 1937–1947). Its ecology has been described by Bodin (1966), who studied the plant in the small, very transparent, dilute, slightly acidic (pH 6.3), and cold Lake Latnjajaure, near Abisko in Swedish Lappland. In this locality *M. emarginata* var. *aquatica* covered about 40% of the lake bottom, reaching down to 32.5 m. At this depth the incident visible light is reduced to about 1.1% of the surface value, the red much more, the violet somewhat less. At depths between 25 m and 30 m where the plant is most abundant, the dry standing crop may be as much as 184 g m^{-2}. The primary productivity of the liverwort population was about 20% of that of the lake as a whole. The height of the plant was strikingly dependent on depth (*C–G* of Fig. 20), the tallest plants, up to 18 cm high, occurring around 30 m; those (*H* of Fig. 20) at 32.5 m were a little shorter.

Jungermannia tristis (*Aplozia riparia*), found mainly in calcareous areas (Schiffner 1931), occurs in several meters of waters in Lake Constance; the aquatic form *rivularis* is larger than the terrestrial but usually sterile.

Blepharostoma arachnoideum, a rather rare North American species recorded from rotten logs in damp woods (Frye and Clark 1937–1947), has been found at a depth of 110 m in Lake Tahoe (Frantz and Cordone 1967), the greatest depth at which a liverwort is known; no information is available as to possible morphological differentiation. *Scapania undulata*, another amphibious species, occurring underwater at the margins of lakes in Scotland, was found by West (1910) in quantity in Loch Skerrow and Loch Grennoch in a moribund condition, apparently as the result of overgrowth by algae (*Ulothrix, Batrachospermum*, etc.).

Naumann (1932) regards *Calypogeia submersa* and *Cephalozia fluitans* var. *gigantea* as characteristic of the infralittoral of the most acid chthoniotrophic lakes of Sweden.

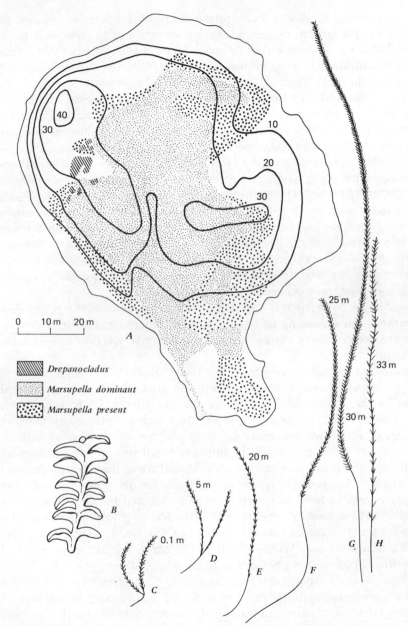

FIGURE 20. *A, Marsupella emarginata* var. *aquatica* in Lake Latnjajaure, Swedish Lappland; a bathymetric map showing the distribution of *Marsupella* and of *Drepanocladus*. *B*, Apex of a stem of *M. emarginata* var. *aquatica* ($\times$4); *C–G*, whole plants ($\times\frac{2}{3}$) from various depths showing an increase in height with increasing depth (or decreasing irradiance) to 30 m, after which, *H*, there is a slight decrease (Bodin, slightly modified, except *B*, after MacVicar).

49

A good many species of liverworts in addition to those mentioned in the last few paragraphs are recorded from springs and streams; it is quite likely that some of these will be found in lakes also. A number of records of the eulittoral occurrence both of some of the species already discussed and of certain other hygrophilous liverworts could certainly be assembled. In view of the very rich liverwort flora of wet tropical forests, and of the considerable number recorded in running waters in Indonesia, it is interesting that Ruttner (1955) found only four species in the eulittoral zone of the lakes of that region and none living permanently below water.

A number of records given by Iversen (1929) seem to suggest that liverworts occur mainly in acidic and neutral lakes and rarely or never in hard water. Vitt and Slack (1975), however, record nine species of Hepaticae on the sedge mats (see p. 58), with a mean pH of 6.7, around their mildly alkaline bog lakes in Michigan, while the comparable mats with a mean pH of 5.3 around acidic bog lakes supported only *Cladopodiella fluitans.* Doubtless the optimum pH for more or less aquatic liverworts is usually circumneutral or slightly acidic; occasional taxa such as *Jungermannia tristis* f. *rivularis* may occur in more alkaline water.

In addition to the plants that have been considered in the preceeding paragraphs, all belonging to benthic taxa in otherwise terrestrial genera, there are two groups of more specialized aquatic liverworts of considerable ecological interest.

Specialized rooted liverworts of the Genus Riella.   The first of these groups, the Riellaceae, containing the single genus *Riella*, is a specialized family of the Jungermanniales. *Riella* is a plant from 1.5 to 6 cm long, consisting of an axis, rooted at one end, to which are attached one or, in the case of *R. bialata*, two platelike wings and a number of small leaflets. The sexes are separate; a limited number of small sporophytes develop on the female plant and produce spores that withstand desiccation. Asexual reproduction by gemmae is important in some of these species. The genus contains at least 16 members; it is distributed in the warmer parts of the world but usually appears to be rare. The largest number of species recorded from any area, namely, seven, is from North Africa, while five inhabit South Africa (Wigglesworth 1937; Arnell 1963); other parts of the world appear to have but one to three species if any.

Riella capensis from Port Elizabeth and *R. paulsenii* from Bokhara were originally described from plants found accidentally in cultures of imported dried mud, to which water had been added to induce the hatching of the resting eggs of Crustacea. *R. purpureospora* from the vleis of the Cape Flats in South Africa was obtained purposefully by Wigglesworth (1937) using the same technique. The success of such methods suggests a life history adapted to temporary or astatic waters. The spores of *Riella* certainly can withstand desiccation for a number of years and can pass through the alimentary tracts of ducks unharmed (Proctor 1961). Members of the genus are thus doubtless dispersed by birds.

R. americana (*A* of Fig. 21) found sporadically in creeks in Texas and New Mexico, from which habitats it is easily washed by floods, is also known in one or two playa lakes, where it can sometimes be very abundant (Studhalter 1933; Griffin 1961), and in the Presa de Hipólito, Coahuila, Mexico, an artificial lake of variable level in semidesert country (Deevey 1957).

Riella affinis (*B* of Fig. 21) from the Canary Islands, South Africa, and western North America has probably provided the most striking lacustrine record for the genus. The plants occur in an artificial lake on the Stanford University Campus, flourishing at a depth of 5–7 m, but less abundant on the shallower parts of the lake bottom and quite absent between the margin and 1.5 m, where the water is likely to be most disturbed. The lake is astatic, being drained for irrigation during May and June, so that in spite of the depths at which *R. affinis* is reported (Thompson 1940) it is nevertheless here, as elsewhere, clearly a plant of temporary waters.

The rather rare European and North African *R. notarisii* was early recorded from a periodically unindated part of the shore of the Lake of

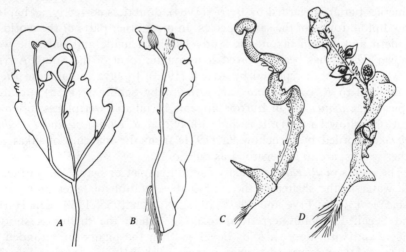

FIGURE 21. Species of *Riella* of limnological interest. *A, R. americana* (×2), female, Texas; *B, R. affinis* (×6.8), Gran Canary, monoecious with sparse marginal antheridia; *C, R. echinospora* (×4.5), Schonker's Salt Pan, Brandford, Orange Free State, male with numerous marginal antheridia; *D*, the same (×4.5), female with oogonia on enlarged fertile leaves (*A, B,* Howe and Underwood; *C, D,* Wigglesworth).

Geneva; a free floating form can arise in culture (Meylan 1924) but it would seem that in general this rather small species is likely to be more eulittoral than other members of the genus. *R. echinospora* (*C*, *D* of Fig. 21) from southern Africa appears to inhabit alkaline or somewhat saline inland waters.

The general distribution and the areas of greatest speciation suggest that *Riella* is a member of the characteristic specialized biota of temporary waters, reaching its maximum development in semiarid areas, paralleling in its distribution certain of the branchiopod and calanoid crustaceans (Vol. II, pp. 559, 560, 688, 690).

Pleustonic liverworts in the family Ricciaceae. The second specialized group of aquatic liverworts consists of the pleustonic members of the Ricciaceae, which are often by far the most important bryophytes in or on a lake. The family belongs to the Marchantiales and often has well-developed air spaces in its thallus. In *Riccia* these spaces are best developed in a small group of species sometimes separated as *Ricciella*, most of which are aquatic; it is very curious, however, that in *R. rhenana*, in which both aquatic and terrestrial ecophenes are known, the terrestrial one has the larger air spaces (*F*, *G* of Fig. 22). It is evident that these spaces were not developed primarily as an adaptation to pleustonic life.

In Europe there are three aquatic taxa of *Riccia*, namely, *fluitans*, *rhenana*, and *duplex* (Müller 1941). The first two certainly occur in North America but are regarded by Berrie (1964), doubtless correctly, as haploid and diploid forms of the same species. In most other parts of the world no modern and critical taxonomic study has been made and only the well-known *fluitans* has been reported. An aquatic form of the South African *R. stricta* has been reported by Arnell (1963). In Java the aquatic *Riccia* is referred to *R. canaliculata* var. *javanica* by Schiffner (1955); nomino-typical *R. canaliculata* in Europe appears to inhabit wet places, often on peat (Grochowska 1971). It is quite likely that *R. cavernosa* and *R. hübeneriana*, recorded by Grochowska (1971) from the margins of lakes and other waters, are to be regarded as eulittoral.

The plants of *Riccia* are usually found living at or below the surface of the water in the shelter of the marginal vegetation of lakes and ponds. (MacVicar 1926; Frye and Clark 1937; Watson 1955, 1968; den Hartog and Segal, 1964) but terrestrial forms in which the thallus is shorter, wider, and with more rhizoids develop when the plants are stranded on mud; such forms are easily produced in culture (*A*, *B*, *D*, *E* of Fig. 22). Asexual reproduction is usual and at least in *R. fluitans* and *R. rhenana* the production of spores is a very rare event. Paton (1973), however, has recently reported the epidemic production of archegonia and sporophytes in a population of *R. fluitans* in England. Plants having antheridia were not

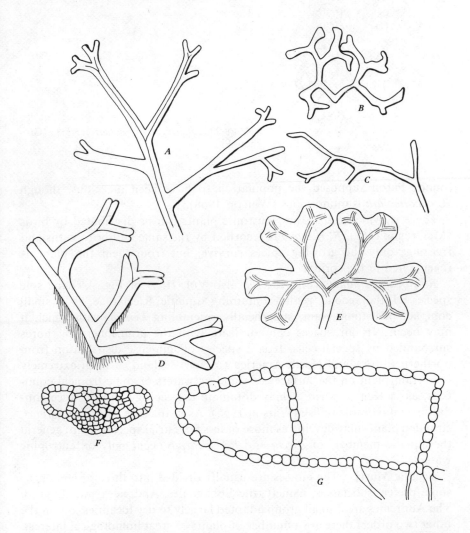

FIGURE 22. *A, Riccia fluitans* typical aquatic form; *B, C, R. rhenana,* typical aquatic forms, from Munich; *D, R. fluitans* terrestrial form; *E,* part of *B* cultivated terrestrially; *F,* cross-section of part of *C; G,* cross-section of part of *E (A–E,* ×3.75; *F, G,* ×7.5, Watson, Müller).

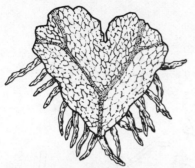

FIGURE 23.   *Ricciocarpus natans* (×5.3, Gro-chowska).

found; Paton supposed the population to have been dioecious, though *R. canaliculata* is monoecious (Watson 1968).

There is evidence that the pleustonic plants can be distributed by birds (McGregor 1961). *R. rhenana* is recorded by the same author to withstand freezing; only the growing apices survive, but from them the plant is regenerated in the spring.

Ricciocarpus natans (Fig. 23; see also Vol. II, *B* of Fig. 4,[10]) the sole species of the second genus containing aquatic Ricciaceae, is a small compact pleustonic plant, superficially resembling *Lemna*, with which it may occur. Its air spaces communicate with the atmosphere by pores surrounded by special cells. It is a species of immense distribution from northern Europe and North America to New Zealand. It is an extremely important plant on the surfaces of standing waters of some tropical countries, as in Kenya, where it may dominate the ecology and produce conditions unfavorable to fish (Watson 1955). As in the case of *Riccia fluitans*, stranded plants may develop as more or less terrestrial specimens. In general the aquatic members of *Riccia* and *Ricciocarpus* occur only on eutrophic waters.

Aquatic Musci.   The mosses are usually divided into three orders or, as some prefer, subclasses, namely, the Sphagnales, Andreales, and Bryales. The Andreales are a small group adapted largely to dry localities, but in the other two orders there are a number of plants of great limnological interest.

Sphagnales.   The order consists of a single family and genus, containing a large number of species living in a variety of calcium-poor habitats ranging from damp clearings in woodland to the infralittoral zone of lakes.

Since all species, as just indicated, tend to be acidophilic, though to varying degrees, and since the water requirements tend to vary also, we may expect the different species to have rather clear-cut niches. This is probably

---

[10] The generic name is given incorrectly in the legend of this figure.

borne out in practice, but much more needs to be done on the autecology of the group.

According to Paul (1931) the European species may be divided into four categories with regard to their water requirements, as set out in Table 5.

Paul indicates that *S. rubellum* and *S. molluscum*, neither of which is among the strongly hydrophilic species, are excessively acidophilic, living at pH 3–4. Most of the other species in the section Cuspidata as well as those of the Acutifolia, Cymbifolia, and Rigida are a little less extremely acido-

TABLE 5. *Water requirements of certain European species of* Sphagnum

---

1. Hydrobiont, living in water with only tip of plant emergent.
   Section Cuspidata: *S. lindbergi, S. riparium, S. jensenii, S. obtusum, S. cuspidatum, S. dusenii*
   Section Subsecunda: *S. rufescens, S. crassicladium, S. platyphyllum*
   Of these species *S. cuspidatum* is of considerable limnological importance, while *S. crassicladium* and *S. platyphyllum* are specifically mentioned by Paul as occurring in the marginal waters of lakes.
2. Strongly to moderately hydrophilic, but able to stand more variation in water level than the members of the previous category.
   Section Cuspidata: *S. recurvum,*[a] *S. balticum*
   Section Subsecunda: *S. subsecundum, S. inundatum, S. auriculatum, S. contortum*
   Of these species *S. subsecundum* is the most important limnologically.
3. Moderately hydrophilic.
   Section Cuspidata: *S. pulchrum, S. molluscum*
   Section Acutifolia: *S. warnstoffi, S. rubellum*[b]
   Section Inophloea: *S. papillosum, S. centrale, S. magellanicum*
   Section Rigida: *S. compactum*
   There is in some species a very wide range of tolerance, with the development of definite aquatic forms such as *S. molluscum* f. *hydrophilum* and f. *immersum* or *S. magellanicum* f. *immersum* and f. *plumosum*.
4. Usually weakly hydrophilic, in moderately damp places, ranging onto fairly dry woodland soil, but sometimes with aquatic forms.
   Section Acutifolia: *S. fuscum, S. acutifolium, S. quinquefarium, S. fimbriatum, S. girgensohnii, S. robustum.*
   Section Polyclada: *S. wulfianum*
   Section Squarrosa: *S. squarrosum*
   Section Inophloea: *S. imbricatum, S. palustre*
   In general of little limnological importance, but *S. squarrosum* has an aquatic f. *immersum*, while there is a similarly aquatic f. *submersum* of the allied but probably more hydrophilic species *S. teres*, not otherwise included in the table.

---

[a] According to Sørensen (1948) this is a composite of two species, of which *S. apiculatum* is more hydrophilic than is *S. angustifolium*.
[b] Included by Vitt and Slack (1975) in *S. capillaceum*.

philic, living in general between pH 3 and 6. According to Sørensen, *S. apiculatum* and *S. cuspidatum* are never found above pH 5.5 in Denmark. *Sphagnum squarrosum* and *S. plumulosum* have a somewhat less strict requirement, living between 4 and 6.5. The members of the section Subsecunda, along with *S. teres*, *S. warnstorfii*, and *S. centrale*, in general need a weakly acid medium of pH 5.0–6.7. It is probable that in all cases calcium is fixed by the organic matter of *Sphagnum*; in less acidophilic species the fixation may perhaps be more efficient, so that even in such cases the plant maintains its own local environment at about pH 4.5–5.0 (Sørenson 1948).

The lacustrine species of *Sphagnum* will naturally be hydrobiont or strongly hydrophilic, usually belonging to categories 1 and 2, or taxonomically to the sections Cuspidata and Subsecunda. Of the species included in these sections, *S. cuspidatum* (*A* of Fig. 24) is probably as common as any other at the margins of small acid lakes (West 1910; Fuchsig 1924), often occurring as a water form (*B* of Fig. 24) with feathery leaves (f. *plumosum*). Feathery forms also occur, as the greenish f. *immersum* and the reddish f. *plumosum*, in *S. magellanicum*. In *S. molluscum* f. *immersum* the branches are widely spaced as in *S. cuspidatum* f. *plumosum*, and in *S. molluscum* f. *hydrophyllum* the leaflets are enlarged. Comparable tendencies are exhibited here and there among other members of the genus (Paul 1931). *S. subsecundum* is clearly able to tolerate slightly less acidic water than is *S. cuspidatum*; it is quite well known in lakes, and though placed by Paul (1931) in a slightly less hydrophilic category, West (1910) implies that in Scotland *S. subsecundum* may occur in rather deeper waters than does *S. cuspidatum*, and Sørensen (1948) mentions a small submersed form, in acidic lakes in Denmark, with a long thin stalk, bearing scattered leaves and a small apical head. The other species of *Sphagnum* at the lake margin are usually associated with a mat growing at the margin of the lake. Such a floating mat may extend centripetally, to form a quaking bog in the terminal phase of the history of a small acidic lake. There are innumerable notes and descriptions of individual floating mats, without chemical or other data permitting much interpretation.

A more intensive approach is afforded by the works of Sobotka (1967), who has described a number of small seepage lakes, locally known as suchars, east of Suwałki, in the neighborhood of L. Wigry in Poland. The pH of the waters of these lakes varied from 5.0 to 6.9; the variation in calcium contents was considerable, from 2.7 to 24.6 ppm. Marginal mats in which either *Carex lasiocarpa* or *C. limosa*, often associated with *Rhynchospora alba*, occur around the lakes, but the presence of one or the other of the two species of *Carex* seems not to be related to the water chemistry as it is in the Michigan localities discussed in the next section. The zonal distributions of the various species of *Sphagnum* encountered are not given

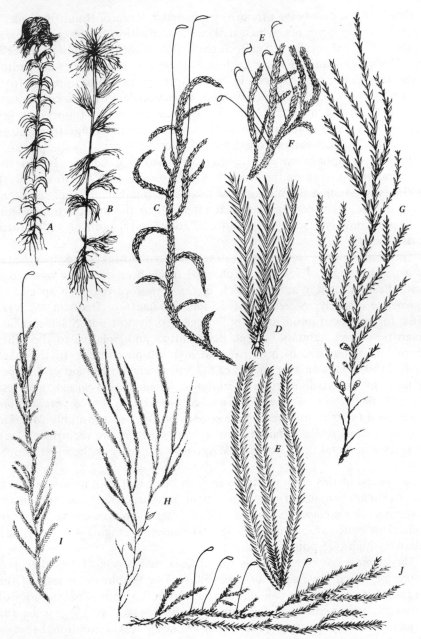

FIGURE 24. Aquatic mosses. *A, Sphagnum cuspidatum; B, S. cuspidatum f. plumosum; C, Scorpidium scorpioides; D, Fissidens julianus; E, F. grandifrons; F, Eurhynchium rusciforme; G, Fontinalis antipyretica* ($\times\frac{1}{2}$); *H, F. dalecarlica; I, Drepanocladus fluitans; J, Amblystegium riparium* (all natural size except G; Paul and Mönkemeyer slightly modified, all presumably based on European material).

in detail, all the data being primarily presented in terms of Braun-Blanquet's phytosociology concepts, which makes the evaluation of the autecologies of the individual species difficult. *S. teres* is recorded from only two localities, having 19.2 and 21.9 mg Ca liter^{-1}; these two occurrences are in line with the behavior of the species in North America, as will be apparent from the next section. *S. magellanicum* and *S. apiculatum* are the two commonest species, occurring in all 21 localities. *S. cuspidatum* was found in seven suchars, but these were distributed throughout the pH range from 5.0 to 6.8 and the calcium range from 5.5 to 16.4 mg Ca liter^{-1}.

Ecology of Sphagnum *in Michigan Senescent Bog Lakes.* By far the most important work on the ecology of *Sphagnum* is that of Vitt and Slack (1975), who studied the marginal ecology of a number of small senescent lakes in Michigan, paying particular attention to the bryophytes present.

They distinguish two types of littoral community, both of which form floating mats.

The *alkaline edge community* is developed around lakes the open water of which has a pH of 7.3–7.8. It forms what has been described as a sedge mat, the dominant plant of which is *Carex lasiocarpa*. Two species of *Sphagnum*, namely, *S. teres* and *S. subsecundum*, are frequent. *S. teres* often forms a continuous mat and is regarded by Vitt and Slack as characteristic of wet habitats of high illumination and, relative to the other species of *Sphagnum*, of high pH and high cation content. In the lakes studied this means an average pH of 6.7 and a calcium content of 7.7 ppm actually in the alkaline edge community. *Sphagnum recurvum* and less often *S. papillosum*, *S. magellanicum*, *S. warnstorfii*, and *S. capillaceum* are present in small numbers. Nine species of liverworts, notably *Moerkia hibernica*, *Cladopodiella fluitans*, and *Pellia epiphylla*, are recorded, as are 11 species of Bryales, of which *Calliergonella cuspidata* is the most important.

Landward of this community there is an open mat community in which the dominant angiosperm is *Vaccinium oxycoccos* and the dominant bryophyte *Sphagnum capillaceum*, which often forms extensive pure red mats. This zone exhibits much lower pH values, averaging 4.9, but is still relatively high (4.5 ppm) in calcium.

The *acidic edge community* is found as a mat around lakes the open waters of which have a pH of from 5.0 to 7.0. Within the mat shelf the mean pH is 5.3 and the calcium concentration 2.3 ppm. The majority of the vegetation consists of *Sphagnum cuspidatum* and *S. papillosum*, the former occurring in wetter places than the latter. Eight additional species of *Sphagnum* are recorded but other bryophytes are rare, only the liverwort *Lophocolea heterophylla* and six species of Bryales being noted. The most important vascular plants are *Cassandra* (= *Chamaedaphne*) *caly-*

culata, *Andromeda glaucophylla*, and the sedges *Carex oligosperma*, *C. limosa*, and *C. paupercula*, the last two being characteristic. Except for the genus *Sphagnum* the number of species and the information-theoretic diversity is less than in the equivalent community of the slightly alkaline lakes.

The open mat community is not typically developed in the acidic bog lakes studied in Michigan. Landward of the acidic mat community there is a shrub–tree mat community which is also developed landward of the open mat in the alkaline bog lakes. It is characterized by *Larix laricina* and *Picea mariana*, with a well-developed ericaceous shrub layer composed of *Ledum groenlandicum* and *Cassandra calyculata*. Two species of *Sphagnum* are found in this zone in large quantities, *S. magellanicum* and *S. recurvum*. The former occurs primarily in the more open drier parts of the community. Still further landward there may be a marginal moat dividing the bog from the surrounding forest. The vegetation of the moat is very variable; in wet conditions *Sphagnum majus* or *S. squarrosum* occur, but where the ground is drier *S. russovii*, *S. recurvum*, *S. girgensonhii*, and *S. magellanicum* are recorded.

The observed zonation leads to a quite complicated arrangement of the species of *Sphagnum* on passing landward from the water's edge. This is expressed diagrammatically by Vitt and Slack (Fig. 25) for their alkaline lakes, typified by Little Lake 16. It must be remembered that in such a series, not only does the water content vary with distance from the lake margin but there is a pH minimum in the open mat. Moreover, the presence of bushes and small trees in the landward zones locally decreases illumination.

The amount of light reaching a *Sphagnum* plant is ecologically at least as important as the water content of the substratum or its chemistry. This factor may well be of significance in determining what species can grow submerged in brown chthoniotrophic waters.

S. teres is in Michigan, as in Europe, one of the least acidophilic species; it is also clearly a hydrophilic sun plant. Its striking development at the edge of the Michigan lakes is presumably due to its developing a floating mat growing out over water just on the alkaline side of neutrality and not excessively poor in calcium. *S. warnstorfii*, which occurs rarely with *S. teres*, is another less acidophilic species, but is evidently a shade plant; its normal habitat in Michigan is in wet wooded situations, notably in *Thuja* forest. The ecological separation of these species is doubtless primarily due to differences in illumination.

S. subsecundum appears mainly at the water's edge in the alkaline lakes; it must be somewhat tolerant of pH values around neutrality and elsewhere is known as an important submersed species.

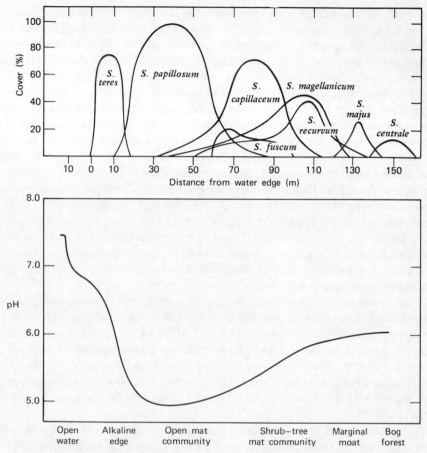

FIGURE 25. Zonation of *Sphagnum* in alkaline edge community (Vitt and Slack).

S. cuspidatum replaces these species as the most hydrophilic *Sphagnum* in the acidic edge community; the difference between *S. subsecundum* and *S. cuspidatum* in pH tolerance observed in Europe evidently also applies in Michigan.

Sphagnum papillosum tends to replace *S. cuspidatum* in the drier parts of the acidic edge community, evidently having a greater tolerance to dry conditions but comparable requirements as to pH and cation content. It is also found landward of the alkaline edge community in some profiles across the mat of mildly alkaline lakes, presumably far enough from the free water for the environment to be quite acidic.

Sphagnum capillaceum is found in quite wet, very acidic, open situations. In the alkaline lake sequence it is the important species of the open mat, which has the lowest pH, though not the lowest calcium content, of any of the communities studied by Vitt and Slack. It can occur in a wide range of water contents, being sometimes found submersed and sometimes on dry hummocks; it evidently requires strong illumination and low pH.

Sphagnum magellanicum, the main species of the shrub–tree mat, is evidently very eurytopic. It is one of the two common species in this landward zone, being found primarily in the more open illuminated areas, often on hummocks, whereas the other species, *S. recurvum*, mainly occurs in hollows and in shaded areas. The main difference between these two species appears to be in the greater water-retaining capacity of *S. magellanicum*. The other species recorded by Vitt and Slack are less common and their ecology largely remains to be elucidated.

Aquatic Bryales. The ordinary mosses make a considerable contribution to the lacustrine flora, at least in soft and moderately hard waters. Fuchsig (1924), for instance, notes no less than 25 species growing submersed in the Lunzer Untersee. As among the liverworts, there are a number of records of terrestrial hygrophilous species growing underwater, often as somewhat differentiated aquatic forms. The most striking case is perhaps that of *Thamnium alopecurus* f. *lemani*, a form of a European species known from wooded ravines and stream banks, which occurs, or used to occur, at a depth of 60 m in the Lake of Geneva (Mönkemeyer 1931). A number of species of the larger genera containing hygrophytes, such as *Bryum* and *Mnium*, may grow in the shallow marginal waters of lakes. *Bryum ventricosum*, a rather elongate and lax species is, for instance, quite important in Lake Fiolen in Sweden down to 4.6 m (see p. 000). Species of *Crateroneurum* such as *C. commutatum* have aquatic forms of some importance in streams.

Certain genera contain well-defined aquatic species or are exclusively found in water. Most of these water mosses are of rather characteristic elongate form (Fig. 24).

A number of species of *Fissidens* are aquatic, more perhaps living in running than in standing water, but *F. crassipes* and *F. adiantoides* occur in the infralittoral of the Lunzer Untersee, and the latter species, which is widespread as a terrestrial moss, reaches to 74 m in Lake Tahoe (Frantz and Cordone 1967), a depth surpassed among identifiable species of mosses only by *F. grandifrons* (*E* of Fig. 24), which occurs at 122 m[11].

---

[11] Unidentified fragments of mosses occurred at 164 m, but may not represent plants growing in situ.

The ecology of *F. julianus* (*D* of Fig. 24) in Scandinavia has been studied in detail by Lohammar (1954b). The species is here at the northern limit of its range, which includes most of Europe and parts of North America and of Africa, and in the north does not reproduce sexually. It is easily killed by being frozen and so occurs only below the level of the winter ice. It is a fairly shade-tolerant species and can penetrate to a depth of up to 4 m in the productive lakes in which it lives. It is found in eutrophic but not heavily polluted waters, growing on rocks, shells, as an epiphyte, and in some cases perhaps on bare mud surfaces. It is extensively eaten by mollusks such as *Lymnaea stagnalis* and *Coretus corneus*. In aquariums these species will feed on *F. julianus* but not on *Fontinalis antipyretica* or *Drepanocladus aduncus*. Lohammar thinks that the rather peculiar distribution of the moss in Scandinavia, primarily in the region around Lake Mälar, is due to this area providing adequately eutrophic waters which are not too abundantly colonized by gastropods.

In the Amblystegiaceae, *Amblystegium riparium* (*J* of Fig. 24), *Scorpidium scorpioides* (*C* of Fig. 24) (cf. West 1910), several species of *Calliergon* and *Hygrohypnum*, and most significantly various members of *Drepanocladus* are aquatic. Like *Fissidens julianus*, *Amblystegium riparium* is extensively eaten by mollusks. In some lakes, such as Lake Erken, it is found only above water level; in such cases apparently the large molluscan populations prevent it from being an aquatic species. Unlike *F. julianus* it can withstand winter conditions out of water, but apart from this capacity the two species are ecologically quite similar and often co-occur (Lohammar 1954b). The most important aquatic species of *Drepanocladus* occurring in lakes are *D. fluitans* (*I* of Fig. 24), *D. exannulatus*, *D. sendtneri*, and *D. aduncus*. All are essentially aquatic, *D. fluitans* perhaps more so than the others; these at times may grow out of water, producing a less elongate, more branched plant. Transfer of the latter to water produces long unbranched stems growing from a branched base, and the water form when growing above the surface may develop the aerial branched habit (Mönkemeyer 1931). The water forms have larger, more widely spaced leaves, larger leaf cells, and larger and more numerous alar cells (Zastrow 1934).

In the Brachytheciaceae, in which there are several species of water mosses mainly in streams and waterfalls, *Eurhynchium rusciforme* (*F* of Fig. 24), though also rheophile, may occasionally be an important member of the lacustrine flora, as West (1910) found at the south end of Loch Doon, Kirkcudbrightshire, Scotland, in 1–1.5 m of water, where it was growing with *Fontinalis antipyretica*. Pearsall (1920) has noticed the same association in the English lakes.

The family Fontinalaceae is now limited (Welch 1960) to contain three genera, all of which are primarily aquatic. *Fontinalis* and *Dichelyma* are

Holarctic, the former reaching south to Ethiopia, the latter possibly to the West Indies; the third genus *Brachelyma* has only two species, in southeastern North America. Welch recognizes 20 species of *Fontinalis;* most of the published records say little about ecology.[12] At least *F. antipyretica* (*G.* of Fig. 25), *F. dalecarlica* (*H.* of Fig. 24), with the doubtfully distinct var. *macounii* from Lake Athabasca and its vicinity, *F. kindbergii, F. novaeangliae, F. hypnoides, F. nitida* if a distinct species, and *F. duriaei* are apparently recorded from lakes, though in all cases the majority of the records are either from rivers or from unspecified localities. Most of these species seem to be eurytopic, but since a number are sympatric, there must be more specific autecology than has been elucidated. *F. squamosa* is a species of rapid streams which at least in the past has been washed into lakes and buried in quantity in the sediments, as occurred in Windermere in early postglacial times (Pennington 1962). *F. antipyretica* is well known in warm and in cold, in still and in flowing, in acidic and in alkaline waters. Pearsall (1917) noted in Esthwaite that it occurred on mud below the mouths of streams, in which twigs and dead leaves were mixed; the organic content of the deposits on which the moss grew in this lake was about 19%. Pearsall suggested that the allochthonous organic matter and better aeration below the stream mouth may have accounted for the distribution of the species. Probably sources of carbon dioxide are involved, but in other lakes, he noted it at times on bare rock (cf. p. 151).

The greatest depth records are from Lake Tahoe, where *F. nitida* occurs at 122 m (Frantz and Cordone 1967), and Crater Lake, Oregon, where Hasler (1938) records *Fontinalis* sp. at 120 m.

All the abundant and eurytopic species are apt to be extremely variable, the forms observed probably being mainly ecophenes. In the extreme case of *Fontinalis antipyretica* very large plants may occur in deep waters; f. *lacustris* from 8 to 25 m in the Lunzer Untersee is over 80 cm long (Fuchsig 1924), and a comparable development is exhibited by f. *gigantea* in various American aquatic localities, not necessarily lacustrine (Welch 1960). Such forms are among the tallest mosses now living.

Brachelyma with two species in southeastern North America may be found floating in quiet waters, and the third genus of the family, *Dichelyma*, contains several species, some of which may grow in places where they become emersed at times; at least the western North American *D. uncinatum* and the Holarctic *D. capillaceum* are recorded from lakes (Welch 1960).

---

[12] This is unhappily true of most large systematic works on cryptogamic botany, where localities are recorded with loving accuracy, but only the geographic and ecological wisdom of the reader enables him to decide if such localities lie at the bottoms of lakes or among the sand hills of deserts.

The other genera formerly placed in the Fontinalaceae, namely, the South African *Wardia*, now in the Wardiaceae, and the South American *Hydropogon* and *Hydropogonella*, now in the Hydropogonaceae, are apparently rheobiont (Welch 1943).

At least in some genera of mosses quite clear-cut ecological differences are apparent between the different aquatic species. Sørensen (1948, cf. also Iversen 1929) has summarized the available data for the Danish species of *Drepanocladus*. *D. fluitans* in Denmark apparently never occurs above pH 5.6, and is usually found below pH 4.5. *D. exannulatus* is also found in acidic waters but exhibits a slightly wider observed range of tolerated pH values, from 3.2 to 6.2. *D revolvens* is a transcursional species ranging from 4.9 to 8.0, and *D. aduncus* is known from pH 5.0 to 9.2. Other records, notably those of Wynne (1944), indicate likewise that *D. fluitans* occurs in the most acidic situations and that *D. aduncus* tolerates more calcareous waters than do the other species; Wynne's remarks on ecology and distribution suggest that in North America *D. fluitans* is not limited to such extremely acidic waters as it seems to inhabit in Denmark. *D. aduncus* is far more tolerant of brackish conditions, up to 2360 mg Cl liter,$^{-1}$ than are any of the other species (Sørensen 1948). There are other ecological differences exhibited by more or less sympatric members of the genus, *D. revolvens* being commonly found only partly submersed, whereas *D. fluitans* appears ordinarily to be fully aquatic, with the other species somewhat intermediate between these two. In the genus *Calliergon*, *C. cordifolium* is found over a wider range of pH values (3.8–8.2) than is *C. giganteum* (5.2–7.4) though their tolerance of bicarbonate alkalinity appears to be about the same. A more complete study would probably permit the definition of quite well defined ecological niches for the species of these and other genera of aquatic mosses.

No bryophytes are known (see p. 000) to be able to utilize HCO_3^- in photosynthesis as a carbon source. This puts the group at a disadvantage relative to the majority of angiosperms in hard water.

It is evident from the extreme depths at which they have been found in Crater Lake, Lake Tahoe, and the clearest Wisconsin lakes, that mosses, like liverworts and the Characeae, can penetrate far more deeply into such transparent lakes than can any freshwater flowering plants. It seems likely, however, that in shallow waters, in which both bryophytes and angiosperms are potentially capable of existing, the former often suffer from competitive exclusion by the latter. Bryophytes may well exist so long as there are bare stones or rock surfaces for them to colonize, but the deposition of fine material, which would not necessarily exclude mosses at great depths, may do so if it permits the establishment of flowering plants; Sayre (1945) specifically noted this for *Fontinalis* in Colorado. These relationships naturally produce ecological succession and zonation.

The eutrophication and consequent decrease in transparency of Furesø have been accompanied by a great reduction in the moss flora of the lake from which *Scorpidium scorpioides*, *Drepanocladus sendtnerii*, and *D. aduncus* have disappeared (Christensen and Andersen 1958). Comparable changes are likely to have taken place, unnoticed or unrecorded, in other lakes.

SUMMARY

The rooted macroscopic vegetation of lakes consists of Charophyceae, Bryophyta, and Tracheophyta. The first two of these groups are presumably more ancient than the third, and although they flourish in quite different circumstances, both today seem to be strikingly limited by competition with the higher plants constituting the third group.

The Charophyceae are best regarded as a class of green algae, though many students of the group remove it from the Chlorophyta and make of it a separate phylum, the Charophyta. There is a single order, the Charales, containing at least five fossil families and a single living one, the Characeae. The group is known from the Devonian and quite likely reached its highest development in the Jurassic.

The plants consist of an upright stem divided into multicellular nodes from which branches arise, separated by long internodal cells which may be covered with filamentous spirally arranged cells derived from the nodes and constituting the cortex. The plant is anchored by rhizoids, one cell thick. The largest species are over 1 m high, the smallest not more than 3 cm. The general level of organization is not much less specialized than that of the Bryophyta but the Charophyceae are haploid throughout almost their entire life history; meiosis occurs at the first or second division of the zygote.

The Characeae consist of two tribes, the Chareae including *Chara*, *Lamprothamnium*, *Lychnothamnus* and *Nitellopsis*, and the Nitelleae containing only *Nitella* and *Tolypella*. *Chara*, *Nitella*, and *Nitellopsis* are the most important genera in lakes. The number of species depends entirely on the taxonomic judgment of the investigator. Wood gives a critical polynomial system which he believes to have biological validity and a binomial system of microspecific names which are convenient to use if not treated too seriously. It is possible that some of his microspecies would satisfy contemporary criteria of specific rank.

Germination of the oospore at least in cool temperate regions apparently takes place after a diapause of some months in cold water. A rising temperature and a low redox potential may be necessary in temperate but apparently not in more tropical species. The role of light is uncertain. Passage through the alimentary canal of a duck does not injure the oospores; ducks enjoy feeding on Charophyceae, and they are probably important agents of dispersal.

In germination a primary protonema is formed, from which the main shoot of the new plant is developed, but accessory protonemata are also formed, so that a number of adjacent individuals may form a clone. Asexual reproduction by bulbils, developed from the rhizoids from nodes low on the stem, is found in some species. In *Chara canescens* in the Old World, ordinary sexual reproduction among dioecious individuals occurs only in Italy eastward to Asia Minor and in equivalent latitudes in China. Further north males are absent and the species is parthenogenetic. This pattern is reminiscent of though not identical with, what happens in some flowering plants such as the water soldier *Stratiotes aloides* and in certain notostracan Crustacea. Many species of *Chara* appear to be perennials, and in cool temperate regions some of them retain their green shoots throughout the year, provided they are not in contact with ice. Such green fields of *Chara* may provide important winter habitats for small animals, notably the Cladocera. Sexual reproduction usually occurs in the summer and autumn, the ripening of the antheridia and oogonia being dependent on the photoperiod. Some species of *Nitella* are apparently short-day plants; their sexual structures may develop as early as the second half of March. In one species, the Japanese *N. imahorii*, there seem to be both vernal and autumnal sexual periods, the plants dying down during the hot intervening time.

The Characeae are mostly freshwater plants, though some are found in brackish waters. They are important in the Baltic but are not found in truly marine habitats. *Chara* usually occur in hard water and most species of *Nitella* in soft or circumneutral water. There is much overlap, but a very rich flora of a number of species of *Chara* seems to develop only in calcareous waters. It is probable that most taxa of *Chara* and some of *Nitella* take up HCO_3^- ions from alkaline water as a source of CO_2 in photosynthesis. The dehydroxylation of the HCO_3^- produces OH^- ions which are pumped out into the surrounding water, increasing the pH locally. In many species of *Chara* and in some other members of the family incrustations of calcium carbonate are deposited on the plant, apparently as the result of this process. Where information exists as to the uptake of HCO_3^- it is evident that $CaCO_3$ is also deposited. In some ecorticate species the outward movement of OH^- ions is limited to particular regions of the plant, so that a banded deposit of $CaCO_3$ is produced.

There is evidence that an excess of phosphate is inhibitory to most or all species of the group and may prove to be a major ecological factor in regulating distributions. Circumstances increasing the phosphorus concentration of a lake, as happened after a catastrophic dry period in Lake Tåkern in Sweden, may cause the disappearance of the Charophycean flora.

Experimental studies in which plants have been hung above mud, with and without rhizoids, rather than allowed to remain rooted in the bottom deposits, clearly indicates the rhizoids to be organs of nutrition. The permeability of such rhizoids may be different from that of the photosynthetic cells. Transport along the stem may be promoted by cyclosis.

The various published chemical analyses of *Chara* and *Nitella* were all made on material determined to genus alone and are probably not really comparable. Part of the variability in these analyses is due to encrusting calcium carbonate. Magnesium seems generally rather high, as in the angiosperms richest in the element. No other generalization is possible at present.

The rhizoids, at least of *Chara globularis*, are apparently able to tolerate 100 times as much H_2S in the mud in which they are rooted, as the green parts are able to withstand dissolved in water.

There is a persistent belief that some species of Charophyceae produce substances inimicable to mosquito larvae, or that they inhibit oviposition by female mosquitoes on the surface film above the plants. The evidence, based on many species of *Chara* and *Nitella* and many of mosquitoes, is conflicting, though some individual experiments seem convincing. Both mechanical impediment by minute gas bubbles produced photosynthetically and the chemical effects of some substance related to those in garlic oil, such as allicin, have been held responsible for these effects.

The nature of the substratum, the radiation flux reaching the plants through the water, and the degree of stillness or disturbance of the latter are presumably the most important physical factors directly or, through their effects on the direction of competition, indirectly controlling the distribution of the Charophyceae within a single chemically homogeneous lake. In no single case is a complete analysis of the action available.

Chara aspera and *Ch. fragifera*, both species with many bulbils, occur primarily in shallow water on sandy bottoms; the bulbils may act as anchors as well as reproductive bodies. *Nitella confervacea* usually lives in, rather than on, shallow mud. *Nitella flexilis* and *N. opaca* in the English Lake District appear to be more tolerant of ongoing silting than is *Isoetes lacustris*, and the distribution of *Nitella* in the neighborhood of islands and estuaries is determined by this. Most species of Charophyceae are obviously shade-tolerant and in transparent lakes extend to much greater depths than do angiosperms. *Nitella opaca* extends to 38–40 m in Lake Vrana, Cherso, and to a like depth of 40 m in Lake Vättern in Sweden. *Chara virgata* f. *barbata* extends to 65.5 m in Lake Tahoe. In such localities angiosperms in general hardly reach to 10 m. The maximum depth of occurrence of *Chara globularis* in Japanese lakes is almost exactly the same as the Secchi disk transparency.

The height of a plant of a given species is clearly inversely related to the illumination that it receives, but the extent of the variation differs from species to species in a way not related to the depth ranges of the taxa under consideration.

Some of the deeper-living species such as *Nitellopsis obtusa* may be limited by a tendency to break when the water is much disturbed, as may happen in the upper infralittoral.

Among the three classes of Bryophyta, the Anthocerotae have but few aquatic members, and none occur perennially submersed in lakes. The other two classes, the Hepaticae or liverworts and the Musci or mosses, contribute almost as much to the freshwater vegetation as do the Charophyceae.

Among the Hepaticae a number of species growing otherwise in wet terrestrial situations may be found living submersed, sometimes at considerable depths. Often, but not always, the submersed plants exhibit special morphological features, or may even be characterized as aquatic vicariant species, being larger, laxer, and sexually sterile. This is well exemplified by aquatic *Marchantia aquatica* compared with *M. polymorpha*. In *Cephalozia bicuspidata* the most extreme terrestrial form is but a few millimeters high, whereas var. *aquatica* can have stems 30 cm long. The deepest record is for *Blepharostoma arachnoideum* at 110 m in Lake Tahoe. *Marsupella marginata* var. *aquatica* can be a very important member of the benthic community, as in Latnjajaure in Swedish Lappland; it covers 40% of the lake bottom, reaching to 32.5 m where the light is reduced to about 1.1% of its surface value. As in other cases the stems are very elongate at such depths. Nearly all the ordinary liverworts that can grow submersed belong to the Jungermanniales. It is probable that they are much more likely to occur in soft, but not extremely acidic, rather than in hard waters. In spite of the abundance of liverworts in tropical rain forests and their frequent colonization of tropical streams, no fully submersed species are recorded from the lakes of Indonesia, the only tropical area properly studied. In addition to the species with close, usually infraspecific, allies on land, two specialized types of aquatic liverwort are known. The first belong to the *Ricciaceae* in the Marchantiales; several species of *Riccia* and *Ricciocarpus natans* live pleustonically in the protected marginal parts, often among reeds, of eutrophic lakes. The second type comprises the genus *Riella* in the Riellaceae, a very specialized family of the Jungermanniales. *Riella* contains at least 16 species of plants, 1.5–6 cm long, consisting of a stem bearing one or, more rarely, two platelike wings, and a number of small leaflets. They seem to be characteristic of the temporary waters of semiarid regions, reaching their greatest development in North and South Africa.

Among the mosses the *Sphagnales*, containing the single family Sphagnaceae and genus *Sphagnum*, are often aquatic and an important part of the flora of acidic lakes, found both fully submersed as in the cases of *S. subsecundum* and *S. cuspidatum* or forming a marginal floating mat, as is often the case with *S. teres*, *S. magellanicum* and *S. rubellum*. Such a mat growing centripetally may be very important in causing the final disappearance of a senescent bog lake. The specific composition of the *Sphagnum* flora varies with the pH and calcium content. It is probable that all species require a quite acidic environment but that some species are more efficient than others in fixing calcium and lowering the pH in the immediate vicinity of their active cells. Of the more hydrophilic species *S. teres* tolerates more calcium, about 7.7 mg liter^{-1} at pH of 6.7 as a mean figure in Michigan, compared with *S. cuspidatum* typically tolerating 2.3 mg liter^{-1} Ca at pH 5.3. On the mat in which at least the tops of the plants are aerial, the water content and degree of shading are important environmental factors. Underwater the transparency, and thus the irradiance, where the mosses are growing may quite probably regulate the specific composition of the *Sphagnum* flora of a lake.

Many ordinary hygrophilous terrestrial mosses have aquatic forms growing underwater, comparable to the facultatively aquatic liverworts. *Thamnium alopecurus* f. *lemani* is a conspicuous example in the Lake of Geneva recorded from a depth of 60 m. Other species occur in the genera *Bryum* and *Mnium*.

Several genera among the Bryales contain well-defined aquatic species or are exclusively found in water. In *Fissidens* there are a number of rheophile species; *F. adiantoides*, a widespread and often terrestrial moss, is found in lakes, going to 74 m in Lake Tahoe, where *F. grandifrons* descends to 122 m. In *Drepanocladus* several species with characteristic calcium and pH optima and ranges are important water mosses, though some of these can also grow aerially. *Fontinalis* is another important genus in freshwaters, *F. nitida* reaching 122 in Lake Tahoe, and an unidentified species to a comparable depth of 120 m in Crater Lake, Oregon.

The very widespread *F. antipyretica*, when growing in fairly deep water, up to 25 m in some European lakes, and apparently under some other circumstances in springs, may reach a height of 80 cm and thus be one of the tallest mosses now living. The commoner aquatic mosses are obviously facultative shade plants and provided adequate light is available can penetrate to depths far below those inhabited by angiosperms. In shallow water on silted bottoms the latter are obviously able to successfully compete with mosses, which are then usually confined to bare stones or rock surfaces.

No bryophytes are known to use HCO_3^- as a source of carbon inphotosynthesis; in hard waters this must put them at a great competitive disadvantage with respect to the Charophyceae and most hard-water angiosperms. Most mosses are apparently not eaten by aquatic snails; this is not true, however, of *Fissidens julianus* nor of *Amblystegium riparium*. The latter species, being resistant to freezing, is apt to live at the water's edge or just above it, where snails cannot go, but *F. julianus*, which cannot survive being frozen, is severely restricted in Sweden at the northern limit of its range, and is confined to lakes poor in gastropod mollusks.

By limiting the extent of the euphotic zone, decline in transparency may be more inimicable to the bryophytes of a lake than to the angiosperms, since the latter are evidently effective competitors in shallower, and the former in deeper water.

CHAPTER 28

The Nature and Diversity of
Aquatic Tracheophytes

The higher water plants are mostly angiosperms, but there are also a few ferns and members of the related groups that often are called fern allies. In this chapter all these plants are considered briefly by systematic categories, in order to indicate what kinds of higher plants may be important in limnology and to call attention again to some fairly well-known if not fully understood general features of the taxonomic composition of the freshwater flora. After this presentation an ecological classification of the life-forms of aquatic plants is attempted, based eclectically on the work of a number of authors. This classification, though primarily of significance when distributions of plants in individual lakes are considered in Chapter 31, is needed occasionally in the two intervening chapters.

AQUATIC MEMBERS OF THE LOWER TRACHEOPHYTA

The number of genera of tracheophytes other than spermatophytes, containing plants inhabiting inland waters is small, but some of the species included in such genera are of great limnological interest. Little is known of the physiological mechanisms of their adaptation to aquatic life, but that little does suggest that the processes are not unlike those involved in the comparable adaptation of the angiosperms.

Lycopsida. In the Lycopodiaceae, *Lepidotis* (*Lycopodium* p.p.) *inundata* is a more or less aquatic plant (Vol. II, *C* of Fig. 4) which may occur as part of the marginal or eulittoral vegetation of lakes in the Holarctic region. Of far greater importance is the family Isoeteaceae which includes the very widespread genus *Isoetes*, and the endemic branched *Stylites* from the eulittoral of lakes in the Andes (Amstutz 1957; Rauh and Falk 1959; Sculthorpe 1967). The family is closer to the Selaginellaceae than to the Lycopodiaceae, but is probably closer still to the Mesozoic Pleuromeiaceae, and may perhaps be a reduced descendant of the well-known Lepidodendrales of the late Paleozoic (Sculthorpe 1967 gives an interesting discussion).

Isoetes is almost cosmopolitan but tends to disappear at low altitudes in the tropics. It has Australian representatives and two endemic species in New Zealand. There are in all about 60 species, most of which are aquatic and often of great limnological importance. All the members of the genus are small and superficially similar plants. The stem is very short and bears a tuft of quill-like leaves from which the vernacular name of quillwort was derived. Spores are produced in two kinds of sporangia on the ventral sides of the leaf bases. Most of the taxonomy of the group depends on the sculpture of the megaspores. *Isoetes lacustris* (Fig. 26) and *I. setacea* (= *echinospora*) are the widespread aquatic species in Europe. When they occur in the same lake they presumably have different ecological requirements, though it is not clear what these requirements are. In Lake Fiolen (see p. 434) *I. setacea* seems limited to eroding bottoms in very shallow water, and *I. lacustris* is commoner in deeper water, growing where neither erosion nor deposition dominate. In contrast to this, Clapham, Tutin, and Warburg (1962) indicate that *I. setacea* occurs in Britain on peaty bottoms and *I. lacustris* only when at most a thin layer of peat covers an inorganic deposit. Jermy (1964) in the *Flora Europaea* (Tutin, Heywood, Burges, Valentine, Walters, and Webb, Eds. 1964) thinks *setacea* occurs in more oligotrophic localities than does *lacustris*. Seddon (1965) gives evidence that the two species are both usually restricted to relatively oligotrophic localities by competition and is unable to indicate any significant ecological differences between them, though *I. setacea* in Wales, as in Sweden, seems a plant of windswept, eroding shores. In addition to these two widespread species a few local endemics are accepted in the *Flora Europaea*. Thus *I. brochonii* is known in up to 4 m of water in some of the mountain lakes of the Pyrenees, *I. boryana* occurs in the shallow lakes of the southwestern coast of France, *I. delilei* occurs in small lakes in southern France and in parts of the Iberian Peninsula, and *I. azorica* is recorded from small lakes in the Azores. In contrast to these species, the very large *I. malinverniana*, with leaves up to 80 cm long, is rheophile, living in irrigation ditches in northern Italy. There are also a number of species known growing in wet ground at the margins of lakes or in depressions that are flooded seasonally.

The aquatic species, as Goebel (1879) noted for *I. lacustris* and *I. setacea* in the Vosges mountains, may become pseudoviviparous in deep water, the sporangia being replaced by plantlets which become detached. This is now known elsewhere, as in *I. lacustris* in Windermere (Manton 1950).

The members of the genus in other parts of the world present an ecological spectrum comparable to that of the European species. Of the mainland North American members of *Isoetes*, *I. braunii* (*I. echinospora* var. *braunii*) is the most widespread and apparently may occur in Iceland, as well as Greenland, where *I. lacustris* is also recorded[1] (Polunin 1959). *I. macrospora* is an important lacustrine species in the Great Lakes region and eastward; *I. bolanderii* in the Rocky Mountains, Cascade Range, and Sierra Nevada and *I. howellii* of comparable range but perhaps in shallower stations, are of some limnological importance. Muenscher (1944) gives notes on the habitats of other species which are often marginally aquatic or even terrestrial; some occur on tidal flats. In temperate South America *I. savatierii* occurs in the infralittoral of the large oligotrophic lake Nahuel Haupi[2] in Argentina (Thomasson 1959), evidently behaving ecologically like *I. lacustris* in Scandinavia. In the Andes *I. lechleri* and possibly other species are found in the smaller and colder lakes that drain into Lake Titicaca but not in the latter lake itself (Tutin 1940).

In Japan *I. asiatica* is lacustrine, and *I. japonica* tends to inhabit slowly running streams (Ohwi 1965). Two species are certainly lacustrine at considerable altitudes in New Guinea, *I. habbemensis* in Lake Habbema and on Mt. Wilhelmina at altitudes of 3223–3660 m, and *I. neoguineensis* in the shallow waters of lakes in eastern New Guinea (Alston 1959). The two New Zealand species, *I. kirkii* and *I. alpina*, both endemic, are found in lakes. They may co-occur, as in Lake Taupo, but nothing seems to be known of their detailed ecological requirements. Though the genus as a whole consists of a rather uniform array of rooted rosette plants, it is clearly capable of considerable autecological, and so presumably physiological, specialization.

Sphenopsida. In the genus *Equisetum*, *E. fluviatile* (= *limosum* auctt.) is often a quite important member of the emergent vegetation of the eulittoral and upper infralittoral of lakes of North Temperate latitudes (Vol II, *D* in

---

[1] Polunin (1959) records "*I. echinospora* s.l. (incl. *I. muricata; I. braunii* of many authors)," as well as *I. lacustris* from Greenland; the former record probably implies *I. braunii*.

[2] In Vol. I, p. 170 a reputed depth of over 1000 m was noted for this lake, but with great reservations as to the validity of the record. Thomasson gives 438 m as the greatest known depth and thinks that a much greater figure is unlikely. Thomasson's paper contains important material on the thermal cycle of the lake.

FIGURE 26. *Isoetes lacustris*. *A*, large individual growing in detritus gyttja; *B*, aged individual from same optimum habitat as *A*, with a tendency to quadripartite root system; *C*, reduced plants from among rhizomes of *Schoenoplectus; D*, small typical specimen from very shallow water; *E*, f, *curvifolium* from same habitat as *D*. All ×⅖, from Lake Fiolen in Sweden (drawn from photographs of Thunmark).

Fig. 4). It can grow in water 1.5 m deep and may reach 1 m above the surface. Hybrids (*E.* × *litorale*) between the more aquatic *E. fluviatile* and the more terrestrial *E. arvense* are not uncommon in Europe.

   Filicineae.   The genus *Ceratopteris* (Ceratopteraceae) contains about six species distributed throughout part of the tropics and adjacent subtropics. Some species, such as *C. cornuta*, are apparently pleustonic, others such as

C. pteridoides (Vol. II, *H* of Fig. 4), *C. thalictroides*, and the tropical American *C. deltoides* usually float submersed, but may attach to the bottom by their roots if stranded on mud.

The distribution of *C. pteridoides* is highly disjunct, the species occurring in the New World from just north of the Tropic of Capricorn in Florida to just south of the Tropic of Cancer in South America, and then again in southeast Asia from near the equator at Singapore northward into southern China and as far as central Honshu in Japan. In its Asiatic range it is largely sympatric with *C. thalictroides*. The latter species can occasionally cover large areas of water, as in the Brokopando Dam on the Suriname River in Surinam (Leentvaar 1966).

In addition to this widespread and highly adapted aquatic genus, a few other homosporous ferns such as *Dryopteris* may occur marginally in lakes. *Microsorium pteropus* can grow underwater; the sporangia may then be replaced by plantlets that become detached (Sculthorpe 1967), as has just been noted in the case of *Isoetes*. *Microlepia speluncae*, a large fern of the family Dennstaedtiaceae, is known as a more or less amphibious species in wet forests and swamps in the warmer parts of the Old World (Wild 1961). A related fern, *Dennstaedtiopsis aerenchymata*, the structure of which shows typical modification for aquatic life (see p. 203), lived in swamps or at the edges of lakes (Arnold and Dougherty 1964; Robison and Person 1973) during the Eocene in the northwestern part of North America.

Heterosporous aquatic ferns. The other aquatic ferns are more specialized and some are very reduced. They are all heterosporous and seem but distantly related to the other Filicinaeae. It has even been suggested (Meeuse 1961) that they are reduced descendants of the glossopterids or pteridosperms of the late Paleozoic. Whatever their origin, some of them are of great limnological importance.

In the Marsileaceae, *Marsilea* has numerous aquatic species with floating quadrifoliate (Vol. II, *A* of Fig. 4) leaves at the ends of long petioles; the genus is chiefly found in the warmer parts of the world. The related *Pilularia* with filiform undivided leaves is generally less aquatic than most aquatic species of *Marsilea* though some species of both genera seem to have submersed, semiaquatic, and usually sterile terrestrial forms. The full life history may depend on the flooding and drying of the habitat, sporocarps maturing as the plants are exposed and the gametophytes developing when the water level again rises. The same sort of life history is exhibited by the rare *Regnellidium diphyllum* in Brazil, the sole member of the third genus of Marsileaceae (Johnson and Chrysler 1938).

The other two genera of heterosporous aquatic ferns are members of related, generically monotypic, families, *Salvinia* in the Salviniaceae and *Azolla* in the Azollaceae. Both genera consist of several species of pleustonic plants (Vol. II, *E, F* of Fig. 4), found mainly, though not exclusively, in warmer latitudes. *Salvinia* can sometimes produce enormous floating populations covering the surfaces of very large bodies of water, particularly when these are artificial, recently filled, and easily invaded by non-native species (see pp. 252, 253). *Azolla* with half a dozen species is of considerable interest as it supports the symbiotic *Anabaena azollae*, a nitrogen-fixing organism; it occasionally can become a nuisance (Wild 1961).

THE NATURE AND DIVERSITY OF AQUATIC SPERMATOPHYTES

Some gymnosperms grow rooted in swamps, where their roots may, for a large part of the year, be covered with water. *Taxodium distichum* of southeastern North America provides an important example. Formally such plants may be regarded as almost as aquatic as some of the reeds. Except where a swamp forest impinges on a lake they are not likely to be of great limnological importance though their existence should not be forgotten. Some swamp forest trees among the angiosperms may have a comparable significance.

Nature and diversity of the angiosperm flora of inland waters.   A number of problems arise as soon as we begin to look at the rooted vegetation of lakes. In this section certain cases of uneven distribution of aquatic species among major taxa are first considered, as this kind of distribution calls attention to various important aspects of the biology of freshwater plants.

Relationship of the number of species of dicotyledonous water plants to that of the monocotyledonous aquatic species.   When any extensive local aquatic flora is examined, the proportion of monocotyledonous to dicotyledonous species is ordinarily at least one to one, whereas in terrestrial floras the proportion is ordinarily one to four or five. Thus in Lake Constance, Schröter and Kirchner (1896) found 40 species of monocotyledons and 38 of dicotyledons. In Indonesia, Ruttner (1933) noted 25 species of submersed or floating-leaved water plants, 15 being monocotyledonous and 10 dicotyledonous. For the whole truly aquatic flora of the United States, as treated by Muenscher (1944), the ratio is almost two to one in favor of the monocotyledonous species. Sculthorpe (1967) in his admirable treatment of the aquatic vascular plants has tabulated the approximate number of genera and species in the characteristically aquatic families of the flowering plants of the world.[3] His table admittedly is distorted by the

---

[3] Sculthorpe gives about 25 for the number of genera of Podostemaceae. The latest edition of Willis's *A Dictionary of the Flowering Plants and Ferns* (Willis and Airy Shaw 1966) gives the family as containing 45 genera and 130 species. The figures have not been changed in reproducing Sculthorpe's table in order to preserve consistency of approach to the problem.

TABLE 6. *Approximate numbers of genera and species of water plants in the Dicotyledones and in the Monocotyledones*

	No. of Genera	No. of Species	Ratio No. Genera /No. Species
Dicotyledones total	51	~391	0.130
Without Podostemaceae	26	~271	0.096
Podostemaceae alone	25	~120	0.208
Monocotyledones total	65	~447	0.126
Ratio of Dicotyledones to Monocotyledones	0.79	0.82	0.96
Ratio of Dicotyledones without Podostemaceae to Monocotyledones	0.40	0.57	0.70

inclusion of the few terrestrial species in certain aquatic families such as the Haloragaceae, and the exclusion of a number of odd aquatic species in otherwise terrestrial families. The first of these distortions probably exaggerates the number of dicotyledonous species, but the second probably does not have any very significant effect. The totals and ratios obtained from Sculthorpe's table are given in Table 6.

The results clearly indicate that even if the rheobiont Podostemaceae are included, the monocotyledonous species outnumber the dicotyledonous. For the groups of which the flora of lakes is composed, the disproportion is even greater. If the ratio of number of genera to number of species can be used as one kind of measure of morphological diversity and so of some kinds of specialization, the two great divisions hardly differ. This, however, is due to the inclusion of the Podostemaceae; without them the generic diversity is greater in the Monocotyledones than in the Dicotyledones, owing largely to the numerous genera of two rather primitive families, the Hydrocharitaceae and Alismataceae.

The comparisons that have just been made appear on further analysis to be a little misleading if they are not qualified. J. Hutchinson (1959) divided the Dicotyledones into two groups, the Lignosae and the Herbaceae.[4] The classification then given by him is used in this work. Hutchinson's two groups are in some respects each coordinate with the Monocotyledones. As appears in a later paragraph, the Lignosae have few aquatic members. A considerable proportion of the aquatic Herbaceae belong to the order Ranales, which is presumably distantly related to the ancestors

---

[4] I am well aware that this division has not found general acceptance among botanists. It is adopted in this book because it appears to correspond to some general, if rather vague, biological difference related to the capacity to colonize water.

of the Monocotyledones. The true situation would therefore seem to be a superdispersed pattern with the probability of occurrence of aquatic species being least in the Lignosae and in some of the higher order of Herbaceae such as the Asteraceae or Compositae, and greatest in the Lythrales (cf., however, p. 89 fn. 6), Ranales, and the Monocotyledones Calyciferae. If the last two groups can be legitimately regarded as related, their higher probability of aquatic adaptation may imply some sort of very generalized ancestral preadaptation, though admittedly one of unknown nature.

The wide distribution of aquatic angiosperms. Although a number of otherwise terrestrial families may contain isolated aquatic genera and species, most of the characteristic lacustrine plants, particularly those that are submersed, belong to a restricted number of specialized families containing few genera of immensely wide distribution, as was pointed out by Darwin (1859) over a century ago. Within such widely distributed genera, there are sometimes, as in *Potamogeton*, very many species, but more usually the number of species is quite small. Arber (1920) supposed that, omitting the Podostemaceae, the range of the average species of water plant is greater than that of the average land plant. Within a genus, large or small, species of immense range, such as *Potamogeton crispus*, *P. perfoliatus*, and *P. pusillus*, or in the very small genus *Ceratophyllum*, *C. demersum*, or again in the hyperhydate *Phragmites*, *P. australis*,[5] may occur in favorable habitats essentially throughout the world.

Dicotyledones Lignosae. Most of the 54 orders of the division consist mainly or exclusively of woody plants, specialized therefore toward vertical extension into the air. However, in a number of the larger orders of the division, which is far more diversified than is the Herbaceae, there are considerable minorities of secondarily herbaceous species which when taken together may well compare with the total number of Herbaceae. Though one would expect few aquatic plants in groups that are primarily arboreal, the number included in the secondarily herbaceous Lignosae does seem small.

In the Euphorbiales, the Euphorbiaceae contain a single pleustonic species of the otherwise terrestrial *Phyllanthus*, *P. fluitans* (Fig. 27). Spruce, who discovered this remarkable plant, wrote of its habitat near Santarem on the lower Amazon. "In the lakes and among the tall grasses, were several small floating plants, chiefly cryptogamic such as a Riccia and Azolla and a Salvinia; but there was also a curious and beautiful Euphorbiad (*Phyllanthus fluitans*, sp. n.) with two-ranked, roundish, heart-shaped leaves, of a pale green colour tinged with rose, a fascicle of white radicles

---

[5] *Phragmites communis* auctt.; this unfortunate but inevitable change of name of the common reed, one of the most widespread of plants, is discussed by Clayton (1968).

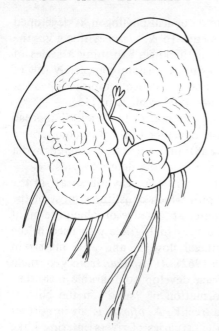

FIGURE 27. *Phyllanthus fluitans* (Euphorbiaceae), lower Amazon south to Paraguay
(Chodat).

from the base of each leaf, and two to four small white flowers in each axil.
Though wide as the poles asunder from Salvinia, it was so like it in external
appearance that I could hardly believe my eyes when I found it to be a
flowering plant" (Spruce, 1908, Vol. I, p. 115).

In his later less detailed work on the phylogeny of flowering plants,
J. Hutchinson (1969) transferred, as the result of "further study" but without any explicit detailed evidence, the Lythraceae to the lignose order
Myrtales. In this work they are retained in their more conventional position
next to the Onagraceae and close to the Trapaceae. If it proves necessary
to transfer the Lythraceae from the Herbaceae, the Lignosae will gain half
a dozen genera of more or less aquatic plants (cf. p. 364).

In the genus *Hypericum*, of the family Hypericaceae, in the order Gutti-
ferales, there are a number of amphibious species of Saint-John's-wort, of
which the aquatic forms such as *H. borealis* f. *callitrichoides* and *H. ellipti-
cum* f. *aquatica* are characteristically aquatic plants looking like *Callitriche*
(Fassett 1940).

In the Rubiaceae, *Limnosipanea* from Central and tropical South America
has seven species, at least some of them being heterophyllous herbaceous
water plants.

In the Mimosaceae, *Mimosa pigra* and *Neptunia oleracea* (*D* of Fig. 87)
are very widespread tropical aquatic sensitive plants in otherwise terrestrial

genera. A true aerenchyma, formed from a cortical phellogen, is developed in the superficial parts of their floating stems. In *N. oleracea* this gives the appearance of "cottony felt of an inch in thickness" forming a series of internodal floats "as buoyant as cork, serving to sustain completely out of water the heads of pale yellow flowers, and the delicate bipinnate leaves, which shrank up at our approach" (Spruce 1908, Vol. 1, p. 115).

Several species of *Sesbania* in the tribe Sesbaniae of the family Fabaceae are more or less aquatic plants that have developed in a way comparable to *Neptunia oleracea* (Scott and Wager 1888); in some cases the aerenchyma forms around adventitious roots that arise from the floating stems.

In a few species of *Aeschynomene*, of the tribe Aeschynomeneae, in the same family, secondary xylem forms a pith which constitutes most of the volume of the shoots that float on the water at the edge of which the plant is rooted. *A. aspera* in India produces a very high-grade pith used in the manufacture of sun helmets, toys, artificial flowers, and as a matrix in cutting botanical sections (Subramanyan 1962). *A. hispidula* from Venezuela and *A. elaphroxylon* from tropical Africa develop comparable pith. The last-named, which takes part in the formation of "sudd" in the Nile, is used for making floats and canoes. The treelike A. *pfundii* is an important element in the marginal vegetation of the estuaries of rivers entering Lake Chilwa in Malawi (Kalk 1974). The plants of all these slightly related genera, *Mimosa*, *Neptunia*, *Sesbania*, and *Aeschynomene*, have a common appearance; like *Mimosa*, *Aeschynomena* and *Neptunia* are sensitive plants. A development of aerenchyma, as in *Sesbania* and *Neptunia*, though far less extreme, can occur in the vetch *Lotus pedunculatus*, in which species a submersed but reduced f. *submersus* is recorded in up to 60 cm of water; such forms may apparently develop in seasonally flooded habitats in autumn and winter (Glück 1936).

In addition to these specialized members of the Fabaceae, *Trifolium resupinatum* is known as a floating-leaved ecophene f. *natans* (*E* of Fig. 58) in North Africa and Europe (Glück 1936), and in the Rosaceae *Potentilla palustris*, usually growing in acidic soil along the banks of small lakes or ponds and streams, may spread out over the water as a floating mat (Ruttner 1962). There may be a few other aquatic Lignosae; the list of at most a few dozen species showing some degree of aquatic specialization, treated in the preceding paragraphs, is certainly a meager one. More study of the relationship of aquatic adaptation to angiosperm descent, considering other phylogenetic schemes, would obviously be desirable.

Dicotyledones Herbaceae. Among the Herbaceae, which consist of only 25 orders, or less than half of the number in the Lignosae, there are, in the most primitive of these orders, the Ranales, several aquatic families containing relatively few species, but of wide distribution and great ecological importance. The Nymphaeaceae include the water lilies of the genera *Nymphaea* (*A* of Fig. 89) and *Nuphar* (Fig. 28). The tropical east Asiatic *Euryale* and South American *Victoria* (Vol. II, Fig. 6) are sometimes separated as a distinct family. *Victoria* produces the largest leaves of any plant. The remarkable architectural supporting system of these leaves was an element in Paxton's design for the tropical greenhouse that he built to accommodate the plant, and later for the Crystal Palace. Lecturing about the latter building to the Fine Arts Society in London on November 13, 1850, Paxton exhibited a leaf of *Victoria* and said "Nature has provided the leaf with longitudinal and transverse girders and supports that I, borrowing from it, have adopted in this building" (Markham 1935; see also Sculthorpe 1967). The structure has thus been placed firmly, if now rather invisibly, into the historical foundation of modern architecture. Miki (1960) has described, from seeds obtained from Pleistocene deposits in Japan, *Eoeuryale*, which he supposes gave rise to *Euryale* by hybridization with *Nuphar*. He also supposes the same fossil genus hybridizing with *Nymphaea* in America to have produced *Victoria*, which seems very unlikely. *Barclaya* from streams in the forests of southeast Asia is sometimes given another family. Yet another generically monotypic family, the Nelumbaceae, is usually recognized for the lotus *Nelumbo* (*C* of Fig. 61). It has peltate leaves raised above the water and develops a remarkable receptacle, shaped rather like the rose of a watering can. The present distribution with one species, the sacred lotus *N. nucifera* in tropical Asia, and the other, *N. lutea* in northern South America, the Caribbean islands, and the southeastern United States, at least to northeastern Indiana and Wisconsin is highly disjunct, but the genus was more widespread in the Cretaceous and early Tertiary. The Cabombaceae, containing *Brasenia* (*A* of Fig. 61) in Asia and America and the heterophyllous *Cabomba* (*B* of Fig. 61) in the warmer parts of the latter continent, have, unlike the previously discussed plants, upright stems rather than long petioles arising from the rhizome. They are believed by J. Hutchinson (1959) to be nearer the Ceratophyllaceae than to the Nymphaeaceae. All the plants so far discussed have fairly large flowers, and are usually entomophilous, pollinated by flies and beetles that are attracted by the odor of the flowers and may eat the stamens. The opening of the flower is sometimes restricted to a limited time of day (Gessner 1960; see p. 89; also Sculthorpe 1967). *Nuphar* and *Nymphaea* in North Temperate latitudes may lose their perfume and become less dependent on cross-fertilization. *Barclaya* and *Euryale* are apparently usually cleistogamous.

The supposedly allied Ceratophyllaceae contains only *Ceratophyllum*, with about six species, of which *C. demersum* is among the most widely

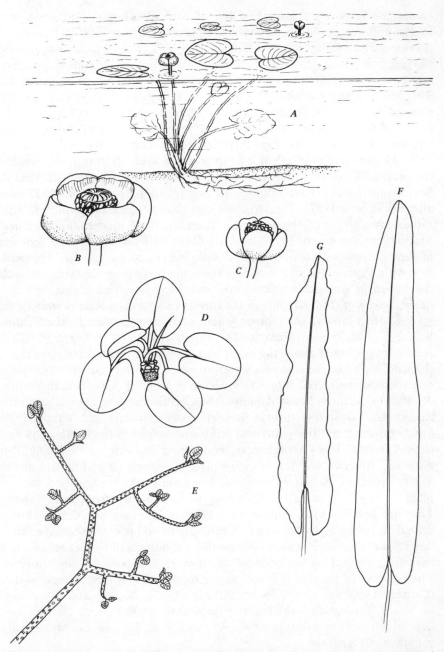

FIGURE 28.   Biology of the yellow water lily *Nuphar* (Nymphaeaceae). *A*, Diagrammatic drawing of the whole plant of *N. lutea* ($\times$ about 7/40), with floating leaves on long petioles that permit these leaves to be quite widely separated, lax submersed water leaves, rhizome, and flowers opening above the water surface; *B*. flower of same, Breslau, Germany ($\times\frac{2}{3}$);

distributed of all water plants. The members of the genus usually have very finely divided leaves (Fig. 29). The flowers are minute and of separate sex, but carried on the same plant; the stamens absciss and float to the surface where pollen is liberated and falls through the water, perchance settling on the stigmas of female flowers. Roots are not developed and the plant is a megaloplanktonic or mesopleustonic, highly specialized and successful water plant. Among the Ranunculaceae, a number of aquatic species of *Ranunculus*, mostly of the subgenus *Batrachium*, are known. They are of great biological interest in relation to leaf form (frontispiece, Figs. 75–77) and heterophylly (see p. 175). Most have aerial entomophilous flowers.

In the Piperales, the small family Saururaceae contains in eastern North America *Saururus cernuus*, the lizard's-tail, an amphibious plant often found growing in water.

The Polygonales contain, in the genus *Polygonum* of the Polygonaceae, certain amphibious species capable of growing in water or on dry land, and often exhibiting slightly differentiated aquatic and terrestrial ecophenes. This is true of the North American *P. coccineum*, which is usually terrestrial but has an aquatic f. *natans* (Fig. 30), and of *P. amphibium*, usually glabrous and aquatic, but with a hairy f. *terrestre*. *P. hydropiperoides* is a quite important aquatic species in North America, and the very variable *P. barbatum*, from tropical Asia south to Queensland, can grow as a water plant as well as on land.

Another family of the Polygonales, the Illecebraceae, usually inhabit dry places in warm latitudes, but *Illecebrum verticillatum* (*C, D* of Fig. 58) provides a striking example of a plant, ordinarily a terrestrial hygrophyte, that can develop underwater into an extremely elongate aquatic form.

Alternanthera, a genus of Amaranthaceae in the order Chenopodiales, contains, among a number of terrestrial species, some that are amphibious or fully aquatic; among these *A. philoxeroides* is an important American species. *A. hassleriana* from open waters in Paraguay (Chodat 1906) is pleustonic (Fig. 31).

The Brassicaceae or Cruciferae in the Cruciales have a few important aquatic species; *Cardamine pratensis* is a good example of an amphibious species (*F, G* of Fig. 32), with a reduced aquatic form capable of producing small plants from detached leaves. Arber (1920) found that in England

---

C, flower of *N. pumila*, Uppsala, Sweden ($\times \frac{2}{3}$), a smaller northern taxon often introgressing into populations of *N. lutea*; *D*, *N. lutea* f. *terrestris* ($\times \frac{1}{6}$); *E*, rhizome system of *N. lutea* with newly forming water leaves; *F*, *N. sagittifolia*, Wilmington, North Carolina, floating leaf ($\times \frac{1}{3}$) of a rheophil taxon; *G*, submerged water leaf ($\times \frac{1}{3}$) of same (*D, E*, after Glück; *B, C, F* and *G*, Herbarium, Yale University).

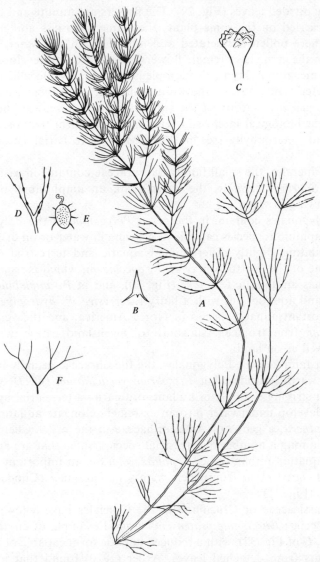

FIGURE 29.   *A, Ceratophyllum demersum*, (Ceratophyllaceae), Twin Lakes, Conn. (×⅔);
B, achene of same (×¾); *C*, turion of same (×⅗); *D*, leaf of *C. echinatum*, New Haven,
Conn. (×⅔); *E*, achene of same (×4/3); *E*, leaf of *C. submersum*, Europe (×2/3) and
(F after Glück; *A*, *D*, and *F*, Herbarium, Yale University).

FIGURE 30. *Polygonum coccineum* (Polygonaceae) showing the slight differentiation be-
tween *A*, the terrestrial form, from along the north shore of Bachmann's Dam, Dallas
County, Texas, and *B*, f. *natans* growing in 2m of water in the Stillwater River, Penobscot
Co., Maine ($\times\frac{1}{2}$; Herbarium, Yale University).

caddis larvae might construct their cases from such leaves, so that they
become "Elegantly crested with tiny adventitious plants of Lady's Smock."
The same family contains the important edible watercresses (*C*, *D*, and *E*
of Fig. 32), the diploid *Rorippa nasturtium-aquaticum*, the very similar but
allotetraploid *R. microphyllum*, and their widely cultivated hybrid × *sterilis*;
the closely related lake cress *Armoracia aquatica* is widespread in North
America. The rather atypical rosulate *Subularia aquatica* (*H* of Fig. 32) is
another crucifer of some limnological importance.

The Lythrales contain sporadically a number of important aquatic plants.
In the Lythraceae the Old World *Peplis portula* and the Holarctic *Didiplis
diandra* are amphibious, with both aquatic and terrestrial forms (*A*, *B*,

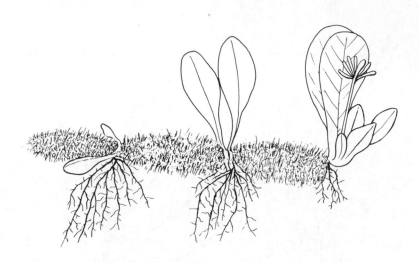

Figure 31.   *Alternanthera hassleriana* (Amaranthaceae), a pleustonic species from Paraguay ($\times \frac{1}{2}$, Chodat).

and *C* of Fig. 33). In the water purslan *P. portula*, the taller sterile aquatic form becomes commoner as one proceeds northward. The swamp loosestrife *Decodon verticillata* is an important American plant, growing out over water and forming aerenchymatous floats where branches curve back to the surface (*A* of Fig. 87). In the same family *Lythrum* can grow in water, as can some species of *Ammania* and *Rotala*. The latter genus which is often eulittoral (*D* of Fig. 33) has in *R. filiformis* and *R. indica* species that are spread in the cultivation of rice (Glück 1936).

Ludwigia and *Jussiaea* (*B* and *C* of Fig. 87), often regarded as a single genus with the former name, are important members of the Onagraceae containing aquatic species, and in the same family *Epilobium* may sometimes be an adventitious emergent water plant. There is a striking tendency for members of both the Lythraceae and Onagraceae to produce aerenchyma, even in casually aquatic genera such as *Epilobium* (Batten 1918).

The very specialized *Trapa*, with about five annual species of water chestnuts or bullnuts, mostly in the warmer parts of the world, constitutes the living part of the family Trapaceae. These plants have a rosette of leaves with buoyant petioles surrounding the flowers, and a long trailing stem bearing adventitious water roots (*A* of Fig. 34). Miki (1959, 1961) concludes that the living *Trapa* is descended from forms comparable

FIGURE 32.   Aquatic Cruciferae. *A, Rorippa nasturtium-aquaticum*, New Haven, Conn., *B*, pod or siliqua (natural size); *C*, seed (×7); *D, R. microphyllum* siliqua (natural size); *E*, seed (×7); *F, Cardamine pratensis*, land form, Simsbury, Conn.; *G*, leaf of water form with adventitious plant at base of apical leaflet, Upware, Cambridge, England; *H, Subularia aquatica*, Newfoundland (×½ unless otherwise indicated; *A, F*, and *H*, Herbarium, Yale University; *B, C, D*, and *E*, diagrammatic drawings after Howard and Manton's photographs; *G*, Arber).

to those surviving into the Pliocene of Japan and probably in contemporaneous deposits elsewhere, described by him under the names *Hemitrapa* and *Eotrapa*; the latter is presumably derived from a *Lythrum*-like ancestor (*B–D* of Fig. 34).

The Haloragaceae, another family of Lythrales, contain the important mermaid weed *Proserpinaca* and especially the water milfoils of the genus

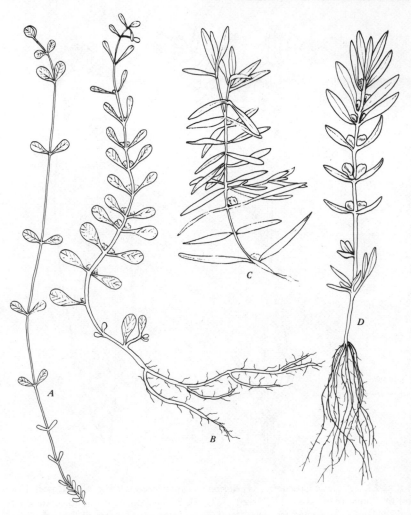

FIGURE 33.   *A, Peplis portula* (Lythraceae), a sterile water form, Europe; *B*, land form with minute axillary flowers, Stockton, Yorkshire; *C, Didiplis diandra*, lakes near St. Louis, Missouri; *D, Rotala ramosior*, gravelly shore of Lake Massapaug, Sharon, Mass. (*A* $\times \frac{1}{2}$, Glück; *B–D* natural size, Herbarium, Yale University).

Myriophyllum (*C–F* of Fig. 35). There are a good many terrestrial species in *Haloragis* and also a few in the smaller genera of the family. The mare's tail *Hippuris* (*A* of Fig. 35) may be allied here, but is sufficiently different to be made the type of a separate family, the Hippuraceae, by modern workers, as is the Callitrichaceae, containing only the cosmopolitan *Calli-*

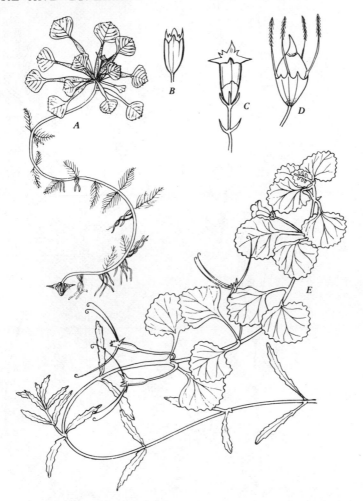

FIGURE 34. *A, Trapa bispinosa* (Trapaceae), India, anchored by original fruit; *B*, fruit of fossil *Lythrum anceps* (Lythraceae); *C*, the same *Eotrapa tetrasepalum*; *D*, the same *Hemitrapa trapelloidea; E, Trapella sinensis* (Trapellaceae), China (*A*, Subramanyan modified; *B, C*, ×1.2, Miki; *D*, ×0.96, Miki; *E*. Oliver).

triche with about 25 species (*B* of Fig. 35). There is no doubt that the Lythrales are an order in which aquatic plants arise rather easily.[6]

The peculiar order Podostemales is regarded by J. Hutchinson as containing two families, the Hydrostachydaceae and the Podostemaceae; the

---

[6] If the Lythraceae belong in the Myrtales, the other families constitute the Onagrales (J. Hutchinson 1969).

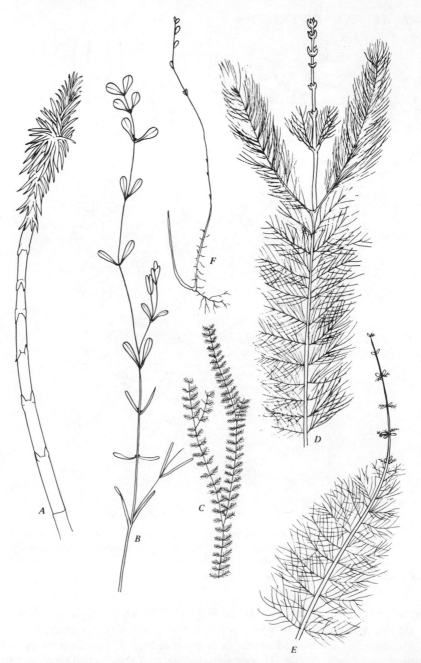

FIGURE 35. *A, Hippuris vulgaris* (Hippuridaceae), pools near Indus, Spitok, Indian Tibet; *B, Callitriche palustris* (Callitrichaceae), Cape Breton Island; *C, Myriophyllum alterniflorum* (Haloragaceae), Lake Champlain; *D, M. exalbescens*, Danbury, Conn.; *E, M. verticillatum*, Uinta, Utah; *F, M. tenellum*, Round Pond, Tewkesbury, Mass., a virtually leafless and often deep-water species ($\times \frac{3}{5}$; Herbarium, Yale University).

evidence that the two families are allied is perhaps not entirely adequate. *Hydrostachys*, the sole genus in its family, contains about 10 species living in Madagascar and the southeastern part of equatorial Africa. Its ecology does not appear to be adequately described, but it is evidently not an obligate rheobiont.

Although *Hydrostachys* is a fairly normal looking angiosperm, the supposedly allied Podostemaceae are usually curious (Vol. II, Fig. 7) thalloid plants, growing like lichens or some seaweeds over stones in running water. There are probably about 130 species distributed throughout the warmer parts of the world and just reaching temperate North America. The generic diversity is much greater and the areas of distribution of the average genus or species doubtless much less than in the other aquatic angiosperms. Since, however, the family occurs only in running water, it must be reluctantly put to one side in a work devoted primarily to lakes.[7]

The Umbellales contain in the family Umbelliferae or Apiaceae several genera which include water plants. *Hydrocotyle* (*F* and *G* of Fig. 36), the water pennywort, with circular or reniform and often floating leaves, is a widespread genus containing 100 species and is often given a family of its own, the Hydrocotylaceae. Among the more typical umbellifers, aquatic species occur in *Berula*, *Oenanthe*, and *Sium* (*A–E* of Fig. 36), which may be strikingly heterophyllous.

In the Convolvulaceae, of the order Solanales, there are one or two species of *Ipomoea*, notably the Palaeotropical *I. aquatica* (*C* of Fig. 37), that appear to be genuine emergent aquatic plants, trailing among other emergent vegetation.

In the order Personales, the Scrophulariaceae contain quite important aquatic members. *Bacopa* (including *Bramia*, *Herpestis*, *Hydrotrida*, and *Macuillamia*) is a genus of mostly tropical plants, with a few aquatic species living on muddy bottoms in shallow water; *B. rotundifolia* extends northward throughout the Mississippi Valley. *Limnophila* (*A* of Fig. 37) contains a number of species of emergent spicate water plants widely distributed in the tropics of the old world; its species are often very heterophyllous. *Glossostigma elatinoides* is amphibious in New Zealand. *Gratiola aurea* can be terrestrial but a very small sexually sterile f. *pusilla* may be quite an important component of the deeper-water flora of temperate North American lakes (*A–C* of Fig. 38). Several species of mudwort *Limosella* (*E* and *F* of Fig. 38) occur in various parts of the world at the

---

[7] The peculiarities of the Podostemaceae greatly influenced J. C. Willis in the formulation of his theory of Age and Area, which was one of the important precursors of the modern statistical study of taxa and their populations. The family, therefore, has an important place in the history of ecology, as has Willis, whose kindness half a century ago remains a pleasant memory.

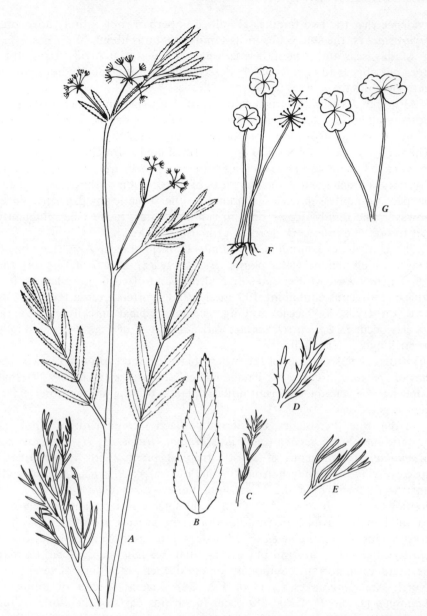

FIGURE 36. Aquatic Umbelliferae. *A, Sium sauve*, whole plant from Bubble Pond, Mount Desert Island, Maine, showing pinnate air leaflets and very dissected water leaflets ($\times \frac{1}{6}$); *B*, large air leaflet and *C*, myriophylloid water leaf from a plant from Wolf Lake, Indiana; *D*, shallower- and *E*, deeper-water dissected leaves of a plant from Randolph, Maine; *F, Hydrocotyle umbellata*, Little Pond, Thompson, Conn.; *G, H. ranunculoides*, Mercersburg, Pennsylvania; in locis aquosis T. C. Porter, August 1836 (all but *A* $\times \frac{1}{2}$; Herbarium, Yale University).

FIGURE 37. *A, Limnophila aquatica* (Scrophulariaceae), Oriental Region; *B, Hydrolea zeylanica* (Hydrophyllaceae), Oriental Region; *C, Ipomoea aquatica* (Convolvulaceae), widespread in Old World Tropics (Subramanyan).

margins of lakes; they are mainly, but not entirely, eulittoral. The monkey flower *Mimulus guttatus* and several species of *Veronica* occur primarily in the shallow waters of springs and ditches. Finally, the peculiar southwest African *Chamaegigas intrepidus* (Fig. 39) is both a typical desert plant and an aquatic, living in the temporary waters of shallow pans (Hickel 1967).

The anomalous family Trapellaceae (Glück 1940), containing only *Trapella*, though originally placed near the Pedalaceae, is believed now (Willis

Figure 38. *A, Gratiola aurea* (Scrophulariaceae), terrestrial form growing on the upper beach of Salmon or Greenville Lake, Yarmouth County, Nova Scota; *B*, the same, moderate submersed form from Winter Pond, Winchester, Mass.; *C*, f. *pusilla*, extreme aquatic form found in many lakes in central parts of North America; *D, Tillaea aquatica* (Crassulaceae), Hummock Pond, Nantucket Island; *E. Limosella subulata*, North Haven, Conn.; *F, L. aquatica*, Pipestone, Maine; *G*, the same, Lake Athabasca, Canada; *H, Littorella americana*, East Worthington, Vermont (all natural size; *C* from Fassett, all others from Herbarium, Yale University.)

94

and Airy Shaw 1966) to be related to the Scrophulariaceae. The genus contains not more than two living species from China and Japan and three fossil species (Miki 1961) from the late Tertiary or Pleistocene of the latter country. A species comparable to the living Japanese *T. antennifera* inhabited western Europe in the Pliocene (Tralau 1965). *Trapella* (*E* of Fig. 34) is a heterophyllous long-stemmed annual with roots that form mats on the bottoms of shallow lakes and ponds; the submersed flowers are cleistogamous, but emergent flowers also occur. The fruits are spinose and parallel in some ways to those of the unrelated genus *Trapa*.

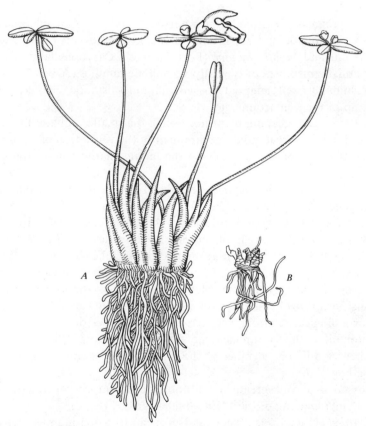

FIGURE 39. *Chamaegigas intrepidus*, a desert aquatic plant of southwest Africa. *A*, adult plant with water leaves and rosettes of four floating leaves and flowers, one of which, on the third rosette from the left, is fully open; *B*, dried plant which revived rapidly when planted in sand and submersed (natural size, Heil).

In the Acanthaceae, *Hygrophila* (including *Cardanthera* and *Asteracantha*) is a genus of tropical plants, some of which evidently grow as spicate emergent aquatic species. *Justicia*, the water willow, is likewise an important emergent genus in tropical and warm-temperate Asia and America.

In the same order, the Lentibulariaceae contain the very important genus *Utricularia*, the bladderworts, with a number of aquatic species in both temperate and tropical regions, as well as terrestrial and amphibious species in wet tropical countries (*A–D* of Fig. 40). The members of the genus possess remarkable traps which catch small animals (Lloyd 1942); they are also favorite substrata for sessile aquatic organisms.

The other aquatic members of the Herbaceae belong to odd genera, usually one or two to a family, scattered about among the remaining orders of the division.

Some species of *Crassula*, often referred to *Tillaea* (Crassulaceae, Saxifagales), are aquatic and are found on brackish mud flats (*D* of Fig. 38). These plants and *Montia fontana* (Portulacaceae, Caryophyllales) are more or less aquatic members of typically xerophytic families (Arber 1920); they are presumably well adapted to withstanding osmotic changes on the drying up of their environments.

Elatine, a small creeping plant not unlike the smaller aquatic Lythraceae in habit, is a widespread minor component of the vegetation of freshwaters. The genus is one of two composing the family Elatinaceae in the Caryophyllales.

Hottonia palustris, the water violet (*B* of Fig. 41) and its curious American congener, *H. inflata* (*A* of Fig. 41) with *Lysimachia vulgaris*, the yellow loosestrife, and *Naumbergia thyrsiflora*, the tufted loosestrife, are aquatic members of the Primulaceae of the order Primulales, *N. thyrsiflora* sometimes being an important plant at the margins of lakes in northern Europe.

Nymphoides (= *Limnathemum*), an important genus with many, mainly palaeotropical, species in the Menyanthaceae, of the order Gentiales, parallels *Nymphaea* in the form of its leaves and flowers (Fig. 42) though the morphological relations between these structures differ radically from those found in the Nymphaeaceae (cf. *A* of Fig. 28, 86). *Menyanthes*, another very different member of the family, is a decorative, more or less aquatic bog plant.

Littorella is a widespread and limnologically important aquatic genus of the Plantaginaceae of the Plantaginales (*H* of Fig. 38).

Aldrovanda (Fig. 43) is a peculiar European free-floating member of the Droseraceae in the Sarraceniales, paralleling *Utricularia* but with a quite different kind of trap.

Lobelia with at least one very important aquatic species *L. dortmanna*

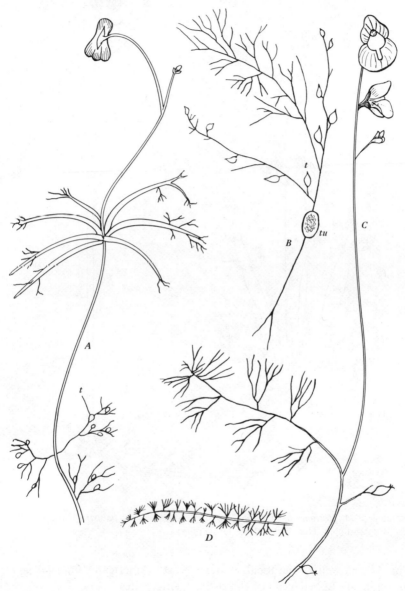

FIGURE 40. *A, Utricularia inflata*, Groton, Conn., with whorl of modified leaves below flower and ordinary divided leaves bearing small traps (*t*); *B, U. intermedia*, Twin Lakes, Salisbury, Conn., May 18, 1916, growing from a turion (*tu*); *C*, the same from the same locality, apex of adult plant bearing flowers, note larger traps (*t*); *D*, the same from the same locality, more or less terrestrial plant growing over quaking bog (all $\times \frac{3}{4}$, Herbarium, Yale University).

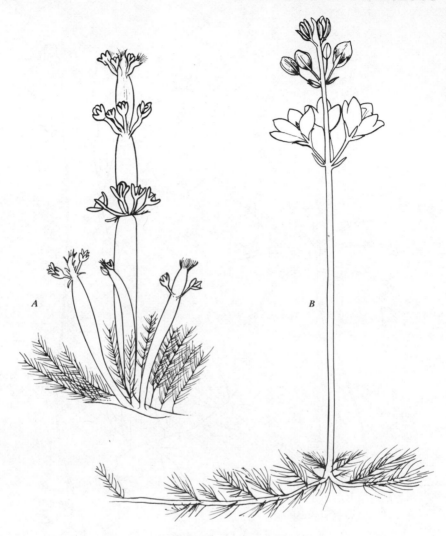

FIGURE 41.   *A, Hottonia inflata*, W. Roxbury, Mass., *B. H, palustris*, Hightown, Lancashire, England ($\times\frac{1}{2}$, Herbarium, Yale University).

(Fig. 44), as well as the local western North American *Howellia aquatica*, belong in the Lobeliaceae of the order Campanales.

Limnanthes and *Floerkea* belong in the Limnanthaceae of the order Geraniales. *Hydrocera triflora* is a remarkable tall emergent aquatic species of the Balsaminaceae of the same order in the Indo-Malayan region. *Hydrolea* in the Hydrophyllaceae and the aquatic form of the dodder

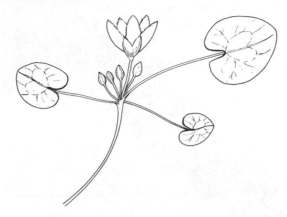

FIGURE 42. *Nymphoides peltata* (Menyanthaceae), Breslau, Germany, showing remarkable convergence with *Nymphaea*, though with a quite different arrangement of leaf petioles in relation to the main axis ($\times\frac{1}{2}$; Herbarium, Yale University).

Cuscuta planiflora (*E, F* of Fig. 58) in the Cuscutaceae, which can parasitize a variety of aquatic plants, belong in the Polemoniales.

Myosotis, the forget-me-not, in the family Boraginaceae of the order Boraginales, contains a well-known swamp species *M. scorpiodes*, which is often found growing as an emergent aquatic plant. Very occasionally, as in the Traunsee in Austria (Morton 1954) and in an influent of Lago Doberdo near Trieste (Seidel 1957), striking populations of this species are found growing and flowering under 50 cm or more of water. The epidermal hairs of the leaves are strikingly modified. These populations have been referred (sub *M. palustris*) to f. *submerse-florens*; it would not be surprising if the form proved to be genetic.

Finally there are a few well-adapted freshwater members of the Asteraceae or composites (J. Hutchinson 1916), the largest family of flowering plants. *Megalodonta* (= *Bidens* p.p.) *beckii* (*B* of Fig. 45), the water marigold, in North America, when not flowering is a typically myriophylloid waterweed; several species of the related genus *Bidens* are marsh plants.

Cotula myriophylloides (*A* of Fig. 45) belongs to a genus reaching its highest abundance in southern Africa, where *C. myriophylloides* occurs. It is a fully adapted water plant with finely divided leaves; some of its relatives grow in salt marshes and in New Zealand *C. coronopifolia*, ordinarily a marsh plant, seems at times to be fully aquatic (Cockayne 1928).

Hydropectis aquatica, (*C* of Fig. 45) from the base of the Sierra Madre, Chihuahua, Mexico, is described as having leaves lacking bristles, unlike the terrestrial members of the related genus *Pectis* (Watson 1888). *Erigeron*

FIGURE 43.   *Aldrovanda vesiculosa* (Droseraceae). *A*, Whole plant; (natural size); *B*, whorl of leaves with traps (×2, Diels).

heteromorphus (*D* of Fig. 45) is another Mexican aquatic composite, apparently rheophile and very heterophyllous.

In addition to these, one terrestrial thistle, *Cirsium dissectum*, usually growing in wet soil, has a very remarkable recurrent elongate fully aquatic form (*A, B* of Fig. 58). Some species of *Lasthenia*, characteristic of vernal pools in California, start their development under water (Ornduff, personal communication).

Monocotyledones.   Among the Monocotyledones, we have in the division Calyciferae two primitive orders, the Butomales and the Alismatales, consisting mainly of aquatic plants, and in the same division five other more specialized orders which contain aquatic genera or are entirely aquatic. The Calyciferae, in fact, include a very large proportion of the important freshwater angiosperms of the world.

The two most primitive orders, the Butomales and the Alismatales, have often been regarded as closely related to the Ranales in the Dicotyledones Herbaceae. *Ranalisma*, perhaps properly referred to as a subgenus of the widespread *Echinodorus*, a member of the Alismataceae growing on mud locally in southeast Asia and Africa, has indeed sometimes been regarded as a monocotyledonous buttercup, representing in morphology and

FIGURE 44. *Lobelia dortmanna* (Lobeliaceae), Monroe, Conn.,
H. L. Beardslee, 1826–1827 ($\times\frac{1}{2}$, Herbarium, Yale University).
Flower in life pale violet.

habitat that kind of plant from which the other monocotyledonous groups
arose. The most recent work on the microscopic anatomy of these plants
(Stant 1964) emphasizes the differences rather than the similarities between
the Alismataceae and the Ranales, the latter group being too advanced to
have given rise to the former. It is, however, reasonable to suppose that if
the monocotyledons are monophyletic and if, as is almost universally
agreed, they are derived from some primitive dicotyledonous plant, this
plant probably resembled more closely the hypothetical ancestor of the
Ranales than any other imaginary taxon.

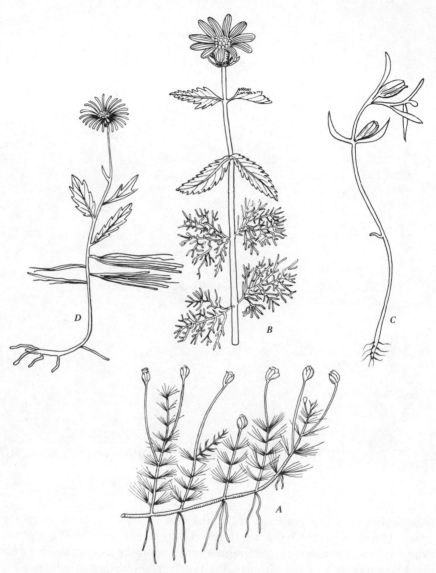

FIGURE 45.   Aquatic Asteraceae. *A, Cotula myriophylloides*, Cape Pennisula, South Africa; *B, Megalodonta beckii*, Canada and northern United States; *C, Hydropectis aquatica*, base of Sierra Madre, Chihuahua, Mexico; *D, Erigeron heteromorphus*, Concepcion River, San Luis Potosi, Mexico (J. Hutchinson).

Whatever their affinities outside the Monocotyledones may be, the Butomales and Alismatales are clearly primitive as monocotyledons and are perhaps not properly separated from each other. The Butomaceae contain in *Limnocharis* an erect marsh plant from South America, adventive (*L. flava*) in tropical Asia. The other four genera are more or less submersed or with floating leaves at least during part of the year. The flowering rush *Butomus umbellatus* is temperate Eurasiatic (*A* of Fig. 46), adventive in North America; the other genera tend to be tropical: *Hydrocleys* (*B* of Fig. 46) in South America, *Tenagocharis* in tropical Africa and Asia, and *Ostenia* from Uruguay.

Tenagocharis latifolia (*C* of Fig. 46) grows in seasonally aquatic localities, flowering when the water recedes. The appearance of the plant when flowering depends greatly on how much vegetative growth has taken place before the water level falls; dwarfed but reproductive individuals have been mistakenly regarded as peculiar taxa (van Steenis 1957).

The second family of Butomales, the Hydrocharitaceae, is the second most generically diversified of all the aquatic angiosperms. Of its 14 genera three are marine; the other 11 contain some of the most important freshwater plants. The family is remarkable for the variety of pollination mechanisms that it exhibits. The well-known Old World temperate *Hydrocharis* (*D* of Fig. 47) and *Stratiotes* (*C* of Fig. 47), most species of *Limnobium* (*E* of Fig. 47), the South American *Egeria*, and the Palaeotropical *Ottelia* have large aerial flowers and are entomophilous. The neotropical *Limnobium stoloniferum* is anemophilous. The other freshwater genera, *Hydrilla*, *Vallisneria*, the African *Lagarosiphon* and Asian *Nechamandra*, the American *Elodea* (*A, B* of Fig. 47), and the marine *Enhalus* show an incipient form of hydrophily in which the female flowers open at the surface film. Further details are found on pp. 230–232.

In the Alismatales there are three families. The Alismataceae are an important family, largely but not exclusively in the Northern Hemisphere. *Alisma* (*A,* of Fig. 48) may be quite significant in the littoral of lakes, and *Sagittaria* (Figs. 66, 68), exhibiting an extreme set of variations in leaf form, occurs in a variety of habitats. *Damasonium* (*C* of Fig. 48), *Baldellia*, *Luronium*, and *Caldesia* are other temperate genera, but *Limnophyton* is Palaeotropical. *Echinodorus*, which may be a swamp plant, is very widespread but has 25 species in Central and South America, mostly restricted in range. The allied and supposedly primitive *Ranalisma* occurs in wet places in a few areas of central Africa and southeast Asia as has previously been noted. *Wiesneria* is Palaeotropical, showing a disjunct distribution in eastern India and Africa. The monotypic *Burnatia* and *Machaerocarpus* occur in Africa and California, respectively.

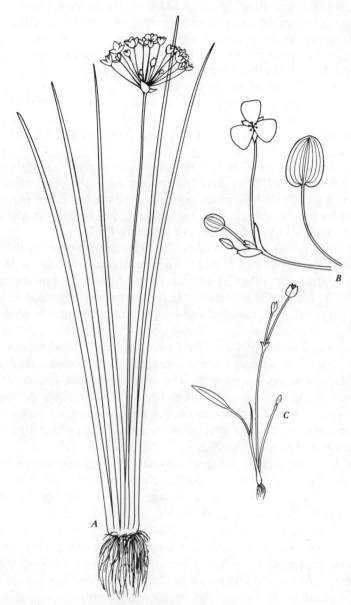

FIGURE 46. Butomaceae. *A, Butomus umbellatus* ($\times\frac{1}{8}$), Lake Champlain, Vermont; *B, Hydrocleys commersonii* ($\times\frac{1}{6}$), Venezuela; *C, Tenagocharis latifolia* ($\times\frac{1}{2}$), Mt. Kordofan, Sudan (Herbarium, Yale University).

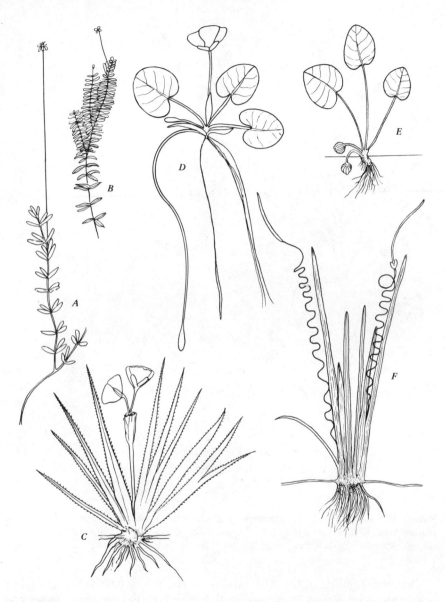

FIGURE 47.   Hydrocharitaceae. *A, Elodea canadensis*, male ($\times\frac{1}{2}$), Lake George, New York; *B, E. canadensis*, female ($\times\frac{1}{2}$), Lake Whitney, Hamden, Conn.; *C. Stratiotes aloides* ($\times\frac{1}{4}$), Breslau, Germany; *D, Hydrocharis morsus-ranae* ($\times\frac{1}{4}$), near Breslau, Germany; *E, Limnobium spongia* ($\times\frac{1}{2}$), Jonesboro, Illinois, a fruiting specimen, with recurrent peduncles, of a species that is often pleustonic; *F. Vallisneria americana* ($\times\frac{1}{4}$), Lake Saltonstall, Conn. (Herbarium, Yale University).

105

FIGURE 48.   Alismataceae. *A*, *Alisma plantago-aquatica*, Yorkshire, England; *B*, *Caldesia parnassifolia*, Khasia Hills, India; *C*. *Damasonium alisma*, Surrey, England; *D. Lophoto-carpus calycinus*, dry lake bed, near Banner, Illinois ($\times \frac{1}{3}$; Herbarium, Yale University).

The other families of the Alismatales are the Scheuchzeriaceae, including a single species *Scheuchzeria palustris* in the North Temperate zone, and the Petrosaviaceae, a monotypic terrestrial family from southeast Asia.

Among the less primitive orders of the Calyciferae, two contain sporadic aquatic species, and the other three are exclusively water plants and of great importance. The Juncaginales contain in the Lilaeaceae the single genus *Lilaea* living in alkaline playa lakes and other mineralized localities in western North America, and in the Posidoniaceae the well-known marine

Posidonia. The Commelinales contain in the Mayaceae the single genus *Mayaca* found in central and eastern South America and in Angola, a distribution that must delight the proponents of the theory of continental drift.

These two small contributions to the aquatic flora having been mentioned, we pass to the Aponogetonales, with the monotypic Aponogetonaceae containing in *Aponogeton* (Fig. 49), 30 or so species in the tropical regions

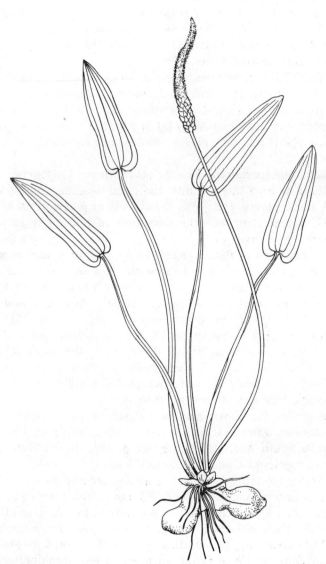

FIGURE 49.   *Aponogeton natans* (Aponogetonaceae), India (natural size, Subramanyan).

of the Old World southward into South Africa, and the marine Zosteraceae with *Zostera* and *Phyllospadix*. The Potamogetonales likewise contain a freshwater family, the Potamogetonaceae, and an almost exclusively salt-water one, the Ruppiaceae. The first of these contains the large genus *Potamogeton* (Figs. 79, 80, 81, 82, 93, 94, 97) with about 90 species, cosmo-politan but mainly in the cooler part of the world, and the largest genus of freshwater angiosperms; its ally *Groenlandia* is monotypic, and occurs in the temperate Old World. *Ruppia* (*A, B* of Fig. 50), though largely marine, has some limnological interest: *R. maritima* occurs in saline lakes, while *R. filifolia* is endemic to Lake Titicaca (Cl 250 mg liter^{-1}), from which *R. spiralis* is also recorded (Tutin 1940).

The order Najadales, includes in the Zannichelliaceae the cosmopolitan *Zannichellia* (*C* of Fig. 50), *Althenia* from the Mediterranean region, and *Lepilaena* from Australia and New Zealand. The other genera are marine. The Najadaceae include only *Najas* (*B* of Fig. 51), reduced but rather im-portant little plants that may play a considerable role in the vegetation of lakes.

Very much more specialized than the other aquatic Calyciferae, the order Eriocaulales includes a single family, the Eriocaulaceae, consisting mainly of tropical marsh plants. The genus *Eriocaulon*, or pipewort (*D* of Fig. 57), is more widespread than the other members of the family and contains truly lacustrine hyperhydates

The other divisions of the Monocotyledones, though very numerous in terrestrial species, are less apt to be aquatic than are the Calyciferae. The Corolliferae include in the Liliales the entirely aquatic family Pontederi-aceae. The members of the family are largely American and African, *Pontederia* (*D* of Fig. 52), the pickerelweed, being widespread in the New World; *Reussia* being found in South America; *Hydrothrix*, a peculiar annual in seasonal waters in Brazil, flowering as the water falls; *Heter-anthera* (*A–C* of Fig. 52) and *Eichhornia*, native in both America and tropical Africa; and *Scolleropsis* in Madagascar. Only *Monochoria* extends into the Asiatic tropics and northward to Japan.

Of these genera *Eichhornia* may be pleustonic, *E. crassipes* (*A* of Fig. 53), the notorious water hyacinth, being a well-known pest when growing away from its South American home (see p. 252). In the Amaryllidaceae at least some species of *Crinum* are amphibious.

In the Arales the family Araceae contains *Acorus calamus*, the sweet flag, native in eastern Asia and (Buell 1935) in North America (see p. 364), but introduced as a medicinal herb into Europe in the sixteenth century (Mücke 1908), *Calla palustris*, the water arum, and the immense *Typho-nodorum lindleyanum* of the standing waters of swamps in Madagascar, Pemba, and Zanzibar (Wild 1961), all more or less amphibious emergent

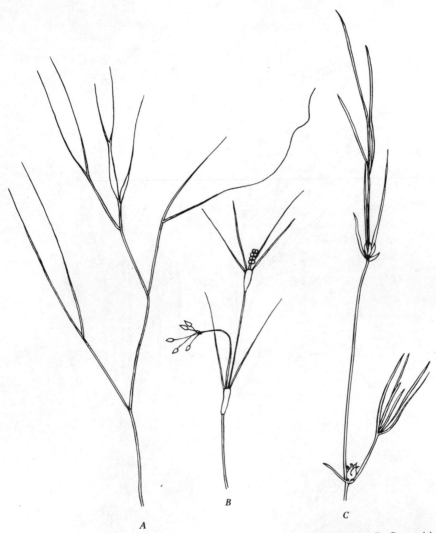

FIGURE 50. *A*, *Ruppia maritima* (Ruppinaceae), Kansas, sterile branch; *B*, *R. maritima* var. *longipes*, brackish water, Barnstable, Mass., with inflorescence of two flowers each with four large stamens, and below fruits on an elongated petiole; *C*, *Zannichellia palustris* (Zannichelliaceae), New Jersey, apical part of a large plant, bearing axillary fruits (natural size, Herbarium, Yale University).

FIGURE 51. *A, Najas flexilis* (Najadaceae), Connecticut, part of plant with a detached piece bearing a minute axillary flower; *B, N. gracillima*, Connecticut, apex of branch; *C, Mayaca fluviatilis* (Mayacaceae), Florida; *D, Lilaea subulata* (Lilaeaceae), California, with basal flowers as well as spicate inflorescences (natural size; Herbarium, Yale University).

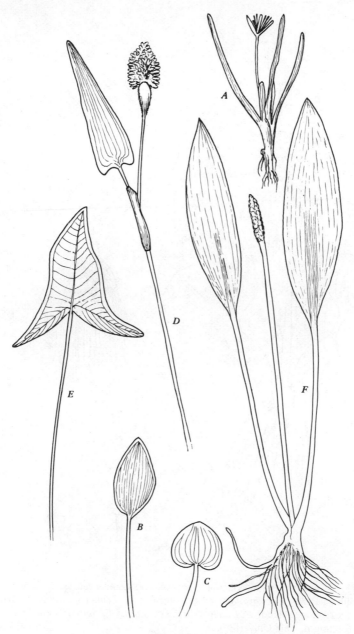

FIGURE 52.   Rooted Pontederiaceae and Araceae. *A, Heteranthera dubia* ($\times \frac{2}{3}$), small specimen, Verde River, Arizona; *B*; *H. limosa* ($\times \frac{2}{3}$), Jalisco, Mexico leaf of specimen growing in alkaline pond; *C, H reniformis* ($\times \frac{2}{3}$), Derby, Conn. leaf; *D, Pontederia cordata* ($\times \frac{1}{3}$), Chester, Conn., inflorescence and leaf; *E, Peltandra virginica* ($\times \frac{1}{3}$), Bethany Bog, Conn.; *F, Orontium aquaticum* ($\times \frac{1}{3}$), Egg Harbor City, New York (Herbarium, Yale University).

111

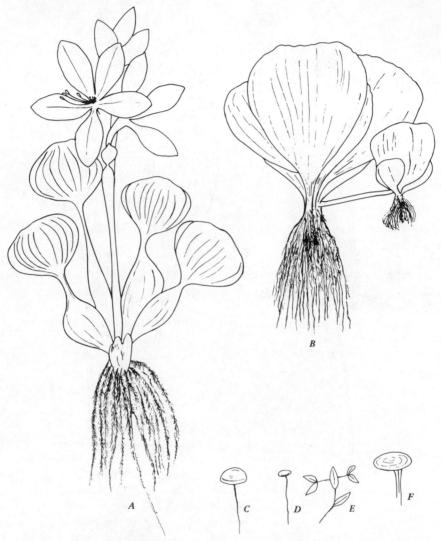

FIGURE 53. Pleustonic Pontederiaceae, Araceae, and Lemnaceae. *A, Eichhornia crassipes* ($\times\frac{1}{2}$), California; *B, Pistia stratiotes* ($\times\frac{1}{2}$), Florida; *C, Lemna gibba* ($\times 2$), Arizona; *D, L. minor* ($\times 2$), Long Island; *E, L. trisulca* ($\times 2$), Illinois; *F, Spirodela polyrhiza* (2), Minnesota (Herbarium, Yale University).

plants. The Indo-Malaysian *Cryptocoryne*, the American *Peltandra* (*E* of Fig. 52) and *Orontium* (*F* of Fig. 52) are well-characterized aquatic forms with emergent leaves, while *Pistia stratiotes* (*B* of Fig. 53), the water lettuce, a pleustonic pantropical species, like *Eichhornia*, can be a serious pest (see p. 000). Allied to the Araceae, though superficially very different, are all the four genera of Lemnaceae, *Lemna* (*C*, *D*, *E* of Fig. 53), *Spirodela* (*F* of Fig. 53), *Wolffia*, and *Wolffiella*, the first two and last two genera often quite reasonably being fused. *Wolffia* (Vol. II, Fig. 5) contains the smallest flowering plants; it is not unlikely that the family represents an extreme paedomorphic reduction of a pleustonic ancestor allied to *Pistia*.

In the same division, the Corolliferae, the Typhales contain the two generically monotypic families Sparganiaceae and Typhaceae. The species of bur reed, *Sparganium* (*C* of Fig. 54), and of reed mace or cattail,[8] *Typha* (*A* of Fig. 54), are of considerable limnological significance.

In the Iridaceae, of the order Iridales, the yellow flag *Iris pseudacorus* is a familiar swamp plant in Europe and often grows in water as a true hyperhydate.

The Glumiflorae, the third division of the Monocotyledones, consisting of the reeds, sedges, and grasses, contains a number of genera of emergent aquatic habit and often of great limnological significance in the eulittoral and upper infralittoral. The important aquatic members of the division belong to *Juncus* in the Juncaceae; *Cyperus*, *Schoenoplectus* (*A* of Fig. 55), *Scirpus* (*B* of Fig. 55), *Carex* (*C* of Fig. 55), *Eleocharis*, and *Rhynchospora* in the Cyperaceae; and *Glyceria* (*A* of Fig. 56), *Hygroryza*, *Phragmites* (Fig. 96), *Vossia*, *Zizania* (*C* of Fig. 56), together with some species of *Coix*, *Echinochloa*, *Hydrochloa*, *Ischaemum*, *Leersia* (*B* of Fig. 56), *Miscanthidium*, *Paspalidium*, *Paspalum*, *Phalaris*, and *Pseudorhaphis* in the Gramineae. A number of these plants are mentioned over and over again in the ecological parts of this volume. The aquatic Gramineae are obviously a very important element in the marginal vegetation of lakes.

Finally, mention must be made of the peculiar and predominantly Austral family Centrolepidaceae, allied to the Juncaceae and including two apparently psammobiont eulittoral species of some limnological interest in Tasmania and New Zealand. *Centrolepis minima* (= *Gaimardia*) is known to grow only in the wet eulittoral sand of Lakes Brunner and Te Anau on the western side of the South Island of New Zealand, and in similar habitats around Lake Pedder in Tasmania. In warmer latitudes, *Hydatella in-*

---

[8] Often called a Bulrush in England, though in that country as in North America, the Bulrush may be one of the larger more aquatic species of *Scirpus* or the allied *Schoenoplectus;* the name is probably most appropriately used for *Schoenoplectus lacustris*.

FIGURE 54. Typhaceae and Sparganiaceae. *A, Typha angustifolia* ($\times\frac{1}{10}$), New Haven, Conn.; *B, T. latifolia* (1/10), Danbury, Conn.; *C, Sparganium angustifolium* ($\times\frac{1}{3}$), New Haven, Conn. (Herbarium, Yale University).

A

B

C

FIGURE 55. Cyperaceae. *A, Schoenoplectus lacustris* ($\times\frac{1}{8}$), Norway; *B, Scirpus subter-minalis* ($\times\frac{1}{3}$), Maine; *C. Carex pseudocyperus* ($\times\frac{1}{5}$), Norway, flower spikes just appearing (Herbarium, Yale University).

FIGURE 56. Aquatic Gramineae. *A, Glyceria borealis* ($\times\frac{1}{5}$), Conn.; *B, Leersia oryzoides* ($\times\frac{1}{10}$), Whitney's Mill Pond, New Haven, Conn., 1858; *C, Zizania aquatica* ($\times\frac{1}{10}$), Vermont, female flowers at top of spike, male on the lower divergent branches (Herbarium, Yale, University).

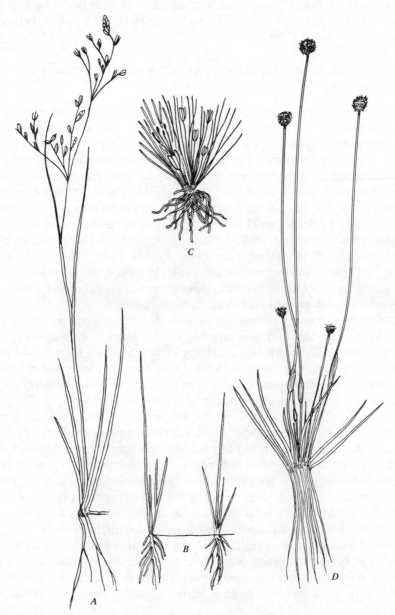

FIGURE 57. *A, Juncus pelocarpus,* Herkimer County, New York, *B, J. pelocarpus* f. *submersus, C, Hydatella inconspicus,* eulittoral of dune lakes, North Island, New Zealand; *D, Eriocaulon septangulare,* Chester, Conn. (all natural size; *B,* after Fassett, *C,* after Edgar, others, Hebarium, Yale University).

117

conspicua (*C* of Fig. 57) occurs on the shores of at least two dune lakes in the North Island of New Zealand (Cheeseman 1907, 1925; Bayly, Peterson, Tyler, and Williams 1966).

LIFE-FORMS AND ECOLOGICAL CLASSIFICATION OF TRA-CHEOPHYTES

On passing from the margin to the deep water of a lake, the higher plants encountered are adapted to an environment that changes gradually; the arrangement of plants, no doubt owing to competitive phenomena (cf. Gause and Witt 1935), often appears rather more discontinuous than the environmental gradient on which it depends, giving rise to easily distinguished zones in which at least the dominant plants are apt to exhibit a limited number of characteristic forms. The classification of these life-forms, begun by Warming (1895, 1923), has been developed by a number of later authors (Fassett 1930; Steenis 1932; Linkola 1933; Wilson 1935, 1939; Iversen, 1936; Dansereau 1945; Luther 1949; Thunmark 1952; Hejny 1960; den Hartog and Segal 1964; Hogeweg and Brenkert 1969). Though there is inevitably arbitrariness in such a classification, some sort of arrangement is essential for descriptive purposes.

Life-forms and growth forms. Two complementary approaches are possible. In the first, formally developed in various ways by Dansereau (1945), Luther (1949), Thunmark (1952), Hejny (1960), and den Hartog and Segal (1964), the aquatic vegetation is divided into a number of broad categories dependent on the relation of the plants to water level and substratum.

In the second approach, formally derived from the work of Du Rietz (1921, 1931), greatly extended by den Hartog and Segal (1964), and most skillfully used by Hogeweg and Brenkert (1969), a number of growth forms are recognized, each consisting of plants of comparable structure and similar relations to the physical environment. These growth forms may be placed in the larger categories that have been defined in the first approach.

The fundamental difference between the two approaches is that the first starts from spatial distributions, whereas the second starts from morphological similarities. A sufficiently able investigator might arrive at the overall broad ecological classification of the first approach by flying over a number of aqueous habitats in a helicopter, without any knowledge of systematic botany, whereas another investigator, shut up in an herbarium, might, with good fortune, make a fairly successful attempt at the second approach.

Major categories of life-forms. There is a good deal of difference between the results of the various botanists who have attempted the broad first approach. This is largely owing to a divergence over the definition of the set of plants to which the classification is to be applied. For the purposes of this work, the plants to be considered are obviously those that inhabit lakes. Attention is primarily given to the plants that grow on, in, or up through the water. Eulittoral plants, which may of course include casual terrestrial annuals, as well as perennials that can withstand some flooding (see p. 207), are considered only when they are of specific limnological interest.

Among the plants growing in contact with the water of the lake, one can distinguish those that live permanently underwater, the *hyphydates* of Thunmark, those that have vegetative parts floating at the surface, the *ephydates* of Thunmark, and those that grow up through the water and have emergent vegetative structures in the air, the *hyperhydates* of Thunmark. These three categories represent in a simple way what one ordinarily sees when looking at the less exposed shores of a small lake. Other authors have tended to group the first two categories as *hydrophytes*, calling the third *helophytes* (Raunkiaer 1934; den Hartog and Segal 1964). Two difficulties attend these initially simple-minded ecological classifications. Firstly, a certain number of amphibious species or *amphiphytes* (Iversen 1936), able to live either rooted in damp soil above the water's edge or completely submersed, may produce persistent clonal populations underwater. Often these populations never produce flowers, though by asexual reproduction they may increase greatly, forming very striking elements in the vegetation of lakes. This is true of *Gratiola aurea* in some North American localities, for instance, and of species of *Juncus* in both the New and the Old Worlds. Such plants are regarded as *pseudohydrophytes* by den Hartog and Segal. They are often morphologically very different from their terrestrial relatives, though the differences are no doubt usually environmentally determined. Since they may form large and characteristic populations of biological importance, it would seem best to regard the ecophenes in question as true hydrophytes even though they belong to amphibious species which can also have terrestrial populations.

The second difficulty arises in the rather numerous cases in which a plant submersed for the greater part of the year produces not only aerial flowers, but a relatively small number of air leaves during the flowering season. This happens in such characteristically aquatic plants as *Myriophyllum* and *Hippuris*. To den Hartog and Segal hydrophytes or water plants are by definition "able to achieve their generative cycle when all vegetative parts are submerged or are supported by water (floating leaves), or which occur normally submerged but are induced to reproduce sexually when their vegetative parts are dying due to emersion."[9] This definition clearly includes

---

[9] The second half of the definition is intended to include the Podostemaceae, which flower and die as the streams they inhabit dry.

such plants as produce aerial flowers, but if rigidly applied excludes any in which the flower or inflorescence is borne on a leafy shoot above water, however insignificant the air leaves may be.

Hejny (1960) insists on rather sharper distinctions. He has developed a classification mainly derived from a study of the vegetation of fluviatile localities, shallow swamps, and rice fields, with few truly lacustrine bodies of water. Cook (1969), however, feels that it provides the best scheme for water plants as a whole.

Hejny employs the following 10 major categories.

The *Euhydatophyta* are the fully submerged species dependent on the water and uppermost sediment layers for all nutrient elements. Hejny defines these as never producing aerial structures or forms. Their root system seldom extends more than 10–15 cm into the sediment, and rhizomes, if present, are not massive. Fully submerged species, whether rooted or rootless, fall in this category.

The *Hydatoaerophyta* are plants growing in permanent water, but with part of the assimilative organs floating with a dry upper surface or emerging above the water. All the pleustonic species at the water surface and all the floating-leaved species belong here; Hejny also includes plants like *Myriophyllum spicatum* and *M. verticillatum*, as leaf-bearing apical shoots emerge late in the season. When rooted the hydatoaerophytes are apt to have a greater development of rhizomes than are the euhydatophytes. At times of low water level they can survive as fully aerial plants rooted in mud.

The *Hydrochthophyta* grow normally in water, producing emergent air leaves or shoots. They are often very heterophyllous and, being more marginal than the preceding category, as well as more often found in small bodies of water, are more likely to have to survive essentially aerial conditions.

The *Ochthohydrophyta* may be fully aquatic when young plants are developing at times of high water level, but normally project as narrowleaved or tubular stems well above the surface; they are ordinarily rhizomatous. The category includes the more important junciform species of lake margins such as *Equisetum fluviatile*, *Typha* spp., *Schoenoplectus lacustris*, and *Phragmites australis*.

The *Euochthophyta* are more terrestrial eulittoral plants differing from the preceding in being smaller and with tap roots. All species belong to the genus *Carex*, including the important *C. elata*, *C. rostrata*, and *C. vesicaria*; it is probable that at least in some parts of its range *rostrata* is as aquatic as any of the Ochthohydrophytes.

The *Teganophyta* are the group of species living in very shallow littoral waters; several important lacustrine plants are included in this category by Hejny, notably *Eleocharis acicularis*, *Juncus bulbosus*, *Littorella uniflora*,

Elatine spp., *Callitriche* spp., and *Limosella aquatica*. Some of these also occur at greater depths.

The other four categories of Hejny's classification, the *Pelochthophyta*, *Pelochthotherophyta*, *Uliginosophyta*, and *Trichohygrophyta* contain less aquatic plants than do any of the previous divisions; these plants are mainly found around shallow swamps, streams, and rice fields. Few if any of their members are, in a strict sense, of limnological importance; such as may occur at the margins of lakes are, at most, eulittoral.

To a limnologist Hejny's scheme may appear unappealing in his failure to distinguish the floating-leaved forms as a primary category. It is also probably impractical to apply the criteria separating the Euhydatophyta from the Hydatoaerophyta to all floras in the present state of knowledge. This should not obscure the scientific interest of the differences involved.

Apart from categories dependent on the emergence or submergence of the plant, its relation to a solid substratum is important. As has been indicated in Vol. II (p. 238), Schröter and Kirchner (1896) introduced the noun *pleuston* as a collective term for all free-floating macroscopic plants whether at or below the surface. Gams (1918) restricted the meaning to include only the association at the surface, and this usage was adopted in Vol. II and has probably been followed by some other limnologists. Luther (1949), however, reverted to the original meaning of the term. He regarded all floating plants as *planophytes* divisible into large *pleustophytes* and small *planktophytes*. Actually the distinction breaks down if we compare a large *Volvox* with a *Wolffiella*. Luther divides his pleustophytes into *acropleustophytes* at the surface, *mesopleustophytes* floating between surface and bottom, and *benthopleustophytes* resting on the bottom but capable of drifting slowly with currents. In spite of the prior use of pleuston, Gams' sense may be sufficiently established for it to be unwise to insist on the original meaning. Acropleustophyte and mesopleustophyte clearly can be used unambiguously.

Luther divides the attached forms into *rhizophytes*, rooted in the substratum, and *haptophytes*, attached to but not penetrating solid surfaces. Apart from the rheobiont Podostemaceae, the attached aquatic tracheophytes are all rhizophytes, but most aquatic bryophytes and many algae are haptophytes. The haptophytic nature of freshwater mosses has already been noted as regulating competition between such plants and angiosperms on the shallow parts of lake bottoms. Luther's terms are clearly useful and some have been incorporated into the formal presentation of the next section. Luther's concept of the separation of the unattached pleustophytes from the attached rhizophytes has in fact been taken as primary, because it involves separating those plants whose distribution as mature individuals can be affected by wind or currents from those where this is not possible.

Den Hartog and Segal employ the term *pleustohelophyte* for such species as *Eichhornia crassipes* and on occasions *Calla palustris*, in which the plant floating at the surface grows up some centimeters or more into the air. Furthermore, Hogeweg and Brenkert use *rhizopleustohelophyte* for a plant rooted on the bank, with a floating stem and vegetative parts growing up from it into the air, as in *Decodon*. In this work the pleustohelophytes are included with the acropleustophytes, and the rhizopleustohelophytes with the hyperhydates or helophytes. Both terms, however, may be useful on occasions.

Subdivisions of the hydrophytes have also been proposed on the basis of the way in which a plant tides over the unfavorable part of the year, a criterion central to the definition of the life-forms of terrestrial plants, at least in temperate latitudes (Raunkiaer 1904). Thus the annual species such as *Subularia aquatica*, *Trapa natans*, and the various species of *Najas* are, according to Braun-Blanquet (1928), *hydrotherophytes*, whereas those plants producing buds on a buried rhizome would be *hydrogeophytes*. Buds produced at the water–sediment interface would qualify their possessors as *hydrohemicryptophytes*, but if they were somewhat higher, in the bottom 25 cm of the lake, their bearers would be *hydrochamaephytes*. These terms have not been extensively used.

Growth forms. The concept of a growth form was developed by Du Rietz (1921, 1931). By a growth form is meant a group of taxa that, though often unrelated, have evolved into morphologically comparable forms as an adaptation to a particular mode of life in a specific habitat. Two very obvious and extreme examples are provided by the lemnid growth form of small acropleustonic plants such as *Lemna minor* and *Ricciocarpus natans*, and the isoetid growth form of benthic plants of oligotrophic lakes which have a very short stem and rosette of stiff leaves, such as *Isoetes lacustris* and *Lobelia dortmanna*. The system was further extended by den Hartog and Segal (1964) who recognize 11 growth forms in the hydrophytes (i.e., hyphydates and ephydates) of Europe and still more by Hogeweg and Brenkert (1969) who, considering both western Europe and India, define 20 such categories. The growth forms of Hogeweg and Brenkert are in general adopted in the formal presentation given in the next section. In order to bring the emergent vegetation, hyperhydates or helophytes, into the scheme, Thunmark's two categories of *graminids* and *herbids* have been adopted. These groups may, however, need further subdivision to make them comparable with the growth forms of the submersed species.

Three new growth forms, the *ipomeids*, *decodontids*, and *aeschynomenids* are introduced for the plants that Hogeweg and Brenkert group as rhizopleustohelophytes, rooted in the bank or in the sediment of very shallow water, but with floating stems, often provided with buoyant structures and with emergent leaf-bearing shoots. They seem best regarded as hyperhydates or helophytes but their admittedly special features may make the term rhizopleustohelophyte convenient if cumbersome.

Two groups of hyperhydates with emergent leaves rather than stems are recognized, the *sagittariids* and the *nelumbids*. The floating-leaved plants with ovate or broadly lanceolate leaves, usually in slightly more exposed habitats than the typical nymphaeids, are separated as *natopotamids*.

Hogeweg and Brenkert's category of peplids is not used because it seems that *Peplis* when growing as a fully submerged hydrophyte belongs as naturally as does *Najas* among the parvopotamids. The same is true, in spite of their very different microscopic anatomy, of the charids. There are thus now 26 growth forms recognizable in the lacustrine flora.

The formal ecological classification adopted. The synthetic classification, set out as Table 7, no doubt has various defects; these can probably be removed only by the work of many investigators in different parts of the earth.

TABLE 7. *Classification of life-forms and growth forms of higher aquatic plants*

A. Free floating, without roots or with roots pendant in the water
  I. At surface, upper part of plant ordinarily dry (Acropleustophyta)
    a. Small, often reduced in structure (lemnids)
      Hepaticae: *Ricciocarpus*, very widespread; *Riccia* (*Ricciella*) spp. often at surface
      Filicineae: *Azolla*, six species native in tropical and subtropical regions but often introduced into temperate waters
      Lemnaceae: *Lemna*, duckweed, most of the 15 species, cosmopolitan; *Spirodela*, Eurasia, America, six species; *Wolffia*, temperate and tropical, 10 species; perhaps some *Wolffiella*
    b. Floating stoloniferous rosettes, with sessile leaves (salviniids, the magnolemnids of Hogeweg and Brenkert)
      Filicineae: *Salvinia*, 10 or more species in warmer parts of the earth, often a pest when introduced. *Ceratopteris*, two species in southeast Asia and in American tropics (*C. deltoides* may be rooted, while *C. pteridoides* often floats submersed)
      Euphorbiaceae: *Phyllanthus fluitans*, tropical South America
      Amaranthaceae: *Alternanthera hassleriana*, Paraguay
      Araceae: *Pistia stratiotes*, water lettuce, throughout the warmer parts of the world and often a pest

TABLE 7 (*Continued*)

   c. Floating stoloniferous rosettes, leaves petiolate (hydrocharids)

     Hydrocharitaceae: *Hydrocharis morsus-ranae*, frogbit, in the Old World, usually floating but occasionally may root. *Limnobium*, three species in the warmer parts of the New World, may be floating or rooted. Hogeweg and Brenkert add *Trionea bogotensis*, the nature of which plant I am unable to ascertain

   d. Floating stoloniferous rosettes, emergent leaves with floatlike petioles (eichhornids)

     Pontederiaceae: *Eichhornia*, seven species in the warmer parts of America; of these *E. crassipes*, the water hyacinth, is the most pleustonic and has been widely introduced to the Old World tropics and to the southeast United States, where it becomes a pest

   e. Floating rosettes of partly emergent narrow leaves (stratiotids)

     Hydrocharitaceae: *Stratiotes aloides*, water soldier, floating in summer, often sinking in autumn, apparently due to photosynthetically deposited $CaCO_3$ (Arber 1920 gives life history); a permanently submersed ecophene, f. *submersa*, is also known

 II. Below surface, plant entirely submerged, floating at mid-depths (Mesopleustophyta or Megaloplankton)

   a. Small, the submersed counterpart of the lemnids (wolffiellids of Hogeweg and Brenkert, ricciellids of den Hartog and Segal)

     Hepaticae: *Riccia* (*Ricciella*) when submerged

     Lemnaceae: *Lemna trisulca*, North Temperate zone, *Wolffiella* tropical, eight species. When flowering, *L. trisulca* rises to the surface; constant occurrence of all *Wolffiella* spp. here seems doubtful

   b. Leaves capillary with traps (utricularids)

     Lentibulariaceae: *Utricularia*, bladderwort, numerous aquatic species of a large genus, also with terrestrial species in humid tropics. Flowers emergent; in some species, which are thus at times pleustonic, supported by floating leaves

     Droseraceae: *Aldrovanda vesiculosa*, warmer parts of Old World

   c. Leaves capillary in whorls, without traps, roots absent but stems sometimes becoming buried (ceratophyllids)

     Ceratophyllaceae: *Ceratophyllum* cosmopolitan, six species. Often free on bottom of lakes, so being benthopleustophytic in Luther's terminology

     [*Ceratopteris* may at times float between bottom and surface or sink to the bottom, as may *Stratiotes* in autumn. Some ordinarily rooted plants such as *Elodea* may at times flourish detached from the bottom or form floating mats with the leaves largely submersed]

B. Rooted in sediment (rhizophytes)

 I. Part of vegetative structures emerging above water surface for most of the year (Hyperhydates of Thunmark; helophytes of many other authors)

TABLE 7 (*Continued*)

a. Elongate emergent stems with long cylindrical or narrow flat leaves; leaves sometimes much reduced and entirely subaquatic, the stem acting as the main photosynthetic organ (graminids)

Equisetaceae: *Equisetum fluviatile*, temperate parts of Northern Hemisphere

Sparganiaceae: Some species of *Sparganium* as *S. multipedunculatum*, but the limnologically more significant species have floating rather than emergent leaves

Eriocaulaceae: *Eriocaulon* widely if sporadically distributed

Cyperaceae: A number of species of the very large and predominantly hygrophytic genus, *Carex*, sedge, a few species of *Cladium*, and of the large genus *Cyperus*; the latter quantitatively very important in warm latitudes, *C. papyrus* in Africa north to the Jordan Valley, *C. giganteus* in Neotropical America, *C. articulatus* and *C. ochraceus* extending into southeast United States. *Schoenoplectus lacustris*, bulrush, widespread in the Old World, *S. tabernaemontani*, Palaearctic, and the allied *S. acutus* and other North American species, in that continent referred to *Scirpus.*[a] *Dulichium arundinaceum*, North America. Very many species of the cosmopolitan *Eleocharis*, the spike rush, some of which are usually eulittoral while others may have fully submerged, rosulate forms

Typhaceae: *Typha*, reed mace or cattail, about 10 species, worldwide except in coldest regions

Juncaceae: *Juncus*, rush, mainly cool temperate regions, some fully aquatic members of a vary large genus; a few species have deepwater forms

Gramineae: A number of genera containing species of water grasses, *Echinochloa*, *Glyceria*, *Hydrochloa*, *Leersia*, *Paspalum*, *Zizania* being among the more important, are not always junciform, but transitional to the next category. *Phragmites*, the reed, however, is a very tall and extremely important lacustrine plant, cosmopolitan, with three species

b. Leaf-bearing stem emerging well above water with air leaves that are usually lanceolate, elliptical, or compound above water, and of vegetative importance through most of the growing season (cf. B.III.a.2 and 3); plant often heterophyllous and in many species with very divided water leaves (herbids)

Saururaceae: *Saururus* in North America; ecological status of Asiatic members of the family uncertain

Polygonaceae: Some aquatic forms of *Polygonum* spp. (see p. 168)

Amaranthaceae: Some species of *Alternanthera*, e.g., the North American *A. philoxeroides*

Brassicaceae (Cruciferae): *Rorippa*, watercress, of wide, partly artificial, distribution; *Armoracia aquatica*, lake cress in North America

TABLE 7 (*Continued*)

Lythraceae: *Lythrum* spp. expecially *L. salicaria* in temperate Eurasia, naturalized in North America, *Peplis*, and *Didiplis* may grow in shallow water, as may the more tropical *Rotala* and *Ammania*; some of these may live fully submersed

Haloragaceae: *Proserpinaca*, mermaid weed (see p. 174), North America, and to a lesser extent the otherwise submersed vittate *Myriophyllum* which puts out aerial tips to the shoots with, in some species, heterophyllous air leaves at flowering

Hippuraceae: *Hippuris*, as in *Myriophyllum* (see p. 172)

Callitrichaceae: *Callitriche*, as in *Myriophyllum* (see p. 171)

Hydrostachydaceae: *Hydrostachys*, Madagascar and southeast Africa, probably belongs here

Apiaceae (Umbelliferae): *Berula, Oenanthe, Sium*, widespread in the Northern Hemisphere and often heterophyllous. *Apium inundatum* is largely floating with capillary water leaves and a few air leaves below the flower

Scrophulariaceae: *Limnophila*, widespread in Old World Tropics. *Mimulus guttatus* and *Veronica americana* in North America, and *V. anagallis-aquatica* in Europe, all adventive elsewhere, mainly in ditches and very small pools

Acanthaceae: Some species of *Hygrophila*, a widespread and mainly tropical genus, often divided into a number of smaller genera, are more or less aquatic, notably *Hygrophila longifolia* in India. *Justicia*, warmer parts of America and Asia

Primulaceae: *Lysimachia* spp., a number of species of loosestrife are more or less aquatic

Menyanthaceae: *Menyanthes trifoliata*, the bog bean, widespread in Northern Hemisphere in soft shallow waters

Hydrophyllaceae: Some species of *Hydrolea*, notably *H. affinis* in the warmer parts of North America

Limnanthaceae: Some species of *Limnanthes* in western North America appear to be more or less aquatic

Balsaminaceae: *Hydrocera triflora*, a striking emergent aquatic in India east to Malaya

Asteraceae: *Megalodonta beckii*, the water marigold of North America, is at flowering emergent and heterophyllous, in general comparable in form to *Myriophyllum*; both genera are transitional to B.III.a.3. The Mexican *Erigeron heteromorphus*, if not the other few aquatic composites, belongs here

Butomaceae: *Limnocharis* in South America and *Tenagocharis* in the Old World tropics grow mainly in swamps and seasonal waters; when submersed they probably belong here

TABLE 7 *(Continued)*

c. Climbing and parasitic emergent plants; two genera which when aquatic
are emergent, but clearly not herbiform (ipomeids)
Convovulaceae: Some *Ipomea* spp. notable *aquatica*, in many places in
the tropics, climbing on other emergent plants
Cuscutaceae: *Cuscuta planiflora*, a south European species of dodder,
parasitizes many aquatic plants including even *Isoetes*; when its host
is emergent it may follow it upward and produce flowers

d. Stem floating, often forming a mat, from which shoots bearing lanceolate leaves arise; some sort of buoyant structure usually developed
(decodontids)
Lythraceae: *Decodon verticillata*, North America growing from the
bank, down onto water where the stem develops a float
Onagraceae: *Ludwigia* and *Jussiaea* widespread, often united; some
Jussiaea spp. have buoyant roots.

e. Stem floating, bearing shoots with compound, usually sensitive leaves,
striking development of buoyant stems (aeschynomenids)
Mimosaceae: *Neptunia oleracea*, widespread in tropical regions, as is
the somewhat less truly aquatic *Mimosa pigra*
Fabaceae: *Sesbania* and *Aeschynomene*, of comparable distribution
and habit
[Rosaceae: *Potentilla palustris* may grow out forming a marginal floating mat, but unlike the other species it does not contain buoyant
tissue]

f. Foliose, petiole extending above water so that the leaf rather than the
whole shoot is emergent; flower stalk or inflorescence ordinarily
emerges above water. Emergent leaf cordate, sagittate, or lanceolate
(sagittariids; permanently vegetative submersed populations may be
pseudohydrophytes)
Alismataceae: *Alisma*, several species, Holarctic extending into
south Asia and Australia. *Sagittaria* spp. most species, Holarctic.
Damasonium californicum, *Lophotocarpus californicus* west North
America, *Limnophyton obtusifolium* India, some species of the
widespread *Echinodorus* spp., as *E. cordifolius* in North America
Pontederiaceae: *Pontederia cordata*, the Pickerelweed of North
America: in *Heteranthera* Africa and America, some species as *H.
limosa; Monochoria* spp. Oriental region
Araceae: *Peltandra virginica*, North America

g. As f, but emergent leaf circular, peltate (nelumbids)
Nelumbaceae: *Nelumbo*, southeast Asia, eastern North America.
[Some nymphaeid petioles may raise the leaves they carry above water]

TABLE 7 *(Continued)*

II. Leaves, or at least some of them, floating but usually not emergent (Ephy-dates of Thunmark; included in hydrophytes in den Hartog and Segal)

    a. Floating leaves cordate, circular or elongate-oblong (nymphoid); if heterophyllous, water leaves not capillary (nymphaeids)

        Nymphaeaceae: *Nymphaea*, *Nuphar* widely distributed water lilies, *Euryale* tropical, *Victoria* South America. Floating leaves may be raised a little above water in some water lilies

        Cabombaceae: *Brasenia* America and Old World tropics to Australia

        Apiaceae: *Hydrocotyle*, very widespread, leaves may be emergent in some plants

        Menyanthaceae: *Nymphoides*, an important water lily-like plant in Holarctic and tropics

        Butomaceae: *Hydrocleys* South America, often introduced elsewhere

        Hydrocharitaceae: *Limnobium*, warmer parts of America, rooted or becoming pleustonic

    b. Floating leaves lanceolate (natopotamids)

        Polygonaceae: *Polygonum*, some forms of several aquatic species, notably *P. amphibium* f. *natans* (see p. 170, fig. 71)

        Potamogetonaceae: *Potamogeton* spp., notably *P. natans*, *P. epihydrus*, *P. gramineus*, widely distributed, mainly in temperate regions

        Aponogetonaceae: *Aponogeton* spp., as *A. natans*, mainly tropical

        Sparganaceae: Several species of *Sparganium*

    c. Floating leaves compound (marsileids)

        Filicineae: *Marsilea*, fully aquatic species, widely distributed

    d. Floating leaves simple or partly dissected; water leaves capillary (batrachids)

        Ranunculaceae: *Ranunculus*, many species of the subgenus *Batrachium* with floating leaves below flower, notable *R. peltatus*

        Cabombaceae: *Cabomba*, water leaves myriophylloid, a few small floating leaves below the flower

    e. Floating leaves a specialized rosette, plant usually heterophyllous (trapids), may be mesopleustonic

        Onagracae: *Jussiaea sedoides*, C. America

        Trapaceae: *Trapa*, water chestnut or bull nut. Old World tropics and warm temperate, introduced in America

III. Plant, except flower or inflorescence, submerged (Hyphydates), perennially (euhydatophytes) or during most of the growing season (hydatoaerophytes)

    a. Vittate, long stems or creeping rhizome with long flexible branches

        1. Large or moderate sized leaves (magnopotamids)

            Trapellaceae: *Trapella*, China and Japan

            Potamogetonaceae: *Potamogeton* spp. as *P. lucens*, Europe and west Asia, *P. praelongus* and *P. perfoliatus*, widespread Holarctic

TABLE 7   (*Continued*)

Aponogetonaceae: *Aponogeton* spp. as *A. crispum*, mainly tropical (leaf may be very long and almost zosteroid)

2. Small leaves (parvopotamids)

Callitrichaceae: *Callitriche*, water starwort, almost cosompolitan (apex may emerge)

Lythraceae: *Peplis* and some other genera when fully submerged (the peplids of Hogeweg and Brenkert)

Hippuridaceae: *Hippuris*, mare's tail, apex may emerge or rarely whole plant terrestrial, cosmopolitan

Elatinaceae: *Elatine* spp., waterwort, cosmopolitan but not all species submerged, *E. hydropiper* in Europe and *E. minima* in North America appear to be lacustrine

Hydrocharitaceae: *Elodea*, mainly America, some species widely introduced. *Lagarosiphon*, Africa and south Asia; *Hydrilla*, Old World

Potamogetonaceae: *Potamogeton* spp., notably *P. pusillus*, *P. berchtoldii*, *P. pectinatus*, *P. filiformis*, widely distributed species with very narrow leaves

Najadaceae: *Najas*, small, often deep water, widespread

Zannicheliaceae: *Zannichellia*, horned pondweed, cosmopolitan

3. Leaf myriophylloid, greatly divided (myriophyllids)

Ranunculaceae: The species of the subgenus *Batrachium* lacking floating leaves

Haloragidaceae: *Myriophyllum*, some species partly emergent, cosmopolitan (cf. B.I.b)

[*Cabomba* in the Cabombaceae, *Apium inundatum* in the Apiaceae, *Megalodonta beckii* in the Asteraceae, before the few floating or emergent leaves develop, are myriophylloid, vittate, submerged plants. The rootless megaloplanktonic *Ceratophyllum* and *Utricularia* are likewise vittate and myriophylloid. The peculiar fenestrate *Aponogeton* (= *Ouvirandra*) *fenestrale* from Madagascar is sometimes regarded as a monocotyledonous equivalent of the myriophylloid dicotyled ons; it appears to be rheophile]

b. Stem very short, leaves in a rosette

1. Leaf zosteroid, elongate and ribbonlike (vallisnerids)

Sparganiaceae: *Sparganium fluctuans* when fully submerged

Alismataceae: *Sagittaria* deep water or flowing water forms as *S. sagittifolia* f. *vallisneriifolia*, *S. kurziana* in Florida

Hydrocharitaceae: *Vallisneria*

2. Leaves (phyllodes) petiolate, wide subapically (otteliids)

Hydrocharitaceae: *Ottelia*, Old World tropics

129

TABLE 7   (Continued)

3. Leaves narrow, not greatly elongate, often stiff (isoetids)
    Lycopsida: *Isoetes*, cosmopolitan except in lowland tropics and
      some hard-water regions
    Plantaginaceae: *Littorella*, Europe, America
    Scrophulariaceae: *Limosella*, cosmopolitan, mainly eulittoral on
      mud
    Lobeliaceae: *Lobelia dortmanna*, cooler parts of Holarctic mainly
      in soft waters
    Hydrocharitaceae: *Blyxa*, Old World tropics
    Alismataceae: *Echinodorus* spp., such as *E. tenellus* in North
      America; *Sagittaria* spp., notably *S. teres* and *S. graminea* in
      North America
    Cyperaceae: *Eleocharis* spp., particularly the submersed forms of
      smaller species such as *E. acicularis*, widespread in the Holarctic
      and the North American *E. intermedia* and *E. microcarpa*
    Eriocaulaceae: *Eriocaulon* spp., a few aquatic species as *E. sep-
      tangulare* in a cosmopolitan family
    Juncaceae: Submerged forms of amphibious species, as *Juncus
      bulbosus* f. *fluitans* in Europe and *J. pelocarpus* f. *submersus* in
      North America.
    [Centrolepidaceae: *Centrolepis minima*, eulittoral on sand, Lake
      Brunner and Lake Te Anau, South Island of New Zealand, Lake
      Pedder, Tasmania. *Hydatella inconspicua* in comparable habitats,
      North Cape district of North Island of New Zealand. The family
      is mainly Austral; most species are bog plants]

---

[a] It has proved impractical to achieve consistency in the use of the names *Scirpus*
and *Schoenoplectus*; I have, therefore, followed the Old World practice in recognizing the latter genus in dealing with Old World species, and of recognizing only
Scirpus in writing of plants from the New World.

The earlier scheme of Fassett (1930), developed by Steenis (1932) and
by Wilson (1935, 1939), has played an important part in American limnology. It may therefore be convenient to compare it with the present treatment and with Dansereau's (1958) linguistically more formal classification,
as has been done in Table 8. Dansereau's presentation played an important
part in the elaboration of the final scheme.

In general, the zonation found in the larger more oligotrophic and exposed lakes will consist of graminid emergent plants (B.I.a) nearest the
shore, some floating-leaved plants (B.II.a, b) in more sheltered places
further out, and a submerged flora largely of isoetid rosulate species
(B.III.b.3). In smaller more eutrophic and sheltered lakes some foliaceous
emergent plants (B.I.f) may also be present marginally, the floating-leaved

TABLE 8. *A comparison of the scheme of ecological classification used in the present work, largely developed from Hogeweg and Brenkert (1969) with the earlier arrangements of Fassett (1930), Wilson (1935. 1939), and Dansereau (1945)*

	Fassett–Wilson	Dansereau
A. Natant (Planophyta)		
I. At surface (Pleuston s.s. or		
Acropleustophyta)	Type 5	Natantia (S)
a. Lemnids		
b. Salviniids		
c. Hydrocharids		
d. Eichhorniids		
e. Stratiotids		
II. At mid-depth (Megaloplankton		
or Mesopleustophyta)	Type 5	Natantia (S)
a. Wolffiellids		
b. Utricularids		
c. Ceratophyllids		
B. Rooted in sediment (Rhizophyta)		
I. Part of vegetative structure above		
water (Hyperhydates)	Type 4	Junciformia (J)
a. Graminids		
b. Herbids		
c. Ipomeids		
d. Decodontids		
e. Aeschynomenids		
f. Sagittariids		Foliacea (F)
g. Nelumbids		Foliacea (F)
II. Leaves mostly floating, not regularly		
above surface (Ephydates)	Type 3	Nymphoidea (N)
a. Nymphaeids		
b. Natopotamids		
c. Marsileids		
d. Batrachids		
e. Trapids		
III. Leaves entirely submerged or almost		
so (Hyphydates)		
a. Vittate, with long stem	Type 1	Vittata (V)
1. Magnopotamids		
2. Parvopotamids		
3. Myriophyllids		
b. Rosulate, stem very short	Type 2	Rosulata (R)
1. Vallisneriids		
2. Otteliids		
3. Isoetids		

plants of various kinds are more prominent, and the vittate submerged plants (B.III.a) largely replace the rosulate. The herbiform emergent species are largely not lacustrine but may occur in very protected bays of lakes. The smaller pleustonic species (A.I.a) are mainly found among the littoral vegetation of eutrophic lakes. Large populations of salviniids (A.I.b) and eichhornids (A.I.d) appear to be transitory if often very undesirable phenomena: the other pleustonic plants (A.I.c, e) are often found on the lakeward edge of floating-leaved plants. The most important distinction from a limnological point of view is certainly that between the rosulate and vittate hyphydates. This may well be a separation into species dependent primarily on the sediment for phosphorus and essential cations and, therefore, having proportionately more root as contrasted with the species that can obtain much of their required nutrients from the water.

SUMMARY

Among the smaller groups of lower Tracheophyta *Lepidotis* (=*Lycopodium*) *inundata* and more commonly the horsetail *Equisetum fluviatile* may occur at the margins of lakes. Of greater importance, in the Lycopsida, is the genus *Isoetes* including a number of fully aquatic species of quillwort which are characteristic rosettelike plants forming part of the flora of unproductive and usually soft-water lakes in the temperate regions of the Holarctic as well as of South America, Australia, and New Zealand. More than one species may occur in a lake but the nature of the ecological separation in such cases is unknown. *Isoetes* is probably excluded from many favorable localities by flowering plants and seems to have a wide but largely unrealized niche.

Among the ferns the homosporous *Ceratopterys* contains about half a dozen mainly tropical mesopleustonic or megaloplanktonic species, but they are of little importance in lakes. The heterosporous *Marsilea* occurs mainly rooted in shallow and often temporary waters. *Azolla* and *Salvinia*, which are acropleustonic, are of far greater importance. They are easily introduced into new habitats, particularly in tropical regions, and once established *Salvinia* may form a covering of vegetation over vast areas of water surface, keeping light from the deeper layers and preventing exchange with the atmosphere, and so severely interfering with the ecology of the lake. On Lake Kariba, formed by the damming of the Zambezi River, a population of $n \times 10^{10}$ individuals of *Salvinia molesta* must have been present in 1962; fortunately this has subsequently declined a little.

In spite of the importance of some of the lower rooted plants, the dominant members of the macroscopic flora of lakes are angiosperms. Taxonomically the various groups are distributed very unevenly. On land there are usually four or five times as many species of dicotyledons as mono-cotyledons in any local flora, whereas among water plants the two groups are more nearly equal; if anything monocotyledons are slightly more nu-merous. Within the dicotyledons the Ranales, which are most likely to be related, though perhaps very distantly, to the monocotyledons, have many aquatic representatives. Some of the largest dicotyledonous families, notably the Asteraceae (Compositae) have very few aquatic members. The herba-ceous families that are clearly related to woody plants seem to have few aquatic members. In any satisfactory classification of flowering plants, we should probably find the aquatic species arranged in a very superdispersed manner. Except in the rheobiont Podostemaceae, the genera of freshwater plants tend to be of enormously wide distribution and some species, such as *Ceratophyllum demersum* or *Phragmites australis*, are essentially cosmo-politan.

Ecologically the tracheophytes of lakes may be divided into *pleustophytes* that float freely and the *rhizophytes* that are rooted in sediment. Among the latter three major life forms exist, the *hyperhydates* with much of the vegetative structure above the water surface, the *ephydates* with leaves floating on the water, and the *hyphydates* that are submerged. Within these major groups 26 growth forms may be recognized as set out in Table 7. Among the submersed forms the most important distinction is between the vittate growth forms, the *magnopotamids*, *parvopotamids*, and *myriophyllids*, most characteristic of eutrophic lakes, and the rosulate *isoetids* of relatively oligotrophic basins.

CHAPTER 29

Biological Characteristics of the Tracheophytes of Inland Waters

Before we turn to more ecological matters, it is desirable to point out certain peculiarities of life history, structure, and physiology shared by many water plants, for these peculiarities are often important in the development of biological communities in lakes. The reader who desires to go further should become familiar with Arber's classical work (1920), the two-volume treatment of Gessner (1955, 1959), which is a mine of information on all aspects of aquatic botany, and Sculthorpe's (1967) more recent and most excellent volume with its splendid bibliography. Without these works the labor of producing even an inadequate summary of the limnologically relevant biology of water plants would have been enormous.

In preparing this chapter on the necessary biological background to the ecology of water plants I have been influenced not merely by what the aquatic naturalist needs, but also by a desire to encourage study of certain aspects of freshwater botany, such as heterophylly, which are of extraordinary potential interest to biologists working in quite other areas such as embryology. Moreover, where a subject is dealt with extensively as is the microscopic anatomy of water plants by Sculthorpe, it has seemed unnecessary to give a great deal of detail. For matters specifically concerning the effect of unidirectional water movements, the reader is referred to the chapter on higher plants in Hynes's (1972) excellent work on the ecology of running waters.

THE CHANGE FROM AIR TO WATER

Adaptation to life in freshwaters, by angiosperms ultimately of terrestrial origin, is probably more reversible, in evolution if not perhaps always in ontogeny, than is the case with any other group of organisms. Certain nineteenth-century writers, notably Regnard (1891), believed the shoots of aquatic angiosperms to be covered with a very thin film of gas; such plants might not strictly be considered as aquatic. Since there are a number of genera such as *Ceratophyllum* and *Utricularia* which are free-floating and rootless but which must obtain all their nutrients from supplies in solution in the surrounding water, and since in many other plants, the HCO_3^- ion, as well as CO_2 itself, enters the leaf during assimilation, the idea of a very thin gas film surrounding the plant is not an attractive one. Such a film may form on submersed terrestrial plants, limiting their absorbtive capacities as Raven (1970) suggests. In the absence of very strong contrary evidence it seems reasonable to assume that water plants really live in water. The ecological significance of the wettability or nonwettability of their surfaces is, however, a problem that might be worth much further consideration. Usually the exposed surfaces of floating leaves have a hydrofuge waxy cuticle. In the pleustonic *Azolla*, *Salvinia*, and *Pistia* and in the North American wild rice *Zizania aquatica* specialized hairs form a pile not unlike that found on some aquatic insects (Sculthorpe 1967, pp. 187, 194, 197; Weir and Dale 1960). The problem of the existence of hydrofuge as well as hydrophilic surfaces on parts of the plant below water may be of significance in any consideration of epiphytic algae. Further work is clearly needed.

Adaptation of land plants to an aquatic existence.   Most terrestrial plants do not grow well when entirely submersed, but isolated individuals of certain species of herbaceous genera, of several different families, may occur in nature growing underwater, though most of the specimens of the species and of its immediate allies are terrestrial. Such isolated individuals may exhibit remarkable morphological modifications. A striking example, already briefly mentioned, is provided by the thistle *Cirsium dissectum* (=*anglicum*), a normally terrestrial though markedly hygrophilous species. When it occurs as the aquatic ecophene f. *diversifolium*, primarily recorded from near Bordeaux, the internodes are greatly elongated and the leaves very long and narrow (*A, B* of Fig. 58); only the tip of the stem, with a well-formed flower bud, emerges in extreme cases.

Another comparable case is that of the western European and North African *Illecebrum verticillatum*, a member of the Caryophyllaceae, which normally grows in moist shady places; again the water form is immensely

FIGURE 58. Aquatic forms of some ordinarily terrestrial plants. *A*, *Cirsium dissectum* ($\times\frac{2}{5}$), normal form, growing in swamps; *B*, f. *diversifolium* ($\times 1/10$), growing underwater with only apex bearing flower emergent, both from Cestas, Bordeaux, France; *C*, *Illecebrum verticillatum* ($\times\frac{1}{3}$), land form; *D*, the same water form, both from Algeria; *E*, the aquatic f. *natans* of *Trifolium resupinatum* bearing the sterile parasite *Cuscuta planiflora* var. *aquatica* f. *submersa* ($\times\frac{2}{3}$), Algeria; *F*, emergent part of *Oenanthe fistulosa* (natural size) bearing flowers of *C. planiflora* var *aquatica* (Glück).

elongate (*C, D* of Fig. 58) but unlike that of *Cirsium dissectum*, it is sterile (Glück 1911).

A third case may be mentioned, that of the Mediterranean dodder *Cuscuta planiflora* which can, as var. *aquatica*, parasitize a variety of submersed plants, including *Isoetes* (Glück 1936). Here there is little to modify morphologically underwater, though the parasite fails to bloom (f. *submersa*) except when it has invaded a part of the host plant emerging as an aerial shoot (*E, F* of Fig. 58). It is possible that in this case *C. planiflora* var. *aquatica* is a genetically determined aquatic form and not an ecophene.

Amphibious plants. Among the large number of typically amphibious plants there is great variation in the relative development of the aquatic and terrestrial forms. Sometimes, as in *Limosella aquatica*, the regularly occurring submersed form is larger than the terrestrial and appears to represent the most vigorous development of the species. *Acorus calamus* is known to flower only when its rhizome is below the water level (Buell 1935). In *Polygonum amphibium*, discussed later (see p. 171) at least some clones cannot flower when grown terrestrially, though the inflorescences of the aquatic form are borne only on the emergent parts of the plant. In *Veronica anagallis-aquatica*, the water form is somewhat more luxuriant than that growing terrestrially, but the plant cannot flower when wholly submersed. *Juncus pelocarpus* and *Gratiola aurea*, though reduced in size (Fassett 1930; Wilson 1935) and sexually sterile when growing underwater, may nevertheless form large, ecologically important, submersed populations which must often be more extensive than those growing, often in the eulittoral, exposed to the air. A peculiar case is provided by *Hottonia palustris*, which when rooted near the banks of a pond may develop a rhizome from which develop both large aquatic shoots, producing inflorescences above water, and smaller entirely terrestrial shoots which are sterile (*B* of Fig. 41). The rhizome may later decay, leaving independent plants growing both on land and in water, though only the latter flower (Prankerd 1911).

A number of details relating to specific aspects of the biology of amphibious plants are taken up later.

Terrestrial forms of normally aquatic species. When cultivated carefully under moist conditions, many of the floating-leaved angiosperms and some of those primarily submersed freshwater species that may produce emergent shoots may be induced to develop into small terrestrial plants. It is probable that the process in general is easier than cultivating terrestrial plants underwater (cf. Allsopp 1965b). It has been recorded as happening in nature (Glück 1936) in various broad-leaved species (Fig. 59) of *Potamogeton*, in *Sagittaria sagittifolia* (*C* of Fig. 68), in *Nymphaea alba* and in *Nuphar lutea* (*D* of Fig. 28), in *Myriophyllum* spp., and in *Utricularia*, as for instance *U. intermedia* (Baumann 1911; see also *D* of Fig. 40). Usually in

FIGURE 59. *Potamogeton natans*, Slovakia. (*a*) Ordinary aquatic form; (*b*) terrestrial form growing on dried mud (Hejny).

such cases the plant starts to grow in an originally wet but rapidly drying environment. The morphology and habit of many such plants have been described by Glück (1911, 1936), who performed numerous experiments in which water plants were cultivated terrestrially. The subject has also been considered by Arber (1920). In view of the ease with which terrestrial forms can be produced, it seems likely that most of the difference between aquatic and terrestrial infraspecific taxa is ecophenic; *Polygonum amphibium* gives a hint (see Fig. 71) of a little genetic adaptation. The plasticity implied, particularly in microscopic anatomy, however, is truly remarkable and deserves even more attention from the developmental biologist than it has been given. In nature the production of terrestrial specimens from aquatic species is usually unimportant ecologically, though in one or two cases such as the occurrence (Heslop-Harrison 1955b) of the terrestrial form of *Nymphaea alba* under very humid conditions in a few localities in western Ireland, the process occurs regularly and is not without interest. The capacity to produce such terrestrial forms is no doubt of value in tiding a species over periods of temporary drought (Hejny 1960; den Hartog and Segal, 1964) in areas much less humid than the extreme west of Europe.

Structural bases of the adaptation. The comparison of terrestrial and aquatic ecotypes of the same amphibious species, no less than the general comparison of the terrestrial and aquatic floras, indicates certain structural corollaries of aquatic life that occur over and over again, not only in angiosperms, but in aquatic ferns like *Marsilea* and even to some extent in bryophytes. Plants developing in water are more elongate, often with long internodes and longer, narrower leaves; these characters mainly express the lower light intensities encountered underwater. Hairs are usually suppressed, though *Veronica anagallis-aquatica* provides a curious exception. Stomata are scarce or absent on the submersed surfaces of leaves. Palisade tissue may not be developed, being replaced by spongy parenchyma with large air spaces; superficial cells which would contain few or no chloroplasts in emergent or terrestrial leaves are often richly chlorophyll-bearing. Such epidermal cells are often more elongate than in a terrestrial leaf. They are doubtless more prone to be wettable, though this important difference has not been stressed. There is a reduction in the development of the vascular system, particularly of the xylem. Cuticularized and lignified supporting structures tend to be absent, whereas lacunar spaces become prominent (Fig. 60). Many examples of these changes are given in the discussion of heterophylly in subsequent pages of this chapter (cf. Fig. 69, 70, 77). Fundamentally the change in passing from air to water may be interpreted as the disappearance of adaptations against water loss to a gaseous environment of negligible buoyancy.

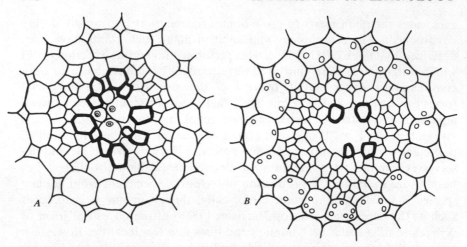

FIGURE 60.   *Callitriche stagnalis.*   *A*, Section of air stem with marked development of xylem and some pith cells; *B*, section of water stem with reduced xylem and central space lacking pitch cells (×475; Arber after Schenck).

Occasionally a species may grow, as does *Isoetes engelmanni* in Mountain Lake, Virginia, both in the water and terrestrially without any striking differentiation of aquatic and terrestrial forms (Parker 1943), though in this case the aquatic form was deeper green and its spores may have had a proportionately larger velum. Though *I. engelmanni* appears ordinarily to be aquatic, Parker records that the specimens growing both in water and aerially at Mountain Lake had stomata and well-developed cuticle.

Functional significance of habit and leaf form.   The emergent species of very protected waters, which may be expected to suffer no more from wind exposure than the plants of sheltered meadows or the edges of woodland, are of various forms, not strikingly modified in adaptation to their habitat. In all the more disturbed habitats the aerial plants rooted in the water tend to be very elongate with cylindrical, or very narrow, or very reduced leaves. This arrangement, in conjunction with suitable microscopic anatomy, permits the plant to bend with the wind. The various truly aquatic species of *Scirpus* (including *Schoenoplectus*) would appear to be better adapted in this respect than is *Phragmites*. Part of the differentiation in distribution of these plants is, however, based on the properties of the rhizome, which at least in *S. lacustris* is harder than in *P. australis*, so that the former plant can grow on a gravelly bottom, while the latter does best rooted in mud (Brand 1896).

When the leaves alone are emergent, there is a strong tendency, appearing independently in several monocotyledonous families (Alismataceae, Araceae, Pontederiaceae), for these emergent leaves to have long petioles bearing cordate, triangular or sagittate blades (Figs. 48, 52, 66, 68). The investigations of Arber (1918) on *Sagittaria* in the first of these three families and on *Heteranthera* and *Pontederia* in the third, confirmed an earlier suspicion of de Candolle (1827) that the blade itself is a pseudolamina, formed by the flattening of the distal part of the petiole.[1] This produces inverted vascular bundles, corresponding to those of the upper perimeter of the petiole, as well as bundles that are normally oriented. The full functional meaning of this arrangement and of the form of the blade itself is not clearly understood, though the sagittate shape, which can be very extreme (*I*, *J* of Fig. 66), may be involved in reducing wind resistance. It is also possible that leaves having approximately the form of an isosceles triangle, when set close together but oriented at random, may provide a maximum surface for uptake of light with a minimum of overlap. An example of this may be provided by *Peltandra*.

In floating-leaved plants the leaves at the surface are generally either ovoid or approximate to an almost circular cordate form, the petiole being inserted at the apex of a cleft. In heterophyllous species in which sagittate aerial leaves are produced, a complete set of transitions between elongate ovoid, floating, and emergent sagittiform leaves may occur. The cleft, characteristic of the subcircular leaves of *Nymphaea* and *Nuphar* (Fig. 28), closed in the evolution of *Euryale* and *Victoria* (Vol. II, Fig. 6), and a similar development occurred in *Brasenia* (*A* of Fig. 61) and the small floating leaves of *Cabomba* (*B* of Fig. 61). In *Nelumbo*, which must have evolved in the same way, the resulting peltate leaf has been thrust up above the level of the water by the growth of the petiole and thus has, presumably secondarily, achieved a purely aerial existence (*C* of Fig. 61).

Sculthorpe (1967) gives a good account of the general adaptation of floating leaves, pointing out the importance of their being able to resist damage by waves and by heavy rain falling on them. Heslop-Harrison (1955a) concludes that the stronger floating leaf of *Nuphar lutea* enables this species to inhabit rather more exposed reaches of the sublittoral than can *Nymphaea alba*. She quotes horticultural experience that *N. lutea* and *N. advena* stand up against mechanical disturbance better than other species of the genus. Pearsall (1920), writing of the English Lake District, says

---

[1] It is, however, convenient to call all such structures leaves when they are being discussed in relation to the biology of the plant bearing them.

FIGURE 61.   *A, Brasenia schreberi* (Cabombaceae), Maine, peltate floating leaves on petioles arising from flower stalk ($\times\frac{1}{2}$); *B, Cabomba coroliniana*, Arkansas, apex of plant with flower, minute peltate floating leaves and submerged myriophylloid leaves (natural size); *C, Nelumbo luteum* (Nelumbaceae), Illinois, peltate leaf ($\times 1/10$), above water surface (Herbarium, Yale University).

that *Nymphaea alba* var. *minor*[2] (sub *Castalia minor*) and *Nuphar* × *spennerana*[3] (sub *Nymphaea intermedia*) are more resistant than either nominotypical *Nymphaea alba* or *Nuphar lutea*. *Nuphar* × *spennerana* is believed to be the hybrid *N. lutea* × *pumila*; *pumila*, however, occurs in Britain only in northern Scotland and in two relict stations in Shropshire and Wales. The hybrid, however, does occur in northern England and southern Scotland, and may well be better adapted to disturbed environments than either parent. Like *Nymphaea alba* var. *minor* it is smaller than its widespread sympatric congener, and this may have something to do with the wave resistance of the two smaller taxa. *N.* × *spennerana* is, however, larger than *N. pumila*, but that species, according to Heslop-Harrison (1955a), is confined to undisturbed localities owing to its less robust rhizome. If Pearsall is correct, his observations are obviously of considerable evolutionary interest; it is possible, however, that not too much emphasis should be placed on his brief remarks.

In general, as in the particular case of the English lakes just discussed, the suborbicular floating-leaved species will be found in less disturbed places than plants such as *Potamogeton natans* with lanceolate or elliptical leaves.

Hiern (1871), about a century ago, examined the mechanical theory of the growth of floating leaves in moving water. He concluded that if the growth potential were constant at any point on the margin of a leaf, the leaf when growing in a constant current would have a mathematically rather complicated oval form, though in still water it would of course be circular. It is, however, extremely unlikely that when floating leaves are not circular, the whole of the departure from circularity is due to external forces. Nevertheless, Hiern's rather elaborate treatment is not without value, for it is probable that when a biological form appears explicable by the operation of external forces, the form actually has developed, through the operation of genetically determined morphogenetic processes, so as to produce a structure on which the external forces will have a minimum

---

[2] Professor T. G. Tutin points out (in litt.) that *N. alba* "grows both in rich lowland waters and in poor upland waters as well as in intermediate habitats. It is now generally agreed that *N. occidentalis* (Ostenf.) Moss (= *N. alba* var. *minor*) represents one extreme of the variation correlated with this range of habitats and does not merit formal recognition." The taxon has been called var. *minor* throughout this work.

[3] Heslop-Harrison thinks *spennerana* refers to a backcross to *lutea* of the hybrid *lutea* × *pumila*, which she refers to × *intermedia;* the Lake District plants which, however clonal, are unlikely to be genetically first-generation hybrids, may well be largely × *spennerana* in this sense.

effect.[4] Hiern does mention that "many floating leaves, as for example in Ranunculus, vary considerably in consequence of, or in association with, the nature of the stream in which they grow," but no further attempt at confirmation of the theory was made.

It is not unlikely that the lanceolate or ovate leaves of some of the less delicate floating-leaved plants are actually adapted in this way, for whenever a wind is blowing, a current will be flowing at the surface and the leaves will tend to orient downstream, presenting minimum resistance to the forces the supposed consequences of which Hiern so elaborately investigated.

Among the submersed limnetic water plants, as has been already discussed (p. 132), there are two fundamental life-forms, the compact or *rosulate* form, typically with an extremely short stem bearing stiff awl-like leaves, and the trailing *vittate* form with very long stems and leaves of varying shape, the whole producing minimum resistance if water is moving past the plant. The rosulate form (Figs. 26, 44, *A* of Fig. 66) characterizes the vegetation of unproductive lakes; these may often be large and windswept, and have but sparse plant populations. The form may be in part an adaptation to marked littoral disturbance accompanied in some cases by the transport of coarse inorganic sediment, but its fundamental significance doubtless lies in the higher ratio of mineral, and possibly even CO_2, uptake by roots from the mud to uptake by the green parts when the water is poor in nutrients. It is however, curious that rosulate plants often seem associated with the most highly leached sediments in a lake (see p. 446).

The leaves of many water plants, as well as the stems, may be very long and trailing. This is apt to happen in its most extreme form when fundamentally rosulate plants evolve into large lax vallisneriid forms giving no resistance to moving water. *Vallisneria* (*F* of Fig. 47) provides a good example of such *zosteroid* leaves in standing water, but more extreme types are provided by some species of *Sagittaria*, notably *S. kurziana* which in rivers may have leaves up to 15 m long! In many such cases in flowing water a direct positive effect of moderate movement on growth seems reasonable (cf. Gessner 1955, p. 306), though rapid flow usually is inhibitory. In con-

---

[4] This argument applies even more to much in D'Arcy Wentworth Thompson's *On Growth and Form* (Thompson 1917, 1942), as has been pointed out elsewhere (cf. Hutchinson 1948, 1953). Thompson does not refer to Hiern's work, but it is conceivable that he had known of it vaguely, as it was done and published in Cambridge a decade before Thompson came up to that University as a highly precocious freshman with a couple of publications to his credit. We know from a footnote on p. 27 of *On Growth and Form* that Thompson was familiar with the contents of the *Proceedings of the Cambridge Philosophical Society* from 1881 onward, so it is not inconceivable that he had seen Hiern's paper, which was published 10 years earlier in that journal.

trast to this type of elongation, the vittate stems of parvopotamids bear either small entire *elodioid* leaves, as in *Elodea*, or in the myriophyllids and some other growth forms, greatly divided leaves. This is true of *Myriophyllum*, of most leaves of *Cabomba, Ceratophyllum*, of the water leaves of most aquatic species of *Ranunculus, Utricularia*, and of many other heterophyllous plants. Great dissection to produce a *myriophylloid* leaf is of course much easier in the dicotyledons than in the monocotyledons.

PHOTOSYNTHESIS IN AQUATIC PLANTS

At sea level and at a temperature of 0°C, air containing 0.033 vol % CO_2 contains 0.65 mg liter^{-1} CO_2, and at 15°C about 0.62 mg liter^{-1} CO_2. The figures correspond to about the amount of dissolved CO_2 in pure water in equilibrium with air at 15–20°C (Vol. I, p. 654); at lower temperatures the quantity is a little greater. Roughly we may equate the equilibrium concentrations in the two media. This provides for the photosynthesizing plant a very different situation to that of any respiring organism, which encounters about 20 times as much oxygen per unit volume in air than in water at 0°C, and a greater inequality at higher temperatures. In spite of this favorable effect of the much greater solubility of carbon dioxide than of oxygen, the assimilating plant is still at a disadvantage in the water, owing to the much lower coefficient of molecular diffusion in a liquid than in a gaseous medium. Submerging a land plant in water in equilibrium with the atmosphere may reduce its photosynthetic rate to a negligible value (Popoff 1941).

Gessner (1955, p. 268) has published posthumously the very interesting results obtained by his student P. Müller, who studied a simple case. Müller determined the rate of photosynthesis, as a function of CO_2 concentration, by the moss *Polytrichum formosum* in both air and water, and found that approximately 10 times as great a concentration of the gas is needed in water as in air to achieve any given rate (Fig. 62). He concluded that in both cases the limiting factor is the passage of the gas through an undisturbed film of water on the surface of the leaves of the moss. In water this layer would be the Prandtl boundary or unstirred layer, outside of which flow is turbulent for all ordinary velocities, and which Müller calculated in his case to be 0.4–0.8 mm thick. A comparable value of 0.5 mm is given by Raven (1970), from a survey of the available literature, for large plant organs, while the unstirred layer around a *Chlorella* cell might be about 0.005 mm in thickness. In air the water film held on the leaf is said by Müller to be about 0.05 mm thick. The rate of entry of CO_2 will be roughly inversely proportional to the thickness of the film or about 10 times faster in air than in water.

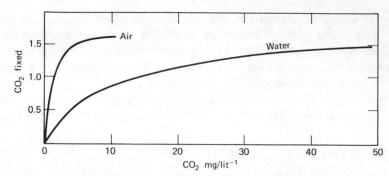

FIGURE 62. Photosynthetic uptake (arbitrary units) of CO_2 by the moss *Polytrichum formosum* in air and in water, plotted against concentration of the gas (Gessner after Müller).

In higher plants the problem becomes more complicated owing to the presence of waxy and dry epidermis, stomata, and other structural complications, which in preventing loss of water are not likely to facilitate entry of CO_2. The fundamental problem will persist, however, though the quantitative contrast may be less great than in the case of *Polytrichum*. That rates of assimilation are more likely to be limited by diffusion of CO_2 in water than they are in air, is indicated by the rather lower discrimination against uptake of ^{13}C in water plants; the diffusivity of $^{13}CO_2$ is only about 1% less than that of $^{12}CO_2$, whereas a considerably greater difference of about 2–3% may be expected in the rates of chemical reactions (Abelson and Hoering 1961; Park and Epstein 1960, 1961; Smith and Epstein 1969).

Morphological adaptation promoting photosynthesis underwater. The considerable difference in the accessibility of CO_2 in air and in water has led to at least two quite different types of major adaptation. One is the morphological elaboration of leaves to increase the area to volume ratio. This can culminate in the production of the extreme myriophylloid form in which a laminar leaf has become dissected into a series of branching cylinders. The area of a thin lamina when dissected into cylinders of the same diameter as the original thickness of the lamina, and without loss of volume, will be twice the original area of the lamina. This is not the only way of achieving such a result. Merely reducing the thickness of the leaf is an even simpler way, and feasible in water, for instance in the case of the water leaves of *Nuphar* (see p. 159), in a manner that would not be possible in air. The transfer of all exchange to the outer surface of the leaf when the problem of water loss ceases to be of any importance, a change reflected in the simple anatomy of many submersed leaves, also increases the ease with which CO_2 can be assimilated.

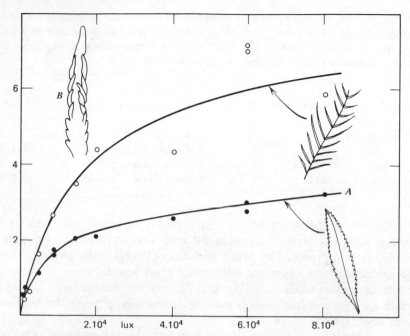

FIGURE 63. *A*, Photosynthesis (arbitrary units), as a function of light intensity, by capillary and by laminar water leaves of *Proserpinaca palustris* (Gessner) with diagrammatic drawings of the two kinds of leaves; *B* indifferent leaf primordium (Burns).

Comparing the dissected with the relatively entire leaf, Gessner (1937) has given some experimental results. His most interesting case concerns *Proserpinaca palustris*, a highly heterophyllous plant in which very slightly and markedly dissected types of leaf can occur underwater on the same plant. Though the slightly dissected leaf has the overall shape of an aerial leaf, the microscopic anatomy is typically that of a water leaf. Comparison of the photosynthetic rates at different light intensities (*A* of Fig. 63) shows that except in a very dim light, the dissected myriophylloid leaf assimilates about twice as fast as the undissected.[5]

Gessner also made the observation that the rate of photosynthesis is dependent on the movement of the water, and that this effect is greater in the case of laminar than in that of myriophylloid leaves (Table 9).

---

[5] As with all Gessner's experiments of this sort, the results are given in volumes of sodium thiosulfate used in titration, 1 ml being equivalent to 0.08 mg O_2, but though time intervals may be given, the amount of photosynthesizing tissue is not; one can merely assume that the amounts are equivalent.

TABLE 9. *Effect of turbulence on increasing photosynthesis by laminar-leaved and capillary-leaved water plants, the figures giving the percentage increase in passing from still to turbulent waters. The experiments on* P. palustris *may have been conducted under rather different conditions from the others*

Almost undivided, laminar	Increase (%)	Much divided, capillary	Increase (%)
Groenlandia densa	36.0	*Myriophyllum heterophyllum*	9.5
P. perfoliatus	34.4	*Ranunculus aquatilis*	19.4
P. crispus	33.0	*Cabomba aquatica*	15.0
Proserpinaca palustris	21.7	*Proserpinaca palustris*	5.4

These observations emphasize that until an adequate theory exists for the uptake of nutrients by leaves of different form in turbulent water, comparable to that provided by Munk and Riley (1952) for the phytoplankton, the problem of the optimum leaf form for an aquatic plant remains unsolved. It is quite likely, however, that for any set of conditions no unique solution exists and that there is more than one way of being the best of all possible leaves.

Since respiration of higher plants is essentially independent of oxygen concentration over 30% saturation, very little effect of turbulence on respiratory rate is ordinarily encountered.

Utilization of bicarbonate ions as a source of CO_2 and other physiological adaptations. The second adaptation is a biochemical one, namely, the uptake of bicarbonate ions rather than that of CO_2 directly. In all but the most dilute waters the quantity of bicarbonate as HCO_3^- present in nature is likely to be several times, and in extreme cases several hundred times, the amount of CO_2 as such. Any plant that can utilize, even rather inefficiently, this bicarbonate as a carbon source is obviously at a great advantage. Since the time of Hassack's (1888) investigation of *Nitella, Chara, Potamogeton,* and *Callitriche* it has been suspected that some water plants could do this, but at the time of his study the chemical equilibria involved were so poorly understood that no valid conclusions could be drawn. In spite of some earlier observations, reviewed by Sculthorpe (1967), the phenomenon was not critically established until the initial study of Ruttner (1921), which has been greatly extended by Dahm (1926), Arens (1930, 1936a, b), Steemann Nielsen (1946, 1947), Gessner (1959), Spence (1967a), and Ruttner (1947, 1948) himself. The simplest way of demonstrating the utilization of bicarbonate is to allow plants to photosynthesize in a closed container filled with ordinary hard water rich in calcium bicarbonate and brightly illuminated. As CO_2 is utilized the pH rises, and since CO_2 is being removed from the system, the absolute quantity as well as the proportion of free CO_2 to carbonate and bicarbonate will fall as the pH rises. If the plant can use only CO_2, photosynthesis will stop when the concentration of the gas becomes negligible, and at this point the rise in pH will also stop and the conductivity, which will have decreased owing to precipitation of $CaCO_3$, will no longer fall. In general this happens when the pH is a little over 9.0. If the plant can use HCO_3^-, the fall in conductivity and rise in pH can continue until the latter is well above 10.0. The method is not quite reliable because pH changes can be produced by assimilation of ammonium or of nitrate ions and possibly by fluxes of H^+ or OH^- ions from the plant; in all the cases to be discussed these possible effects are unlikely to have produced major errors.

In Fig. 64 some of Ruttner's data for experiments with bryophytes, with various immersed land plants, and with several aquatic angiosperms are presented graphically. Neither bryophytes nor submersed land plants can make effective use of bicarbonate, but the higher water plants initially studied were able to do so. Raven (1970), however, points out that it is not certain that the aqueous medium is in contact with a submersed land plant, so that an air film might be interrupting the diffusion of HCO_3^-.

More critical studies, using more elaborate methods, often involving actual measurements of the rate of uptake, have been carried out by Steemann Nielsen (1946, 1947), Gessner (1959), Spence (1967a), and by more recent investigators whose work on the Charophyceae has already been discussed (see pp. 17–20). Consideration of the whole of the available work would suggest that among the flowering plants *Ceratophyllum demersum, Ranunculus aquatilis, R. trichophyllus* (sub *flaccidus*), *Myriophyllum spicatum, Vallisneria spiralis, Elodea canadensis, Egeria densa, Potamogeton crispus, P. lucens, P. pectinatus, P. schweinfurthii, Gidensa Lemna trisulca,* and *Heteranthera graminea* all can use the bicarbonate ion as a source of carbon in photosynthesis. Gessner, comparing specimens of *P. crispus* from standing and from running water, found no difference in bicarbonate uptake. Among the higher aquatic plants, most evidently possess the capacity. The list of those known to lack it is short but very interesting. *Myriophyllum verticillatum,* growing with *M. spicatum* in the Federsee (Gessner 1959) did not use bicarbonate. According to Spence (1967a), *M. spicatum* occurs primarily in hard waters where the faculty would be useful, whereas *M. verticillatum* is more euryionic.

Lobelia dortmanna, so characteristic of the soft-water unproductive lakes of northern Europe, would be suspected of lacking the capacity and in fact cannot use bicarbonate, nor can *Isoetes lacustris* found in the same kinds of habitat. The peculiar South American rheobiont *Apinagia multibranchiata* in the Podostemaceae also lacks the capacity (Pannier, in Gessner 1959).

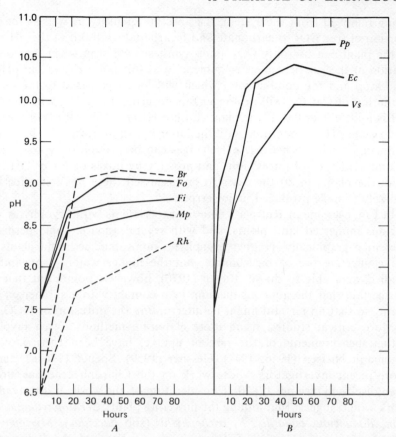

FIGURE 64.   Rise in pH of a hard water initially near neutrality, owing to the photo-synthesis (*A*) of bryophytes (solid lines), *Fo* Fontinalis antipyretica; *Fi, Fissidens rufulus,* and *Mp, Marchantia* cf. *polymorpha*; and of land plants (broken line), *Br, Brassica oleracea*; and *Rh, Rhododendron* sp. cultivar Cunningham's White. (*B*) The same for water plants normally living in hard waters, *Pp, Potamogeton pectinatus; Ec, Elodea canadensis; and Vs, Vallisneria spiralis.* The bryophytes are typical of all the aquatic forms studied; none raise the pH more than does *F. antipyretica.* The land plants represent the extremes of seven species, whereas the water plants are typical of those from hard waters, all raising the pH to well over 9.8.

Gessner found that one specimen of *Callitriche* sp. could not use bicar-bonate but suspected this to be due to the plant in question not having true water leaves (see p. 171); if this supposition is correct it suggests interesting possibilities for investigation.

Ruttner (1921, 1947) studied a number of bryophytes including a liver-wort referred to *Marchantia polymorpha* and the aquatic mosses *Fontinalis antipyretica, Brachythecium rivulare, Fissidens russula,* and *Crateroneuron* spp. without finding evidence of the capacity. Steemann Nielsen (1947) also studied *Fontinalis,* and obtained essentially negative results.

Among benthic algae, however, the faculty appears to be widespread. *Cladophora glomerata* and *Ulothrix zonata* clearly can use bicarbonate (Gessner 1959), as can *Spirogyra varians* (Dahm 1926; Bode 1926), *S. majuscula, S. maxima,* and more doubtfully *S. gracilis* (Bode 1926). Raven (1968) has made an elaborate study of the uptake of bicarbonate by *Hydrodictyon africanum,* which he showed to be an active process, promoted by light. Data on planktonic algae have already been given in Vol. II (p. 309), though since its publication it has become evident that bicarbonate is likely to be an important source of carbon in the photosynthesis of blue-green algae (Morton, Sernau, and Derse 1972). Further critical work on this is badly needed. The important recent studies on the Charophyceae have already been summarized (see pp. 17–20).

In the higher plants, at least as exemplified by *Potamogeton,* when bicarbonate is the carbon source in photosynthesis, bicarbonate ions, balanced by calcium ions, enter both sides of the leaf, while hydroxyl ions, also balanced by calcium, are liberated on the upper or adaxial surface (Arens 1930, 1933, 1936a, b; Gessner 1937; Steemann Nielsen 1944, 1946, 1947; Lowenhaupt 1956, 1958a, b; Raven 1970). The reaction is light dependent, but Lowenhaupt (1956) found that calcium can be taken up in the dark, following exposure of the leaf to light in the absence of calcium. This suggests that a coupling agent is formed photochemically and can be stored in the cell until calcium is available.

Sources of carbon dioxide. It is important to emphasize that the experimental approach to the ecology of photosynthesis in macrophytes sometimes seems to lead to ecologically improbable results. Spence (1967a) points out that *Fontinalis antipyretica* not merely requires CO_2 as such, but appears to need it in the laboratory in quite large quantities, in equilibrium with about 0.01 atm, 1 vol % at sea level of the gas, for photosynthesis to be effective. It is difficult to see how in many of the habitats of this moss it can meet with the required concentrations. In some cases carbon dioxide may be diffusing upward from the more or less organic mud on which the moss is growing. There is, moreover, a suggestion, from the presence of many chloroplasts in the cells around the air spaces in the submersed leaves of *Littorella* sp. and *Isoetes* sp., that conduction of CO_2 from the sediments through the root upward into the leaf is of importance in such plants (Grubb, in Raven 1970). Gessner (1959) indeed finds the same arrangement even in vittate stems of *Myriophyllum.* This structural characteristic of some water plants thus perhaps provides a third specific type of adaptation for obtaining carbon dioxide when living underwater.

It is not unlikely that in a few noncalcareous oligotrophic lakes with very inorganic sediments, a low CO_2 concentration may set limits to the occurrence of rooted vegetation, as Goldman (in Frantz and Cordone 1967) suggests has happened in the infralittoral of Lake Tahoe.

Paths of CO_2 fixation. In land plants there are two main pathways by which CO_2 enters the photosynthetic process. In the simpler and commoner of these two, found in most temperate tracheophytes, the first product of carbon fixation is triphosphoglyceric acid, which then undergoes a series of changes, known, after its discoverer, as the Calvin cycle. Since the initial compound contains three carbon atoms, plants exhibiting this path are usually called C_3 plants. In a number of tropical plants living in full sunlight, and in some temperate species that flourish under hot, bright conditions, there is a different mode of initial fixation, oxalacetic acid being formed and directly transformed into malic or aspartic acids, the preponderance of which depends on the taxonomic position of the plant. Such plants are usually called C_4 plants. They have a characteristic microscopic anatomy, commonly called Kranz structure, correlated with CO_2 being fixed as a C_4 acid in one part of the leaf, the resultant dicarboxylic acid being transferred and decarboxylated in another part, where the CO_2 liberated enters the Calvin cycle. The active transport of C_4 acids away from the fixation site keeps the physiological compensation point at a vanishingly low CO_2 concentration. Photorespiration, which in C_3 plants depends on the production of glycolate, does not occur to a detectable extent. The maximum photosynthetic yield in C_4 plants is usually obtained between 30 and 40°C, while the temperature optimum for C_3 plants is between 10 and 25°C. A further modification of the C_4 or dicarboxylic acid pathway is observed in the Crassulaceae and a few other plants living under dry conditions, in which fixation occurs at night, while the Calvin cycle proceeds by day when the chloroplasts are illuminated but the stomata are closed to prevent water loss. For further details the reader is referred to Downton (1971) and other review articles in Hatch, Osmond, and Slatyer (1971).

It is extremely unlikely, then, that any submersed macrophytes are C_4 plants, though this pathway may occur in *Saccharum*, *Paspalum*, and some species of *Cyperus*, genera that include helophytes growing around lakes. Dr. Walter V. Brown of the University of Texas kindly informs me that although all species so far examined in the terrestrial composite genus *Pectis* are C_4 plants, unlike the great majority of the Asteraceae, the species of the very closely allied *Hydropectis*, containing the hygrophyte *H. stevensii* and the truly aquatic *H. aquatica*, have the C_3 pathway.

Stanley and Naylor (1972, 1973) have obtained evidence that plants of a clone clearly referrable to *Myriophyllum spicatum*, originally derived from Alabama, show a vanishingly low physiological compensation point and a temperature optimum for photosynthesis between 30 and 40°C. Moreover, the presence below the leaf parenchyma of storage cells which become filled with starch, and which are found in various water plants (Wetzel, personal communication), is somewhat reminiscent of the sheath cells storing starch in certain tropical grasses. Though these characters immediately suggest the highly efficient adaptation of such tropical Gramineae as *Zea* and *Saccharum*, detailed biochemical study indicates conclusively that *Myriophyllum spicatum* is a C_3 plant, in which triphosphoglycerate is the first product of CO_2 fixation and in which photorespiration involving glycolate occurs. Glycolate oxidase is known in *Elodea* sp. and in *Lemna minor* as well as in *Myriophyllum* (Frederick, Gruber, and Tolbert, 1973).[6] There is practically no other information about these matters in submersed angiosperms. Hough and Wetzel (1972) have detected photorespiration in *Najas flexilis*. The rate, however, is low except at very high oxygen concentrations of up to 25 mg liter,[-1] much in excess of equilibrium with respect to air, though possible in weed beds on bright afternoons. Among littoral hyperhydates, *Typha latifolia* was found by McNaughton and Fullem (1970) to have a photosynthetic assimilation process almost as efficient as that of *Saccharum* and other cultivated grasses with a C_4 pathway, although it is a C_3 plant. Gifford (1974) believes that in optimal circumstances such C_3 plants have a net photosynthetic efficiency approaching that of C_4 plants, but that the latter on account of their higher temperature optimum and more efficient use of water may prove more effective over the course of a year in warm temperatures and tropical countries than do the C_3 plants.

The HCO_3^- uptake mechanism is in some, if rather remote, ways an aquatic analogy to the C_4-dicarboxylic acid pathway, in that it presumably involves active transport of combined CO_2 to the site of the Calvin cycle and a decarboxylation as the substance enters the latter. In alkaline waters it also permits photosynthesis to reduce the CO_2 concentration to vanishingly low levels. The matter of possible differences in optimum temperature for photosynthesis between plants using only CO_2 and those also using HCO_3^- remains to be investigated.

---

[6] These workers found glycolate oxidase, which also oxidizes *l*-lactate and is cyanide-insensitive, in the lower tracheophytes and such mosses and liverworts as they studied; it was also present in some green algae (*Coleochaete, Klebsormidium, Spirogyra, Netrium*, and in the charophycean *Nitella*). Other green algae (*Chlorella, Dunaliella, Eremosphaera, Oocystis, Protosiphon, Codium, Microspora*, and *Stigeoclonium*) have a different glycolate pathway involving glycolate dehydrogenase, which also oxidizes *d*-lactate and is cyanide-sensitive. The authors point out that these findings may be of considerable phylogenetic interest.

The physiological ecology of photosynthesis at various light intensities and depths. Spence and Chrystal (1970a, b) have studied a number of angiosperms which grow in nature at characteristic depths in the lakes of Scotland. These plants were cultivated in a glass house under extra illumination. The leaves produced were believed to have developed under comparable conditions in the different plants and may be regarded as sun leaves. The depth distributions of the five taxa of Potamogeton which appeared suitable for the detailed experiments, along with the mean photosynthetic rate of isolated sun leaves, or disks cut from leaves, are given in Table 10, prepared by reading off from Spence and Chrystal's graphical representation.

TABLE 10. Photosynthetic rates, under standard conditions, of five taxa of Potamogeton growing over different depth ranges in Scottish Lakes (data from Spence and Chrystal)

Taxon	Depth range in Scotland (cm)	Mean depth in Scotland (cm)	Photosynthesis, under 7.08 cal cm^{-2} hr^{-1} (μl O_2 mg^{-1} dry leaf hr^{-1})
Potamogeton polygonifolius	−38 to 60	8 ± 22	36.8
P. filiformis	4 to 150	53 ± 42	16.6
P. × zizii	18 to 210	121 ± 57	23.6
P. obtusifolius	48 to 310	181 ± 112	29.0
P. praelongus	123 to 250	191 ± 48	22.9

Experiments were done in which photosynthesis was measured under reduced irradiance after an initial run at 7.08 cal cm^{-2} hr^{-1}; the plants were then returned to the original irradiance for a further control run. P. filiformis usually failed to return to a high rate of oxygen production during the second run at 7.08 cal cm^{-2} hr^{-1} and was, therefore, not used in the most critical experiments.

The results can be expressed in various ways. Spence and Chrystal give for their earlier series of experiments the relative decrease under the lower irradiance as a percentage of the mean photosynthesis at 7.08 cal cm^{-2} hr^{-1} during the first and last third of the experiment (Fig. 65A). In later studies they give the actual decrease (Fig. 65B) in oxygen produced as μl $O_2 \cdot mg^{-1}$ dry leaf·hr^{-1}. They do not give the actual values of the O_2 production but only the difference. Ecologically such absolute values at different values of irradiance might be the most interesting figures; they can be roughly ob-

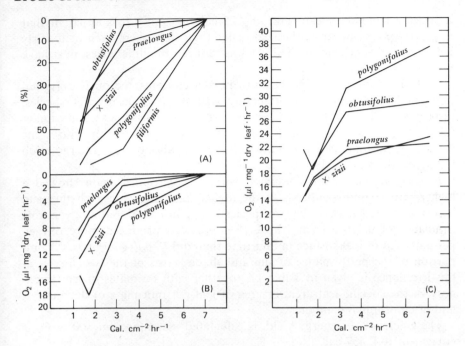

FIGURE 65. Effect of light intensity on photosynthesis of various species of *Potamogeton* studied by Spence and Chrystal. (*A*) Percentage reduction with decreasing irradiance; (*B*) absolute reduction with decreasing irradiance in a second set of experiments; (*C*) data of *B* subtracted from mean photosynthetic rate of 7.08 cal cm^{-2}, hr^{-1}. All experiments conducted on sun leaves adapted to high light intensities.

tained (Fig. 65*C*) by subtracting the differences plotted in Fig. 65*B* from the photosynthesis by sun leaves at 7.08 cal cm^{-2} hr^{-1} given in the last column of Table 10.

Potamogeton polygonifolius, probably the most amphibious member of its genus (*E* of Fig. 80), growing at or above the water's edge, shows the highest rate of photosynthesis in bright light, but this declines strikingly and regularly as the irradiance is reduced. The sun leaves of the deep-water species *P. praelongus* and *P. obtusifolius*, naturally living in 2.5–3 m of water, photosynthesize more slowly than *P. polygonifolius* in bright light but show less reduction in rate as the intensity is reduced. *P.* × *zizii* is somewhat intermediate between these and *P. polygonifolius*.

The actual decline in photosynthetic rate varies in a generally comparable way, being initially greatest in *P. polygonifolius* and least in *P. obtusifolius* and *P. praelongus* with *P.* × *zizii* intermediate. At low irradiances *P. obtusifolius* falls more than *P. praelongus* or *P.* × *zizii*. When these values are subtracted from the mean rates at 7.08 cal cm^{-2} hr^{-1}, it is apparent that *P. polygonifolius* photosynthesized faster than the others even at a fairly reduced irradiance, but as the light was reduced the differences must have become less.

In their second paper Spence and Chrystal concentrated on *P. polygonifolius* and *P. obtusifolius* representing shallow- and deep-water species, respectively. Plants of both species were grown in a glass house, some under full light (sun leaves) with 16 hr supplementary irradiation and some shaded by muslin (shade leaves), which received about 6% of the radiation falling on the sun leaves.

P. polygonifolius when compared with *P. obtusifolius* again showed a higher rate of photosynthesis at the higher light intensities, whether sun leaves or shade leaves of the two species were considered, but at a very low irradiance of 0.216 cal cm^{-2} hr^{-1}, *P. obtusifolius* produced more oxygen per unit area of leaf surface in unit time than did *P. polygonifolius*. A comparison of the performance of sun and shade leaves of the two species at this irradiance is given in Table 11, together with estimates of leaf thickness, of the specific leaf area, or area of leaf per unit mass of dry matter, and of chlorophyll content.

The efficiency, or energy yield, is calculated assuming that 100 μl O$_2$ is equivalent to 0.457 cal.

TABLE *11.* *Mean specific leaf area, leaf thickness, oxygen production, respiration in darkness, gross photosynthesis, and photosynthetic efficiency in a shallow-water* (P. polygonifolius) *and a deep-water* (P. obtusifolius) *species of* Potamogeton (*data from Spence and Chrystal*)

	P. polygonifolius		P. obtusifolius	
	Sun	Shade	Sun	Shade
Mean specific leaf area (Cm^2 mg^{-1})	0.48	1.43	1.91	2.05
Leaf thickness (mm)	0.120	0.040	0.028	0.026
Chlorophyll (a + b) (mg · 100 cm^{-2})	2.38	1.20	1.08	1.33
Net O$_2$ production (μl O$_2$ · 100 cm^{-2} · hr^{-1})	80 ± 2	112 ± 1	116 ± 1	156 ± 103
Respiration in dark (μl O$_2$ · 100 cm^{-2} · hr^{-1})	−149 ± 12	−109 ± 17	−34 ± 6	−1 ± 9
Gross photosynthesis (μl O$_2$ · 100 cm^{-2} · hr^{-1}	229	221	150	157
Gross energetic efficiency (%)	4.8	4.6	3.1	3.3
Gross photosynthesis (mg CO$_2$ · mg^{-1} chlorophyll · hr^{-1})	0.16	0.31	0.23	0.20

The most remarkable feature of these data is the very much lower respiration exhibited by *P. obtusifolius*. This makes possible a larger net rate of photosynthesis at low light intensities than in *P. polygonifolius*, even though the latter has a greater gross rate and a greater energetic efficiency. Presumably decrease in leaf thickness, to a degree that would not be possible in air without a proportional decrease in chlorophyll content, permits the lowered respiration of the deep-water species.

Photosynthesis in emergent vegetation. In spite of these adaptations it remains possible that the most efficient water plants are emergent, using the bottom sediment and water as sources of most nutrients, including water, but obtaining CO_2 and oxygen from the air, thus making the best of all the primary divisions of the biosphere. It is interesting in this connection, and of great practical importance in absolute sedimentary chronology, that emergent plants tend to have ^{14}C contents in equilibrium with the CO_2 of the atmosphere, whereas in very hard water draining from limestone, the internally produced organic matter of a lake, like the bicarbonate of its water, is apt to be deficient in ^{14}C (Table 12).

Table *12. Comparison of ^{14}C content (arbitrary values of specific activities in cpm for the particular apparatus used) of organic carbon of emergent and submersed plants in soft waters in Connecticut and in Queechy Lake, New York, draining from Paleozoic limestone and markedly deficient in ^{14}C (Deevey, Gross, Hutchinson, and Kraybill 1954)*

Plants	Cpm
Mean submersed, soft water	6.13
Mean emergent and marginal, soft water	6.17
Mean submersed (*Potamogeton, Chara*), Queechy Lake	5.08
Mean emergent (*Scirpus, Carex*), Queechy Lake	6.06

HETEROPHYLLY AND COMPARABLE ENVIRONMENTALLY DETERMINED VARIATIONS IN LEAF FORM

The term *heterophylly* strictly denotes the phenomenon of a single plant bearing two or more different kinds of leaf. Since in some cases, in which leaf form is under environmental control, two plants growing in different environments may each bear a uniform and environmentally characteristic type of leaf, while a third individual, growing in an environment that has changed while the leaves developed, is strictly heterophyllous, it is often the practice to regard the term heterophylly as covering any variation in leaf form within a genetically uniform population whether the different types are borne on the same or on different plants. The stricter definition is used in this chapter, the more extended meaning being covered by the phrase *environmentally determined form.*

Heterophylly is of course not confined to water plants. Since juvenile leaves are nearly always at least slightly different from those of more mature plants, a kind of heterophylly is very widespread as a transitory phenomenon, and may in fact be the basic condition from which the more dramatic cases evolved. In herbaceous plants with well-developed basal and cauline leaves, both present in the adult, such terrestrial heterophylly can be quite striking.

Some environmental modification of the shape of almost any leaf is possible. In water plants heterophylly and comparable environmentally determined differences in form are clearly related in many cases to the shoot growing up out of the water into the air, where a different kind of leaf is physiologically appropriate. Within the water, moreover, the upward growth of a shoot over a vertical distance of 0.5 m may in some cases provide the developing leaf rudiments at the apex of the shoot with a much greater change in environment than would occur in 5 or even 50 m of growth on land. Practically all emergent species, unless they are very elongate, reedlike, or junciform, show some degree of heterophylly, and the phenomenon is very common among species with floating leaves. There are, moreover, enough cases of environmentally determined differences in leaf form in completely submersed plants such as various species of *Potamogeton* to show that the passage from water to air is not the only efficient cause of such differences.

It is clearly impossible to consider every case of heterophylly in aquatic plants; those discussed have been chosen either because they involve species of some limnological importance or because they have been subject to some degree of experimental analysis. It is desirable to point out, before proceeding to any actual cases, that two rather different kinds of heterophylly seem to exist among aquatic plants. In the first kind the early leaves are of a specific, juvenile, but not necessarily phylogenetically more primitive type, *whatever the environment in which they may develop*, whereas the later leaves normally start to develop in close proximity to those that appeared earlier and in the same environment as the latter, but grow into an adult structure usually characteristic of a floating or emergent life. These later leaves are, however, not strictly determined as floating or aerial types; extreme environmental conditions may force them to develop a submersed, or in the purely temporal sense, a juvenile form. The early leaves are thus determinate, the later ones labile. This type of heterophylly is exhibited by *Sagittaria* in the Alismataceae and by *Nuphar* in the Nymphaeaceae and probably by other genera in these families. In the second type of heterophylly any leaf rudiment is initially labile and can ideally be modified in the various ways characteristic of the plant that bears it, *the form depending on the environment in which the leaf develops*. Experimental evidence indicates that this is true of the differentiation into aquatic or aerial leaves in *Marsilea drummondi, Proserpinaca palustris, Callitriche* spp., *Veronica anagallis-aquatica, Hippuris vulgaris*, and some of the extremely heterophyllous aquatic species of *Ranunculus*. It is probable that this type of heterophylly is the more frequent kind, though in the majority of heterophyllous water plants really critical evidence is lacking. Cook (1966b) further distinguishes between those cases (*Marsilea, Callitriche, Veronica, Hippuris*) in which air leaves are directly evoked by the plant growing out of water and other cases, as in the majority of the species of the subgenus *Batrachium* of *Ranunculus*, where a change in photoperiod, ordinarily geared to the growth and flowering season, is the environmental stimulus for the change in form.

Heterophylly in the Nymphaeaceae and Cabombaceae. In the genus *Nuphar* (*A* of Fig. 28) and to a rather less extent in *Nymphaea*, a very simple kind of heterophylly exists. The leaves that develop from the apices of the rhizome in winter or early spring are flaccid, translucent, and with wavy margins; in *Nuphar lutea* they are but 0.1 mm thick whereas the floating air leaves are 0.44 mm thick (Grainger 1947). Such water leaves lack stomata. They may be the only type (f. *submersa*) produced by *N. lutea* in running water. Arber (1920) believed that in very hot bright summers only water leaves might be produced; Heslop-Harrison suspects that in such cases young rhizomes, which ordinarily do not produce floating leaves or flowers, are forced into flowering earlier than usual. The water leaves can persist throughout the winter in localities which do not freeze. Ordinarily the floating leaves, opaque, tough, and with regularly rounded margins, are produced in late spring and summer. They are borne on petioles which are rather longer than the depths of water in which the plant is growing, so that the leaves can be spread around, but there is evidently some limitation on petiolar growth (Gessner 1955). They have stomata on their upper sides. Though there is clearly a possibility of the inhibition of floating leaf formation by environmental factors such as running water, both water and floating leaves develop their characteristics underwater in similar microenvironments. Glück (1936) implies that even the small f. *terrestris*, growing abnormally on damp soil in air, starts by producing small leaves comparable in texture to water leaves. There is little doubt that the differentiation between the earlier submersed and the later floating leaves is dependent to a considerable extent on internal factors.

In the fluviatile *Nuphar sagittifolia*[7] from the rivers of Virginia and the Carolinas, both types of leaf are well-developed and both exhibit the very elongated form (*F, G* of Fig. 28) characteristic of the taxon.

The early leaves of *Nymphaea* are also water leaves, but they are less numerous and less persistent than in *Nuphar*; late in the season emergent leaves may be produced in this genus. The earliest leaves, presumably water leaves, in *Victoria* are sagittate (Allen 1854).

In the related family Cabombaceae the genus *Brasenia* (*A* of Fig. 61) bears as an adult plant ovoid peltate leaves, but the earlier leaves are not unlike those of *Nymphaea*. As the plant matures the slit between the posterior lobes is obliterated. This small degree of heterophylly is comparable with what can often be observed on land. In striking contrast, in *Cabomba* (*B* of Fig. 61) itself, though a few very small elongate ovoid peltate floating leaves are associated with the flowers, the submersed part of the plant bears highly dissected myriophylloid leaves not unlike those found in the batrachian species of *Ranunculus*. These highly dissected leaves may in a sense be juvenile, but can hardly be phylogenetically primitive.

Heterophylly in the Alismataceae. Some of the most striking cases of heterophylly occur in various species of the family Alismataceae. Although it has long been realized that these plants can be arranged in a fairly good linear series so far as leaf development is concerned, as was done by Arber (1920), it is reasonably certain that such a series is not a true expression of phylogeny. The fact that the leaves of the Alismataceae appear to be morphologically equivalent only to the petiole, expanded in many species to form a pseudolamina, suggests that the unspecialized linear phyllode is indeed a primitive form in the family; the fact that it occurs in unrelated species, often as a response to low light intensity and perhaps other environmental stimuli, indicates that it may be borne as the sole kind of leaf by plants which have had less primitive kinds in their immediate ancestry. Moreover, although the extreme arrowhead leaf of *Sagittaria longiloba* (*J* of Fig. 66) is clearly very specialized, the capacity to produce the very long ribbonlike leaf with which the series begins may in itself be another sort of specialization.

The simplest condition is perhaps that found in *Sagittaria teres* (*A* of Fig. 66) from Massachusetts southward to New Jersey, a plant regarded by Bogin (1955), in his monograph of the genus, as a geographically defined variety of *S. graminea*, though he admits it comes close to being specifically distinct, as has usually been maintained. In this plant, which has

---

[7] Beal (1956) accords no taxon of *Nuphar* specific rank save *N. lutea*. Most subsequent authors, though acknowledging the great value of his monographic work, recognize at least some of the distinct allopatric taxa as species.

FIGURE 66. Leaves of species of *Sagittaria* illustrating variations in form. *A, S. teres,* Ninemile Pond, Centerville, Mass., a rosulate from with submersed fleshy phyllodes, and emergent flower stalk; *B, S. graminea,* Cherokee County, Kansas, emergent narrow blade; *C,D, S lancifolia,* Jacksonville, Florida, ovoid and lanceolate water leaves; *E, F, G, S. latifolia* f. *hastata,* inundated shore, St. John River, Aroostock County, Maine; *H, S. latifolia,* dwarf plants probably from very shallow water, Great Falls, Montana; *I, S. engelmanniana,* peaty quagmire, Griffith's Pond, Brewster, Mass., emergent and submersed leaf on a mature plant; *J, S. longiloba* ($\times \frac{2}{5}$; Herbarium, Yale University except *J*, after Mason, modified).

a typical rosulate form, the leaves form a rosette of rather fleshy phyllodes, entirely submersed, and when the plant flowers, the emergent inflorescence is borne on a stem considerably longer than the leaves. In the closely allied *S. graminea* (*B* of Fig. 66) found throughout eastern North America, there may be emergent leaves with narrow blades or elongated submersed phyllodes, less fleshy and so perhaps less specialized than those of *S. teres.*

There is evidently a great deal of genetic control of leaf form in *S. graminea* and its allies (Wooten 1970). In another relatively unrelated species, *S. sanfordii*, endemic to the Great Valley of California, the long slender phyllodes usually emerge at their tips, but some may develop narrow apical floating blades. *S. kurziana*, living in Florida and evidently co-occurring with the typical *subulata*, to which Bogin assimilates it as a variety, can in rivers develop with submersed phyllodes up to 15 m long, possibly the longest leaflike structures known in any angiosperm; the inflorescence is also very long (Bogin 1955). Less extreme ribbonlike phyllodes may also develop as the sole leaf type in *S. sagittifolia* f. *vallisnerifolia* (*A* of Fig. 68) in deep water in the humid parts of the Palaearctic region. This form of *S. sagittifolia*, a species which can, under appropriate conditions, produce highly specialized aerial leaves, is clearly an ecophene, but in both this species and *S. kurziana* it is possible that the capacity to produce such very long-leaved ecophenes and to grow where their production is appropriate represents a specialization when compared with plants such as *S. teres* or *S. graminea*.

In the genus *Echinodorus*, in which in fully aquatic species the leaf is usually emergent or floating, ovoid, or cordate, the dwarf *E. tenellus* can have water and land forms occurring together, respectively submersed (*A* of Fig. 67) in the shallowest part of the infralittoral and emergent in the eulittoral or supralittoral (*B, C* of Fig. 67) of small lakes. The submersed form has tapering phyllodes that develop narrow lanceolate blades in the emergent form. Comparable forms of *Sagittaria graminea*, not growing in the same locality, are not only genetically determined but also unable to grow in each other's environments (Wooten 1970). Most of the other genera of Alismataceae have ribbonlike juvenile leaves which can persist for varying lengths of time throughout the summer, followed by ovate, elliptical, or cordate leaves which may be floating or emergent (Fig. 48). *Alisma graminifolium* and *Baldellia ranunculoides* are cited by Arber as examples of plants with persistent ribbonlike submersed leaves and emersed lanceolate leaves produced late in the season. *A. plantago-aquatica* typically does not (*A, B* of Fig. 48) retain the early more elongate leaves.

In *Luronium natans* the submersed leaves are usually not persistent and the broadly elliptical leaves are floating. *Damasonium alisma* has non-persistent submersed ribbonlike leaves and floating and emergent leaves, the blades of the last-named being somewhat cordate. Comparable aerial leaves occur in a number of species of *Echinodorus*. Most of these plants bear large inflorescences and occur mainly in small ponds and other quiet bodies of water.

By far the greatest variety of leaf form is found in *Sagittaria*. The species with narrow phyllodes have already been mentioned. In *S. lancifolia*

FIGURE 67. *Echinodorus tenellus*, Winter Pond, Winchester, Mass. *A*, Shallow water, October 20, 1901; *B*, muddy shore, presumably eulittoral, September 15, 1906: *C*, no record of habitat, probably upper eulittoral, August 27, 1884 (natural size; Herbarium, Yale University).

(*C*, *D* of Fig. 66) from tropical and warm temperate America, the later leaves are ovoid or lanceolate with no basal lobes. The usual specialization, however, is the backward extension of the basal part of the leaf to form lobes which are foreshadowed in the somewhat cordate leaves of other genera such as *Echinodorus*, giving rise in extreme cases to the arrow-shaped leaf from which *Sagittaria* takes its name. In the best studied cases such as *S. sagittifolia*, the earliest leaves are ribbonlike phyllodes (*A* of Fig. 68) formed as such even if a tuber has been stranded by a flood and has started to develop on land (*C* of Fig. 68). It is evident that the form of these phyl-

FIGURE 68. *Sagittaria sagittifolia*, the common arrowhead of the Old World. *A*, Completely submerged, deep-water f. *vallisneriifolia*, retaining ribbonlike leaves throughout life; *B*, typical form, collected on July 16, 1916, presumably near Cambridge, showing sagittate

lodes is internally determined; they are in fact inevitably juvenile leaves. They are normally followed by a series (*D–F* of Fig. 68) of lanceolate and moderately sagittate floating leaves; finally the extreme sagittate emergent leaf appears (*B, G–I* of Fig. 68). The sagittate leaf is very variable in some species, notably in the North American *S. cuneata* and certain populations (*E, F, G* of Fig. 66) of the widespread American *S. latifolia* (Mason 1957). In other species, though lanceolate floating leaves may be produced, the aerial sagittate leaf has a fairly constant and characteristic form as in the eastern North American *S. engelmanniana* (*H, I* of Fig. 66) and still more so in *S. longiloba* (*J* of Fig. 66) from Central America and the southwestern United States, which is distinguished from all other species by having the posteriorly directed lobes of the arrow much longer than the median anterior lobe.

As has just been noted, when *Sagittaria sagittifolia* starts to develop as a land plant in flood jetsam or in the laboratory, the initial leaves are ribbonlike phyllodes (Arber 1920). In water the same kind of initial leaf is produced and in deep water all subsequent leaves are ribbonlike (f. *vallisneriifolia*). Goebel (1895) found that this form persisted under reduced illumination, which presumably explains the occurrence of f. *vallisneriifolia* in nature. Under adequate illumination floating and aerial leaves appear. Since at least the initial lanceolate and sagittate leaves are produced at the same level as the early narrow leaves, they probably have received about the same light flux; the difference in form must therefore be of internal rather than environmental origin, even though reduction in light intensity shows this difference also to be under environmental control.

There is a tendency in *Sagittaria*, well exhibited by *S. sagittifolia*, for the most northern plants in subarctic regions to form not emergent, but only submerged and floating leaves. Such plants in this species (f. *natans*) have smaller achenes than the typical form.

Heterophylly in *Marsilea*. The heterosporous and usually amphibious fern *Marsilea* exhibits a moderate degree of heterophylly. The first leaf to be produced by a sporeling is a simple elongate structure, but a quadrifoliate structure is progressively developed in later leaves. In water leaves

---

leaves and stolons (*s*) terminating in young tubers (*t*); an adult of the metallic green musk beetle *Aromia moschata* characteristically sitting on a leaf, its larva having spent its life in a nearby willow bole, has been added to Arber's figure; *C*, young plant growing in jetsam left on bank of River Cam, Waterbeach near Cambridge, May 31, 1911, from a mature tuber (*t*) and initially producing ribbonlike leaves; *D, E, F*, various forms of floating leaf; *G,H,I*, various forms of emergent leaf (*A, D–I*, Glück; *B, C*, Arber modified by addition of musk beetle posed from memory and based on a specimen in the Museum of Zoology, University of Cambridge; *C* ×$\frac{1}{5}$, others ×1/10).

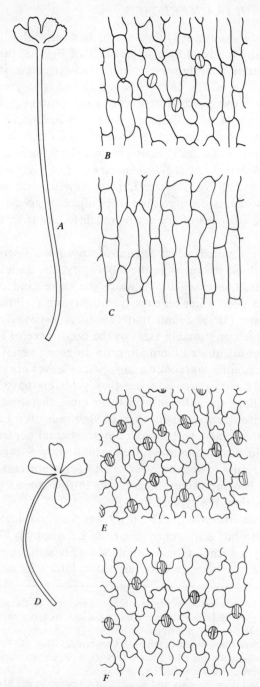

FIGURE 69. Experimentally produced heterophylly in *Marsilea drummondi*. *A*, water leaf grown in 1% glucose; *B,C*, upper and lower epidermis of same; *D*, "air" leaf grown in 5% glucose; *E,F*, upper and lower epidermis of same (Allsopp).

the four lobes are directed upward (*A* of Fig. 69); there are very few stomata in the thinly cuticularized epidermis and these occur only on the morphologically upper leaf surface, and the epidermal cells tend to be elongate rectangular (*B*, *C* of Fig. 69). Air leaves have the four lobes extended at right angles to the stem (*D* of Fig. 69), have many stomata on both surfaces, and well cuticularized irregular epidermal cells (*E*, *F* of Fig. 69). The floating leaves in form are like aerial leaves but with numerous stomata only on the upper surface.

Very extensive experimental studies by Allsopp (1954a, b, 1955, 1963, 1965a, b) on *Marsilea drummondi* have done much to elucidate the nature of the processes producing the heterophylly, but some aspects are still not clearly understood. Allsopp grew his plants in liquid culture medium at a light intensity of 150 ft-candles; at this illumination no growth occurred without the addition of glucose. The addition of progressive amounts of glucose reduced the number of juvenile leaves formed before the adult quadrifoliate form was established. In 2% glucose only water leaves were produced, though growth was very vigorous. When the concentration was raised to or above 4% glucose both the external morphology and microscopic anatomy corresponded to those of land leaves though the plant was fully submerged. Fructose behaved similarly; in the case of sucrose a higher concentration of 10% by mass was needed to produce land leaves, corresponding to the larger molecule of the sugar. Addition of 2% mannitol and 2% glucose produced land leaves; but in 4% mannitol, which the plant cannot use, only stunted water leaves developed. Allsopp concludes that higher osmotic pressure is a determinant of the land leaf but that this operates only in the presence of adequate carbohydrate in solution. Allsopp's view appears to be that the high osmotic pressure in the medium causes a concentration of the cell contents and, if adequate carbohydrate is present, this concentration leads to the production of land leaves. In 4% glucose, addition of 3-indoleacetonitrile, which leads to a great elongation of the cells of the petiole, inhibits the action of the glucose and permits the development of water leaves. Gibberellic acid acts similarly. Allsopp supposes that the rapid elongation reduces the intracellular carbohydrate concentration. Changing the medium from 4% glucose to 2% glucose permits vigorous growth, but only water leaves now appear. Clearly there is no question of the water leaves being merely starved leaves, or the growth would decrease as the change from one type to the other occurred; this does not happen.

Allsopp found that under some conditions metabolic inhibitors, such as 0.01 *M* arsenite, produced land leaves. White (1966), continuing this line of investigation, discovered that when thiouracil, which inhibits protein synthesis, is added to a medium in which water leaves would ordinarily appear, the growth of the sporelings was stunted but the leaves that developed had the microscopic anatomy characteristic of land leaves. Evidently conditions conducive to rapid protein synthesis and rapid growth, with relatively high water content in the cells produced, lead to the development of water leaves, while the reverse processes, in which soluble carbohydrate accumulates in the more concentrated cell sap, lead to the production of land leaves. In spite of the elaborateness and elegance of the research on which such statements are based, it cannot be said that the process is fully understood.

Heterophylly in *Veronica anagallis-aquatica.* The water speedwell, widespread in Europe and adventive in North America, is an example of an amphibious plant, which when growing partly in water and partly in air as it usually does, exhibits rather unspectacular heterophylly morphologically but is found to show very remarkable physiological differences between the aerial and the aquatic parts (Gertrude 1937).

The plant normally grows in shallow water, the upper part emerging above the water level. The leaves borne underwater are larger, broader, less acuminate, and with almost entire margins; the aerial leaves are narrower, more acuminate, markedly thicker, and with slightly serrated margins. The species is quite atypical in that submerged parts tend to be hairy, the emergent glabrous.

The water leaves have a considerably greater water content than do the air leaves, and a much lower osmotic pressure. Photosynthesis proceeds at the same illumination and temperature about as fast in air leaves in air as in water leaves in water when the rate is referred to photosynthesate produced per unit wet weight, but the rate per unit dry matter is inevitably higher in the wetter water leaves. Phosphorus and organic nitrogen are accumulated in greater quantities in the water leaves. Lipogenesis appears to be greater in the water leaves, whereas carbohydrate, to which most of the osmotic pressure is due, accumulates in the aerial leaves. Unless the plant can grow into the air it cannot flower.

The physiological differences which accompany the very moderate heterophylly in *V. anagallis-aquatica* are in some ways comparable to those observed in *Marsilea* and probably are of considerable generality.

Environmental differentiation in *Polygonum.* In several species of *Polygonum*, as has been indicated earlier (see p. 83), land and water forms exist which differ primarily in the land form having narrower pubescent leaves and the water form broader glabrous and usually floating leaves (Fig. 70). The differentiation, as in the preceding case, is very moderate, as is also shown by comparing the extreme forms of the North American *P. coccineum* (Fig. 30).

Turesson (1961) has investigated the matter using 20 clones of *P. amphibium* from 19 Swedish localities. All can grow as either terrestrial or

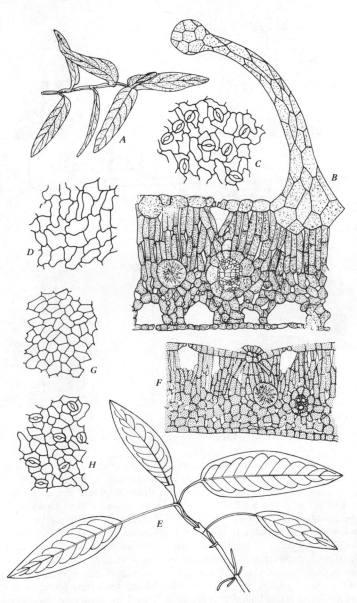

FIGURE 70.   Anatomical changes produced environmentally in *Polygonum amphibium*. *A*, Extreme terrestrial form growing on sand dunes, Coxyde, Belgium; *B*, section of leaf of same; *C* inferior epidermis of leaf of same; *D*, inferior epidermis of leaf of such a plant transplanted and grown under water; *E*, aquatic form, Belgium; *F*, section of leaf of same; *G*, inferior epidermis of leaf of same; *H*, the same from an emergent branch. (Massart, somewhat modified).

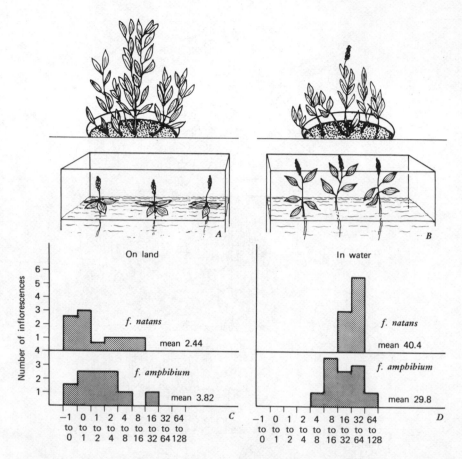

FIGURE 71. *A, B,* Diagrammatic drawings of two clones of *Polygonum amphibium* growing experimentally in pots of soil and in adjacent tanks of water. *A,* From Västervik, Smaland, Sweden, the aquatic form being f. *natans* with floating leaves, the terrestrial tall and luxuriant but sexually sterile; *B,* from Mösseberg, Västergotland, Sweden, the aquatic form being spicate and not unlike the terrestrial in habit, the terrestrial being shorter and less luxuriant than *A* but with an occasional inflorescence. Drawn from photographs in Turesson (1961) but much stylized; these two clones were not side by side in the experiment, which was , however, conduced in the way shown; *C.D,* distribution of number of inflorescences in culture (*C*) on land and (*D*) in water, in clones growing in water as in f. *natans* and in those growing as spicate plants like the terrestrial form *amphibium*; the classes are arranged logarithmically to the base 2, with the zero class divided equally between 0 and 1 and an arbitrary —1 to 0 class; note suggestion of a tendency for f. *natans* to flower less when growing on land than does the typical form.

aquatic plants (Fig. 71). In the aquatic series, however, two different habits were observed. In nine clones the plants developed as typically floating-leaved aquatics (f. *natans*) while 11 clones retained the erect spicate form of f. *terrestris*, with most of the leaves above water. Apart from this dichotomy, which is presumably of genetic origin, the plants grown aquatically showed less variability than those grown terrestrially. In the terrestrial plants there was in particular noticeable variation in the maximum height, and the relative order of height from clone to clone was the same in two summers in which the weather, and so the absolute height of the plants, was quite different. The terrestrially grown specimens of some clones are sexually sterile, and even when inflorescences are produced they are at least three times as numerous on the aquatic as on the terrestrial plants. The clones that produced f. *natans* when growing in water tended to have rather fewer inflorescences on land and rather more when growing in water, than did the spicate form, perhaps suggesting slightly greater aquatic adaptation. Unfortunately no data are given on the pubescence of the leaves, and a finer examination of the leaf form might well have been interesting.

Heterophylly in *Callitriche* and *Hippuris*. The species of *Callitriche* usually occur in shallow standing or slowly flowing water. Floating crowns of emergent leaves develop at the apices of the main stem but axillary shoots also bear numerous submerged leaves. In *C. stagnalis* all the leaves are more or less ovate, with at least a vein on either side of the midrib in the water leaf and usually more than two in the air leaf (*A*, *B* of Fig. 72). In *C. obtusangula* (*C*, *D* of Fig. 72) and *C. intermedia* (Fig. 73) the aerial leaves are ovoid with typically five veins; in *C. obtusangula* and *C. intermedia* the water leaves are long, parallel-sided, and with a single vein. When plants of *C. intermedia* are artificially submerged (Jones 1955a, b), the new leaves formed are linear and the leaf primordia that had started in air tend to change their shape to a more elongate form as they grow. The effect of submergence is said to be greater in running than in still water. Within any set of conditions, growth is heterauxetic with the exponent k hardly greater than unity when ovoid leaves are produced and well over 2 when linear leaves are growing under water (Fig. 73). Leaf elongation does not occur when submersed plants are given only 30 min of light each day. It is apparently inhibited by high temperatures, over 25°C, but this inhibition can be overcome by increasing day length. The elongation on submergence is not immediate. The production of the ovoid shape of the aerial leaves can be induced by growing a submersed shoot in 30% seawater, thus raising the osmotic pressure. Jones thinks the effect is likely to be mediated by auxin production in response to turgor changes. The increase in osmotic pressure does not affect the venation, so that the induced ovoid leaves have a single vein and apparently remain small.

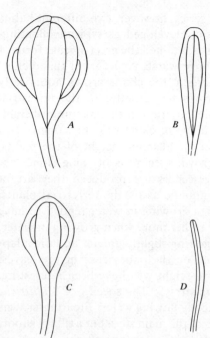

FIGURE 72. *A, Callitriche stagnalis*, ovoid aerial; and *B*, linear aquatic leaves; *C,D*, *C. obtusangula*, the same (Jones).

   The heterophylly of *Hippuris*, which somewhat resembles that of *Callitriche*, has been investigated by McCully and Dale (1961a, b). There are three major leaf types: *rhizome leaves* are minute and rudimentary and do not come into the story; *aquatic leaves* are long with a single vein, no stomata, elongate epidermal cells, and a single layer of mesophyll except along the center of the leaf; and *aerial leaves* are short, a little wider than aquatic leaves, with numerous stomata, irregular polyhedral epidermal cells, and more than one layer of mesophyll throughout (Fig. 74). McCully and Dale distinguish juvenile and mature leaves within both aerial and aquatic series. Differences between the two main types are not apparent till the primordium is 50 μ long.

   Ordinarily when a plant, initially under water, breaks the surface, the new leaves produced are sharply distinguishable as aerial. In the reverse experiment in which aerial parts of shoots are submersed, the transition is less sudden and some intermediates are found. Growing the plant in a mist at high light intensity produced some change to the aquatic form; this was accentuated at low light intensity. Growing the plants in 10% seawater had no effect, but in 30% seawater obovate–obtuse leaves 4 × 3 mm were

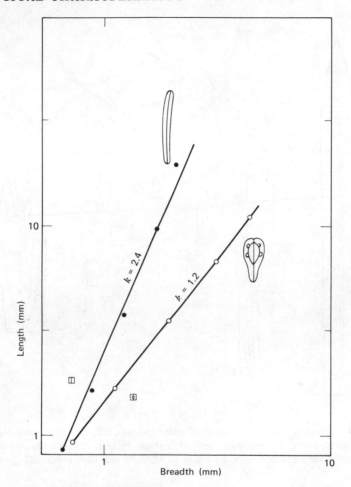

FIGURE 73. Heterauxetic growth of the leaves of *Callitriche intermedia* when submerged (closed circles) and when aerial (open circles) with drawings of young and mature leaves (×1.5) in both series (Jones, modified).

produced in whorls of four to six. These had some stomata, two or more layers of mesophyll throughout the area, and rectangular sinuate epidermal cells. In these characteristics they resembled the aerial leaves of arctic specimens of *H. vulgaris*. They differed strikingly, however, from all aerial leaves in not having lateral veins. The parallelism with Jones' work on *Callitriche* is striking.

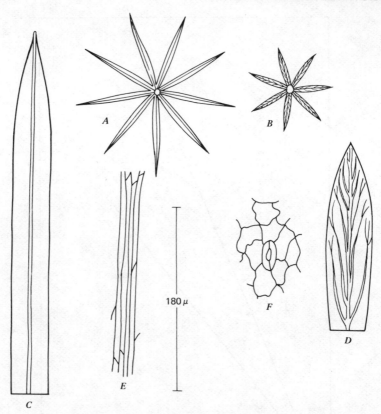

FIGURE 74.   *Hippuris vulgaris.* *A*, General arrangement of a whorl of water leaves; *B*; the same, air leaves; *C*, a single water leaf; *D*, a single air leaf; *E*, epidermis of water leaf; *F*, epidermis of air leaf (scale refers to *E* and *F*, McCully and Dale modified).

Heterophylly in *Proserpinaca palustris*.   The mermaid weed is an important North American emergent aquatic plant belonging to the Haloragidaceae and allied to *Myriophyllum*. *P. palustris* flourishes ordinarily in shallow water, about 30 cm deep, but can grow in water 1 m in depth, or in places which are dry for the greater part of the summer. Typically when growing in water the submersed leaves are extremely dissected while the upper aerial part of the plant bears lanceolate leaves with serrate margins. These leaves differ in microscopic anatomy in much the same way as do the water and air leaves of other amphibious plants (see p. 139).

The natural history of the plant has been considered by Burns (1904), who observed it in Dead Lake near Ann Arbor, Michigan. At the end of the summer the plants that have flowered and produced seed tend to fall over into the water; at such time any new growth produces only water leaves. Underwater axillary buds are produced which start growing into new flowering spikes in the spring. The initial leaves are all of the divided submersed type but later as the plant emerges above water, only lanceolate air leaves are produced. In the summer under very favorable conditions, when the growth of the plant is particularly rapid, lanceolate leaves with serrate or slightly more divided margins may be produced near the surface underwater (*A* of Fig. 63). These leaves are a little larger than aerial leaves which in general they resemble in form, though their microscopic anatomy, in their lack of palisade tissue, is comparable to that of water leaves (Gessner 1938).

Burns found that cuttings from the terrestrial parts made at the end of May continued to produce air leaves. When plants grown from these cuttings were transferred to water in August either the tip was inhibited and lateral branches bearing water leaves were found, or apical growth continued but produced water leaves. However, cuttings made anew from the terrestrial plant set out in May produced water leaves though grown terrestrially. Such cuttings set in water produced little growth in winter, and that only of water leaves. In spring the plants started to grow upward and the emergent spikes bore land leaves. Burns's work suggests that initially the leaves tend to be water leaves and any factor producing slow growth as low winter temperature promotes this juvenile condition. Similarly, rapid summer growth produces aerial gross morphology underwater. The upward spring growth and tendency to fall over in autumn, which one may suspect to depend on the photoperiod, are clearly normally correlated with production of the appropriate leaves.

The leaf primordium is apparently labile until it is 3–4 mm long; at this stage it consists mainly of a midrib with a series of lateral lobes (*B* of Fig. 63). These lobes grow into long filaments as the water leaf develops, but when an air leaf is formed, tissue is intercalated between them except at their tips which form the serration of the margin. McCallum (1902) found that air leaves could be produced in liquid culture medium if the latter had an increased osmotic pressure, just not great enough to produce plasmolysis. This early observation shows that the heterophylly of *Proserpinaca palustris* is physiologically comparable to that in *Veronica anagallis-aquatica, Marsilea drummondi,* and some species of *Ranunculus.*

Heterophylly and similar environmental modifications in *Ranunculus*. The sixteenth-century Belgian botanist Rembert Dodoens (1554) seems to have been the first to notice that different degrees of heterophylly in a water plant might be associated with different habitats, though in his example it is not quite certain that all the plants were conspecific. The existence of heterophylly in *Ranunculus* must of course have often been observed earlier and was the basis of a decorative motif employed by a medieval carver working at Selby Abbey, illustrated in the frontispiece of this book.[8] Dodoens recorded his observations in his Crüÿdeboeck which was almost immediately translated into French by Charles de l'Escluse (Dodoens 1557) and later from the French into English by Henry Lyte (Dodoens 1578). Lyte claimed, in a rhyming commendation of the work at the beginning of his translation, that some of the additions made in his version were communicated to him by Dodoens himself. The passage in English, also quoted by Arber (1920), follows the French text,[9] from which it is derived fairly closely. "Amongst the fleeting herbes, there is also a certayne herbe whiche some call water Lyverworte, [at the rootes whereof hang very many hearie strings like rootes,] the which doth oftentimes change his [uppermost] leaves according to the places where as it groweth. That whiche groweth within the water, carrieth, upon slender stalkes, his leaves very small cut, much like the leaves of the common Cammomill, but before they be under the water (aussi avant qu'elles sont soubs l'eauë), and growing above about the toppe of the stalkes, it beareth small rounde leaves, somewhat dented, or unevenly cut about (un peu crenées tout au tour). That kinde whiche groweth out of the water in the borders of diches, hath none other but the small iagged leaves (n'a autres fueilles que celles menu incisées). That whiche groweth adioyning to the water, & is sometimes drenched or over-whelmed with water, hath also at the top of the stalkes, small rounde leaves, but much more dented than the round leaves of that whiche groweth alwayes in the water."

---

[8] Photographed by C. J. P. Cave and published by him in his *Roof Bosses in Medieval Churches: An Aspect of Gothic Sculpture*, Cambridge, 1948, from which it is reproduced by kind permission of the Cambridge University Press. Cave indicates that a number of bosses fell to safety on the floor of the nave of the church when the roof was destroyed by fire in 1906, the pegs holding the bosses having burned before the bosses themselves were ignited. All the pictures that he gives from Selby seem to be medieval and not the work of modern carvers, who replaced much of the decoration when the roof was rebuilt. The boss figured has undoubtedly been restored, one laminar leaf clearly being modern; this testifies to the authenticity of the rest of the carving. The date, not given by Cave, is presumably the first half of the fourteenth century.

[9] The original text of the *Crüÿdeboeck* "in the Doutsche or Almaigne tongue" was not available; the French text was, however, produced (Arber 1912) under Dodoens' super-vision and presumably represented his views at the time it was prepared. Where there are clear additions in the English version they are given, in the quotation above, in brackets; where there is some uncertainty of meaning, the French text is also quoted in parentheses.

FIGURE 75.   Dodoens' figure of a batrachian *Ranunculus*, which, on account of the length of the peduncle and the shape of the laminar leaf, was probably *R. peltatus*, accompanying his account of environmentally determined leaf form, quoted in the text (from the French edition of 1557).

The figure[10] accompanying this account (Fig. 75) seems to represent *R. peltatus*, which was presumably the species Dodoens found growing in the water. The identity of the other two forms is less clear. The kind growing out of water in the borders of ditches seems to have had only laminar leaves, which is apparently possible in *peltatus*; though *R. hederaceus* could

---

[10] The figures in Dodoens' *Crüÿdeboeck* and its translations are largely derived from Fuchs (Arber, 1912) but this one seems to be original. Dodoens' later work (1583), usually known as his *Pemptades*, was provided with a new set of illustrations by Christopher Plantin, who published the book. Arber believed that this was because Lyte's English printer had acquired the old blocks. The new figure is less clearly *Rannuculus peltatus* and the text makes no mention of heterophylly.

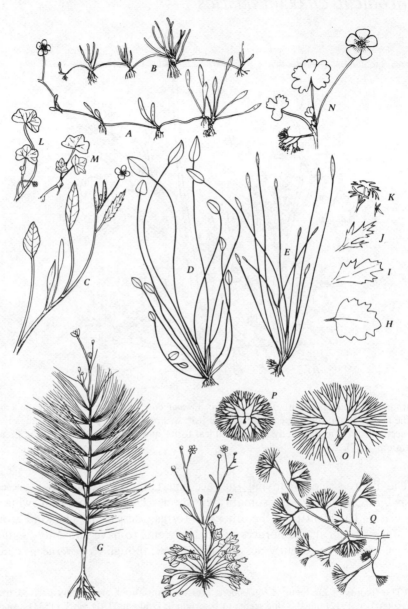

FIGURE 76. Heterophylly and environmentally determined leaf form in *Ranunculus. A, R. reptans* ($\times\frac{2}{5}$), terrestrial; *B*, the same, aquatic form *submersus; C, R. flammula* ($\times\frac{1}{5}$), Breslau, Germany, terrestrial with broader basal and narrower cauline leaves as is usual in land plants of the genus; *D*, the same f. *natans* ($\times\frac{1}{5}$) in shallow water; *E*, f. *submersus* ($\times\frac{1}{5}$), in deeper water; *F, R. polyphyllus* ($\times\frac{2}{5}$), growing on land; *G*, the same f. *submersus* ($\times\frac{3}{10}$), in moderately deep water; *H, I, J, K, R. flabellaris* ($\times\frac{3}{5}$), floor of a dry pond, Meriden, Conn., Oct. 17, 1909, four leaves from same plant showing transitions from laminar to highly dissected, in such plants not necessarily arranged in a regular order; *L,*

have been involved. The more dissected laminar leaves of the third form, however, suggest another species such as *aquatilis*, though that species would be unlikely to produce laminar leaves out of water.

The genus *Ranunculus* contains purely terrestrial species that are moderately heterophyllous, the basal leaves being often rounded or quite wide, though deeply dissected in some species, while the cauline leaves are lanceolate.

Three main groups of aquatic species occur in the genus, namely, (*1*) the members of the section *Flammula* of the nominate subgenus, with the sole member of the allied section *Xanthobatrachium*, (*2*) the members of the section *Hecatonia*, also in the nominate subgenus, and (*3*) throughout the subgenus *Batrachium*.

Broad basal and lanceolate cauline leaves are found in the terrestrial form of *R. flammula*, the lesser spearwort (*C* of Fig. 76). In this species, plants growing in very shallow water (f. *natans*), as Glück records of some in ponds near Erlangen and in the Lac de Jarrie near Grenoble, may have long petioles and somewhat narrowed floating leaves (*D* of Fig. 76), while underwater (f. *submersus*), as at a depth of 30–40 cm in the Schlucksee in Bavaria, and in the Lac de Barterand in Savoy, the leaves are very reduced (*E* of Fig. 76). The related *R. reptans*, a small procumbent plant, rooting at every node (*A* of Fig. 76) has an aquatic f. *submersus* (*B* of Fig. 76) in which the elongate elliptical blade of the terrestrial form is so narrowed that it forms a single linear structure. The aquatic forms of these two species rarely flower; Glück notes abortive flower buds in *R. flammula* f. *submersus*. In the section *Flammula* to which these two species belong, the same author records *R. ophioglossifolius* and *R. lateriflorus* as having floating-leaved as well as terrestrial forms. A very comparable modification in *R. sardous* (sens. lat.) in various parts of North Africa and southern Europe also occurs, as also in the large *R. lingua*, which is often a eulittoral species in lakes.

In some species of *Ranunculus* (s. str.) and in most of the species of the subgenus *Batrachium* very dissected cauline leaves are developed. These are usually, but not always, accompanied by laminar leaves which are associated with the flower-bearing apices of the shoots in the aquatic forms. As well as this very conspicuous differentiation which often involves true heterophylly, the highly divided capillary leaves differ in the aquatic and ter-

---

R. hederaceus ($\times\frac{3}{5}$) aquatic form; *M*, the same ($\times\frac{3}{5}$), growing on mud; *N*, *R. peltatus* ($\times\frac{3}{5}$), Uppsala, Sweden, apex of plant with floating leaves and the topmost capillary leaf, transitional leaves lacking; *O*, *R. circinatus*, winter capillary water leaf ($\times\frac{3}{5}$); *P*, the same, summer capillary water leaf; *Q*, terrestrial capillary leaves from flood plain of Upper Rhine (*A*, *B*, *K*, *L*, *M*, *O*, *P*, and *Q*, Glück; *C*, *H*, *I*, *J*, *K*, and *N*, Herbarium, Yale University).

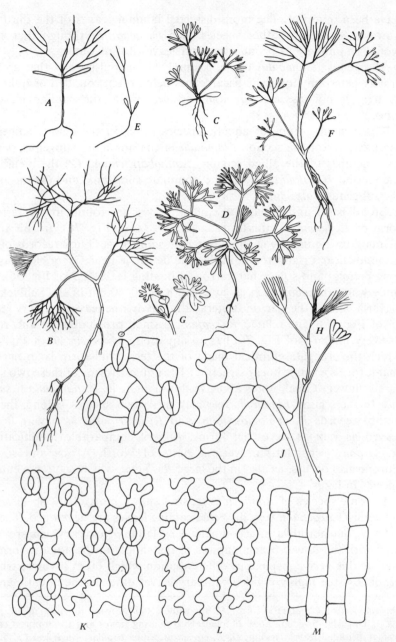

FIGURE 77. *Ranunculus aquatilis*, experimental results of the pioneer work of Askenazy. *A*, Seedling germinated in water, with elongation of all leaves including cotyledons; *B*, the same, older seedling; *C*, seedling germinated in air with broader cotyledons and leaf segments; *D*, the same, older: *E*, seedling germinated in air and transferred to water, cotyledons as in air form other leaves as in aquatic form; *F*, older seedling transferred from

restrial forms of the amphibious species, being a little broader and flatter in the terrestrial form, which has stomata on the upper surface (K of Fig. 77) and very irregular epidermal cells on both surfaces (K, L of Fig. 77), while the whole surface of the capillary leaves in the aquatic forms is covered with rows of rectangular epithelial cells (M of Fig. 77) and lacks stomata (Askenasy 1870). The development of capillary leaves must have taken place at least three times in the genus.

The sole member of the section *Xanthobatrachium, Ranunculus polyphyllus*, is an eastern European plant occurring mainly in slightly alkaline temporary swamps. The typical form has broad aerial basal leaves (F of Fig. 76) and a few lanceolate cauline leaves; the plant is suggestive of the section *Flammula*. When growing in very shallow water the petioles of the basal leaves are elongate and the leaf blades float (f. *natans*). In somewhat deeper water numerous whorls of capillary leaves are developed (G of Fig. 76), giving the f. *submersus* an appearance unlike that of any other member of the genus.

In the section *Hecatonia* capillary water leaves and laminar floating leaves associated with the apical parts of stems bearing flowers are often developed, giving a plant much like the capillary-leaved members of *Batrachium* but with yellow flowers. Here belong the North American *R. flabellaris* and the northern Palaearctic *R. gmelinii* with its Nearctic subspecies *hookerii*(= *R. purshii* auctt.); often there are a few leaves transitional between the fine capillary and the considerably dissected laminar (H, I, J, K of Fig. 76). *R. sceleratus* with lobed, stalked basal leaves and more deeply divided cauline leaves, the uppermost sessile and usually of three segments, also belongs in the section and is usually aquatic but rather less specialized in leaf form than the species just mentioned.

The subgenus *Batrachium* contains a number of species which are primarily aquatic, with flowers which are rarely wholly yellow and are usually mainly white. Many of the species provide difficult taxonomic problems and it is not easy to summarize the details of the variation in leaf form as the published information supposedly about a given taxon may turn out to be partly based on something else. The best treatment of the European forms, which provide most of the difficulties, is that of Cook (1963, 1966b), followed below.

Two species referred to *Batrachium*, namely, *Ranunculus hederaceus*, the ivy-leaved crowfoot of western Europe, apparently adventive in eastern

---

land to water, fourth leaf intermediate, fifth typically aquatic; G, apex of wild plant showing laminar leaves below the flower; H, plant submersed after producing a laminar leaf, returning to the growth of capillary leaves (all natural size); I, J, dorsal and ventral surfaces of laminar leaf; K, L, the same, capillary air leaf; M, uniform epidermis of capillary water leaf (all ×260).

North America including Newfoundland, and *R. omiophyllus*, the moor-land crowfoot found in the same area of Europe but extending less far north and further southeast, lack capillary leaves. They are both primarily terrestrial plants growing in very wet places, but often occur covered by water. Cook (1966a) thinks that they are derived from some member of *Batrachium* that lost its capillary leaves. In *R. hederaceus* the laminar leaves are broadly rounded and divided into lobes, usually three, by shal-low emarginations. Ordinarily the terrestrial plant in summer is compact and has leaves 4–8 mm long and 3–10 mm wide, while the aquatic plant is spreading, with leaves 17–25 mm long and 25–35 mm wide. When the plant is growing under unfavorable conditions, notably in too deep water, in shade, or in dry situations, the leaf tends to be five-lobed. The variation is not marked and Glück (1936) figures as f. *latifolia*, supposedly growing on mud in Ireland, a form which when compared with his aquatic form (*L, M* of Fig. 76) seems to differ from the latter in the same way as the usual aquatic form described by Cook, and figured diagrammatically by Clapham, Tutin, and Warburg (1962), differs from the terrestrial form of these authors. *R. omiophyllus* differs from *R. hederaceus* in having deeper emarginations between the leaf lobes. Though the differences separating them are slight, they are well isolated species, the hybrids being inviable or sterile. Intro-gression into *R. tripartitus* is possible, however. In Britain *R. omiophyllus* is found in localities where the calcium concentration is low while *hedera-ceus* occurs in calcareous and eutrophic localities. Where *hederaceus* is ab-sent, as in Sicily, *omiophyllus* can grow in limy and nutrient-rich stations that would have supported *hederaceus* if the latter had been present. Both species can be cultivated equally well on calcareous and noncalcareous soils. They occasionally occur together in Britain.

The other species included in the subgenus *Batrachium* have, at least in most specimens of each species, capillary leaves. In *R. tripartitus*, which always has laminar suborbicular leaves divided typically into three cuneate segments, there are also always capillary leaves when the plant is growing underwater. Populations referred to this species growing on very wet soil, however, lack such leaves; at least some of these populations (e.g., the "*R. lutarius*" of the New Forest, England) are the result of introgression by *R. omiophyllus* (Clapham, Tutin, and Warburg 1962; Cook 1963).

In nearly all specimens of *R. peltatus* and *R. baudotii*, and in most *R. tripartitus* and *R. ololeucos* and some races of *R. aquatilis, R. pseudofluitans*, and *R. fluitans*, all of which occur in the western part of Eurasia, with some outlying areas of distribution elsewhere in the Old World, and in the western North American *R. lobbii*, both kinds of leaves are produced. Other populations of *R. aquatilis, R. pseudofluitans* and *R. fluitans* with *R. circinatus, R. rionii, R. sphaerospermus, R. trichophyllus*, and certain

North American taxa (*R. subrigidus, R. longirostris*) of uncertain status produce only capillary leaves.

All the Old World species of *Batrachium* mentioned in the preceding paragraphs have been cultivated by Cook (1963), who finds that they can all live as terrestrial plants on waterlogged soils in summer. According to Glück (1936), *R. aquatilis* may produce only capillary leaves either if grown in deep water (f. *submersus*) in which the plant produces a long stem with divided cauline leaves, or if grown on wet soil (f. *terrestris*) when only divided basal leaves are produced. In *R. circinatus* similar terrestrial, but usually sexually sterile, plants (f. *terrestris*) are common in dry years on the mud of abandoned channels of the Rhine (*Q* of Fig. 76).

It is probable that *R. peltatus* is usually the most important to the European limnologist, though *R. aquatilis* is common in ponds; *R. circinatus* may occur in hard-water lakes; *R. pseudofluitans* and *R. fluitans* are rheophile; the latter can be 6 m long. The last three species are long-lived perennials; the other common species may be either annuals or short-lived perennials (Cook 1963).

Experimental Work on Leaf Form in Ranunculus.   Some experimental work has been done on *Ranunculus*, beginning with that of Askenasy (1870), which was one of the first contributions to the analysis of heterophylly. Askenasy found that the early primordia of the capillary leaves were completely labile. Growing the plant in water produced long, thin cylindrical segments with aquatic microscopic anatomy, whereas growth in air produced shorter, flatter segments with aerial microscopic structure (Fig. 77). These differences applied even to the growth of the cotyledons. Much later work by Gessner (1940) indicated that in *R. baudotii* the osmotic pressure of the cell sap is greater in the air leaves than in the water leaves. This difference is not entirely due to sugar as in *Veronica anagallis-aquatica*; the range of concentrations is higher in *R. baudotii*, which as a facultative brackish-water species may exhibit some special features. In general it would seem that in the production of capillary air and water leaves *Ranunculus* behaves in the same sort of way as do the other plants that have been subjected to an experimental analysis.

Cook (1966b) has studied the production of laminar leaves in most of the species of *Batrachium*, and finds surprising differences between some of them. In *R. aquatilis*, the first seedling leaves are always dissected under any conditions, winter or summer, terrestrial or aquatic. In nature the change to entire leaves appears to be seasonally determined, but is rarely synchronous among the different branches of a plant. It is always associated with flowering, but a branch can produce flowers without producing entire leaves. In Cook's experiments such leaves developed only from an apex that was underwater. The effect is not due to shading, as a plant grown aerially beneath a tank of water does not produce aerial leaves. The stimulus to flowering and production of entire leaves underwater is clearly long day length, operating best at high temperatures. Bauer (1952) found that at a high temperature in constant light, laminar leaves could be produced even by terrestrial specimens of *R. aquatilis*. Cook found that at 10°C a photoperiod of 16 hr light produced flowers in winter with accompanying entire leaves in 14 days, whereas at 18°C the effect occurred in 10 days; controls in natural illumination remained sterile with divided leaves. If a plant in which the effect has been produced is returned to natural short-day winter illumination, the entire leaves die and growth occurs only from the part of the plant bearing divided leaves. Cook found *R. baudotii* and *R. peltatus* to behave similarly and in these plants it is known that strains emanating from the Mediterranean region require less increase in day length to evoke flowering and entire leaves than do those from northern Europe. *R. penicillatus* was hard to work with as many strains only flower in running water. Small cuttings when illuminated may not produce flowers or entire leaves, but large plants in natural conditions have the capacity. Cook thinks some true determinate development may be involved. In *B. tripartitus* the seedling leaves are always entire, under any conditions, terrestrial or aquatic. If the plant is grown at more than 10°C only entire leaves are formed, whatever the photoperiod. If it is kept at 4–6°C a short day length of 12 hr will produce divided leaves if applied early enough, but once three or more entire leaves have developed, divided leaves apparently cannot form. In nature divided leaves are produced underwater in winter, but when the temperature rises to over 11°C, with a day length of 12 hr, entire leaves form. If a plant is established at the edge of a pool it may overwinter with entire leaves, whereas underwater in the same pool there are plants with divided leaves. The leaf morphology appears to be entirely under environmental control. *R. lobbii* in North America probably behaves like *R. tripartitus*.

In *R. ololeucos* the first leaf is of intermediate form, entire but deep-lobed under long day length, divided under short day length, whatever the temperature, in both water and air. Entire leaves can form under long photoperiods from emergent buds. If a shoot bearing entire leaves is placed under short day length it reverts to the divided condition rather than dying back as in *R. aquatilis*.

R. saniculifolius, a Mediterranean coastal species, is a short-lived annual found in ephemeral pools. It is determinate, producing three to six divided and then entire leaves as flowering begins, irrespective of the environmental conditions, save that in deep shade or low temperature the plant produces only divided leaves, but under these conditions does not flower and is otherwise not vigorous. It is interesting, though not unexpected, that the one species in which there appears to be a determinate sequence should be the shortest-lived species of the subgenus.

Though the plants of the subgenus *Batrachium* do not normally produce sequential intermediate leaves between the divided and the entire, as occur in the section *Hecatonia* of *Ranunculus* (s. str.), in some species mixed or intermediate leaves are occasionally found. In *R. peltatus* and *R. penicillatus* capillary segments may develop distally from the entire portion, while in *R. aquatilis* entire portions are developed on some of the distal ends of capillary segments. In these species such abnormal leaves occur on plants growing in poor conditions or exhibiting high pollen sterility. In *R. baudoti* a more strictly intermediate rather than a mixed leaf can be produced by the terrestrial cultivation of plants with divided leaves from England and even more so from Finland, but not in an Austrian strain.

Cook believes that the evolution of the heterophylly of *Ranunculus* has proceeded in the following way.

A terrestrial heterophyllous ancestor is believed to have had basal entire leaves, with intermediate and, above them, more or less divided cauline leaves. This sort of condition is found according to Cook in a number of species of *Ranunculus* (s. str.), such as *R. arvensis*. From such a species it is supposed that there developed a condition comparable to that found in *R. gmelini* or *R. flabellaris* of the section *Hecatonia*. Here there is a sequence of leaf form from inferior divided through intermediate to apical entire leaves. Whether this is most reasonably derived by the inversion of the pattern known in some terrestrial species such as *R. arvensis*, or whether it represents the evolution of an entirely new aquatic heterophylly, may doubtless be debated. From this *Hecatonia*-like ancestor, the condition found in the heterophyllous species of *Batrachium* originated by suppression of the intermediate leaves. From this condition the homophyllous divided-leaved species *R. trichophyllus*, *R. rionii*, *R. sphaerospermus*, and *R. flavidus* are believed to have developed by loss of the entire leaves. Cook suspects that in another line, entire leaves were lost first, leaving intermediate and divided leaves. Such a condition is occasionally found in *R. fluitans*, from near which species Cook derives *R. circinatus* and *R. longirostris*. Finally, by the loss of divided leaves from some heterophyllous ancestor comparable to *R. tripartitus*, *R. omiophyllus* and *R. hederaceus* were produced. The two species are regarded as derived from more aquatic ancestors because their leaves are like the entire leaves of the fully aquatic species, with well-developed stipules, and stomata on the upper surface.

An interesting situation was discovered by hybridizing *R. baudotii* and *R. hederaceus*. The former species is a tetraploid ($2n = 32$), and crosses with ordinary *hederaceus* ($2n = 16$) do not produce fertile achenes. When, however, a colchicine-induced tetraploid of *hederaceus* was used, a hybrid which grew quite well and which was fairly fertile resulted. The F_1 generation had leaves for the most part intermediate between the divided and entire type, like the intermediate leaves produced by growing some strains of *baudotii* terrestrially. The leaves had narrower lobes under short photoperiods than under long, but were always somewhat variable. Such plants were fundamentally terrestrial and if grown in 25 cm of water the stems broke off, floating to the surface. The leaf form was not changed by submergence. When inbred, in the first of Cook's experiments, F_2 plants showed segregation into predominantly divided-leaved specimens tolerant of submergence, intermediate-leaved forms like F_1, and dominantly entire-leaved forms like *R. hederaceus*. Cook implies that the first category was less prone to produce entire leaves than *baudotii* and so might be potentially adapted to an environment different from that of either ancestral species. Repetition of the self-fertilization of the F_1 plants three years later produced 50 plants showing no segregation; the F_1 plants presumably had become agamospermic, and now were reproducing apomictically.

In several other cases, intermediate leaves can be produced by hybridization. The weak, slow-growing progeny of *R. hederaceus* ($2n = 32$) and *R. trichophyllus* ($2n = 32$) produced nothing but intermediate leaves like those of *R. flabellaris*. In the F_1 hybrids of *R. tripartitus* and *R. baudotii* there is a suggestion of sequential development in the spring in passing from winter divided, through intermediate, to entire summer leaves. Flowering is not related to leaf form. These hybrids are unfortunately sterile. It is evident that the photoperiodic switch mechanism of control of heterophylly in the various species of the subgenus *Batrachium* easily can be disrupted by small genetic variations. Moreover, the appearance of, for example, essentially homophyllous divided-leaved segregates from the F_2 of *baudotii* and *hederaceus* suggests that in the evolutionary history of the genus a number of discontinuous changes and possibly reversal of evolutionary direction, due to recombination, may have occurred, so that the neat linear evolutionary progression postulated is a little hypothetical. It is reasonable to suppose, however, as Cook has emphasized, that the adoption of a photoperiodic determination enables the plant to adjust more reliably to a seasonally changing environment than would direct reaction to small, inconstant, though seemingly more relevant changes in, for instance, water level, which may always vary one step ahead of the biological adjustment. Cook's argument is, in fact, essentially comparable to that put forward a little later by Levins (1968, pp. 10–14), using bacteriological and entomological examples.

Some interesting experimental work has been done on *R. flabellaris* by Bostrack and Millington (1962). In this species aquatic plants have markedly dissected leaves, and terrestrial plants trilobed laminar leaves, each lobe quite distinct and with three to seven marginal incisions. Unlike what is normally found in the subgenus *Batrachium*, there is here a complete set of transitions between capillary and laminar leaves. Leaf form seems not to vary with light intensity but there appears to be in this species, as in some others, an effect of photoperiod. In terrestrially grown specimens (f. *riparius*), plants on a short day of 8 hr (*A* of Fig. 78) exhibit rather more dissected leaves than those continuously illuminated (*B* of Fig. 78); in aquatic specimens the leaves of the short-day individuals seem a little less dissected (*C* of Fig. 78) than those of land plants at the same photoperiod, but in the water the long-day (17 hr) plants (*D* of Fig. 78) have many more capillary leaves than do the terrestrial plants or the short-day aquatic. Day length acts differently on aerial and aquatic plants, so it is unfortunate that the long days were of different length for the aerial and aquatic experiments. Low temperatures effectively produced a divergence towards the dissected capillary type of leaf (*E–H* of Fig. 78). No evidence was obtained to show that hormonal transport from well-developed adult structures to developing primordia could affect the development of the latter. Apart from the photoperiodic effect, growth in liquid water, or to some extent in saturated air, appears to produce water leaves, whereas air leaves are produced when the plant is exposed to air. There are evidently differences between this plant in the section *Hecatonia* and the heterophyllous species of *Batrachium*.

Heterophylly and related phenomena in *Potamogeton*. The genus *Potamogeton*, which probably is the most important of all the genera containing lacustrine plants, at least in the North Temperate zone, includes a number of heterophyllous species. In general such species develop ovate or elliptical apical floating leaves, while the lower parts of the stem bear more elongate submerged leaves of varying form. The characteristic simplification of the microscopic anatomy of the water leaves can be very extreme.

There are, of course, many essentially homophyllous species of *Potamogeton*, though even in them striking environmental determination of leaf form may occur. Of these species some have ovoid, elliptical, or lanceolate leaves as in *P. perfoliatus* (Fig. 82), *P. praelongus*, *P. crispus* (*D* of Fig. 93), and *P. richardsonii*; in others the leaves are narrow and straplike as in *P. obtusifolius* and *P. friesii*, or very narrow capillary structures as in *P. pectinatus*, *P. berchtoldii*, *P. pusillus*, and *P. trichoides* (*C* of Fig. 93). The water leaves of the heterophyllous species show a like diversity. In *P. alpinus* (Fig. 94) the floating leaves merely differ in being shorter and rather wider than the submerged. In *P. gramineus*, *P. epihydrus*, *P. natans* (Fig. 79), and *P. polygonifolius* (Fig. 80) the submersed leaves are narrow and straplike,

FIGURE 78. *Ranunculus flabellaris*, leaves produced at least in part after beginning of experiment. *A*, Terrestrially grown at day length of 8 hr; *B*, of 24 hr; *C*, aquatically grown at day length of 8 hr; *D*, of 17 hr; *E*, terrestrially grown at 18° C; *F*, at 28° C; *G*, aquatically grown at 16° C; *H*, at 28°C (Bostrack and Millington, modified).

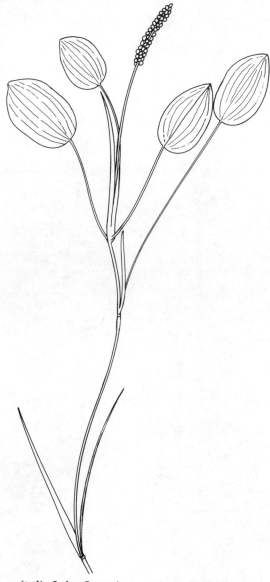

FIGURE 79. *P. natans* ($\times\frac{1}{2}$), Lake Quonnipaug, North Guilford, Conn., very marked heterophylly but flower spikes monomorphic.

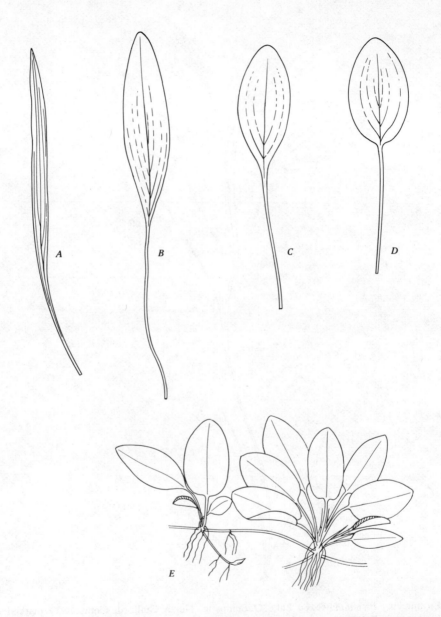

FIGURE 80.   *P. polygonifolius. A*, Extreme submersed leaf of f. *submersus; B*, less extreme form; *C, D*, floating leaves usually in running water; *E*, part of a terrestrial plant (Glück, based on European plants).

while the floating leaves are elliptical or in *P. natans* even subcordate. At
least *P. gramineus*, *P. natans* (Fig. 59), and *P. polygonifolius* quite often
occur in nature as small broad-leaved terrestrial plants growing on damp
mud (Fassett 1957; Glück 1936; Hejny 1960; Spence and Chrystal 1970a).
In *P. spirillus* (*A*, *B* of Fig. 81) and *P. capillaceus* (*C* of Fig. 81) the submersed leaves are capillary and there are both aerial and aquatic inflorescences, the former elongate and entomophilous, the latter smaller and
apparently hydrophilous. Floating leaves may be absent late in the season
or always in some populations (Fassett 1957). The various patterns of
differentiation are repeated through the genus.

In *Potamogeton perfoliatus* and some other widespread species occurring
in lakes very marked environmentally determined variation occurs. In
general, leaves are shorter and broader with thicker peduncles in shallow
water; the internodes are also shorter and the leaves are thicker and of a
less brilliant green, while the reverse of all these characteristics tends to be
exhibited in deep-water plants. Factors other than depth are clearly operating. A representative series of leaf measurements by Pearsall and Pearsall
(1923) for plants from the English Lake District is given in Table 13.
Within a given lake, the depth at which the plant is growing clearly influences the ratio of leaf length to leaf breadth, as is seen in the two examples
from Windermere. Variation with depth and so with light intensity, comparable to that in *P. perfoliatus*, is also recorded by Pearsall and Pearsall
as being shown by *P. praelongus*, *P. alpinus*, *P. crispus*, *P. berchtoldii*

TABLE *13.*   *Variation in leaf form in* Potamogeton perfoliatus

	Leaf length (cm)	Leaf breadth (cm)	Length:breadth ratio
In nature			
1. Esthwaite	2.4	1.3	1.85
2. R. Derwent, Kirkham Abbey	6.8	3.4	2.0
3. Ullswater (f. *macrophyllus*)	9.3	3.6	2.6
4. Windermere 3 m	3.3	1.4	2.4
5. Windermere 6 m (f. *lanceolatus*)	7.0	1.7	4.1
6. Coniston 4 m (f. *lanceolatus*)	6.3	1.4	4.5
Experimental			
Mean of 1, 2, and 6 in well-lighted laboratory	∼3.0	∼1.5	∼2.0
Mean of 1, 2, and 6 in half illumination	3.3	0.9	3.7

FIGURE 81. Extremely heterophylly with dimorphic flower spikes, the larger emergent, the smaller submersed. *A. Potamogeton spirillus* (natural size) Randolph Co., West Virginia, leaves and emergent flower spike from near top of plant; *B*, the same, subcapillary leaves and short submerged flower spike from lower down same plant; *C, P. capillaceus*, Plainfield, Conn. (Herbarium, Yale University and Connecticut Botanical Society).

(sub *pusillus*), and the hybrids *P.* × *zizii* (=*P. gramineus* × *P. lucens*) and *P.* × *nitens* (=*P. gramineus* × *P. perfoliatus*).

In *P. berchtoldii* the deep-water leaves are about 50–70 mm × 0.8–1.0 mm, gradually tapering to an acute apical tip, and are clear translucent green (f. *tenuissimus*), while in shallow water the leaves are not over 30 mm long, 1.4–1.8 mm wide, thicker, more obtuse at the apex, and dull olive green. Pearsall and Pearsall (1921) say that in the typical subspecies most of the variation can be produced experimentally by varying the illumination, the longest, narrowest leaves of extreme *tenuissimus* being produced at 5% of the normal incident surface radiation. In their subspecies *lacustris*, a deep-water taxon with wider paler leaves than in the typical *berchtoldii*, Pearsall and Pearsall find little modification with depth or illumination. Though *lacustris* is less calcicole than typical *berchtoldii*, the two taxa may grow in the same lake, *lacustris* preferring the finer silt. They seem to be biologically distinct though Fernald (1932) placed *lacustris* in *pusillus* var. *mucronatus*, later identified as typical *berchtoldii* (Fernald 1950). Modern opinion (Prof. T. G. Tutin, in litt.) is against the recognition of *lacustris* as a valid taxonomic entity, but the results of the Pearsalls suggest that further experimental study would not be without interest.

Chemical influences on leaf form. At least in *P. perfoliatus*, variations in illumination clearly are not the only determinants of the variation of the leaf. It is possible to find, when several lakes are examined, forms characteristic of a particular depth and illumination in one lake, growing at a different depth and illumination in another, as in the cases of the two samples of f. *lanceolatus*, respectively, from 6 m in Windermere and 4 m in Coniston, although the lakes have essentially equal transparency.

When extreme plants, as those from Esthwaite or the River Derwent on the one hand and those from Coniston on the other, are cultivated together under the same conditions they come to resemble each other very closely. The forms are all clearly ecophenes; at low light intensity the leaf is relatively longer and narrower than at high. It was, however, impossible to produce the full range of variation found in *P. perfoliatus* in nature merely by changing the light intensity. Examination of a limited amount of field data suggested that the short, broad-leaved nominotypical form was characteristic of more calcareous substrata (Esthwaite; 1600 ppm CaO in dry littoral mud), while the extreme f. *lanceolatus* occurred on much less calcareous sediment (Coniston; 90 ppm CaO in dry littoral mud). Pearsall and Hanby (1925) confirmed these conclusions and found that when the calcium content of the substratum is low an even more extreme f. *lanceolatus* can be produced by increasing the potassium content (Fig. 82). They believed that calcium raised the permeability of the dividing cells and promoted cell division, while potassium promoted cell elongation.

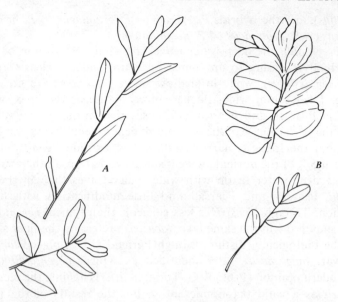

FIGURE 82.   *A*, Extreme variation in leaf form in specimens of *Potamogeton perfoliatus* grown with addition of about 1.5–2.0 g liter K to solution in contact with rhizome; *B*, extreme specimens from same clone grown with addition of 1 g liter Ca as calcium nitrate to solution in contact with rhizome (drawn from photographs published by Pearsall and Hanby).

Leaf form and environment in *Lobelia dortmanna*.   Åberg (1943) has made an elaborate study of the leaf form of this plant, which is a very important member of the flora of relatively unproductive lakes of the cooler part of the North Temperate zone. In this investigation Åberg has mainly been concerned with the ratio of length to breadth of the leaf. Since the width varies much less than the length, the value of the ratio is principally but not entirely a function of length. Studies on the plants collected in a single lake at a given time show an approximately linear increase in the length: breadth ratio with increasing depth of water. The slope of the line expressing this relationship, however, is dependent on the lake and the season. In the lakes studies by Åberg, in the relatively transparent Fiolen (U.S.G.S. col. 9–17), there is only a small and rather irregular variation of the ratio with depth, whereas in the chthoniotrophic Kalven (U.S.G.S. col. 120–182) the effect is very striking. The moderately humic Stråken (U.S.G.S. col. 18–39) gives an intermediate curve (Fig. 83). In some cases of apparent lack of correlation the *Lobelia* plants are shaded by other plants, either vascular, or algal, such as *Batrachospermum*. In other cases, as in Skär-

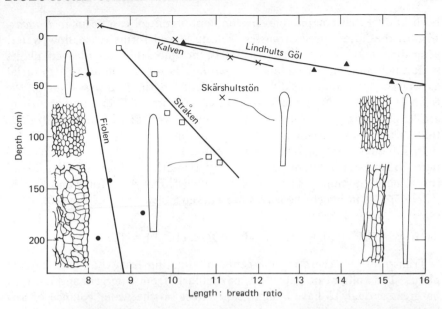

FIGURE 83.   Variation of the mean ratio length:breadth in leaves of *Lobelia dortmanna* from different depths in five Swedish lakes with outline drawings of individual leaves ($\times \frac{1}{2}$) which are fairly representative of the mean values at the points adjacent to these leaves. The elongation with depth is largely dependent on water color, but in Lindhults Göl there is shading by *Batrachosperum*. The single record for Skärshultsjön is of plants shaded at the base by *Isoetes*. For the two extreme leaves surface view (above) of the epidermis and sagittal longitudinal sections (below) are shown, indicating that the elongate form involves elongation of the cells making up the leaf (Åberg).

shultsjön, when the plant is growing in a thick stand of *Isoetes* on which some mud had settled, a microzone of low light intensity at the bottom evidently caused marked longitudinal growth but as the leaves penetrated this thin layer, they grew laterally at the apex, producing a spatulate leaf. Åberg found that seasonal changes and variations in transparency from year to year were reflected in the leaf form of different parts of the plant. There was a little evidence that although most of the elongation is due to low illumination, some other factor is working synergistically in the more chthoniotrophic lakes to promote the growth of the leaf. In the very elongate leaves that had grown at low light intensities, there is a clear elongation of the cells of the leaf, including those of the epidermis, as well as an increase in number of cells on a longitudinal line.

   Leaf form and environment in Isoetes. A very similar picture with elongation of the cells of the leaves in the larger forms is presented by *Isoetes setacea* (sub *echinospora*) in the same lakes (Åberg 1943), and it has long been known that comparable environmental control can occur in *I. lacustris*. In the latter species transfer of long-leaved forms to shallow water, according to Caspary (Luerssen 1889), produces less long-leaved plants with much more divergent leaves (f. *patula*). However, there are also racial as well as environmental differences in leaf length. *I. lacustris* var. *morei* from Upper Bray Lough in Ireland has leaves up to 47 cm long and there are less strikingly long-leaved populations in Wales; Manton (1950) finds that these maintain their characters in culture.

In some lakes the picture is complicated by an apparently genetic (Caspary, in Luerssen 1889) dimorphism, involving the ordinary straight-leaved (presumably nominotypical but often called f. *rectifolia*) form and a form (f. *curvifolia*) in which the leaves are curved outward (*E* of Fig. 26).

THE WATER RELATIONS OF AQUATIC PLANTS

Transpiration occurs in emergent and floating leaves, as in terrestrial plants. The amount of water lost, particularly from emergent species, may be great enough to have a significant effect on the water balance of any body of water in which such plants are growing abundantly.

Evapotranspiration from emergent and floating-leaved plants.   Otis (1914) studied the water loss from tanks, set in a normal aquatic environment in which various water plants had been planted at densities imitating natural stands. He was thus able to estimate the effect of such stands on water loss and at the same time determine the output of water per unit area of the emersed part of the plant. The observations were made in Portage Lake in August 1910, and in the Huron River near Ann Arbor, Michigan, in late August and September 1911; they probably represent typical late-summer results for unispecific full-grown communities in continental humid temperate regions. The results are summarized in Table 14.

It is evident that by day a number of water plants lose water from unit area of the emergent plant surface at least as fast as, and in some cases rather faster than, the evaporative loss from unit area of free water surface. The greatest loss is from the tall culm or stem of *Scirpus*, the least from *Sagittaria latifolia*, which Otis refers to as behaving like a land plant. In all cases the transpiration loss is greatly reduced at night, presumably by the closing of stomata; the average 24-hr rate of all species except *S. validus* consequently is well below that of a free water surface. In *S. validus* the 24-hr rate of 0.169 mm cm^{-2} hr^{-1} is slightly more than that of water surface; presumably the tall plant swinging in the breeze is constantly passed by somewhat unsaturated air.

All the emerged plant stands, simulating those growing in nature, lose water faster than does a free water surface. This is clearly due to the great

TABLE 14. *Water loss from simulated stands and from unit area of component plants floating on or emerging from water* (Otis 1914)

Species	Mean water loss (mm hr⁻¹ cm⁻²) of experimental stand		Ratio of loss from stand to loss from free water surface		Mean water loss ($mm\ hr^{-1}\ cm^{-2}$) of exposed plant (1910)			Ratio of 24-hr loss from plant to loss from free water surface
	1910	1911	1910	1911	Day	Night	Mean	
Nymphaea odorata	0.143	0.135	0.86	0.89	0.176	0.0905	0.133	0.86
Sagittaria latifolia	0.258	—	1.55	—	0.803	0.0058	0.044	0.29
Pontederia cordata	0.329	0.315	1.98	2.09	0.159	0.0096	0.085	0.55
Acorus calamus	—	0.357	—	2.36	—	—	—	—
Sparganium eurycarpum	—	0.342	—	2.26	—	—	—	—
Typha latifolia	0.313	0.462	1.89	3.06	0.147	0.0105	0.074	0.48
Scirpus validus	0.199	0.182	1.20	1.21	0.253	0.0841	0.169	1.10
S. americanus	0.187	—	1.13	—	0.193	0.0490	0.121	0.79
Free water surface (mean of two)	0.166[a]	0.151			0.1535	0.1543	0.154[a]	

[a] The data for a free water surface that can be compared with the artificial stands studied in 1910 refer to a slightly longer period than those that can be compared with loss per unit area of plant surface, thus giving slightly different values.

197

area of plant per unit area of water surface that such stands can provide. Relative to unit water surface, the two species of *Scirpus* remove water less fast than any of the other species. Most of the other stands evaporated and transpired at about twice or occasionally three times (*Typha latifolia* in 1911) the rate of evaporative loss from the free water surface.

Królikowskaia (1971) found values comparable to those of Otis, of 0.09–0.21 mm hr^{-1} cm^{-2} or 2.2–5.0 mg day^{-1} cm^{-2} for the vegetation surrounding Mikołajskie Lake in the Masurian Lake District of Poland.

In *Nymphaea odorata*, the only floating-leaved species studied by Otis, though the leaf transpires more water per unit area by day than an equivalent water surface loses by evaporation, the decline of transpiration at night leads to an area covered with water lilies losing in 24 hr about 90% of what would have been evaporated from a free water surface.

Rodewald-Rudescu (1974) has published a good deal of data for *Phragmites australis* in the Danube delta and has summarized earlier European work, mostly on that species. In general, the results of such investigations agree with those just reported, though occasionally in late summer the ratio of water transpired from German reed beds to that evaporated may be as high as 7.

Gessner (1945, 1955) observed that although the emergent parts of many water plants (*Caltha palustris, Ranunculus lingua, Jussiaea repens, Menyanthes trifoliata, Montrichardia arborescens, Hippuris vulgaris, Alisma plantago-aquatica, Sagittaria sagittifolia*, and *Eichhornia azurea*) when cut and put in water were able to maintain a normal transpiration stream, as would a land plant, this was not true of *Ludwigia palustris, Hydrocotyle umbellata, Heteranthera reniformis, Calla palustris, Pontederia cordata, Bacopa amplexicaulis, Nuphar, Nymphaea, Nelumbo, Eichhornia paniculata*, or *Hydrocleys nymphoides*. These plants lost from 13% in *Ludwigia palustris* to 92% in *Hydrocleys nymphoides* of the total free water content of the leaves in 2 hr. Gessner concludes that in these species, as in the heterosporous fern *Regnellidium diphyllum*, root pressure is forcing water upward. It may be noted that different species of the same genus can behave differently in this respect. It is evident that if such root pressure exists, it could function prior to the emergence of the leaves at the surface. Sculthorpe (1967) is skeptical of these experiments, believing that air locks may have been introduced into the xylem when the petioles were cut or that evaporation took place from the lower surfaces of the leaf under the conditions of the experiment, but not in nature. This last objection would not apply in the cases of *Nelumbo, Pontederia*, and probably some of the other species supposedly exhibiting the phenomenon.

The problem of directional water movement in fully submerged plants. There has been considerable argument for over a century as to whether water movements, analogous to a transpiration stream, in a systematic direction from root to shoot, occur in fully submersed water plants. Though it was often believed in the nineteenth century that the roots of aquatic species were merely anchors of no significance in nutrition, the existence of a stream from root to shoot was first claimed by Unger (1862) over a century ago. The extensive earlier work is well summarized by Arber (1920), who was a strong proponent of the view that such movements do occur and may be of significance in transporting inorganic nutrients, including perhaps CO_2, from the roots embedded in the littoral sediments, to the photosynthetic parts of the plant. The idea is attractive and seemed to have good experimental support. Moreover, Dixon (1898, 1938; Dixon and Barlee 1940) concluded that shoots of terrestrial plants when submerged or placed in a saturated atmosphere exhibited a directional movement of water and of water-soluble material such as eosin, from the cut end toward the apex. Dixon supposed that a water pump, which was partly light dependent, existed in the mesophyll cells. Other more physical and less interesting explanations of the phenomenon have been given and are summarized by Potter and Milburn (1970). The latter investigators concluded from a study of submersed shoots of *Chrysanthemum*, the same genus as was used by Dixon, that the uptake of water observed in potometer experiments is due to the growth of the plant and not to anything comparable to a transpiration stream.

Thut (1932) used an ingenious technique in which the root and shoot of an intact plant lay in two separate vessels joined by a tube through which the plant was threaded. If the vessels are set on the two pans of a torsion balance, any movement of water will alter the position of the center of gravity of the system and the weight needed to adjust the system to the original equilibrium point will be a measure of the water that has passed from the now lighter to the heavier vessel of the pan. Thut found acropetal movements in *Elodea*, *Potamogeton*, *Myriophyllum*, and *Ranunculus* but not in the rootless *Ceratophyllum*. Wilson (1947), however, pointed out that in the only experiment reported in detail, in which there was a movement of 5.5 g of water from the root vessel to the shoot vessel in 22 days, 1.7 g, or 31% of the water movement apparently occurred in the first 9 hr of the experiment. This strongly suggests that adjustment to the experimental conditions led to a quite exceptional flow of water, possibly involving changes in the volume of air spaces in the shoot end of the plant. The results may indicate a small movement, due to root pressure, but it is certainly not dramatic and probably not well substantiated.

In the shoots of fully submersed *Ranunculus fluitans*, Wilson himself, using very careful volumetric technique, was not able to obtain consistent evidence of directional water movements. Some shoots showed such move-

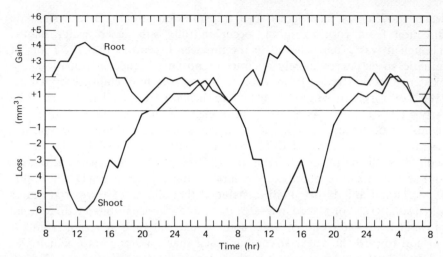

FIGURE 84.   Rate of uptake of water by root and shoot of *Nomaphila stricta* during two complete diel cycles (Höhn and Ax).

ments in the first 10–15 hr of an experiment but later the flow was feeble, undetectable, or sometimes reversed.

Höhn and Ax (1961), studying submersed specimens of *Nomaphila stricta*, an amphibious oriental member of the Acanthaceae, which does not normally grow fully submersed, found that the root took up water continuously while the leafy shoot lost water by day but absorbed it by night. The observed diurnal rhythm is convincing (Fig. 84) even if its mechanism is not clear. The movement is enhanced by light and CO_2, which suggests it is related to photosynthesis. Since the leaves involved are probably typical air leaves it is uncertain whether the effect is relevant to what happens in naturally fully submersed plants. At present we can only reiterate Sculthorpe's position that sustained directional flow has neither been established nor shown not to exist. There can, however, be no doubt about the reality of the transport of dissolved nutrients, or for that matter, herbicides, taken up by the roots into the upper parts of the plant (see pp. 284, 285). This, however, does not necessarily involve a transpiration stream, but may rather be due to cyclosis promoting eddy conductivity through the plant as Bierberg (1908) suggested long ago, and which is the only reasonable explanation of what has been observed in the Charophyceae, as discussed on an earlier page (see p. 26). Bierberg suspected that in water plants with reduced vascular systems, as in *Elodea*, *Vallisneria*, and *Hydrilla*, such cyclosis came into operation only when there was a deficiency of nutrients in the medium and transport from the root became necessary.

Some of the work with herbicides is interesting in indicating the idiosyncratic nature of acropetal translocation in water plants. Thus Funderburk and Lawrence (1963), who studied the fate of eight different compounds in *Heteranthera dubia* found that only simazine (2-chloro-4,6-bis(ethylamino)-1,3,5-triazine) and 2,4-D butoxy ethyl ester (2,4-dichlorophenoxyacetic acid butoxy ethyl ester) were translocated. Moreover, the lack of translocation may evidently be an active process, for Sutton and Bingham (1970), using *Myriophyllum aquaticum*[11] (sub *brasiliense*), found that ordinarily 2,4-D (2,4-dichlorophenoxyacetic acid) was not translocated from root to shoot to any great extent, but that when the plant was treated with dinitrophenol, which is a metabolic inhibitor, striking translocation occurs.

There is an alleged major difficulty in explaining how the water, taken in presumably by the root, leaves the plant if a directional stream exists. Hydathodes or pores are recorded on submerged leaves and it has been claimed that when a leaf of *Callitriche*, *Littorella*, or *Potamogeton* is lifted above the water surface in a saturated atmosphere (von Minden 1899; Weinrowsky 1899) water droplets may appear at the tips of the leaves. The hydathodes or water pores are, however, usually open only in very young leaves; secondary openings are known in some freshwater plants and might function in the discharge of water. That no openings occur in the marine *Cymodocea* or *Posidonia*, as Sculthorpe has noted, may be irrelevant in view of the special osmotic relation likely in such plants. It should be remembered that if ions are freely taken up by leaves, perhaps over special parts of the leaf surface, as must be the case if no directional transpiration stream exists, it could be argued that water could quite easily pass out, as OH^- and H^+ or H_3O^+ do (cf. p. 20), even in the absence of special pores in the macroscopic or optical microscopic size range.

Further research is clearly needed on these matters. The use of tritium oxide in well designed and executed laboratory experiments might prove illuminating.

THE LACUNAR SYSTEM, AERENCHYMA, AND RESPIRATORY ADAPTATIONS

A very remarkable, though far from unique, feature of the anatomy of most water plants is the development of systems of air spaces, which may be continuous from the leaf parenchyma, through the petiole into the stem, and so to the buried rhizome or root. Sifton (1945, 1957) has given excel-

---

[11] For this unfortunate but necessary change of the name of the parrot-feather, as it is called by aquarists, see Verdcourt (1973).

lent reviews of the extensive early work on such systems wherever they occur in vascular plants.

The lacunar system. The primary lacunar spaces are formed either from splits between the cells (schizogeny) or by the disintegration of cells (lysigeny). In general the lacunae of the illuminated part of the plant are schizogenous and those of the buried parts lysigenous, though this is not true of the rhizomes of the Nymphaeaceae (cf. Sculthorpe 1967). In some cases the relative volume of the air spaces can be surprisingly high, up to 60% of the rhizome of *Cladium mariscus* (Conway 1937, 1942) and even more in *Menyanthes trifoliata* (Coult 1964). The spaces form close behind the apex in developing shoots and are said to be enlarged by the pressure of oxygen produced in photosynthesis (Dale 1957). There are usually perforated cellular diaphragms set across the lacunae, at the nodes of the stems, and elsewhere. These appear to be hydrofuge and presumably prevent the system from becoming filled with water if the plant is injured. Although practically all plants of standing water possess lacunae, they have been said to be absent in the rheophile Podostemaceae; Cook (1969), however, found lacunae in *Apinagia richardiana* and *Mourera fluviatilis* but not in the much smaller *Tristica triflora*.

The aquatic fern *Dennstaedtiopsis aerenchymata* (Arnold and Dougherty 1964) and the apparently dicotyledonous plant of unknown affinities *Eorhiza arnoldii* of Robison and Person (1973), both from the northwestern part of North America, testify to the existence of seemingly aquatic plants with large air spaces in the Eocene (Fig. 85).

The physiological significance of the lacunae. The continuity of the air spaces throughout the plant was established by Barthélemy (1874) in *Nymphaea* and *Nelumbo*, who found that by placing a leaf of an intact plant under reduced pressure, air could be drawn in through the stomata of other leaves, down their petioles into the rhizome, and up the petiole of the leaf under reduced pressure. Sifton (1945) records that a like experiment was done in class by an undergraduate using *Sagittaria*. Hartman and Brown (1967) have studied the diurnal changes in volume and in composition of the gas in several limnologically important water plants. In *Elodea canadensis* and *Ceratophyllum demersum* the volume of gas in the submersed plants increased during the morning to a maximum and fell to low values during the night. The quantity of gas present at the time of maximum content was up to 23.4% of the plant volume in *C. demersum*, 37.6% of that of *E. canadensis*, and in some less systematic experiments reached 43% of the volume of *Myriophyllum exalbescens*.

Nygaard (1958) found only 12.75–21.3% by volume of O_2 in the gas in *Lobelia dortmanna* even after exposure to strong indirect-daylight. The gas may contain, however, after a period of photosynthesis, a higher pro-

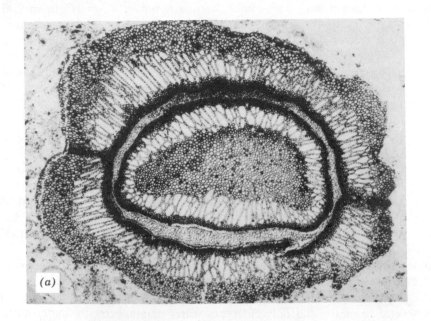

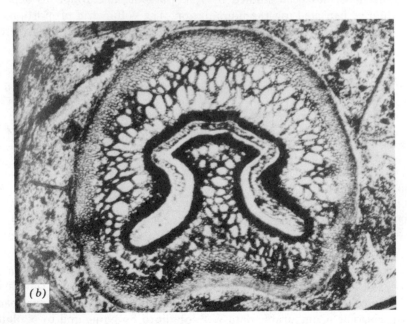

FIGURE 85. Sections of rhizome of the Eocene aquatic fern *Dennstaedtiopsis aerenchymata* showing air spaces (Arnold and Dougherty).

portion of oxygen than does atmospheric air, but in all of Hartman and Brown's observations nitrogen was the major constituent. The CO_2 content was much greater than that present in the free atmosphere, varying from about 0.3% volume at the end of the day to about 0.6% volume during the night. Nygaard (1958) detected 1.01–1.81% by volume CO_2 in the gas of *Lobelia dortmanna*. Since there is a very marked increase in the volume of the internal atmosphere during photosynthesis, and this increment involves a gaseous mixture which contains at least as much oxygen as atmospheric air and often more, the internal CO_2 can be responsible for but an insignificant amount of the oxygen produced. Since the gas remains mostly nitrogen, it is evident that rapid equilibration between the internal atmosphere and the water, which would be in equilibrium with the free atmosphere, must take place. The oxygen in the water around the plant was found to increase, though more slowly than in the internal atmosphere, and in dim light reduced photosynthesis may not produce any detectable external change. Hartman and Brown (1966) found a quantity of methane of the same order of magnitude as the carbon dioxide, in the internal atmosphere of *Elodea canadensis*.

The distribution of carbon dioxide and oxygen in the lacunar systems of several species of partially emergent water plants, growing under natural conditions, has been studied by Laing (1940b) and found to depend, as would be expected, on the illumination. The volumetric proportions of the gases in different parts of a plant of *Pontederia cordata* under different conditions are given in Table 15.

TABLE 15. *Effect of illumination on composition of gas in the lacunar system of* Pontederia cordata (*from Laing*)

	O_2 vol %		CO_2 vol %	
	Dark	Sunny	Dark	Sunny
Upper emergent part of leaf petiole	18.6	19.4	2.1	1.3
Submersed petiole base	10.3	13.1	7.9	7.2
Submersed rhizome	4.6	8.8	15.7	13.5

It is evident that the gradients set up by the assimilation of carbon dioxide and the evolution of oxygen are great enough to cause significant diffusion of the latter gas into and the former gas out of the lacunar spaces of the rhizome. Comparable data were obtained by Laing and by Vallance and Coult (1951; Coult and Vallance 1958) for other plants. The effect in general is least in elongate reed-shaped species and greatest when a large leaf area is developed, as in *Nuphar advena*. In the latter plant, the rhizome is capable of a good deal of anaerobic metabolism when the plant is in darkness, but considerable quantities of oxygen may diffuse downward during photosynthesis (Laing 1940a, b). In one set of determinations the gas of the rhizomal lacunae contained in different parts of the rhizome 0.6–3.9% by volume oxygen in the dark, but the concentration rose to 7.0–11.7% by volume after photosynthesis in sunshine.

Laing (1941) found, rather surprisingly, that the production of shoots in *Nuphar advena* and *Peltandra virginica* occurred best when the rhizome was almost entirely deprived of oxygen and a less strikingly low optimum was found for several other water plants. Root outgrowth in *N. advena*, however, was inhibited by oxygen lack. The young leaves of *N. advena* produce alcohol.

Oxygen diffusing downward may pass from the roots of *Menyanthes* and other bog plants, leading to oxidation of ferrous iron and precipitation of ferric hydroxide in the sediment in which the plants are growing (Armstrong 1964, 1967).

There is a suggestion in the work of Conway (1937) that in *Cladium mariscus* air may enter the spaces by way of dead brown leaves that are beginning to fall apart.

As has been noted earlier (see p. 151) it is by no means improbable that, in rosulate plants of soft waters, movement of CO_2 from the sediments to the roots and thus by the lacunar system into the green parts of the plant is an important additional source of the gas for photosynthesis.

Though the lacunar system may have evolved initially as a respiratory system, wherever it develops to any great extent in a petiole or floating leaf it will add greatly to the buoyancy of such structures. In a few cases, such as the ventral swellings on many of the leaves of *Pistia* (*B* of Fig. 53), the swellings on the petioles of *Trapa* (*A* of Fig. 34) and the bulbous expansions formed from the petioles of *Eichhornia* (*A* of Fig. 53), quite massive structures, consisting largely of lacunar air spaces, have clearly developed primarily as floats. In *Jussiaea sedoides* the leaves of the terminal rosette may take on a remarkable geometrical pattern at the surface of the water (Fig. 86), comparable to the arrangement based on the Fibonacci series found in some land plants (cf. Leigh 1972). Though closely mimicking *Trapa*, these rosette leaves seem to lack discrete floats.

It must be pointed out that Williams and Barber (1961) have claimed that the well-developed lacunar system is primarily skeletal, rather than respiratory in function. They emphasize that the pore area in a cross-partition rather than the cross-section of the lacuna itself will be limiting in respiration and that the mere development of lacunae is therefore of doubt-

FIGURE 86.   Reticulate rosettes of *Jussiaea sedoides* among *Nymphoides humboldtiana* in Laguna Apastupeque, El Salvador, (Armitage and Fassett).

ful respiratory value. Moreover, since the submersed roots of rice plants apparently derive oxygen from the upper part of the plant without a lacunar system, they suspect that diffusion through ordinary intercellular spaces may be adequate in respiration. They believe that the main function of the lacunae with their cross walls is to provide mechanical resistance to bending stresses and to permit the root or rhizome to be large enough to act as an anchor without increasing its metabolism. Whether the consequent decrease in density in the rhizome would promote this function may be doubted. Moreover, what happens in a rice plant may be very different from what happens in a water lily, with its long petiole and massive rhizome. It is, however, reasonable to suppose that the lacunar system has evolved to function simultaneously in more than one way and that its skeletal significance may be quite important.

Aerenchyma.   In addition to the primary lacunar spaces just discussed, secondary spongy tissue with intercellular air spaces may be formed in certain plants through the activity of a cork cambium or phellogen. This tissue is known as *aerenchyma*, though not infrequently that term is somewhat improperly extended to include also the lacunar system.

Aerenchyma may develop in a small way from the lenticles of land plants, such as *Salix, Eupatorium* (Schenck 1889), and *Populus* (Goebel 1893), should they become partially submersed. In such cases there is a presumption that the aerenchyma is involved in the respiratory transport of gases, as lenticles are believed to be. In a few genera, most notably *Jussiaea* (*B* of Fig. 87), submersed horizontal shoots may develop ventral mud roots, which reach the bottom, and dorsal air roots, very largely composed of aerenchyma, which reach the surface and presumably function as respiratory organs. The stem of the plant is also surrounded by aerenchyma.

The development of aerenchyma seems to be particularly characteristic of the Onagraceae and Lythraceae in the order Lythrales and of the sporadic aquatic members of the Mimosaceae (*D* of Fig. 87) and Fabaceae in the order Leguminales. In most of these cases the aerenchyma seems more likely to function in floats than as a respiratory system. In the swamp loosestrife *Decodon* (*A* of Fig. 87), which must be known to the most unbotanical limnologist as one of the most decorative littoral plants of North American lakes, long branches originating from the bank may bend down under their own weight till they touch the water; when this happens they develop aerenchyma which keeps the stems afloat, and permits them to grow upward again for a time. The several cases in the Leguminales have already been discussed (see p. 80), where the anatomically different but functionally similarly secondary xylem of *Aeschynomene* has also been mentioned.

Anaerobic metabolism and tolerance of submersion. It has long been known that some water plants contain ethanol; the popular name "brandy bottle" for *Nuphar* indicates that alcohol can easily be smelled in the tissues of the yellow water lily. Laing found that the rhizomes and corms of a number of water plants, namely, *Nuphar advena, Nymphaea tuberosa, Asclepias incarnata, Sparganium eurycarpum, Sagittaria latifolia, Acorus calamus, Peltandra virginica, Pontederia cordata, Typha latifolia*, and *Scirpus validus* could live anaerobically for long periods of time.

Crawford (1966) studied seven species of *Senecio*. Of these, two, *S. aquaticus* and *S. smithii*, occur in wet ditches and also live in the eulittoral of lakes, where their roots must frequently be flooded. The other species all live in drier situations; of *S. vulgaris* two races were available, one from sand dunes and one from the damper habitat of a garden. The plants were grown in two series under comparable conditions, in one series with a low water table, in the other with a high water table flooding the roots. After 1 month the rate of ethanol production in the roots of the plants was determined, the results being set out in Table 16. It will be seen that in the species not ordinarily liable to flooding, inundating the roots causes an increase

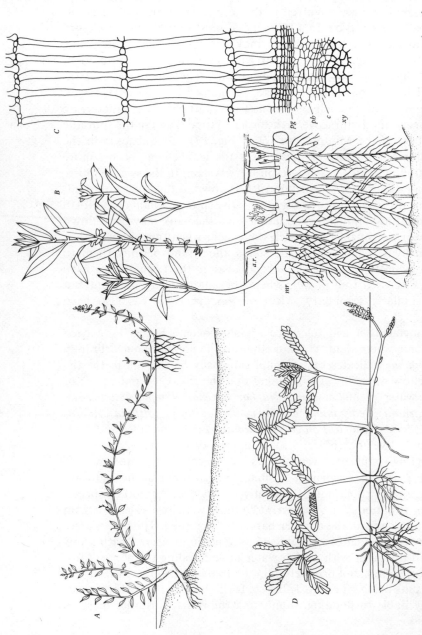

FIGURE 87. Aerenchymatous structures as floats and as respiratory organs. *A, Decodon verticillatus* (Lythraceae) rooted at the margin of a lake with a branch that has grown out and dropped into the water and there has formed a float; *B, Jussiaea peruviana* (Onagraceae), portion of floating stem with upward directed air roots (*a, r.*), which may reach the surface, and downwardly directed mud roots (*m.r.*), which reach the bottom sediments; *C,* the same, section of part of floating stem, (*a*) aerenchyma, (*pg*) phellogen, (*ph*) phloem, (*c*) cambrium, (*xy*) xylem; *D, Neptunia oleracea* (Mimosaceae) with two internodal floats (Arber from Schenk and from Rosanoff, modified).

208

TABLE 16. *Alcohol production in unflooded and flooded roots in five species of* Senecio *from dry situations and in two hygrophytic species of the genus (data of Crawford)*

Species	Alcohol production, low water table, L ($mM \cdot mg^{-1}$ wet $\cdot hr^{-1}$)	Alcohol production, high water table, H ($mM \cdot mg^{-1}$ wet $\cdot hr^{-1}$)	H/L
S. viscosus	0.098	0.366	3.73
S. sylvaticus	0.165	0.490	2.97
S. squalidus	0.260	0.830	3.19
S. jacobeae	0.133	0.320	2.40
S. vulgaris (dunes)	0.153	0.456	2.94
S. vulgaris (garden)	0.400	0.660	1.65
S. aquaticus	0.324	0.320	0.99
S. smithii	0.117	0.123	1.05

in ethanol production, whereas in the two eulittoral species this does not happen.

In later work it was found that the same sort of tolerance was exhibited by a wide group of plants in whose normal habitat flooding of the roots frequently took place, but not in strictly terrestrial species. The rate of action of alcohol dehydrogenase, which converts acetaldehyde to ethanol in the presence of nicotinamide-adenine dinucleotide (NAD):

$$CH_3CHO + NADH + H^+ \rightleftarrows CH_3CH_2OH + NAD^+$$

is greatly increased by flooding in the intolerant species, including not only species of *Senecio* but also unrelated plants such as *Pisum sativum* and *Vicia faba*, whereas it is unchanged (*Senecio aquaticus, Mentha aquatica, Caltha palustris, Ranunculus flammula*) or even decreased (*Juncus effusus, Myosotis scorpiodes, Glyceria maxima, Iris pseudacorus*, and *Phalaris arundinacea*) in a group of plants which include several facultative fully aquatic species. It appears that the apparent Michaelis constant of the enzyme activity falls in the intolerant species on flooding, meaning that for a given stationary concentration of acetaldehyde, conversion to alcohol goes more quickly, but this does not happen in the species in which the roots can adapt to aquatic life. In the latter group of plants the metabolic processes, which lead to enhanced acetaldehyde and alcohol production on flooding intolerant species, are diverted to the production of malate which can accumulate without being toxic. It is found that an otherwise uncharacterized "malic enzyme" that converts malate to pyruvate, from which acetaldehyde is formed by α-carboxylase, is entirely absent in the more aquatic group (*Mentha aquatica*, *Myosotis scorpioides*, *Senecio aquaticus*, *Glyceria maxima*) under whatever conditions they are grown, but is always present in *Senecio jacobeae*, *Hieracium pilosella*, *Senecio viscosus*, and *Pisum sativum*.

When anaerobic metabolism is induced by a rise in water level reducing the rate at which oxygen can diffuse to the roots, two different types of metabolic path may result, one in intolerant or more truly terrestrial species, leading to the ultimately toxic accumulation of ethanol, and the other in tolerant or facultatively aquatic species, leading to the accumulation of the far less toxic malate. These two conditions are expressed by McManmon and Crawford (1971) diagrammatically, as in Fig. 88.

Flood-tolerant species also show a greater capacity for nitrate reduction under anaerobic conditions than do intolerant. The reduction involves the formation of amino acids (Garcia-Novo and Crawford 1973).

In interpreting these most interesting results ecologically, it must be remembered that the malate accumulating in the roots of the flood-tolerant species is available for aerobic metabolism when the water level falls and the roots are well aerated. Crawford's mechanism may, therefore, be primarily developed in eulittoral and other species living in frequently flooded environments and may not be appropriate to the permanently submersed roots or rhizomes of fully aquatic species. Laing's (1940a, b) results seem to suggest that the liquidation of the oxygen debt is mainly likely to take place when photosynthesis is occurring so that oxygen can diffuse downward through the lacunar system. More detailed work on the metabolism of perennially submersed rhizomes is needed.

LIFE HISTORY

Certain critical events in the life histories of water plants are doubtless important in determining their survival in any given set of environmental conditions. Apart from the circumstances of photosynthesis already discussed, the germination of seeds, the events of reproduction, sexual or asexual, and perennation, particularly the survival in the least favorable, usually the winter, season are likely to be paramount, and are considered in detail in the following sections. The material to be presented is chosen for its significance for what we see and study when we examine a lake. Many fascinating details are inevitably omitted; the reader is referred to Sculthorpe (1967) for much of what is not presented here.

Germination of the seeds of aquatic angiosperms. The conditions under which the seeds of water plants germinate in nature are obviously of importance in their ecology. There is much variability from species to species,

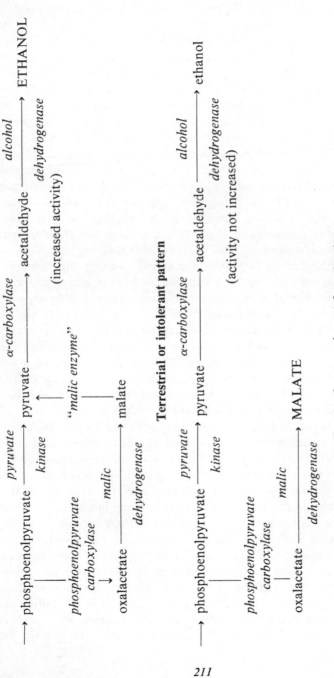

FIGURE 88. Pathways of anaerobic metabolism in flooded roots of terrestrial or flood-intolerant species producing much ethanol under anaerobic conditions and in facultatively aquatic, or flood-tolerant species mainly producing malate anaerobically (McManmon and Crawford); enzymes in italics, substrates roman.

but in very few cases can a fully satisfactory account of what is needed for reproduction in a natural environment be given. The seeds of the majority of aquatic plants fall from the parent individual as fruits in a wide sense, being at least encased in a *pericarp* derived from the wall of the mature ovary. The simplest type of such a fruit is the *achene*, formed by the hardening of the wall of an individual carpel. When the carpels are no longer numerous or separate, the equivalent fruit, containing one or a few seeds, is termed a *nut*; if this secondarily splits into achene-like elements they are termed *nutlets*. This is probably the commonest type of fruit in aquatic plants. Less often the outer parts of the pericarp, termed the *epicarp* and *mesocarp*, remain soft, and are indeed potential food for animals, whereas the inner part or *endocarp* becomes very hard, forming with the seed a *stone*, as in a peach or a plum. Such a fruit, found among aquatic genera in *Potamogeton*, is known as a *drupe*. A fruit containing several seeds may then split into druplets as in *Callitriche*. Though most fully aquatic species produce one or another of these types of fruit, among the more or less emergent species such as *Peltandra* in the Araceae and in the Hydrocharitaceae, berry-like fruits containing many seeds, liberated by slow decay or by bursting of the berries in water, are found. Among the floating-leaved plants, the gynoecium forms a capsule in *Nuphar* and *Nymphaea*. The many seeds are liberated by dehiscence, above water in *Nuphar*, but below water as the result of swelling of mucilage, in *Nymphaea*. In the not too remotely allied *Nelumbo*, the whole receptacle of the flower forms a remarkable seed vessel, in which there are numerous pits containing the one-seeded nuts or achenes, the structure looking like the rose of a watering can. The peduncle bearing it is at first erect but turns over, and the receptacle falls over into the water. Other examples of diversity of behavior in seed production are given when sexual reproduction is discussed. The examples that have just been mentioned are sufficient to indicate that among water plants as among those of the land, there is very great variety in the way in which the seed is protected and, at least for a time, isolated from the external world. This variety may be expected to influence the diversity of conditions that must be met if development of the seed is to be initiated. Moreover, it must not be forgotten that in many large genera achenes, as in *Scirpus*, or the hard parts of drupes, as in *Potamogeton*, or seeds, as in *Juncus*, provide useful taxonomic characters. It can hardly be doubted that in many cases the characters by which species of such fruits or seeds are separated systematically have something to do with the adaptations and niche specificities of the species so separated. We may be almost entirely ignorant as to what effect these differences have in promoting or inhibiting germination under any given circumstances (see, however, pp. 221–3), but the great diversity in structure, whether on a small scale, between species, or on a large scale, when achenes are compared with drupes, berries, or dehiscent capsules, should at least prepare us for great functional differences.

Physiologically the most important factors in germination seem to be the impermeability of the fruit, or at least the hard part of the pericarp, to water, and the consequent necessity for the disruption or decomposition of such impermeable or hard parts; the need in some cases for a reducing environment at the time of germination; and the need for light or darkness, varying with the species. It is also evident that in most water plants of temperate latitudes a period of dormancy, often at a low temperature, is required; in some cases this may be merely coincidentally related to the breakdown of the fruit, but in many others a true diapause must be involved. In a few cases passage through a bird, or an increase in temperature of a kind that might be experienced in the alimentary tract, is known to promote germination remarkably.

The seeds of most species of water plants, though not germinating immediately on liberation from the parent plant, probably ordinarily do so within a period of a few years. Occasional very long survival times are known, however. The most remarkable is that of an achene of *Nelumbo nucifera*, from the collection of Sir Hans Sloane in the British Museum, which was found to germinate in 1942, when it was 237 years old (Ramsbottom 1942a, b; Godwin and Willis 1964). Longer survival for achenes of *Nelumbo nucifera* has been claimed but seems not to be satisfactorily established. It is, however, by no means inconceivable that seeds of a few species of water plants might survive five or six centuries, as appears to be the case for some terrestrial species (Odum 1965).

The significance of hard covering layers and dormancy in clean water. The importance of the fruit, at least the pericarp, or in some cases the seed coat or testa, is probably fairly general. In a few cases it is known that green seeds, detached before hardening and darkening have occurred, can germinate immediately, as was noted by Crocker (1907) for *Eichhornia* and for *Potamogeton natans* and *P. pectinatus*. In Crocker's experience the seeds of none of these plants, once fully ripened, would germinate without some sort of special treatment.

Fischer (1907) gave examples of the fruits or seeds of a variety of water plants remaining ungerminated for many years under pure water. Those of *Sagittaria sagittifolia* were kept under water for 9 yr with only 2.8%, and of *Sparganium emersum* (sub *ramosum*) in a like experiment with only 0.5% germination. Additional observations were made on *Alisma plantago-aquatica, Hippuris vulgaris, Polygonum amphibium, Potamogeton natans, P. lucens,* and *P. pectinatus, Scirpus maritimus,* and *Schoenoplectus lacustris.* This part of Fischer's work is, however, preliminary to a study of the effects of various substances in promoting germination. It is reported in a summary and not very systematic manner and it is not really certain that fruits or seeds of all the additional species had been stored for years in clean water and then had been shown to be viable.

Guppy (1897) did a number of experiments in which the fruits of water plants were left in water or wet mud for years. The conditions are not specified, but seem to have involved some seasonal variation in temperature and to have been fairly uniform from species to species.

Of about 20 species studied, only *Myriophyllum spicatum, Ranunculus repens,* and *Zannichellia palustris* showed some significant germination within the year of the setting of seed. In most species the highest germination rates were observed 1 or 2 yr later. *Sparganium erectum* behaved irregularly, with a tendency for the greatest rate of germination in the third, or for *S. emersum* (sub *simplex*) in the fourth year. *Potamogeton obtusifolius,* grown only on wet mud, hardly sprouted until the third year, when 62% of the seeds germinated. There was considerable but very irregular delay in *P. natans.* The seeds of *Nymphaea alba* tended to germinate after 1 yr, but there was also 6% loss by decay in this period, while those of *Nuphar lutea* both sprouted and rotted more slowly.

Effects of freezing and of seawater. Guppy found that the fruits which he studied in general withstood enclosure in ice or frozen mud for a week or two without significant change in the rate of germination. This was specifically recorded of *Nymphaea alba, Nuphar lutea, Myriophyllum alterniflorum* and *M. spicatum, Sparganium erectum, Sagittaria sagittifolia, Damasonium alisma, Alisma plantago-aquatica, Baldellia ranunculoides,* and *Potamogeton* spp., including *P. natans.* Freezing, however, appears to have accelerated germination in *Nymphoides peltata* and notably in *Calla palustris.* Immersion in seawater increased the subsequent rate of germination in the seeds of *Nuphar lutea* but decreased it in those of *Nymphaea alba.* Flotation of the fruits of *Sparganium erectum* on seawater also appears to have accelerated, but in *Calla palustris* and *Sagittaria sagittifolia* to have delayed germination; in the two last-named species the effect is comparable to that of drying.

Effects of drying. In Guppy's experiments, drying killed the seeds of *Nymphaea alba* and *Nuphar lutea* in about 2 months. The drupes of *Sparganium erectum* withstand being kept dry for 3–4 months, and the nutlets of *Myriophyllum alterniflorum* and *M. spicatum* for at least 1 year. The seeds of *Nymphoides peltata* also withstand prolonged drying. The fruits of *Potamogeton natans* can survive drying for 4 but not for 30 months, and much the same is true of *Groenlandia densa,* in which none survived for 17 months. However, in *P. crispus* germination was possible after 18 months of drying; there may be a genuine specific difference here. The longest period of drying tolerated in Guppy's experiments was 2 years for the fruits of a species of *Callitriche*, but they rotted after being dried $3\frac{1}{2}$ yr and then returned to a wet environment. Drying delays germination in *Calla palustris* but appeared to have accelerated the process in *Ceratophyllum demersum*; such acceleration is clearly unusual in the species studied by Guppy.

Certain early workers, however, had believed that certain seeds or fruits which remained dormant in water germinated after a period of drying. This was recorded by Müller of *Eichhornia, Heteranthera,* and *Mayaca* (in Ludwig 1886). Crocker (1907) indeed found that drying of *Eichhornia* cracked the seed coat and facilitated germination. He also believed that the fruits of *Potamogeton natans* and *P. pectinatus* cracked, on drying, along two creases on the convex side of the embryo and that this promoted development when the fruit was returned to water. Muenscher (1936b), however, found no indication of such an effect in the 21 species of *Potamogeton* that he studied, nor in any of 41 species of North American water plants of other genera (Muenscher 1936a). In *Glyceria striata, Rorippa nasturtium-aquaticum,* and *Veronica anagallis-aquatica* drying appeared neither beneficial or harmful, but in all other cases in Muenscher's experiments it appears to have greatly inhibited and usually prevented development. It is possible that if longer periods of subsequent immersion had been used, the drying would have appeared a little less deleterious. On the whole it would seem unlikely that drying and subsequent wetting play an important part in regulating the reproduction of the water plants occurring in lakes. It is quite possible, however, that among the species found in temporary waters some may exhibit such regulation. In a few cases, such as *Nymphaea* and *Nuphar*, as Guppy points out, the inability of the seeds to withstand drying must prevent the establishment of these plants in any but the most eustatic waters.

McNaughton (1960) in an elaborate study of the biological races of the three species of *Typha* living in North America found that no diapause under cold conditions was necessary to promote germination of any of the seeds. The experiments were conducted on initially dry material which was rinsed with an unspecified detergent followed by water which may have introduced an unnatural circumstance. Most curiously, in each species seeds from the more southern localities were able to germinate at lower temperatures than those from more northern conspecific populations.

In striking contrast to these cases, Spence (1964) observed that the seeds of *Phragmites australis* germinated quite easily on silty sand in pots set in water, the surface of which was 5 or 15 cm below that of the soil surface in the pot, but failed completely to germinate when the soil was covered with 5 cm of water. Spence believes that where *P. australis* is rooted below water level, it has germinated originally on the bank and has colonized down the slope asexually.

Breaking of protective coverings to accelerate germination. Guppy found that baring the stone of the fruit of *Sparganium erectum* produced 40% germination in the first year, as against 6–13% in experiments in which this was not done, but he was unable to induce development in *Potamogeton natans* by such treatment. Crocker (1907) experimented with the ripe fruits or seeds of a number of water plants. He removed all soft material of the fruit, sterilized with 5% formaldehyde, and washed with distilled water. Half of each sample then had the pericarp or testa broken. Each subsample was now incubated in water at 20°C for 2 days in darkness and then kept in diffuse light. In *Polygonum amphibium, Alisma triviale*[12] (sub *plantago-aquatica*), and *Sagittaria latifolia* there was, in the initial 2-day period, at least 85% germination of the broken seeds with apparently complete survival of the seedlings for a further 8 days in the light. In *Potamogeton natans* and *P. pectinatus*, in which many seeds lacked embryos, the experimental samples nevertheless gave germination rates of at least 50%. In no species studied was there any germination of any unbroken sample over the time span of the experiment of 10 days.

Effects of bacterial activity. In nature various processes evidently occur more slowly, but have in the end the same effect as breaking the hard inner part of a fruit or a seed coat. Fischer (1907) observed that in a culture of *Serratia marcescens*, derived from lake mud, in cane sugar with ammonium sulfate, *Alisma plantago-aquatica, Sagittaria graminea* var. *platyphylla, Potamogeton pectinatus*, and *Schoenoplectus lacustris* all easily germinated, and he also obtained germination of some of these species, of *S. sagittifolia*, and even of *Sparganium erectum*, in cultures in which a miscellaneous bacterial and fungal flora had developed.

Fischer believed that the liberation of acid by fermentation promoted germination in these cases. He did many experiments in which germination was brought about by acid or strong alkali. The effect varied greatly with the acids used, being negligible with acetic or formic, moderate with lactic or malic, and very marked with oxalic acid. He concluded that H^+ and OH^- ions were the effective agents. It is obvious that some of the conditions under which Fischer's seeds germinated imitated more closely those in nature than did the conditions of Crocker's experiments. More or less anaerobic environments swarming with bacteria and containing organic

---

[12] Fernald (1950) regards the eastern North American plant as distinct from *A. plantago-aquatica*.

acids are common, while natural agents destroying the inner hard layers of fruits mechanically are comparatively rare, though not unknown. It is, however, very likely that factors other than pH, to which Fischer attributed his results, are operating in anaerobic muds; moreover, his belief in the efficacy of the hydroxyl ion was apparently erroneous (Schaumann 1926).

Stimulation by reduced oxygen tension and low redox potential. A good many aquatic seeds have been shown to germinate under oxygen-deficient conditions. This is true of *Nelumbo nucifera* (Ohga 1926), *Euryale ferox* (Okada 1930), *Alisma triviale* (sub *plantago-aquatica*) (Crocker and Davis 1914), *Trapa natans* (Teresawa 1927), *Peltandra virginica* (Edwards 1933), and *Typha latifolia* (Morinaga 1926). The circumstances of this capacity for at least microaerophilic germination are various, however. In *Alisma triviale* germination can occur in the absence of oxygen if the covering over the seed is removed, but 5 mm Hg pressure of air or 1 mm oxygen are needed for chlorophyll formation, and 10 times that amount for leaf differentiation in the seedling. In *Typha latifolia* the cells of the embryo are full of aleurone grains which swell and vacuolate when the oxygen tension is reduced, thus enhancing germination. In some samples of seed, however, a high oxygen tension produces vacuolation of the cytoplasm rather than the contained grains, thus compensating to some extent for the failure of the latter to swell. The beneficial effect of low oxygen is said by Morinaga to be shown only if the covering of the seed is intact, which is to be expected if low oxygen acts by increasing the internal pressure on such a covering. These results have been confirmed by Sifton (1959). He also found that intact seeds nearly always need light for germination; in some samples, however, sufficiently extensive alternations (15–20°C and 30–35°C) in temperature may produce germination in darkness. Removal of the seed cap or, to a lesser extent, merely pricking the testa obviates the need for light. Light passed through a blue filter, which probably eliminates ordinary red radiation but not the far red (see p. 223), is strikingly inhibitory. It is noteworthy that both Morinaga and Sifton found considerable differences between different batches of seed; a study of the sources of these differences would be interesting.

In *Nelumbo*, seeds pretreated with concentrated sulfuric acid will germinate in atmospheres of either oxygen or nitrogen, but in the latter atmosphere the process is not really anaerobic as each seed has a small oxygen reserve of about 0.22 ml at S.T.P.

Forsberg (1965b) found that the seeds of *Najas marina* would not germinate at the ordinary redox potential of 0.49–0.50 V, usually recorded from naturally oxygenated waters on the bright platinum electrode (Vol. I, p. 693), but did so readily when the potential was lowered to -0.37 V with sodium dithionate; this potential is, however, lower than anything likely to be observed in lake muds in nature.[13] A supposedly comparable effect could also be obtained in this species, in *Alisma plantago-aquatica*, and in *Baldellia ranunculoides* by germinating in agar. For the last two species the germination rate on moist filter paper in air was 5 and 4%, respectively, whereas if the access of oxygen was restricted by agar, in both plants the germination rate was about 95%. Wetzel and McGregor (1968) could not substantiate this effect with *Najas flexilis* but there is a little independent evidence from Muenscher's (1936a) work that these two species differ in their requirements for germination.

Winter dormancy and effect of storage at low temperature. Merely keeping seeds in water so that they experience the natural march of the seasons, as in Guppy's work (1897), or storing them at 1–4°C and then raising the temperature, as in most twentieth-century studies, often promotes germination. Guppy alone seems to have published fairly systematic data on the germination of water plant seeds kept under water for a number of years. His more complete experiments, averaged where this seems appropriate, are summarized in Table 17. Even though this work may now seem rough and inadequately reported, certain interesting conclusions can be drawn from the table.

There is an obvious tendency to delayed germination under conditions that must approximate what happens in nature in pure, well-oxygenated water. In very few experiments was there significant germination in Year 0 of seed set, and in a number of cases much of the germination was delayed till the second or third year. There is clearly well-marked interspecific variation. *Myriophyllum spicatum* usually germinates earlier and the two members of *Sparganium* usually later than the other species studied. In *Potamogeton*, *P. natans* in water tends to be later than *P. polygonifolius*. The data on *Myriophyllum* may perhaps indicate intraspecific genetic variation. In view of the experiments on the promotion of germination by low redox potential, it is curious that there is no systematic difference between germination rates in water and wet mud, in which the redox potential is almost sure to have been lower.

Muenscher (1936b) did a large and more controlled series of experiments on 21 American species of *Potamogeton*. All species except *P. crispus*, *P. filiformis*, and *P. vaseyi* showed some germination after the fruits had been stored for 1 yr in cold water at temperatures of 1–3°C. Over half the seeds of *P. confervoides*, *P. foliosus*, *P. obtusifolius*, *P. berchtoldii* (sub *pusillus*), *P. capillaceus*, *P. epihydrus*, *P. nodosus* (sub *americanus*), and *P. illinoensis*

---

[13] The potential was apparently lowest in his most dilute dithionate solution; in this, at −0.47 V, germination did not occur. Further investigation would clearly be desirable.

TABLE *17. Percentage germination of fruits or seeds in water or wet mud in the experiments of Guppy (1897). Equivalent experiments are averaged; where one set of experiments was discontinued the other set of figures is given. In the case of* Calla palustris *where all experiments ran for 2 years, the actual numbers of germinations were recalculated and averaged*

Species	Conditions of experiment	Germination (%)					
		Year of seed set (0)	Year 1	Year 2	Year 3	Year 4	Year 5
Nymphaea alba	Water unfrozen	0	86	1	0	—	—
	Wet mud unfrozen	0	37	26	20	—	—
	Wet mud frozen (av 2 exp.)	0.5	60.5	0.5	5.5	—	—
Nuphar lutea	Water unfrozen	0	4	13	7	—	—
	Wet mud unfrozen	0	14	13	17	—	—
	Wet mud frozen	0	7	7	7	40	18
Ceratophyllum demersum	Water	0	10	60	10	—	—
	Water after 2 months of drying	0	62	12	—	—	—
	Wet mud	0	23	54	—	—	—
Myriophyllum spicatum	Water (av 3 exp.)	27	38	—	—	—	—
	Water (exceptional exp.)	0	47	12	—	—	—
Nymphoides peltata	Water (av 2 exp.)	0	71.5	19	—	—	—
	Water, after 3 months of drying	0	18	40	—	—	—
	Wet mud (av 2 exp.)	0	31	35.5	12	0	—
Sparganium erectum	Water	0	7.3	7.3	12.3	8.5	2
S. emersum	Water	0	0	8.5	0	33	—
Calla palustris	Water not frozen	0	0	90	—	—	—
	Water frozen	0	77	22	—	—	—
	Water after $3\frac{1}{2}$ months of drying	0	10	45	—	—	—
Potamogeton natans	Water unfrozen	0	1	13.5	28.5	38	—
	Water frozen	0	3	17	13.5	32	—
	Wet mud frozen	0	48	30	—	—	—
Potamogeton polygonifolius	Water	1	37	28.6	—	—	—
	Wet mud	0	42	24	—	—	—
Potamogeton berchtoldii	Water	0	7	14	8	24	—
	Wet mud	0	4	7	4	12	—

(sub *angustifolius*) germinated in tap water in a greenhouse with diurnal temperatures of 18–21°C and nocturnal 13–16°C after only 6 months of storage at 1–3°C, and apart from *P. berchtoldii*, which gave 57% germination, all gave over 80%. In *P. pectinatus, P. zosteriformis, P. pusillus* (sub *panormitanus*), *P. spirillus, P. gramineus, P. natans, P. praelongus, P. richardsoni*, and *P. perfoliatus* var. *bupleuroides*, the germination rate after 6 months was between 12 and 38%. Muenscher pointed out that part of the difference in germination capacity may be due to conditions of harvesting, or in some species to failure to produce an embryo. It is noteworthy that Guppy obtained 68% germination after 1 yr in *P. crispus*, a species that did not germinate at all in Muenscher's experiments, while *P. obtusifolius*, which Guppy found on wet mud not to germinate abundantly till the third year, was one of the species giving very high germination after a year's storage in Muenscher's experiments. Comparable but less extreme differences are exhibited by *P. berchtoldii* in the two series of experiments. Both authors agree with Sauvageau (1894) that *P. natans* is a late germinator.

In other genera Muenscher (1936a) obtained no germination after 7 months in four of the five species of *Sparganium* investigated, nor in either *Sagittaria montevidensis* var. *spongiosa* or *Scirpus acutus*. *Sparganium americanum, Scirpus americanus, S. validus*, and *Eleocharis calva* all had low rates under 15%. In *Najas flexilis* the germination rate was 87% after 7 months in cold water, but in the other species of the genus (*N. gracillima, N. marina*, and *N. minor*) studied the rates were never more than 15%; the difference is of interest in view of the apparent importance of redox potential to *N. marina* but not to *N. flexilis* (see p. 217). *Polygonum amphibium* showed no germination after 5 months and only 26% after 7 months. *Sagittaria latifolia* in one experiment gave 46% after 5 months, but in another no germination until after 7 months, and then only 12% sprouted. Of the other seeds and fruits studied, at least 40% and usually many more germinated after 7 months. Of these the fruits or seeds of *Vallisneria americana, Glyceria striata, Juncus articulatus, Heteranthera dubia, Rorippa nasturtium-aquaticum*, and *Lobelia dortmanna* germinated rather quickly, over 30% sprouting after only 2 months of storage in cold water. *Nymphaea tuberosa, Ceratophyllum demersum, Veronica anagallis-aquatica, Alisma triviale, Peltandra virginica, Pontederia cordata, Calla palustris, Eriocaulon septangulare*, and *Zizania aquatica* required 5 months in cold water before massive germination took place, and in *Nuphar variegata Trapa natans*, and *Acorus calamus* the full 7 months was needed to produce at least 40% germination. These experiments suggest that a winter cold period is of rather general importance to the germination of the majority of temperate water plants but, in view of the uncertainties about all fruits and seeds being collected in equivalent states, it is doubtful how much differences in the length of diapause are correlated with differences in habitat.

Effects of light. Guppy (1897) thought that, though neither darkness nor light were necessary for the germination of *Potamogeton natans*, darkness tended to favor early sprouting. *Iris pseudacorus* also seemed to germinate more readily in darkness than in light. In *Nuphar lutea* the opposite was true, and for the germination of both his species of *Callitriche* and *Ranunculus* (*Batrachium*) spp., darkness appeared to be inhibitory and light stimulatory. A little fluffy mud and good shading by the leaves of emergent plants may be enough, while the leaves last, to prevent the germination of *Callitriche* in nature. Although these experiments are imperfect, they at least suggest a diversity of possible situations.

Later work (Schaumann 1926) indicated that germination in *Alisma plantago-aquatica* is not affected by illumination; this was confirmed by Forsberg (1966), who found the same true of the related *Baldellia ranunculoides*.

In *Najas marina*, however, light is inhibitory (Forsberg 1965b), and this is also the case in the germination of *Najas flexilis* (Wetzel and McGregor 1968). Forsberg (1966) found, in spite of Guppy's statements about the genus, that the seeds of *Potamogeton lucens* only germinated in light.

The only work to go further, and it goes so much further as to make the earlier investigations look rather primitive, is that of Spence (1967b), and particularly of Spence, Milburn, Ndawula-Senyimba, and Roberts (1971), who have studied the physiology of germination of two species of *Potamogeton*, *P. thunbergii*, and *P. schweinfurthii*, in Kigezi, in southwestern Uganda. *P. thunbergii* is mainly found in the shallow water of drainage ditches in *Papyrus* swamps and in lakes rarely grows in more than 50 cm of water, whereas *P. schweinfurthii* may occur in the infralittoral of lakes in water from 0.75 to 6.0 m deep. Locally, as in Lake Bunyonyi, a hybrid, × *bunyonyiensis*, between the two species, grows in quite shallow water (Denny and Lye 1973).

The fruits, usually regarded as drupes, consist of a thin epicarp, an aerenchymatous mesocarp, and a stony endocarp enclosing the embryo. The endocarp is differentiated into a main part enclosing the embryo and a lid or keel attached by a suture of small less lignified cells. The fruits of *P. thunbergii* are large, weighing on an average about 20 mg; those of *P. schweinfurthii* are smaller, weighing about 9 mg. Both kinds of seed float when they are detached from the parent plant. Large chloroplasts are thinly distributed in the cells of the epidermis and mesocarp, and the initially floating seeds are green. In *P. schweinfurthii* they may float for at least 18 months without losing their green color, but ultimately become discolored as they sink. In *P. thunbergii* the still floating fruit becomes reddish brown before sinking.

Kept in total darkness 50% of the fruits of *P. schweinfurthii* become discolored in 23 days, whereas in the control series in natural daylight, half the seeds had discolored in 52 days, and with additional light in 72 days. The seeds in these experiments were weighed weekly and it seems probable that the rapid discoloration compared to what happens in undisturbed seeds was due to this interference. It is, however, quite clear that light inhibits the discoloration. Sinking was similarly affected. After 15–20 days the fruits in darkness began to lose weight, due to disintegration of the pericarp, while this process hardly occurred in the illuminated fruits.

In *P. thunbergii* it was possible to follow the photosynthetic rate of fruits at different stages. Photosynthesis in excess of respiratory uptake of oxygen continues actively in reddish-brown floating fruits, but declines rapidly just as they sink, while the respiratory uptake of oxygen increases. The density of the fruit, which is low (0.848) when it is green, rises as the seed becomes brown to 0.948, the ambient water at 25°C having a density of 0.997. Further increase to 1.012 causes sinking. It was observed in *P. schweinfurthii* that a green floating fruit sank if its mesocarp was deeply incised underwater, and that in the process a gas bubble was lost from the fruit. It is reasonable to suppose that in both species buoyancy, owing to gas in the aerenchymatous mesocarp, is maintained by photosynthesis. When the latter process is inhibited by darkening or by spontaneous aging, the fruit sinks.

Fruits that have sunk apparently germinate only in light. If the epicarp and mesocarp are removed from floating seeds which then are illuminated, germination begins after about 10 days. This occurred in fruits of all ages, freshly shed up to 6 months old. Red light of 659 nm was about 30 times as effective as white light in producing germination of scraped *P. thunbergii* fruits. Following red irradiation with an equivalent amount of far-red (732 nm) light inhibited the germination, as with a number of other plants.

In nature the spectral energy of the stimulatory red band (645–655 nm) and of the inhibitory far-red band (725–735 nm) at the surface will be about 2.0 and 1.4% of the total incident radiation, respectively. Since the pericarp is chlorophyllose, some differential absorption of red light may be expected. Development of fruits floating at the surface will be inhibited by the excess of far-red radiation. On sinking and decay of the chlorophyll, the proportion of red reaching the embryo will increase, as there is proportionately less absorption at this wavelength by the fruit wall and rather more of the far red by the water. Under ideal conditions the germination of *P. thunbergii* fruits might be stimulated down to about 1 m, though in practice, near the shore, seston and colloidal color are likely to decrease this depth. In his earlier paper, Spence (1967b) indicates that the deeper-water *P. schweinfurthii* needs about one-quarter of the light flux required by *P. thunbergii* to produce germination. Preliminary work suggests that phenomena of the kind just described are widespread in the genus *Potamogeton* and will no doubt be found important in regulating depth of germination. Since so much vegetative reproduction occurs in these plants, this may account for depth distributions only in a rather partial manner. The work, however, extends our knowledge of germination in water plants far beyond its previous limits. The results may, however, be compared with the far less detailed observations (see p. 217) on the emergent *Typha latifolia*, by Sifton (1959).

Miscellaneous observations. Frank (1966) found indoleacetic acid to break dormancy in turions of *P. nodosus*, but a comparable treatment of the seeds of *Najas flexilis* by Wetzel and McGregor (1968) was ineffective. The last-named workers noted some differences between experiments conducted in well water and those conducted in synthetic media.

Effects of high temperature and chemical agents in the alimentary tracts of birds. Guppy (1894, 1897) found that fruits of *Potamogeton natans* that had traversed the alimentary tract of a domestic duck (*Anas platyrhynchos*) gave, after winter dormancy, a germination rate of 60% whereas a control sample from the same collection gave only 1%. He also found that *Sparganium* seeds from the alimentary tracts of wild ducks shot for the market germinated much more freely than would have been expected from other experience with the genus. In any such case mechanical trituration in the crop which may contain stones, high temperature, acidity, and the action of pepsin or, in a slightly alkaline intestinal medium, trypsin also must be considered as possible effective agents.

Lohammar (1954a) did a number of experiments in which the fruit stones, usually referred to as seeds and equivalent to the scraped fruits of Crocker's and some of Spence's experiments, of *Potamogeton natans* were treated in various ways to imitate aspects of the passage through the alimentary canal of a bird. They were then held for 1 or 6 months in cold water (1–3°C) and were finally tested for germination in a lighted thermostat at 20°C. The optimum treatment giving germination of over 90%, as against 4% in controls merely stored in cold water, consisted in exposure for at least 8 hr to a temperature of 41–42°C in a medium acidified with HCl to pH 2.0,[14] with or without pepsin. A cold dormancy period of 6 months was better than the shorter period of 1 month. Incubation in distilled water at 41–42°C was fairly effective, while a medium made slightly alkaline with Na_2CO_3, to which 1% pancreatin was added, was better than distilled

---

[14] Farner (1942) gives a pH of 2.33 in the muscular stomach of the domestic duck.

water. When whole fruits were used the germination rates were lower, but the same relative effects of temperature and the chemical environment were observed. Lohammar concluded that the seeds of *P. natans* are adapted to take advantage of the feeding habits and physiology of ducks. Some experiments with *P. lucens* are unfortunately not comparable because the winter dormancy was imitated before rather than after the high-temperature treatment. In this case the latter proved inhibitory. It is, of course, not possible to say if this difference between *P. natans* and *P. lucens* is a specific difference or is merely due to the order in which high and low temperatures were applied.

Wetzel and McGregor (1968) found that heating the seeds of *Najas flexilis* to 35–42°C for 30 hr almost doubled the germination under the conditions of their experiments, but that higher temperatures were deleterious.

In an unpublished thesis, Low (1937) reported a number of experiments on the germination of the seeds of *Scirpus paludosus* and certain other species of the genus. These plants, particularly *S. paludosus*, are important in the marshlands of Bear River Refuge in Utah; on one particular tract surveyed *S. paludosus* covered half the area. The seeds are known to be of significance as food to migrating waterfowl; Low concluded that they were second only to those of *Potamogeton pectinatus* in this respect.[15]

In general the seeds of *Scirpus* germinated very poorly, if at all. Breaking or removing the seed coat had no effect. Acid and alkaline treatment produced 2–3% germination. In one experiment in a fermenting medium 9% germination was achieved. These low germination rates were achieved only in light; practically no seed germinated in the dark. On passage through the alimentary tract of a mallard most of the seeds are broken and in part digested. Some, however, pass through scarified and apparently affected by the digestive secretions of the duck but with intact embryos. Of these relatively uninjured seeds, 94% germinated in experiments. It seems reasonably clear that in nature even if most seeds that are eaten are digested, enough must pass through the duck in a viable state for this process to be of importance in the reproduction and no doubt the local dispersal of the plant.

Sexual reproduction.   The flowers of water plants are in general of four kinds:

1. Conspicuous flowers, *entomophilous* or pollinated by insects, floating at the surface or raised above it, either singly or in inflorescences; flowers usually odorous and with nectar.

---

[15] I am greatly indebted to Dr. Vernon Proctor for an opportunity to study Low's contribution.

2. Less conspicuous flowers, *anemophilous* or pollinated by windblown pollen, raised above water surface and usually in inflorescences; flowers without odor or nectar.

3. Minute submerged flowers, *hydrophilous* or pollinated by waterborne pollen grains which may move at the water surface (*ephydrogamous*) or underwater (*hyphydrogamous*).

4. Flowers of unmodified structure and often of the same genus or even species as those of (1) or (2) that may occasionally or regularly develop underwater where they are self-pollinated, but in some cases may also emerge and undergo anthesis, too late for any further pollination to occur. These flowers are said to be *autogamous* or *pseudocleistogamous*.

The terminology of pollination can become quite formidable; Knuth's three-volume treatise either in the original German (Knuth 1895–1905) or in Ainsworth Davis's English translation (Knuth 1906–1909) provides a guide to this and to the immense body of old literature. Percival (1965), Faegri and van der Pijl (1966), and Proctor and Yeo (1973) summarize much modern work.

The majority of water plants belong to the entomophilous and anemophilous categories, but among the limited number of hydrophilous species there are plants of great limnological importance such as *Ceratophyllum*, the aquatic members of *Callitriche*, *Najas*, *Zannichellia*, a number of species of freshwater Hydrocharitaceae, as well as all the marine angiosperms. The fourth category contains few important species.

A great deal of significant anatomical detail about the flowers of water plants, which would be out of place in this work, is easily accessible in Sculthorpe's (1967) excellent volume.

Support of the emergent flower or inflorescence. Underwater a long stem is generally best adapted if it gives with the current, exerting little resistance. When a stem grows out of water and bears flowers or an inflorescence that is injured if submersed, maximum resistance to wind is desirable. This may result in some difference in structure, the emergent floral axis in *Potamogeton*, for instance (Chrysler 1907; Singh 1965), having a somewhat dicotyledonous arrangement with collateral vascular bundles whereas the fully submersed sterile shoots have a very condensed central cylinder.

When a flower is floating or only slightly emergent it is frequently stabilized by appropriate development of leaves or branches that form floating supports. The whole arrangement of the leaves of *Nymphoides* (Fig. 42) clearly stabilizes the flower. In most species of *Ranunculus* that live submersed but produce aerial flowers, undissected floating leaves evidently maintain the equilibrium of the flower pedicel. A comparable arrangement occurs in *Cabomba*, in the heterophyllous *Heteranthera zosteraefolia*, and very elaborately in some species of *Utricularia* (Fig. 40). In *Hottonia* the floral axis is stabilized by a whorl of branches just below the water surface (Fig. 41). In the hyperhydate umbellifer *Oenanthe aquatica*, the flowering stem is anchored underwater by adventive roots forming a "beautiful system of shrouds and stays to support the stem like a mast in an erect position" (Coleman 1844).

There is probably a tendency for the floating-leaved entomophilous plants to have, in any flora, flowers of greater than average size, culminating in the enormous blooms of *Victoria amazonica*. Such flowers are often, but by no means always, themselves floating.

Phenology. Not much specific information exists beyond the records of flowering times in various regional *Floras*. Grainger (1947) suggests that in general two situations exist in temperate regions. In one, there is probably a determination of flowering by photoperiodic events as on land. This is experimentally substantiated in the batrachian *Ranunculi* (see p. 184) and in *Utricularia* (Harder 1963). In the other, the initiation of flowering depends on the emergence of a shoot above water level, as in *Hippuris*. There is probably more than a hint of an analogy to the determination of air leaves in some heterophyllous species. This is reasonable, for after all the formation of a flower is the most extreme possible kind of heterophylly.

In some cases, notably *Nuphar*, the primordia of all the leaves and flowers are formed the year before they appear as functional organs. In *Nuphar* the production of flower primordia is very likely regulated by photoperiod. Grainger thought that it could not take place if only water leaves were present on the plant because of an inadequate supply of carbohydrate, which he believed to be retained better by the floating than by the submersed leaves, and not to be produced by the floating leaves in adequate quantity till the height of summer. In view of modern knowledge of phytochrome these conclusions may sound naive, but in the light of the work of Allsopp and of Gertrude on the role of soluble carbohydrate in heterophylly (see pp. 167, 168), Grainger's results may prove to be of considerable interest.

In shallow tropical lakes in which there are considerable changes in water level, the successive seasonal appearance of flowers can evidently be striking (see p. 482).

The phenology of flowering in the Lemnaceae (Hillman 1961) has proved rather mysterious. Adequately high temperatures and increasing day length are probably involved but are not the whole story, and the well-known occurrence of flowering of several species in one body of water when the same species may be present but sterile in a pond nearby has led to the unsubstantiated but quite plausible conclusion of some sort of external chemical control. The situation is in fact not unlike what is found in rotifers. *Lemna trisulca*, normally poised in the water, apparently becomes less dense on flowering and rises to the surface (den Hartog 1964).

A number of flowers have rather precise circadian rhythms, usually leading to anthesis by day, but in tropical species of *Nymphaea* and in *Victoria* by night. In the case of the diurnal *Eichhornia crassipes*, anthesis can be delayed by exposure to white light before midnight, but accelerated by exposure after midnight in the previous dark period (Penfound and Earle 1948). Comparable control of the opening of the flowers doubtless occurs in very many species.

Entomophilous aquatic plants. These include a number of herbid hyperhydates of quiet waters. Among the monocotyledons the important members of the category belong to the Alismataceae, Butomaceae, Mayaceae, Pontederiaceae, the rooted aquatic Araceae, and *Hydrocharis* and *Stratiotes* in the Hydrocharitaceae; there are also a good many comparable dicotyledons such as *Sium, Lysimachia, Decodon, Bacopa, Hygrophila, Hydrocera,* and *Menyanthes. Megalodonta*, which is a myriophyllid hyphydate except when flowering, is another conspicuous example. Most if not all of the pleustophytes are entomophilous, as are the floating-leaved *Nymphaea, Nuphar, Nelumbo, Victoria, Brasenia, Cabomba,* and *Nymphoides.*

Nehemiah Grew (1673), just over three centuries before this chapter was completed, noted the marked prevalence of white flowers among water plants. An obvious example is seen when the great majority of species of batrachian *Ranunculus* are compared with the yellow terrestrial species of the genus.

Arber (1920) observes that there are very few blue flowers, though they do occur occasionally, as in the Pontederiaceae. She is uneasy about attributing an adaptive meaning to this scarcity but points out that they might be inconspicuous against a reflected sky (cf. William Barnes's poem on p. *vi*). Colored spots which are supposedly nectar guides and stamens of more than one color, appear in a few species.

Little detailed work has been done on insect pollination, save in a few species of Nymphaeaceae. *Nymphaea* and *Nuphar* appear to be pollinated mainly by beetles or flies, though bees (*Bombus lucorum* and *Apis mellifera*) are recorded visiting *Nymphaea alba* (Heslop-Harrison 1955a, b). The most consistent visitors appear to be beetles of the genus *Donacia* (Chrysomelidae) and flies of the genus *Notiphila* (Ephyridae); some species of both genera, though not necessarily the recorded visitors, feed on *Nymphaea.* The latter genus is regarded by Grant (1950) as one of the plants having ovaries that are difficult for beetles to eat. *Nuphar pumila*, however (Hooker, in Curtis 1817; Heslop-Harrison 1955a), often seems in its Scottish localities to have the carpels completely chewed away. The situation is interesting because the Coleoptera, arising earlier than the Hymenoptera, Lepidoptera, or Diptera, may well have been the first important insect pollinators. The male parts of the flower of *Nymphaea* in which there is a set of transitions between petals and stamens have the most primitive structure now known (Sculthorpe 1967, Fig. 9.6), but the female parts are definitely more specialized.

The European species of *Nymphaea* are diurnal, closing at night, and usually slightly protogynous. In tropical members of the genus nocturnal anthesis is common, and the protogyny may be very striking. On the first night the stamens are held erect and the bowl-shaped stigma is fully exposed and contains a dilute sugar solution (*A* of Fig. 89). In Schmucker's (1932) experiments conducted in a hothouse, insects arriving at this time slid down the stamens and were drowned, presumably pollinating the flower if they bore *N. citrina* pollen. On the second night of anthesis, the stamens bend over the stigma (*B* of Fig. 89) and are presumably visited by pollen-eating

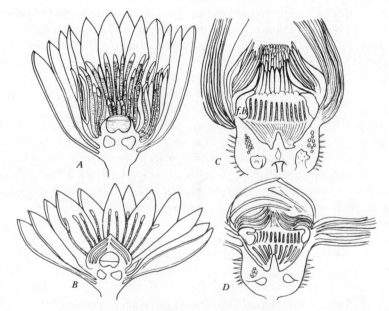

FIGURE 89. Entomophilous mechanisms in Nymphaeaceae. *A*, *Nymphaea citrina* in female state with open crown of stamens and pool of dilute sugar solution in depression in stigma, into which insects allegedly crawl and drown, *B*, in later male phase, with pollen exposed on upward surfaces of stamens; *C*, *Victoria amazonica*, just before anthesis, with open crown of stamens and staminodes; *D*, next morning with cavity above stigma, surrounded by carpellary food bodies (*f.b.*), closed (*A*, *B* after Faegri and van der Rjl from Schmucher; *C*, *D* diagrammatic drawings from Knoch's photographs).

insects. If the visitors of the first night are drowned and cannot escape on the second night, the plant is obviously losing a chance to distribute its own pollen. The artificial circumstances of the observations, probably involving a lack of the natural species of pollinator, may have introduced bias into Schmucker's conclusions. It is, however, evident that detailed further study of pollination in *Nymphaea* would be interesting. Dr. D. A. Livingstone tells me that tropical African species of *Nymphaea* do not produce an odor; they have pillboxlike, rather than echinate, pollen grains.

In *Victoria amazonica* (*C* and *D* of Fig. 89) the immense flower opens in the evening, at which time striking heat production occurs in the carpellary appendices which form a ring in the interior of the flower, raising the latter to a temperature of about 12°C above the ambient air (Knoch 1899). This presumably wafts the fragrance upward, attracting beetles that enter the flower. These are trapped when the flower closes later in the night. Here they feed on the carpellary appendices, which act as food bodies, and doubtless get covered with pollen before leaving the flower as it opens on the second night. The escaped beetles presumably are now attracted to another hot fragrant flower on the first night of opening, when it is in the female phase, and so pollinate it. According to Faegri and van der Pijl (1971) the main beetle pollinator of *Victoria* is the large dynastine *Cyclocephala castanea*.

Among other entomophilous water plants the only case that has been studied in detail is the North American *Pontederia cordata*, which is visited by a monotropic bee *Dufourea* (*Halictoides*) *novae-angliae*, found from Maine to New Jersey and westward to Wisconsin (Viereck 1904, sub *Conohalictoides lovelli*; Michener 1951; Percival 1965). Though this bee visits only *Pontederia*, it is not the only insect visitor of the flower. *Pontederia* and the allied *Eichhornia* are heterostylic and in populations of the latter, spread clonally during recent years, the proportions of the three flower forms are very uneven, differing from place to place (see Sculthorpe 1967 for a review of the scattered records). The relationship of the heterostylism to insect pollinators requires further study.

In all cases of insect pollination of water plants, the insect must fly over the water. Whether this provides a hazard for some species, which could be partly mitigated by a floating carpet of water lily leaves, might be of considerable interest as a subject of study. The possible role of surface-living insects, notably Heteroptera, has been considered only in the vaguest way in relation to the pollination of *Lemna* (Hillman 1961).

Anemophilous water plants.   Transfer of pollen by wind is characteristic of all the graminid hyperhydates (B.I.a, p. 125) in which small flowers are massed in large inflorescences. Anemophilous pollination also occurs in a number of hyphydates in which the flower emerges above the water surface, notably *Myriophyllum, Proserpinaca, Hippuris, Littorella*, most species of *Potamogeton*, and in one species of the Hydrocharitaceae, *Limnobium stoloniferum*.

In most species of *Myriophyllum* the upper flowers are staminate and the lower hermaphroditic or pistillate. A comparable separation, with the very reduced staminate flowers above and the pistillate flowers below, occurs in *Typha*. Although it seems evident that it would be advantageous to have the production of pollen take place as high as possible in an anemophilous species, the arrangement just described is found only in a limited number of anemophilous water plants. When the flower spike, as in *Potamogeton*, rises only a few centimeters above the water surface, the possibility of the transfer of pollen in the surface film must always be present whenever the wind disturbs the water. Ephydrogamous pollination of this kind has been observed in *P. lucens* growing in an aquarium and is of regular occurrence in two species of the subgenus *Coleogeton*, namely, *P. filiformis* and *P. pectinatus* (Daumann 1963). In the latter species pollination can apparently be effected under water (Dandy, in Proctor and Yeo 1973). Sculthorpe, impressed by the relation between hydrophily and the marine habitat, comments on the preference for brackish water of these two species.

Hydrophilous water plants. Transport of pollen by water is relatively rare in freshwater plants, though believed by Sculthorpe (1967) to be a necessary condition for the invasion of the sea by angiosperms. The greatest variety of events occurs in the Hydrocharitaceae.

In *Hydrilla* and *Vallisneria* the male flowers absciss and float to the surface, while the female on long peduncles, also reaching the surface, remain attached. The pollen of *Hydrilla* is discharged explosively by the three anthers of the male flower, which remains dry (Ernst-Schwarzenbach 1945). The female flowers also retain dry styles so that in effect pollination is by a kind of small-scale anemophily and ejected grains falling on the water surface are lost.

In *Vallisneria* the female peduncle (*F* of Fig. 47) becomes greatly elongate by the longitudinal growth of its cells. In European specimens of *V. spiralis* the elongation may be up to 120 cm in water less than 0.5 m deep (Funke 1938), though in India (Kausik 1939) there appears to be a strict relationship between the length of the peduncle and the depth of the water. This elongation brings the female flower (*A* of Fig. 90) to the surface, where it lies on its side unwetted, in a depression in the surface film. The male flowers absciss, and in the form of minute boats (*B* of Fig. 90), sail on the surface. The two stamens carry the pollen which is transferred dry by actual floral contact when a free male flower sails into an attached female (Ernst-Schwarzenbach 1945). There seem to be slight differences in the actual

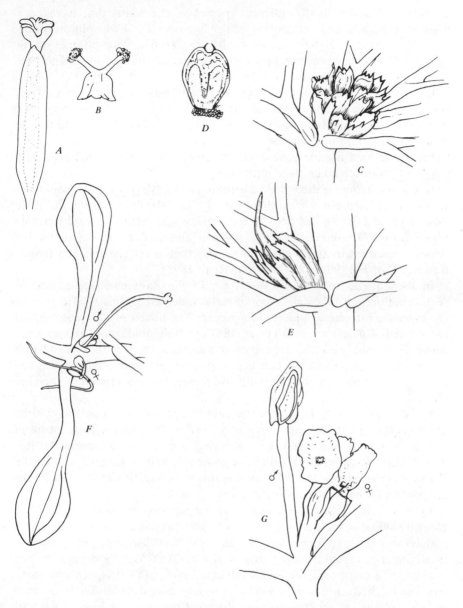

FIGURE 90. Hydrophilous mechanisms. *A*, Female flower of *Vallisneria spiralis; B*, detached male flower of same; *C*, male flower of *Ceratophyllum demersum; D*, mature stamen liberating pollen; *E*, female flower of same; *F*, node of *Callitriche obtusangula* with male (♂) and female (♀) flowers; *G*, adjacent male (♂) and female (♀) flowers of *Zannichellia palustris* (Proctor and Yeo, in part after Kausik).

process of transfer in the different species of the genus that have been studied. For these and many other of the fine points of hydrophilous pollination the reader is referred to Sculthorpe (1967). The pollination of *Lagarosiphon* and *Nechamandra* as well as that of the marine *Enhalus* resembles that of *Vallisneria*.

In *Elodea*, in which both female and male flowers reach the surface, though the males normally remain attached except in *E. nuttallii*, the pollen is liberated explosively onto the surface film, and is carried to the female flowers by random movements.

Finally in two marine genera of the Hydrocharitaceae, *Halophila* and *Thalassia*, transfer takes place underwater.

In *Ceratophyllum*, a dicotyledon with no relationship to the hydrophilous species just discussed, the anthers (*D* of Fig. 90) absciss from the male flowers (*C* of Fig. 90) and float to the surface where they liberate wettable pollen grains. These are denser than water and sink, no doubt being dispersed somewhat by turbulence. Some may then reach the styles of female flowers (*E* of Fig. 90) in the process (Roze 1892).

In the aquatic species of *Callitriche*, in the Zannichelliaceae, and in *Najas*, pollination takes place completely underwater; this is also true of the marine Zosteraceae and Posidoniaceae. The pollen of *Zannichellia* and the related *Althenia* are said (Roze 1887) to be globular and denser than water. Presumably a little turbulence will displace them as they fall so that occasional cross-pollination can occur even when, as in *Zannichellia*, the plants are monoecious and the male and female flowers very close together (*G* of Fig. 90).

In *Callitriche* the pollen grains are said to contain oil drops and to drift at all depths; the flowers are very reduced (*F* of Fig. 90) for the capture of pollen. It is quite likely that if the pollen grains are really practically isopicnal with the water, a condition not obviously easy to achieve, so that the slightest turbulence keeps them afloat, this is as effective an adaptation as any shown by hydrophilous water plants.

In *Najas* the pollen often begins to germinate on liberation and the elongate shape of the pollen tube presumably provides a greater chance of contact with the long-forked stigmas. Bailey (1884) observed "pollen whirled in all directions from the ripe anthers of a plant of *Najas graminea*, by the activity of a colony of vorticellid ciliates." Arber (1920) speculates as to whether in the future some form of zoophily may not ultimately develop in water plants. At the present time the most that one can hope for is that some water plants may survive to exhibit any sort of evolution.

Autogamy or pseudocleistogamy. In a few water plants more or less regular self-fertilization occurs within the air-filled bud, a condition distinguished from true cleistogamy only by the lack of morphological reduction of the flower. Hooker (1847) recorded this process in *Limosella aquatica* under ice in a lake on Kerguelen Island; subsequently the phenomenon has been recorded in almost a dozen genera which are listed by Sculthorpe (1967). The most interesting case, perhaps involving true cleistogamy, is that of *Ottelia ovalifolia* (Ernst-Schwarzenbach 1956), a New Caledonian species, which produced in Switzerland normal aerial flowers under uncrowded conditions in summer, but small aquatic cleistogamous flowers in spring and autumn or when the plants were crowded in summer. Some aquatic species may undergo autogamy and then open, either underwater, as in *Subularia aquatica*, or above water as in some populations of *Lobelia dortmanna* (Faegri and van der Pijl 1966), though others seem to behave like *Subularia* (Thunmark 1931).

Behavior after pollination. There is a curious tendency for the flower peduncle of a number of species (Arber 1920; Crocker 1907) to curve over after pollination, so that the fruit develops underwater. This has been observed in some species of *Ranunculus* (C of Fig. 91), *Victoria, Aldrovanda, Nymphoides, Limnobium* (E of Fig. 47), various species of Pontederiaceae (B of Fig. 91) *Aponogeton, Potamogeton natans* and *P. pectinatus, Peltandra* (A of Fig. 91), and doubtless various other water plants.

Asexual reproduction. In spite of the variety of floral structures involved in pollination that have just been described, it is probable that most reproduction among water plants is asexual. The only striking exception to this generalization is likely to be in the small group of aquatic annuals or hydrotherophytes, notably species of *Najas, Eleocharis microcarpa* and *E. intermedia,* various members of *Elatine, Trapa,* and *Trapella.* The majority of freshwater angiosperms are perennials, but with most of the green parts dying in the winter in temperate latitudes. This cycle of growth and decay in a small lake may have marked effects on the nutrient reservoir in the free water. In such plants any given specimen encountered is much more likely to have arisen by asexual than by sexual processes.

Complete inhibition of sexual reproduction, particularly in species with emergent flowers, when they are growing in deep water, is common. There is a little evidence that hydrostatic pressure may be involved to some extent in this (see p. 420).

It is quite possible that at least in the vittate species with long stems that constitute quantitatively the most important part of the flora of all but the least productive lakes (B.III.a of p. 128), mechanical fragmentation with subsequent regeneration of whole plants from the fragments is as important a method of reproduction as any others. The fragmentation may be caused by breakage during storms or by animals feeding on the plants, or apparently may be spontaneous (Spencer and Lekić 1974).

Rhizomes. There is a striking tendency for water plants to develop horizontal creeping axes or rhizomes, often of great size (E of Fig. 14; Fig. 95) and rich in starch, from which lateral shoots, or the long petioles

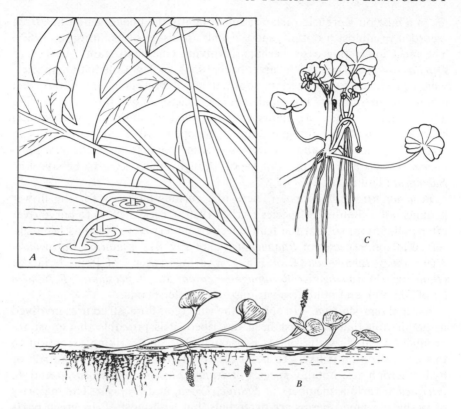

FIGURE 91.   A, *Peltandra virginica*, peduncles bent over with ripening berries in the spathe below water; B, *Pontederia rotundifolia* with submersed infructescences (Arber after Hauman-Merck); C, *Ranunculus hederaceus* with gynoecium turned down to ripen underwater (Arber).

of floating leaves, arise. Mangin (1893) found that 31 of the 40 species of flowering plants and ferns that he recognized in the lakes of the Jura region had rhizomes. Hejny (1960) points out that this development is most characteristic of his group of hydato-aerophytes or water plants mainly submersed but with some of the vegetative organs actually or potentially emergent. Such plants are usually able to exist at least temporarily as terrestrial plants, and the great development of a rhizome, buried in damp mud, would clearly be advantageous in tiding over dry conditions. If the rhizome is growing freely and branching, decay of the older parts automatically leads to reproduction. This is presumably what is happening in reed beds and in some populations of water lilies.

Runners. Among the rosulate or rosette-shaped plants so characteristic of oligotrophic lakes, though not confined to such localities, runners may grow out from a mature plant and establish a number of new individuals. This is well known in *Limosella* (*E–G* of Fig. 38), *Littorella* (*H* of Fig. 38), some of the smaller Alismataceae such as *Echinodorus tenellus* (Fig. 67), and the amphibious species of *Ranunculus* such as *R. reptans* (*A* and *B* of Fig. 76). A comparable development occurs in the pleustonic *Stratiotes*.

Tubers. A few water plants, notably the larger species of *Sagittaria*, produce tubers (*B* and *C* of Fig. 68).

Turions or winter buds. The production of specialized buds or turions which survive the winter when the rest of the vegetative parts of the plant have decayed is very characteristic of the water plants of temperate regions. Such structures may, as has been pointed out in Vol. II, be regarded as the botanical equivalent of the gemmules of freshwater sponges or the statoblasts of freshwater Ectoprocta, which are also specialized buds adapted to

FIGURE 92. *Caldesia parnassifolia* with floating leaves, and two reproductive stalks, one bearing emergent inflorescences and other submersed turions (Glück).

carry the species over unfavorable periods. Such buds are very widespread at least in the water plants of temperate regions, and some, notably in *Utricularia*, are highly modified (Glück 1908) in structure (*B* of Fig. 40).

As in *Isoetes*, some Alismataceae, when in deep water, may replace sexual by asexual reproduction, forming turions in the place of flowers on inflorescence-like stems, as for example in *Caldesia parnassifolia* f. *natans* (Fig. 92).

Even within a single genus, notably in *Potamogeton* (Fig. 93), there is great variety in the nature of the turions (Sauvageau 1894; Raunkiaer 1896). Raunkiaer recognizes six types of turion in *Potamogeton* and *Groenlandia*. Of these, the first four are produced from the rhizome and the other two are modifications of the ordinary buds borne on the stems.

1. In *G. densa*, after flowering, a new shoot may be produced which grows from the rhizome horizontally or obliquely, avoiding the surface. Growing in fairly deep water during the part of the year when the light flux is declining, the shoot may become somewhat etiolated. From such a shoot the new plant develops in the subsequent spring.

2. In *P. natans* there are comparable, hardly modified overwintering shoots which may form and then lose their floating leaves, the shoot later producing only narrow water leaves.

3. In a number of species, *P. praelongus*, *P. perfoliatus* (*A* of Fig. 93), *P. gramineus*, *P. lucens*, and probably a good many more, several resting buds develop serially from the apex of the rhizome at the end of the vegetative season, and produce the next year's shoots in the spring. In *P. alpinus* comparable buds may be formed on thin rhizome-like shoots that grow from the axils of the lower leaves (Fig. 94).

4. In the subgenus *Coleogeton* containing *P. filiformis*, *P. pectinatus* (*B* of Fig. 93), and some other less well-known taxa, all partial to mineralized water, the resting buds produced from the rhizome are swollen and of characteristic form, being well filled with starch.

5. In *P. crispus* (*D–F* of Fig. 93), in which the rhizome persists throughout the winter producing an overwintering shoot like that of *P. densus*, there are also curious detached turions formed by the development of special axillary buds at the bases of groups of modified leaves. The stems bearing these leaves dehisce and fall to the bottom, new plants forming the following spring from the axillary buds. In this case the process is certainly as important as a reproductive phenomenon as it is in overwintering.

6. In the narrow-leaved species of *Eupotamogeton*, notably *P. compressus*, *P. acutifolius*, *P. obtusifolius*, *P. friesii*, *P. berchtoldii*, *P. rutilus*, and *P. trichoides* (*C* of Fig. 93), and presumably other species, turions are formed

FIGURE 93.   Overwintering in the genus *Potamogeton. A, P. perfoliatus,* apex of rhizome
with two leaf-bearing branches which will die late in the year leaving the thickened end
with three winter buds from which the plant will be regenerated in the subsequent spring;
B, P. pectinatus, rhizoids bearing specialized turions on winter buds enriched in starch;
C, P. trichoides, turions (*t*) like ordinary buds but larger, darker green, stiffer, and more
compact *D, P. crispus,* turions (*t*) formed from highly modified parts of apical branches
in a plant also bearing infructescences (*i*); *E,* leaf and much slenderer turion formed
basally on same plant; *F, P. crispus,* turion germinating. (Sauvageau; *B* after Irmisch).

FIGURE 94.   *Potamogeton alpinus* with turions (Raunkiaer).

as rather compact but otherwise not greatly modified buds which become detached from the parent plant. The whole of the latter may decay at the end of the season so that such plants are in effect asexual annuals growing anew each spring from buds that may be carried around to new sites by the water much as if they were seeds or fruits.

Clonal populations.   As a result of the frequency of asexual reproduction and the inhibition of flowering in deep water in many aquatic plants, large clonal populations are likely to be very common in lacustrine angiosperms (Fig. 95).

The most detailed study of lacustrine clonal populations is that of Björk (1967) on *Phragmites australis* in a number of Swedish localities (Fig. 96). The plant is quite variable in total height, panicle size, and a number of minor characters. Part of this variation is due to differences in the substratum; sediments rich in exchangeable cations and localities somewhat fertilized by sewage produce larger reeds than do less base-rich unfertilized stations.

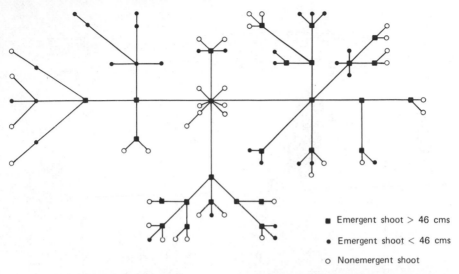

■ Emergent shoot > 46 cms

● Emergent shoot < 46 cms

o Nonemergent shoot

FIGURE 95. Schematic plan of rhizome of *Typha latifolia* developed after 1 yr from a single seedling (Yeo).

In two lakes it was possible to study two clones living under essentially identical conditions, and in one fluviatile locality four clones, two tetraploid and two hexaploid, exist as populations over a short distance of about a quarter of a kilometer (Fig. 96). In both the lakes, Tystrup Sö and W. Ringsjön, one member of each pair of clones was clearly shorter than the other and tended to flower about 2 weeks earlier than the taller clone. In these two lakes the panicle sizes were variable and hardly characteristic of the clones.

In the Norjesund channel connecting the drainage channels of the former Lake Vesan with the Baltic Sea, two of the clones were of the rare hexaploid variety, one (A) taller, later flowering, and producing smaller panicles than the other (B). In the two tetraploid clones the taller, later flowering population (A) produced the larger panicles. The leaves of the hexaploid clone (A) had soft watery tissue and were more attacked by aphids than were the harder, less watery leaves of the hexaploid clone (B). The leaves of the latter are proportionally broader than are those of clone (A). All four clones are probably derived from natural reed beds formerly surrounding the drained lake. Their present habitat is artificially eutrophic. Transplanted to the less eutrophic environments of Lake Orlunden and Lake Sträken, and set in the sandy sediments at the margins of these lakes, the dimensions of the shoots of the hexaploid clones decreased, and after a year no panicles

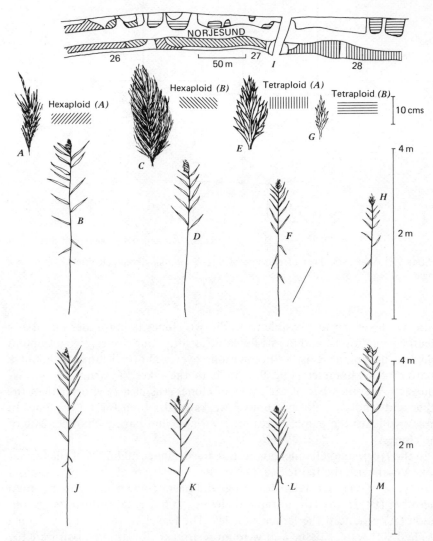

FIGURE 96.   Morphologically differentiated clones of *Phragmites australis* in Sweden. *A*, Hexaploid clone (*A*) and (*B*), its panicle, from Norjesund, a channel draining the bed of the old lake Vesan to the Baltic; *C* and *D*, the same of hexaploid clone (*B*); *E* and *F*, the the same of tetraploid clone (*A*); *G* and *H*, the same of tetraploid clone (*B*); *I*, map of a section of Norjesund showing distribution of the populations of the four clones; *J*, *K*, Late flowering large and early-flowering small clones, Tystrup Sö; *L*, *M*, early-flowering small and late-flowering large clones, W. Ringsjön (Björk).

were produced, though in the indigenous tetraploid population in Lake Orlunden 60–80% of the individuals ordinarily bear panicles. The hexaploid clones of Norjesund are clearly adapted to a eutrophic environment and do less well on minerogenic sediment, which can support its own sexually reproducing population successfully, however. The characteristic textural differences between the leaves of hexaploid (A) and (B) are retained by the transplanted plants.

Another interesting situation was studied at the head of Pukavik Bay, an inlet of the Baltic in Blekinge, south Sweden. Here two tetraploid clones lived side by side with a sharp line of demarcation. One clone was slightly shorter, with a much larger panicle and dark green leaves, the other slightly taller with a very small panicle and light green leaves. There was evidence that during the period 1959–1965 the boundary between the clones moved northward, the first clone tending to displace the second. It is obvious from these examples that biological differences exist between the several clones and that natural selection between them may be expected to occur.

Lohammar (1965) implies that in *Butomus umbellatus* genetically different populations occur in different lakes in Sweden, but his study of this problem has as yet not been published. Faegri and van der Pijl (1966) point out that populations of this plant are known in Scandinavian lakes in which seed is apparently never set. They believe it quite likely that the whole population in any lake may consist of a single self-incompatible clone. In such a case selection would act in favor of any dominant mutation suppressing flowering. This might conceivably have happened in a few cases such as *Elodea nuttallii* in Esthwaite Water, though the plant has recently flowered in its Irish locality (Scannell 1974).

Vegetative reproduction leading to immense clonal populations undoubtedly occurs in *Potamogeton*. Of particular interest is the plant found in the deeper water of most of the English lakes, which was described as a subspecies of *P. berchtoldii* (sub *pusillus*) by Pearsall and Pearsall (1921) and named by them subsp. *lacustris*. It differs in having, at any depth, constantly broader, more delicate, and paler green leaves than typical *berchtoldii*, which is said by these authors to produce very long narrow leaves in deep water (see p. 193). The plant ordinarily reproduces solely by turions and was found by its describers only once to flower, in Esthwaite during an abnormally hot summer, and then not to form mature fruit. Both Fernald (1932, 1950) and Clapham, Tutin, and Warberg (1962) regard it as but a form of *berchtoldii*; Pearsall and Pearsall seem to have had evidence that the differences are genetic. Whatever its taxonomic status,

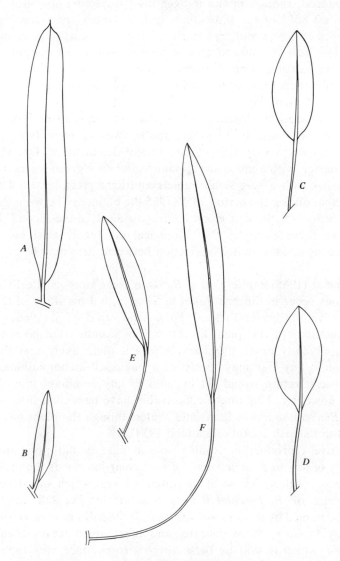

FIGURE 97.   *A, B, Potamogeton schweinfurthii*, submerged leaves, Lake Bunyonyi; *C, D,*
P. thunbergii coriaceous floating leaves, Lake Mutanda; *E, P.* × *bunyonyiensis* submerged,
and *F*, floating leaf, from Lake Bunyonyi (Denny and Lye).

lacustris is clearly an important asexually reproducing element of the flora of the English lakes (see p. 443).

Clonal populations of hybrids. Other interesting cases are provided by the numerous hybrids of *Potamogeton* spp., which may exist (Fig. 97), reproducing asexually, after one or both parents have disappeared from a lake. Thus Lohammar (1938) notes *P.* × *zizii* (= *gramineus* × *lucens*) as present in Lake Ensen, Dalarna, where only one of its parent species, namely, *P. lucens*, was also growing and in Glisstjärn, Dalarna, the same hybrid was present but both the parent species were absent. In the extreme south of Sweden, Lundh (1951) found *P.* × *nitens* (= *gramineus* × *perfoliatus*) to be present in 7 out of 31 lakes studied, but in two of them, Sövdesjön and Vombsjön, *P. gramineus* was missing. The trihybrid *P.* × *torssandri* (= *gramineus* × *lucens* × *perfoliatus*) was identified from two lakes, Levrasjön and Siesjön, about 26 km east and a little north of Kristianstad. In the first of these lakes all three of the parent species occurred with *P.* × *nitens* but no other dihybrid; one may suspect that the × *torssandrii* arose by a cross between *P. lucens* and a rare fertile *P.* × *nitens*. In the very small Siesjön only *P. gramineus* and *P. lucens*, with no dihybrids, were observed.

In the English Lake District, Pearsall found *P.* × *zizii* in Derwentwater, with *P. gramineus* but without *P. lucens*. In view of the widespread occurrence, and at least in the case of *P.* × *nitens*, the frequent abundance (e.g., Koch 1926) of the hybrid, it is probable that comparable phenomena occur all over Europe.

An extraordinary fluviatile case is recorded by Hagström (1916) in the Gudenaa at Kongensbro in Jutland, where five other hybrids, *P.* × *sparganifolius* (= *gramineus* × *natans*); *P.* × *undulatus* (= *crispus* × *praelongus*); *P.* × *decipiens* (= *lucens* × *perfoliatus*); *P.* × *babingtonii* (= *lucens* × *praelongus*), and *P.* × *subrufus* (= *lucens* × *nodosus*) all occurred mixed up together, though *nodosus* now does not grow on the island of Jutland. It is evident that in such a case the hybrid clones must be remarkably persistent.

A case comparable to the last one mentioned is provided by *P.* × *suecicus*, the hybrid of *P. pectinatus* and *P. filiformis*, which occurs in England well south of the present range of the last-named species, though in late glacial times both parents were probably found throughout England. In the case of the isolated populations of *suecicus* the hybrids have obviously persisted for up to about 10,000 years (Dandy and Taylor 1946; Bance 1946; Godwin 1956; Sculthorpe 1967).

In Lake Bunyonyi (see p. 478) Denny and Lye (1973) find *P.* × *bunyonyiensis* in the shallow infralittoral down to about 2–5 m; one of its parents, *P. schweinfurthii*, tends to occur in rather deeper water and may reach 6 m, but the other parent, *P. thunbergii*, is found only in protected pools of the marginal swamp.

In all these cases one may expect the hybrids to be better adapted to certain niches than are their parents, a matter of some evolutionary interest. This is clearly the case for the three taxa in Lake Bunyonyi.

Clonal populations and anomalous geographical distribution of the sexes. A few rather peculiar cases in which the two sexes of dioecious plants may have fairly different though overlapping distributions are known. *Stratiotes aloides* in northern Europe is entirely female; in Britain rare specimens with hermaphroditic flowers have been recorded (Clapham, Tutin, and Warberg 1962) but fruiting seems not to occur. In southern Europe only male plants occur but there is an intermediate zone, in which sexual reproduction is possible.

A comparable case in *Chara canescens* has already been noted, though here the female populations are parthenogenetic, as of course they are in the Crustacea that exhibit somewhat comparable phenomena (see p. 12). In cases where a species has been introduced, as *Elodea canadensis*, only one sex may occur; in this species almost all the European specimens are female. The various phenomena involving clonal reproduction that have just been discussed could doubtless be illustrated by many other comparable cases recorded in scattered papers and books.

DISPERSAL OF WATER PLANTS

The very wide distribution of many species of freshwater angiosperms would suggest that such plants have efficient means of dispersal. It is, moreover, obvious that since most bodies of freshwater are geologically speaking transitory, efficient dispersal is necessary for survival. It may indeed be supposed that the wide distribution of many kinds of water plant is a corollary to the necessity of an efficient dispersal system for survival in a rather uncertain habitat.

Transport of actively vegetative plants or plant fragments. Dispersal in general can be of two sorts, that of whole plants or viable fragments, in an active vegetative condition, and that of dormant stages, mainly seeds, but occasionally perhaps turions. Accidental transportation on the bodies of birds is possible for whole small plants, such as *Riccia* (see p. 54), *Riccocarpus, Azolla, Lemna,* and *Wolffia,* or for viable fragments of long-stemmed or vittate plants, such as *Potamogeton, Elodea, Ceratophyllum, Utricularia, Myriophyllum,* or *Callitriche.* Woodruffe-Peacock (1917) observed ducks flying with pieces of pondweed draped over their backs and necks. In one case he specifically indicated the plant to be *Potamogeton perfoliatus,* and in another either this species or *P. praelongus*; in a third case a duck was shot and found to be carrying *Potamogeton crispus.* Woodruffe-Peacock also recorded two ducks shot while transporting *Elodea canadensis*. Ridley (1930) found that a fragment of *E. canadensis*, left in the open air lying on a feather for 23 hr, recovered completely in a few hours from this degree of drying when placed in an aquarium. Weddell (1849) noted *Wolffia braziliensis* to be carried on the feathers of a water bird called "Camichi"[16] in Brazil. *Lemna* has been observed on the breast feathers of wildfowl exposed for sale in French markets (Duval-Jouve 1864), and Woodruffe-Peacock (1918) concluded that *Gallinula chloropus* carries *L. minor* and *L. trisulca* in this way in England. Ridley found that *Lemna minor*, after having been left dry on a feather in the open air for 12 hr, recovered completely in a few hours when placed on water and at least some specimens were able to survive 22 hr out of water. The important aspect of this sort of dispersal of water plants is that, provided the plant can survive transport, when it arrives it is in a medium in which growth can start, at least by day, immediately. There is no difficulty, as there would be in the case of similar random dispersal of most herbaceous land plants or their fragments, of setting the plant in the soil of its new home. It is also quite likely that, as the stems of most water plants are laxer than those of herbaceous land plants, owing to the lack of supporting tissue, pieces of water plant would be more easily draped over a bird than would fragments of land plants. It is quite possible that this very simple situation, followed by extensive asexual reproduction after establishment, is involved to a major extent in the movement of many water plants from one aquatic locality to another over humid land surfaces. It cannot be the whole story; it is unlikely to be involved in the dispersal of small rosulate plants, nor are birds apt to transport living, moist, actively metabolizing plant fragments over the long distances involved in transoceanic dispersal.

All the pleustonic plants, and those with floating but easily detached branches such as *Neptunia oleracea*, can be transported at the surface by water movements, and most vittate and occasionally detached rosulate plants likewise can be moved by currents underwater, but in all ordinary circumstances such movements will involve only dispersal within a lake or downstream in a river.

Transport of resting stages. The problems of the dispersal of seeds and other resting stages are more complex. Many aquatic seeds and fruits, particularly of monocotyledons, float. This is usually due to aeriferous tissue in the pericarp, as in *Sparganium, Pontederia, Alisma, Lophotocarpus, Sagittaria, Potamogeton* (see pp. 221–2), and *Ranunculus scleratus*, or in the seed testa, as in *Iris pseudacorus, Scheuchzeria, Lemna*, and *Pemphis* and *Menyanthes*. In a few cases the seeds may sink but on germination produce

---

[16] According to F. C. Novaes of Belem, the name Camichi refers to species of the family Anhimidae (personal communication through Dr. T. E. Lovejoy.)

a floating seedling. This occurs in *Baldellia ranunculoides*, in some species of *Juncus* and in *Hottonia*. Occasionally, as in *Iris pseudacorus* and *Ranunculus sceleratus*, the seed may sink after floating for a short period and then produce a floating seedling. The seedlings of many riparian plants float, but in none of such cases is transportation normally possible except downstream. Ridley (1930), whose work can be consulted for additional cases, suggests that some of the divergence in the records of sinking or floating seeds, notably in *Polygonum*, may be explicable in terms of variability or seed polymorphism; the evidence is inadequate, but the idea is interesting enough to merit investigation.

Transportation of resting stages by wind is rare in aquatic macrophytes. In *Ruppia maritima*, growing in coastal lakes, detached fruits embedded in decaying pericarp may form balls that can be rolled along the shore by the wind. Ridley suggests that "the plant growing in such masses as it does in New Zealand might readily be blown in this manner across open spaces from lake to lake."

Aerial dispersal of seeds by the wind certainly occurs in a few tall emergent plants such as *Typha* and *Phragmites* and doubtless in other aquatic Gramineae.

There can be little doubt that the major way in which seeds can be carried from lake to lake, across watersheds, and from one river system to another, is by birds, either stuck to their feet in mud or in the alimentary tract.

The most important observations of the seeds of water plants on birds are those of Kerner von Marilaun (1895), who found in mud taken from the beaks, feathers, and feet of a variety of birds 21 species of seed. The majority of these species are marsh plants or amphibious, the following being often, if not always, aquatic: *Glyceria fluitans*, *Limosella aquatica*, *Veronica anagallis-aquatica* (sub *anagallis*), *Lythrum salicaria*, and *Elatine hydropiper*. It is obvious that the wet and sticky mud of damp localities would facilitate this method of transport. Although the proportion of birds carrying viable seeds on long migrations may be extremely small, the number of birds migrating is so enormous that viable transportation by one bird in a million[17] would, in the long run, explain many more introductions than have actually been observed.

The transport of seeds in the alimentary canals of birds has been the subject of some special studies. In order to be effective as a transporting

---

[17] Paynter (1953), for instance, concludes that over a million migrants may reach the Yucatan Peninsula annually during the autumn migration. Mac Arthur (1972) estimates a thousand times this number may leave North America for the New World tropics as a whole.

agent, the bird must take seeds into its alimentary tract and retain them in a viable state over a sufficient length of time to permit it to carry the seed considerable distances. Although a variety of birds may take in seeds which they do not fully digest and in some cases may actually promote, by partial digestion (see pp. 223–4), the germination of the seed, this does not mean that any bird that has eaten a seed will carry it great distances. Seeds that might be passed through the alimentary tract alive have obviously little further value to the bird and may be systematically regurgitated. Proctor (personal communication) believes that any really long transoceanic transport is likely to be due only to a relatively few species of Charandriiformes. The suitable birds must be those that migrate, and which do not regurgitate the whole crop contents in a single pellet. Proctor believes that of the species so far studied the least sandpiper (*Erolia minutilla*) is the most probable species to be involved. Though this species is not likely to ingest seeds purposefully,[18] Ridley quotes records of the accidental occurrence of small seeds in the crops of various other species of Calandriidae in India, so that very occasionally almost any species might bear such propagules.

Certain cases of the occurrence of isolated populations of northern species in the southern hemisphere have been recorded and can hardly have any explanation other than that of avian transport. The most dramatic is that of *Ranunculus rionii* which occurs in the Palaearctic from Austria eastward to Japan and may also occur in western North America. In the southern hemisphere it is known only in a number of localities in the eastern part of the Union of South Africa (Cook 1966b).

Adventive species. During the past century and a half a number of water plants have been accidentally introduced into areas far from their native homes and have undergone a vast if often only temporary expansion.

Sculthorpe lists 71 species that are known to have become at least locally established in continents to which they are alien, and at least one further addition, *Myriophyllum spicatum*, must apparently be made to his list.

In many of the cases the adventive plants constitute small and geographically limited populations, but in a few cases the invaders have been so successful that they have become serious pests. Sculthorpe (1967) and Holm, Wheldon, and Blackburn (1969) give excellent reviews of the problems raised by these species; the literature on them consists largely of ephemeral official reports and these two reviews are, therefore, of great value. Where no authorities are given in the following account the information has been derived from these sources.

Acorus calamus, introduced purposefully from Constantinople into Eu-

---

[18] Gardner Stout, personal communication.

rope in the sixteenth century (Mücke 1908; Grigson 1955), has undoubtedly spread widely, often with human help. Though perhaps the first of the adventive water plants it never seems to have been a problem.

Adventive hyphydates. The earliest well-documented case of an accidentally introduced species of water plant becoming a major economic problem is that of the North American *Elodea canadensis,* first in Europe and later in other parts of the Old World. This case is of particular importance as it is the only one as yet in which the history can be followed over a long period, and in which that history was not complicated by the use of herbicides.

The introduction of the species into Ireland and Great Britain has been discussed by Babington (1848), Marshall (1852, 1857), Siddall (1884), and Walker (1912). Because some of these papers are not easy to consult, the review of the whole problem by Sculthorpe (1967) is most useful.

Elodea canadensis seems to have been first found in Ireland in 1836, probably in two localities, in one of which it was said to have occurred in association with *Aponogeton* and other exotic species. It perhaps appeared at Watford Locks, Northamptonshire, in England in 1841, and certainly at Duns Castle, Berwickshire, Scotland, in 1842. All these cases, up to four in number, must have been separate introductions. The next records, both in 1847, are from Leigh Park, Hampshire, where it may have been accidentally imported with the rhizomes of *Nymphaea odorata*, and at Foxton Locks, Market Harborough, Leicestershire. The basins containing the plant at the latter locality were cleaned in 1845; the plant must, therefore, have been introduced between 1845 and 1847. There is, however, hydrographic connection by way of the Grand Union Canal from Watford Locks to Foxton Locks, so that if the Watford record is reliable the Foxton plants may represent the same population. From Foxton, plants were sent both as herbarium specimens and alive to Babington in Cambridge, who believed that they represented a new species (Babington 1848), closer to *E. nuttallii* than to *E. canadensis*. It is certain that some of the living plants at Cambridge were put in Hobson's Conduit by a Mr. Murray, the curator of the then new Botanic Gardens of the University of Cambridge. From this brook they could easily have reached the River Cam, either in floodwater or conveyed by ducks over a very short distance, into a stream tributary to that river. Once in the Cam the species rapidly multiplied and spread into the great system of drainage canals of the Fenland. At this time transport of goods by horse-drawn barges was an essential part of the economy of Britain. Marshall records that extra horses had to be used to pull the barges through the mass of *Elodea* in the Cam. About the same time the Trent was invaded (Brown 1849), probably from the Foxton population, and soon also became full of the weed. Not only was barge traffic greatly impeded when the weed appeared in a new waterway, but water levels rose and fishing and boating became impossible.[19] This happened over most of England as the plant spread. Fortunately, after about 5–7 yr in any locality the populations declined. By 1912 (Walker 1912) few were still expanding and many were greatly reduced. At the present time *E. canadensis* is no particular problem in Britain.

The same sort of story occurred in continental Europe; the species entered France in 1850 and finally reached western Siberia in this century.

Throughout the enormous Old World range now occupied by *E. canadensis*, the flowers are almost all female and seeds are never set. Male flowers were found once, near Edinburgh in 1879, perhaps as the result of a separate introduction, though possibly through some genetic anomaly. It is quite possible that the greater part, if not all, of the female plants of the Old World are part of the Foxton Locks clone.

The decline in the population of *E. canadensis*, which has fortunately occurred since its rapid nineteenth-century spread, was early attributed to a loss of vitality owing to lack of sexual reproduction. This sounds old-fashioned today; it cannot conceal a valid genetic explanation because the asexually produced propagules were still vigorous when they entered a new territory. Salisbury (1961) suggested that some nutrient deficiency now limits the plant. The work of Olsen (1954) indicates that it is particularly sensitive to a lack of ferrous iron, though it seems most unlikely that such a limitation would explain the observed reduction and stabilization of the population. Walker, however, evidently thought that some change on the bottom was involved which of course could involve a change in the availability of iron. He raised the interesting question as to whether there were cases in which a population completely disappeared from a body of water which was then reinvaded in full force. To this writer the phenomenon looks much more likely to have involved as yet unrecognized biotic rather than physicochemical factors, even though the plant is rejected by nearly all phytophagous aquatic insects (Gajevskaia 1958). The question is an important one, not only because its solution might give hints as to methods of control of current outbreaks by other species, but also because of the obvious evolutionary implications of the observed events.

---

[19] When the writer was an undergraduate, in the 1920s, some of the older Cambridge biologists still spoke of *Elodea canadensis* jokingly as *Babingtonia damnabilis*, though by that time the species had declined in numbers and had become an ordinary denizen of ponds and rivers. Chapman (1970), in New Zealand, still writes of Babington's Curse. However, Babington, an excellent botanist, does not seem to have introduced the plant into the River Cam himself and the introduction would have certainly occurred even in the absence of Mr. Murray's activities.

Elodea canadensis reached Australia and New Zealand in the 1860s partly as a result of purposeful introduction (Chapman 1970; Chapman, Brown, Hill, and Carr 1974). The invasion of New Zealand was less aggressive than in England, partly perhaps because the watercress, *Rorippa nasturtium-aquaticum*, had been brought to New Zealand earlier and was something of a competitor. Later *E. canadensis* may have been limited by the introduction, in or before 1946, of *Egeria densa*[20] from tropical America and, in or before 1950, of *Lagarosiphon major* from southern Africa. These two plants are now widely spread throughout the warmer parts of the temperate zones. In much of New Zealand temperatures are more nearly optimum for them than for *E. canadensis* (Mason 1960). At the present time they, with *Ceratophyllum demersum* which arrived in 1961, are important pests in the lakes, natural and artificial, in the North Island between Auckland and Lake Taupo. They are particularly noxious in artificially dammed lakes used in the generation of hydroelectric power. Chapman (1970) likens the history of these weeds in New Zealand in the twentieth century to that of *Elodea canadensis* in nineteenth-century Europe.

Apart from the four species just discussed as producing massive populations in the parts of the Old World that they have invaded, *Hydrilla verticillata* from the warmer parts of the Old World has recently appeared in southeastern North America and is likely to become an increasingly serious problem, possibly the worst of such problems in North America (Holm, Weldon, and Blackburn 1969).

In addition to these cases there is a probability that *Myriophyllum spicatum* is another adventive water plant that is developing huge populations. In the last decade an enormous development of this or closely allied taxa has been recorded in the Chesapeake Bay area, in coastal North Carolina, in the Tennessee Valley, in the Gulf states, and in Wisconsin if not elsewhere in the central part of North America (Smith, Hall, and Stanley 1967; Holm, Weldon, and Blackburn 1969; Stanley 1970, and references therein). Unfortunately there is great taxonomic confusion about the plant, which makes it difficult to ascertain what has really happened.

In the older accounts of the flora of North America *Myriophyllum spicatum*, found throughout a large part of the Palaearctic, was regarded as American. In 1919 Fernald separated the American plants as *M. exalbescens* and in this he has been followed by most subsequent taxonomists. Patten (1954), who was investigating populations in New Jersey which had greatly increased and had become a nuisance to fishermen, swimmers,

---

[20] Often included in *Elodea*.

and boatmen and were preventing free flow of water used industrially, came to the conclusion that two forms of *Myriophyllum* were present, one approximating to *M. exalbescens*, the other closer to the European *spicatum*, though in some characters intermediate. He concluded that the evidence for the introduction and establishment of *M. spicatum* and subsequent introgression of *exalbescens* into such populations was inadequate. He believed intermediates occurred in northwestern Europe and in eastern Asia and suspected that they represented incomplete separation of two subspecies during the Pleistocene. A. Löve (1961), however, criticized Patten's conclusions, believing *M. spicatum* and *M. exalbescens* to be distinct species, the latter being native only to North America. Springer (in Beaver 1962) considered *M. spicatum* to have been introduced into eastern North America late in the nineteenth century, perhaps around 1880. This view seems now adopted by investigators involved with the economic problems presented by the species (Smith, Hall, and Stanley 1967; Holm, Weldon, and Blackburn 1969). Smith, Hall, and Stanley record *M. spicatum* from Wisconsin and Illinois, in a more central region of North America than did Patten, thus suggesting a recent spread of the invader; they also believe the presence of the species in the Tennessee Valley to be quite recent. Though far more critical taxonomy is needed, it seems probable that the economically serious developments of *Myriophyllum* populations in North America are due to *spicatum*, perhaps in some cases more or less introgressed by *exalbescens*. The invader may well be able to take special advantage of increasing eutrophication. Quite small pieces of *M. spicatum*, only 5 cm long abscissed from the tip of the plant, may under favorable circumstances lose buoyancy, sink, put out roots, and grow to a length of 3–5 m in the first season, and the multiple stems produced in the next season may have an aggregate length of 7–13 m. Some insects feed on the plant and may actually or potentially act as controlling agents (Spencer and Lekić 1974).

In the next chapter, in which chemical analyses of *Myriophyllum* are reported from regions in which massive populations have recently developed, these are referred to *M.* cf. *spicatum* with the understanding that the adventive species is probably involved but that some introgression may well have occurred.

Adventive pleustophytes. The most celebrated twentieth-century introductions, producing overwhelming populations, are those of the water hyacinth, *Eichhornia crassipes.* Two other very serious invasions of recent manmade lakes in Africa by pleustophytes may be comparable, but in both cases either phytogeographical or systematic difficulties complicate the story.

Eichhornia crassipes is a South American plant found everywhere east of the Andes, southward to about latitude 30°S or near the coast a little further. Northward it is now found in Central America and the Caribbean islands and may be native in part of these areas. Owing to its beautiful violet-blue flowers it was early prized as an ornamental water plant. This led to its introduction into botanic gardens, as at Buitenzorg or Bogor, in Java in 1894, and into private pools in and around New Orleans 10 years earlier. When the species flourished, covering the whole pool, surplus individuals were often thrown out into watercourses in which they could multiply. *E. crassipes* is now found throughout the humid tropics, northward into Japan in the Old World, and Virginia in the New. It is a serious pest in Florida and Louisiana, in the Congo basin and the White Nile, in northeast India eastward through Malaya, Cambodia, Vietnam, and Java, Sumatra, and Borneo, the Philippine Islands, and northwestern Australia. Reproduction is both vegetative and sexual, but in some areas in which clones of a single form of this heterostylous plant are found, the setting of seed does not occur. Several species of *Eichhornia* other than *E. crassipes* are found in South America but none have so far traveled to become pests in other countries.

Among the other pleustonic flowering plants, *Pistia stratiotes* may form enormous populations in warm regions, particularly on newly filled impoundments. Whether it is to be regarded as adventive is uncertain, as it seems now to be tropicopolitan. An immense development of the species occurred at the margins of Lake Volta, the largest man-made lake so far in existence (Ewer 1966; Holm, Weldon, and Blackburn 1969). The development of a mat formed of this species is a very serious matter as it provides an optimum habitat for the larvae of mosquitos of the genus *Mansonia*, the vector of rural filariasis and of encephalomyelitis.

Understanding of the problem of the spread of the pleustonic fern *Salvinia* is complicated by taxonomic questions. Plants of the genus have been known for a quarter of a century as a serious weed in rice paddies in Ceylon and have been referred to *S. auriculata*. Sculthorpe, who gives a good account of the infestation, indicates that the South American plant was introduced from Germany by way of Calcutta for botanical study and then accidentally was disseminated. *Salvinia* also became a major problem on Lake Kariba, the artificial lake on the Zambezi between Zambia and Rhodesia. The population reached its maximum in 1962, when about 1000 km² of the lake was covered by a mat of the plant, underneath which the water became deoxygenated. In subsequent years the area occupied (Fig. 98) has decreased but later increased again (Mitchell, in Little 1966; Mitchell 1969; Mitchell, in Bowmaker 1973). It is probably limited by the area of reasonably quiet water. At the height of the population, assuming from 1 to 10 cm² of water surface was occupied by a single average plant, the population must very conservatively have consisted of $n \times 10^{10}$ individuals. It is now believed that the species of *Salvinia* that occurs as a pest is not simply an old South American member of the genus, but represents a new taxon, *S. molesta*, probably of hybrid origin (Mitchell 1972). The ecology of the plant in relation to its associated flora and fauna has been well studied and is of great interest, as will appear in Vol. IV.

The wide distribution of water plants. Though as Sculthorpe points out, there are many endemic species of water plants in various parts of the world, the immense distribution of a number of genera and of a few species is as striking as it was in Darwin's day. The very wide distribution of some adventive species probably gives a model of the process by which these wide natural distributions were achieved, though one in which the process is greatly accelerated. There are evidently two aspects of the matter to be considered, the actual distribution mechanisms and the fate of the distributed propagules. The great acceleration of introduction in recent times involves the former aspect. Distribution either purposefully or accidentally by man has replaced the very slow but probably ultimately very effective distribution by birds. In either case the newly germinated seed of a water plant finds itself in a medium, either water or wet mud, which is far more favorable for continuous growth and subsequent asexual reproduction than are most terrestrial habitats. Water plants have largely depended on asexual reproduction. Almost any minor disturbance of the plant may become an occasion for propagation; moreover, many species have become specialized to reproduce in this way. Though clearly not all water plants have the capacity to be opportunistic colonizers, those that do presumably take advantage of the favorable environment provided by water and mud for rapid asexual spreading. It is reasonable to suppose that this is why there are such striking examples of worldwide distributions. This explanation is in accord with the fact that for large organisms the phenomenon is almost exclusively a botanical one. The only zoological analogues would probably be provided by the Ectoprocta which produce, as statoblasts, reproductive bodies that can be dried and are comparable in size to small seeds but that, being produced asexually, permit not only dispersal but rapid occupation of a new site by the descendants of a single introduction. Several cosmopolitan genera and a few species occur in the group. The other cosmopolitan freshwater organisms are all much smaller, being analogous to widespread algae more than to flowering plants, but at least in the rotifers and Cladocera the concatenation of small easily distributed resting eggs with rapid parthenogenesis provides a comparable situation.

Quantitative aspects of colonization. An interesting case has been considered by Godwin (1923) of a group of ponds of comparable size, situa-

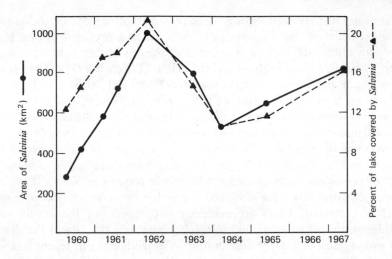

FIGURE 98. Variation in population of *Salvinia molesta* on Lake Kariba; the decline after the major peak appears to have been due to continued rise in the water level increasing the fetch of the wind and so the maximum possible height of the waves. After the water surface was stabilizeo at a slightly lower level there was some increase in *Salvinia*, mainly in bays (Mitchell).

tion, and surrounding soil in the vicinity of Trent Junction, south of Long Eaton, Derbyshire, England.[21] The dates of origin of all the ponds are known, though for the oldest, a natural oxbow, only approximately. The entire macroscopic flora of the ponds, including hygrophytes that are not strictly aquatic but depend for their local existence on the presence of the ponds, consists of 59 species. The oldest pond, formed about 222 yr before the study was made, contained 44 species, and the youngest pond, 12 years old when examined, only 8 species. The other ponds contained intermediate numbers of species, the number being roughly dependent on age. The graphical presentation by Godwin, here reproduced (Fig. 99) suggests two series; one (Forbes', 1852; Stenson's, 1836; and Oxbow, ca. 1700) being very close to or connected to streams, the other (Farmer's, 1902; Rifle-Range, 1898; and Fletcher's, 1836) being more isolated. At any age the former series appears to be richer in species than the latter. Only *Alisma plantago-aquatica* and *Potamogeton natans* occurred in all ponds; 22 species occurred in only one pond apiece.

---

[21] The ponds themselves appear to lie partly in Derbyshire and partly in Nottinghamshire, very close to the place where these two counties and Leicestershire meet.

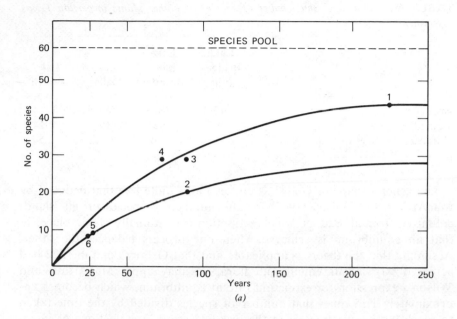

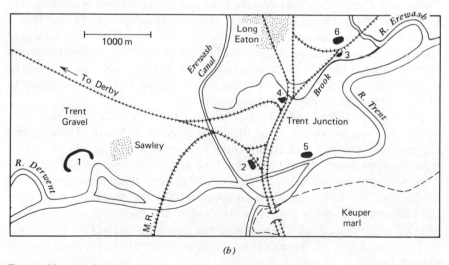

FIGURE 99. (A) Relationship of number of species of higher plants to age of ponds in two series of localities around Tent Junction, Long Eaton, Derbyshire, England. The species pool of 59 species is indicated by a broken line. (B) Map of the localities. One series of ponds, consisting of Oxbow (1), Stenson's (3), and Forbes' (4), are connected with or very close to the River Trent or its tributaries; the others, Fletcher's (2), Rifle-Range (5), and Farmer's (6) are less likely to receive plants from watercourses (modified from Godwin).

TABLE *18.*   *Area, age, and number of species of higher plants in certain Texas reservoirs*

	Lake Bridge- port	Lake Eagle Mountain	Lake Dallas	Lake Worth
Area (Rm²)	42.1	38.9	44.2	15.4
Year filled	1935	1934	1927	1914
Number of species of higher plants	9±	16	52	54

The general shape of Godwin's curves looks quite like that deduced by MacArthur and Wilson (1967) for the number of species on an island, colonized from abroad, on which extinction is continually taking place, so that an equilibrium is achieved when one process balances the other. Assuming that the theory is applicable and that Oxbow Pond in 1922 had achieved 90% of its equilibrium flora, we may apply MacArthur and Wilson's expression for extinction rate at equilibrium, which becomes approximately 1.15 times that number of species divided by the time taken to reach 90% saturation, or in the present case 0.23 extinctions or introductions per year when the pond is connected with a stream. Assuming that Godwin's extrapolation of his lower curve is roughly correct and that a pond in the area studied isolated from a stream would be 90% saturated with 30 species in 222 yr, we should have an extinction and introduction rate of about 0.16 yr.$^{-1}$ These conclusions seem reasonable. In view of the great difficulty of finding data of this sort, it would be most interesting to restudy any of these ponds that may still exist.

The data of Harris and Silvey (1940) for four artificial lakes in Texas, which they studied primarily in 1937, are given in Table 18. These figures suggest very roughly that equilibrium is approached in 10–25 yr, which would correspond to 2.5–6.1 introductions and extinctions per year at equilibrium, numbers an order of magnitude greater than those implied by Godwin's data. It is reasonable to suppose that the much greater size of the colonizable areas is primarily involved in the difference as the species pool of aquatic macrophytes is clearly not markedly greater in Texas than in England. Even so, the turnover implied in the Texas reservoirs seems extremely high.

SUMMARY

Most land plants cannot grow underwater, presumably because carbon dioxide cannot diffuse through a liquid medium fast enough to support effective photosynthesis. A few terrestrial species are, however, known to produce striking occasional aquatic ecophenes, such as the immensely elongate aquatic form of the swamp-dwelling thistle *Cirsium dissectum*.

A great number of species are regularly amphibious; *Polygonum amphibium*, *Veronica anagallis-aquatica*, and *Gratiola aurea* provide important examples. These species must produce shoots in air if they are to flower, but in *P. amphibium* some clones can flower only if rooted in water. In such amphibious plants the microscopic anatomy of the parts of the plant growing under water differs strikingly and characteristically from that of the aerial parts. The epidermal cells are much more elongate under water and are often chlorophyll-bearing, palisade tissue is reduced or absent, stomata are rare or lacking, the vascular bundles are less well developed, the xylem is particularly reduced and gas-filled lacunae are almost always present. This kind of change occurs in quite unrelated plants including ferns and must represent a fundamental response that has permitted the evolution of aquatic species in many groups of angiosperms. Floating-leaved aquatic species and even a few fully submersed plants, as *Utricularia*, can usually be grown with care as terrestrial plants on wet soil; this may happen to species such as *Potamogeton natans*, *P. polygonifolius*, and *Nymphaea alba* in nature. On the whole the adaptation to fresh water is more clearly reversible in the case of aquatic angiosperms than in any other group of organisms.

The herbid emergent species (B.I.a, p. 125) of protected waters, such as small ponds, ditches, and to a limited extent the less disturbed parts of the lake margin, may be expected to suffer no more from wind exposure than the plants of meadows or the edges of woodland and are not strikingly modified. In all windswept habitats if emergent plants are present they are very elongate with cylindrical or narrow or reduced leaves (B.I.b, p. 125), and can easily bend with the wind. Among foliose monocotyledons the emergent leaves are often sagittate, a form perhaps reducing wind resistance and thus breakage.

Ephydates usually have subcircular or ovoid leaves, the latter probably being characteristic of more disturbed localities. Within the Nymphaeaceae there is evidently a good deal of variation in capacity to withstand disturbance, which plays a part in regulating distributions.

Though the CO_2 concentration in water in equilibrium with the atmosphere is of the same order of magnitude as the concentration in normal air, the rate of diffusion of the gas is very much less, so that photosynthesis is more difficult underwater. This is offset to a considerable extent by the water plants not needing to guard against water loss, so that the photosynthetic tissue can be more exposed than in an aerial leaf. Two main adaptations promoting photosynthesis exist. One is morphological, involving the modification of the leaf either into a very thin lamella that would be too lax under aerial conditions, or the subdivision of the leaf into a compound capillary structure. These arrangements produce a higher surface to volume ratio than would be feasible where evaporation is a problem. Where direct comparison is possible, as in dissected and more or less entire water leaves of *Proserpinaca*, the dividing of the leaf may double the rate of photosynthesis. Reduction in volume per unit area also decreases respiration and so increases the net, if not the gross, photosynthetic activity.

The second adaptation is physiological and involves the development of mechanisms whereby bicarbonate ions, in addition to molecules of CO_2, can be taken up by the plant and used in photosynthesis, though with reduced efficiency. This mechanism confers an enormous advantage in hard water and is found in nearly, but not quite all, angiosperms living in hard-water lakes and in some algae, though not in bryophytes. The development of the bicarbonate uptake mechanism has some slight analogy to that of the C_4 dicarboxylic acid pathway in many plants of hot and dry habitats. In both cases a decarboxylation precedes photosynthesis, a special arrangement of storage cells may be observed, and efficiency is increased.

Emergent plants probably obtain most of their CO_2 from the atmosphere.

Very many emergent and floating-leaved plants are heterophyllous, the upper leaves exposed to the air having a different form from those fully submerged. The latter, as might be expected, tend to exhibit the kinds of morphological adaptation, possible underwater, that increase the surface to volume ratio, or in some cases are long trailing structures, whereas the emergent leaves are more compact. There is one hint that air leaves may lack the mechanism for bicarbonate uptake, which is of course not present in terrestrial plants. The microscopic anatomy of air and water leaves on the same plant differs in the same ways as have been described in comparing allied land and water plants. There are great physiological differences, air leaves tending to cell contents with higher osmotic pressure, usually due to carbohydrate accumulation. There is evidence that the increase in osmotic pressure is primary and is partly involved in determining the occurrence of air leaves. In some plants as in *Sagittaria* the initial leaves are inevitably water leaves, even if the plant is growing on wet soil in air; in other plants as in most aquatic species of *Ranunculus* the nature of the leaf is entirely determined environmentally, some modification even of the cotyledons being possible.

Transpiration occurs in emergent and floating-leaved aquatic plants much as in terrestrial species. By day the rate of water loss from unit area of an emergent or floating leaf is usually not very different from the rate of loss at an exposed natural water surface, though some species as *Sagittaria latifolia* may lose less, and some such as *Scirpus validus* may lose more. By night the rate falls off greatly owing to stomatal closure. In fairly dense stands in summer, owing to the great area of leaf per unit area of water, the average rate for night and day for the association as a whole may be greater, by a factor of two or three, than the loss from a comparable free water surface.

There is some evidence that in a number of floating-leaved or emergent plants the aerial and aquatic parts detached from the root or rhizome cannot maintain a full transpiration stream. There has been much discussion as to whether there is an analogue to a transpiration stream in fully submersed plants, dependent on root pressure. The most recent direct evidence seems not to establish a well-marked unidirectional movement of water from root to stem apex. It is, however, clear that various solutes, both natural nutrients and artificial substances, such as dyes and herbicides, can be transported from the roots upward. Though the mechanisms involved still need elucidation, there is evidently no physiological difficulty in accepting the close dependence of water plants in nature on the chemical characteristics of the sediments on which they grow.

Almost all water plants have a well-developed system of air spaces which may be continuous from the leaf parenchyma through the petioles and stems to the rhizomes and roots. Its volume can be surprisingly great, in some cases over 60% of the rhizome. In general this lacunar system is formed as spaces between cells (schizogeny) in the green parts, while in most species it is formed by cell disintegration (lysigeny) in the buried parts.

The quantity of the gas in the lacunae of the green parts of a submersed plant increases during the day as the result of photosynthesis, but in all cases that have been studied nitrogen remains the chief component. There is clear evidence of a fall in oxygen and rise in carbon dioxide in the lacunar gas in passing from the illuminated parts of a plant to the buried parts. However, even in the latter the oxygen is higher when the plant is illuminated, so the system does provide a respiratory mechanism transporting oxygen to the unilluminated structures of the plant.

As well as serving a respiratory function, the lacunar system may develop in expansions of leaves or petioles which become floats as in *Pistia, Eichhornia*, and *Trapa*. Secondary spongy tissues with intercellular air spaces known as aerenchyma develop in certain hyperhydates, notably in the Lythrales and in the limited number of aquatic genera in the Leguminales; in these plants various kinds of floats are developed.

The rhizomes of some water plants, notably *Nuphar*, metabolize anaerobically and may produce considerable quantities of alcohol. In certain eulittoral plants a flood-tolerant biochemistry is developed whereby the final product of anaerobic metabolism is malate rather than the more toxic ethanol. In such plants the malate can be oxidized when the water level falls. The ultimate fate of the alcohol in water lilies presumably involves oxidation when photosynthesis is proceeding actively in bright light and oxygen can diffuse down the petiole. There is some upward movement of the ethanol which perfumes the "brandy bottle" flower. The growth of shoots from the petiole proceeds optimally at very low oxygen tensions in *Nuphar, Peltandra*, and to a lesser degree in other rhizomatous water plants.

The seeds of water plants are generally liberated as small fruits with hard pericarps (achenes, nuts, or nutlets), or with a soft epicarp and mesocarp (drupe) and a hard, seedlike stone. In general, the seed does not germinate until the hard impermeable fruit wall is broken or decomposed. In nature germination during the year of seed set is unusual though known occasionally. The longest recorded period of dormancy in any water plant is for *Nelumbo nucifera*, seeds of which have remained viable for at least 237 yr.

In the water plants of temperate regions it is usual to find that a period of dormancy in cold water greatly promotes the ability of seeds to germinate. Breaking the protective coverings of the fruit or seed nearly always promotes early germination. In some cases it is probable that bacterial decomposition in mud has this effect. Reduction of oxygen concentration and lowering of redox potential also may accelerate development. The effect of light is often important but varies from species to species.

In *Potamogeton thunbergii*, the only species studied in the light of modern concepts of the action of light on plants, it is found that the drupe floats for some time while the outer tissue of the pericarp is still photosynthetic. As this tissue decays photosynthesis stops and the fruit sinks. At the surface it is apparently prevented from germinating by the action of far-red light (732 nm) which, unlike red light (659 nm), is not absorbed by the chlorophyllose pericarp. When the seed sinks into water a few tens of centimeters deep, the ratio of red to far-red light received by the embryo is increased, as the chlorophyll absorbing far-red has decayed and the depth of the water, which is more transmissive for red than far-red, has increased. This change in the relative amounts of the two wavelengths promotes, at least in water up to 1 m deep, germination. In *P. schweinfurthii* growing sympatrically with *P. thunbergii*, the absolute sensitivity to light is greater so that a comparable mechanism may operate at greater depths.

Studies of a few seeds indicate that the condition of passage through the alimentary canal of a bird, particularly prior to winter dormancy, may greatly increase the germination rate when the temperature rises.

The pollination of water plants may take place by transport of pollen on insects (entomophily), by wind (anemophily), or on or in water (hydrophily). The first type is characteristic of the herbid plants of very sheltered bays or small ponds and streams, with showy perfumed flowers, and of the large flowers of many floating-leaved species. Specialized relations with insects, mainly beetles, which are trapped by the newly opened flower in a female condition and may later be liberated when covered with pollen as the flower goes over to a male state, occur in some night-blooming Nymphaeaceae.

Anemophilous flowers are found among many submerged species that produce a short inflorescence above water, as in *Myriophyllum* and *Potamogeton*, and in the graminid hyperhydates such as *Phragmites*, *Scirpus*, *Typha*, and *Cyperus*.

Hydrophilous flowers are not very common in freshwaters but occur in a few species of *Potamogeton*, in *Najas*, in the important isolated genera *Callitriche* and *Ceratophyllum*, and in a number of members of the Hydrocharitaceae. Several of the freshwater members of the last-named group liberate pollen on the water surface and it may in fact never be wetted.

There are a few species that are autogamous or pseudocleistogamous on occasion, the submersed flower being self-fertilized when underwater though with a gas bubble in its interior. Such flowers may open later but by that time all ovules may have received pollen tubes. *Lobelia dortmanna* seems to be a regular member of this ecological group of plants.

There is a tendency found in many unrelated water plants for the flower peduncle to bend over when the flower has been pollinated, thus immersing the developing fruit in the water.

It is probable that, except for a very limited number of annuals, most reproduction in water plants is asexual. The mere mechanical breaking of plants by violent water movements in storms or by the feeding activities of animals may be a major mode of propagation. A very large number of water plants produce large rhizomes. If these branch and the older parts tend to decay, their growth inevitably leads to reproduction. A few species produce tubers, and from the rosette-shaped plants, common in unproductive lakes, runners often grow out and establish a series of daughter plants, easily detached from the parent.

Many water plants in temperate regions perennate by the formation of turions, winter or resting buds, formed late in the year and dormant during the coldest season. In some of the Alismataceae these may be produced in place of flowers when the plant is not growing in very shallow water. In structure the turions may be very diversified, even within a genus. In *Potamogeton* they are usually produced from the rhizome in the broad-leaves species. In the subgenus *Coleogeton* the turions derived from rhizoids are swollen, of characteristic shape, and filled with starch. In *P. crispus* specialized parts of the shoot with resting buds in the axils of modified leaves are shed from the plant in autumn. In the narrow-leaved species of *Eupotamogeton* they are large dense buds which fall off as the rest of the plant decays in the autumn. In such plants everything save these turions may disappear, so that the species is essentially an asexual annual, the turion being equally involved in reproduction and perennation.

In view of the great importance of asexual reproduction, many lacustrine populations of water plants are probably clones. This is best known in *Phragmites australis*, in which species a lake may be fringed by one or two such clonal populations. Cases are known where natural selection is clearly involved in one clone displacing another. The striking occurrence of hybrids in the genus *Potamogeton* in lakes in which one or even both parent species are absent, again suggests clonal populations, which, though largely infertile sexually, may be better adapted than either parent to the particular niche provided by some body of water. A comparable phenomenon is provided by cases in which only one sex of a dioecious species exists over a wide range, or where no flowering has ever been reported in a lacustrine population. It has also been noted that occasionally lacustrine monoecious populations, though they flower, never set seed; such populations are probably derived asexually from a single self-incompatible ancestor.

A number of genera and a few species of water plants have an enormous distribution; *Phragmites australis* is perhaps the most cosmopolitan angiosperm. Since nearly all bodies of freshwater are, in a geological time scale, very transitory, it is evident that water plants must have very good methods of dispersal. In spite of more than a century of active research, the nature of these dispersal mechanisms is inadequately understood.

Accidental transport of living whole plants on the bodies of flying birds, as in the Lemnaceae, or of viable fragments of vittate water plants, such as *Potamogeton* and *Elodea*, is well documented and provides a way by which new localities can be invaded, provided the lakes between which transport takes place are not far apart. Such fragments on reaching a new body of water would be able to start growth immediately.

Transportation of seeds by migrating birds seems to be the only reasonable explanation of such very long range transoceanic migration as has occurred. Though the probability of any individual bird carrying a seed accidentally is apparently very low, the number of birds involved in migration is so enormous that transportation by one bird in a million might well be more than adequate to explain the observed distributions. Asexual reproduction would allow any such seed that germinated successfully to start a clonal population, and successful sexual reproduction in a dioecious or self-sterile monoecious species might not occur for a very long time, until another introduction occurred. There are a few distributions, notably *Ranunculus rionii* in eastern Europe eastward to Japan and perhaps to western North America, and then again in eastern South Africa, with no intervening tropical records, that strongly suggest transport by birds migrating from Europe to South Africa.

In the past 130 years various accidental or unthinking introductions of water plants into alien environments have led to massive proliferation of certain species which have proved very harmful to human activities involving natural waters. Such evidence as exists suggests that ordinarily the very large populations that develop after a region has been invaded are temporary and may be expected to decline naturally, though the reason is not known. This happened with *Elodea canadensis* in Europe and to some extent with *Salvinia molesta* in Lake Kariba. Other important invaders are *Eichhornia crassipes* throughout the Tropics, *Egeria densa, Lagarosiphon major*, and *Ceratophyllum demersum* in New Zealand, *Hydrilla verticillata* and *Myriophyllum spicatum* in North America. The successful spreading of such plants presumably provides a model of what happened much more slowly to the naturally distributed water plants. Asexual reproduction is obviously of great importance in the process.

In the very few cases where adequate floristic analysis of a group of ponds or lakes of known ages has been made, the entire species pool is not represented in any one lake. The total number of species in each body of water seems to reach a saturation value, of about 44 in an English study and 54 in Texas. The MacArthur–Wilson theory of colonization and extinction on islands suggests between 0.16 and 0.23 introductions and extinctions per year in the English ponds, but in the much larger Texas reservoirs a rate of about an order of magnitude greater.

CHAPTER 30

The Chemical Ecology of Freshwater Macrophytes

The occurrence and luxuriance of the various species of higher plants in lakes is clearly regulated to a considerable extent by chemical factors. The interrelations of such factors in nature are complicated, and in spite of a great deal of work, understood only in a rather unsatisfactory way.

In this chapter three major topics are considered, primarily as they are related to tracheophytes. Discussions of some comparable aspects of the Characeae and the Bryophyta have already been given (see pp. 14–29, 58–61, 64), though in view of the ease with which they are studied, extended reference to *Chara* and *Nitella* is necessary in any discussion of ionic uptake.

The first topic is the uptake of materials by water plants from their environment. In considering this matter it is impossible to avoid a brief treatment of various physiological problems, though as far as possible the ecological aspects of the physiology will be kept in the foreground.

The second topic is the elementary composition of the plants as found in nature. This is of potential interest not only in a consideration of what plants take from their environments and may in fact actually need, but also in relation to their value as food for animals (see p. 293). A large amount of information exists about elementary composition in the form of analyses of varying quality. Very little effort, Cowgill's work (1973a, b, 1974a, b), providing the most important exception, has hitherto been made to coordinate this material and to disclose such regularities as the data contain.

The third topic is the distribution of plants in relation to the chemical properties of the waters and sediments in which they grow. Here again, there is a great deal of data, but considerable care must be taken in interpretation, as it is very difficult to distinguish effects mediated directly from those involving competition under varying environmental conditions.

THE PASSAGE OF DISSOLVED MATERIALS INTO WATER PLANTS

The uptake of various substances by plant cells immersed in aqueous solutions involves a number of different processes, which, insofar as they have been unraveled, present a complicated picture. In this work only the most basic physiological concepts that apply directly to ecological and biogeochemical processes in freshwaters are considered. For summaries of the vast amount of additional detail, the reader may consult some of the excellent reviews, fortunately prepared by the leading workers in the field, that are now available, notably those of Dainty (1969), Laties (1969), MacRobbie (1970, 1974), Epstein (1972), and Higinbotham (1973).

Passive and active transport.   Whenever there is a concentration gradient, and no completely impermeable barrier set across it, diffusion of any substance under consideration will result in a net transport from the more concentrated to the less concentrated region, or down the gradient. If an electrical potential gradient is imposed on the concentration gradient of an electrolyte, the cations present will tend to move toward the negative and the anions toward the positive pole. As the concentration of, say, cations increases toward the negative pole, the concentration gradient will come to balance the electrochemical gradient, producing an equilibrium distribution of cations so long as the potential difference is maintained, the tendency for net diffusion down the concentration gradient being balanced by net diffusion in the opposite direction down the electrochemical gradient. Any movement involved in producing this sort of situation is spoken of as *passive* because, the potential gradient being given, no additional work is needed to produce the movement resulting in equilibrium. It is of course obvious that for passive movement to occur at all across any cell membrane, that membrane must be permeable to the substance under study. Some investigators, notably Epstein (1972), are skeptical of this being true of the bounding membrane of healthy plant cells, and so tend to regard all movements of dissolved substances, into or out of plants, as active. The concept of a passive equilibrium distribution is, however, useful in providing a standard to which other distributions can be compared.

Active transport is any transport which would not occur without the direct supply of energy derived from some metabolic process. The mechanisms by which particular substances are moved actively into, within, or out of a cell are called *pumps*. MacRobbie (1970) has given a good account of the more elaborate and abstract ways of considering active transport. For the purpose of this discussion, only the simpler aspects of the process need be treated.

Michaelis–Menten kinetics. Epstein and Hagen (1952), working on the uptake of rubidium by barley roots, suggested that in active transport a carrier substance united with the ion under consideration on one side of the cell membrane and dissociated on the other. Such a process could give rise to kinetics comparable to those found when an enzyme unites with and later dissociates from a substrate, which in that case is of course altered.

Epstein and Hagen concluded that the Michaelis–Menten equation,

$$V_t = \frac{C_o V_m}{C_o + K_m} \tag{1}$$

where V_t is the rate of entry at time t, V_m the maximum possible rate of entry, C_o the external concentration, and K_m the Michaelis constant, would apply in cases of active transport. K_m is the concentration when the rate of entry is half the maximum possible value. In experiments large volumes of medium and short periods of time are best used, to avoid decrease in external concentration throughout the course of a single set of observations. Radioactive tracers are ordinarily employed in determining V_t.

Since from (1)

$$\frac{V_m}{V_t} = 1 + \frac{K_m}{C_o} \tag{2}$$

a plot of $1/V_t$ against $1/C_o$ should give a straight line (Lineweaver and Burk 1934). This type of approach has been little used in the lower macrophytes except *Hydrodictyon africanum* (Raven 1967) but has proved most illuminating in studies on higher plants, including a few habitually found growing in freshwaters. It has also been useful in the study of the uptake of phosphorus (Fuhs, Demmerle, Canelli, and Min Chen 1972) and of CO_2 (Allen 1969, 1972) by phytoplankton.

The Nernst equation. It is found that when a plant cell is in an aqueous medium, there is ordinarily a potential gradient across the boundary of the cell, the interior of which is negative to the medium. More refined study indicates differences in potential within the cell; in particular there is usually not only a fall in crossing the *plasmalemma* or outer membrane, but also a slight rise in crossing the *tonoplast* or membrane delimiting the vacuole. The active cytoplasm is thus slightly negative to the vacuole as well as strongly negative to the environment. These internal differences are not considered here, since the available analyses mostly refer to vacuolar contents and the main limnological interest of transport problems lies in overall movements into and out of the plant. The reader desiring more information will find it in the reviews already mentioned, MacRobbie (1970) being intellectually the most satisfying.

The negative potential just discussed could be set up in a variety of ways. Anions in solution may be produced metabolically within a cell the plasmalemma of which is impermeable to the anion in question but not to cations; a similar situation could arise from immobile anionic groups on structural components of the cell. Alternatively an electrogenic pump could force one anion, say, chloride, into the cell, thus setting up the potential, which would control the distribution of all other ions. It is important to realize that a concentration of an ion in the cell in excess of that of the same ion in the environment does not necessarily imply an active process of accumulation. In some cases, in fact, there may be a higher concentration inside than outside, but at the same time evidence of active transport of the ion outward to compensate for a passive movement inward down the potential gradient.

If we have an ion j in solution at concentration C_o in the medium and C_i inside the cell, and inquire into the condition for a passive flux equilibrium, we find that for such an equilibrium, the potential across the cell boundary E_N, which is of the kind called a Nernst potential, is given by

$$E_N = \frac{RT}{Z_j F} \ln \frac{C_o}{C_i} \tag{3}$$

where R is the gas constant, T the absolute temperature, F the Faraday or charge carried by 1 g-equiv, and Z_j the algebraic valency or charge of the ion j. For a temperature of 20°C the equation becomes

$$E_N = \frac{58}{Z_j} \log \frac{C_o}{C_i} \quad (mV) \tag{4}$$

For a monovalent cation ($Z_j = +1$), if the potential of the cell relative to the medium were held at -116 mV, net inward movement of cations would take place until the concentration inside were 100 times that outside. If the potential were dropped to -58 mV, the equilibrium ratio of the concentration of any positive ion present within the cell to the concentration outside would fall to 10. When observed ratios differ radically from those calculated from (4), it is evident that a mechanism must exist actively transporting substances into or out of the plant. If, for any constant value of C_o, the value of C_i calculated from a measurement of the potential drop

TABLE 19. *Vacuolar contents of sodium, potassium, and chloride, in various Characeae, compared with contents of the same ions in medium and with the passive equilibrium vacuolar concentration calculated by taking E_{obs}, the potential difference between medium and vacuole as a Nernst potential (data from various sources collected by MacRobbie)*

	Na^+ (mM)	K^+ (mM)	Cl^- (mM)	E_{obs} (mV)
Nitella translucens				
Medium	1.0	0.1	1.3	
Vacuolar content and potential difference	65	75	150–170	−122
Vacuolar content at passive equilibrium	127	13	0.01	
Implied direction of active flux	Efflux	Influx	Influx	
N. flexilis				
Medium	0.2	0.1	1.3	
Vacuolar content and potential difference	28	80	136	−155
Vacuolar content at passive equilibrium	94	47	0.003	
Implied direction of active flux	Efflux	?Slight influx	Influx	
N. clavata				
Medium	3.0	0.1	3.1	
Vacuolar content and potential difference	36–34	75–83	120–124	−106 to −120
Vacuolar content at passive equilibrium	350–200	12–7	0.03–0.05	
Implied direction of active flux	Efflux	Influx	Influx	

Tolypella intricata				
Medium	1.0	0.4	1.4	−120 to −140
Vacuolar content and potential difference	3–10	90–110	110–136	
Vacuolar content at passive equilibrium	260	110–119	0.005–0.01	
Implied direction of active flux	Efflux	None	Influx	
Chara australis				
Medium	1.0	0.1	1.6	−152 to −159
Vacuolar content and potential difference	66	54	100–150	
Vacuolar content at passive equilibrium	525–420	42–53	0.003–0.004	
Implied direction of active flux	Efflux	None	Influx	
Lamprothamnium succinctum				
Medium	289	6	337	−100
Vacuolar content and potential difference	136	250	373	
Vacuolar content at passive equilibrium	14,900	310	7	
Implied direction of active flux	Efflux	?None	Influx	
Nitellopsis obtusa				
Medium	30	0.65	35	−120
Vacuolar content and potential difference	54	113	206	
Vacuolar content at passive equilibrium	3500	76	0.3	
Implied direction of active flux	Efflux	?Influx	Influx	

269

between the outside and the inside of the cell is significantly lower than the observed concentration of the ion under investigation, there must be a pump maintaining this concentration by producing an influx into the cell; on the other hand, if the interior concentration calculated from the potential is significantly higher than that observed, the pump must be operating to produce an efflux.

Uptake of ions by Characeae. The most important studies employing the concept just indicated relate to the movement of sodium, potassium, and chloride ions into or out of the large cells of the Characeae and of the green alga *Hydrodictyon africanum.* The experimental data have been well summarized by MacRobbie (1970); a simplified version of her presentation, relating only to the vacuolar contents and the overall potential drop from the medium to the vacuole in the Characeae, is given in Table 19.

Examination of the table indicates that there is clear evidence of strong active movement of chloride into and of sodium out of the cell in all the species studied. There is evidently active transport of potassium into the cells of *Nitella translucens* and *N. clavata.* No such transport is needed to explain the potassium contents of *Tolypella intricata* and *Chara australis,* and in the other three species that have been studied the differences are not great enough to permit valid judgment. *Hydrodictyon africanum* behaves like *Nitella translucens* and *N. clavata* in having a clear active potassium influx.

It has long been known that the uptake of ions by green plant cells is greatly stimulated by illumination (Fig. 100). Hoagland and Davis (1923) found this to be true of the uptake of chloride, bromide, and nitrate by the cells of *Nitella clavata.* In *Nitella translucens* the maximum rate of

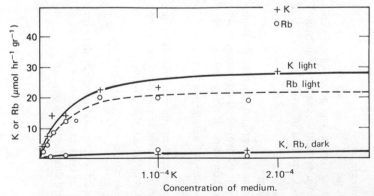

FIGURE 100.   Uptake of ^{42}K and ^{87}Rb from various concentrations of potassium by *Egeria densa* leaves in light and darkness (Jeschke, modified).

potassium and chloride influx is 10–20 times, and for sodium efflux 2–3 times, the rates in the dark (MacRobbie 1962). The difference between the effects of light on the potassium influx and sodium efflux implies that the ratio of potassium to sodium transported, though in opposite directions, must be lower in darkness than in light. In *Hydrodictyon africanum* the action spectrum for the transfer of chloride, and of chloride-linked Na^+ and K^+, corresponds to that of photosynthesis (Raven 1969).

In *Hydrodictyon africanum* Raven (1967) found from the composition of the medium and vacuolar fluid and the potential difference between them that there would be a passive efflux of potassium and chloride and an influx of sodium. Tracer experiments indicated that the observed influx of potassium and chloride and the efflux of sodium were temperature dependent, whereas the efflux of potassium and chloride and the influx of sodium were practically temperature invariant. The temperature-dependent fluxes are presumably active and chemically mediated, whereas the movements in the opposite direction are passive, owing to diffusion, and much less sensitive to temperature changes. In these experiments the net transfer of potassium was very small at 14°C in the light, while chloride was increasing internally and sodium decreasing.

At 3°C transport is probably entirely passive. In light at 14°C, though not in darkness, the sodium efflux is dependent on the external potassium concentration, just as in the active influx of potassium. The data suggest identical Michaelis constants for the two fluxes which are probably the result of a single process. The potassium influx and sodium efflux are inhibited by ouabain which, however, does not act in the dark or at low temperatures. This drug competitively combines with adenosine triphosphatase and so prevents adenosine triphosphate from acting as an energy source. The same kind of situation exists in *Nitella translucens* (MacRobbie 1970, and papers quoted therein). The reasonable interpretation of these findings is that the active influx of potassium and active efflux of sodium, by which the ordinary cationic proportions are maintained in chlorophyll-bearing cells of aquatic plants, depend on a photophosphorylation. Though the energy source of comparable processes in animal cells cannot involve the direct use of light, it is reasonable to suppose that the pumps involved are comparable to those of like action in animal cell membranes, which also depend on ATP (see Keynes 1969 for review).

In *Nitella clavata* (Spear, Barr, and Barr 1969), in *Ch. australis* (Smith 1970), and doubtless in other Characeae in which there is localized uptake of HCO_3^- ions, there is also evidence of the efflux of H^+ ions, in the intermediate regions between the areas of calcium carbonate deposition. Smith (1970) believes that the separation of H^+ and OH^- at the plasmalemma is the fundamental process involved in ion uptake, the other movements being a matter of ion exchange. The energy requirement is presumably for the primary separation. Such a unifying hypothesis is attractive but it provides little or no explanation of the detailed differences that have been reported between the absorption of the various ions that have been studied intensively.

Though it has often been supposed (see Smith 1970 for a critical summary) that the influx of chloride is related to that of cations, notably potassium, the energetics of the principal process at least in the Characeae seem to differ strikingly from what is found for sodium or potassium. Chloride uptake is not inhibited by ouabain in these plants, so it presumably does not involve ATP as an energy source. In *Hydrodictyon* chloride uptake, unlike that of potassium and sodium, is less efficient in far-red than in ordinary red light (Raven 1969); this is interpreted as due to the dependence on photosystem 2 in photosynthesis, in which ATP is not involved. There is more than a suggestion of reduced nicotinamide–adenosine nucleotide ($NADH_2$) being the energy source, but other components of the electron transfer system may also be implicated.

The chloride flux is, however, depressed by the complete absence of monovalent cations in the medium. This suggests that perhaps after all some chloride uptake is, indeed, linked to cation influx. The chloride influx is greatly increased by the presence of ammonium sulfate (Smith 1970) and by imidazole (MacRobbie 1966; Smith 1970), though the latter material inhibits potassium uptake. MacRobbie (1971) finds that bromide is taken up less rapidly than is chloride, though once within the cell the two halide ions are transported similarly.

A bicarbonate pump certainly exists in a number of Characeae (see p. 17); its action appears to resemble that of the chloride pump but it is more active. Phosphate is also clearly actively absorbed (Smith 1966) by *Nitella translucens*, but its influx is much less light dependent than is the case with the other ions studied, the rate of uptake in darkness being at least 60% of that in light. In other ways the phosphate flux seems to resemble that of potassium and is clearly dependent on ATP.

Active transport of sulfate in the Characeae has been studied by Robinson (1969a, b). The relation of the process to illumination is more complicated than in the cases previously discussed because there is evidence not merely of greater uptake in the light than in long continued darkness, but also a transitory stimulation of uptake in passing from light to the dark. In the light there is no inhibition of uptake by carbonyl cyanide *m*-chlorophenylhydrazone (CCCP), a substance which in the concentration used suppressed photosynthesis; it is an inhibitor of transfer of energy from ATP, so photophosphorylation seems not to be involved. In darkness, however, there is inhibition, presumably implying a role for ATP in the uptake. The heat of activation above 15°C is given as 3400 J or 813 cal mol⁻¹, while below 15°C the values are 22,600 J or 5400 cal mol⁻¹ in the light and 18,400 J or 4400 cal mol⁻¹ in darkness. The values above 15°C are extremely small and presumably exclude any chemical rate-dependent process.

It will appear from this very condensed review that although there are a good many well established facts about ionic uptake by the Characeae and *Hydrodictyon* there is as yet no coherent body of theory to explain these facts. If the chloride pump is a major factor in setting up the negative potential in the cell, the observed correlation of chloride and potassium in the analytic results to be reported (see p. 349) becomes reasonable.

Uptake of ions by angiosperms. The uptake or release of ions by higher plants is a more complicated process than in the single large cells of the Characeae and *Hydrodictyon*, and is also more difficult to investigate. The plant is differentiated into a chlorophyll-bearing and a nonphotosynthetic part, which are clearly likely to differ in the energetics of uptake. Moreover, there is internal transport from one part of the plant to another, so that a single cell cannot be regarded as a sink for incoming material. Most of the work has been done with parts of terrestrial crop plants, immersed in laboratory solutions. In such plants uptake is likely to be confined in nature to the roots. In aquatic plants it has commonly been supposed that much of the uptake of nutrient materials is through the green parts of the plant. Although it is now evident, as will appear in the next section, that there is great diversity in this respect, the roots often being important organs of absorption, in many water plants the leaves are certainly very significant in mineral nutrition. The few studies that have been made on such plants will be considered in detail, but it is necessary to supplement such work with information derived from terrestrial plants studied under artificial conditions. All the original sources of this information are summarized in the reviews mentioned on p. 265.

The most striking aspect of ionic uptake in higher plants is that there is very generally a multiple mechanism involved. This is apparent from experiments in which the rate of uptake of a given ion, marked with a radioactive tracer, is studied at different external concentrations. The general result, as indicated in Fig. 100, is that at low external concentrations a high-affinity system saturating at about 0.5 mM operates, and that when the external concentration is further increased, the second or low-affinity system saturating at about 50 mM comes into operation. The high-affinity system is more specific and less influenced by the nature of other ions present than is the low-affinity, high-concentration system. The existence of a multiple system has been demonstrated over a great taxonomic range of plants, including the moss *Mnium cupsidatum*, for both roots and leaves in angiosperms and for K^+, Rb^+, Na^+, Ca^{2+}, Mg^{2+}, Fe^{2+}, Cl^-, $H_2PO_4^-$, SO_4^{2-}, and $H_2BO_3^-$ in at least some species.

It is quite likely that the multiple system is also widely distributed among algae, which usually have been studied without taking into account such a possibility. It appears to exist in the uptake of rubidium, and so probably of potassium, in *Chlorella* (Kannan 1971) and Nissen (1972), reanalyzing the results of Jeanjean, Blasco, and Gaudin (1970), concludes that this is true of phosphate uptake also.

Very careful work indicates at least in some cases that the low-affinity, high-concentration mechanism is actually complex, as a number of inflections may occur when plots of numerous good data are made. There has been much discussion as to whether the two mechanisms are situated in parallel in the plasmalemma, or whether the low-affinity, high-concentration mechanism is actually in the tonoplast, coming into action only when a sufficiently high concentration is built up in the cytoplasm.

In natural situations in inland waters only the high-affinity system, operating at low external concentrations, is likely to be of any significance.

Uptake of potassium by an aquatic angiosperm. Jeschke (1970) studied the uptake of potassium by shoots of *Egeria densa*, finding a typical multiple system. The uptake under all conditions of temperature and concentration is much greater in light than in darkness (Fig. 100). The temperature dependence differed somewhat, being greatest between 5.4 and 13°C in light but at higher than 13°C in darkness. In the regions of strongest temperature dependence, the activation energy was 32,000 cal mol^{-1} in the light and 28,000 cals mol^{-1} in darkness, perhaps implying identical rate limiting mechanisms. The rate of uptake of rubidium is somewhat less than that of potassium.

Uptake of phosphate and other anions by aquatic angiosperms. Gessner (1933) studied *Egeria densa* and *Cabomba australis*. The uptake of phosphorus in the former appears to have been independent of nitrate concentration, and it was also shown that in *C. australis* nitrate uptake was independent of phosphate concentration. At least in the latter plant the uptake of phosphorus was two or three times more rapid in water containing 100 mg SO$_4$ liter^{-1} than in water not containing sulfate; this is perhaps reminiscent of the effect of ammonium sulfate on chloride uptake by *Chara australis*. Light seems to have been slightly inhibitory, or (Gessner and Kaukal 1952) to have had no effect on phosphorus uptake.

Jeschke and Simonis (1965) also studied phosphate uptake as well as that of sulfate by *Egeria densa*. They found that the effect of light depended on both the temperature and the concentration of phosphate in the medium. The ratio of rate of uptake in light to rate in darkness was maximal at both 3.4°C (1.3) and 16°C (1.5), with lower values at intermediate temperatures, when the external concentration of phosphate was 10^{-4} M. As this concentration was reduced to 10^{-6} and 10^{-7} M the ratio also fell, so that at 16°C uptake was as fast in the dark as in the light, and at 3.4°C light actually inhibited uptake at these low concentrations. It is to be noted that such concentrations are in fact in the range to be expected in nature, where values of 10^{-6} M or 3.1 mg m^{-3} are common. Increasing the concentration above 10^{-4} M also reduces the effect of light, which is unimportant at 10^{-3} M. It is evident that as with the Characeae the effect of light is far less important in the uptake of phosphate than of potassium, and in fact under natural conditions is probably often negligible. Sulfate behaved like phosphate at 16°C, but at 3.4°C the effect of light was much greater in dilute solutions; at 10^{-6} M, light doubled the rate of uptake.

The heats of activation were maximal at intermediate concentrations at which the high-affinity mechanism is probably approximately saturated, being 15,800 ± 2800 cal mol^{-1} for phosphate and 24,800 ± 2800 cal mol^{-1} for sulfate. It is evident from all of this that the mechanisms for the uptake of these two ions show clear differences.

Normann (1967), working with *Ranunculus fluitans* over the range from 10 to 20°C, found a very low Q_{10}, not greater than 1.1, corresponding to an Arrhenius activation energy of less than 1000 cal mol^{-1}. At low concentrations of phosphate in the medium (<0.03 mM or 0.9 mg P. PO$_4$ liter^{-1}) the Q_{10} was higher, reaching about 1.3, which corresponds to an activation energy of the order of 5000 cal mol^{-1}, which is still very low. Normann concludes that no single system underlies the observed differences of rate throughout the whole concentration range employed. The temperature relations suggest the inherently reasonable conclusion that at high concentrations the rate is set by diffusion, but as the external concentration is reduced, ultimately becoming less than that of the interior of the cell, an active transport mechanism becomes increasingly important. These findings presumably suggest the type of multiple mechanism now well established in other plants.

There seem to be considerable differences in the capacity of different species to absorb phosphate from the water. Schwoerbel (1968) finds that *Callitriche intermedia* (sub *hamulata*) is much more effective in high (>1 mg P. PO$_4$ liter^{-1}) concentration than is *Ranunculus fluitans*, though at low concentrations the rate of uptake was about the same in each species. A difference at high concentrations might be important if plants are being used to remove excess nutrients from polluted streams or lakes. In *C. intermedia* the process is highly temperature dependent. Between 5 and 15°C the rate of uptake is essentially proportional to the temperature with $Q_{10} = 2.8$. At higher temperatures the rate of uptake increases less and less fast, the uptake being maximal at about 25°C and declining as higher temperatures are encountered. Between 10 and 20°C the apparent Q_{10} would be about 1.5. These experiments were done at high concentrations of phosphate, well over 1 mg P. PO_4 liter^{-1}. A good deal more work on many other species, primarily using the sort of external concentrations likely to occur in nature, would obviously provide interesting and probably ecologically significant results.

Uptake of nutrients from the sediments by rooted submersed plants. Though it was widely believed during the latter part of the last century that the roots of completely submersed water plants acted only as holdfasts, it is increasingly becoming apparent that a number of such plants obtain mineral nutrients from the sediments in which their roots are growing.

Pond (1905) did a series of experiments in which plants were rooted either in natural subaqueous sediments or in pure sand, or were suspended above such substrates in either lake water or tap water. In each experimental series 10 cuttings were used, the sediment employed was described as "suitable soil from the bed of a stream," and in the most quantitative experiments the water was Ann Arbor tap water. Pond's more complete results are summarized in Table 20.

It is evident that in *Potamogeton perfoliatus*, *Elodea canadensis*, and to some extent *Myriophyllum exalbescens*, the specimens rooted in the natural stream sediment did much better than the others. Comparable but less complete results were obtained for *Vallisneria americana* (sub *spiralis*), *Potamogeton obtusifolius*, and *Chara* sp. but, as would be expected, apparently not for the rootless *Ceratophyllum demersum*.

In the cases of *Myriophyllum exalbescens* and *Ranunculus trichophyllus*, rooting in sand is to some extent advantageous, for Pond indicates quite clearly that contact with sand promotes root growth in *R. trichophyllus* and implies that this is also true of *M. exalbescens*, though the green parts of the plant are not benefited in his experiments. In *R. trichophyllus*, though the main axis grew no better when rooted in soil than under the other conditions, numerous quite long lateral branches were produced on soil; their mean length is added to that of the main axis to give the figure in parentheses in Table 20.

Pond did an experiment using three different kinds of soil on which *Vallisneria americana* and *Chara* sp. were grown. The proximate compositions of the soils were as follows:

Mixture 1   Organic 6.50%, gravel 8.78%, sand (0.05–1 mm) 21.46%, silt 47.9%, clay 14.26%

Mixture 2   Organic 8.02%, gravel 0.84%, sand 34.22%, silt 47.56%, clay 8.05%.

Mixture 3   Organic 4.22%, gravel 1.54%, sand 26.42%, silt 36.10%, clay 31.04%.

TABLE 20. *Growth of various submersed water plants rooted in or suspended above soil or sand*

Species	Investigator	Experiment duration (days)	Growth rooted (cm)		Growth suspended (cm)	
			In soil	In sand	Over soil	Over sand
Potamogeton perfoliatus						
Mean length of rhizome formed	Pond	49	69.9	20.5	18.3	21.2
Mean length of secondary shoots formed	Pond	49	23.8	0.6	0.8	0.5
Groenlandia densa						
Mean length of shoot and side branches, the former originally 15 cm	Snell	40	459	129	102	90
Myriophyllum exalbescens (sub *spicatum*)						
Mean length, cutting originally 15 cm	Pond	31	67.8	35.0	46.3	39.8
Elodea canadensis						
Mean length, cutting originally 10 cm	Pond	31	154.2	38.4	35.0	33.6
Mean length including side branches, cutting originally 6 cm	Snell	28	30.8	17.8	11.4	11.4
Ranunculus trichophyllus						
Mean length, cutting originally 15 cm	Pond	61	53.6 (92.4)	31.3	56.7	33.7

277

Both plants grew best on mixture 1, a result to be expected in the case of *Vallisneria* which ordinarily grows on this kind of soil. *Chara*, however, at Put-in Bay on Lake Erie, where the experiments were done, tends to grow on a sandy sediment like mixture 2. Pond concludes that *Chara* is competitively excluded by *Vallisneria* from the best sites.

Essentially comparable results were obtained by Snell (1908) on *Groenlandia densa* and *Elodea canadensis*, using a soil composed apparently of a mixture of sand, loam, and humus, and Munich tap water. These results are also reported in the table. Snell found that in *Lemna minor* and *Spirodela polyrhiza* the roots had no nutritive function. Plants kept rootless by continual amputation grew as fast as unoperated controls. Snell considered, as some earlier authors also had done, that the roots of the Lemnaceae act solely as mechanical stabilizers. In *Pistia stratiotes* the root is an essential organ for uptake of water in the adult plant, in which the leaves are more or less emersed. Young plants with small leaves in contact with water, at least on their ventral sides, can use these leaves to obtain water and nutrients.

In striking contrast to the experiments of Pond and Snell on *Elodea canadensis*, Brown (1913) found that the difference in growth rates of this plant in the four kinds of culture supposedly copied from Pond and from Snell could be completely abolished by bubbling CO_2 intermittently through the cultures. Using a soil derived from the decomposition of granite, and supposedly of high inorganic nutrient and low organic content, Brown found without CO_2 no better growth than on sand. In this experiment the plants floating above the substratum did better than either of those rooted; Brown supposes this is due to the atmospheric supply of CO_2. It is evident that in Brown's experiments, in which an ordinary soft water from the vicinity of Baltimore was used, CO_2 limitation occurred readily; in some cases he records plants in his aquariums dying from lack of CO_2. It is therefore probable that his experiments are not comparable with those of Pond and of Snell; this is particularly likely to be true of a plant capable of using bicarbonate ions. An inadequate carbon source probably became limiting long before other materials were exhausted. Some CO_2 production from an organic soil would certainly have been advantageous in such a case, but Brown's work clearly does not invalidate that of his two predecessors. Bourne (1932) reinvestigated the matter and obtained results with *Potamogeton* and *Najas* comparable to those of Pond and Snell.

Roll (1939b) grew *Lobelia dortmanna*, *Littorella uniflora*, and *Isoetes lacustris* in natural sand from the Grosser Plöner See covered with hard water that had, during the course of the experiments, a rather complicated history. Ten good specimens of *Lobelia dortmanna* were planted in the middle of August; only two were surviving in really fine condition 2 months later.

Plants of *Isoetes lacustris* had survived throughout the period, and *Littorella* did less well than *Isoetes* though better than *Lobelia*. These experiments and the next investigation to be reported, along with information (e.g., Seddon 1965) about the distribution of *Isoetes*, strongly suggest that though *I. lacustris* and *L. dortmanna* are frequently associated in nature, the incidence of the latter species is more directly determined by chemical conditions, whereas that of the former is due to environmental regulation of the direction of competition.

Moyle (1945) did two series of experiments in which *Lobelia dortmanna* and *Ruppia maritima* were grown in the waters of five very different lakes in Minnesota, using in one series the natural lake sediment below its own water and in the other a clean natural silica sand. Six plants were rooted for each experiment. The results are summarized in Table 21.

Lobelia appears to be able to survive, but not to grow, rooted in clean sand in any water within the wide range studied. It could grow only on the low organic sand of Big Lake, and was evidently killed or severely inhibited by the extreme organic sediment of Farley Lake and by the sediments of the alkaline sulfate-rich prairie lakes, though not by their waters.

Ruppia did least well where *Lobelia* did best, and grew best, though with an unexplained low survival, in the two prairie lake waters when rooted in their own substrates. On the whole it withstood unfavorable conditions better than *Lobelia*. In both cases it seems likely that full development requires both the appropriate water and appropriate substrate. To establish this precisely, however, would involve more elaborate experiments in which the plant but not the ambient water could be influenced by the substrate. Nevertheless, Moyle's experiments are of great importance and suggest a whole field of interesting and significant research.

Lemna minor apparently grew well only on the water over the Dead Coon Lake mud, and showed no appreciable growth on any water over washed sand.

Mulligan and Baranowski (1969) have returned to this type of experiment, finding that *Myriophyllum exalbescens* rooted in sand produced only 12.1% of the growth exhibited by the plants rooted in soil. Mixtures of sand and soil gave intermediate results. Fertilization of the water over the sand with ammonium nitrate and calcium dihydrogen phosphate approximately doubled the growth, but it was still only a quarter of what is found on soil. The water employed seemed to have contained about 75 mg HCO_3^{-1} liter^{-1}; CO_2 limitation is therefore unlikely. Possibly iron or minor trace elements are involved.

Denny (1972c) conducted a number of experiments with Central African aquatic plants, set out in small artificial ponds on the bottoms of which plots of washed sand from Lake Victoria alternated with a synthetic nu-

TABLE 21. *Survival and growth of* Lobelia dortmanna *and* Ruppia maritima *on various sediments and in various Minnesota lake waters (Moyle)*

		HCO$_3^-$ (mg liter^{-1})	SO$_4^{2-}$ (mg liter^{-1})	pH	Solid phase	Lobelia dortmanna			Ruppia maritima		
						Survivors after 11 weeks	Increase in wt wt (g[a])	Length root (cm)	Survivors after 11 weeks	Increase in wet wt (g[a])	Length root (cm)
Lake and type of sediment	Water										
Big Lake, Carlton Co., low organic red sand	Clear	24	2	7.2	Lake sediment	6	0.09	9.0	5	−0.03	1.5
					Clean sand	6	−0.02	7.0	6	0.04	0.5
Farley Lake, Itasca Co., semifluid organic sediment	Brown	65	2	6.8	Lake sediment	0	—	—	5	0.20	3.7
					Clean sand	6	0.0	7.0	6	0.17	3.7

280

Location					Substrate						
Snail Lake, Ramsay Co., calcareous sand with organic matter	Clear	198	5	8.7	Lake sediment	5	−0.17	1.7	5	0.17	4.0
					Clean sand	6	−0.09	4.4	6	0.50	4.3
Dead Coon Lake, Lincoln Co., black organic alkaline sediment	?	235	216	8.8	Lake sediment	0	—	—	1	1.29	4.0
					Clean sand	6	−0.23	2.0	4	0.10	1.8
Big Stone Lake, Big Stone Co., calcareous organic sand	?	204	318	8.6	Lake sediment	2	−0.09	1.5	4	0.63	4.8
					Clean sand	6	−0.19	0.6	6	0.05	5.4

[a] Given in the original as cms., presumably in error.

281

trient-rich mud made of equal volumes of sand, horticultural soil, and sieved leaf mold. The plants were grown from small cuttings set in the two substrata. Some upward diffusion of nutrients from the synthetic mud must have occurred, with subsequent quite incomplete lateral mixing, for the rootless *Ceratophyllum demersum* over mud produced a mean crop just over twice that produced over sand. The mean rate of growth of the plants up to the time of harvest is given in Table 22. As can be seen from the table there is great variation in the effect of a richly nutrient sediment, the origin of which variation is not entirely clear. The high dependence of *Hydrilla* on its relatively small root system is curious.

TABLE 22. *Growth rates of various African plants set over or in nutritious mud or clean sand (Denny)*

Species	Growth rate (mg plant^{-1} day^{-1})		Ratio of growth rates, mud:sand
	On mud	On sand	
Ceratophyllum demersum	9.5	4.6	2.1
Potamogeton schweinfurthii	43.1	15.8	2.7
P. × bunyonyiensis	26.5	8.9	3.0
P. thunbergii	63.3	16.7	3.8
Vallisneria aethiopica	33.1	7.1	4.6
Hydrilla verticillata	81.5	11.0	7.4

Within the three taxa of *Potamogeton* the picture is fairly clear and most instructive (Table 23). *P. thunbergii* with cutinized coriaceous floating leaves is obviously more dependent on the substratum than is the fully submersed *P. schweinfurthii* with its ribbonlike leaves with feebly developed cutinization, if any at all. The difference between the two species is clearly indicated in the growth of the shoot, but hardly at all by that of the root, as may be seen by comparing column 6 with column 4. The hybrid between the two species, with both coriaceous and uncutinized leaves, is in general intermediate between its parents though variable in both form and physiology. The taxa studied are said to have had more penetrating roots, with more root hairs, when growing on sand than on mud.

Denny's work clearly confirms the conclusion of earlier investigators that both the sediments and the water can supply nutrients. The relative quantities entering from these two sources clearly depend largely on the species of plants under consideration. Within a limited taxocene there is a

TABLE 23. *Growth of shoot and root in relation to substratum in the three taxa of Potamogeton used by Denny*

1	2	3	4	5	6	7	8	9	10	11	12
	Mean growth rate of shoot (mg plant^{-1} day^{-1})			Mean growth rate of root (mg plant^{-1} day^{-1})						% Root in plant at harvest	
Taxon	On mud	On sand	Ratio 2:3	On mud	On sand	Ratio 5:6	Ratio 5:2	Ratio 6:3	Ratio 9:8	Mud	Sand
P. schweinfurthii	37.6	12.3	3.1	5.5	3.5	1.6	0.15	0.29	2.0	12.0	17.6
P. × *bunyonyiensis*	23.4	6.7	3.5	2.8	2.3	1.2	0.12	0.37	3.1	10.7	17.2
P. thunbergii	59.7	10.7	5.6	3.6	6.0	1.7	0.06	0.56	9.3	5.2	25.4

reasonable relationship between structure and function with respect to the uptake. One would moreover expect the vittate plants of eutrophic lakes to depend more on the nutrient supply of the water and the rosulate plants of oligotrophic lakes on that of the sediment. It is, however, also clear that in a comparison of fairly diverse plants such as *Vallisneria*, *Hydrilla*, and fully submersed species of *Potamogeton* such as *P. schweinfurthii*, there may be large unexplained differences between what is expected and what is actually found.

Further insight into the nutritive role of the root in water plants has come from the more analytical approach of Bristow and Whitcombe (1971), who studied the uptake of phosphorus in *Egeria densa*, *Myrioplyllum exalbescens*, and *M. aquaticum* (sub *brasiliense*). The plants were grown in Erlenmeyer flasks with funnels, the stems being led up from the flask through the short tube of the funnel at the top of which tube the stem of the plant was embedded in an inert plastic plug. Above this the upper part of the plant grew in the aqueous solution placed in the funnel. Phosphate containing ^{32}P could be introduced into the solution surrounding the roots in the lower compartment or flask, or into that surrounding the shoots in the upper compartment or funnel.

In short-term experiments lasting 6 hr, removal of roots reduced the uptake of radiophosphorus from the lower compartment and its translocation into the part of the plant in the upper compartment by 33% in *M. exalbescens*, by 88% in *E. densa*, and by 98% in *M. aquaticum*.

In experiments lasting 10 days the roots always took up more radiophosphorus from the solution in the lower compartment than did equivalent amounts of shoots when the radiophosphorus was put in the upper compartment. In *M. aquaticum*, four and a half to six times as much radiophosphorus was translocated into the shoot from the root when the latter was treated with the radioisotope than was absorbed when the isotope was added to the upper compartment. In the other two species the shoot obtained considerable amounts of phosphorus from the root by translocation but not more than it could obtain by direct uptake.

In one experiment with *M. aquaticum* in which roots were very well developed, 90% of the phosphorus found in the axillary shoots that grew out of the upper part of the plant during the 10-day experiment was derived by translocation from the roots, though in the other two species the proportion was only about 20%. It is evident that the two species of *Myriophyllum* studied differ in their capacity to take up phosphorus through the roots and transport it upward. Bristow and Whitcombe reasonably correlate this with the vascular system being less reduced in *M. aquaticum* than in *M. exalbescens*.

There was no evidence of translocation downward from the shoot when the latter was supplied with radiophosphorus. Such basipetal movement is, however, well established for *Zostera* (McRoy and Barsdate 1970) and has more recently been found in other experiments with *Myriophyllum exalbescens* (De Marte and Hartman 1974).

Bristow and Whitcombe, in experiments not reported in detail, found that the rate of upward movement of phosphorus in *Egeria densa* is not dependent on the concentration of phosphate in the water surrounding the shoot into which the element is being translocated. They also found that the shoot of *M. aquaticum* could continue to grow when immersed in distilled water in the upper compartment, provided the root in the lower compartment was surrounded by a nutrient solution. Evidently all essential nutrients may, like phosphorus, enter by the roots and then be translocated acropetally. De Marte and Hartman (1974) found that both iron and calcium behaved in this way though less actively than phosphorus. These investigators also found that some of the phosphorus coming from the roots into the leaves of *Myriophyllum* was lost to the water, becoming available to other plants such as *Elodea* growing juxtaposed to the *Myriophyllum*. This effect was greatly enhanced by injury to the donor plant, as by removal of leaves or buds in much the way that might result from the feeding of an herbivorous fish. The net result would certainly be an acceleration of the rate of the lacustrine phosphorus cycle.

Nutrient uptake by carnivorous plants. A third source of nutrients, in addition to the sediments and the water, is exploited by the few aquatic carnivorous plants belonging to *Utricularia* and *Aldrovanda*. At least in *Utricularia exoleta* growing autotrophically (Pringsheim and Pringsheim 1962; Harder 1963) animal matter, which in experiments may be in solution, must be added if flowering is to occur. Lollar, Coleman, and Boyd (1971) found that radiophosphorus introduced into *Cypridopsis* sp., which was fed to *Utricularia inflata*, appeared later in the plant. Since in the experiments on *U. exoleta* the phosphorus content in the medium was more than 4 mg P liter^{-1}, it is clear that an animal source of this element is not involved in the production of flowers. In oligotrophic waters it is quite likely that the animals caught in the traps of aquatic carnivorous plants are a significant source not only of phosphorus but of nitrogen and perhaps some minor elements (cf. p. 292).

ELEMENTARY CHEMICAL COMPOSITION OF AQUATIC ANGIOSPERMS

Data have been obtained on the elementary composition of freshwater angiosperms, partly as the result of purely limnological studies (Schuette and Hoffman 1921; Birge and Juday 1922; Schuette and Alder 1927, 1929a; Harper and Daniel 1934; Lawrence 1968, 1971; Bernatowitz 1969; Petkova and Lubyanov 1969; Boyd 1970a; Varenko and Chuiko 1971; Cowgill[1] 1973a, b, 1974a, b), and partly in relation to the consumption of such plants by wild (Botkin, Jordan, Dominski, Lowendorf, and Hutchinson 1973) or domestic mammals (Nelson and Palmer 1938; Riemer and Toth 1968, 1969, 1970; Lancaster, Coup, and Hughes 1971). Estimates of the mean contents of a number of elements in aquatic plants have been prepared by Denton (unpublished M.S. thesis 1965), partly from the literature and partly from his own analyses; these means have been published by Guadet (1973). Some of the work was stimulated by a desire to find a use for excess aquatic plants. It may be noted that such a use as fodder (Sculthorpe 1967; cf. also Boyd 1972) is traditional in various parts of the world, as in the Vale of Kashmir. Part of the information obtained in the applied investigations is of considerable ecological and botanical interest, though hitherto no adequate attempts to analyze these data have been made.

In this section the available information is summarized, using broad chemical categories of a conventional kind. However, nitrogen and phosphorus, the concentrations of which in plants may give important information as to nutrient limitation, are treated separately, at the end of the discussion of the other elements. A few data are added on organic compounds in water plants, a subject about which little is known.

Some additional information has been published by Adams, Cole, and Massie (1973). Unfortunately for several important elements their data are limited by the technique employed to the lower part of the range, and all the data are presented in a way that makes interpretation difficult. Their results, however, do seem to confirm some of the conclusions of this chapter.

Water and ash content.   Straškraba (1968) has summarized the available determinations of water content in fresh aquatic plants. The quantities are

---

[1] Dr. Cowgill most generously permitted me to use all the data that she had obtained in 1971 from her study of the water plants of Linsley Pond, Connecticut, in the preparation of this account, prior to the publication of these very important papers. When my tables are compared with hers it should be borne in mind that her ranges refer to the analyses of individual samples, and mine to the mean analyses of individual species, which were again averaged to give a mean content for any element in the plants of a particular body of water or area. Arguments for either usage could be made; the differences in procedure change nothing of the general conclusions that may be drawn. A mean of Cowgill's means for Linsley Pond 1971, Linsley Pond 1972, and Cedar Lake 1971 has been given in all appropriate tables after the 1971 mean based on my procedure. Some 1972 data for Linsley Pond plants have been used in special tables on the distribution of elements in different parts of water lilies; when mean analyses are specifically credited to Cowgill 1973a or 1973b, they are means of the Linsley 1971 and 1972 and Cedar Lake 1971 averages, as given in her tables.

very variable, but average less in emergent species, with a mean of 79%, than in floating-leaved, with a mean of 82%, or in submersed species, with a mean of 88%. Very roughly, for the fully submersed species, an estimate of 10% dry matter in the fresh plant is reasonable. The dry matter appears to contain more ash in the submersed species, namely, a mean value of 21%, than in the floating-leaved, with a mean of 16%, or in the emergent species, with 12%.

The alkalies.   Most of the available analyses naturally relate to sodium and potassium (Table 24), which, though evidently playing very different roles, are most conveniently considered before the small amount of information about lithium and the two rare heavy alkalies is summarized.

Potassium.   Potassium is ordinarily though not universally the more abundant of the two common alkalies in plant tissues. The lowest mean concentration for any aquatic species in a regional collection is 0.39% dry[2] in *Typha latifolia* from Lake Warniak in the Masurian lake district of northeast Poland (Bernatowicz 1969). Lawrence (1971) found the lowest mean value for a submersed species, namely, 0.62% in *Myriophyllum* cf. *spicatum*[3] from Lake Seminole, but elsewhere the plant may have more than twice this concentration; the New Jersey material studied by Riemer and Toth (1968) gave a range of 1.20–2.10% with a mean value of 1.68%. The lowest mean value for a New Jersey species studied by the last-named authors was 0.89% for five samples of *Phragmites australis*.[4] The latter species contained only 0.42% in Lake Warniak, whereas *Schoenoplectus lacustris* had 0.48%. Boyd (1970a) in South Carolina found the mean of five samples of *Juncus effusus* to be 0.89%. It is interesting that *Typha latifolia*, which in Poland contained so little potassium and which is roughly equivalent ecologically to *Phragmites australis*, should in New Jersey have been much richer (2.98% K) in potassium than is the latter plant, though their low sodium contents, of 0.11% and 0.10%, respectively, are comparable (Riemer and Toth 1968). In spite of obvious exceptions the junciform emergent plants evidently tend to be low in potassium. High values are consistently found in *Heteranthera* (mean *H. dubia* 5.03%) and commonly in *Vallisneria*, *Ceratophyllum*, and some of the Lemnaceae. The greatest recorded concentration appears to be 6.58% in *Elodea canadensis* from Lake Warniak (Bernatowicz 1969).

There seems to be, at least when Riemer and Toth's data are studied statistically, a slight but significant correlation (0.2933, $P < 0.01$) between

---

[2] All determinations quoted in this chapter refer to dry matter unless otherwise stated.
[3] See p. 251.
[4] Not all specimens were growing in water.

TABLE 24. *Distribution of potassium and sodium in aquatic angiosperms and in some terrestrial collections*

Study	K (%) Range[a]	K (%) Mean	Na (%) Range[a]	Na (%) Mean
Aquatic				
Florida, Georgia, Alabama: 14 spp. (Lawrence)	0.62–4.09	1.98	0.13–1.50	0.37
South Carolina: 18 spp. (Boyd)	0.89–4.04	2.26	0.12–1.87	0.72
New Jersey: 37 spp. (Riemer and Toth)	0.89–5.75	2.92	0.06–2.60	0.56
Connecticut: 6 spp. (Cowgill)	1.74–3.52	2.30 (2.46)[b]	0.13–1.56	0.81 (1.08)[b]
Isle Royale, L. Superior: 6 spp., submerged or floating (Botkin, Jordan, Dominski, Lowendorf and Hutchinson)	—	—	0.353–0.938	0.65
Isle Royale, L. Superior: 14 spp., emergent (Botkin, Jordan, Dominski, Lowendorf, and Hutchinson)	—	—	0.0002–0.171	0.055
Lake Warniak, Poland: 16 spp. (Bernatowicz)	0.39–6.58	2.24	—	—
Rotorua dist., New Zealand: 3 spp. (Lancaster, Coup, and Hughes)	2.52–5.91	3.85	0.68–0.97	0.87
Mean of the above	—	2.59	—	0.66[c]
Mean for water plants (Denton)	—	2.48	—	0.56
Terrestrial				
Maryland: 26 spp. (Robinson, Steinkoenig, and Miller)	0.25–7.19	2.21	0.01–0.47	0.10
Isle Royale: 9 spp., woody plants (Botkin, Jordan, Dominski, Lowendorf, and Hutchinson)	—	—	0.0003–0.0028	0.0012
Northwestern Europe, 36 samples mainly cultivated (Baumeister)	—	3.07	—	0.24
Polish Gramineae and Fabaceae (Klapp, see Bernatowicz)	—	0.88	—	—
Mean for terrestrial vegetation (Bowen)	—	1.2	—	0.12

[a] Range of means for individual species, as in all later tables of this form.

[b] In parentheses, mean of Cowgill's (1973b) means for Linsley Pond 1971, Linsley Pond 1972, and Cedar Lake 1971, weighted equally, as in all later tables of this form (see p. 286, footnote 1).

[c] Botkin, Jordan, Dominski, Lowendorf, and Hutchinson's emergent species, which are clearly largely amphibious, are not included; inclusion of these analyses would lower the overall mean to 0.58% dry.

the potassium content of the plant and that of the water in which it is growing. The overall mean potassium content of aquatic angiosperms based on the material in the table is very little higher than that which can be obtained from the data of Robinson, Steinkoenig, and Miller (1917) for land plants; Bowen's (1966) estimated mean for terrestrial vegetation, namely, 1.4%, is considerably lower, though the mean given by Baumeister (1960) is distinctly higher; Bernatowicz concluded that his Polish water plants are usually richer in potassium than are herbaceous plants from Polish meadows, analyzed by Klapp (1962).

Sodium.   The sodium contents are more variable than the potassium and are nearly always lower. Statistical study of Riemer and Toth's data shows no significant correlation (-0.1730) between the two elements in the plant nor between the sodium in the plant and that in the ambient water (0.0185).

The functional significance of sodium is problematic in the majority of the higher plants. It has recently been found that the element is an essential minor nutrient for a considerable number of species having the C_4 dicarboxylic acid pathway in photosynthesis (Brownell and Crossland 1972). Certain hygrophytes such as *Saccharum officinarum* and some, but not all, species of *Cyperus* are in this category, but it is most improbable that fully submersed plants would belong here. Sodium appears to be of importance in photosynthesis in *Najas*, a plant not having the C_4 pathway (Wetzel 1969a) (see pp. 153, 390).

It is evident that in most aquatic species there is a characteristic and fairly narrow range of sodium contents. This is strikingly demonstrated by the data collected in Figure 101. The very high sodium content (mean 2.60%) of *Cabomba caroliniana* is evident in the figure, even though the plants were living in waters containing about the same amounts of alkali metals (Na 4.5–13.5 mg liter^{-1}, K 0.4–3.1 mg liter^{-1}) as those (Na 4.8–10.0 mg liter^{-1}, K 0.6–3.8 mg liter^{-1}) in which the allied *Brasenia schreberi*, containing much less sodium (mean 0.66%), was growing. Similarly, the two species of *Myriophyllum*, *M. heterophyllum*, and *M.* cf. *spicatum*, are almost completely separated by their sodium contents.

In some groups of plants the specificity of the sodium content is less marked than in others. *Nuphar advena*, which can be very low in sodium, certainly often contains less than do the species of *Nymphaea*, but in both genera there is much wider variation than in *C. caroliniana*, *B. schreberi*, or the species of *Myriophyllum*.

Inadequate attention has been given to the distribution of the alkalies within the plant. Lawrence has found more (Na 1.07%, K 4.24%) of both metals in the shoot than in the root (Na 0.77%, K 1.47%) of *Vallisneria*

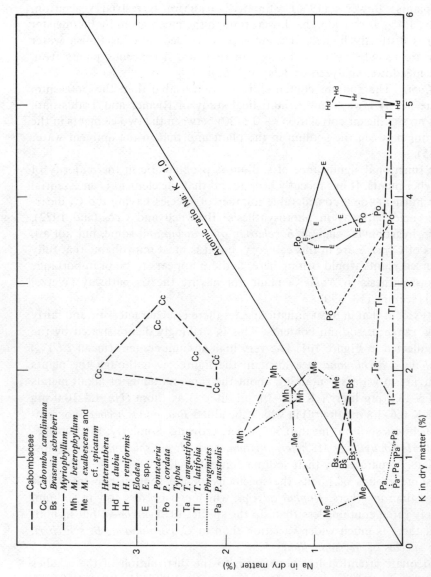

FIGURE 101. Relationship of sodium and potassium concentrations in dry matter of those water plants for which several analyses exist.

TABLE 25. *Distribution of sodium, potassium, and chlorine in various parts of the Nymphaeaceae (Riemer and Toth 1968; Cowgill 1973b, 1974a)*

Study	Na (%)				K (%)				Cl (%)			
	Leaf petiole	Leaf	Flower stalk	Flower	Leaf petiole	Leaf	Flower stalk	Flower	Leaf petiole	Leaf	Flower stalk	Flower
Nuphar advena												
New Jersey	0.04	0.01	—	—[a]	3.00	1.97	—	—[b]	2.02	1.11	—	—[c]
(Riemer and Toth)	0.11	0.07	—	—	5.37	2.15	—	—	4.42	1.33	—	—
	0.33	0.06	—	—	2.20	1.35	—	—	1.88	1.00	—	—
Connecticut	1.86	0.88	1.11	0.22	2.90	2.50	2.74	2.68	1.75	1.37	2.90	0.53
(Cowgill)	1.65	0.41	0.93	0.72	1.71	1.39	2.91	2.49	1.26	0.68	2.26	0.62
Nymphaea odorata												
New Jersey	0.92	0.60	—	—	2.80	1.50	—	—	2.11	1.33	—	—
(Riemer and Toth)	1.09	0.70	—	—	2.82	0.90	—	—	2.96	1.14	—	—
	1.50	0.70	—	—	3.60	1.50	—	—	4.08	1.18	—	—
Connecticut (Cowgill)												
1971	2.15	1.12	1.60	0.40	1.11	1.08	1.72	2.33	1.49	0.69	1.99	1.03
1971	3.63	0.21	3.00	0.36	1.96	1.42	1.84	2.43	4.06	1.59	2.76	1.47
1972	2.82	0.32	3.17	0.26	2.59	2.24	2.86	3.25	3.19	1.36	2.88	1.42
N. tuberosa												
New Jersey	1.00	0.52	—	—	2.97	1.05	—	—	2.75	0.96	—	—
(Riemer and Toth)	0.86	0.50	—	—	3.27	1.55	—	—	2.70	1.04	—	—
	1.50	0.86	—	—	2.10	0.80	—	—	3.04	1.09	—	—

[a] Rhizome 0.10% Na.
[b] Rhizome 3.10% K.
[c] Rhizome 2.04% Cl.

291

americana; two analyses showed the reverse pattern for sodium in *Eichhornia crassipes* but the results for potassium were inconsistent. Far too few analyses, in fact, exist to permit any conclusions save in the Nymphaeaceae (Table 25), where the petioles always contain more, often very much more, than do the leaves that they bear. It is possible that some of the irregularities that are observed within any collection of data are due to differences in the age of the material studied. No very obvious correlation with taxonomic position is apparent, but *Phragmites australis*, consistently deficient in both elements (mean Na 0.10%, K 0.89%, Riemer and Toth 1968), is a member of the Gramineae, which appear in general to be a little poorer in potassium and much poorer in sodium than the average angiosperm (see, for instance, Robinson, Steinkoenig, and Miller 1917).

Comparison of the sodium contents of land and freshwater plants.   Botkin, Jordan, Dominski, Lowendorf, and Hutchinson (1973), working on material from Isle Royale in Lake Superior, give data on a number of emergent species and of more or less amphibious hygrophytes. They found that these plants contained less sodium than the fully aquatic species which they studied. The generally higher sodium content of aquatic as opposed to terrestrial plants, noted originally for *Vallisneria* by Nelson and Palmer (1938) and very apparent when the data of other more recent workers are compared with those of Robinson, Steinkoenig, and Miller (1917) for land plants, is fully confirmed and much extended by this investigation. They found as little as 2 ppm or 0.0002% Na in the hygrophytic grass *Calamagrostis canadensis*; *Iris versicolor* contained 28 ppm or 0.0028%, and *Juncus gerardii* 44 ppm. In a group of *Carex* spp., in *Potentilla palustris*, *Polygonum* sp., and *Menyanthes trifoliata* values from 0.022 to 0.089% were found; *Calla palustris* with 0.17% approached more nearly, in its sodium content, the obligate water plants. In the six fully aquatic species studied, *Callitriche* sp., *Myriophyllum tenellum*, *Nuphar* sp., *Potamogeton gramineus*, *P. richardsonii*, and *Utricularia vulgaris*, the sodium content was always over 0.35%. In the last-named plant, which contained no less than 0.805% of the element, the sodium must have been ultimately derived from the water, the content implying a concentration factor of about 500. Miss Susan R. Craig (verbal communication) suggests that part of this very large quantity may have been derived from ingested zooplankton.

Part of the difference between the emergent and fully aquatic species may be due to taxonomic differences such as the prevalence of Cyperaceae in the former group, but this is clearly not the whole explanation. Taking all the data together, it seems clear that aquatic life, even in freshwaters containing little of the element, predisposes angiosperms to high sodium contents.

By comparing the theoretical Nernst potentials set up by the differences of concentration of sodium, potassium, magnesium, and calcium on the one hand and chloride, sulfate, and phosphate (HPO_4^{2-} + $H_2PO_4^-$) on the other, in the medium and in the cells of leaves of *Potamogeton schweinfurthii*, Denny and Weeks (1968) concluded that the anions are actively taken up by the leaf but that the cations are probably lost to the water. This obviously implies some other source of cations for the whole plant.

Using a comparable experimental approach, Shepherd and Bowling (1973) found evidence of active accumulation of potassium and to a less marked but quite definite degree of sodium also, but not certainly magnesium and calcium, by the roots of two swamp or eulittoral plants (*Equisetum palustre, Ranunculus flammula*) and of three floating-leaved or emergent aquatic species (*Potamogeton natans, Menyanthes trifoliata*, and *Equisetum fluviatile*). In all cases there is evidence suggesting uptake of potassium, sodium, chloride, and nitrate, but not of calcium or magnesium. These findings, taken with those of Denny and Weeks, suggest a movement of alkali metals from the root or rhizome upward into the leaves.

There is good evidence that at least in some land plants, such as *Phaseolus* (Jacoby 1965) and *Helianthus* (Bowling and Ansari 1972), sodium may likewise be taken up actively by the root, but stored there or in the lower part of the stem rather than being translocated to the upper region of the stem and the leaves. In *Helianthus* the element is apparently also pumped from the xylem sap into the root tissue. It is possible that at least the fully submerged water plants have dispensed with the mechanism by which this separation is achieved, though it may be indicated in the distribution of sodium in the petiole and leaf of the water lilies (Table 25). It has recently been suggested by Arms, Feeny, and Lederhouse (1974) that the low concentration of sodium in the exposed parts of terrestrial plants is an adaptation, reducing the nutrient value of the plant to phytophagous insects, which often seem to suffer from extreme sodium deficiency. There are far fewer phytophagous insects in fresh water than on land and many of the herbivorous animals found on water plants doubtless eat mainly epiphytic algae, so that in lakes and streams, the kind of selection involved in producing the adaptation may be relatively unimportant.

The rather general high sodium contents of water plants may, however, make them, as Botkin, Jordan, Dominski, Lowendorf, and Hutchinson (1973) point out, important occasional sources of sodium for any herbivorous animal that has access to these plants as food.

Lithium. Of the rarer alkalies, the analyses of Cowgill seem to constitute the only significant collection (Table 26). She found that the mean lithium contents for five of the species studied in Connecticut in 1971 lay between 0.22 ppm for *Decodon verticillatus* and 0.28 ppm for *Potamogeton* cf. *praelongus*, with a mean for the five species of 0.24 ppm. The range for individual samples varied from 0.11 ppm in a sample of the leaves of *D. verticillatus* to 0.33 ppm in one of the leaves of *Nuphar advena*. The mean of 0.1 ppm for terrestrial vegetation (Bowen 1966) is of the same order of magnitude. In contrast to these figures *Pontederia cordata* accumulates lithium in its leaves, which in two different samples contained 4.2 ppm dry, though the rest of the plant had about the same amount as the other species analyzed. If this species is included, the overall mean becomes 0.45 ppm, or using also 1972 data, computed according to Cowgill's method, 0.50 ppm. The ratio of the mean lithium to the mean sodium contents for 1971 of all plants in the Linsley Basin except *P. cordata* is 3.0×10^{-5}, whereas for the leaves of the latter plant it is 3.7×10^{-4}. In the rocks and soils of the basin it is 3.2×10^{-4}, so that relative to the sodium of the ultimate source material all plants save the leaves of *Pontederia* are excluding lithium.

TABLE 26. *Distribution of lithium* (*ppm*) *in Nymphaeaceae and in* Pontederia (*Cowgill*)

Study	Leaf petiole	Leaf	Flower stalk	Flower
Nymphaea odorata				
Cedar Lake 1971	0.17	0.29	0.23	0.27
Linsley Pond 1971	0.16	0.27	0.23	0.27
Linsley Pond 1972	0.15	0.30	0.15	0.20
Nuphar advena				
Cedar Lake	0.29	0.33	0.27	0.30
Linsley Pond	0.19	0.25	0.20	0.26
Pontederia cordata				
Cedar Lake	—	4.19	0.34	0.24
Linsley Pond	—	4.20	0.31	0.25

Rubidium and cesium. These elements were determined by Cowgill (1974a) in the same plants and from the same localities as the other alkalies and many other elements. The ranges of her analyses, averaged for each species, and the overall means are given in Table 27, from which it may be seen that the range of interspecific variation is not great. The quantities found are of the same order of magnitude as in terrestrial vegetation.

TABLE 27.   *Rubidium and cesium in plants of Cedar Lake and Linsley Pond* (*Cowgill*)

Study	Rubidium (ppm)		Cesium (ppm)	
	Range	Mean	Range	Mean
Cedar Lake 1971	17.1–27.3	22.9	0.50–0.72	0.61
Linsley Pond 1971	15.2–26.7	20.8	0.36–0.71	0.53
Overall mean	—	21.9	—	0.57
		(24.3)		
Terrestrial vegetation (Bowen)	—	20	—	0.20

Cesium has been determined in material from a Polish fishpond by Włodek, Bysiek, and Grzybowska (1970) who analyzed *Phragmites australis*, containing 0.0069 ppm Cs wet, and *Elodea canadensis* containing 0.085 ppm Cs wet. These values, if converted to dry weight, would be about 0.03 ppm and 1.1 ppm, with a mean of about 0.6 ppm. Though the range is greater, the Polish figures embrace those of Cowgill; the practical identity of the means is of course fortuitous. Of the six species analyzed by Cowgill, *Decodon verticillatus* with a mean content of 0.72 ppm Cs contains consistently a little more cesium than do the other five; no such slight enrichment is exhibited by rubidium.

In the various parts of water lilies the rubidium is more evenly distributed than is the potassium (Tables 25 and 28), and there is in general little correlation between the two elements when the various analyses of water plants are compared.

In the source materials of the Linsley basin the ratios (Table 29, Fig. 102) Rb:K and Cs:K do not depart greatly from the ratios of the mean concentrations in the accessible lithosphere. There is some enrichment of rubidium relative to potassium in the waters of Linsley Pond and Cedar Lake (Cowgill 1970) when comparison is made with the rocks and soils of the basin. In the plants, however, the ratios are always lower than in the source materials, suggesting that rubidium is to some extent excluded from the plant and so perhaps accumulates in the water. This is of interest as it is often supposed (e.g., Läuchli and Epstein 1970, who give a useful review) that under normal conditions, with adequate calcium, rubidium is taken up by plants very much as if it were potassium.

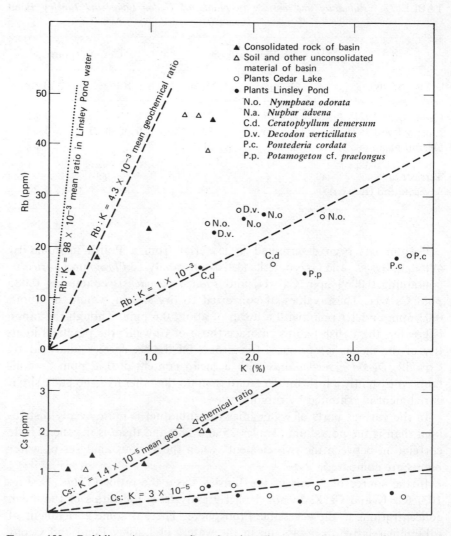

FIGURE 102. Rubidium (upper panel) and cesium (lower panel) concentrations plotted against potassium concentrations in source materials and in the water plants of Linsley Pond and Cedar Lake, North Branford, Conn. Note that both elements are excluded relative to potassium, though rubidium appears to be concentrated in the water.

TABLE 28. *Distribution of rubidium and cesium in the various parts of* Nymphaea *and* Nuphar *(Cowgill)*

Study	Rubidium (ppm)				Cesium (ppm)			
	Leaf petiole	Leaf	Flower stalk	Flower	Leaf petiole	Leaf	Flower stalk	Flower
Nymphaea odorata								
Cedar Lake	23.7	21.9	23.1	31.1	0.67	0.75	0.54	0.64
Linsley Pond	24.7	24.2	25.1	29.0	0.46	0.67	0.48	0.58
Nuphar advena								
Cedar Lake	26.2	24.6	24.8	30.4	0.60	0.63	0.67	0.68
Linsley Pond	23.6	22.7	29.2	31.4	0.62	0.66	0.58	0.69

TABLE 29. *Contents of potassium, rubidium, and cesium and ratios of rubidium and cesium to potassium (mainly based on Cogwill 1974a)*

Study	K (ppm)	Rb (ppm)	Cs (ppm)	Ratio Rb:K	Ratio Cs:K
Mean accessible lithosphere (Taylor 1964)	20,900	90	3	4.3×10^{-3}	1.4×10^{-4}
Source materials Linsley Basin	10,000	31.6	1.7	3.2×10^{-3}	1.7×10^{-4}
Surface water Linsley Pond (mean)	0.97	0.009	—	9.3×10^{-3}	—
Aquatic plants, Linsley Pond and Cedar Lake	23,000	21.9	0.57	0.95×10^{-3}	0.25×10^{-4}

Alkaline earths. Magnesium is a major nutrient element in all green plants, being an essential constituent of chlorophyll. Calcium is much less well understood physiologically. Ecologically it may be regarded as of greatest importance as a scenopoetic or stage-setting element, directly or indirectly regulating the occurrence of calcicole or calcifuge species by its high or low concentration. It is, however, certainly involved in the activation of certain enzymes in plants and is quite probably essential in maintaining the integrity of cell membranes and controlling permeability in plants as well as in animals.

Of the three other stable alkaline earths, beryllium is rather peculiar in its geochemistry, following the hydrolysate elements such as aluminum.

Strontium and particularly barium are proportionately somewhat more enriched in the more acidic rocks of the continents, but otherwise behave very similarly to calcium. These rarer alkaline earths are conveniently treated after the more abundant ones have been considered.

Magnesium. The ranges for the mean contents of individual species, and the overall means derived from these, are summarized in Table 30 for the same five sets of modern analyses as were used for the alkalies.

Boyd's analyses are on plants from a very dilute water containing 1.04 mg liter^{-1} Mg and 2.64 mg liter^{-1} Ca; nearly all of Riemer and Toth's plants and all those studied by Cowgill came from waters containing more of both alkaline earths than this. Both Riemer and Toth and Cowgill found that *Ceratophyllum demersum* contains more magnesium than any other water plant analyzed, individual specimens in New Jersey and Connecticut being found to contain as much as 1.09% and 1.14%, respectively. Moreover, in the older analyses of Nelson and Palmer (1938) one of their specimens of this plant from Minnesota contained 1.49% Mg, though their other specimen with 0.83% is overlapped by some examples of *Potamogeton amplifolius* and *Najas flexilis*. Boyd, studying plants from a locality containing much less magnesium, found *C. demersum* to be relatively rich in the element, compared with his other species, the mean content being 0.41%, just exceeded (0.47%) by *Najas guadalupensis* and by *Hydrocotyle* sp.; 14 additional species had mean contents of less than 0.4%. In the Rotorua district of New Zealand, Lancaster, Coup, and Hughes found more magnesium in *C. demersum* than in two other species analyzed. Presumably the high concentrations in *C. demersum* from New Jersey and Connecticut represent luxury consumption, as they are more than twice the mean concentration found by Boyd, or by the New Zealand investigators.

Riemer and Toth found *Najas* sp. to have the next highest mean (0.61% dry) after *C. demersum*, and Lawrence, who did not analyze *Ceratophyllum*, found a maximum of 1% Mg dry in *Najas minor* with 1.28% Ca; his analyses of *Hydrocotyle*, giving a mean of 0.25% dry, are not specially high. His minima were 0.075% in *Potamogeton crispus* with 3.81% Ca and 0.08% in *Bacopa* sp. with 4.46% Ca, both calcium contents being high for his waters. Schuette and Alder (1929a) found 1.21% Mg dry in *Najas flexilis* in Wisconsin, while Nelson and Palmer record 0.77–0.96% dry in the same species in Minnesota. It is evident that both *Ceratophyllum demersum* and *Najas* spp. tend to be higher in magnesium than the other water plants associated with them. None of the published analyses of *C. demersum* indicate large quantities of calcium, the highest being 4.47 in Minnesota (Nelson and Palmer 1938), whereas *Najas* may, though does not always, accumulate massive amounts of that element.

TABLE 30. *Magnesium, calcium, and strontium in various collections of water plants*

Study	Mg (%)		Ca (%)		Sr (ppm)	
	Range	Mean	Range	Mean	Range	Mean
Florida, Georgia, Alabama (Lawrence, 14 spp.)	0.075–1.00	0.33	0.20–5.28	1.93	1–23	13
Oklahoma (Harper and Daniel, 10 spp.)	—	—	0.46–9.30	2.66	—	—
South Carolina (Boyd, 18 spp.)	0.10–0.47	0.25	0.20–1.85	0.92	—	—
New Jersey (Riemer and Toth, 37 spp.)	0.08–0.84	0.32	0.19–14.75	1.78	—	—
Connecticut (Cowgill, 6 spp.)	0.22–0.93	0.37 (0.31)	1.37–6.51	2.56 (1.91)	17–117	62 (46)
Canada (Ophel and Fraser, 19 spp.)	—	—	0.11–3.34	0.98	5–134	69
Poland (Bernatowicz, 16 spp.)	—	—	0.05–5.90	1.10	—	—
New Zealand (Lancaster, Coup, and Hughes, 3 spp.)	0.29–0.43	0.39	0.66–2.61	1.67	—	—
Overall mean	—	0.33	—	1.70	—	48
Mean water plants (Denton)	—	0.48	—	2.11	—	—
Mean terrestrial vegetation (Bowen)	—	0.32	—	1.80	—	14

In one of Riemer and Toth's analyses for *Ceratophyllum demersum* the magnesium content (1.09% dry) was actually just in excess of the calcium (1.07% dry). Such a ratio of about unity occurred in none of the plants analyzed by Nelson and Palmer, by Boyd, or by Cowgill. Lawrence noted a little more magnesium (0.27% dry) than calcium (0.24% dry) in the aquatic grass *Paspalum fluitans*; here the ratio in excess of unity is due to the low calcium rather than the high magnesium content.

In the analyses (Table 31) in which the various parts of the plant are considered separately, little variation between the magnesium contents of these parts has been noted; what variation there is does not conform to any systematic pattern.

Calcium. Calcium is the only major cation present in freshwaters that is likely to be precipitated by the removal of CO_2 in photosynthesis. The precipitation of $CaCO_3$ consequently occurs frequently when photosynthesis is taking place in macrophytes in hard waters; calcite, or much more rarely aragonite, is produced and often accumulates on the surfaces of plants as a calcareous incrustation. When really large amounts of calcium are reported in analyses, such as the 20% found in one sample of *Najas* sp. and in one of *Potamogeton natans* by Riemer and Toth (1968), quantities that would correspond to 50% $CaCO_3$ if all the calcium were present as carbonate, they are doubtless always due to this phenomenon. Such photosynthetic precipitation makes the higher values given in analyses, and any average values based on them, somewhat meaningless. The species on which large quantities of calcium carbonate are apt to accumulate natu-

TABLE 31.   *Mean contents of magnesium (% dry matter) in different parts of water plants (Riemer and Toth, Cowgill)*

Study	Leaf petiole	Leaf	Flower stalk	Flower
Nuphar advena				
New Jersey	0.24	0.19	—	—
Connecticut	0.21	0.30	0.25	0.31
Nymphaea odorata				
New Jersey	0.17	0.12	—	—
Connecticut 1971	0.19	0.24	0.20	0.25
Connecticut 1972	0.22	0.29	0.22	0.25
N. tuberosa				
New Jersey	0.17	0.14	—	—
Pontederia cordata				
Connecticut	—	0.33	0.17	0.29

rally tend to occur in those genera, some species of which are commonly found in hard waters. Pia (1933) lists *Ranunculus*, *Nymphaea*, *Ceratophyllum*, *Sisymbrium*, *Myriophyllum*, *Justicia*, *Elodea*, *Stratiotes*, *Vallisneria*, and *Potamogeton* as likely to contain lime-precipitating plants, and *Najas* clearly must be added to the list. The supposed role of the precipitate in the life history of *Stratiotes* has already been mentioned (see p. 124).

Wetzel (1960) has made a study of the acid-soluble precipitate of alkaline earth carbonate on various macrophytes in four lakes in Michigan in which the alkalinity varied from about 170 to about 200 mg HCO_3 liter^{-1}. The emergent species (*Scirpus acutus*, *Decodon verticillatus*, *Pontederia cordata*) and those with floating leaves (*Nymphaea odorata*, *Nuphar variegata*), in which the main photosynthetic structures are in contact with the atmosphere, in general have a small and very variable deposit of calcium carbonate on their submersed surfaces. Such deposition as was observed was apparently correlated with the abundance of epiphytic organisms, no doubt mainly algae.

Chara sp., which was present in all the lakes studied, always had more calcareous deposit than did any other water plant. The mean quantity of acid-soluble carbonate in the dry material of this plant, growing in all four lakes, was 36.5%, the greater part, if not all, being external. *Potamogeton pectinatus*, the only other species present in all four lakes, had 23% acid-soluble carbonate in the dry matter. The other submersed species had almost as much (*Myriophyllum verticillatum*, *Utricularia vulgaris*) or slightly less (*P. illinoensis*, *P. gramineus*, *Najas flexilis*) carbonate than *P. pectinatus*. Except for *Chara*, it is doubtful if the differences in calcium contents between any of these species, taken in pairs, are significant.

Wetzel points out that the dissection of leaves, increasing the area for precipitation, may well be involved in the differences that are discovered.

When the deposition of calcium carbonate by the same species growing at different depths in the same lake (Fig. 103) is considered, it is found that the plants in very shallow water have a lesser mean load, but greater variation in their incrustation, than those at greater depths. This is believed to be due to the greater but very irregular water movements in really shallow water. There is a little evidence that the precipitation can be deleterious; Ball (1948) found that cleaned water plants survived longer under ice than did those carrying a full load of calcareous matter.

It is possible that in polluted waters, certain specific materials such as methyl cellulose, used in detergents, may inhibit calcareous deposition (Edwards and Haywood 1960). There is some evidence (Hastings, Murray, and Sendroy 1927, van Wazer and Callis 1958, Eyster 1958) that quite small amounts of orthophosphate in solution prevent precipitation of calcium carbonate from supersaturated solutions.

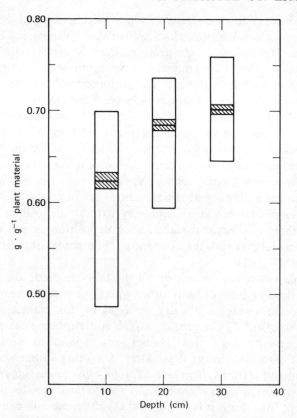

FIGURE 103.   Mean (solid bar), standard deviation (hatched), and range (open rectangle) of calcareous incrustation of *Potamogeton gramineus* in Michigan (Wetzel).

Ordinarily the material deposited, as has been indicated, is *calcite*. Müller (1971) has recently described the deposition of *aragonite* on the leaves of *Potamogeton* sp. in Lake Balaton, Hungary; at the same time a magnesian calcite was precipitating in the open water as the result of planktonic photosynthesis. Though recorded only once (Rowlands and Webster 1971) in Holkham Lake, Norfolk, England, and then apparently dispersed in the free water as a product of the photosynthetic activity of the phytoplankton, the possible presence of the third form of $CaCO_3$, *vaterite*, should not be forgotten. It is conceivable that its occurrence may be due to pollution with taurates, condensed phosphates, or other surfactant substances (Nathan 1971).

Though the formation of hydroxyl when HCO_3 is used in photosynthesis is doubtless often important in the precipitation of calcium carbonate, the process clearly occurs when only CO_2 is being taken up, as very many species of mosses and a few liverworts have been recorded as producing travertine in calcareous waters (Pia 1933).

In addition to the precipitation of calcium carbonate, Cowgill (1974b) has observed the frequent occurrence of calcium oxalate, both as the monohydrate *whewellite* mostly associated with emergent and floating leaved plants and as the dihydrate *weddellite* largely in or on submersed species.

Supposed internal calcium concentration. The range of calcium contents (Table 30) recorded by Boyd in his plants from Par Pond, none of which plants belong to supposedly calcifuge species, presumably indicates the sort of values to be expected before luxury consumption or photosynthetic precipitation occurs in hard waters; many of the analyses given by Riemer and Toth, whose plants came from a number of different waters, half of which contained less than 8 mg liter^{-1} Ca, fall in the same range, with a mean that, in spite of a few individual high values, is slightly below that of Boyd.

Bernatowicz (1969), studying plants from Lake Warniak, in which the calcium content falls from 32 mg liter^{-1} in May to 19 mg liter^{-1} in August, doubtless as a result of photosynthetic precipitation, found values from 0.05 ppm in *Potamogeton compressus* to 5.90 ppm in *P. pectinatus*. The fairly high content of the latter plant doubtless involves some photosynthetic precipitate; it is, however, lower than the values recorded for *P. pectinatus* in very hard waters in Michigan by Wetzel (1960). Bernatowicz found that *Chara vulgaris* contained 26.0% Ca in Lake Warniak, a value much higher than those given by angiosperms growing in the same water. The mean calcium content of all the phanerogams in Lake Warniak was 1.10%, hardly higher than the means obtained by Boyd and by Ophel and Frazer for plants growing in much softer water. In spite of Shepherd and Bowling's (1973) failure to find evidence of active transport of calcium into the roots of the water plants that they studied (see p. 293), it is clear that some regulation must take place.

The distribution of calcium in the various parts of water plants is evidently somewhat irregular. Riemer and Toth found no systematic differences between the petiole and the leaf of the Nymphaeaceae that they analyzed. Cowgill's data suggest that the flower is rather poorer than are the green parts of water lilies, but this is not true of *Pontederia cordata*. The quantity of calcium, namely, 1.66%, in the flowers of the last-named plant, indicates that the slightly higher values sometimes noted in parts of plants that otherwise contain only a moderate amount of the element, do not have to be due to photosynthetic precipitation.

Ophel and Fraser (1970) observed considerable differences in the calcium contents of the floating and submersed leaves of two species of *Potamogeton*

TABLE 32. *Calcium and strontium content of submersed and floating leaves of two species of* Potamogeton *in Perch Lake, Chalk River, Ontario (data from Ophel and Fraser)*

Species	Submersed leaves		Floating leaves	
	Ca (%)	Sr (ppm)	Ca (%)	Sr (ppm)
P. amplifolius	0.56	54	1.17	138
P. gramineus	1.71	157	1.06	90

that they studied; in one species it is the floating and in the other the submersed leaves that are richer in the element (Table 32).

Strontium. The strontium content of water plants has been studied primarily by Ophel and Fraser (1970), Lawrence (1968, 1971), and Cowgill (1974a). Some other analyses have been published by various investigators interested in the movements of ^{90}Sr in the environment, but these determinations throw little light on the general distribution of the element; they are mentioned in Ophel and Fraser's work.

It is evident that the strontium content of any species of water plant may be regarded as depending on three factors, namely, the quantity of strontium in the environment of the plant, the tendency of the latter to take up calcium, and its tendency to discriminate in favor of or against strontium. The operation of these factors is evident in Fig. 104 in which the mean quantity of strontium in various water plants is plotted against their calcium contents.

In Fig. 104A the data are derived from those of Ophel and Fraser,[5] based on 19 species of angiosperms growing in Perch Lake, a small chthoniotrophic lake described by Ophel (1963). Its water contained (Ophel 1963) 7 mg liter^{-1} Ca and 0.03 mg liter^{-1} Sr; later a mean ratio Sr:Ca of 5.7×10^{-3} was given for the water of the lake by Fraser and Ophel. There is quite a wide range of calcium concentrations in the plants of Perch Lake, as has already been noted; strontium varies proportionately even more so, from 5 ppm in *Nymphaea odorata*, to 194 ppm in *Nuphar variegata*. Most points fall on a line having a slope corresponding to a Sr:Ca ratio of about 8×10^{-3} by weight or 3.7×10^{-3} by atomic proportions. Most species, therefore, concentrate strontium relative to calcium to a slight extent. This is, however, not true of *Eriocaulon septangulare, Brasenia schreberi*, and

---

[5] In the original the calcium concentration and the Sr:Ca atomic ratio alone are given; the strontium contents have been recalculated from these.

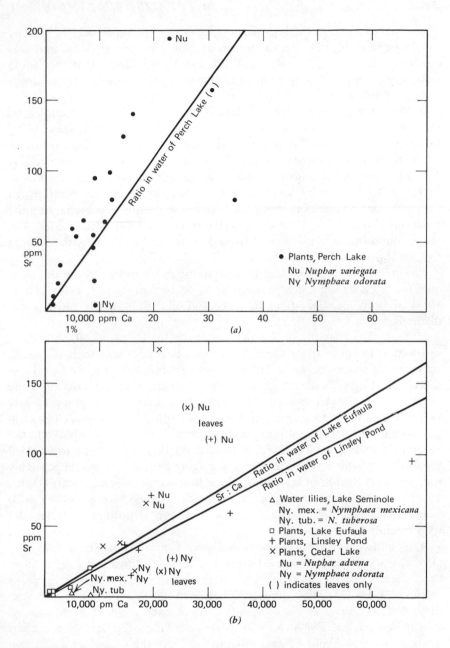

FIGURE 104. Concentration of strontium in dry matter of plants plotted against calcium. (*A*) In Perch Lake, Ontario. (*B*) In Eufaula Lake, Georgia–Alabama and the Linsley Basin, Connecticut. Note the great differences between the Sr:Ca ratio in the leaves of *Nuphar* and *Nymphaea* in both cases in which these genera were analyzed (data of Ophel and Fraser, Lawrence, and Cowgill).

Nymphaea odorata. In the last-named species the low ratio (0.53×10^{-3} by weight or 0.25×10^{-3} by atomic proportions) is very striking, and was confirmed by repeated analyses. There can be no doubt that this white water lily differs strikingly from the yellow *Nuphar variegata* in its strontium metabolism.

In Fig. 104B, the same kind of data is plotted for the plants studied by Lawrence in Lake Eufaula and by Cowgill in Linsley Pond, these being localities for the water of which there are both calcium and strontium analyses. In Lake Eufaula the mean calcium content in the summer was 3.33 mg liter^{-1} and the mean strontium 8.2×10^{-3} mg liter^{-1}, giving a ratio Sr:Ca of 2.5×10^{-3} by weight or 1.17×10^{-3} by atomic proportions. In the creeks or tributaries entering the lake the strontium was higher and the ratio was about 5.7×10^{-3}, comparable to that of Ophel and Fraser. The range found in the plants varied from 0.88×10^{-3} in *Zizaniopsis miliacea* to 2.48×10^{-3} in *Polygonum*.

Cowgill's data refer to a locality containing much more (spring and summer, mean Ca 29.7 mg liter^{-1}, mean Sr 61×10^{-3} mg liter^{-1}; ratio 2.06×10^{-3}) of both elements than in Lake Eufaula, though the ratio is not dissimilar.

It is obvious that the Sr:Ca ratio is lower in the plants of both these series than in those from Perch Lake; this is concordant with the lower ratio in the waters of Lake Eufaula and of Linsley Pond. Neither Lawrence's nor Cogwill's data suggest a preponderance of species concentrating strontium relative to calcium. The relative uptake of strontium clearly varies from species to species, and the mean value for the water plants in any lake would depend on the species present. If the relative uptake in the vegetation of Perch Lake were calculated on the basis of the total plant biomass rather than with each species weighted equally, it would probably indicate an exclusion of strontium, since *Brasenia schreberi* appears (Ophel 1963) to be by far the commonest angiosperm in the lake. Gaudet (1973) found that in culture *Salvinia minima* took up strontium preferentially over calcium.

It is quite clear from both Ophel and Fraser's and from Cowgill's (1974a) work that there is a great difference between *Nuphar* and *Nymphaea*, the former concentrating and the latter excluding strontium relative to calcium (Table 33). The difference between the two plants may be expressed as the ratio of the concentration of each element in *Nuphar* to that in *Nymphaea*. For strontium in the leaf, the only part of the plant analyzed by Ophel and Fraser, this ratio is 39 in the Canadian and 5.8 in the Connecticut material; the ratios for calcium are 2.4 and 1.3, respectively. Thus relative to calcium, strontium is taken up from 4.5 to 16.2 times as actively by *Nuphar* as by *Nymphaea* (Table 33). The phenomenon is shown in the Connecticut material most strikingly in the leaves and least in the flowers.

It may be noted that in *Potamogeton amplifolius* and *P. gramineus*, Ophel and Fraser found the same kind of difference between the strontium content of floating and submerged leaves as they found for calcium (Table 32).

TABLE 33. *Calcium, strontium, and barium contents, the last two both absolute (ppm) and relative to calcium, of some Nymphaeceae from Connecticut (Cowgill)*

Study	Petiole	Leaf	Flower stalk	Flower
Nuphar advena				
Ca (ppm)				
Cedar Lake	21970	25170	16450	8200
Linsley Pond	22970	29500	16920	6570
Sr				
Cedar Lake	71.7	133.9	28.7	27.6
Linsley Pond	65.9	115.8	42.4	31.7
Sr:Ca (by weight)	3.06×10^{-3}	4.57×10^{-3}	2.13×10^{-3}	4.01×10^{-3}
Ba (ppm)				
Cedar Lake	44.7	68.2	47.3	47.6
Linsley Pond	71.5	77.6	47.5	48.0
Ba:Ca	2.59×10^{-3}	2.67×10^{-3}	2.84×10^{-3}	6.47×10^{-3}
Nymphaea odorata				
Ca (ppm)				
Cedar Lake	18980	19780	18790	7320
Linsley Pond	16120	22570	13260	10230
Sr				
Cedar Lake	18.6	19.1	17.5	17.1
Linsley Pond	14.3	23.8	15.3	13.4
Sr:Ca	0.94×10^{-3}	1.01×10^{-3}	1.02×10^{-3}	1.74×10^{-3}
Ba (ppm)				
Cedar Lake	45.1	40.5	48.4	40.0
Linsley Pond	43.3	40.2	48.1	38.1
Ba:Ca	2.52×10^{-3}	1.91×10^{-3}	3.01×10^{-3}	4.45×10^{-3}
Ratio of mean content in *Nuphar advena* to that in *Nymphaea odorata*				
Ca	1.28	1.29	1.04	0.84
Sr	4.18	5.82	2.17	1.94
Ba	1.31	1.81	0.98	1.22

Barium. The only data on barium appear to be those derived from Cowgill's investigation. Averaged over the whole plant the quantities varied from 42.4 ppm dry in *Nymphaea odorata* from Linsley Pond to 66.8 ppm in *Ceratophyllum demersum* from the same locality, the mean being 49.4 ppm. The range of variation within plants is small. As with strontium, the ratio Ba:Ca, namely, 1.93×10^{-3} in the plants, is lower than is the mean geochemical ratio or the ratio in the source materials, but is almost identical with that observed in the water, namely, 2.07×10^{-3}. Barium is far less concentrated in the leaf of *Nuphar* than is strontium (Table 33). It is much less impoverished in the flower of water lilies than is calcium, leading to high Ba:Ca ratios in this part of the plant.

Beryllium. Beryllium has also been determined by Cowgill (Table 34). The mean quantity present varied from 0.22 ppm in *Decodon verticillatus* from Linsley Pond to 0.80 ppm in *Pontederia cordata*. In *Pontederia* the leaves are richer in beryllium than the stems or flowers, but in the Nymphaeaceae (Cowgill 1974a) the stems tend to be richer in the element than do the other structures.

The enrichment of both beryllium and lithium in the leaves of *Pontederia cordata* is remarkable, but there is no trace of a relationship between the two elements when the smaller quantities found in other plants are compared. Moreover, as will appear in later paragraphs, the leaves of *P. cordata* accumulate a few other elements, notably vanadium and cobalt, though the array accumulated as yet makes no apparent sense.

TABLE *34.* *Beryllium content (ppm) of various parts of Nymphaeacea and of Pontederia*

Study	Leaf petiole	Leaf	Flower stalk	Flower
Nuphar advena				
Cedar Lake	0.48	0.29	0.45	0.28
Linsley Pond	0.41	0.30	0.47	0.25
Nymphaea odorata				
Cedar Lake	0.51	0.32	0.45	0.25
Linsley Pond	0.47	0.36	0.53	0.42
Pontederia cordata				
Cedar Lake	—	1.10	0.65[a]	0.44
Linsley Pond	—	1.68	0.52[a]	0.40

[a] Main axis.

The mean content in the six species analyzed by Cowgill was 0.42 ppm Be or, for 1971–1972, 0.46 ppm; the former figure implies a ratio Be:Mg of 114 $\times$ 10^{-6} and a ratio Be:Ca of 16.4 $\times$ 10^{-6}. In the source materials of the basin, the ratios would be 5.25 $\times$ 10^{-6} and 5.3 $\times$ 10^{-6}, respectively. If the Be:Li ratio is considered, we have for the plants (including *Pontederia cordata*) 1.1, while for the source material the ratio is 0.03. Beryllium seems able to pass more easily from the source materials to the plant than does lithium, and is also enriched relative to magnesium and slightly so relative to calcium.

Boron. The boron content of a number of water plants has been studied by Boyd and Walley (1972), mainly using material from Par Pond, a reservoir on the AEC Savannah River Plant, Aiken, South Carolina. The mean boron content of the water was 5.2 mg m^{-3}. The sediment of the lake is sandy and contains less than 0.1 ppm boron. The boron content of the 22 species studied varied tenfold from 1.2 ppm dry in *Eleocharis equisetoides* to 11.3 ppm dry in *Nymphaea odorata*, the mean value being 6.4 ppm; assuming the dry matter is 10% of the wet, this figure implies a concentration in the living plant about 100-fold that of the ambient water. In *Ceratophyllum demersum* and *Utricularia inflata*, in which the plants are rootless and all constituents must come from the water, the values were 4.3 and 7.6 ppm, respectively, with a mean of 6.0 ppm, implying the same sort of enrichment over the medium. In general, monocotyledonous plants contained less boron (1.2–8.1 ppm; mean 4.3 ppm) than did dicotyledonous (7.6–11.3 ppm), as has also been observed among terrestrial species. The boron uptake of *Typha latifolia* was found to be faster than dry matter production in the spring and early summer, but less rapid in July. Plants collected over a wide range of localities in eastern North America showed great variation in boron, containing from 5.2 to 100 ppm with a mean of 19.8 ppm for *T. latifolia*, and 4.6 to 51.0 ppm with a mean of 18.8 ppm for *Juncus effusus*. In both species the modal contents lay between 10 and 20 ppm, suggesting that the range of values in Par Pond is rather low.

Ahl and Jönsson (1972) found a range of boron contents of 21 to 114 mg m^{-3} in Swedish rivers and a range of 3.7–19 ppm B in plants in Lake Mäler. These results evidently fall between Boyd and Walley's for Par Pond and the results for Connecticut published by Cowgill (1974a), next to be considered.

Cowgill, working in the Linsley Basin, in which the water contains about 485 mg B m^{-3}, or nearly 100 times the concentration in Par Pond, obtained consistently higher values for the plants than those of Boyd and Walley, but all her analyses fall within their range for *Typha latifolia* sampled over a wide area. Her mean value, weighted for each species equally in 1971, was 32.1 ppm, or averaging all determinations for 1971 and 1972, 40.6 ppm. Her extremes were 13 ppm for *Potamogeton* cf. *praelongus* and 62 ppm for *Nymphaea odorata*. In the relatively boron-rich water of the Linsley Basin, the average enrichment factor must have been only about seven, as compared with about 100 in Par Pond. It is interesting that although *Nymphaea odorata* in the Linsley basin contained about five and a half times as much boron as in Par Pond, in both localities this species had the highest content of the element. The distribution of boron in the various parts of *Nuphar advena*, *Nymphaea odorata*, and *Pontederia cordata* analyzed by Cowgill is given in Table 35; in *Decodon verticillatus* the distribution was much less regular, the leaves being very low in one specimen and very high in another.

Boyd found that dense stands of *Typha domingensis*, which formed populations averaging 1483 g dry m^{-2}, contained 6.8 mg B m^{-2}, and stands of *Pontederia cordata* contained 5.7 mg B m^{-2}.

Aluminum, gallium, scandium, yttrium, and the lanthanide rare earths. The amount of reliable data is very limited, but as far as it goes suggests most interesting relationships that deserve much further study.

Aluminum. Stoklasa (1922) believed that hydrophytes contain more aluminum than ordinary terrestrial plants, but the high contents that he recorded have not been confirmed by later workers (Levy, 1931; Hutchinson and Wollack, 1943), though Schuette and Hoffmann (1921) and Schuette and Alder (1927) obtained some fairly high values that they at-

TABLE 35. *Distribution of boron (ppm) in three species of plant from two Connecticut localities*

Study	Leaf petiole	Leaf	Flower stalk	Flower
Nuphar advena				
Cedar Lake	33	37	23	38
Linsley Pond	11	31	26	44
Nymphaea odorata				
Cedar Lake	20	94	57	83
Linsley Pond 1971	21	92	48	82
Linsley Pond 1972	20	90	54	90
Pontederia cordata				
Cedar Lake	—	74	34[a]	47
Linsley Pond	—	75	39[a]	49

[a] Main axis.

tribute to contamination. Most modern investigators have not considered the element. Cowgill found mean values from 250 ppm in *Potamogeton* cf. *praelongus* to 785 in *Ceratophyllum demersum*. The overall mean for the Linsley Basin is 366 ppm (Cowgill, 1973a), which falls between the 200 ppm given by Hutchinson (1943) and the 500 ppm given by Bowen (1966) as the most acceptable values for terrestrial vegetation. Within the plant body of both *Nuphar* and *Pontederia* the leaves appear to be richer than the stems. In *Nymphaea odorata* the flower may be rich in aluminum; the occurrence seems irregular and may depend on the state of development of the flower (Table 36). The rhizomes of these species have not been analyzed. In *Decodon verticillatus* roots, or more probably rhizomes, contained 410 ppm, and the leaves had 230–260 ppm; a concentration of aluminum in the underground parts of terrestrial plants is very common.

Gallium. Gallium varies from 0.37 ppm in *Potamogeton* cf. *praelongus* from Linsley Pond to 0.68 in *Decodon verticillatus* from Cedar Lake (Cowgill 1973b, 1974a). The mean value for 1971 is 0.55 ppm corresponding to a ratio Ga:Al of 1.25×10^{-3}; if the 1972 data computed by Cowgill (1973b) are included the content is 0.67 ppm and the Ga:Al ratio $1.83 \times$

TABLE 36.   *Aluminum and gallium (ppm) in water lilies (Cowgill)*

Study	Leaf petiole	Leaf	Flower stalk	Flower
Nuphar advena				
Al				
Cedar Lake	230	510	260	270
Linsley Pond	300	390	330	340
Ga				
Cedar Lake	0.64	0.68	0.65	0.67
Linsley Pond	0.58	0.55	0.56	0.68
Ga:Al	2.3×10^{-3}	1.1×10^{-3}	2.1×10^{-3}	2.2×10^{-3}
Nymphaea odorata				
Al				
Cedar Lake	420	730	180	1250
Linsley Pond 1971	180	610	370	1730
Linsley Pond 1972	199	179	188	194
Ga				
Cedar Lake	0.63	0.69	0.60	0.65
Linsley Pond 1971	0.55	0.67	0.60	0.62
Linsley Pond 1972	0.82	0.92	0.71	0.78
Ga:Al	2.5×10^{-3}	1.5×10^{-3}	2.6×10^{-3}	0.65×10^{-3}

10^{-3}. These figures are about 10 times greater than the best value for terrestrial plants (Bowen 1966). In the water of the lake the ratio is much higher (Cowgill 1973b), around 38×10^{-3}, but in the source material of the basin it is lower, around 0.3×10^{-3}, the ratio for the accessible lithosphere being 0.18×10^{-3}. Evidently the water is enriched in gallium relative to aluminum but the whole of this enrichment is not passed on to the plants. The supposed functional significance of the element in plants has apparently not been confirmed (Bowen 1966).

Scandium and Yttrium. In spite of the almost identical contents of the mean source material in the Linsley Basin, namely, 24.5 ppm scandium and 20.8 ppm yttrium, which may be compared with the mean values for the accessible lithosphere, namely, 22 and 25 ppm (Taylor 1964), Cowgill (1973a) found an immense difference between the scandium and the yttrium contents of the water plants that she analyzed. The mean scandium content for each species varied from 0.26 ppm in *Decodon verticillatus* to 0.98 ppm in *Potamogeton* cf. *praelongus*, with an overall mean of 0.38 ppm (Cowgill 1973a), and the yttrium varied from 60.5 ppm in *Ceratophyllum demersum* to 82.5 ppm dry in *Decodon verticillatus*, with an overall mean of 69.4 ppm. There is a suggestion of a negative relationship between the two elements when the mean contents of each species are compared.

If the ratios of the aluminum, gallium, scandium, yttrium, and total lanthanide rare earths in the plants to the amounts in the source materials are considered (Table 37), it becomes apparent that the first three elements are absorbed to a very moderate extent, while yttrium and the lanthanides are taken up in quantity, giving an enrichment of about 100-fold relative to the other three.

Within the plants of which various parts were analyzed, there is often a tendency for greater concentrations of both scandium and yttrium to occur in the leaves than elsewhere.

TABLE 37. *Mean quantities of aluminum, gallium, scandium, yttrium, and lanthanide rare earths in plants of the Linsley Basin, related to source materials*

	Al	Ga	Sc	Y	Rate Earths
1. Mean in plants	366	0.67	0.38	69.4	210.5
2. Mean in source materials	57,800	17.4	24.5	20.8	175
Ratio *1/2*	0.63×10^{-2}	3.85×10^{-2}	1.55×10^{-2}	3.42	1.20

Lanthanide rare earth elements. As has just been indicated these elements relative to the source materials of the basin are taken up by plants roughly 100-fold more than is aluminum. All the lanthanides of even atomic number were detected by Cowgill (1973a); of the odd-numbered members of the group only lanthanum and praseodymium were found (Fig. 105). The others presumably occurred in amounts of less than 1 ppm. Cerium appears rather less concentrated than do the other detectable lanthanides. Samarium is present in excess of neodymium in most samples. The rather high concentration of erbium in most of the plants may be a local peculiarity of the basin, the rocks of which seem a little higher in the element than is the accessible lithosphere (Table 38).

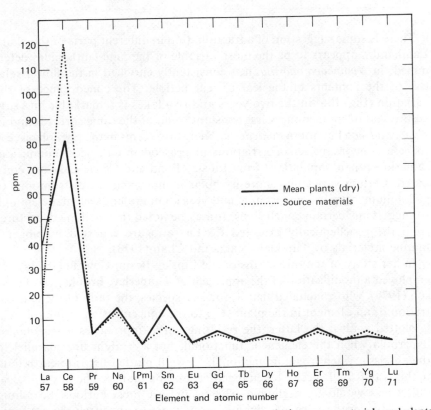

FIGURE 105. Distribution of mean quantity of rare earths in source materials and plants of the Linsley Basin (data of Cowgill).

TABLE 38.   *Distribution of rare earth elements (ppm) in Linsley Pond; the shallow-water sediment determinations are the means of Cowgill's values for the materials actually below the plants; the plant determinations are the averages of her means for Linsley Pond 1971 and 1972. Note enrichment of lanthanum and samarium and slight depauperation of cerium in plants as compared to any sediments of source materials*

Study	La	Ce	Pr	Nd	Sm	Gd	Dy	Er	Yb
Earth's crust (Taylor)	30	60	8.2	28	6	5.4	3.0	2.8	3.0
Source materials, Linsley Basin	20	120	4.0	12	7	3.2	1.1	4.1	3.7
Shallow-water sediments, Linsley Pond	26	93	3.9	14	10	2.5	1.9	1.5	1.8
Deep-water sediments, Linsley Pond	49	112	5.0	20	11	4.5	5.2	2.7	3.1
Plants, Linsley Pond	40	90	4.6	14	16	5.0	2.8	4.5	1.5

There is some suggestion of a fractionation in different parts of the plant. Lanthanum appears to be the most variable of the nine lanthanides determined; in *Nymphaea odorata*, it is consistently enriched in the flower relative to the contents of the leaf or leaf petiole. The concordance of the variation (Fig. 106) in the two years and two lakes is remarkable and suggests a real phenomenon. A less constant trend of the same sort is found in *Nuphar advena* but not in *Pontederia*. There also seems in the Nymphaeaceae to be a concordant set of variations in praseodymium, neodymium, and samarium when populations from Linsley Pond and Cedar Lake are compared. Cerium varies in a more irregular manner and the distributions of gadolinium, dysprosium, erbium, and ytterbium are not systematic enough to suggest any certain conclusions. It may be noted that striking departures from the geochemically expected Ce:La ratio are reported in biogenic marine materials by Turekian, Katz, and Chan (1973).

In her study of the rare earths of the Linsley Basin, Cowgill (1973a) has employed a modification of the approach of Timperley, Brooks, and Peterson (1970), who concluded that if, for any species, the ratio of the concentration of an element in the plant (C_p) to the concentration in the soil (C_s) is plotted against the latter, the resulting curve approaches a rectangular hyperbola when the element is functional, but a straight line, parallel to the abscissa, when it is nonfunctional. Cowgill plotted her rare earth data in this way for all species taken together, hoping that specific physiological differences would be negligible. The results are most curious. Scandium and, of the lanthanides, neodymium alone seem to approach the nonfunctional pattern, though in the case of the latter element this may merely be because no sediment contained little enough of the element to disclose the

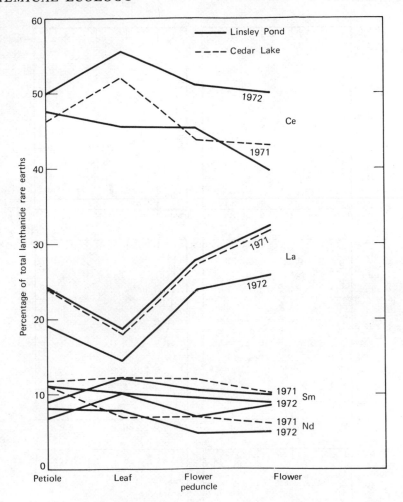

FIGURE 106. Proportion of cerium, lanthanum, neodymium, and samarium in the total rare earths in various parts of *Nymphaea odorata* (data of Cowgill).

rising branch of the hyperbola, asymptotic to the ordinate. Dysprosium, by such a criterion, seems almost as functional an element as phosphorus. The other rare earths fall between these two extremes (Fig. 107) but in general approach hyperbolic distributions. All the plot really indicates is that in the case of the nonfunctional element accumulation is proportional to external concentration, whereas in the case of a biologically significant element the quantity incorporated tends to be independent of the supply.

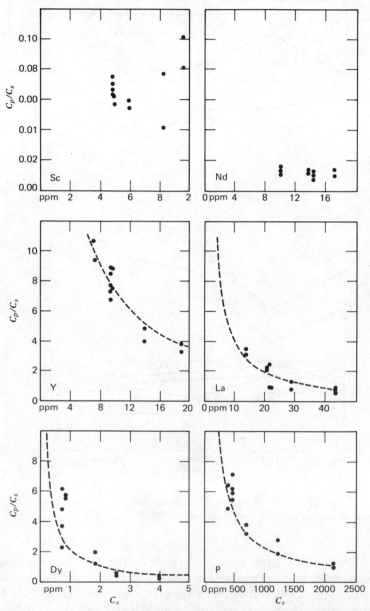

FIGURE 107.   Ratio of element in plant (Cp) to content in sediment (Cs) in or on which it is growing, plotted against latter quantity, giving an hyperbolic relationship if the element is more efficiently concentrated from low external contents than from high.

This of course might be as true of a poisonous element, kept out at high external concentrations, as of an essential one actively transported in when the external supply is low. The approach of Timperley, Brooks, and Peterson may well be naive in view of the complexity of the processes by which elements enter plants; their hyperbolic plot is certainly not the simplest, though it is possibly the most dramatic, way of handling the data. In spite of such criticisms it would be hard to deny that Fig. 107 is interesting.

Silicon, germanium, titanium, zirconium, hafnium, and thorium. These elements, of which the oxides and other compounds are among the most insoluble materials of the lithosphere, are conveniently treated together. Of the other quadrivalent elements, carbon, constituting about half the mass of organic matter, is treated implicitly throughout any consideration of lake biology and will be considered explicitly in connection with primary productivity. Tin and lead are more usually bivalent and geochemically belong with the bivalent transition metals.

Silicon and Titanium. Silicon is given as SiO_2 in many of the older analyses, often distinguished from sand left behind as an insoluble residue when the plant ash is dissolved.

The quantities recorded are quite variable even within a single species. Thus Birge and Juday (1922) found 0.24% Si in *Vallisneria americana* in Wisconsin and Schuette and Alder (1927) 2.54% from the same plant in the same state. Many of the more extensive modern series of analyses do not give data for the element, and where it is recorded there is always doubt whether it is present as a mineral contaminant, as the frustules of epiphytic diatoms, or as silicon actually present in plant tissue.

Silica of course occurs as opaline phytoliths, formed in many cases by the silicification of individual cells, in the Gramineae, Cyperaceae, and some other plants. In the aquatic grasses such as *Phragmites australis* and *Oryza sativa*, bulliform cells in the leaves may become silicified (Parry and Smithson 1958, 1964; Sangster 1970), but a great number of different types of silicification are known and some opaline phytoliths are of micropaleobiological significance, though they seem not yet to have been studied in lake sediment. In addition to support, silica accumulation may protect plants against attack by snails (Stahl 1888). Little is known of silica deposition in fully aquatic species, though it occurs in the Podostemaceae. The older literature on phytoliths is reviewed by Haberlandt (1914, note 266), while the more recent papers may be found through references given by Blackman (1971).

Apart from the determinations of Cowgill (1974a) there are practically no data for any of the other elements. Her ranges and means based on six species of water plants growing in Linsley Pond and Cedar Lake, North

Branford, Connecticut, are set out in Table 39, together with the mean contents of the source materials and the most acceptable (Taylor 1964) estimate of the concentrations of the elements in the accessible lithosphere.

Titanium is probably the least soluble and least mobile of the common elements of the earth's crust. It therefore forms a convenient standard by which contamination by solid, relatively unchanged, mineral matter may be judged. In Table 39 the expected quantities of the other elements, assuming they accompany titanium in the proportions found in the source materials, are given in column (5); and in column (6) the difference between the observed quantities (2) and these expected quantities, as percentages of the former, give a measure of the accumulation of these elements independently of titanium. Since the assumption that all the titanium is present as solid contamination by a material having the composition of the source material, and that none of the element enters into any biological cycle, is an extreme and not very probable hypothesis, it is likely that column (5) overestimates the nonbiological and column (6) underestimates the biological uptake of the elements. In the case of silicon, however, some nonbiological accumulation may take place on plants as clays, not containing any titanium.

It is evident that at least 83% of the silicon is not associated with titanium as a contaminant having the mean composition of the source materials. This may be an overestimate of the biological silicon because contamination by clay not containing titanium is likely. The maximal silicon contents are in two samples of *Ceratophyllum demersum* containing 23,130 and 15,560 ppm Si, respectively. These also had the highest titanium contents of 54.6 and 108.3 ppm Ti, respectively, which with the Si:Ti ratio of the source material would correspond to 2560 ppm and 5060 ppm SiO_2, leaving 20,570 ppm and 10,500 ppm Si unaccounted for as titanium-containing contaminants. The aluminum contents of 730 ppm and 940 ppm suggest that less than 1520 ppm and 1750 ppm, respectively, of the silica is present as clay. Much of the remaining silicon may well be present as epiphytic diatoms.

There is considerable irregularity in the distribution of both silicon and titanium in the different parts of the plants in which leaves, flowers, and stems have been analyzed separately (Table 40), but in the water lilies the ratio Si:Ti is consistently high in the leaf.

In addition to Cowgill's data, Petkova and Lubyanov (1969) have given some determinations of titanium, but of none of the other elements, in water plants from the Ukraine. Most of their data are referred to ash, but for some species the analyses can be recomputed to dry weight. For *Nymphaea alba* they give a titanium content of 45 ppm and for *Nuphar*

TABLE 39. *Distribution of quadrivalent lithophile elements in plants and source materials of the Linsley Basin, and estimates of the percentage (6) not accompanying titanium in supposed contaminants*

Element	(1) Range in species of plants (1971) (ppm)	(2) Mean in plants (ppm)	(3) Mean in source materials (ppm)	(4) Mean in accessible lithosphere (ppm)	(5) $\dfrac{(3) \times 29.1}{6035}$	(6) $\dfrac{[(2)-(5)]100}{(2)}$ %
Silicon	1910–19,350	7920 (4320)	279,000	281,500	1345	83
Germanium	0.15–0.40	0.31 (0.33)	2.1	15	0.010	97
Titanium	12.9–81.5	29.1 (16.4)	6035	5700	29.1	(0 by definition)
Zirconium	23.8–31.5	27.3 (22.3)	175	165	0.843	97
Hafnium	0.030–0.051	0.037 (0.030)	2.5	3	0.012	67
Thorium	1.0–1.8	1.5 (1.43)	2.4	9.6	0.012	99

319

TABLE 40.   Distribution of silicon and titanium in the Nymphaeaceae and in Pontederia cordata *in the two lakes of the Linsley Basin, North Branford, Connecticut* (*ppm or ratios, data of Cowgill*)

		Leaf petiole	Leaf	Flower stalk	Flower
Nuphar advena					
Cedar Lake	Si	1,760	5,600	2,210	2,640
	Ti	20.3	13.8	12.8	13.0
Linsley Pond	Si	4,320	4,660	3,030	5,630
	Ti	11.6	11.4	12.5	7.4
	Si:Ti	191	407	207	41
Nymphaea odorata					
Cedar Lake	Si	4,780	9,020	2,810	14,640
	Ti	21.5	37.4	11.2	91.2
Linsley Pond 1971	Si	1,830	10,640	3,630	11,780
	Ti	13.4	11.5	17.0	8.0
	Si:Ti	189	402	228	266
Pontederia cordata					
Cedar Lake	Si	—	5,680	2,740[a]	2,120
	Ti	—	48.7	13.2[a]	12.4
Linsley Pond	Si	—	3,120	2,880[a]	1,800
	Ti	—	11.1	10.9[a]	9.1
	Si:Ti	—	147	233[a]	182

[a] Main axis.

lutea of 35 ppm, quantities two or three times as great as the American figures for these genera. Other water plants contained considerably more titanium, the greatest quantities being in the emergent junciform species, *Typha angustifolia* having a mean content of 411 ppm, *Phragmites australis* of 759 ppm, and *Schoenoplectus lacustris* of 1120 ppm. The titanium in the ash of fully submersed species suggests contents in the dry matter between these reeds and the water lilies.

The available data on the titanium content of water plants would clearly average above the 11 ppm regarded by Bowen (1966) as the best mean for terrestrial vegetation.

Germanium.   This element, as is to be expected, is present in quite small amounts. It shows very little variation between species or when different parts of the plants are compared. It is, however, present in quantities that represent a considerable enrichment relative to titanium and is most unlikely to be an external contaminant.

Zirconium and Hafnium. The most remarkable feature of these elements is the very considerable quantity of zirconium found in the Connecticut water plants. The mean quantity present in soils, mainly derived from glacial till, and rocks in the Linsley Basin, is within 6% of the most acceptable value for the mean accessible lithosphere, and the analyses therefore can be received with some confidence. Relative to titanium, zirconium is enriched about 35-fold. The only considerable series of analyses of herbaceous angiosperms are those of Lounamaa (1956) on the terrestrial plants of Finland, which contain a mean quantity of about 12 ppm in the ash, corresponding to about 1 ppm of the dry plant. Only further work can decide if the element is in general concentrated in water plants.

Hafnium most curiously seems not to show the great enrichment exhibited by zirconium, but the quantities are very small and hard to estimate. Both elements appear to be slightly more concentrated in leaves than in other parts of the plants of which different structures were analyzed separately (Table 41).

TABLE *41. Distribution of zirconium, hafnium. and thorium (ppm) in the Nymphaeaceae of the Linsley Basin, North Branford, Connecticut (data of Cowgill)*

Study	Leaf petiole	Leaf	Flower stalk	Flower
Nuphar advena				
Zr				
Cedar Lake	32.1	41.5	28.7	31.1
Linsley Pond	30.7	41.5	22.8	23.9
Hf				
Cedar Lake	0.033	0.040	0.018	0.027
Linsley Pond	0.033	0.040	0.027	0.027
Th				
Cedar Lake	1.48	1.82	1.58	2.18
Linsley Pond	1.54	1.70	1.52	1.82
Nymphaea odorata				
Zr				
Cedar Lake	22.3	25.9	19.4	23.5
Linsley Pond	19.1	41.9	18.2	20.4
Hf				
Cedar Lake	0.024	0.042	0.027	0.027
Linsley Pond	0.027	0.042	0.027	0.027
Th				
Cedar Lake	1.14	1.46	1.20	2.50
Linsley Pond	1.48	1.60	1.12	2.30

Thorium. Thorium, which on the basis of radiochemical studies on *Lemna* was believed by Vernadsky, Brunowsky, and Kunasheva (1937) to be essentially absent from living matter, appears to exist in the Connecticut plants analyzed and in fact to be strikingly enriched relative to titanium. Iskra, Kulikov, and Bakhurov (1970) found in experiments using thorium isotopes, studied radiochemically, that water plants concentrated the element 970–15,800 times over the environmental concentration.

Compared with silicon and titanium, which exhibit at least a tenfold variation between the highest and lowest values, the rarer elements appear much more constant in concentration. No function has been suggested for any of the elements treated in this section except silicon, but Cowgill's results clearly make a prima facie case for far more research on their occurrence and possible biological significance.

Arsenic, bismuth, vanadium, and niobium. The quinquevalent elements that exist, when fully oxidized, as oxides of the form R_2O_5, include nitrogen and phosphorus which, being the most important limiting nutrients, are discussed separately in a later section, and six other stable elements, namely, arsenic, antimony, bismuth, vanadium, niobium, and tantalum. Antimony and tantalum are unstudied in freshwater organisms. Of the other four, both arsenic and vanadium are at least potentially of considerable importance.

Arsenic. Arsenic has been studied by a few investigators and is evidently accumulated in some water plants.

The information for environments not specially enriched in arsenic appears to be limited to one set of analyses in New Zealand and Cowgill's (1974a) study on Linsley Pond and Cedar Lake. In these two localities the mean arsenic content of water plants varied from 2.8 ppm in *Nuphar advena* to 20.0 ppm in *Ceratophyllum demersum*, the overall mean being 7.0 ppm (3.6 ppm). One specimen of *C. demersum* contained 26.0 ppm; *Potamogeton* cf. *praelongus* with 9.9 ppm was also quite rich in the element. It is noteworthy that the highest values are found in the plants least likely to obtain the element from the bottom deposits. Within the plant the distribution is fairly uniform, save that in the Nymphaeaceae arsenic is slightly more concentrated in the leaves than in the flowers or stems.

In the waters of certain of the lakes, both natural and artificial, in the vicinity of Rotorua, Province of Auckland, in the North Island, New Zealand, rather high arsenic concentrations, of geothermal origin, are known. In the water plants of such lakes considerable amounts of arsenic have been found. Fish (1963) noted concentrations of 19.4–76.0 ppm dry in the introduced South African *Lagarosiphon major* and 58.5 in *Nitella hookeri*. Though these values are low compared with what was found in

TABLE 42. Arsenic contents (ppm) of New Zealand water plants

Species	Lake Okakuri (Lancaster, Coup, and Hughes 1971)	Waikato River (Reay 1972)	Hastings (Reay 1972)
Nitella hookeri	—	182	13
Ceratophyllum demersum	825	650	1.4
Myriophyllum propinquum	456	—	—
Elodea canadensis	374 (48–700)	307	3.0
Lagarosiphon major	924 (315–1450)	251	—
Potamogeton	436 (crispus)	178 (sp.)	<6 (sp.)
Lemna sp.	—	30	2.5

other material from the region by later investigators, Fish suspected that the weeds had acquired a resistance to arsenic as a herbicide.

In Lake Okakuri, New Zealand, in material collected in spring and summer (October–February, 1969–1970), Lancaster, Coup, and Hughes (1971), found the mean values and ranges given in the first column of figures in Table 42.

In other lakes two further species were studied by the same authors, Egeria densa containing 266 and 310 ppm, and Potamogeton cheesemanii with 45 ppm. At Whinnaki Bridge, apparently another locality on Lake Okakuri, Elodea canadensis contained 91 ppm, Lagarosiphon major 119 ppm, Ceratophyllum demersum 20, and Potamogeton crispus 11 ppm. The last two figures are almost identical with those of Cowgill for C. demersum (mean 20.0 ppm) and P. cf. praelongus (9.9 ppm). It is evident that at least Ceratophyllum demersum, which can contain 1060 ppm, and Lagarosiphon major, with up to 1450 ppm, are efficient concentrators of arsenic.

Reay (1972), studying a number of plants in the artificial lakes on the Waikato River draining from Lake Taupo, and which receives geothermal water a short distance below its origin from the lake, obtained the mean values given in Table 42. He analyzed, in addition, samples of five plants from water containing only 0.4 mg m^{-3} total arsenic, of which 0.3 mg m^{-3} was in solution, from Hastings, southwest of Lake Taupo and in a region free from arsenic-bearing influents. These analyses are given in Table 42, and are roughly comparable to, or rather lower than those of Cowgill.

Reay gives some graphical data for the concentration of total and soluble arsenic at different points on the Waikato River and the concentration factors for several plants growing at these stations. Since the concentration factors are given as the ratio of arsenic in the dry plant to the concentration in the water, they do not really represent the increase in going from unit volume of water to unit volume of plant. Lancaster, Coup, and Hughes (1971) found that fresh *Ceratophyllum demersum* contained 8.5% and *Lagarosiphon major* 5.8% dry matter. Using these values, the data given by Reay suggest the concentration factors given in Table 43.

TABLE *43.* *Concentration of arsenic by water plants in New Zealand*

Species	As in dry plant (ppm)	As in water mg m^{-3a}	Concentration factor[b]
Ceratophyllum demersum	524	40	1,100
	971	45	1,700
Lagarosiphon major	32	7	270
	405	77	310

[a] Calculated from As in plant and Reay's concentration factor and checked against his graphical presentation; at least three-quarters in solution.
[b] Arsenic in living plant divided by total arsenic in water; calculation assumes 8.5% dry matter in *Ceratophyllum* and 5.8% in *Lagarosiphon*.

It is probable from Table 42 that *Myriophyllum*, *Elodea*, and *Potamogeton* would have concentration factors rather below that of *Lagarosiphon*, and that of *Lemna* is doubtless lower still. The green alga *Enteromorpha* sp., which, growing in water containing 7 mg m^{-3} As, contained 20 ppm dry, accumulates arsenic to some extent, but at a higher concentration of about 50 mg m^{-3} in the medium, the content of the plant rose only to 40 ppm dry. The rhodophycean *Compsopogon hookeri*, recorded as containing up to 550 ppm As dry, seems to behave like *Lagarosiphon*. *Scirpus* sp. and *Typha orientalis* containing but 12 ppm and 8 ppm, respectively, appear not to take much arsenic from the sediments in which they grow.

It is evident that waterweeds enriched in arsenic might be sources from which the element could enter the food chain. Fish (1963) noted that snails, mainly *Potamopyrgus corolla*, occurring in the beds of *Lagarosiphon* in Lake Rotorua, contained 17.3–24.0 ppm dry As. It is of course uncertain if these snails obtained their arsenic from the plant, from the water, or from small organisms living on detritus ultimately derived from the waterweeds.

Since the use of excess waterweeds for feeding stock has been so often suggested, the arsenic content of such plants may be of practical as well as theoretical interest. Lancaster, Coup, and Hughes (1971) found that sheep fed for 3 weeks on *Lagarosiphon* containing 288 ppm As, accumulated over

1 ppm wet in their muscles, up to 3.38 ppm wet in the liver, and 3.76 ppm wet in the kidney, though after a further 4 weeks on different food, practically all the arsenic was eliminated. Quantities up to 15 ppm were present in the wool. The sheep were apparently quite healthy, though containing more arsenic than the British[6] statutory limit of 1 ppm in meat that may be offered for sale. It is, however, not impossible that prolonged ingestion of arseniferous waterweeds would have deleterious physiological consequences.

The source materials of the Linsley Basin, studied by Cowgill, contained an average of 570 ppm phosphorus and 3.55 ppm arsenic, giving a ratio As:P of 6.2×10^{-3}. Only in the case of *Ceratophyllum demersum* (7.7×10^{-3}) is the ratio in a plant as high as this; in *Nuphar advena* it is as low as 0.93×10^{-3}, and for the mean contents it is 2.6×10^{-3}.

Bismuth. Although antimony has not yet been recorded in water plants, Cowgill found them to contain bismuth. The concentration varied from 0.79 ppm in *Ceratophyllum demersum* to 5.4 ppm in *Pontederia cordata*, the mean being 3.0 ppm. In *Pontederia* the element was rather evenly distributed, whereas in *Nymphaea odorata* there was some concentration in the flower which contained 5.1 ppm, as against 2.7 ppm in the rest of the plant.

The mean quantity of arsenic in the source materials, 3.5 ppm, is higher than the 1.8 ppm given by Taylor, while the mean quantity of bismuth, 0.06 ppm, is lower than Taylor's figure of 0.17. These differences between the local and general occurrences are, however, not unreasonable. In general arsenic is evidently present in the accessible lithosphere in concentrations of at least an order of magnitude greater than the concentration of bismuth. It is therefore curious to find that relative to the source materials, bismuth is concentrated about 24 times as much as is arsenic in the plants. There is no proportionality between the elements in the different species, *C. demersum* being richest in arsenic and poorest in bismuth. The problem of bismuth in water plants clearly needs further study.

Vanadium and *Niobium.* Vanadium has been determined by Petkova and Lubyanov (1969) in plants from lakes in the steppe zone of the Ukraine, and by Cowgill (1974a) in six species from Connecticut. Petkova and Lubyanov refer their data to ash or to wet weight,[7] while Cowgill's are referred to dry weight, though ash contents can be calculated from her data. In the case of *Typha angustifolia, Schoenoplectus lacustris, Phragmites australis, Nuphar lutea,* and *Nymphaea alba,* it is possible to calculate the vanadium content referred to dry weight, as Petkova and Lubyanov esti-

---

[6] The authors indicate that in the United States the limit is 2.6 ppm.

[7] There seem to be some discrepancies; notably the sample of *Ceratophyllum* sp. with the highest vanadium in the ash has the lowest content referred to wet weight.

mate the ratio of the content in the plant to that in the sediments on wet, dry, and ash bases, so that a conversion factor can be obtained. In Table 44, the available data referred to dry weight, with relevant geochemical information, are summarized.

Though Cowgill's figures for the water lilies are not very far from those deduced from the data of Petkova and Lubyanov, there is much less good accord when the species known only on the contents in the ash are compared. Petkova and Lubyanov found from 92 to 260 ppm vanadium in the ash of *Ceratophyllum* sp., with a mean value of 120 ppm, 60 times Cowgill's mean of 2.0 ppm. Even more strikingly, Petkova and Lubyanov found marked accumulation in two species of *Potamogeton*, 1650 ppm in the ash of *P. pectinatus*, and 1300 ppm in the ash of *P. perfoliatus*, while Cowgill's *P.* cf. *praelongus* contained but 2.1 ppm in the ash; this species, with *C. demersum*, was much the poorest in vanadium in her collections. These curious discrepancies are accentuated by the fact that although the mean vanadium in Linsley source materials was low, the sediments of the Ukrainian localities were uniformly much lower.

TABLE *44.* *Concentration of vanadium and niobium in earth's crust, mean terrestrial vegetation, and water plants*

Study	Vanadium (ppm)	Niobium (ppm)
Accessible lithosphere (Taylor 1964)	135	20
Mean source materials, Linsley Basin (Cowgill 1974a)	35.1	6.4
Mean source materials, Ukraine (Petkova and Lubyanov 1969)	9.1	—
Terrestrial vegetation (Bowen 1966)	1.6	0.3
All water plants, Linsley Basin (Cowgill)	7.4 (8.0)[a] 0.4–32	13 (14)[a] 8.7–15
All water plants except *Pontederia*, Linsley Basin (Cowgill)	2.5 0.4–4.8	—
Five species from Ukraine (Petkova and Lubyanov)	23 7.2–57	—
Mean *Nuphar* and *Nymphaea* (Petkova and Lubyanov)	9.7	—
Mean *Nuphar* and *Nymphaea* (Cowgill)	3.4	14.8

[a] Figures in parentheses are from Cowgill 1973b, including 1972 data.

Cowgill's greatest accumulation occurred in the leaves of *Pontederia cordata*, in which she found 79.5 ppm in the dry matter or 871 ppm in the ash; the rest of the plant contained quantities comparable to those of her other species. Though the *Pontederia* leaf is not as rich as either of the species of *Potamogeton* analyzed by Petkova and Lubyanov, it is richer in vanadium than any of their other plants. The distribution of vanadium referred to dry matter in two samples of *P. cordata*, collected in 1971, is given in Table 45.

TABLE 45. *Vanadium and niobium in two collections of* Pontederia cordata (*Cowgill*)

	Vanadium (ppm)			Niobium (ppm)		
	Stalk	Leaf	Flower	Stalk	Leaf	Flower
Cedar Lake	8.0	79.0	9.0	13.4	11.8	13.4
Linsley Pond	6.3	80.0	10.3	14.2	13.4	14.8

It may be remembered (see pp. 294, 308) that *P. cordata* also accumulates lithium and beryllium in its leaves. Cowgill's mean value, excluding *P. cordata*, of 2.5 ppm seems much more in line with the work of previous investigators studying terrestrial plants, than does the mean derived from the five Ukrainian species for which reference to dry weight is possible.

Niobium appears to have been studied only by Cowgill. Though the amount in the source materials of the Linsley basin is low, the V:Nb ratio of 5.5 in such materials does not depart greatly from the mean ratio for the earth's crust of 6.8. It is very surprising to find that all the plants of Cedar Lake and Linsley Pond appear to contain much more niobium than vanadium, except in the case of the leaf of *Pontederia*. The lowest niobium concentration is in *P.* cf. *praelongus* and the highest in *Nymphaea odorata*, but the range is not great and the distribution within the plants fairly uniform. Both elements clearly deserve much further study.

Chalcophile transition metals. These predominantly bivalent elements, which tend to occur in the earth's crust as sulfides, include copper, zinc, and probably tin, biologically significant trace metals, and cadmium, mercury, and lead, three elements that have recently presented serious environmental problems owing to their use in various technological processes from which they are apt to escape into the biosphere. Silver, though hardly a typical chalcophile element, is often concentrated in lead sulfide or galena and is most conveniently considered after copper. It is not believed at present to have any biological function, and so far deleterious effects of its

TABLE 46. *Distribution of copper, silver, and the bivalent chalcophile metals in water plants and relevant comparative materials*

Study	Cu	Ag	Zn	Cd	Hg	Sn	Pb
Accessible lithosphere (Taylor 1964)	55	0.07	70	0.2	0.08	2	12.5
Source materials							
Linsley Basin (Cowgill)	99.7	0.013	96.1	0.45	0.029	0.74	47.6
Water, Linsley Pond (Cowgill 1970)	0.016	—	<0.003[a]	0.0015	—	6×10^{-6}	0.013
Water, Par Pond, South Carolina (Boyd)	—	—	0.008	—	—	—	—
Water, mean Bartlett's Ferry, Lake Eufaula, and Lake Seminole (Lawrence)	0.061	—	0.15	0.0023	—	—	0.011[b]
Water, mean New Jersey (Riemer and Toth)	0.014	—	0.045	—	—	—	—
Par Pond, South Carolina (Boyd) 16 species, range and mean	20–60 40	—	30–267 69	—	—	—	—

Linsley Basin, Connecticut (Cowgill), six species,							
range and mean	39–52	.040–1.41	103–150	4.4–10.0	7.7–22	3.1–10.2	8.5–13
	46 (44)[c]	0.86 (0.76)	134 (128)	6.5 (6.0)	12 (11)	5.5 (6.0)	11 (11)
Chattahoochee Basin (Lawrence),	26–243	—	75–600	2.6–28	—	—	2.0–53
14 species, range and mean	119		168	9.4			27
New Jersey (Riemer and Toth),	2.5–74	—	27–792	—	—	—	—
37 species, range and mean	25		136				
Dneprodzerzkinsk Reservoir (Varenko and Chuiko),	8.4–25	—	26.5–1000	—	—	—	—
seven species, range and mean	17		209 (66)[d]				
Ukraine (Petkova and Lubyanov),	19–52	—	—	—	—	—	2.2–30
five species,[e] range and mean	38						15
Mean aquatic plants (as above)	48	0.86	143 (115)[d]	8.0	?	5.5	11
Mean terrestrial plants (Bowen)	14	0.06	100	0.6	0.015	<0.3	2.7

[a] Zinc is recorded as often not detectable, though occasionally 0.003 ppm were present.

[b] Suspended lead only; the dissolved is presumably small.

[c] Figures in parentheses based on Cowgill's means including Linsley Pond 1972 data.

[d] Figure in parentheses without *Spirodela polyrhiza*, containing 1000 ppm Zn dry.

[e] Only species that can be referred to dry matter.

329

accidental artificial enrichment have not been noted; it must, however, be borne in mind that almost nothing is known about its biogeochemistry.

The range of mean values for various species of flowering plants and the overall mean, each species weighted equally, are given, from the more recent[8] determinations of these elements, in Table 46, together with certain other data of interest. In Table 47, data are given for copper and for zinc for those plants that have been studied by several different analysts working in quite different regions.

TABLE 47. *Copper and zinc contents of species of water plants that have been analyzed by several investigators in more than one geographical region*

Study	Mean Cu in day matter	Mean Zn in dry matter
Nuphar advena		
South Carolina (Boyd, 2 samples)	35	50
New Jersey (Riemer and Toth, 3 samples)	10.2	32.2
Connecticut (Cowgill, 2 samples)	51.6	129.3
N. lutea		
Ukraine (Petkova and Lubyanov, 1 sample)	31.0	—
Nymphaea odorata		
South Carolina (Boyd, 5 samples)	36	32
New Jersey (Riemer and Toth, 3 samples)	8.6	34.5
Connecticut (Cowgill, 2 samples)	46.1	122.9
N. tuberosa		
New Jersey (Riemer and Toth, 3 samples)	10.8	31.7
N. alba		
Ukraine (Petkova and Lubyanov, 1 sample)	38.0	—
Brasenia schreberi		
South Carolina (Boyd, 4 samples)	32	267
New Jersey (Riemer and Toth, 3 samples)	15.0	85.3
Ceratophyllum demersum		
South Carolina (Boyd, 4 samples)	30	100
New Jersey (Riemer and Toth, 3 samples)	15.2	164.1
Connecticut (Cowgill, 2 samples)	38.8	174.2
Myriophyllum heterophyllum		
South Carolina (Boyd, 4 samples)	44	54
New Jersey (Riemer and Toth, 3 samples)	39.5	451.6
M. cf. spicatum		
Georgia–Florida (Lawrence)	117.7	142.0
New Jersey (Riemer and Toth)	25.5	307.0

[8] A few analyses by Nelson and Palmer (1938) for copper gave results about two orders of magnitude greater than those of more recent investigators; these determinations are not further considered.

TABLE 47   (*Continued*)

Study	Mean Cu in dry matter	Mean Zn in dry matter
Potamogeton crispus		
Florida–Georgia (Lawrence)	58.0	156.5
New Jersey (Riemer and Toth, 4 samples)	45.5	97.1
Potamogeton pectinatus		
New Jersey (Riemer and Toth, 2 samples)	74.3	80.5
Dneprodzerzhinsk Reservoir (Varenko and		
Chuiko, 3 samples)	8.4	60.8
Potamogeton diversifolium		
South Carolina (Boyd, 1 sample)	36	60
New Jersey (Riemer and Toth, 1 sample)	25.0	73.5
Pontederia cordata		
South Carolina (Boyd, 1 sample)	60	67
New Jersey (Riemer and Toth, 3 samples)	16.3	26.5
Connecticut (Cowgill, 2 samples)	47.5	126.1
Vallisneria americana		
Louisiana (Lawrence)	85.0	233.0
New Jersey (Riemer and Toth, 1 sample)	39.0	625.0
Typha latifolia		
South Carolina (Boyd, 4 samples)	37.0	30
New Jersey (Riemer and Toth, 3 samples)	6.3	50.5
Typha angustifolia		
New Jersey (Riemer and Toth, 1 sample)	5.0	23.5
Dneprodzerzhinsk Reservoir (Varenko and		
Chuiko, 4 samples)	24.3	33.4
Ukraine (Petkova and Lubyanov, 6 samples)	19.1	—
Phragmites australis		
New Jersey (Riemer and Toth, 5 samples)	26.1	37.8
Dneprodzerzhinsk Reservoir (Varenko and		
Chuiko, 3 samples)	25.0	40.3
Ukraine (Petkova and Lubyanov, 1 sample)	52.4	—

Copper.   The highest copper content recorded for an individual sample of an aquatic angiosperm is 243 ppm in *Alternanthera philoxeroides* analyzed by Lawrence, but even this is low compared with the 725 ppm noted by the same author in *Chara* sp. Riemer and Toth found 135 ppm in one specimen of *Cabomba caroliniana*, growing in the water of the Millstone River, Somerset County, New Jersey; the same plant also contained large quantities of zinc, as this species does elsewhere. The amounts of copper and zinc in the water of the river, namely, 0.009 mg liter^{-1} Cu and 0.024 mg liter^{-1} Zn, are certainly not extraordinary and indeed are below the mean values for the New Jersey waters analyzed. In the same locality *Lemna minor* contained 32.5 ppm Cu. In the South Branch of the Raritan River a much higher copper concentration of 0.034 mg liter⁻¹ was encountered; the six species of water plants growing here contained 21.5–31.5 ppm dry, in the middle of the range for flowering plants.

The lowest copper contents are 2.5 ppm dry recorded by Riemer and Toth for *Wolffia* sp. and for one specimen of *Cabomba caroliniana*; the latter species therefore spans the entire range of values recorded for aquatic flowering plants in New Jersey, or indeed anywhere, except for Lawrence's *A. philoxeroides*. The six analyses for *C. caroliniana* give no hint of a relationship between copper contents of the plant samples and those of the ambient water. The very high values might be due to high copper contents of artificial origin in the sediments in which the plant is rooted, rather than in the water.

All Lawrence's values for copper are consistently high, though fairly variable, and the quantities of the element recorded from the waters that he analyzed are also considerably greater than from the localities studied by the other investigators. Of the 14 species for which mean data are given in his table, the copper content exceeds the zinc in five species. In the 107 individual analyses given by Riemer and Toth and by Cowgill, in only three cases is the copper in excess of the zinc; such a situation is evidently very unusual and suggests that some special circumstance accounts for Lawrence's data.

It is reasonable to suppose that all the higher values, whatever their cause, represent luxury consumption; this is emphasized by the great range of values for different individual samples of the same species, as in the case of *Cabomba caroliniana* or the wide variation in average content from area to area, as in *Pontederia cordata*, *Potamogeton pectinatus*, *Typha angustifolia*, or *T. latifolia* set out in Table 47.

In the cases of a few species that are either pleustonic or megaloplanktonic, and so must get all their copper from the water, it is possible to estimate roughly the concentration factor or ratio of the concentration of copper in the living plant to that of the water. The dry weight has been assumed, arbitrarily but with an approximation to realism, to be 10% of the wet weight (Table 48).

The concentration factor evidently falls with increasing copper concentration in the water, as would be expected of an essential element.

The data of both Riemer and Toth and of Cowgill indicate little difference in the copper contents of the various parts of plants of which leaves, petioles, and flowers were analyzed separately.

Chiaudani (1969) has investigated the distribution of copper in specimens of *Phragmites australis*, growing in various lakes in northern and central

TABLE 48. *Copper content of water, copper content of dry plant, and concentration factor, assuming a 90% water content, of species likely to obtain all their copper directly or indirectly from the water*

Species	Mean Cu in water (mg liter⁻¹)	Mean Cu in dry plant (ppm × 0.1)	Concentration factor
Ceratophyllum demersum			
Riemer and Toth	0.0083	1.52	183
Cowgill	0.016	3.23	202
Utricularia sp.			
Riemer and Toth	0.017	4.01	236
Eichhornia crassipes			
Lawrence	0.049	4.34	89
Lemna minor			
Riemer and Toth	0.012	3.58	298
Allenby	0.044	3.06[a]	70
L. gibba			
Allenby	0.047	3.00	64
Spirodela polyrhiza			
Varenko and Chuiko	0.0036	1.56	433
Allenby	0.02	1.65	83

[a] Allenby's eight analyses range from 0 to 110 ppm dry and show no clear dependence on external concentration.

Italy. These lakes include Lago d'Orta, which was for many years so badly polluted with cuprammonium compounds of industrial origin that except for *P. australis* all macrophytes formerly living in the lake were killed. As with grasses such as *Agrostis tenuis* (Bradshaw, McNeilly, and Gregory 1965), growing on soil containing copper derived from mining operations, the excess uptake of copper by the reeds of Lago d'Orta is largely confined to the buried parts. Even in plants growing in almost or quite unpolluted areas, there is some indication that the quantity of copper present in the rhizomes[9] depends on the copper content of the sediments in which the plants are rooted.

The behavior of the element in the stems and leaves appears to indicate three groups of populations (Fig. 108). In plants from Lago Maggiore and

[9] In the original "radici" and in its English summary "roots," but presumably rhizomes with attached roots were analyzed.

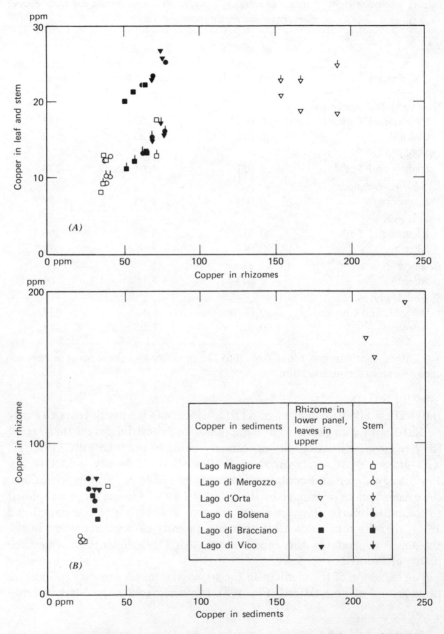

FIGURE 108. Distribution of copper in the rhizomes, stems, and leaves of *Phragmites australis* and in the sediments in which the plants were growing in the lakes of Latium and subalpine Italy (data of Chiaudani). (*A*) leaf. (*B*) rhizome.

the neighboring small Lago di Mergozzo, the contents of the stems (8.7–12.8 ppm) and leaves (11.8–17.5 ppm), though apparently dependent on the amount in the rhizomes (37.5–72.0 ppm), are lower than in other populations; the highest value in each case came from a slightly polluted locality. In the lakes of Latium (L. di Bolsena, L. di Bracciano, L. di Vico), though the copper contents of both sediments and rhizomes (51.5–78 ppm) widely overlap the values given by the material from the first group of lakes, the amounts in the stems (10.5–17.2 ppm), and particularly in the leaves (19.9–26.5 ppm) are systematically higher than in the plants from the northern localities; within the group these amounts appear to be linearly dependent on the rhizomal concentrations. In both regions the leaves contain more copper than do the stems. In the third group, consisting of only the reeds from the grossly polluted sediments of Lago d'Orta, the concentrations in the rhizomes are very high (211–237 ppm) but in spite of this the concentrations in the leaves (18.1–20.7 ppm) fall between those from the relatively unpolluted subalpine lakes and the lakes of Latium. The concentrations in the stems, however, are higher than in the leaves. It is reasonable to suppose that genetically different physiological races are involved in producing the observed phenomena.

Silver. The amount recorded by Cowgill is small, usually less than 1 ppm, though greater than the mean for terrestrial vegetation. Rather higher values, around 1 ppm, occur in the flowers and leaves of *Nuphar advena* and in the stems and flowers (mean 1.01 ppm) of *Pontederia cordata*, and the leaves of the latter plant, containing a mean quantity of 2.2 ppm, evidently accumulate silver very slightly.

Zinc and Cadmium. Zinc, as has been indicated, seems normally to be more abundant in the tissues of flowering plants than is copper. The means for different areas range from 69.3 to 209.0 ppm dry with an overall mean of 143.2, which is comparable to the value of 100 ppm given by Bowen (1966) for land plants.

Emergent junciform monocotyledons in general are low in the element. *Typha latifolia* was found by Boyd to have a mean content of 37 ppm and by Riemer and Toth a mean content of 50.5 ppm; the zinc content of *T. angustifolia* varied from 22 to 45 ppm in Varenko and Chuiko's study with a mean of 33.4 ppm, and Riemer and Toth found for a single sample of the same species 23.5 ppm. *Phragmites australis* in New Jersey analyzed by Riemer and Toth contained from 12.5 ppm, their lowest figure, to 65.0 ppm, with a mean of 37.8 ppm, while the concentration in the same species in the Dnieper Valley was found by Varenko and Chuiko to vary between 18 and 53 ppm with a mean of 40.3 ppm, much as in the American material. In Boyd's series, the sedge *Eleocharis quadrangulata* and the grass *Panicum hemitonom* contained 20 and 26 ppm, respectively, but in another grass, *Zizaniopsis miliaceae*, Lawrence records 97 ppm, more than in several fully submersed dicotyledons.

The highest values recorded are from *Spirodela polyrhiza* with 1000 ppm (Varenko and Chuiko 1971) and from *Cabomba caroliniana* with 750–1,000 ppm (Riemer and Toth 1968). Such plants, with about 0.1% zinc in their dry matter, are clearly accumulators of the element, living in water not particularly rich in zinc, 0.004 mg liter^{-1} in the case of *S. polyrhiza*, and 0.024 mg liter^{-1} in that of the sample of *C. caroliniana*, richest in the element; there is, however, no information about the content of the sediment in which the latter plant was rooted. Some specimens of *Lemna minor* analyzed by Riemer and Toth contained 500 ppm, the mean for the plant being 370 ppm; not all Lemnaceae accumulate the element, as the same investigators found only 58 ppm in *Wolffia* sp.

Though all the samples, from six localities, of *Cabomba caroliniana* analyzed by Riemer and Toth were very rich in zinc, the allied *Brasenia schreberi* seems quite variable in its content, Boyd finding a high mean value of 267 ppm, while Riemer and Toth give a range of 29–116 ppm with a mean of 85.3 ppm. Comparable variability is found in *Myriophyllum heterophyllum* and less strikingly in *Vallisneria americana* and in the Nymphaeaceae as set out in Table 47.

Cowgill found the quantity of zinc to be consistently slightly higher in the leaves than in the leaf petioles of the Nymphaeaceae and in the leaves, as contrasted with the stem and flowers, of *Pontederia cordata*. Riemer and Toth found the zinc content to be greater in the leaves than in the petioles of *Nuphar* but the reverse to be true in *Nymphaea*.

The pleustonic or megaloplanktonic species for which water analyses exist (Table 49) exhibit higher concentration factors than in the case of copper.

Cadmium is known from the studies of Lawrence and of Cowgill, whose analyses indicate mean cadmium contents of freshwater flowering plants to be 5.6% and 4.8%, respectively, of the zinc content. In Cowgill's analyses of the source materials in the Linsley Basin the ratio Cd:Zn is 0.47×10^{-2}, suggesting a tenfold enrichment of cadmium relative to zinc in going from the lithosphere to the plants. Unfortunately, the zinc content of Linsley Pond appears to be very variable; on many occasions the element could not be detected at all. Two analyses of cadmium, namely, of *Eichhornia crassipes* in Lake Seminole with 16.2 ppm dry in the plant and 0.0024 ppm in the water (Lawrence 1971) and of *Ceratophyllum demersum* in Linsley Pond with 9.12 ppm dry in the plant and 0.0015 ppm in the water, suggest concentration factors of 600–700 for plants not rooted in the sediments.

TABLE 49. *Mean Zn contents of water, of dry plants, and concentration factor assuming a water content of 90%, of species likely to obtain all their zinc directly or indirectly from the water*

Study	Mean Zn in water mg/liter^{-1} (*1*)	Mean Zn in dry plant × 0.1 (ppm) (*2*)	*2/1*
Ceratophyllum demersum (Riemer and Toth, 3 samples)	0.009	16.4	1,820
Utricularia inflata (Boyd, 4 samples)	0.008	10.8	1,350
Utricularia sp. (Riemer and Toth, 3 samples)	0.034	15.7	406
Eichhornia crassipes (Lawrence, Lake Seminole mean)	0.126	21.0	166
Lemna minor (Riemer and Toth, 3 samples)	0.017	37.0	2,140
Spirodela polyrhiza (Varenko and Chuiko, 1 sample)	0.004	100.0	25,000

Lawrence gives some data for the zinc and cadmium concentrations of lake sediments, termed by him soils or hydrosols.[10] He did no complete analyses but determined the elements either in ammonium acetate or in aqua regia extracts. The former gives the exchangeable zinc or cadmium, the latter an approach to the total zinc or cadmium. The two analyses were done on separate samples; occasionally the exchangeable zinc is higher than that extracted with aqua regia which in such cases cannot represent total zinc. The means of the figures for the sediments of Lake Seminole are as follows: mean Zn; exchangeable 53 ppm, aqua regia extraction 227 ppm. Mean Cd; exchangeable 1.55 ppm, aqua regia extraction 21.5 ppm. All these figures are extraordinarily high. The ratio Cd:Zn in the exchangeable fraction, namely, 2.02×10^{-2}, is not very different from that in the water

---

[10] This word appears to be a transliteration or adaptation from the Russian. It is etymologically unsound and also confusing, in that it has an accepted meaning that might well occur in limnological discourse. It should therefore be avoided as denoting a sediment. Though lake sediments have many properties of soils, and terrestrial soils can be, geologically, sediments in the widest sense, it is often necessary to differentiate between *soils* in the drainage basin of a lake and *sediments* underwater. Pragmatically little confusion is likely to arise from this usage.

of the lake, namely, 1.87×10^{-2}. The much higher value of the ratio in the aqua regia extraction, namely, 9.5×10^{-2}, may be due to some of the zinc determinations being much too low. In view of the concordance of Lawrence's and Cowgill's results for plants in spite of great apparent environmental differences in chemistry, and of the marked toxicity of cadmium, the matter obviously requires much further study.

Mercury. Mercury has been determined by Cowgill; the results are extremely high, as indicated in Table 46. The determinations on *Pontederia cordata* leaves and on stems of *Decodon verticillatus* were repeated by a different technique by F. Breck but gave almost identical results; 35 ppm for *P. cordata* in which Cowgill herself found 33 ppm, and 10 ppm for *D. verticillatus* in which Cowgill had found 10.1 ppm. Whatever the cause of these immense values they can hardly be typical of aquatic vegetation in general. As Cowgill points out they are most peculiar in that there is no hint of enrichment of mercury in the source materials; though in most species analyzed there is little variation in the different parts of the plant, the leaves of *P. cordata* contain about twice as much of the element as do the flowers or stems.

Tin. This element seems to be known only from Cowgill's (1974a) study. The quantity present represents a much greater enrichment relative to the source materials than is the case with copper or zinc, and apparently an enormous concentration over the minute amount in the water. This may be of interest in view of the growing evidence that tin has a metabolic significance in some organisms (Schwarz, Milne, and Vinyard 1970).

Lead. The lead content of freshwater angiosperms is known from the work of Lawrence (1971) and of Cowgill (1974a). Lawrence's values vary from 2 ppm in *Bacopa* sp. to 52.5 ppm in *Eichhornia crassipes*. In the case of the latter plant growing in Lake Seminole with a mean suspended lead concentration of 0.0327 ppm, the concentration factor would be of the order of 160; it might be lower if appreciable soluble lead were present but all lead could be utilized, or much higher if little soluble lead was present but only that fraction could be taken up.

Cowgill's values all lie in a restricted part of Lawrence's range; her analysis of *Ceratophyllum demersum* in Linsley Pond implies a concentration factor, relative to total lead in the water, of about 70. There seems to be very little tendency for the different parts of the plant to differ significantly in lead content. The values recorded today may well be considerably influenced by pollution.

The ferrides. This term was applied by Landergren (1943) to the elements of atomic numbers 22–28 inclusive, namely, titanium, vanadium, chromium, manganese, iron, cobalt, and nickel. Owing to the progressive incorporation of electrons into the deeper shells of their atoms, their chemical properties are fairly similar, though much less so than in the case of the lanthanide rare earths. The differences that are observed between these elements are, however, apt to be very important biogeochemically. Titanium, one of the least biologically active elements, and vanadium, which is probably quite active though little understood, have already been discussed. The other elements are now conveniently considered, beginning with the two that are commonest in the biosphere.

Iron and manganese. These two elements are apt to go into solution, in quantities of the order of tenths of milligrams or milligrams in reduced environments, being precipitated either chemically or by chemotrophic bacteria if the environments subsequently become oxidizing. Their high availability in reduced lake sediments is probably responsible for the variable but often high values (Table 50) of both elements in water plants, as Mayer and Gorham (1951) have emphasized. It is also quite likely that some analyses are based on plants on which precipitation of the elements has occurred, perhaps as a result of the action of epiphytic bacteria. Mayer and Gorham found no obvious evidence of this, even in those plants richest in the elements, such as *Sparganium minimum* with 0.562% Fe and 0.378% Mn. Occasional examples of very much greater concentrations have been recorded by other workers.

The variability exhibited by both elements makes it difficult to make any significant general statements. In most analyses of water plants iron is somewhat in excess of manganese, as is ordinarily the case in the inorganic materials of the lithosphere. The series of emergent junciform plants studied by Mayer and Gorham has a higher Mn:Fe ratio than do their submerged and floating-leaved plants, and in this respect are more like land plants, in which manganese is usually in excess of iron (Robinson, Steinkoenig, and Miller 1917; Mayer and Gorham 1951; Bowen 1966). This difference between land and water plants may well be due to the latter being more often rooted in highly reduced sediments in which the proportion of ferrous and manganous ions differs little from the ratio of the total quantity in the lithosphere. In soils, in which there is a far greater opportunity for water to be replaced by air, and vice versa, variations in the availability of the two elements may well be more rapid and more complicated. On the whole iron is likely to be relatively less available than manganese; Mn^{2+} is stable at higher values of the redox potential than is Fe^{2+}.

In Riemer and Toth's (1968) study, the water lilies are consistently low in both elements; no specimen of the nine that they studied had more than 0.21% Fe and 0.15% Mn in the leaf blade. Mayer and Gorham's material of *Nuphar lutea* with 0.026% Fe and 0.076% Mn was likewise very low in both elements. Cowgill, however, found that in *Nuphar advena* and *Nymphaea odorata* in Linsley Pond and the adjacent Cedar Lake, the leaves

TABLE 50. *Iron and manganese in the earth's crust, source materials, and water plants, as % dry matter, and in water as ppm*

Study	Fe	Mn	Mn:Fe
Accessible lithosphere (Taylor)	5.63%	0.095%	0.017
Source materials, Linsley Basin (Cowgill)	7.22%	0.259%	0.036
Water, Linsley Pond, mean	0.30 ppm%	0.29 ppm	0.97
Plants, Linsley Pond and Cedar Lake (6 spp.)[a]	0.456–9.60%; 3.04 (0.102)%	0.020–0.31%; 0.092 (0.029)%	0.030 (0.284)
Water, Chattahoochee River Reservoirs mean (Lawrence)	0.736 (0.226) ppm[b]	0.124 (0.058) ppm[b]	0.168 (0.255)[b]
Plants, Chattahoochee River Reservoirs (14 spp.)	0.094–0.890%; 0.284%	0.012–1.07%; 0.193%	0.680
Water, Par Pond, South Carolina mean (Boyd)	0.29 ppm	0.002 ppm	0.069
Plants, Par Pond (16 spp.)	0.012–0.292%; 0.092%	0.012–0.097%; 0.035%	0.382
Water, New Jersey mean (Riemer and Toth)	0.413 ppm	0.088 ppm	0.213
Plants, New Jersey (37 spp.)	0.02–3.15%; 0.717%	0.01–1.19%; 0.228%	0.312

Plants, Minnesota (3 spp., Nelson and Palmer)	0.045–0.408%; 0.173%	0.039–0.513%; 0.294%	1.71
Submerged and floating plants, English Lake District (10 spp., Mayer and Gorham)	0.007–0.562% 0.148%	0.038–0.378%; 0.146%	0.99
Emergent junciform plants, English Lake District (19 herbaceous spp., Mayer and Gorham)	0.007–0.065%; 0.024%	0.011–0.148%; 0.062%	2.56
Water, Dneprodzerzhinsk Reservoir (Varenko and Chuiko)	—	47 ppm	—
Plants, Dneprodzerzhinsk Reservoir	—	0.061–0.570%; 0.188%	—
Plants, Ukraine (5 spp., Petkova and Lubyanov)	—	0.046–2.31%	—
Mean aquatic plants (Denton)	0.190	0.180	0.94
Mean aquatic plants from data above[c]	0.317	0.238	0.71
Mean terrestrial vegetation (Bowen)	0.014	0.063	4.5

[a] Without *Ceratophyllum* and *Potamogeton* the means would be Fe 0.674%, Mn 0.037%; Mn:Fe 0.054. Figures in parentheses are Cowgill's (1973b) means including 1972 when the great enrichment in these two genera was not observed.

[b] Figures in parentheses refer to dissolved, the others to dissolved and suspended material.

[c] Using the data omitting *Ceratophyllum* and *Potamogeton* in the Linsley Basin.

always contained at least 0.60% Fe though the manganese was very low, never in excess of 0.037%.

Riemer and Toth found *Phragmites australis* to contain 0.01–0.05% Fe and 0.00–0.02% Mn, essentially confirming the low values of 0.023% for both elements given by Mayer and Gorham.

Elodea (sp., 0.95–2.90% Fe, 0.25–0.55% Mn, Riemer and Toth; *E. canadensis*, 0.132% Fe, 0.244% Mn, Mayer and Gorham; 0.408% Fe, 0.331% Mn, Nelson and Palmer), *Heteranthera dubia* (0.85–0.95% Fe, 0.38–1.00% Mn, Riemer and Toth), *Myriophyllum heterophyllum* (0.20–3.80% Fe; 0.047–0.58% Mn, Boyd, Riemer, and Toth), *M.* cf. *spicatum* (1.10–3.20% Fe; 0.73–2.00% Mn, Riemer and Toth),[11] and *Utricularia* sp. (1.0–2.50% Fe, 0.01–0.09% Mn) are examples of plants of which at least three samples have been analyzed and which usually exhibit high, sometimes very high, iron contents.

The very high iron values recorded by Cowgill for *Ceratophyllum demersum* (8.2%, 11.0%) and for *Potamogeton* cf. *praelongus* (5.9%) are almost certainly due to precipitation of hydrated ferric oxide on the plants.

Chromium. Though important in vertebrate metabolism, chromium is little known in plants. The available data for aquatic angiosperms (Table 51) are derived from the studies of Petkova and Lubyanov (1969), Lawrence (1971), and Cowgill (1974a). Unfortunately, though they agree on the amount of chromium to be found in lake waters and in the sediments or source materials in lakes or their basins, the quantities that they found in aquatic plants are not at all concordant.

Cowgill's figures for chromium are consistently low and not very different from the mean for terrestrial plants given by Bowen. All Lawrence's values are very high, his mean being nearly two orders of magnitude greater than Cowgill's. The data of Petkova and Lubyanov tend to bridge the gap between the two American series, though none of their values are as low as Cowgill's. In that part of their series which can only be referred to ash weight, the very high value of 780 ppm in *Utricularia* sp. would probably be rather greater than the 108 ppm dry found by Lawrence in *Limnophila* sp. in Lake Seminole. The mean value of this part of their series is 177 ppm ash, which would correspond to about 20 ppm dry. There is evidently no systematic difference in the mean contents of the submersed species referred only to ash and the emergent and floating-leaved species for which the analyses can be referred to dry weight. The individual samples of the

---

[11] Nelson and Palmer (1938) give values as low as 0.064% Fe and 0.047% Mn for *M. spicatum*, but, working in Minnesota in the 1930s, they probably were analyzing *M. exalbescens*.

TABLE 51. *Chromium and molybdenum in the earth's crust, source materials, waters, and water plants*

Study	Cr (ppm)	Mo (ppm)
Mean accessible lithosphere (Taylor)	100	1.5
Mean sediment, Chattahoochee Lakes (Lawrence)	97.5	—
Mean source materials, Linsley Basin (Cowgill)	86.6	0.1
Mean sediments, Ukraine Lakes (Petkova and Lubyanov)	76.4	2.0
Mean water, Chattahoochee Lakes (Lawrence)	0.0092	—
Mean water, Linsley Pond (Cowgill)	0.017	—
Means for species and overall mean for aquatic macrophytes		
Chattahoochee Lakes (Lawrence)	8.0–108 45.2	—
Linsley Basin (Cowgill)	0.47–0.69 0.60	0.085–85 (0.61)[a] 24 (0.31)[a]
Ukraine Lakes (Petkova and Lubyanov)	1.7–50 18.3	4.0–87 (7.7)[b] 21.5 (5.1)[b]
Mean for terrestrial vegetation (Bowen)	0.23	0.9

[a] Figures in parentheses omit *Ceratophyllum* and *Potamogeton;* Cowgill's means for 1971–1972 are Cr 0.62 and Mo 5.5, the latter figure including these genera.
[b] Figures in parentheses omit *Phragmites.*

species analyzed several times varied very greatly. Thus in five analyses of *Typha angustifolia* the range was from 13 to 380 ppm ash, probably corresponding to about 1.7–50 ppm dry, while in *Ceratophyllum* sp. the content varied from 27 to 540 ppm ash, which would be equivalent to about 5–110 ppm dry. These very wide ranges, which span the greater part of the whole range of values given by Petkova and Lubyanov, or for that matter all the investigators of chromium in water plants, suggest that if the technique used was adequate, under some circumstances very large amounts of chromium can be associated with water plants, though probably without any biological function. It is evident that the whole subject is in considerable confusion.

Molybdenum. This element, which plays an essential role in nitrogen fixation in procaryotes and in nitrate reduction in many organisms, is probably required by all plants. It has been little studied in aquatic angiosperms.

The available data are summarized in Table 51. Although the element is much rarer in nature than is chromium, the quantities present in organisms are little less and imply much more active concentration. Cowgill's values fall into two groups. In the emergent or floating-leaved species the content is low, ranging from 0.085 ppm in *Nuphar advena* to 0.61 ppm in *Decodon verticillatus*. In specimens of *Ceratophyllum* and *Potamogeton* the amounts found were very high, from 60 to 90 ppm. The plants exhibiting these excessive values also contained very much larger amounts of iron than did the other species studied. The high molybdenum contents were not found in material from the same localities a year later. It is reasonable to suspect that when very large amounts of molybdenum are recorded, as the 240 ppm ash or 87 ppm dry in *Phragmites australis* noted by Petkova and Lubyanov, the element was associated with extraneous deposition of iron. Apart from such cases of very high molybdenum content, the range in either Cowgill's or Petkova and Lubyanov's series is small, though the results of the latter workers are greater by an order of magnitude than Cowgill's figures; the mean value for terrestrial vegetation appears to fall between the two groups. Since Petkova and Lubyanov's mean for sediments is slightly greater than and Cowgill's mean for source materials is much less than the mean content of the accessible lithosphere, it is possible that the Connecticut plants were less well supplied with molybdenum than were the Ukranian. However, when conditions for fixation of molybdenum prevail, very large amounts can clearly be deposited in the Connecticut lakes. It is noteworthy that Gorham (1964) found molybdenum to be associated with ferric iron in oxidized lake sediments.

As has been noted in Vol. II (p. 312), Goldman (1960) obtained evidence that the presence of *Alnus* bushes along the shore of a lake may reduce the input of molybdenum, because the alders, which have nitrogen-fixing bacteria in their root nodules, remove the element from superficial groundwater entering the lake.

Nickel and Cobalt. The distribution of these two elements in freshwater macrophytes is inadequately known, such data as exist (Table 52) being far from concordant. Since Petkova and Lubyanov's figures for nickel in the ash of submersed plants (*Ceratophyllum* sp., *Elodea canadensis*, *Utricularia* sp., *Potamogeton* spp., *Lemna trisulca*) average 24.5 ppm, whereas the mean content in the ash of the emergent and floating-leaved species represented in Table 52, is 9.8 ppm, it is probably legitimate to conclude that their whole assemblage would have a mean of about 3 ppm dry, in satisfactory concordance with Cowgill's mean figure. The latter investigator did not observe any striking differences in nickel content between submersed and emergent or floating-leaved species. Where direct comparison on a dry weight basis is possible, as between *Nymphaea alba* with a mean of 1.05

ppm Ni in the Ukraine and *N. odorata* with 3.08 ppm in Connecticut, or *Nuphar lutea* with a mean of 1.26 ppm in the Ukraine and *N. advena* with 3.18 ppm in Connecticut, it is clear that Cowgill's values are higher. In contrast, if her figures for *Ceratophyllum demersum* and *Potamogeton* cf. *praelongus* are referred to ash, they are 11.6 ppm and 10.8 ppm, respectively, definitely lower than the mean of 52 ppm in the ash of Ukrainian *Ceratophyllum* sp., though comparable with the 12 ppm in the ash of *Potamogeton pectinatus* and 20 ppm in that of *P. perfoliatus* analyzed by Petkova and Lubyanov. It is doubtful if the recorded differences between the observations of Cowgill and those of Petkova and Lubyanov are of any significance, though it is possible that in some circumstances *Ceratophyllum*, which the latter workers found to contain up to 100 ppm Ni in the ash, may be a mild facultative accumulator of nickel.

TABLE 52. *Distribution of nickel and cobalt in aquatic angiosperms with relevant geochemical data*

Study	Ni (ppm)	Co (ppm)	Ni/Co
Mean accessible lithosphere	75	25	3
Mean source material, Linsley	52.6	6.9	7.6
Water, Linsley Pond	0.0021	—	—
Plants, Linsley Basin[a]	2.0–3.6	0.075–1.12	
	2.9	0.37 (0.22)	7.8 (13.2)
Water, Chattachoochee Lakes (Lawrence)	0.0083	0.0034	2.4
Sediments, Chattahoochee Lakes (Lawrence)	284	115	2.5
Plants, Chattahoochee Lakes	17.7–44	0.2–32.5	
	25.4	12.6	2.0
Mean sediment, Ukraine (Petkova and Lubyanov)	35	—	—
Emergent and floating plants, Ukraine	1.1–4.7 2.0	—	—
Mean sediments Dneprodzerzhinsk Reservoir (Varenko and Chuiko)	—	9.1	—
Mean water, Dneprodzerzhinsk Reservoir	—	0.0002	—
Plants, Dneprodzerzhinsk Reservoir	—	0.27–8.30 3.0	—
Mean terrestrial plants (Bowen)	3	0.5	6

[a] Figures in parentheses omit *Pontederia cordata;* Cowgill's means for 1971–1972 are Ni 2.8, Co 0.32.

The very high values recorded by Lawrence, though matched by Petkova and Lubyanov's higher figures for *Ceratophyllum*, refer to a number of species for which there are no other analyses. In view of the general concordance of Cowgill's and of Petkova and Lubyanov's means with that of Bowen for terrestrial vegetation, Lawrence's determinations remain somewhat problematical, even though they are in line with the high values for the nickel content of the sediments in the basins that he examined and to some extent of the waters of those localities in which plants were growing.

Within the plants of water lilies there is in Cowgill's work a slight tendency for the leaf petioles and flower stalks to contain less nickel (Table 53) than the organs which they bear.

Varenko and Chuiko (1971) found 0.27 ppm cobalt in *Phragmites australis*, 0.30 ppm in *Schoenoplectus lacustris*, and 0.56 ppm in *Typha angustifolia*, but considerably more, from 2.8 ppm in *Potamogeton pectinatus* to

TABLE 53. *Distribution of nickel and cobalt in the various parts of plants of the family Nymphaeaceae in the lakes of the Linsley Basin (data of Cowgill)*

	Leaf petiole	Leaf	Flower stalk	Flower
	Nickel (ppm)			
Nymphaea odorata				
Linsley Pond	2.4	2.8	2.76	3.1
Cedar Lake	3.1	3.6	3.0	3.87
Mean	2.8	3.2	2.8	3.5
Nuphar advena				
Linsley Pond	3.1	3.4	2.9	4.5
Cedar Lake	2.7	3.0	2.6	3.1
Mean	2.9	3.2	2.8	3.8
	Cobalt (ppm)			
Nymphaea odorata				
Linsley Pond	0.07	0.08	0.05	0.13
Cedar Lake	0.07	0.11	0.02	0.13
Mean	0.07	0.095	0.035	0.10
Nuphar advena				
Linsley Pond	0.04	0.11	0.08	0.09
Cedar Lake	0.07	0.15	0.03	0.10
Mean	0.055	0.13	0.05	0.095
	Ratio Mean Ni to Mean Co			
Nymphaea odorata	40	34	80	35
Nuphar advena	53	25	56	40

8.3 ppm in *Spirodela polyrhiza*, in submersed or floating plants. Only the three determinations from emergent plants are concordant with the analyses of Cowgill based on submersed, floating, and emergent species, which, however, included no junciform species. Cowgill found low values, both absolutely and relative to nickel, in the Nymphaeaceae, definitely more in *Ceratophyllum demersum* (mean 0.34 ppm) and *Potamogeton* cf. *praelongus* (0.30 ppm), and some accumulation relative to other parts of the plant or to other species in the leaves of *Pontederia cordata* (Table 54). In these leaves the amount of cobalt can exceed that of nickel. As with some other elements, Lawrence's values for cobalt are extremely high and present the same kind of problem that arises from his determination of nickel.

TABLE 54. *Distribution of nickel and cobalt in the various parts of* Pontederia cordata *from the two lakes of the Linsley Basin* (data of Cowgill)

Lake	Stem	Leaf	Flower
		Nickel (ppm)	
Linsley Pond	3.9	4.0	2.8
Cedar Lake	2.7	3.9	2.9
Mean	3.3	4.0	2.9
		Cobalt (ppm)	
Linsley Pond	0.10	1.7	0.10
Cedar Lake	0.14	4.6	0.06
Mean	0.12	3.2	0.08
		Ni/Co	
	27	1.3	36

Sulfur and selenium. Sulfur has been determined by a number of investigators, notably Riemer and Toth (1968), Boyd (1970); and Cowgill (1973b, 1974a). The data of the first-named workers, which cover a wider range of sulfur contents than those of the later investigators are summarized in Table 56. The distribution of values is very skewed about the mode; only a single plant of *Phragmites australis*, collected from a dry locality, contained less than 0.1% S, though the petioles of water lilies, but not the leaves, might contain such low concentrations. Boyd's mean of 0.25% for plants growing in water containing but 0.34 mg S liter^{-1} is a little below the 0.29% of Cowgill and the 0.31% of Riemer and Toth, figures which are certainly not significantly different. None of these means are very different from that of 0.34% given by Bowen (1966) for terrestrial plants. Cowgill found rather more sulfur in water lilies than did Riemer and Toth, her *Nymphaea odorata* containing 0.26%, while from New Jersey the same species contained 0.14% S. This difference is curious in that the Connecticut habitats of the water lilies contained but 2.5–3.3 mg liter^{-1}, while those from New Jersey came from water with 15–25 mg S liter^{-1}. There is some indication of rather greater sulfur contents in the leaves than in the petioles.

The ratio of mean sulfur to mean nitrogen in Riemer and Toth's analyses is 0.114; the equivalent ratio in mean vegetable protein (Mathews 1927), is about 0.038, or one-third of that in whole water plants. Presumably in the latter a good deal of the sulfur is in inorganic form, as sulfate.

Selenium has been determined by Cowgill (1973b, 1974a), who found little variation between different species, the range being 1.3–2.6 ppm, with a mean of 2.2 ppm. The ratio of Se:S in the source materials of the Linsley Basin is 14×10^{-4} while in the plants analyzed the ratio of the means was 7.6×10^{-4}. It was not possible to detect selenium in the water, but it is clear that no differential accumulation of the element is occurring in the plants.

The halogens.   The halogens have been determined less frequently than the common cationic elements with which they tend to be associated in nature, and when studied usually analyses have been made only for chlorine, though there are enough data for the other elements of the group to suggest interesting possibilities.

Fluorine.   Cowgill determined fluorine for the six species of plants analyzed from the two small lakes of the Linsley Basin in North Branford, Connecticut. The quantity present ranged from a mean of 263 ppm in *Decodon verticillatus* to 516 ppm in *Pontederia cordata*, the overall mean being 356 ppm or 428 ppm using Cowgill's means that include 1972. The ratio of fluorine to chlorine varied from 8.0×10^{-3} in *Nymphaea odorata* to 32.6×10^{-3} in *Potamogeton* cf. *praelongus*. In *Ceratophyllum demersum* the ratio varied from 24.5×10^{-3} to 31.3×10^{-3}; this plant must take up the halogens from the water. It seems therefore probable that the observed ratios in the plants, which are considerably higher than the 3.8×10^{-3} found for the ratio of the means in various analyses of the surface waters of Linsley Pond (Cowgill 1970), are due to the preferential uptake of fluorine, at least when it is present in small quantities, from 22 to 24 mg m^{-3}, in the water. It must, however, be noted that the mean amount in the source materials of the basin, namely, 351 ppm, is somewhat greater than the chlorine content of 189 ppm. Most of the halogens in inland waters are from rain and so ultimately from the ocean. High fluorine seems to limit *Cyperus papyrus* in East Africa (Kilham and Hecky 1973).

Chlorine.   The most significant data are those of Riemer and Toth (1968), who found a range of from 0.24% in one specimen of *Potamogeton natans* to 3.47% in one of *Typha latifolia*. The same two species give the lowest and highest means, namely, 0.31 and 2.87% for the whole New Jersey series, of which the overall mean was 1.67%. There is no significant relationship with the sodium in the plant ($r = 0.1775$), or with the chlorine in the water in which it was growing ($r = 0.0097$), but there is a moderate but highly significant correlation ($r = 0.5935$, $P < 0.001$) between the chlorine and potassium contents of the plants. A comparable correlation ($r = 0.6024$, $P = \sim 0.01$) is given by the chlorine and potassium contents of terrestrial plants studied by Robinson, Steinkoenig, and Miller (1917). These correlations are of some interest in view of the possibility that passive movement of potassium may depend on the activity of a chloride pump (see p. 273).

The other published data for chlorine, such as the range from 0.85 to 2.48% for the means of the six species studied by Cowgill in Connecticut, giving an overall mean of 1.50%, or 1.64% including the 1972 data, or the range for means of individual species from 0.58 to 2.01%, with a mean of 1.31% in the three species studied by Lancaster, Coup, and Hughes in New Zealand, are clearly comparable to those of Riemer and Toth. As with fluorine, the chlorine content of leaves is rather lower than that of stems or petioles, but there is some variation in the other parts of the plant (Table 55).

Allenby (1968) gives a few curious analyses of *Lemna minor* living on water with a wide range of chloride concentrations, which suggest an inverse relationship between the chloride concentration of the plant and that of the environment. *Spirodela polyrhiza*, over a narrower range of external concentrations, exhibited a direct relationship.

Bromine. The only important data are those of Cowgill, who found from 17.6 ppm in *Potamogeton* cf. *praelongus* to a mean of 42.0 ppm in *Nymphaea odorata*. The mean content of all six species was 31.5 ppm, or 32.3 ppm averaging in Cowgill's 1972 data. The ratio of the mean chlorine to mean bromine was 473, which differs little from the ratio of the mean quantities in the water, namely, 440:1. There seems, however, to be systematic variation among the plants. *Pontederia cordata* gave values of 620:1 and 625:1, while *Decodon verticillatus* gave 285:1 and 251:1. In the water lilies the ratios lay between 398 and 538, while in *Ceratophyllum* there is great variability.

Iodine. In the same material that Cowgill analyzed for the other halogens the iodine contents varied from 0.25 ppm in *Potamogeton* cf. *praelongus* to 0.49 in *Nymphaea odorata*, with an overall mean of 0.39 ppm or 0.46 averaging in the 1972 data. There is little systematic variation, but since *Ceratophyllum demersum* with 0.32 ppm is the next to lowest, the species with large rhizomes or roots come in the upper part of the range.

TABLE 55. *Halogen content of water lilies from the Linsley Basin*

Halo-gen	Petiole			Leaf			Flower stalk			Flower		
	Cedar Lake	Linsley Pond		Cedar Lake	Linsley Pond		Cedar Lake	Linsley Pond		Cedar Lake	Linsley Pond	
		1971	1972		1971	1972		1971	1972		1971	1972
Nymphaea odorata												
F	401	309	538	192	226	450	266	274	595	424	339	427
Cl	14,900	40,600	31,900	6,900	15,900	13,600	19,900	27,600	28,800	10,300	14,700	14,200
Br	30	63	45	26	38	26	30	54	41	30	66	31
I	0.58	0.53	0.56	0.55	0.58	0.54	0.54	0.38	0.52	0.33	0.37	0.52
Nuphar advena												
F	472	457		375	272		361	257		372	336	
Cl	17,500	17,600		13,700	6,800		29,000	22,600		5,300	6,200	
Br	31	35		25	30		36	44		30	25	
I	0.42	0.37		0.50	0.44		0.49	0.35		0.58	0.43	

Nitrogen and phosphorus.   As the two elements most likely to be limiting, nitrogen and phosphorus are of special importance.

Experimental studies.   Experimental work by Gerloff and Krombholz (1966), using cuttings of *Vallisneria americana* grown in alga-free culture in a modified Hoagland's solution as medium, shows the relationship of yield to the amount of the element present when all other requirements are met. The amount of the plant produced increases almost proportionately with the amount of the element supplied (solid line of Fig. 109A) until the latter ceases to be limiting; further addition then causes no further increment in yield, though the quantity incorporated into the tissue continues to increase, a phenomenon known as *luxury consumption* in agronomy. This means that when the plant is being limited by either of the elements, the concentration in the tissues will tend to correspond to the fundamental quantity required for metabolism, while the yield of the plant increases; when the element is no more limiting further increase produces no greater yield but only storage of the element. The transition point, at which this storage without additional growth starts to occur, defines a critical concentration so that if plants are found in nature containing less of the element, it is a reasonable presumption that they are limited by the element in question. Presumably critical concentrations of this kind could be worked out experimentally for any nutrient.

Gerloff and Krombholz conclude that for *Vallisneria americana* the critical content of nitrogen is 1.3% N and for phosphorus 0.13% P. Actually the nitrogen content appears to start rising in the tissue with the smallest increment in nitrogen supplied; the data clearly give some leeway in interpretation, though the critical figure of 1.3% N is obviously reasonable, as is the value of 0.13% for phosphorus, for which element the full data are not given (Fig. 109c). Gerloff and Krombholz concluded from experiments on *Elodea nuttallii*, *Ceratophyllum demersum*, and *Heteranthera dubia* that the same critical values applied over a wide range of water plants. Such uniformity has not been observed by investigators making similar studies of agricultural and horticultural terrestrial species. Gerloff and Krombholz conclude that the uniformity that they observed is due to submersed water plants varying much less in the amount of nonprotoplasmic supporting structures, low in nitrogen, than would an assemblage of diverse land plants. It is not unlikely that different, presumably lower, critical concentrations would be derived from the study of emergent plants such as *Phragmites* or *Decodon*.

Field data on both elements.   Since the field data for the two elements determined on the same samples suggest that now one, and now the other, can fall below the critical level, as just defined, it is convenient first to dis-

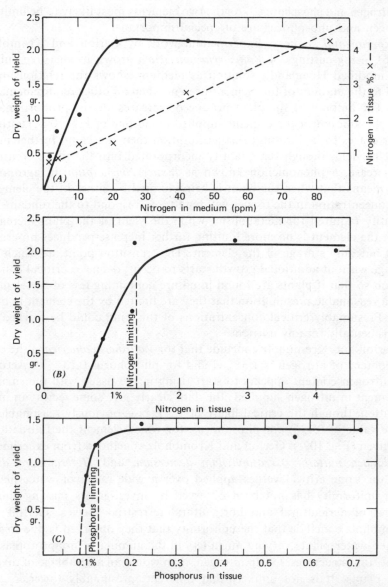

FIGURE 109. Relationship of yield, composition of plant and of medium in axenic cultures of *Vallisneria americana* from the data and graphs of Gerloff and Krombholz. (*A*) Yield (solid line) and percentage nitrogen content (broken line) of plants grown at different nitrogen concentrations; (*B*) yield as a function of percentage nitrogen content in plants grown in otherwise complete media containing varying amounts of nitrate; (*C*) yield as a function of percentage phosphorus in plants grown in otherwise complete media containing varying amounts of orthophosphate. The broken vertical lines (*B*) and (*C*), indicating varying amounts of orthophosphate. The broken vertical lines in (*B*) and (*C*), indicat-

cuss cases for which data on both elements exist. Certain further aspects of nitrogen are then discussed, and finally a few recent data on phosphorus unaccompanied by nitrogen determinations are considered.

Gerloff and Krombholz give data for six kinds of water plants growing in Lake Mendota, Wisconsin, collected on four occasions during the summer. All plants appear to contain more than the critical quantities of both elements, though *Ceratophyllum demersum* during the middle and *Vallisneria americana* at the end of the season contain only about 2% N, which is getting close to the quantity indicating a limitation by nitrogen (Fig. 110). These two species showed striking seasonal variation in nitrogen content, but of a different kind. *Myriophyllum* spp. and *Potamogeton zosteriformis*, however, varied very little. The changes in phosphorus content are less striking and less regular, though *C. demersum* exhibits the same qualitative pattern for both elements. This species, being rootless, is probably more in competition with the phytoplankton than are the other water plants analyzed, which may explain the low nitrogen concentration during the warmest part of the year when nutrient demand due to phytoplankton production is likely to be greatest. A later study in Lake Wingra, also in the Yahara River drainage, by Adams and McCracken (1974) indicates that in spring and autumn the phosphorus content of *Myriophyllum* cf. *spicatum* is not less than 0.135% whereas in July it is between 0.113 and 0.132%. Here phosphorus may well be limiting in summer.

In the much more oligotrophic Nebish Lake, Wisconsin, all plants contain lower concentrations of both elements, *Potamogeton epihydrus* having most and *Lobelia dortmanna* least. If the value of 0.13%, indicating phosphorus deficiency, applies to the plants of oligotrophic waters as well as to the more eutrophic species used in experiments, *L. dortmanna*, with a minimum content of 0.10% P in August, and *Eriocaulon septangulare*, with the same content in September, are presumably limited by the supply of the element. Somewhat similar distributions suggesting phosphorus limitation were noted in the plants of other mesotrophic or somewhat oligotrophic lakes in northeastern Wisconsin, also studied by Gerloff and Krombholz.

Riemer and Toth give 92 analyses of the vegetative parts of 37 species of angiosperms. Their ranges, modes, and means are set out in Table 56. The highest values for both elements are given in *Lemna minor*, but *Wolffia* sp. (N 4.18%, P 1.00%) is almost as rich; the Lemnaceae are ordinarily

---

ing the concentrations at which nitrogen or phosphorus became limiting, are based on the estimates of Gerloff and Krombholz and presumably involve much more experience than the single experiments on which the curves are based.   The intercepts of the extrapolated lower ends of these curves with the abcissae, at about 0.6% N and 0.08% P, presumably indicate the minimal concentrations in the plant that permit some growth.   The comparable intercept for the broken line drawn by eye, in (*A*) gives 0.7% N.

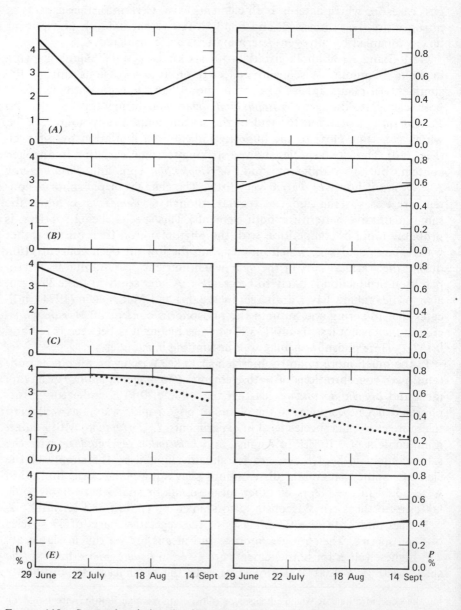

FIGURE 110.   Seasonal variations in nitrogen and phosphorus contents of water plants in Lake Mendota (data of Gerloff and Krombholz). (*A*) *Ceratophyllum demersum.* (*B*) *Heteranthera dubia.* (*C*) *Vallisneria americana.* (*D*) solid line, *Potamogeton zosteriformis;* dotted line, *P. richardsonii.* (*E*) *Myriophyllum* spp.

found on eutrophic water. The lowest nitrogen content was in a single plant of *Phragmites australis* growing in a dry locality; but a specimen of *Utricularia* sp. with 0.87% N was almost as low. The three plants of *Decodon verticillatus* analyzed (1.10–1.83% N mean 1.52%) seem systematically low in nitrogen; this may merely be because of a greater amount of non-nitrogenous supporting tissue in the material studied than in most of the other plants, the same being possibly also true of *P. australis*. These plants, and a single specimen of *Najas* sp. with 1.06% N (not the same specimen that was deficient in phosphorus), alone suggest nitrogen limitation if Gerloff and Krombholz's criterion of 1.3% N be strictly applied.

The lowest phosphorus content is in *Phragmites*, the smallest concentrations being in two plants growing in dry localities. These two plants, with 0.10% and 0.12% P, alone among the 89 samples show clear limitation by phosphorus by Gerloff and Krombholz's criterion, though single specimens of *Potamogeton natans* and *Najas* sp. with 0.15% and of *Callitriche* with 0.17% approach the critical value. With both nitrogen and phosphorus the validity of such critical values derived from experiments with submersed water plants, in studying emergent species like *Decodon* and *Phragmites* with much supporting tissue, is obviously very doubtful.

Histograms for both nitrogen and phosphorus using Riemer and Toth's individual analyses look roughly normal when plotted on an arithmetic scale (Fig. 111). When a semilogarithmic plot is used the two curves are slightly skewed in different directions.

The ratio of the mean nitrogen to the mean phosphorus is 6.04:1 by weight or 13.4:1 by atomic proportions. In *Lemna minor*, the proportion is 2.72 or in atomic terms 6.02:1, phosphorus being accumulated relative to nitrogen about twice as effectively as in the average water plants.

TABLE 56. *Sulfur, nitrogen. and phosphorus distribution in the water plants of New Jersey*

Sulfur		
Range of individual analyses	0.05–0.78%	Mode 0.1–0.2%
Range of means for species	0.13–0.71%	Mean 0.31%
Nitrogen		
Range of individual analyses	0.71–5.29%	Mode 2.5–3.0%
Range of means for species	1.52–5.09%	Mean 2.73%
Phosphorus		
Range of individual analyses	0.10–1.95%	Mode 0.3–0.4%
Range of means for species	0.16–1.87%	Mean 0.45%

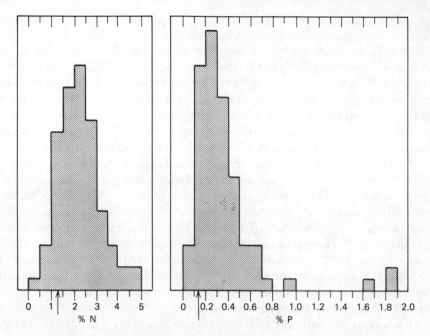

FIGURE 111. Distribution of nitrogen and phosphorus in water plants of New Jersey; arrows indicate limits of deficiencies according to Gerloff and Krombholz (data of Reimer and Toth).

Analyses of the water plants of Lake Warniak, given by Bernatowicz (1969) suggest a rather different picture.

	Range	Mean
Nitrogen, 15 spp.	1.18–2.82%	1.82%
Phosphorus, 16 spp.	0.01–0.61%	0.17%

Only *Typha latifolia* (1.18% N) and *Phragmites communis* (1.23% N) contain less than 1.3% N, but there is a strong suggestion of limitation by phosphorus, for 12 species out of 16 contain less than 0.1% P, the lowest content being 0.01% in *Phragmites australis*. The highest nitrogen contents were in *Elodea canadensis* (2.51% N) and *Nymphaea alba* (2.82% N), while the greatest phosphorus concentrations were in *Elodea canadensis* (0.59% P) and *Ceratophyllum demersum* (0.61% P). The low phosphorus concentrations in most of the plants of Lake Warniak make the ratio of mean nitrogen to mean phosphorus high, namely, 10.5 by weight or 23.3 in atomic proportions.

Further data on nitrogen and its forms in water plants. A number of analyses have been made by Boyd (1968) of the nitrogen content of plants collected in spring in a variety of habitats in Alabama. The data are given as crude protein, but can easily be reconverted to Kjeldahl nitrogen, or total nitrogen less nitrate nitrogen, by multiplication by 0.16, when they are presumably comparable to the figures given by Gerloff and Krombholz.

Twelve submersed species contained from 1.36 to 3.65% N with a mean of 2.30%; only one species, *Myriophyllum heterophyllum*, contained less than 1.50%. Twenty species of emergent and floating plants gave an almost identical range from 1.49 to 3.79% N, with a mean of 2.30%; again only one species, *Nymphoides aquatica*, fell below 1.50%. The modal class for the entire group was 1.5–2.0%. Although probably few species were limited by nitrogen, many must have been growing in places in which the supply was only just adequate to permit utilization of the other available nutrients.

The forms of nitrogen present in water plants have been little studied. The figures published for crude protein, derived by multiplying the Kjeldahl nitrogen by 6.25, are obviously always in excess of the true protein, but by a very variable amount. Boyd (1968) found that leaf extracts of various aquatic species contained from 42.4% of the nitrogen as protein, in a sample of *Hydrocotyle* sp., to 96.9% in one of *Nymphaea odorata*. In most species in which several samples were analyzed, about two-thirds of the nitrogen was in protein, the ratios of the means being for *Justicia americana* 64.0%, *Alternanthera philoxeroides* 60.0%, *Sagittaria latifolia* 57.7%, and *Orontium aquaticum* 70.8%. In *Nymphaea odorata* the proportion always appeared greater, from 72.8 to 96.9% with a mean value of 88.0%; a single specimen of *Nuphar advena* with a protein nitrogen content of 86.5% falls in this range.

Boyd (1969b) has published analyses of the composition of the nitrogen of whole plants of *Justicia americana* collected throughout the growing season. During this time the proportion of both total and protein nitrogen declined, while the nonprotein nitrogen varied rather less regularly (Table 57).

TABLE 57. *Seasonal variation of crude protein, true protein, and nonprotein nitrogen in* Justicia americana

	May 16	June 14	July 10	August 19
Crude protein (N $\times$ 6.25)	17.69	12.62	10.69	10.19
True protein (Σ amino acids)	10.76	7.94	6.98	5.93
Difference	6.93	4.68	3.71	4.26
Proportion of N not as protein	39.2	37.1	34.7	41.8

Wick and Sandstrom (1938) found about 4.0% of the nitrogen in a sample of *Elodea canadensis* to be amide; it is quite likely that when, as in Gerloff and Krombholz's experiments, large amounts of nitrogen accumulate, much of it will be present as asparagine and glutamine, in which forms nitrogen is usually stored in angiosperms.

Boyd observed that the amount of true protein in specimens of *Typha latifolia* collected at 11 different sites varied from 4.0 to 11.9%. This corresponds to a difference of 1.26% N between the highest and lowest values. He suspected that the differences were environmentally determined, but as it is quite possible that more than one clone was involved, some genetic differences may also be involved. It is at any rate clear that some nitrogen in excess of the basic physiological needs of the plant can be stored as protein.

Boyd (1969a, b) has also studied the amino acid composition of water plants. In Table 58 some of his data relating to the extractable leaf protein of three pleustonic or floating-leaved species are given, as well as data for the emergent *Justicia americana* and *Typha latifolia*. He also analyzed a number of other plants from Par Pond, Aiken, South Carolina, but did not publish the data as they were within the range of variation of the other species. The amino acid composition of plants from a stand of *T. latifolia* was studied throughout the summer. Though the protein content of the plant decreased with aging, the amino acid composition of this protein showed little variation. (Boyd 1970c).

In a few additional analyses in which only the amino acids essential in mammalian nutrition were studied (Boyd 1968), thus not permitting an estimate of true protein by summation, it was found that the extractable leaf proteins of *Alternanthera philoxeroides* and of *Sagittaria latifolia* are deficient in phenylalanine, only a trace being detectable, whereas in all the other species analyzed the protein contains about 5% of this amino acid. This difference, if real, seems to be the only major one, between species, in the quantities of amino acids so far found in water plants.

Further data on phosphorus. Boyd (1970a) found the plants of Par Pond varied from 0.10% P in *Eleocharis quadrangulata* to 0.40% in *Nuphar advena*; the mean content was 0.20%. Out of 18 species five had mean phosphorus contents below 0.15%; low phosphorus concentrations may well limit these plants.

Cowgill gives for her various samples, values from 0.188% P in *Decodon verticillatus* from Linsley Pond to 0.341% P in *Nuphar advena* from the adjacent Cedar Lake, North Branford, Connecticut. The mean of her determinations, each species weighted separately, is 0.268% P.

It is of interest to compare the data that exist on the phosphorus contents of the leaves of such water lilies as have been analyzed several times

TABLE 58. *Amino acid composition of proteins derived from the extraction of green parts of five water plants (Boyd 1969a, 1969b, 1970b)*

	Justicia americana (Boyd 1969b)	Eichhornia crassipes (Boyd 1969a)	Pistia stratiotes (Boyd 1969a)	Hydrilla sp. (Boyd 1969a)	Typha latifolia (Boyd 1970b)
Mean true protein	7.90%	19.45	17.63	13.6	8.0
Proportion of N not protein	38.2	25.0	23.4	20.5	—
Aspartic acid	14.9	14.0	11.9	12.6	14.5
Glutamic acid	13.5	13.5	13.4	11.9	15.4
Proline	5.1	4.8	5.0	4.8	5.2
Glycine	6.0	6.0	6.5	8.6	5.8
Alanine	6.2	6.9	7.1	6.4	6.2
Valine	6.1	6.0	6.3	6.2	6.2
Leucine	7.7	9.1	9.2	9.3	9.2
Isoleucine	3.6	5.1	5.2	5.1	5.0
Phenylalanine	4.9	5.5	5.8	5.9	5.6
Tyrosine	3.6	3.9	4.2	4.7	3.3
Tryptophan	n.d.	n.d.	n.d.	n.d.	n.d.
Serine	5.8	4.7	5.0	5.6	4.9
Threonine	5.0	5.0	5.0	4.6	5.3
Cysteine	0.2	0.3	0.4	0.1	<0.1
Methionine	1.6	1.8	1.7	2.1	1.5
Lysine	5.8	6.3	6.9	5.1	4.6
Histidine	2.7	2.2	2.2	1.8	2.4
Arginine	5.8	6.1	4.6	5.2	5.0

(Table 59). In the case of these two species it seems clear that *Nymphaea odorata* contains rather less phorphorus than does *Nuphar advena*, even when, as at Par Pond, Linsley Pond, or Cedar Lake, the two species are growing in the same water. Even though the general level of phosphorus in water plants must be set by the quantity available in the environment, it is reasonable to conclude that genetic differences between species also regulate the amount of the element that is absorbed.

There seem to be no studies in which the nature of the phosphorus, stored after luxury consumption, has been elucidated; by analogy with terrestrial plants one might expect phytin or calcium magnesium inositol hexaphosphate to be one compound in which the element is present.

Ether extract and cellulose. The most useful work is that of Boyd (1968), who determined ether extract or crude fat, cellulose, and tannin in a num-

TABLE 59. *Phosphorus content of water lily leaves from various localities*

Locality	*Nuphar advena*	*Numphaea odorata*
Par Pond, S. C. (Boyd)	0.40	0.18
New Jersey (Riemer and Toth)	0.40	0.30
New Jersey (Riemer and Toth)	0.46	0.35
New Jersey (Riemer and Toth)	0.32	0.25
Linsley Pond, Conn. (Cowgill)	0.30	0.24
Cedar Lake, Conn. (Cowgill)	0.39	0.24
Mean	0.378	0.260

ber of different species in Alabama, an array that should demonstrate any differences between fully submersed plants and those with floating or emergent parts.

The mean ether extract was 3.62% in the submersed species and 4.70% in the emergent and floating-leaved plants, in which 30% of the samples gave greater ether extracts than did any submerged species. Though this might be naturally interpreted as due to waxes on the surface of the leaves exposed to the air, expressing the data on an ashfree basis reduces the difference somewhat to 4.41% in the submersed and to 5.23% in the emergent and floating species. The highest values of 9.14% of the organic matter in *Orontium aquaticum* and 9.15% in *Sparganium americanum* are considerably greater than the 6.00% of the organic matter found in the submersed *Cabomba caroliniana*, but the lowest values of the emergent series, 2.99% in *Polygonum pennsylvanicum*, 2.96% in *Hydrochloa carolinensis*, and 2.59% in *Myriophyllum aquaticum*, are all lower than any value recorded in Boyd's analyses of submerged species.

As far as the data go, the ether extract therefore appears to be less variable in the submersed than in the floating or emergent species.

Straškraba (1968) gives rather lower means for emergent (2.1%) and submersed species (2.2%) with the floating-leaved plants containing almost twice (4.0%) as much material extractable with ether.

Cellulose, on an ashfree basis, was determined by Boyd (1968) and by Bernatowicz (1969). Grouping the plants into those living entirely underwater, and those with floating or emergent leaves and vegetative stems, Boyd's data seemed to suggest a great cellulose concentration in some of the submerged plants, though Bernatowicz did not confirm this (Table 60).

Straškraba found slightly more crude fiber (32%) in the emergent species than in the floating-leaved or submersed plants, which both gave means of 27%.

TABLE 60.   *Cellulose in vegetation of Par Pond, and of Lake Warniak, estimated on an ashfree basis*

	Range(%)	Mean (%)
Submersed (Boyd), 12 spp.	23.2–44.3	34.8
Submersed (Bernatowicz), 6 spp.	25.2–33.7	28.5
Emergent (Boyd), 20 spp.	22.8–40.5	28.5
Emergent (Bernatowicz,) 9 spp.	13.6–41.2	29.4

The analyses collected by Straškraba (1968) suggest that the nonfibrous carbohydrate is a little lower in ephydates (42%) than in emergent (50%) or submersed (51%) species.

The pentose D-*apiose* (*A* of Fig. 112), which is found as the carbohydrate moiety of a number of glycosides occurring in unrelated plants, occurs in the Lemnaceae (*Lemna minor, L. gibba, Spirodela polyrhiza*), in various marine monocotyledons, and in the euryhaline *Potamogeton pectinatus*, as a polysaccharide component of the cell wall (van Beusekom 1967). It is not found in the freshwater allies of the marine genera in which it has been detected nor in *Potamogeton natans, P. crispus,* or *P. "pusillus."* A disaccharide of D-apiose, termed by Hart and Kindel (1970) *apibiose,* has been isolated from galacturonans obtained from the cell wall of *Lemna minor.*

It may also be noted that in *Littorella uniflora* 85% of the soluble carbohydrate stored in the roots and stems is the tetrasaccharide *stachyose,* a galactobiosylsucrose (Bourdu, Cartier, and Gorenflot 1963); sucrose and raffinose make up the remaining 15%. This is consistent with the membership of *Littorella* in the Plantaginaceae, but might raise some enzymological problems for any unadapted herbivore that tried to live on the plant.

Boyd also determined tannin, the mean content being 5.4% in the submersed and 6.8% in the emergent plants. If the nitrogen is supposed to be present in a crude protein containing 16.0% N as in a true protein, the sum of the mean quantities of this crude protein, ether extract, cellulose, and tannin will be 62.4% in the submersed and 56.6% in the emergent and floating-leafed group. The unidentified non-nitrogenous organic matter thus appears to have a mean value of 37.6% in the submersed and 43.4% in the emergent group.

Alkaloids and other secondary compounds. An examination of any of the large surveys of phytochemistry, notably Hegnauer (1962–1973), Gibbs (1974), and the Lynn Index (Farnsworth, Blomster, Quimby, and Schermerhorn 1974), indicates that the water plants have been unduly neglected by organic chemists; when they have been studied, secondary compounds,

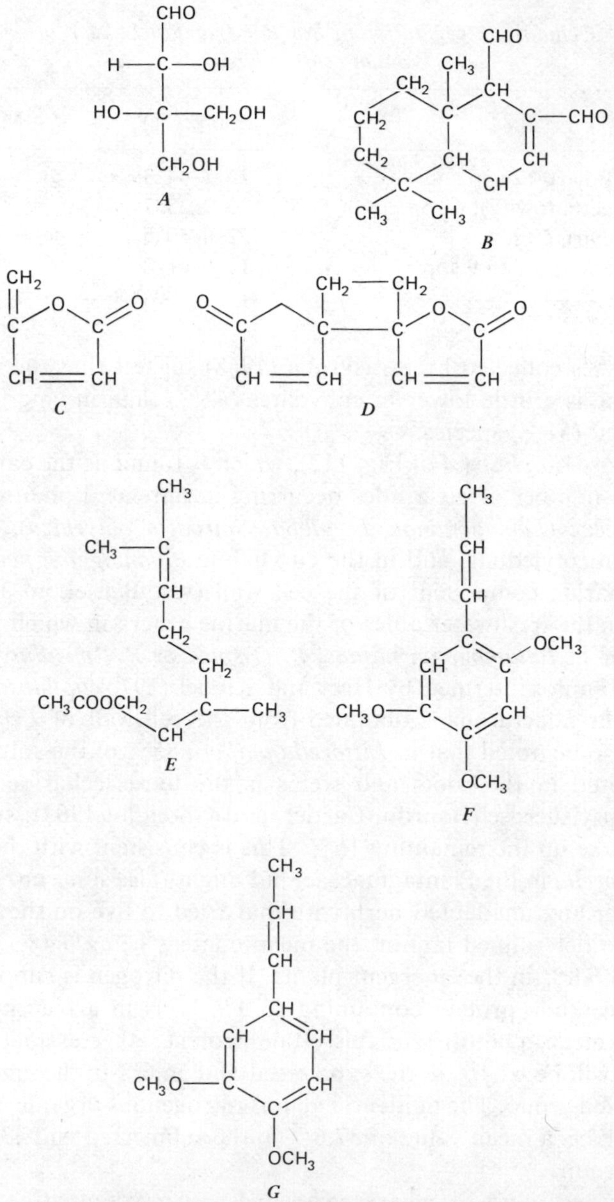

FIGURE 112. Some secondary compounds in aquatic angiosperms. *A*, apiose, present in a polysaccharide in cell walls of *Lemna* and in various marine and brackish-water angiosperms; *B*, the aldehyde polygodial from *Polygonum hydropiper*; *C*, protoanemonin, and *D*, anemonin, in various species of *Ranunculus* (s. str.) including the amphibious *R. lingua*; *E*. geranyl acetate which, with geraniol or geranyl alcohol, constitutes about 80% of the oil of the leaf of the diploid *Acarus calamus* var. *americanus*; *F*, asarone, the main constituent of the equivalent oil in the triploid variety of *A. calamus* brought from

particularly those such as alkaloids, glycosinolides, cardenolides, and cyanogenic substances, which may constitute chemical defenses against herbivores, are rarely found.

The only systematic survey of secondary compounds is that of Su, Staba, and Abul-Hajj (1973). They studied 24 species collected from Minnesota lakes and found small amounts of substances giving the Dragendorff reaction, which may indicate the presence of alkaloids though it is not fully specific, in ethanol or chloroform extracts of *Sagittaria latifolia*, *Ceratophyllum demersum*, *Carex lacustris*, *Elodea canadensis*, *Lemna minor*, four of five species of *Potamogeton*, and *Sparganium fluctuans*, as well as the water lilies that contained larger quantities. These records cannot be regarded as clearly indicating the presence of alkaloids in these plants but are suggestive for further research. *Lemna minor*, *Nuphar variegatum*, *Potamogeton amplifolius*, and *Sparganium fluctuans* certainly contained saponins and a number of other species may do so. Tannins are fairly generally present. Beta-sitosterol was present in *Ceratophyllum demersum*, *Nuphar variegatum*, *Potamogeton amplifolius*, *P. richardsonii*, *P. zosteriformis*, *Sparganium fluctuans*, *Typha angustifolia*, and *Carex lacustris*. No 3- or 17-oxosteroids were found, nor were cardenolides present.

Among the emergent herbid hyperhydates the lack of significant secondary compounds, as might be expected, is not so obvious as in the more fully aquatic plants. The amphibious species of *Polygonum* such as *P. hydropiper* appear to have a quite complicated set of secondary compounds, including *polygodial* (*B* of Fig. 112), which is said by Hegnauer (1969), who summarizes the work done on this and other members of the genus, to be the source of the pungent taste from which the species derives its name.

The somewhat amphibious and often eulittoral *Ranunculus lingua* may contain both *protoanemonin* (*C* of Fig. 112) and *anemonin* (*D* of Fig. 112); these lactones occur in many terrestrial species of the genus and in allied plants. Nothing seems to be known about the occurrence of any secondary compounds in the fully aquatic members of the genus. Among the lower hyperhydates at least the hygrophyte *Equisetum palustre* yields the quite poisonous alkaloids *palustrin* and *palustridin*, with empirical formulas $C_{17}H_{31}O_2N_2$ and $C_{18}H_{31}O_3N_3$ (Eugster, Griot, and Karrer 1953), but nothing seems to be known about *E. fluviatile*. *Lepidotis inundatum* in the Lycopodiaceae contains a mildly poisonous (Muszynski 1948) alkaloid *inundatin*, of uncertain nature.

India and grown in Europe since the sixteenth century; *G*, isoeugenol methyl ether found with asarone in both the triploid and the Far Eastern tetraploid var. *spurius* and in some of the latter plants the major constituent of the leaf oil.

Among the emergent angiosperms a number of alkaloids occur in *Decodon verticillatus*. Seven have been isolated by Ferris (1962, 1963), who finds them to constitute about a quarter of the total mass of alkaloids in the plant. The three most abundant are *verticillatin*, $C_{25}H_{27}O_5N$, *decodin*, $C_{25}H_{27}O_5N$, and *decinin*, $C_{26}H_{31}O_5N$. They contain two aromatic rings, a lactone group, and three, in part methylated, hydroxyl groups. It is interesting that Hegnauer, considering all the chemical evidence, regards the Lythraceae, which contains (see pp. 85, 86) a few submersed species, to belong in the Myrtales (cf. p. 79) and so far from the other water plants. In the family there is another group of alkaloids in *Heimia*, which may be chemically related to the *Decodon* group.

Before we leave the emergent species the case of the oils of the sweet flag *Acorus calamus* must be mentioned, as they are extremely interesting biologically even if of little specific limnological importance. The plant was introduced into Europe from Turkey in the sixteenth century as a source of a sweet-smelling oil and a rhizome widely used in medieval and later pharmacy. Modern investigation discloses three cytologically distinct taxa, a North American var. *americanus* which is diploid, the triploid Indian form through which the species was first known in Europe, and a tetraploid var. *spurius* from eastern Asia.

The leaves of the diploid var. *americanus* yield an oil which consists mainly of *geranyl acetate* (*E* of Fig. 112), with some geranyl alcohol and about 20% sesquiterpenes. The oil from the leaves of the triploid is mainly *asarone* (*F* of Fig. 112) with only a trace of geranyl acetate, but with some *isoeugenol methyl ether* (*G* of Fig. 112). One tetraploid strain resembled the triploid chemically, but in another isoeugenol methyl ether was more abundant than the asarone (Wulff and Stahl 1960; see also Hegnauer 1963). The oil derived from the roots is also very poor in asarone in the diploid *americanus*, but much richer in this compound in the polyploid forms.

Schultz and Gmelin (1952) record from the water cress *Rorippa nasturtium-aquaticum*, the glycosinolide *gluconasturtiin*, a glucoside of a phenylethyl mustard oil; the compound also occurs in *Brassica* and *Reseda*.

Among the floating-leaved water plants some saponins of uncertain structure occur in *Hydrocotyle* (see Gibbs 1974). The most remarkable feature of the organic chemistry of the ephydates in the noteworthy collection of alkaloids produced by the water lilies. Of the six genera included in this assemblage of plants, only *Nymphaea*, *Nuphar*, and *Nelumbo* have been studied by organic chemists. *Nuphar* and *Nelumbo* are particularly well-known, probably because they have traditionally been regarded as medicinal plants, the embryos from the seeds of *Nelumbo* being particularly important in Chinese pharmacy. The information about the alkaloids of *Nymphaea* is meager and unsatisfactory. A number of nineteenth-century papers listed in the Lynn Index (Farnsworth, Blomster, Quimby, and Schermerhorn 1974; see also Hegnauer 1969) suggest that the rhizome of the plant may contain a collection of alkaloids related to those of *Nuphar*. Bures and Hoffmann (1934) obtained a compound which they called *nympheine* from *Nymphaea alba*. They gave its empirical formula as $C_{14}H_{23}O_2N$. It is said to be an hypnotic drug and powerful fish poison.

The much more extensive information available about the alkaloids of *Nuphar* has been admirably summarized by Wróbel (1967), more recent work being noted by LaLonde (1970) and LaLonde, Wong, and Cullen (1970). The rhizome of *N. lutea* is said to have been used in folk medicine, and the existence of alkaloids in it has been known for almost a century. No adequate chemical investigation was made until that of Arima and Takahashi (1931). Subsequent studies initially by Japanese workers on *N. japonica* and by Polish investigators on *N. lutea* established the existence of a series of furan derivatives of quinolizidine (*A* of Fig. 113) in *N. japonica*, *N. lutea*, *N. variegata*, and *N. advena* (sub *N. luteum* var. *macrophyllum*).[12] The simplest of these compounds are *deoxynupharidine* (*B* of Fig. 113), *nupharidine* (*C* of Fig. 113), and *nupharamine* (*D* of Fig. 113). In the first two the quinolizidine structure remains intact, but in the third it is broken, forming a piperidine skeleton. Both nupharidine and deoxynupharidine are widespread in *Nuphar*, but nupharamine is so far known only in *N. japonicum*. Several other compounds closely related to these three have also been isolated.

It is interesting that castoramine, occurring in the scent gland of the beaver *Castor canadensis*, is an hydroxyl derivative (*E* of Fig. 113) of deoxynupharidine (Valenta and Khaleque 1959). With Valenta and Khaleque, one may suspect that it is formed from one of the alkaloids of yellow water lily plants eaten by the beaver. Dr. R. A. Paynter tells me that beavers in New Hampshire eat much *Nuphar* in summer. Castoreum apparently contains a number of other compounds derived from the bark and buds of trees.

One most surprising discovery in the chemistry of the alkaloids of *Nuphar* was made by Achmatowicz and Bellen (1962), who isolated from *N. lutea* four compounds in which two molecules having the basic structure of deoxynupharidine are linked through two CH_2 groups and a sulfur atom, an arrangement having no analogue in any other alkaloids. Several further compounds of this kind have now been identified (LaLonde 1970; LaLonde, Wong, and Cullen 1970) the best understood (Achmatowicz

---

[12] LaLonde follows Beal (1956) in admitting only one species in the genus *Nuphar*.

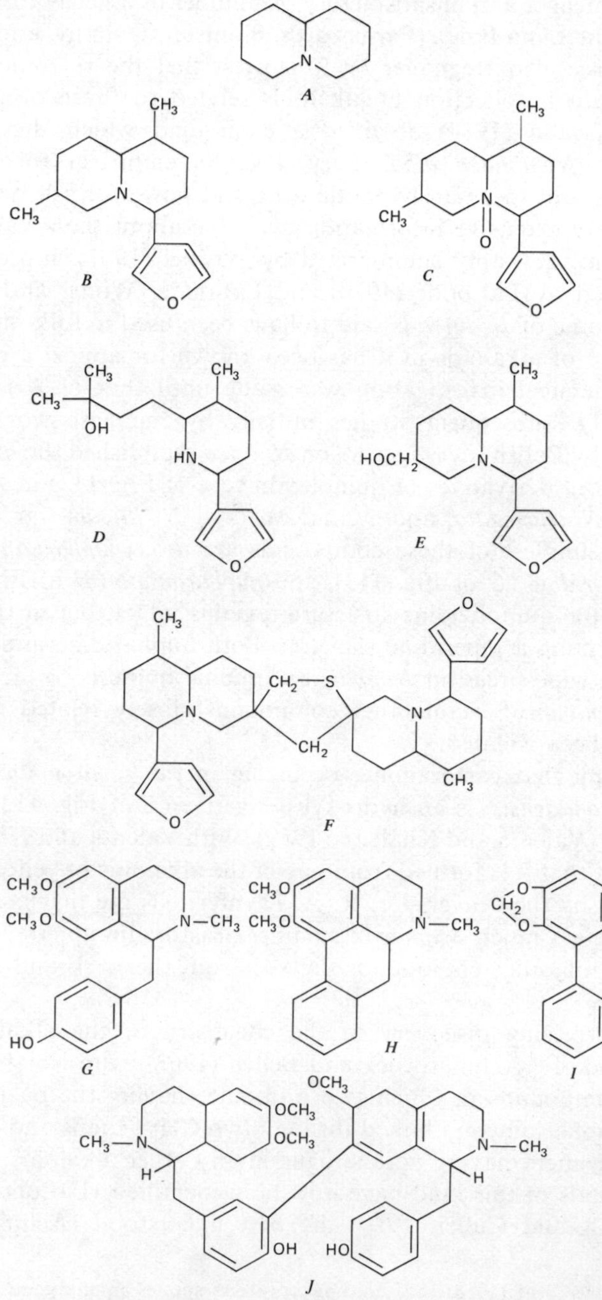

FIGURE 113. Alkaloids from *Nuphar* and *Nelumbo* with some related compounds. *A*, quinolizidine; *B*, deoxynupharidine; *C*, nupharidine; *D*, nupharamine; *E*, castoramine;

and Wróbel 1964; Achmatowicz, Banaszeh, Spiteller, and Wróbel 1964; Wróbel 1967) being neothiobinupharidine (*F* of Fig. 113). LaLonde found that such compounds are bacteriostatic when tested on species of *Corynebacterium* and some other plant pathogens, though not on bacteria isolated from the neighborhood of *Nuphar* plants. Nupharidine and deoxynupharidine showed no bacteriostatic properties. It is reasonable to suspect with LaLonde that the bacteriostatic compounds may play some part in the ecology of inland waters or their sediments.

The alkaloids of *Nelumbo* are unrelated to those of *Nuphar* and belong to the isoquinoline group, mostly being 1,1'-benzylisoquinolines, a group of compounds widely distributed in the more primitive dicotyledons (see Gibbs 1974). The available information on the alkaloids from *Nelumbo* has been well summarized by Hegnauer (1969), on whose account this treatment is based. The alkaloids are found mainly in the leaves and in the embryo, but not in the starchy rhizome and cotyledons. In *N. nucifera* there is very great variation in the occurrence and quantities of the dozen compounds that have been identified in samples from various sources. The American *N. lutea* appears to contain fewer alkaloids than does *N. nucifera*, but it has been less investigated than the latter plant. It seems to lack the *liensinine* (*J* of Fig. 113) alkaloids in which two *armepavine* (*G* of Fig. 113) skeletons are joined together; several such compounds are found in *N. nucifera*. Two alkaloids of the latter plant, though clearly related to the other compounds present, belong to the aporphine group of isoquinolines, the structures of these two, which also are found in other plants, being indicated in I of Fig. 113. *Annonain* occurs also in the custard apple *Annona*, a plant totally unrelated to the water lilies, while *roemerine*, or methylannonain, is found in both *Roemeria* and some species of *Papaver* among the poppies, and in certain species of Lauraceae. In view of the great difference between the alkaloids of *Nelumbo* and *Nuphar*, study of the compounds found in the other genera of water lilies would be most interesting. It is of interest to note that the rhizomes of both *Nuphar* and *Nymphaea* have been very widely used as sources of human food; Core (1967), Turner and Bell (1972), Wilken (1970) may be mentioned among many records.

F, neothiobinupharidine (Wróbel).   *G*, armeparine, from *N. nucifera* and *lutea*, substitution of —H for the —CH$_3$ giving *N*-norarmeparine from *N. lutea;* *H*, nuciferine, from *N. nucifera* and *N. lutea*, substitution of —H for the —CH$_3$ likewise giving *N*-nornuciferine from *N. lutea; I*, annonain from *N. nucifera*, also known from *Annona*, the custard apple, substitution of —CH$_3$ for the —H attached to the nitrogen atom giving roemerine, also from several poppies and members of the Lauraceae; *J*, liensinin from *N. nucifera*, several other alkaloids with this general structure but with —CH$_3$ substituted for —H or vice versa being known from this species (Hegnauer).

In the fully submersed water plants very little has been recorded. According to Gibbs (1974) *Myriophyllum aquaticum* (sub *brasiliense*) contains a cyanogenic compound. None of the other more toxic classes of secondary compounds seem to be reported. A few may have been missed, as in the subgenus *Batrachium* of *Ranunculus* which, as has been noted earlier, appears not to have been studied, even though some terrestrial species of the nominotypical subgenus are quite poisonous. Whether the apparent rarity of substances that might have been evolved as a means of discouraging aquatic herbivores from eating submersed plants in inland waters is real is a question of considerable interest. It has already been noted (p. 293) that difference in sodium content between land and water plants may depend on the relative lack of selection pressure exercised by herbivorous animals on angiosperms growing under water. Later it will be suggested that the almost universal presence of microscopic epiphytes growing on macrophytes has tended to divert herbivores from the latter as food (see p. 548). Perhaps chemical defenses are less important where this sort of biological protection is available. A few cases, such as the general unpalatability of *Elodea canadensis* to aquatic insects (Gajevskaia 1958), do perhaps suggest chemical protection and clearly require further study.

Possible antibiotic and repellent effects of submersed vegetation. Many investigators have concluded that there is some suppression of phytoplankton by macrophytic vegetation when the latter is very abundant (Embody 1928; Bennett 1942; Hasler and Jones 1949). According to Schreiter (1928), who also found a striking inverse correlation between the abundance of *Elodea* and phytoplankton in a large pond in Czechoslovakia, Langhans had suggested that the effect might be due to some substance inhibiting phytoplankton growth, produced by the plants. It is obvious, however, that competition for nutrients might take place and, as Hasler and Jones indicate, this could be responsible for the inhibition. Massive fertilization is apt to inhibit rooted vegetation (Smith and Swingle 1942; Swingle 1945) by increasing the phytoplankton populations and in extreme cases reducing very greatly the light available for higher vegetation. It is evident that in principle competition for light and nutrients could explain the observations that have been made; this, however, does not rule out the possibility of some antibiosis or allelopathy also operating.

Hasler and Jones (1949) found that rotifers as well as phytoplankton appeared to be inhibited by water plants, but no effect was observed on planktonic Crustacea. It is presumably possible that the effect on rotifers is due to a reduction in their food supply.

Su, Abul-Hajj, and Staba (1973) found that ethanol extracts of *Nymphaea* and *Nuphar* are moderately active against *Staphylococcus aureus* and *Mycobacterium smegmatis* and Skellysolve-F extracts of *N. variegata* and *Sponganium fluctuans* against *Candida albicans*. The materials in *Nymphaea* active against *M. smegmatis* were identified as tannic acid (pentagalloyl-α-D-glucopyranose), gallic acid, and methyl gallate, the latter being apparently the most important.

Stangenberg (1968) has demonstrated the production of an antibiotic in *Lemna minor*, effective against the well-known filamentous bacterium *Sphaerotilus natans*, but not against *Escherichia*, *Sarcina*, and *Staphylococcus*.

A somewhat different type of effect has been reported by Pennak (1973), who observed that individuals of *Daphnia rosea* were repelled by various macrophytes. In this case, since it is very unlikely that the cladoceran could have an adverse effect on such plants, it is probable that the planktonic *Daphnia* is using materials diffusing from the plant as chemical signals indicating that it has strayed too far from the open waters, rather than reacting to a material produced as a repellent.

CHEMICAL FACTORS IN THE ENVIRONMENTS OF HIGHER AQUATIC PLANTS

It has long been known that certain water plants are primarily found in the soft waters of lime-poor areas and others mainly in the hard waters of regions underlain by calcareous sedimentary rocks. *Lobelia dortmanna* and *Isoetes* spp. immediately come to mind as species of the first kind of region, and *Ceratophyllum demersum* and various species of *Potamogeton* as characteristic of the second. It was also early realized (West 1910) that the harder and, in general, more calcareous waters were likely to contain more inorganic nutrients than the acid waters draining off igneous rocks. Not only is it evident that somewhat hard waters are more likely to be eutrophic in the strict sense of the word (Vol. II, pp. 379–380) than are dilute soft or acid waters, but the biological significance of hardness itself may involve bicarbonate, calcium, or hydrogen ions acting on quite different physiological processes. The simple-minded division of plants into those of soft and of hard water obviously hides something complicated, even if we study only the relations of the assimilative parts of the plant to the chemistry of the ambient medium, and not any influence that a lake sediment may have on a plant rooted in it.

Considering only the composition of the water, two major groups of interrelated chemical variables may be taken up, namely, pH, alkaline earth content, and bicarbonate on the one hand, and the two main limiting nutrients phosphorus and combined nitrogen on the other. Total electrolyte content, chloride, and sulfate must also be considered, and in practice are best treated along with the alkalinity. There is some evidence of effects of iron, manganese, and brown humic materials, substances which are often interrelated. Other minor elements may well prove as important to macro-

TABLE 61. *Distribution of Danish water plants in lakes arranged according to pH categories*

	I	II		III	IV		V	
	Strongly acidic, pH always ≤5.3	Variable, acidic, pH in any lake 4.4–6.9	% of acidic waters with species	Variable, usually though not always acidic	Circum-neutral	% of variable or neutral waters with species	Always alkaline, pH 7.0–9.0	% of alkaline waters with species
No. of lakes	10	7		9	5		19	
Characteristic soft-water species								
Sparganium angustifolium	7	1	47	2	1	21	0	0
Juncus bulbosus	7	4	65	7	3	71	0	0
Littorella uniflora	4	6	59	8	5	93	4	21
Lobelia dortmanna	3	5	47	4	4	57	1	5
Isoetes lacustris	2	5	41	6	2	57	1	5
Euryionic species								
Polygonum amphibium f. natans	2	2	24	7	4	69	11	58
Utricularia minor	1	2	18	1	2	21	0	0
Nymphaea alba	1	2	18	1	3	29	12	63
Nuphar lutea	1	1	12	2	4	43	13	68
Lemna minor	1	1	12	3	2	36	15	79
Elatine hexandra	0	2	18	3	2	36	0	0
Apium inundatum	0	2	18	4	3	50	1	5
Potamogeton natans	0	2	18	5	3	57	13	68

Moderate hard-water species							
Myriophyllum alterniflorum	0	0	4	5	64	5	26
Potamogeton berchtoldii	0	0	2	1	21	6	32
Eleocharis acicularis f. *submersa*	0	0	1	1	14	3	16
Potamogeton perfoliatus	0	0	1	1	14	10	53
Ranunculus aquatilis	0	0	1	2	21	5	26
Potamogeton gramineus	0	0	1	3	29	4	21
Hydrocharis morsus-ranae	0	0	1	1	14	11	58
Potamogeton alpinus	0	0	0	1	7	4	21
P. crispus	0	0	0	2	14	13	68
Lemna trisulca	0	0	0	2	14	14	74
Elodea canadensis	0	0	0	1	7	4	21
Characteristic hard-water species							
P. compressus	0	0	0	0	0	5	26
P. pectinatus	0	0	0	0	0	10	53
Stratiotes aloides	0	0	0	0	0	7	37
Ceratophyllum demersum	0	0	0	0	0	12	63
Ranunculus circinatus	0	0	0	0	0	14	74
Myriophyllum spicatum	0	0	0	0	0	14	74

scopic vegetation as to the plankton, but we know little or nothing about them in the present context.

Alkalinity, pH, and the alkaline earth elements. The elementary theory of the relationships between these variables and CO_2 pressure has been discussed in Vol. I (pp. 668–683). Few attempts have been made to separate their ecological effects. The CO_2 tension of a natural water is regulated by photosynthesis and respiration as well as by the atmospheric partial pressure of the gas. At low pH values sulfuric or organic acids may be present. Calcium may be present in equilibrium with sulfate, or bicarbonate in equilibrium with magnesium and sodium as well as calcium. The correlation between the three variables under discussion is therefore not absolute. Because they are separable to some extent, enough field data ideally could give some information as to which factors are ecologically operative. Experimental studies are obviously likely to be of great value, but it is important to remember that there is evidence to show that the final results in nature may be due to the chemical parameters controlling the direction of competition, so that experiments on the tolerances of single species might be quite misleading.

Distribution of water plants in lakes of varying composition. The earliest detailed work is that of Iversen (1929), who studied a number of Danish lakes and ponds, the waters of which provided a wide range of pH values. Since in any lake there is always some seasonal variation, Iversen classified his localities in five categories, without giving the individual pH values. The summarized data for all plants which occurred in at least five localities are given in Table 61, the species being arranged in order of decreasing acidity of their habitats in four convenient if arbitrary groups.

Iversen found little correlation between pH and calcium concentration in his most acidic waters. The distributions of plants appeared to follow pH more closely than calcium. He concluded, therefore, that the former variable is the effective determinant. This seems reasonable at the low pH values of his most acidic lakes.

Moyle (1945) has given an extensive series of data for New World species based on his experience in Minnesota. The lakes he studied are mainly hard water; he investigated no really acidic localities. He arranged his species in a series of categories, depending on their pH, and alkalinity and sulfate tolerances and requirements. Unfortunately there are a great many inconsistencies in his formal treatment, so that for a summary presentation it has been necessary to rearrange his categories and data to a considerable extent, though the fundamental idea of his classification is certainly illuminating. The present arrangement of the data is given in Table 62, to which a few records of total salinity are added from Metcalf's (1931) work in the lakes of North Dakota.

TABLE 62. *Range of alkalinity, pH, sulfate, and total salinity for some North American water plants (mainly after Moyle 1945)*

	Alkalinity range as HCO_3^- (mg liter^{-1})	pH range	SO_4^{2-} range (mg liter^{-1})	Salinity range (mg liter^{-1}) (Metcalf 1931)

I. Dilute water group: alkalinity <60 mg HCO_3^- liter^{-1}, lowest pH ≤ 7.0; sulfate ≤ 10.0 liter^{-1}. (Moyle's soft-water subgroup 1)

Isoetes braunii	10–55	7.0–8.0	0.0–4.5	—
Sparganium fluctuans	24–55	7.0–7.3	0.5–6.0	—
Potamogeton spirillus	22–56	7.0–8.3	0.0–3.0	—
Scirpus subterminalis	10–52	6.8–7.5	n.d.	—
Eriocaulon septangulare	12–54	6.7–7.8	0.0–5.8	—
Lobelia dortmanna	15–51	6.8–7.5	0.0–10.2	—
Nuphar microphylla	9–50	6.8–7.3	0.5–6.0	—
N. rubrodisca	0.6–39	6.8–7.3	0.5–1.0	—

The following species, for which there are inadequate data, probably may be placed in Group I: *Isoetes macrospora, Sparganium angustifolium, S. minimum, Najas gracillima, Nymphaea tetragona, Ranunculus trichophyllus* var. *eradicatus* (? = *R. trichophyllus* subsp. *lutulentus*), *Callitriche hermaphroditica, Elatine minima, Myriophyllum alterniflorum, M. farwelli, M. tenellum, Littorella americana.* Other experience with most of these species does indeed indicate that they belong in the group.

II. Eurytopic intermediate group: ranging from dilute (<15 mg HCO_3^- liter^{-1}) to farily hard (<100 mg HCO_3^- liter^{-1}) water (Moyle's soft-water subgrout 2, with some changes)

a. Lowest alkalinity <1 mg HCO_3^- liter^{-1}; sulfate variable, often high

Potamogeton gramineus	0.6–186	7.0–8.5	0.0–17	—
Sagittaria latifolia	0.6–363	6.3–8.8	0.0–199	—
Eleocharis palustris	0.6–273	6.3–9.0	0.0–396	—
E. palustris var. *major*	0.6–223	6.8–8.8	0.0–155	—
Phragmites australis	0.6–363	6.3–9.0	0.5–396	—

b. Lowest alkalinity 9–15 mg HCO_3^- liter^{-1}; sulfate usually low

Equisetum fluviatile	9–363	6.8–8.8	0.0–16	—
Potamogeton alpinus	15–141	7.0–8.6	0.5–4	—
P. epihydrus	12–148	6.7–8.6	0.6–6	—
P. praelongus	13–375	7.1–9.0	0.0–143	—
Glyceria borealis	10–229	6.8–8.8	0.5–17	—

Calla palustris, Potentilla palustris, Callitriche palustris, and *Myriophyllum verticillatum,* with perhaps *P. obtusifolius,* and *Glyceria neogaea* also seem to belong here.

373

TABLE *62*   (*Continued*)

	Alkalinity range as HCO_3^- (mg liter^{-1})	pH range	SO_4^{2-} range (mg liter^{-1})	Salinity range (mg liter^{-1}) ((Metcalf 1931)

III.   Hard-water group: alkalinity always >15 mg HCO_3^- liter^{-1}.

   a.   Lowest alkalinity 15–30 mg HCO_3^- liter^{-1}; sulfate <75 mg liter^{-1}.

Pontederia cordata	22–113	7.2–7.9	0–10	—
Potamogeton amplifolius	15–255	7.1–8.8	0–28	—
P. natans	23–376	6.8–9.0	0–50	—
Sagittaria cristata	23–223	7.2–8.8	4–24	—

   a′.   Lowest alkalinity 15–30 mg HCO_3^- liter^{-1}; sulfate <600 mg liter^{-1}

Heteranthera dubia	28–299	7.6–9.0	0–318	—
Ceratophyllum demersum	28–458	6.3–9.0	0–332	—
Myriophyllum exalbescens	28–458	7.2–8.9	0–317	350–1465
Utricularia vulgaris var.				
americana	20–363	6.8–8.9	0–318	458–1089
Elodea nuttallii	27–247	7.3–8.8	0–282	—
Nymphaea tuberosa	23–363	6.3–9.0	0–178	—
Nuphar variegata	9–268	6.8–8.6	0–178	—
Potamogeton zosteriformis	22–299	6.9–9.0	0–282	501
Najas flexilis	23–375	7.2–9.0	0–318	—
Sagittaria cuneata	24–458	7.3–9.0	0–317	—
Vallisneria americana	23–338	7.0–8.9	0–318	—
Eleocaris acicularis	23–458	7.0–8.9	0–318	—
Acorus calamus	24–247	7.3–8.8	4–318	—

   a″.   As above but sulfate can be very high

Typha latifolia	12–458	6.3–9.0	0–1296	—
Scirpus acutus	21–273	7.2–9.1	0–1296	—

   b.   Lowest alkalinity > 30 mg but <150 mg HCO_3^- liter^{-1}; sulfate <75 mg liter^{-1}

Potamogeton friesii	87–458	7.7–8.8	1–62	—
P. gramineus f. *myriophyllum*	37–207	7.0–8.8	0–39	—
P. illinoensis	40–200	7.7–8.8	0–18	—
P. robbinsii	40–176	7.2–8.4	0–18	—
P. berchtoldii[a]	38–228	7.0–8.8	0–17	—
P. strictifolius[b]	39–321	7.4–9.0	0–18	—
Sagittaria rigida	40–363	7.4–8.8	0–26	—
Elodea canadensis	43–363	7.0–8.8	0–37	501

   b′.   Lowest alkalinity > 30 mg HCO_3^- liter^{-1}; sulfate <600 mg per liter^{-1}.

Sparganium eurycarpum	43–460	7.2–8.8	2–199	—
Potamogeton foliosus	45–279	7.2–8.8	0–282	458–1431

TABLE 62 (Continued)

	Alkalinity range as HCO₃⁻ (mg liter⁻¹)	pH range	SO₄²⁻ range (mg liter⁻¹)	Salinity range (mg liter⁻¹) (Metcalf 1931)
P. nodosus	49–380	7.3–8.8	5–199	—
P. richardsonii	38–451	7.0–9.1	0–318	—
Najas guadalupensis	92–195	7.2–8.6	36–177	—
Alisma triviale	39–364	7.3–8.5	5–199	—
Leersia oryzoides	37–338	7.2–9.0	0–178	—
Zizania aquatica	46–364	7.2–8.6	3–282	—
Scirpus heterochaetus	50–243	7.3–8.6	12–282	—
Lemna minor	50–320	6.3–9.0	0–254	—
Lemna trisulca	50–363	7.2–8.8	0–332	—
Wolffia columbiana	104–268	7.2–8.4	20–178	—
Polygonum coccineum	91–253	7.7–8.8	16–178	—
P. natans	37–317	7.7–8.8	3–282	—
Hippuris vulgaris	37–362	6.8–8.8	0.5–199	—
b″. As above but sulfate can be very high				
Potamogeton pectinatus	39–458	6.3–9.0	0.5–1297	350–35,873
Zannichelia palustris var. *major*	92–412	7.6–9.0	8–1297	458–1465
Scirpus fluviatilis	37–268	7.0–9.1	0.5–630	—
S. americanus	107–338	7.4–8.9	3–1296	—
Spirodela polyrhiza	60–363	6.3–8.8	1–619	—

IV. Alkali water group: in water with at least 150 mg HCO₃⁻ liter⁻¹ and 50 mg sulfate liter⁻¹, tolerances usually much higher (Moyle's alkali water group)

	Alkalinity range as HCO₃⁻ (mg liter⁻¹)	pH range	SO₄²⁻ range (mg liter⁻¹)	Salinity range (mg liter⁻¹) (Metcalf 1931)
Ruppia maritima	179–458[c]	8.1–9.0	50–396	457–77,386
Najas marina	179–458	8.2–9.0	50–1297	624–1089
Scirpus paludosus	179–241	8.4–9.0	254–395	—

[a] Sub *pusillus*.
[b] Including var. *rutiolides* as well as typical var. *strictifolius*.
[c] Moyle's records sub *R. occidentalis*, which is usually not regarded as distinct from *R. maritima*.

Little can be learned about the separation of the effects of bicarbonate and of pH from this table. It is, however, evident that some plants are likely to be able to tolerate fairly high alkalinities provided the overall concentration of other electrolytes is not too high. This seems to be true of *Potamogeton strictifolius* and *P. friesii* and to a rather less extent of many other species, all of which may be contrasted with *P. pectinatus*, which has a far greater sulfate tolerance than any of the other Minnesota species, and in other areas a capacity to tolerate salinities at least up to 3.5% (Metcalf 1931).

Spence (1967a) arranges the commoner submersed plants of the lochs of Scotland in the categories of Table 63.

Seddon's ordination procedure in the lakes of Wales.   Seddon (1972) in a study of the macrophytes of 70 lakes in Wales has adopted a more elaborate procedure than those of the preceding paragraphs. Using a principal component method of ordination developed by Orloci (1966), each lake is represented by a point in a three-dimensional space, the distance between any two points representing floristic dissimilarity between the two lakes. The

TABLE 63.   *Distribution of plants in Scottish lochs according to Spence's classification*

Poor waters, alkalinity less than 0.4 mequiv or 24.4 mg HCO_3^- liter^{-1}
  Elatine hexandra
  Eleogiton fluitans
  Isoetes lacustris
  Subularia aquatica
  Ranunculus flammula
  Juncus bulbosus f. *fluitans* (once to 1.1 mequiv or 67 mg liter^{-1})
  Lobelia dortmanna (once to 1.1 mequiv or 67 mg liter^{-1})
  Sphagnum subsecundum var. *auriculatum*
Moderately rich and often slightly saline, alkalinity more than 0.4 mequiv or 24.4 mg HCO_3^- liter^{-1}
  Potamogeton filiformis (alkalinity >0.74 mequiv or 45 mg HCO_3^- liter^{-1})
  P. pectinatus (alkalinity 0.74 mequiv or 45 mg HCO_3^- liter^{-1})
  P. praelongus
Rich water, alkalinity more than 1.2 mequiv or 73 mg HCO_3^- liter^{-1}
  Ceratophyllum demersum
  Chara papillosa
  Cinclidotus fontinaloides
  Myriophyllum spicatum
  Potamogeton lucens
Ubiquitous
  Chara aspera
  C. virgata
  Fontinalis antipyretica
  Myriophyllum alterniflorum
  Littorella uniflora
  Potamogeton gramineus
  P. perfoliatus

---

interested and adequately prepared reader should consult Orloci's paper for the mathematical technique used. The points are plotted relative to three axes at right angles; these are initially uninterpreted but their position in the space is not arbitrary. The first axis (I) is chosen so that the two floristically most diverse lakes lie on the axis on either side of the origin. A second axis (II) at right angles to I is now obtained in the same way, lying in a plane that gives maximum dispersion at right angles to the first axis. The third axis (III) is, in an ordinary three-dimensional Euclidean space, defined by the other two.

There is nothing to prevent a hypervolume being used, but in Seddon's example the third axis is relatively unimportant and is used in discussion of only one detail.

Nearly all of the discussion is in terms of the projection of the points on the plane defined by I and II. In this projection (Fig. 114) the points corresponding to the lakes are seen to be grouped more or less naturally into three sets. That in the left-hand lower quadrant primarily consists of mountain lakes lying at altitudes between 137 and 701 m. The set in the lower right-hand part of the field consists largely of lowland lakes at altitudes between 6 and 290 m; the third set lying on either side of axis II in the two upper quadrants consists largely of lakes at intermediate altitudes from 30 to 305 m. If the conductivities are entered on the diagram it can be seen that the lower left-hand set consists of lakes with dilute waters, and the lower right-hand set of lakes with concentrated waters, the set around axis II in the upper quadrants tending to be intermediate. The pH is on the whole above 7.0 in the right-hand part of the diagram and below 6.0 in the bottom left-hand part.

The ratio of the sum of the calcium and magnesium precipitated as carbonates to the elementary sodium and potassium is called by Seddon the *hardness ratio*. This chemically somewhat inelegant quantity is minimal in the bottom left quadrant and maximal in the lower part of the upper right quadrant. The product of the conductivity and the hardness ratio is somewhat unhappily called by Seddon (1967) the *trophic index*, but is little used in his more recent paper. On the whole the lakes on the right-hand side of the projection would ordinarily be regarded as eutrophic and those on the left oligotrophic. Seddon speaks of dystrophic (i.e., chthoniotrophic) localities, but they are not specified nor is there any indication as to whether color was measured.

Seddon concludes that there are three types of distribution of submerged and floating-leaved plants in Wales. Firstly, there is a group of eurytopic species occurring in localities scattered all over the diagram. These tolerant species are *Potamogeton natans*, *Nuphar lutea*, *Nymphaea alba*, *Glyceria fluitans*, and *Littorella uniflora*. Within this group there is some differenti-

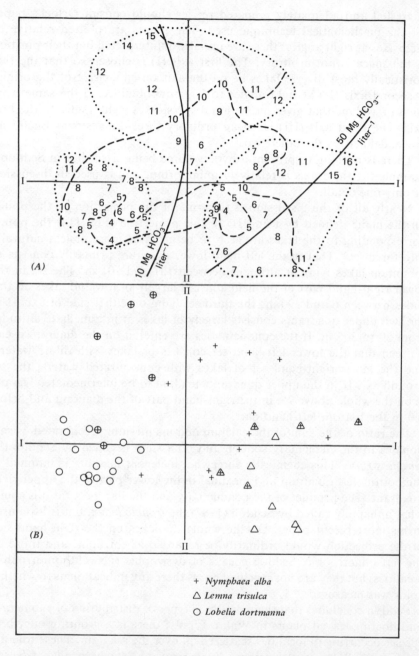

FIGURE 114. Ordination of Welsh lakes by resemblance and difference of floristic composition; projection of plane of the two most important axes I and II. (*A*) Number of species in each lake, with contours (broken line) for 5, 10, and 15 species; isopleths (solid line)

ation, *Nymphaea alba* being commoner in the more concentrated waters, *Littorella uniflora* in the more dilute.

The second group is described by Seddon as consisting of eutraphent species, and includes in order of increasing tolerance of low conductivity (minimum tolerated, in micromhos, in parentheses) *Potamogeton pectinatus* (200), *Myriophyllum spicatum* (200), *Lemna trisulca* (170), *P. crispus* (150), *P. lucens* (100), *Ranunculus circinatus* (100), *Lemna minor* (100), *Polygonum amphibium* (100), *Potamogeton obtusifolius* (100), *Ceratophyllum demersum* (75), *R. aquatilis* and *peltatus* (60), *Apium inundatum* (50), *Elodea canadensis* (50), *Potamogeton berchtoldii* (50), and *P. perfoliatus* (38). Some of these species such as *Apium inundatum* are absent from the more concentrated localities and may legitimately be regarded as mesotraphent.

The third or oligotraphent group consists of *Isoetes lacustris*, *Lobelia dortmanna*, *Luronium natans*, *Sparganium angustifolium*, and *Juncus bulbosus* var. *confervaceus*. These species are ordinarily found in waters of conductivity well below 100 μmhos. There are, however, several species common in such waters, such as *Isoetes setacea*, *Callitriche intermedia*, and *Myriophyllum alterniflorum* which are capable of living in waters of conductivity over 200 μmhos, though they rarely do so.

Seddon suspects that the eutraphent plants are limited by their nutrient requirements, whereas the oligotraphent species have potentially a wide fundamental niche from much of which they are usually excluded by competition. These conclusions seem reasonable.

Seddon has undoubtedly made a very important contribution to the chemical ecology of an aquatic macrophytic flora, even though some of the conclusions with regard to individual species merely confirm what was already known. Evidently much more data are available than have been used in his paper. Such data may permit getting away from the total concentration and the ratio of alkaline earth to alkali cations as indirect measures of trophic potential. Phosphorus, combined nitrogen, and sometimes other elements must also be involved. Treatment of the kind employed in the next sections of this chapter, perhaps refined by the use of discriminant functions or comparable statistical techniques, might be applied to the full body of Seddon's data with interesting results.

One feature of Seddon's ordination should be mentioned, though its significance is uncertain. If the number of species per lake is entered on the ordination projected onto I–II, a very definite pattern is obtained with the

---

for 10 and 50 mg HCO_3^- liter^{-1} (not based on the whole series); and boundaries (dotted line) of the three more or less distinct groups of lakes. (*B*) Ecological distribution relative to the ordination of *Nymphaea alba*, a eurytopic species; *Lemna trisulca*, a hard-water or eutraphent species; and *Lobelia dortmanna*, a soft-water or oligotraphent species (data and diagrams of Seddon, modified).

lakes with most species appearing peripherally, whereas the lakes with fewest species occupy a field on either side of axis II in the two lower quadrants. This pattern, however, is quite unrelated to lake chemistry and may in fact be partly an artifact of the ordination technique. The localities that are floristically richest are likely to have a greater number of rare species and so are likely to differ from each other more than those which are floristically relatively poor differ among themselves. This might lead to an accumulation of floristically poor lakes in the center with the very rich ones scattered round the periphery of the diagram.

The relationship of macroscopic plants to calcium, bicarbonate, and pH in Swedish lakes. Apart from Iversen's paper, little seems to have been done to elucidate the relative significance of the different aspects of hardness. The very fine body of chemical and floristic data given by Lohammar (1938) for the lakes of the provinces of Uppland and Dalarna and for a number of basins in north Sweden does permit some further analysis of the problem.

In using Lohammar's observations, it is important to remember that the north Swedish localities lack a number of species, presumably on account of climatic and biogeographical reasons; for the most part it is safer to consider the two areas that he studied separately.

Lohammar's account moreover can be supplemented by the floristic studies of Lundh and the concomitant chemical investigations of Almestrand (Almestrand and Lundh 1951) in the predominantly hard waters of the southern extremity of Sweden (Provinces of Kristianstad and Malmöhus), though the mode of study was not quite identical in the two investigations. Detailed analysis is best made within genera represented in the flora by several species which are likely to have much the same life-form and general physical requirements. In Lohammar's collection of data, species of *Potamogeton*, *Myriophyllum*, and *Carex* are particularly suitable for this kind of study.

Edmondson (1944) introduced a useful method for the study of the limitation of organisms by pH and by the concentration of any of the substances on which pH depends. Each occurrence of an organism is plotted as a point, the coordinates of which are pH and one of the other chemical variables, in the present case calcium, on which pH partly depends. The envelope of all possible points for a collection of localities will surround an ideal curve relating pH to the concentration of calcium as bicarbonate or carbonate under the natural atmospheric pressure of CO_2. The presence of other cations and anions will displace the points on either side of the curve so that the envelope may be quite wide. Within the envelope points are marked according to the species inhabiting each locality. For any given species a second envelope within the first one may now be drawn, indicating the area in which there is a high probability that the species occurs. Allowing for some fuzziness at the border, around which we could draw a series of confidence limits, the area within the envelope of each species is really a projection of its niche space on the pH–calcium plane. Ideally, if high pH were the sole determinant of limitation to soft or hard water, a clear horizontal boundary to the envelope would be apparent if pH is plotted on the ordinate, whereas if calcium were the determinant alone a clear vertical boundary would be obtained. Since the distributions are often far from normal the Wilcoxon rank order test (Tate and Clelland 1957) has been applied to determine significance (Table 65). Since the test is known, for a normally distributed array, to be a little weaker than the Student t test, the highly significant results may be accepted with fair confidence, and some of the less significant differences may be regarded as suggestive.

In a few cases, the two species of *Typha* providing a striking example, there appears to be no chemical differentiation of the waters inhabited by two sympatric species, which may occur in the same lake, apparently achieving ecological separation by different substratum preferences, *T. latifolia* growing on less and *T. angustifolium* on more organic bottoms. In the other genera considered there seem to be some eurytopic species, with others differentiated as hard, alkaline, or as dilute, acidic water species, though members of the two categories often co-occur in approximately neutral localities.

In general, among the species of *Potamogeton* studied by Lohammar as well as by Almestrand and Lundh, *natans*, *perfoliatus* (Fig. 115), and *praelongus* are eurytopic, at least with respect to calcium and pH. *P. obtusifolium* and *P. compressus* (sub *zosterifolius*) are rather more limited to the less calcareous waters in central Sweden, and this is still more true of *P. gramineus* (Fig. 117); in the extreme south of Sweden there is, however, no trace of this limitation. *P. alpinus* (Fig. 116), which does not occur in the lakes studied by Lundh, appears in central Sweden to be definitely less calcicole than the other species just mentioned. In no case does there seem to be any clear upper limit set by pH. A group of species (Fig. 116), *P. crispus* (Ca $\geq$ 7.5 mg liter^{-1}), *P. filiformis* (Ca $\geq$ 18 mg liter^{-1}), *P. pectinatus* (Ca $\geq$ 25 mg liter^{-1}), and *P. friesii* (sub *mucronatus*, Ca $\geq$ 36 mg per liter^{-1}) are clearly limited to water containing moderate to relatively high concentrations of calcium; no effects of pH have to be postulated to explain their distributions but such effects cannot be ruled out by the available data. It would seem likely, from the very low calcium concentrations of the order of 1.5 mg liter^{-1} which the eurytopic and less calcicole species can tolerate, that the lower limit of such species in calcium-poor, acidic water is set by pH rather than by calcium. Iversen (1929) found no species of *Potamogeton* in his really acidic (pH < 6.0) lakes, though some of these lakes are likely

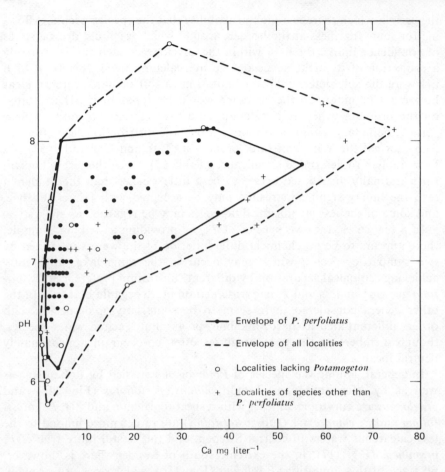

FIGURE 115.   Distribution of *Potamogeton perfoliatus* relative to mean pH and to mean calcium concentration in all the Swedish lakes studied by Lohammar with points for those lakes containing other members of the genus but not *P. perfoliatus* and for the lakes containing no species of *Potamogeton* (data of Lohammar).

to have contained up to 2 mg Ca liter^{-1}. In Lohammar's data *P. perfoliatus* occurs to pH 6.1, *P. gramineus* to pH 6.2, and *P. alpinus, P. compressus, P. obtusifolius,* and *P. praelongus* all to pH 6.5. At least tentatively it may be suggested that the absence of such species in the more acidic lakes studied by Iversen is, as he believed, a real limitation by low pH.

In the case of *Potamogeton gramineus* and *P. lucens*, which produce a widespread hybrid $\times$ *zizii*, the chemical data in central Sweden (Fig. 117*b*) indicate that *lucens* is tolerant of calcium concentrations in excess of about

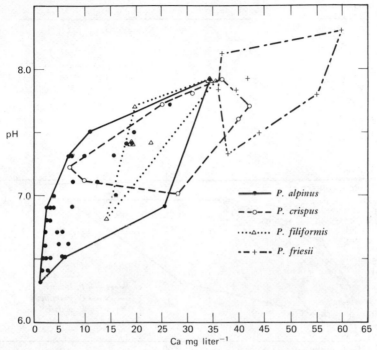

FIGURE 116.   Distribution, relative to mean pH and mean calcium concentration of the water, of *Potamogeton* species in the Swedish lakes studied by Lohammar.

35 mg liter^{-1}, which are not tolerated by *gramineus*, the difference being highly significant ($P < 0.005$). The tendency ($P = 0.0125$) of *P. lucens* to occur at slightly higher pH values is probably not independent of its tolerance of calcium. The hybrid usually occurs where both species grow, but this is not an absolute restriction; it can sometimes be found where only one, or neither, parent now survive. Its occurrence in very slightly more alkaline ($P = 0.05$) and at slightly higher pH values ($P = 0.05$) than *gramineus* is only of marginal significance, while there is no significant distinction in such respects from *P. lucens*. In view of the apparently highly significant lower tolerance of *P. gramineus* to calcium in central Sweden, it is most curious (Fig. 117*c*), as has just been mentioned, to find that in southern Sweden this species occurs in the highly calcareous lakes inhabited by *P. lucens* without any suggestion of a chemical separation of the species.

The four species of the genus *Carex* found growing in the lakes of central Sweden provide a comparable set of examples (Fig. 118). *Carex rostrata*

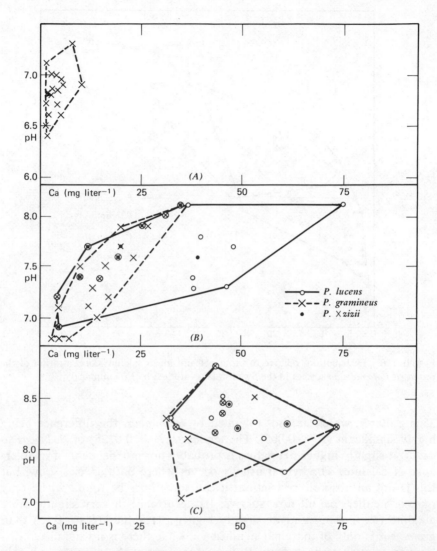

FIGURE 117. Distribution, relative to mean pH and mean calcium concentration of the water, of *Potamogeton gramineus*, *P. lucens*, and their hybrid *P. ×zizii* in (*A*) the lakes of north Sweden, (*B*) those of central Sweden (Uppland and Dalarna), and (*C*) those of the extreme south of Swedish; note the apparent difference in behavior of *P. gramineus* in (*B*) and (*C*) (data of Lohammar and of Almestrand and Lundh).

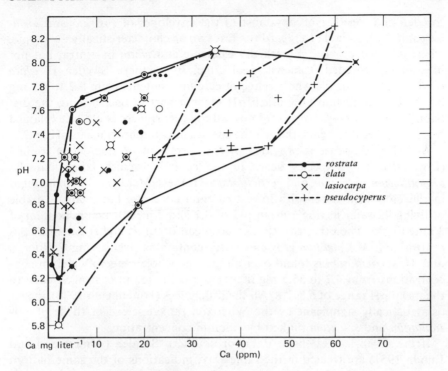

8.2
8.0
7.8
7.6
7.4
7.2
pH
7.0
6.8
6.6
6.4
6.2
6.0
5.8

Ca mg liter⁻¹   10   20   30   40   50   60   70
                              Ca (ppm)

rostrata
elata
lasiocarpa
pseudocyperus

FIGURE 118.   Distribution, relative to mean pH and mean calcium concentration of the water, of *Carex* species in the Swedish lakes studied by Lohammar.

is a eurytopic species of wider distribution in Sweden than the other three, occurring in the lakes in the north studied by Lohammar, which the other species did not. *C. lasiocarpa* is less common but seems to have pH and calcium requirements comparable to those of *C. rostrata*. Spence (1967a) finds that in Scotland, where *C. rostrata* is often the most important junciform emergent plant, the species can grow in up to 95 cm of water, but *lasiocarpa* is more marginal, associated with *Myrica*, in up to 20 cm of water. *C. elata* (sub *hudsonii*) seems to be found in less calcareous waters than either of these species, though the difference is not statistically significant in Lohammar's data. *C. pseudocyperus* occupies the calcium-rich end of the envelope of *C. rostrata* and *lasiocarpa*, the differences in the distribution of calcium between the habitats of the first and of the second and third species being significant ($P < .01$). There is also a significant ($P < .01$) difference in the calcium distribution between *elata* and *pseudocyperus*. As these two species have hardly overlapping envelopes in central

Sweden and together occupy most of the envelopes of *rostrata* and *lasio-carpa*, it is reasonable to regard the last two as characteristically eurytopic, whereas *pseudocyperus* is markedly calcicole and *elata*, in central but not in southern Sweden, somewhat calcifuge. In southern Sweden *C. elata* occurs throughout the whole range of calcium contents from 8.7 to 73 mg liter^{-1}. It is uncertain how much pH plays a part in determining the distribution of *C. pseudocyperus*; almost all the occurrences could be explained by calcium requirements, though the species may require a mean pH $\geq$ 7.2.

An interesting case is provided by the species of *Myriophyllum* studied (Fig. 119). Three species occur in the central Swedish lakes, namely, *alterniflorum*, *spicatum*, and *verticillatum*. Of these *M. alternifolium* is found in the most acid water with lowest calcium contents, but is also capable of living in water having a mean pH of 8.1 and a mean calcium content of 35 mg liter^{-1}. The other two species both can occur at higher calcium concentrations; *M. spicatum* grows in water containing over 25 mg Ca liter^{-1}, and *M. verticillatum* is found over almost the whole range of calcium concentrations from 4.2 to 55.5 mg liter^{-1}, but is limited in central Sweden to the mean pH range of 6.8–7.8. All the differences (Hutchinson 1970) appear as statistically significant by the Wilcoxon rank test except those of *verticillatum* and *spicatum* ranked by calcium concentrations.

If the much less extensive data for southern Sweden (Almestrand and Lundh 1951) are treated in the same way, indications of the same pattern are disclosed. *M. alterniflorum* occurs in the softer waters containing not more than about 35 mg Ca liter^{-1}, and *M. spicatum* is found in water containing more than 25 mg Ca liter^{-1}. *M. verticillatum* seems to occupy the lower part of the envelope of *M. spicatum* as before, but all the pH values involved are much higher. It must be noted that Almestrand gives only pH ranges; the means used are the midpoints of these ranges and may well be greatly weighted in favor of the high values. This is evident from any of the diagrams involving both his and Lohammar's data, the southern Swedish pH values at any calcium content tending to be higher than those of central Sweden.

The differences in pH preferenda seemingly implied by Lohammar's data are in line with Gessner's observations that *M. verticillatum*, unlike *M. spicatum*, does not use HCO_3^- as a carbon source. Consequently it would be at less of a disadvantage at low pH values than at high in the presence of any competitor using bicarbonate. The possible, though by no means certain, inconsistency of the data on pH tolerances in central and south Sweden may imply that the whole argument rests on statistical accidents or, alternatively, that there is something much more interesting involved. The case clearly deserves further study. Dr. Lohammar (in litt.) kindly informs me that the soft-water north Swedish form referrable to *N. spicatum*

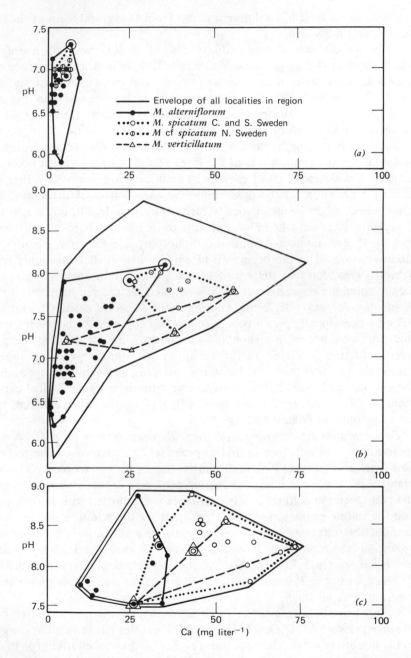

FIGURE 119. Distribution, relative to mean pH and mean calcium concentration of the water of *Myriophyllum* species in (*A*) north Sweden, (*B*) central Sweden (Uppland and Dalarna), and (*C*) south Sweden (data of Lohammar and of Almestrand and Lundh).

in a wide sense is clearly a different taxon from the typical form of the species in central Sweden.

Quite apart from the probability that the only way of averaging Almestrand's pH data gives too high a result, there is clearly a marked difference between some of Lohammar's results and those of Almestrand and Lundh. This is most obvious in the case of *Potamogeton gramineus*, but also is suggested by the data for *Carex elata* and to a lesser extent by that for *P. obtusifolius*, which occurs at or below 38.5 mg Ca liter^{-1} in central Sweden but in the south may live at 61 mg Ca liter^{-1}. One gets a strong impression that the components of the flora of the central Swedish lakes, inhabiting a wide spectrum of chemical conditions, are behaving rather differently from those of the predominantly hard waters of the south. The whole effect might be a statistically rather improbable illusion; if it is real it suggests that even when plants appear to be obvious hard- or soft-water species, the phenomena behind the dichotomy are far from obvious, as already appeared at the beginning of the discussion. It is probably justifiable to conclude that pH below about 6.0 can limit some species, that locally there are characteristic ranges of tolerable calcium concentrations, *P. alpinus*, for example, being calcifuge and *P. friesii* calcicole, and that pH may occasionally play a role in regulating competition between species that can or cannot use bicarbonate as a carbon source. No doubt competitive interaction involving all the variables is important and, as appears below, the fact that fairly hard water is often highly nutrient water adds to the confusion. It is a relief to turn to two situations where critical experiments indicate that on the one hand pH, and on the other calcium, may act as genuine ecological factors.

Determination of occurrence of tropical pleustophytes by pH. A very clear-cut case of influence by pH appears to be provided by the work of Chadwick and Obeid (1966) on the cultivation of the two tropical pleustonic plants *Eichhornia crassipes* and *Pistia stratiotes*. These investigators grew the two species in cultures in which the pH was adjusted with sulfuric acid, and the sulfate content maintained constant by the addition of equivalent amounts of sulfate as sodium sulfate in the less acid cultures. Under such conditions the biomass of *P. stratiotes* was maximal at pH 4.0 and that of *E. crassipes* at pH 7.0. The size of the individual plants varied little in *E. crassipes* but in *P. stratiotes* the very numerous individuals on an acidic medium were all small.

Competitive displacement of *P. stratiotes* by *E. crassipes* has often been observed (Parija 1934; Gay 1958). In the localities where this happens the pH is doubtless nearer the optimum for *E. crassipes*; the rapid growth and asexual reproduction of the plant probably crowds out the *Pistia* at least in some circumneutral waters.

In an extensive study of *E. crassipes* in the Congo Basin, Berg (1961) found that the plant is present in significant quantities only where the pH is greater than 4.5 and is absent at pH 4.2 and below. In the waters that he studied, low pH is associated with high color, usually from 100 to 400 U.S.G.S. units. When the plants were cultured in water from the Congo River, which had been acidified with sulfuric acid to pH 4.0, they grew more slowly than at pH 7.0 but survived, though plansts in natural brown water at pH 4.0 died. Berg concludes that the limitation is due not only to some direct effect of pH but to a marked mineral deficiency, potassium and other ions being absorbed by the humic acids of the brown waters.

Adaptation of Lemnaceae to variations in the calcium content of the medium. Some extremely interesting results have been obtained by Jefferies, Laycock, Stewart, and Sims (1969) on the effects of variation in the calcium content of the medium on the growth of *Wolffia arrhiza* and on both the growth and certain enzymatic activities in *Lemna minor*. If comparable situations occur in other water plants a much more refined analysis of the ecological role of calcium will become possible. It is already evident that such a role, independent of pH or bicarbonate concentration, must exist in the Lemnaceae.

In the clones of both species that were studied, growth rates were higher in media containing relatively low concentrations of calcium, between 0.5 and 1.0 mM or 20–40 mg liter^{-1}, than at 4.0 mM. Most natural waters would contain no more of the element than the lower concentrations used.

Transferring *W. arrhiza* from a medium containing 0.5 mM Ca to one containing 4.0 mM Ca as Ca Cl$_2$ led to an initial decline and then to a rapid rise in the potassium content of the plant which was stabilized in the growing population at about one and a half times the original concentration. Meanwhile the sodium content was decreased and was stabilized at about a third of the original concentration when the plant was growing on a low calcium medium. The process of adjustment is obviously not an instantaneous one based solely on the kinetics of uptake. Data are not given on calcium concentrations but it is implied that they increased.

Further remarkable light is thrown on the process of regulation by studies on the effect of calcium on the activity of the enzyme malic dehydrogenase in *Lemna minor*. Plants of a single clone grown on media of different calcium concentrations for two weeks showed that the specific activity of the enzyme decreased with increasing calcium in the medium, whereas the total protein content increased. When the relationship between activity and the calcium content of the enzyme preparation was studied, it was found that the enzyme from plants grown on the high calcium medium was far more sensitive to activation by calcium ions and had a slightly higher calcium optimum than did the enzyme from plants grown on a medium low in calcium. The malic dehydrogenase from plants grown on medium containing 1 mM Ca proved to be mostly the dimer of a fundamental compound of molecular weight about 17,000, with a small amount of the tetramer. The enzyme from plants grown at the very high calcium concentration of 25 mM was a mixture of dimer, tetramer, and octomer. Isolation of these three isozymes showed that the dimer is very insensitive to changes in calcium concentration, while the octomer is very sensitive, with the tetramer occupying an intermediate position. The type of adaptation to high calcium concentrations just described occurred in a clone draining clay at Gillingham, Dorset; a clone from a pond on chalk at Milton Abbas, Dorset behaved similarly, but a third clone from a ditch at Minehead, Somerset, in sandstone did not show the effect at all and exhibited very little variation in growth rate on media of different calcium concentrations. A fourth clone from peaty water at Shapwick, Somerset was intermediate between the Minehead clone and the other two. It seems likely that the effect of calcium on the enzyme is primarily exhibited in clones from calcareous water; the possible adaptive significance is not clear. The Lemnaceae, though a member of the Arales, includes plants that tend to behave like large microorganisms, which is no doubt part of their attraction to experimental biologists. This, however, does not exclude the fascinating results just discussed from having a wide application, perhaps in very modified ways, throughout the aquatic angiosperms.

Effect of common cations on photosynthesis. Wetzel (1969a), working with *Najas flexilis*, a plant which though characteristic of hard waters does not use HCO_3^- as a carbon source, found striking effects on photosynthesis and on the excretion of organic matter, of varying the concentrations of the major cations (Fig. 120).

Increase in potassium had very little effect on either photosynthetic rate or the excretory loss which remained high at all concentrations. Increase in sodium, however, had a striking effect causing a very marked increase in photosynthetic rate between about 3 and 4 mg Na liter^{-1}, while the proportion of organic matter lost was minimal between about 2 and 3 mg Na liter^{-1}. This sodium dependence is reminiscent of what is known in terrestrial plants showing the C_4 dicarboxylic pathway.

Magnesium becomes strikingly inhibitory as the concentration rises to between 10 and 15 mg liter^{-1}, with a minimum proportional loss of organic matter around 6–10 mg liter^{-1}. There is a low optimal concentration of calcium for photosynthesis around 20 mg liter^{-1}, with a steady decline in the proportion of organic matter lost as the calcium content increases.

Much more work is clearly needed to determine how far these remarkable results are duplicated in other water plants.

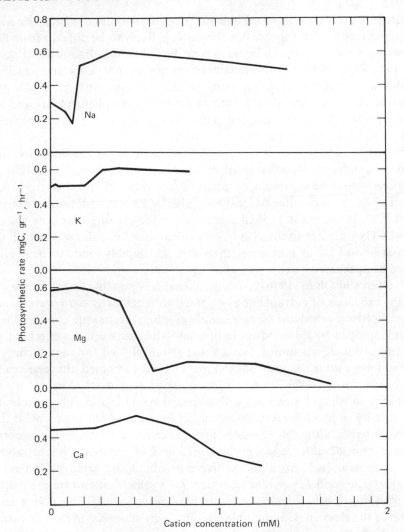

FIGURE 120.   Effect of increasing the four common cations individually on the rate of photosynthesis by *Najas flexilis* (data of Wetzel).

Combined nitrogen and phosphorus as ecological factors.   The two nutrients most likely to set limits to the development of any species of higher plant are combined nitrogen and phosphorus. The experimental aspects of this matter have already been discussed (see p. 351). It has long been recognized (Weber 1907; West 1910) that at least moderately hard waters are likely to contain greater quantities of these and other nutrients than are the dilute soft waters, draining off igneous rocks, or for other reasons generally impoverished in electrolytes. It is thus always likely to be difficult from field observations to distinguish between what Weber called oligotraphent plants characteristic of low ambient concentrations of nutrients and calcifuge plants characteristic of water poor in calcium and with an acidic pH; likewise the equivalent discrimination between eutraphent plants and calcicole plants is likely to be equally hard. In actual practice very few investigators have tried to make the distinction.

We have already seen that in the Characeae there is evidence that high concentrations of phosphate can prove deleterious, though such concentrations would be optimum or perhaps suboptimum to other freshwater species. At the same time at least a number of species of *Chara* seem to do best in quite hard water. Such species are evidently oligotraphent but calcicole. They are apt to flourish in very calcareous localities where such dissolved phosphate as may enter the water presumably tends to be precipitated as apatite.

Iversen and Olsen (1946) pointed out that it is possible to gain some idea of the existence of eutraphent as opposed to specifically hard-water plants from Lohammar's data, using a simple graphical technique comparable to that employed by Edmondson in discriminating between the effects of pH and bicarbonate alkalinity. Iversen and Olsen plotted for each locality in Lohammar's table the total phosphorus or total combined nitrogen against pH. Then for each species under investigation they marked the points for localities in which it occurred with a special symbol, using open circles for the totality of localities and closed circles for stations for the plant. It then appeared that although the commoner species of *Potamogeton* occurred over a considerable range of both pH and of nutrient concentrations, *P. compressus* (sub *zosterifolius*) living at about the same pH values as *P. praelongus* and *P. perfoliatus*, is definitely somewhat eutraphent relative to phosphorus and does not grow in hard waters containing only a minimum of the element. Comparable relations were observed in the two littoral species *Ranunculus lingua* and *Sium latifolium* and in the planktonic *Lemna trisulca*.

In view of the fact that except at very low pH values of the order of 6.0 or less, members of the genus *Potamogeton* appear to be influenced more by the concentration of calcium than by pH, it has seemed desirable to plot the total combined nitrogen and total phosphorus of Lohammar's localities also against calcium, for the various common species of the genus, in the hope of detecting further chemical characteristics of these species.

Almestrand and Lundh (1951) give no values for total nitrogen. Their determinations for phosphorus, called soluble, but made after oxidation of organic matter, gave very high results which they believed to be due to low water levels permitting leaching of littoral sediments. Such values would be irrelevant to the earlier growth of the plants and it has seemed justifiable not to consider them.

The results based solely on Lohammar's data are given in Figs. 121–123, and the relevant statistics permitting comparison between the species are given in Tables 64 and 65. All estimates of significance are based on the Wilcoxon rank order test, which seems to be a useful procedure when one is most interested in the significance of a certain degree of nonoverlapping on the part of two largely overlapping populations, differing little in their

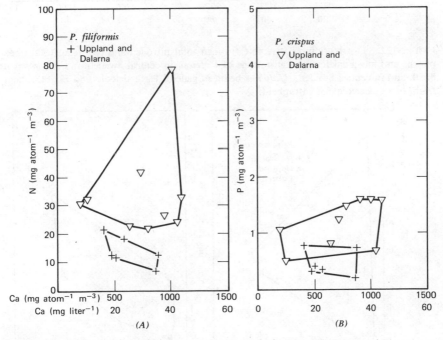

FIGURE 121. Distribution relative to (A) mean total nitrogen (B) mean total phosphorus and mean calcium concentrations of *Potamogeton filiformis* and *P. crispus* in central Sweden, both species being moderately calcicole but differing in their relation to nitrogen (data of Lohammar).

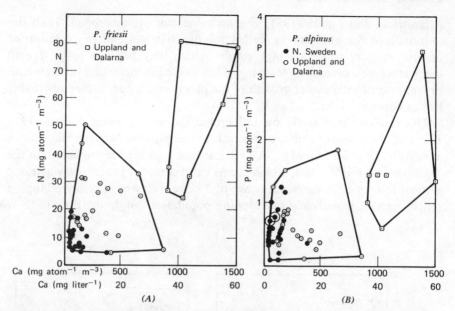

FIGURE 122. Distribution, relative to (A) mean total nitrogen and (B) mean total phosphorus and mean calcium concentrations of *P. friesii* in central Sweden and *P. alpinus* in north and in central Sweden, *P. alpinus* being in general less calcicole and oligotraphent, *friesii* more calcicole and eutraphent.

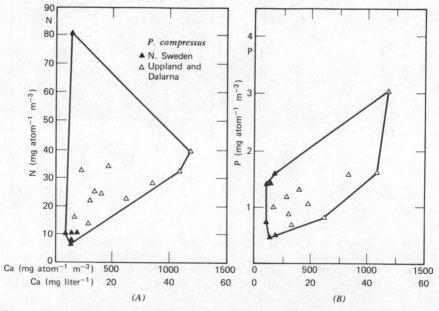

FIGURE 123. Distribution, relative to (A) mean total nitrogen and (B), mean total phosphorus and mean calcium concentrations of the generally eurytopic *P. compressus*.

TABLE 64. *Mean and variance of calcium, total phosphorus, and total nitrogen in localities for various common species of* Potamogeton *in Central Sweden*

Species	Ca mg liter^{-1}		P mg m^{-3}		N mg m^{-3}	
	Mean	Variance	Mean	Variance	Mean	Variance
All southern lakes 84	17.6	252	27.8	360	386	99,867
P. compressus 11	20.9	183.6	35.6	369.3	367	11,982
P. crispus 6	28.3	165.4	32.1	114.7	482	62,523
P. filiformis 9	24.2	69.5	11.2	17.7	186	4,864
P. friesii 9	42.6	74.2	47.2	1,036	598	69,151
P. gramineus 28[a]	13.3	98.3	18.5	80.2	262	17,432
P. lucens 19	28.0	309.9	27.0	347.8	544	213,761
P. × zizii 9	20.4	138.8	15.7	43.3	258.6	21,948
P. pectinatus 9	41.0	115.9	43.1	1,176	549.8	96,036
P. perfoliatus 50[b]	16.7	171	26.4	340	373.5	88,451
P. praelongus 32	21.4	266.0	27.5	298.8	359.5	38,852

[a] 27 for total nitrogen.
[b] 47 for total nitrogen.

mean values for some measurable variable. In some cases the variance ratio and its significance (Bailey 1959, Appendix 5) is of interest.[13]

The two commonest species found by Lohammar in the lakes of central Sweden, *P. praelongus* and *P. perfoliatus*, are chemically eurytopic and occur throughout the greater part of the ranges of concentration of com-

---

[13] It is important to remember that although the geochemical properties of lakes, as of other collections of matter, are likely to be distributed log normally, negative values being impossible, biological reactions to such properties are likely to involve quite different types of distribution. In dealing with variance and the variance ratio the safest procedure would seem to be to limit comparison to those cases where the mean concentrations are nearly the same and to assume in such cases a normal distribution.

TABLE 65. *Significances of Wilcoxon rank order separations (top right) and variance ratios (bottom left) for the mean calcium, total phosphorus, and total nitrogen contents of waters inhabited by various species of Potamogeton in central Sweden (data of Lohammar). The variance ratios are significant to <0.02 but are only given where the ratio of the means is less than 1.5; where the variance ratio is given in bold type the ratio of the means is less than 1.05.*

Species	*P. compressus*			*P. crispus*			*P. filiformis*			*P. friesii*			*P. gramineus*		
	Ca	N	P	Ca	N	P	Ca	N	P	Ca	N	P	Ca	N	P
P. compressus	—	—	—	—	—	—	—	<0.01	<0.01	<0.01	—	<0.01	—	—	—
P. crispus	—	—	—	—	—	—	—	—	—	—	—	—	0.02	—	—
P. filiformis	—	—	—	—	—	—	—	—	—	—	—	—	—	—	—
P. friesii	—	—	—	—	—	—	—	—	—	—	—	—	—	—	—
P. gramineus	—	—	—	—	—	—	—	—	—	—	—	—	—	—	—
P. lucens	—	—	—	—	—	—	—	—	—	—	—	—	—	4.3	—
P. × zizii	—	—	—	—	—	10.3	—	—	—	—	—	—	—	—	—
P. pectinatus	—	8.0	—	—	—	—	—	—	—	—	—	—	4.2	5.1	—
P. perfoliatus	—	**7.4**	—	—	—	—	—	—	—	—	—	—	—	3.7	—
P. praelongus	—	—	—	—	—	—	—	—	—	—	—	—	—	—	—

Species	*P. lucens*			*P. × zizii*			*P. pectinatus*			*P. perfoliatus*			*P. praelongus*		
	Ca	N	P	Ca	N	P	Ca	N	P	Ca	N	P	Ca	N	P
P. compressus	—	—	—	—	—	—	—	—	—	—	—	—	—	—	—
P. crispus	<0.01	—	—	—	—	—	—	—	—	0.02	—	0.02	—	—	—
P. filiformis	—	—	—	—	—	—	<0.01	<0.01	<0.01	<0.01	<0.01	0.01	<0.01	—	—
P. friesii	—	—	—	—	—	—	<0.01	—	—	—	—	—	—	—	—
P. gramineus	<0.01	—	—	—	—	—	—	—	—	0.02	—	—	—	—	—
P. lucens	—	—	—	—	—	—	—	—	—	0.02	—	—	—	—	—
P. × zizii	—	—	—	—	—	—	<0.01	—	—	<0.01	—	—	<0.01	—	—
P. pectinatus	—	—	—	—	—	—	—	—	—	—	—	—	—	—	—
P. perfoliatus	—	—	—	—	—	—	—	—	—	—	—	—	—	—	**2.2**
P. praelongus	—	—	—	—	—	—	—	—	—	—	—	—	—	—	—

bined nitrogen, total phosphorus, and calcium observed in the waters of the region. When the distribution of total combined nitrogen is compared for the two species, the variance ratio is found to be significant, *P. perfoliatus* occurring throughout a greater range of concentrations than *P. praelongus* though the means for the habitats of the two species are almost identical. This presumably provides a hint, though at present not an interpretable one, of differences in ecological tolerance between the two species. There is no comparable effect when the phosphorus or calcium distributions are considered. It is possible that Lohammar's data for total combined nitrogen reflect something more complicated than merely the potential supply of an important nutrient. Pearsall concluded that in the English Lake District, where the two species often occur in the same lake, *P. praelongus* tends to grow in rather deeper water on finer silt than does *P. perfoliatus*. It is reasonable to suppose that the two species tend to be separated ecologically by factors other than water chemistry. *P. alpinus* (Fig. 122) appears both moderately calcifuge and moderately oligotraphent, but in this situation it is obviously not possible to determine which of these characteristics is primary.

P. filiformis seems to be oligotraphent, but definitely is a species of fairly hard waters. In this it may provide an analogy with some of the Characeae. Though it occurs in only six of Lohammar's well-analyzed central Swedish localities, the association with low total combined nitrogen or low total phosphorus is significant, whatever comparisons are made. It is interesting that Koch (1928) found the species in high alpine lakes in Switzerland which are likely to be rather deficient in nutrients, while Krausch (1964) comments on its association with Characeae in north Germany and Finland. In Scotland it is partial to slightly saline water (Spence 1964).

P. compressus (sub *zosterifolius*) is a much less oligotraphent species (Fig. 123) than is *P. filiformis*, though the calcium concentrations of the habitats of the two species do not differ significantly, those for *P. filiformis* actually being a little higher than those for *P. compressus*. The latter species is significantly associated with high phosphorus when comparison is made between its habitats and all the central Swedish lakes in which it does not occur. Comparison with localities for *P. perfoliatus* points in the same direction, but less significantly, there being much overlap. The mean total combined nitrogen concentrations are about the same for the localities for *P. compressus* as for those for *P. perfoliatus* and *P. praelongus*. The variance, however, in the case of *P. compressus* is significantly lower than for *P. praelongus* and *a fortiore* for *P. perfoliatus*. It is possible that *P. compressus* is actually somewhat mesotraphent relative to combined nitrogen when compared, say, with *P. friesii*; this might explain its disappearance from Furesø and its becoming rarer in Lake Mendota during a period when eutrophication must have been taking place (see p. 467). There is, however, one anomalous record of the species in a water very high in combined nitrogen in north Sweden.

P. crispus appears to have approximately the same calcium requirements or tolerances as *P. filiformis* and *P. compressus*; its phosphorus requirements are much as in the last-named species, but it may be characteristic of waters containing much combined nitrogen. The differences in the habitats of *compressus* and *crispus* in this last regard are, however, not statistically significant, but Patrick (personal communication) notes *crispus* as being specially characteristic of rivers below influents of sewage so that some kind of eutraphent character is not unlikely.

P. friesii (Fig. 122), as has been indicated, requires more calcium than *P. filiformis*, *P. compressus*, or *P. crispus*. With regard to nutrients it behaves like *P. crispus*, but here the difference in the nitrogen concentrations of its habitats compared with those of *P. compressus* is moderately significant, though the difference in phosphorus concentrations is not.

P. pectinatus is like *P. friesii* in its high calcium requirements; in its relationship to nutrients it is somewhat more eurytopic than either that species or *P. crispus*. It is, of course, well-known as a plant of mineralized water (see p. 375).

P. gramineus appears to be a species confined in central Sweden to rather low calcium concentrations, as has been already noted (see p. 383). It may be compared with *P. lucens* which is much more likely to occur in hard water, though it is markedly eurytopic and overlaps most of the range of *P. gramineus*. The equivalent differences in phosphorus and combined nitrogen are much less striking.

It is clear from this discussion that within a given range of calcium concentrations, species of *Potamogeton* may be characteristic of water containing potentially low or high supplies of phosphorus and nitrogen, that the behavior of such plants is not the same relative to the two elements, and that at least in the case of total combined nitrogen, plants may grow in sets of localities with a high variance of the concentrations for one species and low for another, even when the mean concentrations for each species are essentially the same. Such conclusions indicate that a statistical separation, on the basis of field data, between calcicole and eutraphent plants is by no means impossible, even though it has so far been achieved in a very fragmentary way.

Little can be said about the possible specific effect of other elements. Lohammar (1938), however, suspected that the occurrence of *Potamogeton compressus* and *P. obtusifolius* is favored by the presence of detectable iron in the water, whereas *Ceratophyllum demersum* usually occurred in waters in which the iron content in summer was below the limit of detection.

SUMMARY

The interior of the typical cell of a freshwater plant is electronegative to the medium. The potential may be maintained in various ways such as by the presence of anionic groups attached to nondiffusible materials or structures, or as the result of an electrogenic pump, such as that which actively transports chloride ions into the cell. If the outer membrane of a cell is permeable to a cation, the latter will move into the cell until a sufficient concentration is built up so that the tendency to diffuse outward down the concentration gradient exactly balances the tendency to move in along the electrochemical gradient. An anion will behave in the opposite manner, the electrochemical gradient causing it to leave the cell. Although it is by no means certain that cell membranes are ever indiscriminately permeable to any dissolved substance, the pattern of ionic equilibrium distributions achieved by the process of passive transport just described provides a convenient standard by which actual distributions of ions may be judged. It is described quantitatively by the Nernst equation

$$E_N = \frac{RT}{Z_j F} \ln \left(\frac{C_o}{C_i} \right)$$

where E_N is the Nernst or equilibrium potential, R the gas constant, T the absolute temperature, F the Faraday or charge per gram equivalent, Z_j the valency of the ion j, and C_o and C_i are the external and internal concentrations. E_N is ordinarily taken as given by experimental determination of the potential between the cell vacuole and the medium. When the concentrations are determined it is then possible to calculate a value for E_N, and if it differs markedly from that observed, it is clear that the observed concentrations depend on active transport involving mechanisms ordinarily described as pumps.

The most critical work on the uptake of ions has involved the use of the easily isolated internodal cells of *Nitella* and of the ecorticate species of *Chara* as well as the large cells of the green alga *Hydrodictyon*. In these there is clear evidence of a sodium pump working to remove the ion from the cell and often, but not always, a pump bringing potassium into the cell. A chloride pump moving this anion in against both the electrochemical and diffusion gradients is always found. The active movement of potassium and chloride in and of sodium out of the cell is strongly light dependent. The light-dependent movement of potassium and sodium, though in opposite directions, are both inhibited by ouabain, a drug which combines with adenosine triphosphatase, and so prevents adenosine triphosphate from being an energy source for the transfer. The active movement of chloride, though largely light dependent, is not inhibited by ouabain. It is less efficient in far-red than in ordinary red light, whereas the opposite is true of the uptake of the two alkalies. The energy source for the chloride pump is clearly not ATP but perhaps may be nicotinamide-adenosine nucleotide. There is, however, a suggestion that since active chloride uptake is depressed in the complete absence of sodium and potassium, some part of the transport of chloride may be linked to that of these two ions.

There is evidence of a bicarbonate pump in those Characeae in which this ion is used in photosynthesis; it appears to have properties comparable to the chloride pump but may be more active. Active uptake of phosphate is well established; it appears in the Characeae, as elsewhere, to be far less light dependent than the other mechanisms just enumerated. There is also evidence of active uptake of sulfate; the relations of this mechanism to light appear complicated. There is at present no evidence that the uptake of either calcium or magnesium is anything but passive.

It is generally supposed that the active transfer of any ion or other simple molecule across a cell membrane involves combination with a carrier on one side and dissociation from the carrier on the other. According to this hypothesis the Michaelis–Menten kinetics developed in enzyme chemistry should apply, V_t, the rate of entry of any substance per unit area, being given by

$$V_t = \frac{C_o V_m}{C_o + K_m} \quad \text{or} \quad \frac{V_m}{V_t} = 1 + \frac{K_m}{C_o}$$

where V_m is a maximal rate and K_m is the Michaelis constant characterizing the process.

In some lower plants and in a number of angiosperms either naturally aquatic, or as tissue slices of terrestrial species in liquid media, the relationship between V_t and C_o fits the equation well and permits calculation of K_m. In many cases, however, as the value of C_o increases there is a change in V_t, corresponding to a new value of K_m. In nature the concentrations of most significant substances are within the range characterizing the low concentration high-affinity process.

As with the lower plants the uptake of potassium by *Egeria densa* is light dependent. Phosphate uptake by the same plant varies much less with light, and in a complicated way, so that at low temperatures and very low but natural concentrations, light may be inhibiting. The rather fragmentary information suggests that in different water plants the uptake of phosphorus depends on environmental factors in different ways.

There has been much argument as to the importance of the roots of rooted aquatic plants as organs of nutrition by which required substances are obtained from lake sediments. It is now clear from a considerable number of experiments that this process does occur. There is, however, clearly great variation in this matter. Although the rootless *Ceratophyllum* obviously does not need roots and like the pleustophytes must obtain all its nutrients from the water, *Lobelia dortmanna* can survive, but cannot grow, in the water in which it is found without being rooted in the appropriate sediments. Comparable differences in the relative importance of the uptake of phosphorus from root and shoot have been found within the genus *Myriophyllum*. At least in some cases leakage of phosphorus derived from the sediments into water from the shoot, particularly after injury, has been observed. This may be significant in the phosphorus cycle of lakes. It is interesting parenthetically that the carnivorous *Utricularia* cannot flower without animal food, and is known to obtain phosphorus from such nutriment.

A good deal of information exists as to the chemical composition of water plants. Some quite striking differences between aquatic and terrestrial plants seem to exist and curious dissimilarities between fairly closely related species are well documented. The potassium content of aquatic angiosperms is little greater than that of terrestrial. The content is weakly but very significantly correlated with the external potassium concentration and quite strongly with the internal chloride concentration. The sodium content is rather variable, usually but not always less than the potassium, and clearly higher than in ordinary land plants growing in the same regions as the water plants studied. Thus the mean potassium content for water plants from a variety of localities in the eastern half of North America is 2.59% dry matter, and the mean sodium 0.66%; a long series of terrestrial plants from Maryland gave 2.21% K and 0.10% Na. The sodium contents in some cases seem to be species specific; in the Cabombaceae *Cabomba caroliniana* in New Jersey had a mean sodium content of 2.60% but *Brasenia schreberi* contained only 0.66%. The environments of the two plants did not differ significantly in their alkali concentrations. Comparable though less striking differences occur among the species of *Myriophyllum*.

In regions in which the sodium content of vegetation on land is very low, the aquatic flora may provide an accessible source of sodium for terrestrial herbivores.

The rarer alkalies are little known; the leaves of *Pontederia cordata* concentrate lithium to a moderate extent. Relative to potassium, cesium and rubidium are ordinarily slightly excluded.

The mean magnesium content of water plants (0.33%) appears not to differ significantly from that of terrestrial vegetation. There is a persistent tendency for *Ceratophyllum* to be high in the element, which may occasionally be present in excess of the calcium concentration. Calcium carbonate, ordinarily as calcite but very occasionally as aragonite, is apt to be deposited during photosynthesis by plants growing in hard water. Though this can occur by simple removal of CO_2 and a consequent shift in the equilibria depending on the latter gas, deposition takes place much more actively if HCO_3^- ions are being used as a source of carbon. The extent of the deposition depends not only on this aspect of photosynthetic metabolism but on the texture and the relation of the plant to water movements. Such deposition is maximal in *Chara*, in which over half the dry plant may be $CaCO_3$, but considerable quantities are also deposited on species of *Potamogeton* such as *P. pectinatus*. Smaller amounts of the calcium oxalate minerals whewellite and weddellite may occur in or on water plants. All such deposits make an estimate of the quantity and distribution of calcium in water plants difficult; a mean value of around 1.8% as in terrestrial plants is probably reasonable.

The enrichment or partial exclusion of strontium relative to calcium is variable. Within the Nymphaeaceae *Nuphar* markedly concentrates the element and *Nymphaea* excludes it. It has been supposed that a mild enrichment relative to calcium is commoner than exclusion, but the data are not yet numerous enough to permit a sound judgment. Barium, in the only cases in which it has been studied, seems to behave essentially like calcium; it is not strikingly enriched in *Nuphar* nor depauperated in *Nymphaea*.

As with lithium, there seems to be a slight enrichment of beryllium in the leaves of *Pontederia cordata*.

The boron content of aquatic plants is very variable. Within a single species, *Typha latifolia*, it ranges from 5.2 to 100 ppm of the dry weight. The variation presumably depends on the availability of the element. In the two best-studied localities *Nymphaea odorata* is the species richest in the element (11.3–62 ppm dry); it was not analyzed from the localities giving much higher values for *T. latifolia*.

The aluminum content of water plants, contrary to an earlier opinion, seems comparable to that of terrestrial plants. The small amount of information on scandium indicates that this element behaves like aluminum while yttrium and the various rare earth elements are concentrated relative to that element. Apart from lanthanum and praseodymium only the even-numbered lanthanide rare earths have been detected. In general they follow a typical geochemical distribution based on the Oddo–Harkins rule, but lanthanum is enriched over cerium, and samarium is usually rather more abundant then neodymium, unlike what is found in the source materials in the locality studied.

The silicon content of water plants is difficult to determine as not only may extraneous mineral matter be entrapped by finely divided leaves, but numerous epiphytic diatoms are associated with all sorts of aquatic vegetation. Opaline phytoliths occur in the Cyperaceae and Gramineae, but though they may make highly diagnostic microfossils they do not seem to have attracted palaeolimnological studies. If titanium, probably the least reactive biologically of the common lithophile elements, is assumed to be present solely as a contaminant, in material having a mean composition comparable to the source materials in a lake basin, the quantity of silica not present as such materials can be calculated. The amount of such silica may be quite high, of the order of 1–2% of the dry weight. Some of this may be present as quartz sand, some as clay, roughly estimable from the Al_2O_3 content, and some as diatom frustules. How much is really present within plant cells is uncertain.

There are observations which suggest that emergent junciform plants such as *Schoenoplectus lacustris* are particularly rich in titanium; if this proves valid it can hardly be entirely due to contamination. Minute quantities of germanium, about 0.3 ppm of the dry matter, have been recorded in the few plants analyzed for the element. Relative to the titanium of these plants, the germanium is much enriched. Further study might be interesting.

Zirconium appears to be more abundant in at least some water plants than might be expected, the mean amount from Connecticut material being 27 ppm dry. Hafnium seems to be proportionately much less enriched but the available figures for this element are inadequate.

There is a little data on thorium which suggests some enrichment.

Arsenic is accumulated in some water plants. Most species contain but a few parts per million, but *Ceratophyllum demersum* may have up to 26 ppm dry in ordinary water. When there is any increase in the arsenic of the environment, as from geothermal waters in New Zealand, this plant may contain over 1000 ppm As dry. *Lagarosiphon major* is known to contain even more of the element and some species of *Potamogeton* may exhibit definite enrichment. Compared with the environmental concentration the enrichment factor in *C. demersum* is over 1000. Antimony is not known in water plants but small amounts of bismuth have been recorded; there is no accumulation in *C. demersum*. There are some analyses for vanadium but they are not concordant; the mean value would seem to be about 2.5 ppm dry. There are indications of striking accumulation in the leaf of *Pontederia cordata* and perhaps in some species of *Potamogeton*. The only information on niobium indicates that it is concentrated more than vanadium.

Among the chalcophile transition metals copper is always detectable. The amount recorded for the whole range of species varies from 2.5 to 243 ppm dry, but the higher values are clearly exceptional; a mean value of about 40 ppm would be reasonable. Apart from a single analysis of *Alternanthera philoxeroides*, *Cabomba caroliniana*, varying from 2.5 to 135 ppm, covers the whole range.

Silver is hardly studied but the amount present seems rather under 1 ppm dry.

Zinc is ordinarily more abundant than copper, as is also true in terrestrial plants, the quantities for individual species ranging from 27 to 1000 ppm dry. The highest values are from *Spirodela polyrhiza* and *Cabomba caroliniana*, which may both contain 1000 ppm dry and seem to be zinc accumulators. The mean value in aquatic vegetation is about 140 ppm.

In plants in which the copper is likely to have all been obtained from the water, concentration factors of about 200 appear to be usual. Study of the accumulation of copper from normal and polluted sediments in the Italian lakes has disclosed the existence of populations of *Phragmites australis* differing in their copper metabolism. In normal localities the plants accumulate some copper in the rhizomes, the amount apparently depending on the supply. In the lakes of Latium the amount transferred to the stems and leaves is linearly dependent on the amount in the rhizome, though more is found in the leaves than stems. In plants from unpolluted sediments of the Italian Alps, the quantities in the leaves and stems are less, though again they are linearly dependent on the rhizomal contents. When growing on the sediments of Lago d'Orta, grossly polluted by copper, the rhizomes contain massive amounts of copper, but the concentrations in the leaves, which are lower than those of the stems, fall between the leaf concentrations of the plants from the other two populations.

In plants in which the zinc is likely to have been derived from the water, concentration factors of the order of 1000 seem usual, though in *Spirodela polyrhiza* a factor of about 25,000 is recorded.

Cadmium has been little studied. In the two investigations of the element, the Cd:Zn ratio in water plants was about 0.05, or nearly 20 times what might be expected from the terrestrial abundances. In view of the toxic properties of cadmium the matter needs further study, as does the occurrence of mercury in water plants for which the available data, though reliable, are clearly exceptionally high.

Lead appears to be present in amounts of the order of 10 ppm dry and tin is perhaps about as abundant. The concentration factor may well be greater for tin; this is interesting as tin is more likely to be a biological element than is lead.

Water plants tend to contain more iron (mean around 0.3%) than manganese (mean around 0.2%), whereas in terrestrial plants the opposite tendency is observed, where the quantities of both elements are much smaller and the manganese content typically several times that of iron. This is probably mainly due to the mobility of ferrous iron in reduced waterlogged sediments. Occasionally heavy incrustation of iron, probably of bacterial origin, may cover water plants. The chromium content of water plants is very uncertain; the best data appear to give a low mean, of about 0.6 ppm, not greatly different from terrestrial plants. The amounts of molybdenum present are typically of the same order of magnitude, though the element can be greatly enriched when externally deposited iron is present.

Nickel and cobalt are also inadequately known; again the best data seem to be concordant with what is known in terrestrial plants. There is, however, clear evidence of accumulation of cobalt in *Pontederia* leaves, along with lithium, vanadium, and to some extent, beryllium and silver.

The fluorine content of water plants is little known; it appears to be of the order of several hundred parts per million dry and to represent a definite enrichment over chlorine when compared with lake water, though not with freshwater sediments, in which fluorine may be expected to be more abundant than chlorine. In *Ceratophyllum* in one locality the F:Cl ratio was about six to eight times as great in the plant as in the water, implying definite concentration. Chlorine varies from about 0.25 to 3.25%. There is no significant relationship with ambient chloride in freshwaters nor with the sodium in the plant, but a quite strong and highly significant correlation with potassium in the plant, which probably would be expected from the physiological information on ion uptake.

The limited amount of data available on bromine suggests that it is distributed in relation to chlorine much as in the biosphere, but there seem to be systematic differences in the ratio between different plants which presumably reflect discrimination, which is, however, evened out in the vegetation as a whole. In the only study of any significance iodine appears to be excluded from the plants relative to bromine, the Br:I ratio being about 60:1 in the plants and about 3.4:1 in the ambient water.

Phosphorus and nitrogen are generally believed to be the most important limiting elements in freshwaters. Experimental studies suggest that when the nitrogen content of the dry matter is below 1.3% the element is limiting in the presence of abundant phosphorus, and when the phosphorus content is below 0.13% phosphorus is limiting in the presence of adequate nitrogen.

In plants collected in nature the quantities of both elements are generally higher than these limiting values, the means being 2.73% N and 0.45% P in one long series of analyses. The Lemnaceae appear to be very high in both elements, whereas *Phragmites* is typically very low. These differences are partly explicable in the absence or presence of nonliving supporting structures.

The proportion of total nitrogen that is present as true protein varies from 42% in *Hydrocotyle* sp. to 97% in *Nymphaea odorata*; it is usually around two-thirds. The amino acid composition is usually normal though *Alternanthera philoxeroides* and *Sagittaria latifolia* among the species analyzed are very deficient in phenylalanine.

There are clearly specific differences in the concentration of phosphorus among allied plants, *Nuphar advena* containing more than *Nymphaea odorata* even when they are growing together.

The most interesting feature of the carbohydrate chemistry of water plants is the occurrence, in cell wall polysaccharides, of the pentose apiose in the Lemnaceae, and in a number of brackish-water and marine monocotyledons but not in their freshwater allies.

There is a slight difference in ether extract observable when emergent and floating-leaved plants are compared with submersed species, but when this is expressed as a percentage of the ashfree dry matter, 5.23 % in emergent or floating-leaved species to 4.41 % in submersed plants, the difference, though not unexpected, is unimpressive.

Aquatic plants are apparently less likely to contain secondary substances liable to render them unpalatable to herbivores than are terrestrial. A number of alkaloids occur in *Decodon* among the emergent species, and in the water lilies a very remarkable set of compounds belonging to various groups of alkaloids are known. Some of these from *Nuphar*, which are peculiar in containing sulfur, are antibiotic, and one more normal compound is sequestered by beavers, hydroxylated, and appears in castoreum, the product of their scent glands.

The submersed water plants may not produce alkaloids and are perhaps less in need of chemical defenses than are terrestrial plants.

The most important chemical dichotomy in the ecology of the plants of freshwaters is that of soft and hard waters. An idea of the species involved at least in the North Temperate zone can be obtained from Tables 61, 62, and 63.

The dichotomy involves a complex situation. Soft waters are low in all dissolved salts, may have more alkalies than alkaline earth elements, have a low pH and low bicarbonate content, and often are deficient in nutrients, whereas the reverse is true of hard waters. The limitation, however, of any particular species may be due to any of these more or less correlated factors, the significances of which are hard to separate.

It is probable that in soft waters pH does play an important role. This has been shown critically in the case of *Pistia stratiotes* compared with the less acid-tolerant *Eichhornia crassipes*. Species of *Potamogeton* appear not to occur in water perennially more acidic than pH 6.0, whatever the calcium content. In hard waters most of the available observations can be explained by variations in calcium tolerance from species to species. There is experimental evidence from the Lemnaceae that the environmental calcium can influence the enzyme systems of the plant. There is a little evidence suggesting that some plants not able to use bicarbonate ion as a source of carbon are at a disadvantage in nature when the pH is too high. Curious regional differences in calcium tolerance, notably by *Potamogeton gramineus*, seem to exist and require further study. The total salinity and chlorinity of waters certainly affect their flora, there being a definite group of facultative brackish species of which *Potamogeton pectinatus* is an important example. There are hints from the field data that in such waters the proportion of sulfate may be a significant ecological factor. There are angiosperms such as *Potamogeton filiformis* which seem to be characteristic of hard, or sometimes slightly saline, water poor in nutrients. This situation, so far as phosphorus is concerned, has earlier been encountered in the Characeae. There are also some species such as *P. compressus* which tolerate low calcium concentrations but not the extremely low total phosphorus and nitrogen characterizing most soft water. Some of the common more eurytopic species such as *P. perfoliatus* appear to occur in a wider range of nitrate concentrations than do others such as *P. praelongus*, though the mean values are almost the same. It is likely that most of the soft-water species have wider fundamental niches than they can occupy in the face of competition by hard-water species in the less dilute habitats.

CHAPTER 31

The Distribution of Macrophytes
in Lakes

H aving considered in the preceding chapters a good deal of autecology and some other matters that provide a background to ecological studies, we now turn to the central theme of this volume and give an account of the distribution of the macrophytes in lakes. The subject may be divided naturally into three parts. In the first the working of the various external forces in producing vertical zonation is considered. In the second the resulting patterns of distribution in as many kinds of lakes as possible, spread over the surface of the earth, are described. In the third part an attempt is made to summarize the various approaches that have been made toward an intellectual categorization of these patterns.

THE VERTICAL EXTENT OF THE VEGETATION

In all considerations of the vertical variation of the biota of a lake the great steepness of the environmental gradients must always be kept in mind. In a small stratified and productive lake in a temperate landscape, the march of the seasons may cause a change of 25°C in the temperature of the surface water, but an increase or decrease of only 2 or 3°C at a depth of 15 m. Stratification will often produce striking chemical gradients. At the surface the annual variation in illumination will be much the same as affects the marginal supralittoral plants, but at 15 m, virtually no light may be present at any season. The pressure at the surface will be, at low altitudes, about 1 atm, but at 15 m an additional 1.5 atm due to the water will raise the total pressure to 2.5 atm. Disturbance due to wind, waves, and currents will die out rapidly with depth so that in a small stratified lake some ingenuity may be needed to detect water movements at 15 m. On land, for example, on a hillside sloping down to the lake, at a point 150 m above the lake surface, there might be at any season an average temperature perhaps three-quarters of a degree lower than around the lake. The difference in illumination at the top of the vegetation layers at the lake level and 150 m up the hillside will be negligible, as air is very much more transparent than water. The pressure difference at moderate elevations will be about 0.02 atm. The effect of wind may increase a little but the range in disturbance of the medium will be far less than in the lake. The enormous difference made by descending 15 m into the water compared with a vertical movement of 10 times that distance on land must always be kept in mind.

The restriction of tracheophytes and the wide range of bryophytes and algae. With the single, very doubtful, exception of records (Dangeard 1925) of *Najas marina* from 12–15 m and *Elodea canadensis* from 10–12 m in the Lac d'Annecy in the French Alps,[1] no angiosperms are known to grow at depths of over about 11 m, and in nearly all lakes they do not extend below a depth of 9 m. In Lake Titicaca (Tutin 1940), *Potamogeton strictus* occurred down to just over 11 m, *Chara* spp. to 14 m, and the moss *Hygrohypnum* to 29 m. These depth records are evidently highly reliable. Hill (1969) noted *Lagarosiphon major* almost to 10 m in Lake Aratiatia, Auckland, New Zealand. Ruttner (1933) found *Ceratophyllum demersum* at 8–9 m in Lake Ranau in Sumatra, but the presence of the plant at such depths is almost certainly due to drift and sinking of specimens initially growing in shallower water. In Lake Toba the same author noted *Hydrilla verticillata*, *Potamogeton malayanus*, *P. maackianus*, *Najas falciculata*, and *Myriophyllum spicatum* all able to reach to 5 m but not further; *Chara* occurred, at least sporadically, down to 12 m. In Lake Tahoe (Frantz and Cordone 1967) vascular plants are scarce but appear to extend to 6.5 m, whereas *Chara virgata* (*C. globularis* var. *virgata* sub *delicatula* var. *barbata*) was found at 75.5 m and broken Characeae at 164 m, at which depth

---

[1] Dangeaud also records *Nitella flexilis* from 23 m. The plants were obtained with a four-pronged grapple on a 50-m line, and doubts may be entertained as to the reliability of the depths, particularly as Roux (1907) had earlier found no plants in the lake below 8 m. Dr. Daniel Livingstone has called my attention to the existence, in the Brussels Botanic Garden Herbarium, of a shoot of *Hydrilla verticillata* alleged to be from 180 m in Lake Tanganyika. The specimen, Kiner A6, is a very poor one, probably a fragment that has drifted into deep water and has sunk there, according to Professor J. Leonard who most kindly examined it.

bryophytes evidently also occurred. In Lake Vrana, Cherso (Cres), Golubić (1963) noted no angiosperms below 7.7 m, where *Myriophyllum spicatum* occurred, though *Nitella opaca* could grow at depths as great as 38 m and *Spirogyra* penetrated to 50–52 m. In Crystal Lake, Wisconsin (Fassett 1930), angiosperms and *Isoetes macrospora* occurred in the top 4 m, with a sterile zone from 4 to 15 m, below which mosses covered the bottom to the maximum depths of 20 m. Examples from deep transparent lakes could probably be multiplied almost indefinitely.

In Lake Tahoe it appears that about 2% of the incident radiation flux is still present at 75 m, whereas in Crystal Lake the corresponding depth would be 14 m, in both cases well below the deepest flowering plants. In Titicaca, the 2% isophote usually lies at 12–14.5 m, a little below the maximum depth of occurrence of *Potamogeton strictus*. Yet in the English Lakes (Pearsall 1920), *Potamogeton berchtoldii* and *P. praelongus*, probably the most shade-tolerant of the common aquatic angiosperms, can live at this relative intensity, though at depths of only 6.5 m or less. Elsewhere, as at Trout Lake, Wisconsin, *Ceratophyllum demersum* occurs at similar depths and light intensities. It is evident that there is a very marked difference in reaction to depth between the angiosperms and the lower macroscopic plants and that the difference depends on something other than light intensity.

ZONATION, DEPTH DISTRIBUTION, AND COMPARATIVE LIMNOLOGY OF AQUATIC TRACHEOPHYTES

At the margin of the lake, mechanical action of wind and water movements are likely to be the most important environmental factors. In deeper water, illumination is clearly not the only factor of importance, though it may be a paramount one. Much of the difference between the tracheophytes and the lower plants is apparently due to different capacities to withstand increasing pressure. Finally edaphic differences in the sediments in which most of the aquatic plants are rooted may be almost as important as variation in illumination.

Exposure and resistance to wind and waves. Most large lakes, at least on the shores receiving the full force of the wind and waves, lack any visible higher plants. That small lakes may have such vegetation along equally exposed and similarly directed coastlines may be explained by the relationship of wave height to the fetch of the wind (Vol. I, pp. 355–356). Very shallow areas of considerable size may also be fringed with emergent vegetation even though parallel but less flat parts of the shoreline lack such vegetation. In very shallow water of any extent the waves may become translatory, losing energy to the bottom.

Emergent plants. Except in the most protected bays, the emergent vegetation of lakes is junciform; the herbiform emergent plants such as the larger Alismataceae are primarily species of ponds.

Where emergent vegetation exists and is not confined to particularly sheltered inlets, it is nevertheless apt to be much better developed on the sheltered side of the lake upwind, than on the exposed opposite shore. This phenomenon appears wherever vegetation maps have been made in regions of a strongly prevalent wind; it is very conspicuous in Sweden (Thunmark 1931), Denmark (Boye-Petersen 1917), and north Germany (Klinge 1890; Sauer 1937), where the prevalent wind is from the southwest. Spence (1967a) thinks that the coarse, unfavorable sediment of the exposed shores is a major factor in this type of distribution, though it seems unlikely that the direct buffeting by wind and breaking waves is not equally significant.

In the more eutrophic lakes of these European countries, the marginal reed association or *Phragmitetum* provides striking examples of the detailed ecological effects of exposure. The association is nearly always developed best along the southwestern shores, except where locally there is a very shallow bay, as at the northeast corner of Furesø; here the protection of the headland defining the bay and the shallowness of the whole region permit more emergent plants than would otherwise occur on a northeastern shore. *Phragmites* can grow in soil the surface of which is a little above the water table; the outermost plants thus are eulittoral, or even supra-littoral, but the species can also be rooted in up to 2 m of water in the infralittoral. Under optimally eutrophic conditions as in Holstein, the stems of such deep-water emergent reeds can be up ot 5 m tall. In general *P. australis* grows on hard bottoms.

Two other characteristic species of the *Phragmitetum* may replace *P. australis*, largely or wholly in some reed beds. *Schoenoplectus lacustris* ordinarily grows in 0.5–2.0 m of water, often, though not always, in a softer sediment than that colonized by *Phragmites*, and usually on the lakeward side of the latter (*A* of Fig. 124, section *f*), thus giving rise to some zonation. Since the terete leafless stems of *Schoenoplectus* are better able to withstand wind and wave action than is *Phragmites*, this zonation, when it occurs, is adaptive. It is, however (Koch 1926), often possible to find inverted zonation with the reeds growing lakeward of the bullrushes; even more frequently the two grow together. Several species of reed mace of the genus *Typha* are certainly more easily injured by wind or waves than *P. australis* and are usually found only in well-protected places. Wilson (1935) concluded that in northern Wisconsin, *Typha latifolia* disappears from lakes as their margins become smoothed by erosion and the locally quiet parts of the shoreline lose their protection. *Typha* grows from the

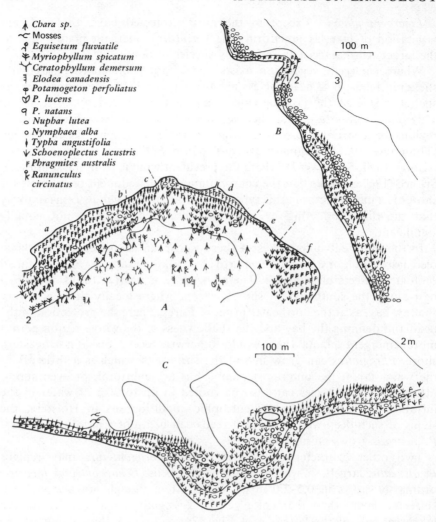

ʎ Chara sp.
ᴄ Mosses
ʄ Equisetum fluviatile
ψ Myriophyllum spicatum
Ψ Ceratophyllum demersum
Ⴈ Elodea canadensis
φ Potamogeton perfoliatus
♥ P. lucens
ϙ P. natans
o Nuphar lutea
o Nymphaea alba
ι Typha angustifolia
ψ Schoenoplectus lacustris
ғ Phragmites australis
ʔ Ranunculus
circinatus

FIGURE 124.   Distribution of emergent and floating leaved plants in the shallow marginal waters of *A*, Storekalv, the northeast bay of Fureso; *B*, part of western shore of Bagsvaerdso; and *C*, part of southern shore of Farumso (Boye-Petersen, slightly modified).

sandy margins of some lakes to a depth of about 2 m. Where *Phragmites* is present, either by itself or mixed with *Schoenoplectus*, the species of *Typha* may grow in protected places lakeward of such plants (*A*, of Fig. 124 section *a*, and *B*), but occasionally the order from the land lakeward may be *P. australis*, *Typha angustifolia*, *Schoenoplectus lacustris* (*A* of Fig. 124, section *d*). It is probable that edaphic factors as well as differences in exposure are involved in the separation of the two last-named species, though it is difficult from the literature to gain a clear idea as to what the determinants may be.

In North America *Typha latifolia* is the most widespread of the three species of the genus, *T. angustifolia* tending to be rather more northern and *T. domingensis* definitely more southern. McNaughton (1960) finds experimentally that *T. latifolia* is ecologically the most tolerant of the three. All species are composed of populations that must be largely clonal and are genetically adapted to specific environments. Kalk (1973) records that *T. domingensis* forms an almost pure stand around Lake Chilwa in Malawi, which would not be expected from the behavior of the other species. An extensive account of the autecology of *Schoenoplectus lacustris* is given by Seidel (1955), and of *Phragmites australis* by Rodewald-Rudescu (1974).

It should be noted that the existence of reed beds provides an environment in which the surface of the water is much less disturbed by wind than it is in open areas and which is thus suitable for populations of lemnid pleustophytes. Some account of their ecology, particularly the relation to competition, will be given when the associations of the surface film are taken up in Vol. IV.

Floating-leaved plants. In the zone of floating-leaved vegetation there is a good deal of evidence of the regulatory effect of disturbance, though it is not easy in the present state of knowledge to separate this factor from others. Pearsall found that although *Nymphaea alba* var. *minor* and *Nuphar* × *spennerana* (sub *intermedia*) commonly occurred on more organic sediments than *Nymphaea alba* and *Nuphar lutea*, he also had evidence, as has been indicated earlier (p. 143), that the former two taxa might occur on less organic sediment in the more disturbed areas within the range of ephydates. *N.* × *spennerana* is a persistent hybrid of *N. lutea* and *N. pumila;* it is therefore interesting to find it showing superior adaptation in some circumstances outside the contemporary range of the boreal parent *N. pumila*. The latter plant according to Heslop-Harrison (1955a) is less adapted to disturbance, owing to the small size of its rhizome.

As might be expected, species with smaller ovate leaves like *Potamogeton natans* are usually found under more disturbed conditions than are the water lilies (see p. 144).

Submerged plants. In lakes with exposed shores the shallowest zone is one of erosion; below this there is a neutral zone where erosion is balanced by sedimentation, whereas further out in deeper water sedimentation prevails. In relatively mature basins the actual amount of erosion may be small, all easily erodable inorganic material having long since been removed. However, the water plants are themselves subject to the eroding action. These plants are mostly small and rosulate, having the isoetid growth-form. They have been best studied in certain Swedish lakes such as Fiolen (see p. 434), where *Isoetes setacea, Subularia aquatica,* and *Ranunculus reptans* are characteristic of the zone of erosion, whereas *Isoetes lacustris* and *Lobelia dortmanna* become common as the neutral zone is approached. In the English Lakes *Littorella* appears as an important plant in the uppermost, disturbed zone.

Illumination. The maximum depth at which autotrophic plants can grow, irrespective of their nature, clearly does depend on the transparency of the water. An admirable example of this very general and elementary limitation is shown in Fig. 125, based on 27 Finnish lakes considered by Maristo (1941), for which the Secchi disk transparency and the maximum depth of macroscopic phytobenthos is recorded. It will be seen that the relationship is approximately linear. The apparent interception of the regression line with the depth of vegetation axis is doubtless due to the spectral composition of such light as reaches the depth of disappearance of the disk in the less transparent lakes, being redder than in the more transparent waters and thus more favorable for photosynthesis. This results in the limit of vegetation exceeding the transparency when the latter is low, but falling far short of it when the transparency is high. In 17 cases out of the 27, the plants penetrating furthest were mosses, usually *Fontinalis antipyretica* (four cases), or *Drepanocladus sendtneri* (eight

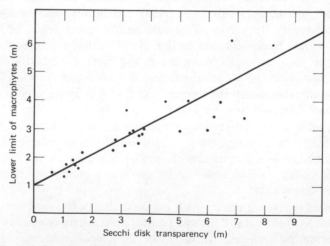

FIGURE 125. Relationship of maximum depth of macrophytes to Secchi disk transparency in 27 Finish lakes (Maristo). Note that the line of best fit (by eye) appears to intersect the ordinate.

cases). The latter species occurred at 6.3 m, and *Isoetes lacustris* at 6.0 m; no other plants were found below 5 m.

The fact that no autotrophic plants will occur below their biogeochemical compensation points does not mean that the zonation is necessarily determined solely by light penetration. Nevertheless, there can be no doubt that some of the details of zonation, as well as the depth range within which zonation can develop, are determined by light penetration. Pearsall (1920), who most strongly supported the view that edaphic factors are of major importance, concluded that the lower limit of illumination permitting successful colonization varies among the deep-water species of *Potamogeton* in the English Lakes, as indicated in Table 66.

TABLE 66.   *Environmental conditions permitting growth of* Potamogeton *spp. in the English Lakes*

Species	Normal range of light as % of surface intensity	% Fine silt and clay in substrate		% Organic matter in substrate	
		Range	Mean	Range	Mean
P. berchtoldii	2–15	12–46	23	12–26	16.4
P. praelongus	2–20	15–26	20	10–21	14.8
P. alpinus	4–40	—	—	20–44	33.4
P. perfoliatus	4–30	10–21	15	13–19	20.3

It is evident that *P. berchtoldii* and *P. praelongus* can extend deeper than *P. alpinus* or *P. perfoliatus;* of the first two species apparently *P. berchtoldii* is more likely to occur on the finest and supposedly most nutrient rich silts. *P. obtusifolius* seems to have an intermediate position, tolerating a light penetration of 3–20%. *Nitella flexilis* and *N. opaca* are often associated with and have similar light requirements to *P. berchtoldii*, but *Isoetes lacustris* seems not to penetrate quite so deeply. *Sparganium minimum* behaves very much like *Potamogeton alpinus*, both with respect to light intensity and the high tolerance of organic soils. *Juncus bulbosus* f. *fluitans* does not grow at depths with less than 5% of the surface illumination.

Most of the submersed shallow-water plants recorded by Pearsall doubtless habitually grow at greater relative intensities, but no data are given. Owing to Pearsall's mode of presentation in terms of communities rather than species, it is impossible to ascertain the limits for a number of the plants he discusses; it would obviously be incorrect to assume that all the species listed as forming a community would have precisely the same ecological tolerances.

More extensive data, based on better determinations of the penetration of light than were available to Pearsall, have been published by Wilson (1941) as a result of his studies on Trout Lake, Wisconsin. It must be realized, however, as Wilson himself makes clear, that the vertical distributions, which he gives certainly depend in part on factors other than illumination. Thus *P. pectinatus*, which Bourne (1932) found naturally limited by 4% surface illumination, seemed in Trout Lake to require 14%. In Table 67, Wilson's figures for the percentage light penetration at the bottom of the ranges of the higher plants studied have been converted to values based on the angular altitude of the mean sun, rather than the less realistic zenith sun used by Birge and Juday (1931) in the diagram from which Wilson obtained his optical data. This is done by multiplication by 0.89 or the mean of the cosines of the angles of refraction given by Birge and Juday (1929). The order within any optical category in which the plants appear is that of Wilson; it is clearly not taxonomic but is not explained.

There can be little doubt that many, if not most, of the plants in the infralittoral are limited in their downward extension by factors other than light. *Lobelia dortmanna*, for instance, in the less transparent Lake Fiolen in Sweden (see p. 435) is found in 2.6 m of water where the light intensity is certainly less than 10% of that incident on the surface, rather than the 62% of Table 67. Nevertheless, some of the deeper records are probably determined by illumination. *Potamogeton berchtoldii* extends about as far into the shade here as in the English Lakes and only *Ceratophyllum demersum*, in other lakes often the deepest species of flowering plant, goes deeper. In Trout Lake *P. praelongus* reaches to less great depths than *P. berchtoldii*, though in the English Lakes they both grow at the level of 2% isophote.

Little is known about the mechanisms by which various degrees of tolerance to low illumination are evolved. In the clearest lakes the light reaching to greatest depths will be predominantly blue, but where organic color is present, the deepest penetrating light, reaching only a few meters, will be red. Some adaptation on the part of *Elodea* to the spectral quality of the available light has been claimed (Harder, Döring, and Simonis 1936) and the frequent occurrence of reddish benthic Myxophyceae suggests chromatic adaptation.

It has already been pointed out that the work of Spence and Chrystal (1970a, b) indicates that *P. obtusifolius*, one of the species going to greatest depths in Trout Lake, owes some of its apparent capacity to photosynthesize at reduced light intensity to the low respiratory needs of its leaves, so that while gross photosynthesis may be no more efficient than in less shade-tolerant species, the proportion of energy usefully fixed is clearly larger.

TABLE 67. *Depth distribution of the higher plants of Trout Lake, Wisconsin, with light intensities at the lowest depth for each species as percentage of the incident radiation*

Lower limit (m)	% Surface illumination	Species
0.25	62	*Sparganium angustifolium*
		Potamogeton epihydrus
		Ranunculus reptans
		Gratiola aurea f. *pusilla*
		Potamogeton spirillus
		Lobelia dortmanna
		Littorella americana
0.5	45	*Equisetum fluviatile*
		Juncus pelocarpus f. *submersus*
		Eleocharis palustris
		Scirpus acutus
1	25	*Nymphaea odorata*
1.25	22	*Sagittaria cuneata*
1.5	20	*Eleocharis acicularis*
1.75	18	*Potamogeton natans*
2	16	*Ranunculus trichophyllus*
2.5	14	*Myriophyllum alterniflorum*
		Isoetes macrospora
		Potamogeton pectinatus
3.5	10	*Megalodonta beckii*
		Myriophyllum verticillatum
4	5.9	*Myriophyllum tenellum*
		Sagittaria graminea
4.5	4.5	*Potamogeton gramineus*
		P. praelongus
		Vallisneria americana
		Elodea canadensis
5	3.8	*Potamogeton amplifolius*
		P. richardsonii
5.5	3.1	*Najas flexilis*
6	2.4	*Potamogeton obtusifolius*
		P. berchtoldii (sub *pusillus*)
		P. robbinsii
6.5	1.8	*Ceratophyllum demersum*

The work of Spence, Milburn, Ndawula-Senyimba, and Roberts (1971; see also Spence 1967b), which strongly suggests that the drupes of *Potamogeton schweinfurthii* are adapted to germinate in deeper water than are those of *P. thunbergii*, indicates that some of the differentiation between deep- and shallow-water species might depend on where the seeds can best germinate rather than where the adult can best live. In view of the probable predominance of asexual reproduction in perennial water plants this source of additional spatial differentiation may prove unimportant. Spence (1964) himself has pointed out that *Phragmites australis* when growing underwater is living under conditions in which its seeds cannot germinate. The observed pattern of distribution of the species round a lake must be due to asexual reproduction, and this may well be true of a number of other plants.

The ecological role of pressure.   Schimper (Lauterborn 1934; Gessner 1952), in an academically exuberant Natursonett, written in 1854, attributed heterophylly to the magic of water pressure, and many years later Glück (1905) concluded from experiments with *Sagittaria* and other water plants that some such action of pressure may exist, though in his work other factors were not fully excluded. Subsequently the possible effects of pressure on higher water plants were ignored, probably because of the small range of pressures available within the ordinary depth span of freshwater angiosperms. Almost a century elapsed after Schimper's initial poetic insight before Gessner (1952) clearly demonstrated that pressure differences within the range of depths commonly encompassed by the euphotic zone of a transparent lake could have profound effects on higher plants. Some inhibition on the growth of *Nuphar* in c. 3 m of water contrasted with growth in c. 1.5 m had already been noted by Laing (1941) but excited little interest.

Experimental Studies.   Gessner examined the growth of *Hippuris vulgaris* in closed illuminated bottles in which the pressure in excess of 1 atm could be varied by the setting of mercury manometers. When the excess pressure did not surpass 0.5 atm, corresponding to 5 m of water, growth in length was normal, but the thickness of the axis of the newly formed main shoot was about 30% less than that of the control. At an excess pressure of 0.75 atm, growth in length stopped completely (Fig. 126). *Myriophyllum aquaticum* grew normally between 0 and 0.3 atm excess pressure, but at 0.5 and 1.0 atm there was a moderate inhibition, about as much at the higher as at the lower of the two pressures that give the effect. Inhibition was also observed using *Cabomba*, and Gessner quotes results of Fricklinger showing inhibition in *Cryptocoryne;* in later figures (Gessner 1955) there is perhaps a suggestion that the leaves of the small plants, grown at an excess pressure of 0.6–1.0 atm, were proportionally narrower

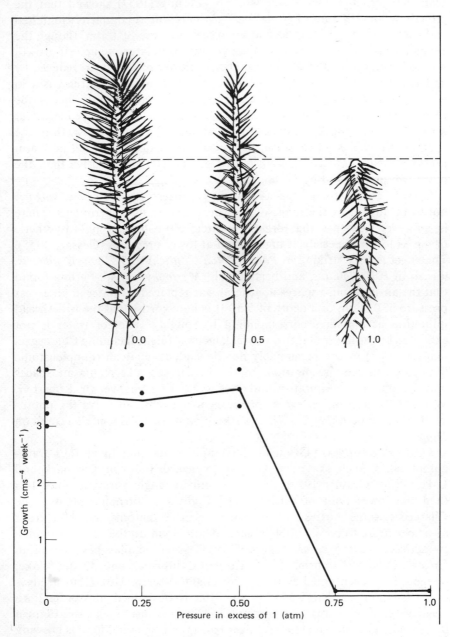

FIGURE 126. Plants of *Hippuris vulgaris* regenerating a cut tip under varying pressures, and relationship of growth rate to pressure (Gessner).

than the normal leaves. Later work by Ferling (1957) showed that the growth of lateral shoots of *Groenlandia densa* is almost completely inhibited and root growth much reduced at an excess pressure of 1 atm, though the elongation of the main shoot was apparently stimulated, while leaf growth was somewhat inhibited and the number of flower buds formed reduced by half (Fig. 127). It is therefore conceivable that in some of the cases in which plants growing in deep water are sexually sterile, the sterility is due to pressure. In *Ranunculus circinatus*, 1 atm excess pressure reduced leaf formation by about 25% and 2 atm by about 75%, but the growth of the roots was much more sensitive, being only 20% of the normal at 1 atm excess pressure. *Elodea canadensis* was somewhat less sensitive than the other two plants used by Ferling (1957).

Gessner (1952) found the assimilatory processes of *Hippuris vulgaris* not to be altered by the range of pressures used in his experiments. There is, however, evidence that organic matter, ultimately of photosynthetic origin, is lost more easily at higher than at lower pressures (Gessner 1955). The effect is very striking in *Potamogeton* × *nitens* and *Hippuris vulgaris*, less so in *P. perfoliatus*, and negligible in *Myriophyllum* sp. Ferling found that the air in lacunar spaces in general was replaced by water at an excess pressure of 0.5 atm or a depth of 5 m. It is noteworthy that the widespread inhibition at pressures corresponding to roughly 10 m of water is not exhibited by the lower plants which lack lacunae (algae including Characeae, many mosses) or are presumably not dependent on them (nonpleustonic liverworts) in their respiration. In the higher vascular plants air spaces may facilitate both respiratory and photosynthetic exchange. Dr. Robert G. Wetzel tells me that an excess pressure of 0.5 atm can halve the photosynthetic rate of *Najas flexilis*, in striking contrast to Gessner's results on *Hippuris*.

Field Observations. Gessner (1961) points out that in various transparent lakes, such as Grane Langsø (Nygaard 1958) in Denmark and Lake Ohrid (Gessner 1959), the lower limit of angiosperms is much less than the lower limit of other kinds of green autotrophic plants. The Characeae, some mosses and liverworts, benthic diatoms, and blue-green algae penetrate to considerably greater depths than do the vascular plants. In addition to the cases discussed by Gessner, similar phenomena in Crystal Lake, Wisconsin, Lake Tahoe, California, and Crater Lake, Oregon, have been noted earlier in this chapter (see p. 410). It must, however, be observed that wherever zonation is developed mosses tend to occur at greater depths than angiosperms, as for instance in the Finnish lakes studied by Maristo (1941); this is true even if the total flora is growing within the depth limits under 10 m, and thus in a range in which pressure is unlikely to be of any importance. Clearly the deep-water mosses and

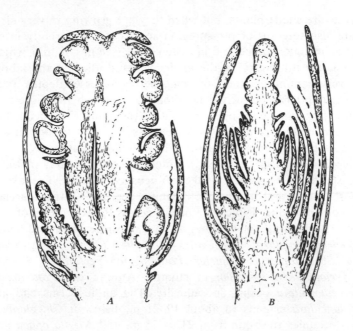

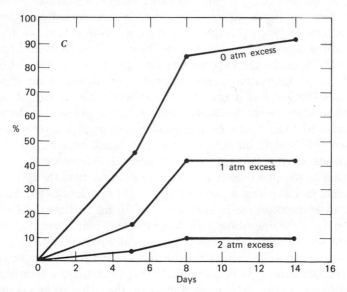

FIGURE 127. *Groenlandia densa* grown at varying pressures. *A*, At 1 atm with no excess pressure, section showing numerous flower buds; *B*, at 3 atm, equivalent to 2 atm excess pressure or 20 m of water with no certain flower buds; *C*, graphical representation of percentage incidence of visible flower buds at different pressures (Ferling, modified).

liverworts are shade plants, but when they are growing in very clear water they are also tolerant of pressures, in some cases apparently in excess of 10 atm as in Lake Tahoe and in Crater Lake (see pp. 48, 63), which would be completely inhibitory to the angiosperms studied in the laboratory.

The very common pattern of angiosperms at lesser depths and mosses at greater depths can clearly depend on the mosses being more tolerant of both low light and high pressure, but at the same time being much less adequate competitors on soft sediments (see p. 64) within the range of light intensity and pressure tolerated by vascular plants.

Golubić (1961, 1963) has made a most interesting study of Lake Vrana on the island of Cherso (Cres) off the Yugoslavian coast. The lake is one of the most transparent in Europe, having a Secchi disk transparency of up to 23 m on occasions. Typically a profile across the vegetation of the muddy part of the littoral zone shows from the shore lakeward successively *Holoschoenus vulgaris, Phragmites australis, Typha angustifolia, Najas marina, Schoenoplectus triqueter, Potamogeton perfoliatus, P. pectinatus,* and *Myriophyllum spicatum* in clumps. Among the *Potamogeton* spp. *Chara pedunculata* occurs sporadically. The angiosperms end at 7.7 m, *Ch. pedunculata* extends to about 19–21 m, below it *Ch. globularis* (sub *fragilis*) occupies the zone from 21 to 26 m, and *Nitella opaca* grows still more deeply, from 26 to as much as 38–40 m in some years. *Spirogyra* sp. occurs even deeper, to 50–52 m; this plant extends upward to 10 m.

Experiments indicate *C. globularis* had a compensation point, with photosynthesis balancing respiration over a 20-hr period, at 42 m; the corresponding depth for *Myriophyllum spicatum* was 36 m and for *Chara pedunculata* 35 m. In the experiments with the two species of *Chara* the depth of the compensation point under the conditions of the experiment is 1.6 times the greatest depth of colonization, whereas for *M. spicatum* the corresponding factor would be about 4.7. The bottom of the range of *M. spicatum* in Lake Vrana corresponds moreover to a level where about one-quarter of the light incident at the surface is still present. The comparative evidence of the experiments and general experience of the depth distribution of the plant make it extremely unlikely that the lower limit of *M. spicatum* in Lake Vrana can be due to light deficiency. The lake has in summer an epilimnion freely circulating to 10 m, so that the lower limit cannot be due to temperature. Golubić, however, points out that the lower limit of the species corresponds to an excess water pressure of about 0.8 atm, which is about the magnitude of the pressures found to be somewhat inhibitory in the laboratory. It is quite likely that in nature, where permanent colonization, perhaps in competition with the Characeae, is involved, rather lower excess pressures than are found to permit some development of *Myriophyllum* in the laboratory would be effectively exclusive. It would therefore seem that in Lake Vrana the lower limits of *Nitella* and *Chara* are likely to be set by light penetration, and that of *Myriophyllum* most probably by pressure. The limitation of rooted angiosperms, with the doubtful exception of those growing in the Lac d'Annecy, to water not over 9–10 m deep in low-altitude lakes, is evidently general and is clearly likely to contribute to the ability of the Characeae and the Bryophyta to occupy the otherwise unvegetated deeper zones of the bottom in transparent lakes.

It is of great interest that in Lake Titicaca at an altitude of 3815 m, *Potamogeton strictus* descends to a depth of a little over 11 m, probably the greatest reliable depth for an angiosperm, while *Chara* reaches to 14 m and the moss *Hygrohypnum* to 29 m (Tutin 1940). The pressure at the lake surface would be about 485 mm Hg, or 275 mm Hg less than pressure at sea level. This difference would correspond to 3.7 m of water, so that at the lower limit of the range of *P. strictus* in the lake the pressure would be about the same as at a depth of 7.5 m in a lake at sea level.

It must, however, be noted that in the sea, the flowering plant *Posidonia* has been found growing at a depth of 50 m (Gessner 1961) so that in some cases the difficulties presented to angiosperms by high pressure have been overcome.

Relation to substratum.   Whereas permanently pleustonic or megaloplanktonic species must obtain all their nutrients from the water alone, rooted plants can apparently take up mineral nutrients from the sediments in which they grow (see p. 276). Although the effects of the chemical composition of the ambient water, especially as a source of carbon dioxide or bicarbonate, but also no doubt as a source of phosphate and other nutrients, is likely to be of great importance when comparisons are made between lakes, it seems likely that underwater, as on land, the sediment or soil in which the plant is rooted is also of great physiological importance to the plant and plays a determining role in its autecology within a given body of water.

The most significant work on this matter, and the foundation of all the investigations that have followed, was that of Pearsall (1917, 1918a, 1920, 1921) on the vegetation of the English Lakes. Pearsall's studies suggested that within rather broad limits of depth or light intensity, the main factor determining differences in vegetation is the physicochemical nature of the sediment. The relevant characters involved appear to be texture, chemical composition, and rate of sedimentation, but they are interrelated. In the English Lake District fine sediments tend to be richer in potassium than do coarse, and the fine material is of course deposited further from the shore in deeper water. In a typical profile, running out from the exposed shore of one of the English Lakes, there is usually first a zone of wave-

TABLE 68.   *Typical distribution of sediments and plants in Ullswater*

Depth (m)	Sediment
0–1.6	Bare loose gravel
1.6–2.5	Sand, *Littorella uniflora*
2.5–3.5	Boulders washed clean
3.5–4.5	Thin silt on stones, *Isoetes lacustris*
4.5–~6	Mud with *Nitella*

washed gravel, then a zone of unaltered glacial clay or of boulders, and finally a zone of silt of increasing fineness as the depth increases. The vegetation follows this zonation in general, as in the profile for Ullswater given in Table 68.

Though this zonation could in the absence of further investigation be attributed to direct effects of erosion in shallow water and below this a decline of light intensity, such further investigation shows that it is certainly dependent on the detailed nature of the deeper depositional substratum. Cases are known, as for instance in Ennerdale Water, where the *Nitella* zone occurs above rather than below the *Isoetes*. When detailed studies of disturbance of the physical zonation in the neighborhood of shoals or islands or by the presence of influent streams are made, the plants are found to follow the sediment pattern rather than depth per se. Thus, in Derwentwater, there are small islands on the lee side of which silt has been deposited in a part of the lake where the bottom is largely rocky and bare. In the case of Rampsholme (Fig. 128) the greatest deposition of silt lies to the northeast where the wind drift is most reduced by the presence of the island, with less to the east and west. Here *Littorella* grows at about 2 m, but in the zone between 2 and 4 m *Isoetes* grows on the east and west sides, and *Nitella* to the north and northeast, curving round into deeper water below the *Isoetes* at between 4 and 6 m.

In Wastwater where Nether Beck has built a small arcuate delta of gravel on the northern shore of the lake, the combined action of the stream and the prevalent wind drift, running southwest to northeast, has carried silt along the shore within the 4-m contour. Here the quantity of silt is greatest nearest the outlet of the stream, and the vegetation parallel to the shore consists of *Juncus bulbosus* f. *fluitans* where sedimentation is greatest, then *Nitella opaca*, and finally *Isoetes lacustris* where the rate of deposition is least (Fig. 129).

In the first of these examples *Littorella*, as in all the English Lakes, is a shallow-water plant able to colonize the sand of highly disturbed areas. *Isoetes lacustris* can establish itself on sand but more usually on stones

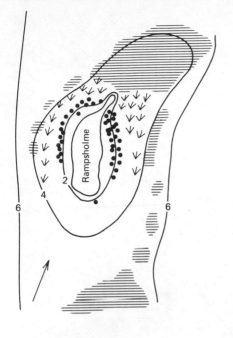

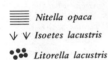

≣≣≣ *Nitella opaca*

↓ ↓ *Isoetes lacustris*

•••• *Litorella lacustris*

FIGURE 128.   Distribution of rooted vegetation in the neighborhood of Rampsholme, a small island in Derwentwater. Between 2 and 4 m *Nitella opaca* grows in the lee of the island where silting may be supposed to be more rapid, while in the same depth zone *Isoetes lacustris* grows at the sides where silting is less rapid (Pearsall).

with a thin layer of silt or on boulder clay where no erosion or deposition are occurring. If the bottom is organic, the peaty layer present is very thin. *Isoetes* is essentially a plant of areas undergoing little modification from their primitive state either by erosion or by rapid deposition of silt. Pearsall notes that it is very easily smothered, especially when young, by deposition of sediment, and it apparently can not alter its root level. It is therefore excluded from areas where silting is occurring moderately fast. *Nitella* and *Juncus bulbosus* f. *fluitans* evidently characterize localities of progressively more rapid silting. The nature of the silt as well as its abundance are clearly also significant. In Windermere between 2 and 4 m, *Isoetes* may give place to *Potamogeton perfoliatus* rather than to *Juncus bulbosus* f. *fluitans* in passing from an exposed part of the shore to a small bay behind an island where sedimentation is much increased. Pearsall finds that in such cases the proportion of the clay fraction and the amount of potassium is greater where *P. perfoliatus* is growing than at the *Juncus bulbosus* f. *fluitans* stations. Evidently, as might be suspected, properties of the finer sediments

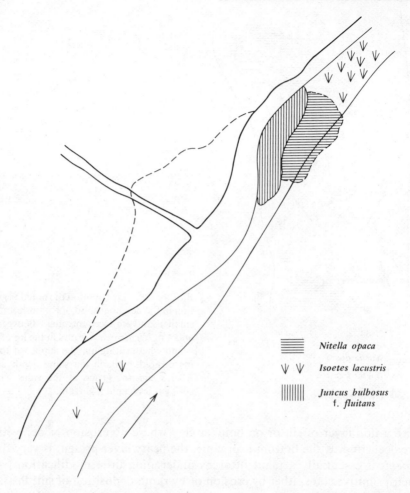

FIGURE 129.   Delta of Nether Beck, Wastwater, showing distribution of *Isoetes lacustris*, *Juncus bulbosus* f. *fluitans*, and *Nitella opaca* in relation to wind drift and deposition of silt from the beck.

and not only their rate of deposition are important. In an ideal case, in passing from the shore toward deep water, we would travel first across a zone of erosion, then a more or less neutral zone, and finally a zone of sedimentation in which the material deposited increased in its fine fraction and so in some cases at least in nutrient content. We could easily have here the basis for a quite elaborate zonation of vegetation independent of light intensity. With the possible exception of the most shallow-water species, this is in fact the way that Pearsall tended to interpret zonation.

It is not unlikely that Pearsall overestimated the direct effects of the rate of sedimentation along parts of the shore distant from the actual point of entry of streams (see p. 497). His conclusions on the effect of the qualitative nature of the sediments rather than of the speed at which they accumulated have received confirmation by other investigators.

Misra (1938) has studied in detail the substrata required by various submersed plants in the English Lakes. Three types of mud were used (Table 69) in his experiments. When *P. perfoliatus* seedlings were planted in these muds in jars which were submersed at a depth of 1.5 m in a small bay of Lake Windermere the growth was found to be greatest on the mud (type II) ordinarily supporting this species, and least on the more highly organic mud of type III. Laboratory experiments using the same muds, but after they had lain covered by distilled water for 6 months, gave comparable results in that *P. perfoliatus* could grow permanently only on mud II; *Sparganium minimum* did best on mud III and least well on mud I, whereas *Potamogeton alpinus*, though it did best on mud III, its natural habitat, did least well on mud II and produced on mud I a greener, more narrow-leaved form than is found in the lake. All three species clearly react differently to the substratum, even though two are ordinarily associated.

Misra concluded that the mud optimal for *P. perfoliatus* is a mixture of organic material and silt, with a minimum C:N ratio (Fig. 130), a high capacity to produce ammonia, and a low redox potential, suggesting much bacterial activity, and a high content of exchangeable cations. The latter characteristic seems established on rather inadequate evidence. It is, at any rate, clear that moderately organic muds fairly rich in nitrogen and exchangeable calcium are more suitable for this species and perhaps for

TABLE 69. *Growth of* Potamogeton perfoliatus *on three different sediments*

	Mud type	Vegetation	Organic matter ("humus") (%)	Dry weight of two plants of P. perfoliatus (g)
I	Inorganic coarse brown silt	*Isoetes lacustris*	8.04	0.467
II	Moderately organic black flocculent mud	*Potamogeton perfoliatus*	12.26	0.778
III	Highly organic brown mud	*Sparganium minimum* and *P. alpinus*	24.00	0.298

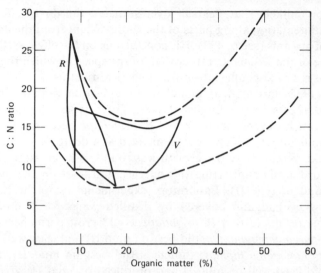

FIGURE 130. Envelopes of occurrence of two rosulate (*R*) species of plants, *Littorella uniflora* and *Isoetes lacustris*, and of two vittate (*V*) species, *Potamogeton perfoliatus* and *P. praelongus*, in relation to organic content and the C:N ratio in the organic matter. The broken lines define the possible occurrences in the English Lake District, though many localities lying on the right of the diagram lack plants (Misra, modified).

P. praelongus than are very inorganic muds, and much better than extremely organic muds, even though the latter can be paralleled in their high exchangeable calcium or hydrogen by the moderate or intermediate samples. The favorable nature of a mud for a particular species in a laboratory experiment or even in experimental jars in nature is, however, no guarantee that mud of this type will support the plant in the wild. *Isoetes lacustris* in experiments in jars placed in the lake grew best in brown mud with 26.3% organic matter. In nature, however, in the localities studied the plant did not occur on mud containing more than about 17% organic matter. Misra, following Pearsall, concludes that the more highly organic muds are formed by too rapid sedimentation to permit growth of a plant that seemingly cannot raise itself in the mud as the latter accumulates. Later work by Seddon (1965) has indicated that *Isoetes* is to a large extent restricted to bare and sometimes unfavorable localities, and in general to rather oligotrophic lakes, by its inability to compete with angiosperms under more favorable conditions. With this additional limitation, the findings of Pearsall and of Misra with regard to *I. lacustris* are certainly largely correct.

An aspect of the sediments not often considered in discussions of the distribution of rooted vegetation is their oxygen content. Dabbs (1971), studying *Scirpus validus* and *S. acutus*[2] in the lakes (Big, Egg, Wapisew, and Bloodsucker) of the estuarine plain of the Saskatchewan River, found *validus* never to occur in more than 65 cm of water with a mean depth of occurrence of 43 cm, whereas *acutus* was found between 60 and 150 cm with a mean depth of 109 cm. Dabbs believed from the studies of Laing (1941) that *S. validus* might be limited by decreasing oxygen in the sediments under increasing depths of water. No independent information existed suggesting *S. acutus* to be more tolerant of low oxygen concentrations. There is doubtless some competitive interaction between the species. Occasional irregularities in the distribution are attributed to changing water levels.

It is possible that competition between *Glyceria* and *Phragmites* may be regulated in a comparable manner, the latter plant tolerating less aerobic conditions (Buttery, Williams, and Lambert 1965).

DISTRIBUTION AND ZONATION IN VARIOUS KINDS OF LAKES

Having indicated the chief types of plants and the principal factors involved in determining their distribution in lakes, we may consider a number of cases of different kinds in which the operation of these factors is exemplified. These examples have been chosen on account of their inherent diversity, the adequacy of their description, and the diversity of approach on the part of the investigators examining them.

It has proved convenient first to consider a number of very oligotrophic lakes in the North Temperate zone, which exemplify the characteristic vegetation, dominated in the deeper part of the euphotic zone by rosulate plants, of nutrient-poor or primitive (Pearsall 1921, 1930; see Vol. I, frontispiece: Vol. II, p. 418) lakes. After considering these, the series of somewhat more eutrophic lakes in the English Lake District, the subject of Pearsall's fundamental studies, and a few lakes of comparable character in North America are described. Another very extensive series, namely, the 135 Finnish lakes investigated by Maristo, in which the transition is mainly from brown humic or chthoniotrophic to more eutrophic water, is then taken up, as is an important series of hard-water lakes in Poland. With these groups as a basis, a number of other lakes or groups of lakes in the North Temperate zone are next considered, and the section

---

[2] These two species are very close to *lacustris* and *tabernaemontani*, which in Europe, where they are abundant, are referred to *Schoenoplectus*. The two American taxa have been regarded as conspecific by some authors but Dabbs finds that their hybrid exhibits striking sterility.

is completed by an indication of what is known about the vegetation of lakes in other, mainly tropical, parts of the world.

It must be realized that even though a great deal of materials is covered by such a summary, nearly all the detailed studies considered were preceded by a series of earlier works, by other investigators whose results are implicit in the material summarized, and whose papers are easily found in the bibliographies of the contributions that form the basis of the present account. Anyone working on any of the regions considered will naturally have to turn to these earlier studies.

Oligotrophic transparent and relatively unsilted lakes, mainly with rosulate plants. The flora of the oligotrophic lakes which Pearsall would have regarded as unevolved, with little or no silting and transparent uncolored water, is characterized by plants of rosulate form. It is possible that in such plants, the ratio of nutrient uptake by the roots to that by the rest of the plant is greater than in vittate species, making the rosulate form more suitable in oligotrophic waters. However, this would not account for the observed restriction of such plants within a lake to the most leached sediments (Wilson 1935; see p. 446). It is also possible that the rosulate form is better adapted mechanically to live on sparsely colonized areas along exposed coasts.

Small oligotrophic lakes in Wisconsin. Fassett (1930) describes briefly the flora of three small glacial lakes in northeastern Wisconsin, namely, Weber, Crystal, and Clear Lakes, with sandy bottoms and very transparent (Secchi disk 8.0 m in Weber, 10.7 m in Crystal), soft (pH 5.8–6.8; HCO_3^- 1.2–4.8 mg liter^{-1}) water, in which apart from rare or very localized specimens of *Sparganium angustifolium*, all the angiosperms present in the lake proper exhibited the rosulate or comparable form.

In all three lakes *Isoetes macrospora*, *Eriocaulon septangulare*, *Juncus pelocarpus* f. *submersus*, *Elatine minima*, *Gratiola aurea* f. *pusilla*, and *Lobelia dortmanna* occurred, with *Sagittaria graminea* and *Ranunculus reptans* var. *ovalis* in Clear Lake, *Eleocaris acicularis* in Crystal, and *Myriophyllum tenellum*, regarded by Fassett as rosulate, in Crystal and Weber Lakes. These plants grow on the littoral shelf at depths from about 0.5 to 4.0 m. Below this the bottom of Crystal Lake down to 15 m is unvegetated sand, with a very thin, slightly irregular layer of decayed organic material. Still deeper the mosses *Fontinalis flaccida* and *Drepanocladus fluitans* var. *submersus* f. *filiformis* cover the bottom to its deepest point at 20 m, to which 1–4% of the solar radiation at the surface may penetrate. The depth of Clear Lake was not studied, but Weber Lake had the same kind of moss flora in the deepest water, apparently at 13.5 m. These three lakes appear to present the simplest kind of lacustrine macroscopic vegetation recorded from moderate altitudes and latitudes (cf., however, Latnjajaure in Lappland, p. 48) on any continent. Clear Lake, though the least dilute of the three, seems to have had quantitatively the least developed vegetation.

Both Weber and Crystal Lakes had marginal lagoons separated from the lake proper by an ice rampart. In these lagoons *Juncus brevicaudatus*, *J. canadensis*, *J. effusus* (Crystal only), *Scirpus atrovirens*, and *S. cyperinus* var. *pelius* grew, with *Bartonia virginica, Gratiola aurea* f. *pusilla*, and *Habernaria clavellata* in the Weber lagoon, and a little *Sphagnum* and *Utricularia* in the Crystal lagoon.

A decade after the publication of Fassett's paper, Potzger and Van Engel (1942) restudied the vegetation of Weber Lake. Meanwhile the lake had been fertilized in 1932–1939 with superphosphate, lime, ammonium sulfate, potassium chloride, cyanamide, soybean meal, and cottonseed meal, in an experimental attempt to increase phytoplankton and fish production. In spite of all the fertilization, the flora encountered by Potzger and Van Engel was the same as that found by Fassett with the possible exception of *Carex* sp. found mainly at the shore. The vegetation is said to disappear completely at 5 m; the deepest record given is at 4.63 m for *Isoetes macrospora*. This is comparable to Fassett's observations before the fertilization. Potzger and Van Engel describe zonation, passing from the shore downward, as follows: *Gratiola aurea* f. *pusilla* (to 2.8 m)–*Juncus pelocarpus* f. *submersus* (to 3.8 m) association with *Eriocaulon septangulare* (to 1.8 m); then the *Sparganium angustifolium* (to 2 m)–*Elatine minima* (to 2.25 m) association; and finally the *Myriophyllum tenellum* (to 3.25 m)–*Isoetes macrospora* (to 4.63 m) association with *Lobelia dortmanna* (to 2.75 m). Unfortunately no further observations on mosses were made.

Mountain Lake, Virginia, were its vegetational history better known, would have probably provided, in its pristine condition, an even simpler situation than do the Wisconsin lakes just described. The lake is surrounded by virgin hemlock forest, and has extremely dilute water, which in 1931 contained 18.9 mg litre^{-1} of which 10.4 mg litre^{-1} were inorganic; the pH varied from 6.4 to 6.6 (Hutchinson and Pickford 1932). Its macroscopic flora in 1890 is said to have consisted only of a few mosses underwater, with *Parnassia asarifolia* (Saxifragaceae) growing in small numbers on old logs. *Isoetes engelmannii* invaded the lake and its basin sometime between 1980 and 1921 (Parker 1943). Even more restricted floras presumably may be found in lakes in rock basins above the tree line in various mountain ranges.

Oligotrophic lakes in the English Lake District. In the English Lakes, we have in Wastwater and Ennerdale Water, two examples of rocky, essentially primitive lakes with transparent water, and a deep-water vegetation largely composed of *Isoetes lacustris* and *Nitella opaca* down to about 8 m. The maximum abundance of both plants at about 5–5.5 m appears to correspond to the middle of the region (3.5–6.5m) in which silt is deposited, though in these lakes very slowly. *Myriophyllum*, mainly *M. spicatum*, is the next most abundant plant below 2 m and very small amounts of *Potamogeton berchtoldii* and *Callitriche intermedia* also occur. In somewhat shallower water there is a feeble development of *Juncus bulbosus* var. *fluitans* at 2–3 m and this plant is said to occur on sand near stream mouths. *Littorella uniflora* occurs mainly, but in Ennerdale not entirely, on gravel in the shallowest water of both lakes; in Ennerdale it is accompanied by *Equisetum fluviatile* (sub *limosum*) and *Carex inflata*, which are very usual eulittoral species. The vegetation of Buttermere and Crummockwater, not described in detail, seems to be similar to that just discussed, as would be expected from the rockiness of their basins and transparency of their waters. The processes by which *Isoetes* and *Nitella* tend to be displaced in some of the other English Lakes have been already indicated (see pp. 424, 425).

   Grane Langsø.   A comparable condition to that encountered in Crystal Lake is found in the small and very transparent Grane Langsø, studied by Nygaard (1955, 1958). The vertical distribution of plants, based on the mean dry weight per unit area for two profiles from the eastern margin towards the center of the lake, taken in 1945 and 1955, is presented in Fig. 131. The important higher plants in the shallower water are *Lobelia dortmanna*, *Littorella uniflora*, and *Isoetes lacustris*, arranged in that order in a striking zonal distribution. The liverwort *Riccardia sinuata* var. *submersa* also forms a modest part of this infralittoral vegetation, and *Elatine hexandra* occurs rarely. At a depth between 5 and 6 m all these plants disappear and at 6 m the vegetation consists only of scattered and quantitatively insignificant colonies of *Nostoc minutissima*. Below this almost unvegetated zone, beginning at about 7 m, there is a rich flora of mosses, consisting of *Fontinalis* sp., *Sphagnum subsecundum*, and *Drepanocladus exannulatus*. It is noteworthy that both the second and third species occur in water both shallower and deeper than the 6-m level where they are absent. The shallow-water form of *D. exannulatus* is described as robust; presumably the deep-water form is more elongate. Nygaard says that 1% of the incident green light would be found at 28 m in a lake of the same transparency as Grane Langsø, but adequately deep. Nygaard tentatively attributes the vegetation minimum to lack of plants adapted to the light regime at 6–7 m; in view of the distribution of *S. subsecundum* and *D. exannulatus* this seems very unlikely. It will be noted that the minimum corresponds to the maximum slope of the lake bottom. Whatever its explanation, the occurrence of a minimum in Grane Langsø as well as in Wisconsin suggests that the phenomenon has a certain generality (see also p. 470).

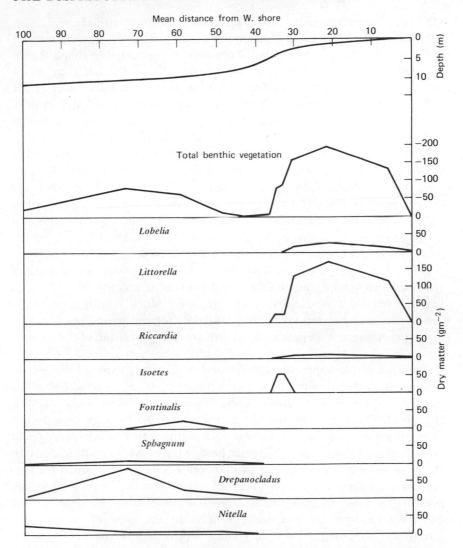

FIGURE 131. Profile of west shore of Grane Langsø (note vertical and horizontal scales are identical) and distribution of vegetation in the lake (data of Nygaard).

Two Swedish examples. A rather different situation is provided by two very well studied lakes in Sweden, in less rocky basins than the English Lakes just discussed, though with soft but, unlike the previous examples, somewhat colored water. Both the lakes lie in a calcium-poor glaciated landscape and are evidently typical of a vast number of north European basins.

Fiolen (Thunmark 1931), with its surface at a mean altitude of 228 m, has an area of 1.6 km², and a maximum depth of 10 m. The western shore of the lake is straight, the eastern shore more complicated in shape. There is an island near the western shore separated from the latter by water under 2 m deep. The water is clear but yellow-brown in color; only about 20% of the incident light penetrates to a depth of 1 m, and at 7 m only 0.5% is present. The phytoplankton is poorly developed quantitatively, and is qualitatively characterized by the abundance of desmids.

Associated with ice ramparts a fairly rich vegetation can develop locally in the eulittoral zone, which is of course dry at the lowest seasonal water level. The infralittoral along the exposed eastern shore can be divided into three subzones. There is a region about 50 cm deep in which the bottom suffers from erosive disturbance by ice during the winter; below this is a neutral zone where sediment is collecting no faster than erosion is occurring; and below about 3.75 m sediment begins to accumulate.

On the less exposed western side, the effect of ice is evident as throughout the rest of the shore, but sediment is deposited at a depth of 1.25 m, so that the neutral zone is very much narrower. Much of this sediment is diatomaceous ocher and lake earth, materials formed by the precipitation of iron-rich humic materials with subsequent decomposition of the organic matter.

The flora of the uppermost infralittoral of the more exposed shore consists of *Naumbergia thyrsiflora*, *Carex rostrata*, *C. lasiocarpa*, *Equisetum fluviatile*, *Phragmites australis*, and *Eleocharis palustris* (sub *Scirpus*) (Fig. 132). These grow mainly in water less than 0.5 m deep; they do not form closed communities of any size. No plants with floating leaves occur on the exposed shores and the greater part of the higher vegetation down to the lower limit at 4.6 m consists of plants of rosulate form, which are also scattered through the communities of open reed beds where these are present. Of these rosulate plants *Isoetes setacea* (sub *echinosporum*) and *Subularia aquatica* are practically limited to the zone of erosion, the latter species tending to occur at greater depths than the former. Both are accompanied by *Ranunculus reptans* which reaches a depth of just over 1 m, and by *Isoetes lacustris* and *Lobelia dortmanna* which become far more common quite suddenly lower down, as the neutral zone is reached where *Littorella uniflora* also appears. The vegetation cover of the deeper bottom down to a lower limit of 4.6 m consists primarily of communities of these rosulate plants, with the mosses *Bryum ventricosum* and *Drepanocladus fluitans* from 2.8–3.0 m downward. *Bryum ventricosum* actually occurs a little deeper than any other benthic species, at 4.6 m; *Isoetes lacustris* is found down to 4.4 m.

The main communities are formed either by *Isoetes lacustris* (extending to 4.4 m), or by *Littorella uniflora* (extending to 4.5 m) and *Lobelia dortmanna* (extending to 2.6 m). Patches of the *I. lacustris* community seem to alternate with those of the *Littorella uniflora–Lobelia dortmanna* community. In the lower part of its range *Isoetes* may be accompanied by *Nitella opaca;* as would be expected from Pearsall's findings, *Nitella* occurs where sediment, described as fine detritus gyttja, is accumulating. The *Isoetes lacustris* in very shallow water can be either the typical straight-leafed form *lacustris* or the form *curvifolia* with recurved leaves, but in the deeper water only the former occurs. There is, however, considerable variation, presumably ecophenotypic, within the typical f. *lacustris*, very well developed plants occurring where there is some sedimentation and where no other species occur, while very reduced plants grow among the rhizomes of *Schoenoplectus* (sub *Scirpus*) *lacustris* on the less disturbed western side of the lake. When the plant is well developed, groups of individuals with short more or less bent leaves and very large quadripartite rhizomes may occur; they may be very aged specimens (Fig. 26).

The relationship of *Lobelia dortmanna* and *Littorella uniflora* is interesting. In the zone of erosion *Lobelia dortmanna* occurs, alone or with *Isoetes setacea* or *Subularia aquatica*, as has been indicated. The *Lobelia* plants are well developed and produce inflorescences above water. Between the zone of erosion and that of sedimentation *Littorella uniflora* is usually the dominant plant. In the upper part (40–80 cm) of this neutral zone, where the lake bottom is composed of sand mixed with clay and a little organic material, the development of *Littorella* is maximal, from 80 to 140 cm on purer sand it is less luxuriant. In both regions, though the conditions are not optimal, *Lobelia* is present but it does not flower. Still deeper, from 140 to about 260 cm, both *Littorella* and *Lobelia* occur on bottoms receiving sediment; here *Lobelia* is again well developed, flowering under water (Fig. 133). Thunmark thinks that the sterile plants of *Lobelia* in the zone where *Littorella* is dominant are derived from seeds which have been dispersed from the uppermost infralittoral as a result of disturbance by ice.

On the less exposed western shore there is a greater variety of marginal plants including *Alisma plantago-aquatica* and *Menyanthes trifoliata* among the herbiform, with *Eleocharis palustris* and *Schoenoplectus lacustris* among the junciform emergent species; *Utricularia intermedia* and *U. vulgaris* also occur in the quieter marginal water under 50 cm deep. There

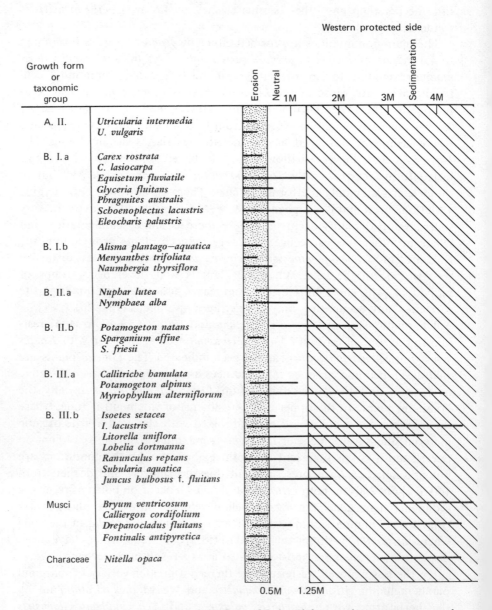

FIGURE 132. Mean depth ranges of the flora of Lake Fiolen on the western protected and eastern exposed shore of the lake, showing the greater extent of the neutral zone and much poorer flora on the exposed side.

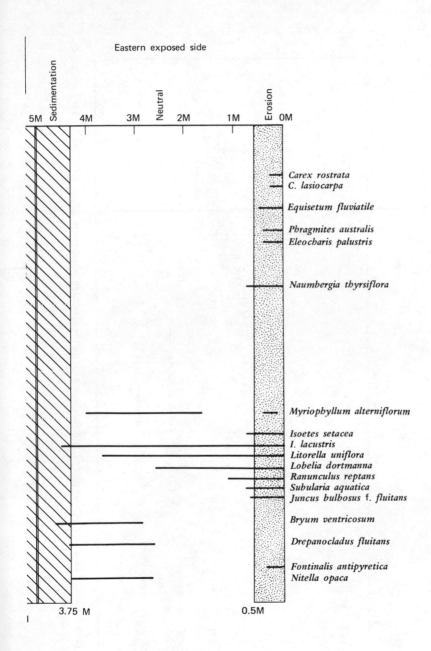

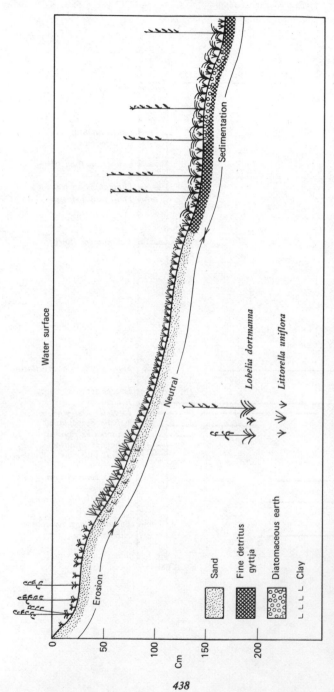

FIGURE 133. Distribution of *Littorella uniflora* and of *Lobelia dortmanna* on the protected western side of Lake Fiolen. Note the two zones of flowering of *L. dortmanna*.

Water surface

Neutral

Erosion

Sedimentation

Lobelia dortmanna

Littorella uniflora

Sand

Fine detritus gyttja

Diatomaceous earth

Clay

Cm

0

50

100

150

200

is a floating-leaved community in some places composed of *Nymphaea alba,* *Nuphar lutea, Potamogeton natans, Sparganium* spp. The submerged flora is essentially like that of the more exposed shore, save for the presence of *Callitriche hamulata* and *Potamogeton alpinus; Myriophyllum alterniflorum* and *Juncus bulbosus* f. *fluitans* occur more freely than on the eastern shore.

The neighboring less transparent and more humic Lake Stråken has been studied by Blomgren and Naumann (1925). The eulittoral vegetation is quite rich and varied and there seem to be reed beds around most of the shore. The more important of these upper infralittoral communities consist of *Phragmites australis* and *Eleocharis palustris* growing in up to 1.8 m; *Equisetum fluviatile,* in up to 2.2 m, is also of some significance. There are quite well-developed floating-leaved communities, but only in limited areas, the most important having *Nuphar lutea* as dominant and *Equisetum fluviatile* as subdominant; *Potamogeton natans* and *Nymphaea alba* communities are also recorded locally. The deeper vegetation consists largely of *Isoetes lacustris* (to 3.0 m), *Lobelia dortmanna* (to 2.4 m), *Littorella uniflora* (to 2.2 m), and *Ranunculus reptans* (to 2.1 m); *Subularia* is of little importance. There are more isolated plants of *Potamogeton natans* (to 2.3 m) *Myriophyllum alterniflorum* (to 3.1 m), *Nuphar lutea* (to 3.2 m, but sterile at this depth), and *Sparganium friesii* (to 3.2 m). *Fontinalis antipyretica* also occurs to 3.2 m, but below this no macroscopic vegetation is recorded though the lake is 12 m deep.

A number of fairly small lakes in Finland (see p. 450) associated with sand or *os* deposits, have a flora comparable to that just described (Maristo 1941), and the type is not uncommon in other parts of northern Europe.

Comparison of lakes from different lake districts. It is instructive to consider the depth ranges of some of the more important plants occurring in the limnologically well-studied lakes containing rosulate vegetation (Table 70).

Although in a general way the distribution of macroscopic vegetation in these lakes is clearly determined partly by light, the obvious operation of other factors is apparent. The sterile zones in Crystal Lake and Grane Langsø are clearly not due to light limitation. They can hardly be due, in view of the deeper occurrences of a fairly closely allied species of *Isoetes* in the English lakes, entirely to pressure, and either the slope or some other physical peculiarity of the substratum is likely to be involved. Spence (1967) notes that in lakes in Scotland the slope below the littoral shelf may be devoid of plants.

Intermediate or less primitive lakes. A number of lakes studied by Pearsall in the English Lake District and three investigated by Wilson in Wisconsin are profitably compared with the basins just discussed. In all lakes studied by Pearsall the conclusions as to causal factors are his own;

TABLE 70.   *Depths of occurrence of certain plants in lakes with primarily rosulate higher vegetation*

Lake	Depth of 2% of surface illumination[a] (m)	Depth of Isoetes (m)	Depth of Littorella uniflora (m)	Depth of Nitella (m)	Depth of Musci (m)
Grane Langsø, Denmark	<22[b]	5 (*lacustris*)	4	11.5 (*flexilis*)	11.5
Crystal, Wisconsin	~14	4 (*macrospora*)	—	—	20
Weber, Wisconsin	9.5	4 (*macrospora*)	—	—	Deepest water ?13.5
Wastwater, England	10	~7 (*lacustris*)	1 (local)	~7 (*opaca*)	?
Ennerdale Water, England	9.3	8 (*lacustris*)	4	5 (*opaca*)	?
Derwentwater, England	6.5	4–6 (*lacustris*)	2	6–7 (*opaca*)	?
Windermere, England	6.5	4 (*lacustris*)	3	7 (*opaca*)	?
Fiolen, Sweden	6.5	<~1 (*setacea*) 4.4 (*lacustris*)	4.5	4.2 (*opaca*)	4.6
Ullswater, England	6.4	5 (*lacustris*)	2.5	6 (*opaca*)	?
Stråken, Sweden	5.0	3 (*lacustris*)	2.2	—	3.2

[a] Wisconsin figures (Birge and Juday 1930; cf. Vol. I, Fig. 118) refer to transmission not corrected to zenith sun, and are probably comparable with the other data.
[b] 1% green light would penetrate to 28 m if lake were deep enough; this would correspond to 2% at 22 m. The lake has 11.5 m maximum depth.

some are more likely to be correct than others, but the subject is still not sufficiently well studied for intelligent criticism to be possible.

The less primitive lakes of the English Lake District.   In Derwentwater the transparency is definitely less than in the rocky lakes discussed previously; 2% of the incident radiation reaches to 6.5 m rather than to at least 8.0 m, as in the four rocky lakes, and the lower limit of vegetation is in consequence not so deep. *Nitella* extends further than any other plant. It is abundant to about 3–3.5 m, which is about the upper limit of sedimentation in the lake. *Isoetes*, though occurring to between 5 and 6 m, is abundant only in the neutral zone between 2 and 3 m, where both erosion and sedimentation are minimal; below this zone there is probably rather too much silting for successful competition with *Nitella*, while above 2 m it is replaced by *Littorella* on gravel and sand. *Juncus bulbosus* var. *fluitans* and *Potamogeton perfoliatus* occur on areas of sediment near stream mouths. The latter is characteristic of somewhat finer silts than occupied by *J. bulbosus* var. *fluitans; P. praelongus* grows better on still finer silts (15–26% fine silt and clay) than *P. perfoliatus* (10–21% fine silt and clay) and so appears in Derwentwater in deeper water than the latter, at between 3 and 5 m. In Windermere the sedimentation is greater than in Derwentwater, and in consequence the processes just described have become more pronounced. *Littorella* is well developed in the shallowest water, and *Nitella* in the deeper well-sedimented zone; between them there is little space for *Isoetes* and none for *Juncus bulbosus* var. *fluitans. Potamogeton perfoliatus* occurs from 1 to 5.5 m and *P. praelongus* in 2.3–7 m, with *P. berchtoldii* in the lower part of the range of the latter species.

Ullswater presents a complex picture because part of the infralittoral bottom consists of an impenetrable glacial till on which only *Isoetes* grows. The lake, however, has received a large amount of sediment as the result of mining operations in some of the tributary valleys. This has led to a rather general distribution of fine silt below 3–4 m, providing an exceptionally favorable environment for *Potamogeton berchtoldii*, which appears to require a fine silt bottom but is evidently more tolerant of low light intensities than the other species of macrophytes present in the lake. In Ullswater it has largely taken the place of *Nitella* as the plant going furthest into deep water.

In all three of these lakes a more conspicuous zonation in the lower infralittoral has developed than in the unevolved rocky lakes, and in every case a major factor in this development is clearly the increase in deposition of inorganic sediment, mainly silt and water-borne clay. Pearsall attributes much of the importance of this material to its nutrient content and shows that in general the fine silts lying in deeper water contain more potassium than do the other sediments of the English Lakes. In particular he regards organic matter as a diluent tending to reduce the nutrient value of the fine silt and clay fractions. The shallow-water vegetation of the three lakes under discussion consists in the upper infralittoral of either an *Equisetum fluviatile–Carex rostrata* community or a *Phragmites australis–Schoenoplectus lacustris* community, the former predominating in Derwentwater, the latter in Windermere. Further out, *Potamogeton natans* occurs in all three lakes, with water lilies in Derwentwater and Windermere. In addition to the fully submersed species already discussed all three lakes have *Myrio-*

phyllum spicatum and *Ranunculus peltatus*. The occurrence of the *Equisetum–Carex* community as contrasted with the *Phragmites–Schoenplectus* community seems to be determined by the former occurring more on high organic substrata low in potassium, the latter on low organic substrata high in potassium. A comparable dichotomy seems to regulate the occurrence of *Potamogeton natans* on high organic substrates and water lilies on low. It is not impossible that these dichotomies may actually chiefly reflect the variation in mechanical disturbance.

Apart from the three well-described lakes just mentioned, several others of the English Lakes were found by Pearsall to give support to his general conclusions on the relationship between vegetation and substratum.

Esthwaite Water, which is one of the smaller and least oligotrophic of the group, was studied in great detail by Pearsall and described in a paper (1917, 1918a) antecedent to his main account of the region. The lake is elongate, with its long axis lying NNW–SSE. The shore has a well-defined wave cut and built terrace, the submerged part of which slopes gradually to 0.9 m, and then falls off as a mont to 1.2–1.47 m, below which the gradient is again gentle. The main influent is at the north end and most of the inorganic sediment deposited in the lake is laid down in the northern and central parts of the basin, so that the southern littoral is largely siltfree. The interpretation of the distribution of the vegetation given by Pearsall depends primarily on the interaction of light distribution as a function of depth, on sediment type determining the degree of inorganic silting and organic deposition, and on the antithesis between exposed and protected parts of the shoreline. The following fairly detailed summary shows these influences interacting.

On the most exposed parts of the littoral of Esthwaite, higher vegetation, if present at all, is confined to a narrow band of *Myriophyllum alterniflorum*, rooted at the foot of the slope or mont of the littoral terrace in 1.25–1.5 m of water, but reaching up to near the surface. The well-developed root system and the finely divided leaves probably permit the existence of this plant in spite of considerable wave wash, though the amplitude of the waves never exceeds 30 cm in the lake. *M. alterniflorum* tends to follow the base of the slope even where the shore is less exposed and where a quite complex zonation has developed. It usually lacks associated species, but may occur with *Potamogeton alpinus* on the more sheltered shore, and with *P. gramineus* var. *longipedunculatus* on the more exposed eastern shore. The latter plant may form a carpet of small vegetative shoots from which a few flowering shoots with long stout peduncles arise; there are no floating leaves in these circumstances.

Above the zone of the roots of *M. alterniflorum*, a *Littorella uniflora–Lobelia dortmanna* community develops, usually from 0.3 to 1.2 m on a gravelly substratum which may, however, be covered with black peaty mud, but never by inorganic silt. The latter is clearly removed by wave action, but it is not clear from Pearsall's account why the peaty mud can accumulate. Odd *Littorella* plants unrooted by ducks may be washed onto any newly formed gravelly shore and, if they can become established, put out runners and form asexual clones which ultimately coalesce to form a carpet among which *Lobelia* seeds are caught.

Where the lower infralittoral is unsilted, as at the south end of the lake, *Isoetes* develops below the *Myriophyllum*, at a depth of 1.5–2.7 m. Here the general zonation is not unlike that already described for the more oligotrophic lakes of the region.

Where there is a good deal of silting the deeper communities may be dominated by *Najas flexilis*, *Potamogeton berchtoldii* (sens lat.), or *Nitella flexilis*, the first-named in the purer inorganic silts with less than 9% ignitable matter, the last-named in the more organic soft infralittoral sediments with more than 15% ignitable matter.

The *P. berchtoldii* or linear-leaved community characteristically includes also *P. crispus* var. *serratus*, *P. obtusifolius*, *Najas flexilis*, *Callitriche hermaphroditica*, *Elodea canadensis*, and *E. nuttallii* (sub *Hydrilla verticillata* var. *pomeranica*). The last named, mainly North American, also occurs in one Irish station, and perhaps also in Pomerania. All these plants have pellucid linear leaves and delicate stems; they are in general bright green and translucent. *Nitella flexilis* is evidently more shade-tolerant and so can colonize slightly deeper water, down to 3.6 m, than can the other plants of the linear-leafed community. If, however, the sediment is more nearly optimal for *N. flexilis* above the linear-leaved community, which may well be the case, it can occur also above the latter community.

In the most sheltered regions the upper parts of the infralittoral develop a striking emergent and floating vegetation. Pearsall thinks that when the linear-leaved association is well developed it causes an increase in organic sedimentation, thus reducing the depth of the water from more than 2 to less than 2 m. The area is then colonized by *Nymphaea alba*, and the abundant organic debris of this plant raises the bottom further. Reed swamp then tends to replace the *Nymphaea*, invading all or almost all of the built-up terrace in the process and increasing the declivity at its edge. *Nymphaea alba* var. *minor* occurs in shallower water than typical *N. alba*, colonizing organic mud that has accummulated in undisturbed places on littoral gravel. Since typical *N. alba* appears to require inorganic silt, which *N.* var. *minor* does not, Pearsall supposes that the latter has lower nutrient requirements than the former, for in this region high organic matter seems to imply nutrient deficiency. Many botanists now would regard *minor* merely as somewhat starved *alba*. Outside the *Nymphaea alba* community, which in addition to the dominant may contain *Nuphar lutea* near the influents, and species of *Ranunculus* as well as *Lobelia dortmanna* and *N. alba*. var. *minor*, there is usually found growing on gray or yellowish-gray mud, largely compose of plant fibers, a scattered populaton of a small submersed form of *Sparganium minimum*, sometimes associated with *Potamogeton obtusifolius* and more rarely *Elodea canadensis*. The reed swamp which replaces *Nymphaea alba* and which may be very well developed in the mouths of bays where conditions for its formation seem optimal, consists of *Schoenoplectus lacustris* dominant toward the water and *Phragmites australis* dominant toward the land. The smooth elastic shoots of *Schoenoplectus* are probably far better adapted to withstand injury in a high wind than is *Phragmites* and so the former plant tends to survive in the more open areas (see p. 411). At the south end where there is little silting, *Nymphaea alba* var. *minor* may fringe a *Carex* community (*C. lasiocarpa, C. rostrata. C. vesicaria*, and a hybrid between the last two).

If Pearsall's work is considered as a whole, it is clear that he makes a consistent picture of the vegetation in terms of substratum as well as light intensity. However, apart from Misra's (1938), Roll's (1939b), and Moyle's (1945) experiments, there is still very little direct evidence of specific effect of different sediments on the plants rooted in them. It must also be borne in mind that there seem to be some discrepancies when Pearsall's findings are compared with those of workers outside the English Lake District. Thunmark noted clearly that sedimentation occurred at a lesser depth on the west than on the east shore of Fiolen, but this appears not to affect greatly the plant zonation; in this lake it seems as though *Isoetes lacustris* is less restricted by the deposition of sediment that Pearsall thought. Though much of Pearsall's argument looks convincing, the whole problem requires a new and deeper study, as Spence (1967a) strongly suggests.

Three less oligotrophic lakes in Northern Wisconsin.   Wilson (1935) has described the vegetation of three lakes in northern Wisconsin which are somewhat less acidic and less dilute than the three already described.

Silver Lake, just south of Trout Lake, has an area of 0.87 km² and a maximum depth of 19 m. The water is just on the alkaline side of neutrality, pH 7.6–7.8. The shoreline is reniform and rather regular; former-bays seem to have been cut off by the building of bars that were afterwards modified by ice action, as often happens in this region.

On the north and west sides of the lake the shore is mainly formed by embankments of very rocky drift, whereas on the east and southeast sides there is a gentler slope and more sandy and less rocky bottom in the very shallow water. Along the quieter parts of the shore where the sediment is not constantly renewed by wave erosion and current action, it is described as leached and acidic, but elsewhere the finer sediments are, though sandy, neutral or slightly alkaline.

On the gentle beach on the eastern side a eulittoral vegetation of *Eleocharis palustris* had developed, extending into 0.75 m of water, the plant being the most abundant species in the lake. It is of considerable importance in binding sand, and may protect the developing bars that tend to cut embayments off from the main lake. Where the shore is steep and composed of rocky drift, there is a littoral shelf formed mainly of gravel with pockets of sand and pieces of rock. Vegetation is sparse but the shelf bears a bushy form of *Najas flexilis*, *Potamogeton spirillus*, *Isoetes macrospora*, and *Chara* sp. Below 1 m, where there is a slight drop from the shelf, the sediment becomes more sandy; here *Vallisneria americana* and *Potamogeton gramineus* var. *graminifolius* occur, in addition to the species just mentioned. *V. americana* flowers abundantly at depths down to just over 2 m, and is present but sterile to 4.5 m; *Potamogeton gramineus* also was observed fruiting to 3 m, but forming only water leaves from 3 m to its limit at 4 m, where the plants are but a few centimeters high. *Najas flexilis* also extends to 4.5 m, the plants in deep water being more flexuous than the bushy specimens nearer the water's edge; it is in general the most widely distributed species in the lake. *Potamogeton berchtoldii* (sub *pusillus*), an unimportant member of the flora of the lake, nevertheless occurs locally at greater depths than the other species, to 6 m, where the zenith transmission is 6.8% corresponding to a vertical transmission of about 4.5%. It is presumably here, as often elsewhere, the most oligophotic vascular plant present. Wilson points out that *P. amplifolius* occurred locally on silted parts of the bottom at depths up to 1.75 m where the zenith transmission is 40%, but not where such sediment occurred at much greater depths. However, in Muskellunge Lake it occurred on organic soils at 5 m where the zenith light transmission is 10.4%. The species may well be less oligophotic than *P. berchtoldii* as Wilson implies, but it is clearly not really polyphotic.

Where the beach is gently sloping and sandy, the species found along the steeper and more gravelly shores occur between the root stocks of *Eleocharis palustris*. In some places in the eulittoral, *E. palustris* is replaced locally by *Carex* spp. and *Juncus* spp., while in the water it is associated with *Eleocharis acicularis*, *Equisetum fluviatile*, and *Polygonum natans* f. *genuinum*, the only important floating-leaved species in the lake. *Typha latifolia* was present very locally; the water level of the lake was known to have fallen during the period of the investigation, and as this happened the stand, colonizing the shallowest water from the newly formed eulittoral, increased from 6 to 89 plants from 1932 to 1935. Lateral spread of the colony was apparently prevented by wave action on either side of the favored region of the shore where the plants could occur. Wilson believes that in northern Wisconsin *Typha* usually disappears as the shore matures and quiet embayments are filled.

In the regions where leached acidic sand is found, the sediment not being continually renewed by currents carrying freshly eroded material, a typical rosulate flora, consisting of *Eleocharis acicularis, Isoetes macrospora, Gratiola aurea* f. *pusilla, Lobelia dortmanna,* and *Ranunculus reptans* f. *ovalis* tends to develop. The somewhat protected area where this flora was best developed suffered a change in shoreline when the lake level fell, which is said to have led to redistribution of sediments. The rosulate flora tended to become less abundant and its place was to some extent taken by *Vallisneria, Najas,* and *Potamogeton gramineus.* At least initially there was little change in acidity.

Wilson gives detailed quantitative estimates for the total mass of plants in the lake, and the percentage of each species in 0–1, 1–3, and 3–8 m. Rearranging his data in order of decreasing abundance we have the figures set out in Table 71, for 14 of the 15 species present, *Typha latifolia* not being sampled.

TABLE 71. *Estimated biomass of water plants in Silver Lake, Wisconsin, and its percentage distribution in three zones*

Species	Estimated mass in lake (kg air dried)	Percentage distribution 0–1 m	1–3 m	3–8 m
Eleocharis palustris	5.15	100	0	0
Vallisneria americana	3.79	19	46	35
Potamogeton gramineus	3.14	59	37	4
Polygonum natans var. *genuinum*	1.34	100	—	0
Najas flexilis	1.12	31	36	33
Isoetes macrospora	0.62	77	21	2
Lobelia dortmanna	0.47	100	0	0
Juncus pelocarpus var. *submersus*	0.41	97	3	0
Gratiola aurea f. *pusilla*	0.35	100	0	0
Potamogeton amplifolius	0.14	43	57	0
Renunculus reptans var. *ovalis*	0.13	100	0	0
Chara sp.	0.09	35	65	0
Potamogeton berchtoldii	0.08	8	16	76
P. spirillus	0.01	50	50	0
Total mass	17.07			

The area of the lake is 872,000 m², but of this only 23% is within the depth range colonized. In this area the biomass of macroscopic vegetation appears therefore to be 0.085 g dry:m⁻², which is astonishingly low. In spite of this small figure the lake clearly shows some of the features that Pearsall regards as signs of evolution, though in northern Wisconsin the transparent, dilute, relatively colorless, slightly acidic seepage lake with rosulate vegetation actually may represent a later stage than does the somewhat silted and intermittent drainage lake basin with neutral water exemplified by Silver Lake.

A second lake studied by Wilson, Muskellunge Lake, is larger (3.72 km²) and deeper (z_m = 21 m) than Silver Lake. It has a much more complex shoreline with a large shallow bay running east from its southern end and containing several islands. The littoral sediment along most of the shore is sand and gravel with increasing silt in the deep water. The profiles studied showed a curious maximum in pH at about 2 m; above this the sediments are evidently more leached. In the large shallow bay there is a considerable accumulation of well decomposed organic matter, while locally in a small bay relatively undecomposed organic matter occurs.

The shallow leached sediment, as in Silver Lake, supports a rosulate flora; the less leached sediments are clearly very rich in submersed *Potamogeton* spp., whereas where organic sediments are accumulating there is a tendency for the more exclusive persistence of floating-leaved plants such as *Nymphaea odorata* and *Potamogeton natans*. The rosulate vegetation seems to have played a prominent role in the shallow water of the large bay, becoming more conspicuous in summer when the water level dropped and *Littorella americana* flowered but produced no seed. Below this there was a junglelike growth of *Megalodonta beckii, Nymphaea odorata, Myriophyllum alterniflorum, Najas flexilis*, also *Nuphar variegata, Polygonum natans* f. *genuinum, Potamogeton amplifolius, P. epihydrus, P. natans, P. gramineus* var. *graminifolius, P. praelongus, P. pusillus, P. robbinsii, Scirpus acutus, Sparganium angustifolium*, and *Vallisneria americana*. This richly vegetated area was reduced to about one-tenth of its former extent in 1934 when a drop in the water level of the lake caused a redistribution of organic sediment, which completely smothered great areas of these plants.

Away from the bays, the vegetation in the open water of the lake resembled that of the less leached deposits of Silver Lake, though in deeper water well-decomposed organic soil supports *P. amplifolius* and *P. robbinsii* to 5 m in Pearse Bay, with *P. berchtoldii* to 6 m and *Nitella* to 7 m.

The total flora consisted of 30 species of vascular plants, *Chara* sp., *Nitella* sp. with *Nostoc* sp. as an important macroscopic benthic blue-green alga. The sizes of the populations of the different species are not presented relative to the very different parts of the lake and so are of little comparative significance.

The total mass of plants estimated per unit mass of colonized lake bottom was 0.45 g dry·m^2. The high value is largely attributed to the favorable conditions in the large shallow bay. The diversity of the flora moreover is clearly attributable to the diversity of bottom sediment; indeed Wilson indicated that in profiles in which the pH of the superficial sediment varies markedly in passing from the margin to deeper water, the vegetation varies concomitantly, but he gives no details.

Wilson's third lake, Little John, though chemically like Muskellunge, is smaller (0.67 km^2), shallower (6 m), and with rather browner (U.S.G.S. col. 14–22) water. Low light penetration probably causes the restriction of vegetation to the area of the lake not deeper than 3 m, where the zenith transmission is 4%; *Najas flexilis* and *Potamogeton berchtoldii* reached this depth. There are no leached shallow-water sediments and most of the specialized rosulate plants (*Lobelia dortmanna, Gratiola aurea* f. *pusilla, Juncus pelocarpus* f. *submersus, Ranunculus reptans* var. *ovalis*) are absent, though *Isoetes macrospora* occurs. The flora is relatively poor, consisting of 13 species, but the total crop of 0.52 g dry·m^2 on the colonized areas is very slightly greater than that of Muskellunge.

It is evident that in these lakes as in those studied by Pearsall, the slight variation in water chemistry is of no obvious significance in explaining the occurrence and distribution of the plants; illumination presumably limits overall occurrence of the flora and may determine the nature of the species to penetrate furthest, but it seems much less significant than the sediment types and the degree of exposure to which the plants are subjected. In particular, it appears that here, as elsewhere, the rosulate flora is characteristic of the more leached sediments and the more vittate plants of the areas of silting. In general Wilson's work seems reasonably in line with that of Pearsall.

The vegetation of the lakes of Finland.   Maristo (1941) has considered the higher vegetation of 135 Finnish lakes which he classified in 11 vegetation types, seven being regarded as oligotrophic and four as eutrophic.

The Equisetum, Equisetum–Phragmites, *and* Phragmites *types.*   In the oligotrophic category three types form a more or less linear series, passing from very small highly chthoniotrophic lakes in the headwaters of river systems to large and more transparent lakes of the central parts of the valleys. The small yellow-brown or dark-brown lakes in general have an area less than 8 km^2, most of the shores are peaty, the Secchi disk transparency is 0.15–2.0 m with a mean value of 1.3 m, and the pH lies between 5.8 and 6.5. Hyperhydates are the most conspicuous elements in the vegetation of such lakes, with *Equisetum fluviatile* (sub *limosum*) dominant;

Phragmites australis is ordinarily present with *Eleocharis palustris* more often than *Schoenoplectus lacustris*. *Nuphar lutea* is the most usual floating-leaved plant, but *Nymphaea candida* is recorded in 60% of the lakes. Vittate submersed species are almost absent, *Potamogeton alpinus* and *Callitriche platycarpa* appear as minor constituents in, respectively, one-fifth and one-third of the lakes of this kind. Rosulate submerged plants are commoner; *Lobelia dortmanna* and *Ranunculus reptans* occur in about half. The lakes with *Isoetes* are rather less frequent; *Littorella uniflora* is absent, but *Elatine triandra* and *E. hydropiper*, ordinarily not very frequent in Finland, may occur. Pleustonic macrophytes are absent. Maristo refers these lakes to his *Equisetum* type. Part of the poverty of the flora can be attributed to the low transparency restricting higher plants to small depths, at which the loose peaty sediment is frequently disturbed by ice in winter.

Somewhat larger and less chthoniotrophic, brown or greenish-yellow lakes, 0.68–29.0 km² in area, with yellow water, a Secchi disk transparency of 1.2–3.0 m with a mean of 2.7 m, and a pH range of 6.2–7.0, are grouped as the *Equisetum–Phragmites* type. *Phragmites australis* is slightly more important than *Equisetum fluviatile*, followed by *Schoenoplectus lacustris* and *Eleocharis palustris*.

The lakes of the *Phragmites* type are generally large, 31–2,600 km² in area. The transparency varies between 2.5 and 7.0 with a mean value of 3.9 m, the lake in general is yellow-green. The pH lies between 6.6 and 6.8. *Phragmites* can occur in populations of moderate or low density along exposed shores. Its form would appear less adapted to withstanding wind than the strictly cylindrical *Schoenoplectus lacustris;* the capacity of *Phragmites* to invade harder, coarser sediments explains its greater development on open shores, whereas *S. lacustris* is commoner in protected bays. *Eleocharis palustris* is commoner than in the two previous categories because the *Phragmites* lakes provide more sandy littoral areas. The lakes of this type tend to occupy basins in the middle reaches of the river systems, receiving their water from small and varied lakes upstream. As Järnefelt (1938) pointed out, the humic color and thus the chthoniotrophic character of the water and lake tend to vary inversely with the size of the lake and the length of its influent.

The floating-leaved vegetation is more varied, *Potamogeton natans*, *Sparganium friesii*, and *Nuphar lutea* being the most important species. There is a fair representation of vittate submersed plants, *Potamogeton perfoliatus* and *Myriophyllum alterniflorum* being much the most important. *Isoetes lacustris*, *Lobelia dortmanna*, and *Ranunculus reptans* are the most significant rosulate species; *Juncus bulbosus* var. *fluitans* and *Elatine triandra* sometimes are found but *Littorella uniflora* is absent. *Lemna minor* occurs occasionally. The emergent-leaved hyperhydates are rather more abundant than in the more chthoniotrophic lakes, *Alisma plantago-aquatica* almost always and *Sparganium simplex* usually occurring; in the previous two types they occurred only in a large minority of lakes. *Sparganium friesii* is the most characteristic floating-leaved form and finds its optimal habitat in this kind of lake. *Nuphar lutea*, *Polygonum amphibium*, and *Potamogeton natans* are usually present, and *Glyceria natans* is definitely more common, but *Nymphaea* is less so, than the two previous types.

Other oligotrophic types. Outside this regular sequence of decreasing chthoniotrophy downstream, Maristo distinguishes four other oligotrophic vegetation types of less wide distribution. The first of these, the *Lobelia* type, is in Finland, as elsewhere, characterized by relatively high transparency (4.0–12.5) and yellowish-green to greenish-blue water. The Finnish examples lie in sand or material derived from eskers, locally termed *os*. As elsewhere, *Phragmites* occurs but is not important, and the vegetation is dominated by rosulate species, *Lobelia dortmanna* and *Isoetes lacustris* being the most important.

The other three oligotrophic types are primarily of regional occurrence in north Finland. The first is the *Carex* type, occurring north of latitude 68°N, but represented only by three lakes of widely different areas, high transparency (6.0–7.3), yellowish-brown to green color, and usually acidic (pH 6.8–6.9). All have *Equisetum fluviatile*, and one *Eleocharis palustris*, but *Schoenoplectus lacustris* and *Phragmites* are absent. There is, however, a well-developed more marginal vegetation of *Carex* spp., notably *C. lasiocarpa*, *C. rostrata*, and *C. aquatilis*, but much of the margin can be rocky and without plants. *Sparganium affine* is present in two of the lakes and *Myriophyllum alterniflorum* in all three, with *Potamogeton perfoliatus*, *P. berchtoldii* (sub *pusillus*), and *Ranunculus trichophyllus* (sub *confervoides*) in two. *Isoetes lacustris*, *Scirpus acicularis*, and *Ranunculus reptans* are always present but *Lobelia*, *Littorella*, and *Elatine* are absent.

Between the area to the far north supposedly characterized by the *Carex* type, and that of the *Equisetum* and *Equisetum–Phragmites* lakes of central Finland, there is an area largely within the Arctic Circle comprising much of Finnish Lappland where lakes apparently characterized by a richer development of submersed vittate vegetation occur. Over the greater part of this area the lakes are designated by Maristo as the Elodeid type. They vary in area from 0.3 to 19.3 km²; the mean area is 6.2 km². The water is brown to yellow-green; there is a tendency for the northern lakes to be less chthoniotrophic than those of southern Lappland. The transparency varies from 1.0 to 3.3 m, with a mean of 2.3 m; the pH varies from 6.7 to 7.5 with a mean of 7.1.

Equisetum fluviatile is always present, and *Phragmites australis* usually so; *Eleocaris palustris* is unimportant. *Sparganium friesii* and *Nuphar lutea* are the most important floating-leaved species with *Nuphar pumila* present in three-quarters and *Nymphaea candida* in two-thirds of the lakes. The type differs from the *Equisetum–Phragmites* type mainly in the far greater development of the submersed vittate plants. *Potamogeton perfoliatus* is always present and *P. berchtoldii* usually so; *P. filiformis*, however, is absent. *Nitella flexilis* occurs in three-quarters of the lakes but *Chara* is absent. The rosulate species are rather less well represented in most cases than in the other oligotrophic types, but *Isoetes lacustris* is usually present and *I. setaceum* also in over half the lakes. *Eleocaris acicularis*, *Ranunculus reptans*, and *Subularia aquatica* are usually present, with *Lobelia dortmanna* in a quarter of the lakes. Pleustonic species are absent.

To the east of the area of the Elodeid type there is a small region of somewhat more alkaline water, in which Maristo studied nine lakes, which constitute his *Potamogeton filiformis–Chara* type. They vary in area from 0.1 to 227.5 km² with a mean of 29.2 km². The transparency is fairly high, 4.5–6.5 m, with a mean of 5.5 m; the color is greenish yellow to blue-green. The pH varies from 7.3 to 7.9 with a mean of 7.5. *Equisetum fluviatile* is always present, *Phragmites* occurs in over three-quarters of the lakes; *Schoenoplectus* is in general much less important. *Nuphar lutea* is the commonest floating-leaved plant, but does not occur in quite all the lakes. Among the submersed vittate plants *Potamogeton filiformis* as well as *P. perfoliatus* and *P. praelongus* and *Myriophyllum alterniflorum* are usually present, while *Chara strigosa* (*C. globularis* var. *aspera* f. *strigosa*) is always found. The rosulate species are roughly comparable to those of the last category, though *Lobelia* is common. These lakes are referred by Maristo to the *Potamogeton filiformis–Chara* type. Comparable slightly saline lakes occur in Scotland (Spence 1964).

Eutrophic types. A fourth northern type occurring in a small area within that of the Elodeid type is represented by four small alkaline (pH 8.2–8.3) lakes, yellow-green in color and with a transparency of from 1.5 to 3.0 m. The emerged flora is not unlike that of the two previous types; *Potamogeton filiformis* appears again among the vittate submersed species and *Myriophyllum spicatum* is also important, but the most significant plant is *Stratiotes aloides*, abundant in all four. This clearly eutrophic but Arctic group of lakes are placed by Maristo in a *Stratiotes* type.

In southern Finland Maristo delimits several discontinuous areas forming a southern eutrophic region in which two kinds of vegetation types occur, designated as the *Scirpus lacuster* (i.e., *Schoenoplectus lacustris*) type and the *Typha–Alisma* type. The *Schoenoplectus lacustris* type of lake appears to be moderately eutrophic and moderately chthoniotrophic, being in fact mixotrophic in Järnefelt's (1930) terminology. The area varies from 0.84 to 16.0 km², with a mean value of 6.0 km². The transparency is low, from 0.4 to 1.4 m, with a mean of 1.0 m; the lake appears yellow-brown or brown. The pH lies between 6.6 and 7.5 with a mean of 6.9. *Equisetum fluviatile* and *Phragmites australis* are always present but the main obvious feature of the type is the great development of *Schoenoplectus lacustris*. *Typha angustifolia*, absent in the oligotrophic lakes, is present in about a fifth of the *Schoenoplectus* type. *Alisma plantago-aquatica* is always present but unimportant. Floating-leaved plants are abundant, the most important being *P. natans*. The submersed species are poorly represented, the commonest being *P. perfoliatus*, found in only 60% of the lakes of this type. *Isoetes* and *Lobelia* are absent; *Eleocaris acicularis*, a relatively unimportant component of the vegetation in about half the lakes, is the only significant rosulate species.

The more definitely eutrophic lakes of the same areas are classified by Maristo as belonging to his *Typha–Alisma* type. The lakes are mostly small, from 0.45 to 7.0 km² in area with a mean of 3.0 km². They are also very shallow, usually not over 2 m deep. The transparency is low, from 0.2 to 2.3 with a mean of 1.5. The lakes are often turbid with plankton and suspended clay; the color may be greenish or yellowish but humic stain is largely absent. The pH varies from 6.8 to 7.7 with a mean of 7.1. *Equisetum fluviatile*, *Schoenoplectus lacustris*, and *Phragmites australis* are always present, the last-named being the most important; *Eleocharis palustris* and one or both of *Typha latifolia* and *T. angustifolia* usually occurs. *Alisma plantago-aquatica* is almost always conspicuous. *Potamogeton natans* and *Nuphar lutea* are the most important floating-leaved species. Both vittate and rosulate submersed species are commoner than in the previous type. *P. perfoliatus* is the commonest of the former, but *P. obtusifolius* often occurs. *Lobelia* and *Isoetes* are found in a minority of lakes of this type. Seventy percent of the lakes supported *Lemna minor*.

A small group of four Karelian lakes richer in rosulate plants, with the vittate forms less well developed and with considerable representation of *Sparganium minimum*, is separated as the Kannas variant of this type.

The final eutrophic type, termed by Maristo the *Potamogeton* type, is represented by three very shallow ponds less than 1 km² in area and with depths of about 2 m, on the island of Alo, in the extreme southwest of Finland, but perhaps representative of the lakes of this area. The water is alkaline, with pH values of 8.0–8.2. The emergent vegetation is very rich and the whole floor is carpeted with submersed plants so that Secchi disk readings could not be obtained. *Typha latifolia* is constantly present. *Potamogeton berchtoldii* is the most important submersed plant, *P.*

perfoliatus, *P. obtusifolius*, and *Callitriche hermaphroditica* also always occurring, as does *Lemna trisulca*. No rosulate species are present.

The lakes of Northeastern Poland. Bernatowicz and Zachwieja (1966), in a very important paper, have given an account of the zonation observed in the basins of some of the lakes of the more or less contiguous Masurian and Suwałki Lake districts of northeastern Poland. Their approach is a little different from that of other investigators, as they have attempted a typology of the littoral zone in terms of both lake morphology and vegetation. The resulting classification, suitably amplified, may well provide the most convenient way of characterizing the littoral region of any lake.

The area in which the lakes studied by Bernatowicz and Zachwieja lie is a little south of the Baltic and rarely attains an altitude over 200 m. The lakes are primarily of glacial origin, usually lying in basins of till, and in their natural state, nearly all were presumably mesotrophic or moderately eutrophic. The calcium concentration in these waters is quite high, over 2 mequiv, or 40 mg liter^{-1}, and the pH is ordinarily between 7.8 and 8.4. The vegetation thus lacks the characteristic soft-water plants such as *Lobelia dortmanna*, found in many more oligotrophic lake districts. It is also to be noticed that *Elodea canadensis* is a very important member of the deeper-water flora of these lakes, but there seems to be no information as to what, if anything, took its place before the plant was accidentally introduced into Europe in the nineteenth century.

The important variables that produce the various types of littoral are as follows:

1. The form of the original basin, particularly its slope in the vicinity of the shore line and several meters below.

2. The material of the basin, either unconsolidated rock, or clastic materials of various average sizes.

3. The aspect of the shore, the winds as elsewhere in Europe being predominantly westerly, so that the effect of waves is greater on the eastern than on the western coast of a lake.

4. The size of the lake determining the fetch of the wind and thus the amplitudes of the waves breaking on the shore.

Bernatowicz and Zachwieja distinguish 10 types of littoral. Of these, one is the result of experimental and aquicultural disturbance and, though very interesting, does not belong in the natural sequence. One is found only where submerged shallow banks, away from the lake margins, permit the development of emergent vegetation in the middle of the lake. The other eight types form a natural series which is believed to be successional, though it is most unlikely that the localities exhibiting the late stages ever went through all the early ones.

Bernatowicz and Zachwieja distinguish three fundamental types of littoral. In the *litholittoral* the beach and the shelf at the margin of the lake are either cut in rock or are formed of boulders with some gravel but, in the shallowest water, no sand or silt. In the *psammolittoral* the beach and shelf are sandy, though some of the latter may be carpeted with macrophytes. In the *phytolittoral* the whole littoral is covered with plants or the results of their decay; five types of phytolittoral may be distinguished; a well-marked transition to the phytolittoral from the psammolittoral is conveniently treated with the latter.

Litholittoral. In this type the beach, if there is one, and the shelf, which is usually narrow, are composed either of rock in situ or of boulders. In the most extreme cases in which there is a vertical cliff face going down into the water, nothing much is eroded because incoming waves are largely reflected. With a less vertically sided basin, or particularly where boulders of various sizes are present, a little erosion on the beach and building on the shelf may occur. Bernatowicz and Zachweija figure as an example the littoral profile of the eastern shore of Lake Hańcza (Fig. 134a) in the Suwałki Lake District, a lake they consider to be oligotrophic. There may be a few feeble plants of *Phragmites* and more numerous specimens of *Equisetum palustre* among the stones near the water's edge. There is no continuous vegetation on the shelf but at the top of the slope some *Potamogeton perfoliatus* is present and beyond this from 2 to about 9 m *Elodea canadensis* is common.

A comparable litholittoral must be developed around mountain and some other lakes in rock basins in many parts of the world, but in most such lakes, containing soft water poor in nutrients, the plants present will be different though their arrangement, insofar as it is based on the physical properties of the lake margin, will be similar.

Psammolittoral. The psammolittoral is characteristic of the exposed shores of large mesotrophic and eutrophic lakes in Poland, but it is also probably developed in some oligotrophic basin in unconsolidated material.

The beach tends to be composed of gravel and sand, the bottom of the shelf is predominantly sandy with 2–3% organic matter, and the slope beyond the shelf has a covering of mud increasing in thickness with depth.

The type is of particular interest in view of the special biological, mainly animal, association, the *psammon*, occupying the interstitial water between sand grains; this association will be considered in detail in the next volume. In the example figured (Fig. 134b) from the eastern shore of Lake Dargin, the landward part of the shelf is sufficiently disturbed by waves to be bare, whereas the lakeward part with a slightly deeper bottom supports an association of small low-growing Characeae (see pp. 40, 489) which form a *Parvocharacetum*. *Potamogeton perfoliatus* and *P. pectinatus* occur at

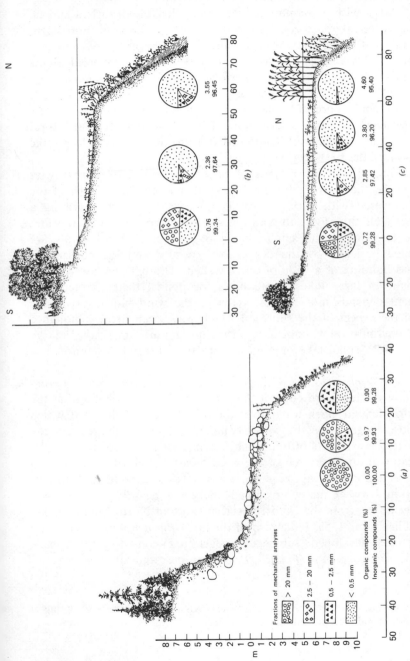

FIGURE 134. Profile across littoral region of (*A*) eastern shore of Lake Hańcza, a typical litholittoral; a little *Potamogeton pectinatus* rooted at about 2 m, and below if *Elodea canadensis* to about 9 m. (*B*) eastern shore of Lake Dargin, a typical psammolittoral; *Parvocharacetum* on sand in up to 1 m of water, *P. pectinatus* and *P. perfoliatus* at top of mont rooted in about 1 m of water, *E. canadensis* and Charophyceae at greater depths. (*C*) protected southern shore of same lake with psammolittoral bearing a narrow belt of *Phragmites australis* at the lakeward edge of the shelf, with *P. compressus, P. perfoliatus, P. lucens,* and *Ranunculus circinatus* rooted in 2–4 m water.
  Sectored circles refer to the composition of the sediments at the points immediately above their centers (Bernatowicz and Zachwieja).

455

the top of the slope, beyond which, down to 5 m, there is *Elodea canadensis*, and large Characeae, forming a *Magnocharacetum*.

In some lakes with a psammolittoral, along the less disturbed shores, the bottom at the lakeward edge of the shelf, perhaps 0.8 m or more deep, may be sufficiently undisturbed to permit the development of emergent vegetation, notably *Phragmites*, as a narrow belt, with submersed plants such as *Potamogeton compressus, P. perfoliatus, P. lucens,* and *Ranunculus circinatus* a little lower down the slope. The example figured (Fig. 134*c*) is from the southern shore of Lake Dargin, where one would expect less disturbance than along the eastern shore of Fig. 134*b*. This type of littoral in which a sandy beach is still retained is transitional to the large-lake phytolittoral of the next section.

Phytolittoral. In all other types of littoral described by Bernatowicz and Zachwieja, the entire eulittoral, the shelf, and the upper part of the slope are covered with more or less continuous vegetation, forming a phytolittoral. Of this, five subtypes are distinguished. Of these, the first three, the large-lake,[3] the small-lake, and the pond phytolittorals are distinguished basically by the degree of exposure and the consequent cutting and building of a wide or narrow shelf. Though they are roughly characteristic of large lakes, small lakes, or ponds, their characteristic development depends more on the fetch of the wind blowing over the water and the aspect of the shore on which waves can break. Though a large-lake phytolittoral will not occur at the margin of a small lake, a large lake may have a small lake or even a pond phytolittoral developed in a protected bay.

The *large-lake phytolittoral* is characterized by having a zone of *Phragmites* both at the lakeward edge of the very broad littoral shelf and at the water's edge, leaving open water over the middle part of the shelf which here is too deep to damp the waves completely and too shallow for the latter not to disturb the bottom. Such a broad shelf develops where the shore is exposed and the fetch of the wind great enough to ensure a long history of active cutting above mean water level and building below it. In the bottom between the two reed beds there may be a *Parvocharacetum*, as in the example, from the exposed eastern shore of North Mamry Lake, illustrated in Figure 135*a*. Lakeward of the inner *Phragmitetum* there is on the slope well-developed submersed vegetation consisting of *Elodea canadensis, Potamogeton perfoliatus, Lemna trisulca,* and tall Characeae.

---

[3] Bernatowicz and Zachwieja use the term "great-lake", which would be confusing at least to American and African readers.

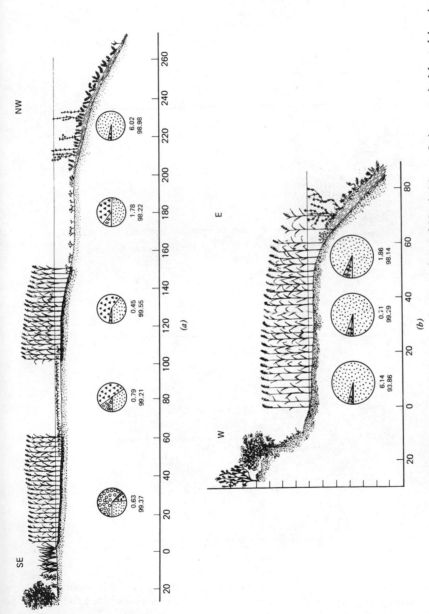

Figure 135. Profile across littoral region of (A) the exposed eastern shore of North Mamry Lake, a typical large-lake phytolittoral; *Acorus calamus* in the eulittoral, *Phragmites australis* forming two belts with a *Parvocharacetum* on the shelf between them, and to lakeward a little *Lemna trisulca*, more Charophycea, *P. perfoliatus*, *Elodea canadensis*, and in deep water *Fontinalis antipyretica* (Bernatowicz and Zachwieja). (B) the exposed eastern shore of Lake Kisajno, a typical small-lake phytolittoral; *P. australis* from the water's edge to the lakeward edge of the shelf and Charophycea, *Ranunculus circinatus* and *E. canadensis* in deeper water (Bernatowicz and Zachwieja).

457

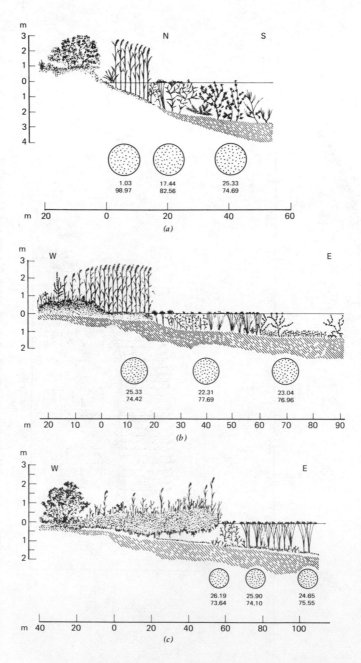

FIGURE 136.   Profile across littoral region of (*A*) a bay on an island in the southern part of Lake Kisajno, a typical pond phytolittoral, with little trace of a discrete shelf and mont;

458

A subtype, called by Bernatowicz and Zachwieja the *midlake phytolittoral*, may develop in large lakes in which isolated shoals almost reach the water surface and can carry emergent vegetation. *Schoenoplectus lacustris*, which tends to grow on softer muddy bottoms than does *Phragmites*, but which is very resistant to injury by wind, is often found in this situation. This subtype of course does not belong in the supposed successional sequence.

The *small-lake phytolittoral* is characterized by the coalescence of the two reed beds of the preceding type, to give a single band of reeds from above the mean water level across much of the shelf; there may be a *Characetum* lakeward of the reeds, with *Elodea canadensis* and *Ranunculus circinatus* on the slope as on the eastern shore of Lake Kisajno (Fig. 135*b*).

The *pond phytolittoral* has floating-leaved vegetation, notably *Potamogeton natans* and some *Nuphar lutea* lakeward of the reed bed, and a more varied flora of submersed plants than in the previous types. Organic matter tends to accumulate, but as the fetch is small and the waves low, little removal of such matter occurs and the distinction between shelf and slope may be obliterated. The example illustrated (Fig. 136*a*) is from a bay in an island in the southern part of Lake Kisajno.

A further stage is found in the *marsh phytolittoral* found on very sheltered shores with a very wide zone of floating-leaved vegetation. In the example (Fig. 136*b*) from a part of the eastern shore of Lake Kisajno, protected by a group of islands, *Stratiotes aloides* is well developed landward of the broad *Nupharetum*.

Finally the tangle of rhizomes of *Phragmites* and other emergent plants may extend lakeward from the margin over the water, shading and ultimately killing the submersed species and forming what Bernatowicz and Zachwieja call on *atrophic phytolittoral*, illustrated by an example from the small Lake Wojsak (Fig. 136*c*).

Artificial phytolittorals. When a lake has rather turbid water and a well-developed *Phragmites* zone in the shallow upper infralittoral there are often practically no submersed plants. Removal of the *Phragmites* permits some erosion to occur, producing a narrow sandy beach. In a case studied

---

Phragmites australis at the water's edge, *Nuphar lutea* and *Potamogeton natans* just below the reeds and *Ranunculus circinatus*, *Myriophyllum spicatum*, *Elodea canadensis* and *P. compressus* in up to 3 m water. (*B*) of a protected part behind islands of the same lake, a typical swamp phytolittoral, with a very gentle gradient; various amphiphytes and *P. australis* above or at the margin, *Stratiotes* and a broad belt of *Nuphar lutea* and *Ranunculus circinatus* lakeward of the reeds with Charophyceae, *E. canadensis* and *Potamogeton* spp. (*C*) Lake Wojsak, a typical atrophic phytolittoral; *Carex* and *Phragmites* growing out as a mat over the lake and shading the landward part of the bottom, with *Potamogeton natans*, *Nuphar lutea* and *Fontinalis antipyretica* growing in the unshaded part (Bernatowicz and Zachweija).

by Bernatowicz and Zachwieja, small numbers of *Potamogeton perfoliatus*, *Ranunculus circinatus*, and *Ceratophyllum demersum* developed below the beach, the last-named plant being abundant in 0.8–0.9 m at the edge of the shelf. Deeper, on the gentle slope, the vegetation declined. Left without further disturbance, an emergent flora of *Sagittaria sagittifolia*, *Schoenoplectus tabernaemontani*, and *S. lacustris* began to appear at the margin.

The continual removal or poisoning of emergent plants now practiced in many lakes probably increases the growth of submersed species at least where transparency is low, and may increase the invertebrate fauna on which fish feed. The consequences of continuing such practices for a long time have, however, not been fully studied and undesirable long-term effects might conceivably arise if the removal of emergent vegetation is too drastic.

Finally it may be noted that the average chemical composition of littoral sediments becomes poorer in insoluble siliceous material and richer in all other constituents in progressing from the litholittoral towards the extreme senescent atrophic phytolittoral. The big change begins to occur in passing from a small-lake to a pond phytolittoral (Fig. 137).

Mesotrophic and eutrophic lakes in Northern Germany. Sauer (1937) has considered the vegetation of a number of the lakes of Holstein in north Germany. These lakes are of interest as apparently providing examples of how the surrounding terrain may influence the macroscopic plants of a lake; further study along these lines might be interesting.

In general the junciform emergent vegetation of the more exposed shores, if it is present, consists of *Schoenoplectus lacustris*. There is an association of *Potamogeton pectinatus* var. *tenuifolius* and *P. filiformis* in 5–30 cm of water growing on sand and gravel on some exposed shores, but the most characteristic community of such areas is composed of *Chara aspera*, *Ch. vulgaris*, and *Ch. globularis* (sub *fragilis*). Some algal associations are also present, and in the Bültsee there is an *Isoetetum*, composed of *Isoetes* with varying amounts of *Littorella uniflora* (sub *juncea*), *Lobelia dortmanna*, *Myriophyllum alterniflorum*, and some other species. In the same lake and in the Kollsee a shallow-water association dominated by *Eleocharis acicularis* occurs, and fragments of this association may be found in the shallowest water of some of the more eutrophic lakes.

On the sheltered coasts *Phragmites australis*, *Schoenoplectus lacustris*, and *Typha angustifolia* occur much as elsewhere in Europe. Lakeward there may be a *Nupharetum* with *Nuphar lutea*, *Nymphaea alba*, *Polygonum amphibium* var. *natans*, *Potamogeton natans*, *Hydrocharis morsus-ranae*, *Stratiotes aloides*, *Myriophyllum verticillatum*, and *M. spicatum*. Within this there are associations of different species of *Potamogeton* and the *Magnocharacetum* already discussed (see p. 40). Though the local associa-

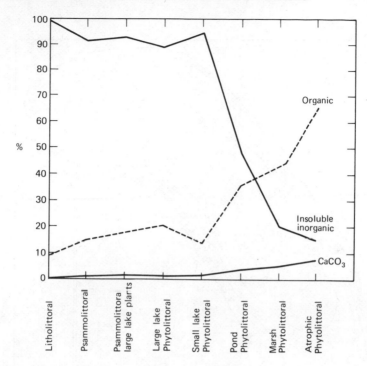

FIGURE 137. Calcium carbonate, insoluble inorganic matter, mainly SiO_2, and organic matter in the different types of littoral deposit in the lakes studied by Bernatowicz and Zachwieja.

tions of *Potamogeton* and other submersed species at particular stations are listed in detail, in only one case, the Krummensee, a lake of maximum depth 13 m, about 800 m long and 150 m wide, is there full information about the distribution of individual species throughout a lake (Fig. 138). The Krummensee is surrounded by woodland and is greatly influenced by fallen leaves. It is a kidney-shaped lake with its concave margin on the southwest side. The vegetation is best developed in the southeastern and northwestern parts of the shoreline. *Phragmites* and *Typha*, with *Carex* locally, form the emergent zone, patches of *Nuphar*, *Nymphaea*, and *Menyanthes* are the most important features of the floating-leaved vegetation. There is a little *Potamogeton obtusifolius* between 2.5 and 5 m on the northern exposed shore and *P. crispus* var. *gemnifer* in from 4 to 7 m in the southwest corner of the lake. *Elodea canadensis* occurs between 2.5 and 5 m on the southern shore and there is a good deal of *Fontinalis antipyretica* and some *Nitella* between 2.5 and 7.5 m. Two patches of *Stratiotes aloides* are conspicuous in the southeastern bay and against the northwestern coast.

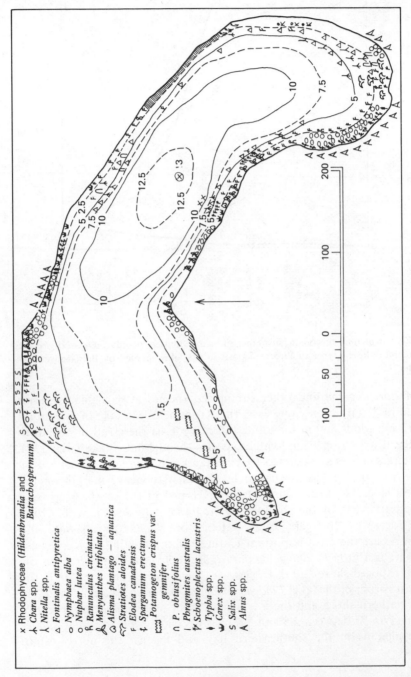

x Rhodophyceae (*Hildenbrandia* and
     Batracbospermum)
λ *Cbara* spp.
λ *Nitella* spp.
Δ *Fontinalis antipyretica*
o *Nympbaea alba*
o *Nupbar lutea*
ℛ *Ranunculus circinatus*
⌀ *Menyantbes trifoliata*
⌀ *Alisma plantago — aquatica*
⌇ *Stratiotes aloides*
F *Elodea canadensis*
ɬ *Sparganium erectum*
⫘ *Potamogeton crispus* var.
     gemnifer
∩ *P. obtusifolius*
∨ *Pbragmites australis*
Ⅴ *Schoenoplectus lacustris*
▮ *Typba* spp.
⥥ *Carex* spp.
S *Salix* spp.
Λ *Alnus* spp.

FIGURE 138.   Map of vegetation in the Krummensee.

462

Sauer arranges his lakes in four types: The *woodland humic type* (Wald-humusseetyp), first characterized by Koppe (1924), has sediments of low mineral content, mainly formed from the leaves of trees. The deep-water flora is reduced both qualitatively and quantitatively, and among higher plants is dominated by *Potamogeton crispus* var. *gemnifer*. There is a good development of floating-leaved vegetation. In the emergent zone *Carex acutiformis, Menyanthes trifoliata, Naumbergia thyrsiflora*, and *Equisetum fluviatile* occur. The Krummensee described in the previous paragraph is an example of this kind of lake.

The *herbaceous humic type* (Krauthumusseetyp), also characterized by Koppe (1923), has a reduced emergent flora, a very well-developed floating-leaved association, and massive amounts of *Ceratophyllum demersum*. There may be a tendency toward formation of a quaking shore. The type is regarded as having a chthoniotrophic type of sediment with fairly eutrophic water, supposedly more eutrophic than the woodland humic lakes. Sauer gives as examples the upper and lower Ausgrabensée and the Kleiner Madebröken See; all are small lakes. Both these humic eutrophic types of lake have moderately calcareous (Ohle 1934) waters (15–35 mg Ca liter^{-1}).

The *Potamogeton* type, comparable to lakes in Sweden described by Samuelsson (1925), is the typical vegetation type of the larger, hard water (Ca > 35 mg liter^{-1}), eutrophic lakes of the Baltic countries. The reed zone is largely occupied by *Schoenoplectus lacustris*. In the shallow water of the exposed shores a *Parvocharacetum* is developed, consisting of *Chara vulgaris*, either with *Ch. aspera* and *Ch. globularis* or with *Potamogeton perfoliatus*. In the intermediate shores between the windswept and sheltered reaches, *Potamogeton lucens, P. perfoliatus*, and some less important plants are recorded, and below them *P. berchtoldii* (sub *pusillus* var. *acuminatus*) and *P. friesii* (sub *mucronatus*). On the least exposed shores within a reed girdle of *Schoenoplectus* and *Phragmites* in varying proportions and with varying associations, there may be a well-developed zone of floating-leaved species and then an association of *Potamogeton perfoliatus* and *Ranunculus circinatus*. Below this a *Magnocharacetum* is developed. The margins of these lakes are stable.

The final type recognized by Sauer is the *quaking meadow type* (Wiesen-schwingenseetyp) which he regards as a eutrophic development of the *Potamogeton* type in basins, surrounded by hills, that have undergone succession uninterrupted by littoral erosion. There is a great development of a quaking littoral with *Phragmites* and behind it stages of hydrarch succession beginning with *Alnus glutinosa* and including some bog plants. The floating-leaved vegetation is well developed. Hydrogeophytes of the *Potamogeton perfoliatus–P. lucens* association are unimportant; the associations dominated by Characeae are abundant. In some respects this type represents a eutrophic version of a small senescent bog lake. It is neatly exemplified by the Blinkersee near Plön of which Sauer gives a photograph.

The changing vegetation of very eutrophic lakes. Two studies have been made of the vegetation in eutrophic lakes, one in Denmark and the other in Wisconsin, which include investigations, repeated at widely separated intervals, of two lakes of great importance, namely, Furesø and Lake Mendota, that have undergone a good deal of artificial eutrophication. These cases are presented in the following sections along with some comparative data from several other Danish lakes and from Green Lake, Wisconsin.

Eutrophic lakes in Denmark. The vegetation of several eutrophic lakes (Furesø, Bastrupsø, Farumsø, Bagsvaerdsø, and Lyngbysø) was mapped by Boye-Petersen (1917) and that of Furesø described in greater detail by Seidelin-Raunkiaer and Boye-Petersen (1917), on the basis of work done in 1911–1912. Furesø was again investigated in 1950–1951 (Christensen and Andersen 1958), though somewhat less completely.

All lakes tend to have a girdle of *Phragmites australis.* Lakeward of this there may be *Schoenoplectus lacustris* or *Typha augustifolia;* occasionally all three species can occur in the order *Phragmites, Typha, Schoenoplectus.* Sharp zonation is best developed where the depth increases moderately fast on leaving the shore and the zone of emergent vegetation is narrow; where there is a very flat shallow infralittoral, the zonation is much less striking (*C* of Fig. 124). *Phragmites* can be rooted on land, or in water down to 2 m in depth, and *Typha* and *Schoenoplectus* grow in from 0.5 to 2 m of water. They both occur on softer sediment than does *Phragmites; Typha* is more easily damaged by waves than is *Schoenoplectus* and occurs in the most sheltered parts of the shore.

Nuphar lutea, Potamogeton natans, and usually in somewhat deeper water, *Nymphaea alba* are the chief floating-leaved species, whereas the submersed flora consists mainly of Characeae, *Potamogeton* spp., and *Ceratophyllum demersum.* The extent of the submerged weed beds is very variable. In Bastrupsø there is no submersed vegetation at all in spite of the well-developed girdle of reeds; Boye-Petersen attributes this to the steepness of the littoral and the disturbed condition of the water, though the low transparency and high plankton productivity are suggested as general causes for the existence of unvegetated areas of moderate depth in most of these Danish lakes.

Farumsø has rather more submersed vegetation, *Ceratophyllum demersum* reaching 7 m, and *Fontinalis antipyretica* 6.5 m. A very large part of the shallow water below 1.5–2 m is, however, without plants of any kind.

Bagsvaerdsø has a *Phragmites* girdle and very large beds of *Nymphaea alba* along the more protected southwest shore. In a few places *Typha* alternates with *Nymphaea* as one goes along the waterward edge of the reed bed in which *Schoenoplectus* as well as *Phragmites* occur. Isolated large patches of *Potamogeton lucens* and *P. crispus* made up the submersed vegetation; much of the bottom even in quite shallow water, 2–3 m deep, is quite bare of higher plants.

Lyngbysø has the same sort of *Phragmites* girdle as the other lakes with *Nymphaea* and *Nuphar* along the southwest shore and locally in other sheltered stretches of shore. Much of the bottom is covered with *Potamogeton lucens*.

Furesø has a comparable *Phragmites* girdle to those just mentioned, but in the very limited part of the shore where there is clear zonation of the three major emergent species, *Typha* lies between the more littoral *Phragmites* and the more open water *Schoenoplectus*. *Potamogeton lucens* tended to occur below the reed girdle in the shallow northeast parts of the lake. The main deep-water plants were *Nitellopsis obtusa* and *Chara* spp. with some *Ceratophyllum demersum*, *Elodea canadensis*, and *Potamogeton perfoliatus*. A number of species of *Chara* and five species of mosses were recorded, some extending below the flowering plants to 11 m.

Since the investigations of 1911–1912, the lake has become considerably more eutrophic, at least partly on account of pollution by sewage. As a result the transparency had decreased considerably (Berg and Røen 1958). Casual observations between 1901 and 1925 indicate that the maximum Secchi disk transparency in the colder part of the year lay between 9 and 12 m, and the minimum in the summer at about 5 m. In 1951–1952 the maximum values, in the colder seasons, were about 7 m; the minimum values, in the summer, were about 2 m. The change seems to have occurred largely between 1939 and 1947. As a result, the depth to which rooted vegetation extends has been considerably reduced (Table 72).

The depth ranges of all species have evidently decreased (Table 72) and some qualitative changes have occurred. It seems probable that *Nitellopsis obtusa*, *Potamogeton lucens*, and *Elodea canadensis* have become less important and the other species listed more important. *P. compressus* (sub *zosterifolius*) recorded earlier in the present century has disappeared (see p. 397). It is interesting that *P. zosteriformis*, the American vicariant ally of *P. compressus*, has become rare in Lake Mendota, but even after massive eutrophication has not disappeared.

The changes in the Charophyceae, other than in *N. obtusa*, and in the mosses are less well documented. Of the latter group *Scorpidium scorpioides*, *Drepanocladus aduncus*, and *D. sendtnieri* all disappeared, though the last-

TABLE 72. *Lower limit, depth of maximum frequency, and value of the latter of various plants in Fureso before and after considerable artificial eutrophication*

Species	1911–1912			1950–1951		
	Lower limit (m)	Depth of maximum frequency (m)	Maximum frequency (%)	Lower limit (m)	Depth of maximum frequency (m)	Maximum frequency (%)
Nitellopsis obtusa	8	2.0–2.5	38	3.5	1.5–2.0	20
Ranunculus circinatus	7	3.0–3.5	10	5	2.5–3.0	41
Myriophyllum spicatum	7	2.0–2.5	8	5	1.5–2.0	31
Ceratophyllum demersum	7	3.0–3.5	13	6	3.5–4.0	53
Potamogeton perfoliatus	7	3.5–4.0	14	4	2.5–3.0	36
P. pectinatus	7	5.0–6.0	7	5	1.5–2.0	17
P. lucens	7	1.5–2.0	20	3.5	1.5–2.0	11
Elodea canadensis	7.5	2.0–2.5	33	3.5	2.0–2.5	28

named was earlier the commonest moss in the lake, leaving only *Fontinalis antipyretica* and scattered specimens of *F. kindbergii*.

Although too much emphasis should probably not be placed on the comparison of the depth distribution of frequencies, as the comparable nature of the two sets of observations is not entirely certain, it seems likely that in the case of *P. pectinatus* there has been a striking change; in 1911–1912 the species was not common and was most frequent just above its maximum depth, whereas in 1950–1951 it was much more abundant and most frequent in shallow water, declining rapidly with depth. Since the distribution of any species is likely to depend not only on light, but on the distribution of kinds of sediment, hydrographic factors, and competition, it is reasonable to suppose that the distribution of any species will react in essentially a nonlinear manner to a change in any environmental variable.

Lake Mendota, Wisconsin. Three studies have been published, one based on work done in August 1912 by Denniston (1922), the second reporting a more quantitative study, done about 1920 by Rickett (1922), and the third limited to a part of the lake examined by Lind and Cottam (1969) in 1966. The last two authors had access to unpublished information obtained by Andrews in 1939–1941 (cf. Andrews and Hasler 1943). There are certain differences to be noted between the first two accounts which probably represent real changes in the vegetation of the lake. The more recent study indicates that quite drastic alterations have taken place during the past half century.

Denniston found an almost continuous girdle of submersed vegetation, extending downward in most places to 5–5.5 m; in a few places in the eastern half of the lake the presence of a rocky bottom limits the depth distribution of the plants. There is little emergent or floating vegetation; that developed occurs only in bays and behind bars. In University Bay *Scirpus validus* grew on a sandy bar, behind which were found *Ranunculus trichophyllus*[4] (sub *aquatilis*), *Nuphar advena*, *Nymphaea odorata*, *Lemna minor*, *L. trisulca*, and *Wolffia columbiana;* a rich fully submersed flora of the same species as occur in the open lake was found in deeper water of the bay. At the mouth of Pheasant Branch Creek the same kind of zonation was apparent.

Rickett's quantitative data show a similar general distribution as found by Denniston, but insofar as the two investigations are comparable, they suggest certain dramatic changes in the distribution and abundance of some of the commoner species. Both authors found *Vallisneria americana* (sub *spiralis*) to be the commonest plant in the lake; Rickett's data, however, show that below 3 m, *Potamogeton amplifolius* was locally slightly more abundant and that this species was of great importance in zone 2, from 1 to 3 m; it actually had become the second most abundant plant in the lake, a position given by Denniston to *Najas flexilis*. *P. zosteriformis*, Denniston's fourth most abundant plant, seems to have become much less abundant, particularly in shallow water. *Potamogeton illinoensis* (recorded by both authors sub *lucens*) appears to have undergone a restriction in its depth range between the two investigations, as Denniston found it to more than 5 m deep and Rickett only in the top 1 m; in neither study was it important quantitatively. It has now disappeared, at least from University Bay.

There was some difference between the flora of the sandy and gravelly bottoms and those covered with mud in the top 3 m, but it is much less than would have been expected from Pearsall's studies. *Ceratophyllum demersum*, *Myriophyllum exalbescens*, and *Potamogeton illinoensis* seem to be mud plants, *Ranunculus trichophyllus* a sand plant. In zone 1, from 0 to 1 m, the colonization per square meter was about the same on mud and sand. In zone 2 it was about one and three-quarters as great on mud as on sand; this is due primarily to the preference of *P. amplifolius* for mud in this zone, but the small population of this species in zone 1 is largely on sand.

In zone 3 the sandy bottom was absent. It is probable that the much lower population density in this zone than in zone 2 on mud is partly due to including areas down to 7 m which lacked vegetation. Rickett is not

---

[4] Lind and Cottam use this name; *R. aquatilis* is western in North America, according to Cook (1966b).

explicit on this point; Denniston says that *Ceratophyllum* occurred to a depth of 6 m. Because his collecting rake had a handle 6 m long, the depth limit recorded may be an artifact, though he states clearly that in most places plants were not found growing below 5.0–5.5 m.

The more recent study of Lind and Cottam (1969), though limited to University Bay, clearly indicates the changes that have occurred since Rickett's investigation in the early 1920s. Lind and Cottam recognize six plant communities. The *Scirpus validus* community still occupies water less than 1 m deep on the sandbar that crosses the head of the bay; this community is not described in detail but evidently *Myriophyllum exalbescans* and *Vallisneria americana* are the only other plants present. The floating-leaved community, apparently on an organic ("muck") bottom in less than 1 m of water, now consists mainly of *Nymphaea tuberosa* rather than *N. odorata* (if it was correctly determined) with *Ceratophyllum demersum* below it. *Nuphar advena* present in Denniston's time is not now recorded, but *Nelumbo lutea* and *Potamogeton nodosus* occur locally near a small inlet. *Myriophyllum exalbescens*, unlike *C. demersus*, occurs in this community only where the *Nymphaea* leaves do not form a complete canopy.

Four fully submersed communities are recognized. There is a shallow-water submersed community in which *Vallisneria americana* is dominant and *Myriophyllum exalbescens* and *Ceratophyllum demersus* are frequent; *Elodea canadensis*, *Najas flexilis*, and *Zannichellia palustris* not found in the other communities are all present, as are seven other species, making this the most diverse part of the vegetation of the bay. A *Vallisneria* community, almost lacking *M. exalbescens* and *R. trichophyllus*, is developed locally in the same depth zone as the shallow-water community just described.

There is a transitional *Vallisneria–Myriophyllum* community in water between 1.5 and 2.0 m in which *Ceratophyllum demersum* and *Potamogeton richardsonii* are moderately frequent. Below this from 2.0 m to the limit of macrophytic vegetation, now apparently around 3 m, there is a *Myriophyllum exalbescens* community on fine sediment; *C. demersum* is the only other significant plant in this zone.

Vallisneria now never occurs below 2.5 m and is almost confined to sandy bottoms. In Rickett's time this plant was a subdominant, not greatly less abundant than *Potamogeton amplifolius* on mud in the zone from 3 to 7 m of water. Its present restriction to less fine sediments is presumably due to competition with *M. exalbescens*.

Comparison with earlier work can be made, though there are differences in technique which may limit recognition of the finer differences. Rickett estimated the biomass of each species. Lind and Cottam determined frequency of occurrence in 0.5-m line segments along one of 21 transects across the bay. They give the result as the percentage frequency, defined as the percentage of line segments, within any community, in which the species occurs. They also give relative frequency or the percentage, in the total number of records for all species, in which a given species occurs, though this measure is less useful and is not employed in Table 73.

It is clear that great changes have taken place. The most significant of these is the enormous increase in *Myriophyllum exalbescens*, now much the most important plant, constituting from half to three-quarters of the plants present, though in 1922 its biomass was about 2% of the total quantity of vegetation. Lind and Cottam are aware of the problems of *M. spicatum* in America but do not discuss the finer points of the taxonomy of the plant present in Lake Mendota. Correlative with the rise of *Myriophyllum*, *Vallisneria americana*, the second most important species in 1922 has declined markedly, and *Potamogeton amplifolius*, once the third most important species, has disappeared. In all, there were 14 species other than *Scirpus validus* in the bay in 1922. This had increased by the addition of *Zannichellia palustris*, *Potamogeton crispus*, *P. natans*, *P. nodosus*, and *P. praelongus* in 1945. The last three species along with *P. amplifolius* and *P. illinoensis* have now become extinct in the bay, but *P. foliosus* has been added to the flora, the number of species having fallen from the 18 present in 1945 to 14; the same number as found in 1922. It is, however, reasonably certain that diversity as measured by any of the acceptable methods (Levins 1968; Pielou 1969; see also Vol. II, pp. 360–374), which take into account not merely the number of species but also the number of individuals of each species, would have declined greatly, owing to the tendency of *Myriophyllum exalbescens* to form unispecific communities over much of the bottom of the bay.

Green Lake, Wisconsin. A comparable though less complete study of Green Lake in Wisconsin was also made by Rickett (1924). The lake is more transparent than Lake Mendota, as is indicated in Table 74. The emergent vegetation is noted very briefly; it was mainly developed at the southwest corner of the lake and consists of *Typha* sp., *Carex* spp., *Megalodonta beckii*, *Sagittaria latifolia* at the water's edge, and *S. heterophylla* in slightly deeper water. *Nuphar advena* also occurred in sheltered shallow water and *Nymphaea odorata* locally in somewhat deeper water. The two floras are not dissimilar qualitatively, but quantitatively Green Lake differs from Mendota in the much greater importance of *Chara* (unfortunately not determined) and the much less great importance of *Potamogeton amplifolius* and *Vallisneria*. It is not unlikely that competition between *Chara* and these two species is important.

The details of the depth distributions differ somewhat from the contemporary accounts of Lake Mendota. *Potamogeton pectinatus* was commonest on sand in water less than 1 m deep in Mendota and even on mud became rarer with increasing depth; there is little sand in Green Lake and *P. pectinatus* on mud was commoner in the deeper water. *P. richardsoni* was a specifically shallow-water species in Lake Mendota but is commoner in Green Lake in zone 2 (1–3 m) than in zone 1. It is not unlikely that such differences are due to stronger wave action in Green Lake. Rickett notes that where the slope of the bottom is very steep the benthic macrophytes occur only to 4–5 m, but where the slope is very gentle some stunted vegetation persists to 10 m. In most parts of the lake at "about 6 meters the slope usually becomes much steeper and the outer strip of vegetation hangs, as it were, to the base of a hill." Rickett used a diving bell and here is clearly writing from direct visual experience. It seems from this work that the steepness of the slope of the bottom is a real ecological factor, which may explain certain puzzling cases of vegetationless zones within the euphotic region, as in Crystal Lake and Grane Langsø (see p. 432). It is unfortunate that the species descending deepest in Green Lake is not specified; it may well have been the moss *Drepanocladus pseudofluitans*.

New Zealand. Though no very complete study of a single natural lake seems to have been published, Mason (1969) has given a general account of the aquatic vegetation of the Canterbury district of South Island. This account shows the great potential interest of further study of the lakes of the large and isolated pair of islands, enjoying a temperate climate comparable to those of the areas most intensively investigated in the Northern Hemisphere but with a very restricted native aquatic flora.

In the clear permanent waters of lakes with little or no silting, *Isoetes alpinus*, *Limosella lineata*, *Ruppia polycarpa*, which is a short and delicate freshwater species, and a number of species of characeae may occur. *Myriophyllum elatinoides*, with the introduced *Elodea canadensis*, may occur below these species; *E. canadensis* is in fact said to go deeper than any native plant. Where silting occurs *Potamogeton cheesemani* is dominant. The latter species evidently has a very wide tolerance and can occur in a depauperate reddish form in some mountain lakes. Mason suggests that in the absence of much floristic diversity, some of the New Zealand species are prone to produce remarkable ecophenes filling many niches. *Myriophyllum propinquum* can grow as a mosslike subaerial plant on wet mud, as a submersed plant up to 45 cm long with uniformly dissected leaves in streams, as a lacustrine and very heterophyllous plant up to 3 m tall in coastal ponds, or apparently as a swollen leafless plant in some mountain localities.

TABLE 73. *Comparison of the submersed vegetation of Lake Mendota at different times during the years 1912–1966*

| | Depth range 1912 (Denniston) (m) | Biomass ~1920 (Rickett) (wet plant gm^{-2}) | | | | | Total in lake (kg) |
| | | Zone 1, 0–1 m | | Zone 2, 1–3 m | | Zone 3, 3–7 m | |
Species		Sand	Mud	Sand	Mud	Mud	
Chara spp.[a]	0.3–2.8	65	61	103	43	0	477,000
Ranunculus trichophyllus	0.3–1.8	126	0	0	0	0	328,000
Ceratophyllum demersum	0.3–6.0	1	19	5	157	36	476,000
Myriophyllum exalbescens	0.3–5.8	2	35	1	225	44	659,000
Utricularia vulgaris var. *americana*	0.4–0.8	—	—	—	—	—	—
Vallisneria americana	0.6–5.3	419	730	878	1191	503	7,213,000
Elodea canadensis	0.3–1.2	0	1	0	0	(1)	<4,000
Potamogeton pectinatus[b]	0.3–4.5	305	158	103	63	25	1,380,000
P. crispus	—	—	—	—	—	—	—
P. zosteriformis	0.3–5.7	0	0	2	21	80	288,000
P. foliosus	—	—	—	—	—	—	—
P. amplifolius	0.9–3.8	50	0	171	830	683	4,171,000
P. nodosus	—	—	—	—	—	—	—
P. illinoensis[c]	0.3–5.1	1	69	0	0	0	88,000
P. alpinus	2.0–3.0	—	—	—	—	—	—
P. praelongus[d]	—	—	—	—	—	—	—
P. richardsonii	0.3–3.7	265	158	170	142	40	1,572,000
Zannichellia palustris	—	—	—	—	—	—	—
Najas flexilis	0.4–5.3	93	57	25	13	2	395,000
Heteranthera dubia	—	31	8	54	17	<1	201,000
Lemna trisulca	0.3–1.7	4	0	0	21	0	56,000

471

TABLE 73 (Continued)

	Presence (+) or absence (−) ~1940 (Andrews)	Relative frequency in different communities,[e] 1966 (Lind and Cottam)						Rank order of abundance		
		Sv	FIL	ShS	V	MV	M	1912[f]	~1920	1966
Chara spp.[a]	+	Not indicated						(6)	6	15
Ranunculus trichophyllus	+	—	0.4	14.1	2.7	—	0.3	(13.5)	9	5
Ceratophyllum demersum	+	—	26.2	8.9	15.5	8.7	14.0	(7)	7	3
Myriophyllum exalbescens	+	36.3	7.8	24.5	1.7	48.0	81.9	(8)	5	1
Utricularia vulgaris var. americana	−	—	—	—	—	—	—	—	—	—
Vallisneria americana	+	18.4	0.1	37.4	74.6	38.1	0.7	1	1	2
Elodea canadensis	+	—	3.1	3.2	—	—	—	(13.5)	14	10
Potamogeton pectinatus[b]	+	—	<0.1	2.3	0.3	0.8	0.6	5	4	7
P. crispus	+	—	—	—	—	—	—	—	—	14
P. zosteriformis	+	—	0.2	4.0	0.3	—	—	4	10	11
P. foliosus	−	—	—	0.2	1.0	—	—	—	—	9
P. amplifolius	+	—	—	—	—	—	—	(9)	2	—

P. nodosus	+	—	—	—	—	4.5	—	—	8
P. illinoensis[c]	+	—	—	—	—	—	(10)	12	—
P. alpinus	−	—	—	—	—	—	(11)	—	—
P. praelongus[d]	+	—	—	—	1.7	—	3	3	4
P. richardsonii	+	2.1	2.7	0.9	—	0.1	3	—	13
Zannichellia palustris	+	—	—	0.4	—	—	2	8	12
Najas flexilis	+	—	—	0.7	—	—	—	—	—
Heteranthera dubia	+	1.7	1.6	3.3	0.7	0.5	11	11	6
Lemma trisulca	?	—	—	—	—	—	(12)	13	—

[a] Given as *Chara crispa* by Rickett.

[b] Includes some *P. filiformis* (sub *interior*).

[c] Includes in Rickett's sample a little *alpinus*.

[d] Recorded by Lind and Cottam as having occurred in 1906.

[e] Sv, *Scirpus validus* community (*S. validus* relative frequency 53.8%); FIL, Floating-leaved community (*Nymphaea tuberosa* relative frequency 45.3%); ShS, shallow-water submersed community; V, *Vallisneria americana* community; M, *Myriophyllum exalbescens* community; MV, *Myriophyllum exalbescens–Vallisneria americana* community.

[f] Numbers in parentheses refer to rank order estimates made from Denniston's table of distributions, assuming an abundant species twice as common as a common species, which is taken as twice as common as one present in small numbers. Other modes of treatment would give roughly the same order; the figures not in parentheses are those given by Denniston for the five commonest species.

473

TABLE 74. *Optical properties and depth of vegetation in Green Lake and Lake Mendota at the times of Rickett's studies*

	Depth (m)	
Optical property	Green Lake	Lake Mendota
Range Secchi disk transparency	2.75–6.25	1.73–3.80
Mean Secchi disk transparency	~4.25	~2.25
Mean depth of 1 % of surface illumination (mean sun, from Birge and Juday 1929)	9.3	4.4
Maximum depth of macroscopic plants	10	6

In small lakes with a very gently sloping margin, a littoral flora composed mainly of *Glossostigma elatinoides* (Scrophulariaceae), *Myriophyllum elatinoides*, *Lilaeopsis novae-zealandiae*, and *Pilularia novae-zealandiae* grows on firm soil, while on softer finer sediment *Glossostigma submersum*, *Tillaea sinclairii*, *Montia fontana*, *Utricularia monanthos*, *Callitriche petriei*, *Myriophyllum propinquum*, *Elatine gratioloides*, *Eleocharis pusilla*, and *Juncus pusillus* occur. All these marginal plants may grow underwater but some, such as *Utricularia monanthos* and *Liliaeopsis novae-zealandiae*, do not flower when submersed.

The characteristic eulittoral psammobiont members of the Centrolepidaceae in New Zealand and Tasmania have already been mentioned (see p. 113), as has the occurrence of two sympatric species of *Isoetes* in Lake Taupo (Allan 1961).

The great ease with which exotic species become established and produce enormous noxious populations in New Zealand (see p. 250) may in part be due to the impoverished nature of the native aquatic flora.

Lakes of tropical latitudes. There is fairly good information on the vegetation of a few of the lakes of Central Africa and of Indonesia and studies are beginning to be made by Indian limnologists on the lakes of that country. In the New World by far the most important investigation is of the lakes of the Titicaca Basin, which though it lies within the tropics is primarily of interest on account of its altitude.

Lake Bunyonyi. The most completely described (Denny 1972a, b, c) lacustrine vegetation in Africa is that of Lake Bunyonyi, a fairly large lake of area about 60 km², lying at an altitude of 1950 m, and formed by the volcanic damming of a deep branching valley about 18,000 years ago (cf. Vol. I, p. 41). The lake has a complicated form with many small inlets. It is meromictic with a chemocline lying rather above 15 m; the thermal and chemical structure of the lake above this depth varies seasonally and the water is sometimes deficient in oxygen up to 7 m.

There are two distinct plant communities. On the steep exposed shores there is a zone of firmly rooted *Phragmites australis* which can extend outward into water 4.2 m deep. On its landward side there is typically a zone of *Cyperus papyrus* 1–4 m wide. This is absent behind the *Phragmites* of Habukara Island, a small island near the middle of the lake, made the subject of detailed study, probably as a result of artificial disturbance by people formerly living on the island. Rhizomes of *Typha latifolia* occur among the *Phragmites* and there may also be isolated patches of *Typha* between the reeds and the papyrus, or along the shore where the last-named plant is absent. As elsewhere, *T. latifolia* rarely occurs at the lakeward edge of the zone of emergent plants. Floating rafts of *Cladium jamaicense* occur lakeward of the *Phragmites* or may to some extent be incorporated into the *Phragmites* zone. Along parts of the shore there is a narrow zone of floating-leaved vegetation, composed of *Nymphaea caerulea* and *Potamogeton* × *bunyonyiensis* (see pp. 242–244).

The detailed study of Habukara Island (Fig. 139) indicates that the floating-leaved plants occur mainly in less than 2 m of water along those stretches of shore where *Phragmites* does not extend into deep water. *Nymphaea lotus* was also found contributing to the floating-leaved association around the island, in more exposed places than are occupied by *N. caerulea*. It does not occur elsewhere in the lake, or for that matter in other localities at comparable altitudes in southwestern Uganda; it may well owe its presence around Habukara Island to human introduction.

The fully submersed vegetation of the lake consists mainly of *Chara* sp., *Potamogeton pectinatus*, *P. schweinfurthii*, *Hydrilla verticillata*, and *Ceratophyllum demersum*. The mean distribution of these plants around Habakura Island, calculated as percentage frequency of occurrence at a given depth (Fig. 140) revealed an average zonation obscured by the patchiness of the vegetation when only a small part of the coast is examined.

Denny believes that light is the most important factor in producing the observed distribution. Experiments indicated that in the laboratory *P.* × *bunyonyiensis* required brighter light than *P. schweinfurthii*, an irradiance of 2.24 cal cm^{-2} hr^{-1} being optimal for the former but supraoptimal and inhibitory for the latter species. There appeared to be no correlation between the occurrence of any plants in the lake and any property of the sediment except its carbon content. Pure *Ceratophyllum* stands tend to lie over sediment of high (10.4–20.9%) carbon content whereas floating-leaved plants grew in sediment containing less than 3.2% carbon. This correlation is probably not causal but due to depth and

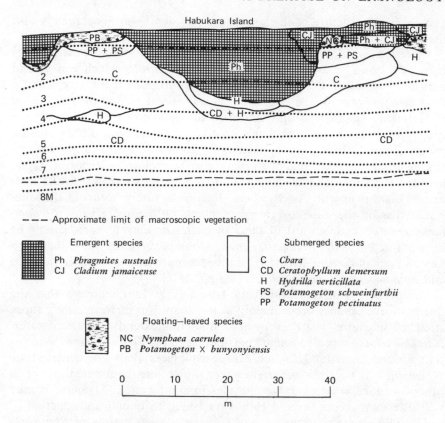

FIGURE 139. Part of southern shore of Habukara Island, Lake Bunyonyi, showing irregular disposition of vegetation (Denny).

water movements affecting both plants and sediments. The distribution of *Chara* when compared with that of *Ceratophyllum demersum*, *Hydrilla verticillata*, and *Potamogeton pectinatus* suggests that these three flowering plants are suppressed competitively by the *Chara* in the zone between 2 and 3 m.

In general, *Phragmites australis* is, of all the emergent species in the lake, the one able to withstand most disturbance. Along the most exposed shores it is the only plant, other than fully submersed species, to be found. It always remains anchored to the bottom by its rhizomes ramifying in the sediment, and may be so rooted in a depth of 4.2 m of water. This is considerably deeper than is usual in Europe (see p. 411, however), where is some places, such as the Danube Delta, massive floating rafts are formed. A single small patch of *Phragmites mauritianus*, described as more robust

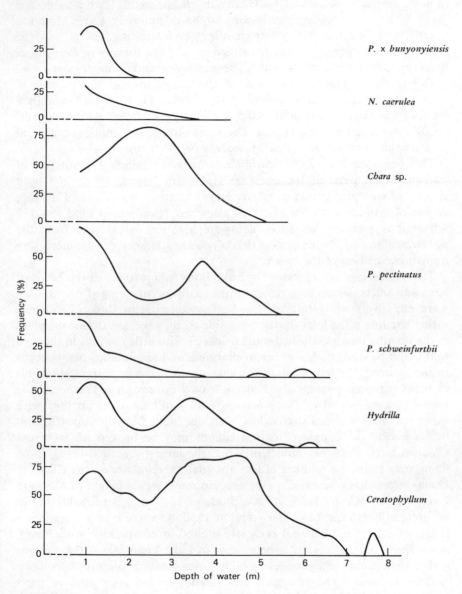

P. x *bunyonyiensis*

N. caerulea

Chara sp.

P. pectinatus

P. schweinfurthii

Hydrilla

Ceratophyllum

Depth of water (m)

Frequency (%)

FIGURE 140. Mean distribution of plants around Habukara Island (Denny).

than *P. australis*, was noted by Denny in an apparently rather protected place in an inlet; the species is said to be common in Lake Mutanda nearby, and its competitive relations might be interesting.

In the less disturbed parts of the shoreline of Lake Bunyonyi, *Phragmites* is presumably in competition with *Cyperus papyrus* and *Cladium jamaicense*.

Denny thinks that a good deal of the irregularity of the pattern of colonization in the shallow waters of the lake is due to chance establishment of vegetative propagules. After a plant is established its fate is ordinarily determined by competition. This seems likely, but implies occasional catastrophic removal of plants by storms or other disturbances.

The occurrence of *Typha latifolia*, which is abundant landward of *Phragmites* on parts of the coast of Habukara Island, which had been cleared of emergent plants in relatively recent times, may suggest a slight degree of artificial eutrophication, as elsewhere (Beadle and Lind 1960) in Africa it is a species of eutrophic swamps. There is evidence from the pollen profile of Lake Bunyonyi that *Typha* has increased with increasing human occupation of the basin.

The second type of vegetation in Lake Bunyonyi is found at the heads of bays and inlets, where papyrus swamp usually occurs fringed on its lakeward edge by floating rafts of *Cladium jamaicense*. In Bugoroba Bay, a rather shallow silted inlet on the west side of the lake, the dominant plant in the floating mat was the last-named species with little papyrus in the area that could be studied. A number of marginal and amphibious plants occur in the swamps, the fern *Thelypteris squamigera* being important. In pools in these marginal swamps the floating-leaved *Potamogeton thunbergii*, the floating-leaved parent of *P.* × *bunyonyiensis*, still survives; analogy with other localities suggests that it has been displaced from the open littoral by its hybrid descendant. Floating islands may be broken off from the *Cladium* rafts, and when sufficiently big, the largest recorded being 75 × 65 m, may support a number of less abundant species among the *Cladium*. Denny notes that whereas *Cyperus papyrus* may reach a height of 4–5 m in Lake Victoria (Carter 1955) at an altitude of 1240 m, it is probably not in an optimal habitat in Lake Bunyonyi at 1950 m, where it rarely reaches a height of 3.5 m, and where it is clearly limited by competition with *Phragmites* and *Cladium*. It is noteworthy that in Lake Victoria it is *Cy. papyrus* rather than *Cladium jamaicense* which forms floating islands.

Lake Victoria. The emergent and floating-leaved vegetation of parts of the shores of Lake Victoria have been well described by Eggerling (1935) and by Carter (1955). Both authors were mainly interested in papyrus or comparable swamps and the completely submersed flora is far less well known.

Where the slope of the basin is very gentle, as is usual around Lake Victoria, the prevalent terrestrial grassland gradually passes into a grass swamp, which is eulittoral, being dry except during the rainy season. Within this there is a papyrus swamp, ordinarily dominated by *Cyperus papyrus* with the grasses *Miscanthidium violaceum* and less commonly *Panicum chionachne*, and the fern *Dryopteris striata*. Eggerling also records among frequent species *Cissampelos mucronata* (Menispermaceae) and *Dissotis rotundifolia* (Melastomaceae). In shallow water the papyrus tends to disappear leaving a *Miscanthidium* swamp, developed particularly on local shallow areas. There is also a deeper water variant, the *Limnophyton* swamp, in which *Limnophyton obtusifolia* (Alismataceae) is an important subdominant. The papyrus, except in very shallow water, has a layer of interwoven roots forming a mat which lies well above the bottom, covered with 15–30 cm of water. The plant grows in clumps set up to 1 m apart and may reach a height of 5 m. The differentiation of the papyrus swamp into variants, such as that in which *Limnophyton* is subdominant, is passed over by Carter. Lakeward of the papyrus zone there may be a narrow fern and sedge zone, up to about 20 m across, in which the fern *Dryopteris striata*, several sedges (*Cyperus haspan, Fimbistylis subaphyllus, Fuirena pubescens, F. umbellata*) and the grass *Leersia hexandra* occur. This fern and sedge zone may capture detached pieces of papyrus drifting in the lake, producing a secondary narrow *Cyperus* zone on the lakeward side of the fern and sedge. Still further from land there is often a prominent zone of ephydates, mainly *Nymphaea* cf. *heudolotii, N. lotus, Nymphoides nilotica*, and *Trapa bispinosa* var. *africana*, with *Ottelia ulvifolia* and *Eleocharis* sp. *Ceratophyllum demersum* and *Utricularia thonningii* may occur in this zone and doubtless in deeper water also. The entirely submersed vegetation is not fully described but certainly includes *Potamogeton schweinfurthii* in water up to 6 m deep (Spence 1967b). The available accounts do not make quite clear the relationship of the fern and sedge zone to the bottom, and whether it is founded on a floating mat of roots, as is the more lakeward part of the papyrus zone.

Tanganyika. Van Meel (1952) gives a general account of the vegetation of the basin, but few details regarding submerged plants. Though the vegetation below water is said not to be greatly developed, along the extensive sandy section of the shoreline, where the sand continues into the sublittoral, there may be considerable beds of water plants, the most important species being *Potamogeton*, probably *pectinatus*[5] (sub *filiformis*), *Najas horrida, Vallisneria* sp., and *Chara zeylandica*. The last-named is recorded at least to 6 m (Wood 1955).

---

[5] Dandy records only *P. pectinatus* and *P. schweinfurthii* from the lake and indicates that the older African records of *filiformis* refer to the former species. No critical account of the genus from the Belgian studies has yet been published.

The lakes of Indonesia. Ruttner (in van Steenis and Ruttner 1933), in the course of his work on the German Limnological Expedition of 1928–1929, made a number of observations on the macrophytic vegetation of lakes in Java, Sumatra, and Bali. The flora of the deeper water usually includes *Hydrilla verticillata*, which occurred in 9 out of 12 lakes studied, generally as a dominant and was the most widespread aquatic angiosperm encountered. It reached a depth of 8 m in Lake Singkarak in Central Sumatra and to rather less great depths in others of the more transparent lakes of the region. It is associated with *Najas falciculata* in four lakes, with *Potamogeton malayanus* in three and with *Potamogeton pectinatus* and *Ceratophyllum demersum* in two lakes. The most extensive submersed flora occurs in Lake Toba, the largest lake in these Indonesian islands. Angiosperms are, however, recorded only to 5 m, where *Hydrilla verticillata*, *Potamogeton malayanus*, *P. maackianus*, *Najas falciculata*, and *Myriophyllum spicatus* may all be found. Ruttner believed, because at least *H. verticillata* occurs in greater depths in rather less transparent lakes, that the deepest occurrences of angiosperms in Lake Toba remain to be discovered. Off the western shore, near Samosir, opposite a solfatara field, *Blyxa oryzetorum* occurred fully submersed in 1.5 m of water.

The marginal vegetation is very diverse. On flat sandy shores it consists of sparse *Panicum repens* with *Nymphoides cristata*. A submersed sterile and so underterminable species of *Eleocaris* is also characteristic. In contrast to this, there is on less exposed parts of the shore a floating bog composed of tussocks of considerable complexity (*Vaccinium littoreum*, *Ficus diversifolia*, *Ilex cymosa*, and a number of species of Rubiaceae) with large swamp ferns (*Nephrolepis biserrata*, *N. radicans*, *Pleopeltis longissima*, and *Stenochlaena palustris*) and several species of *Nepenthes*. Lakeward this gives place to an association of *Pistia stratiotes* and *Dryopteris gongyloides* with *Polygonum barbatum*.

In Lake Singkarak, another quite large lake in Central Sumatra, *Hydrilla verticillata* occurred to 8 m; *Potamogeton malayanus* grew in less deep water, while in quite shallow areas, from 0.5 to 1.0 m deep, there was a reduced form of this species, clearly influenced by mechanical disturbance, and only 20 cm tall compared with the 3-m long shoots in rather deeper water. The shallow-water form of *P. malayanus* was associated with a reduced form of *Eleocharis acicularis*, 3–5 cm high. A single record of *Najas falciculata* may be based on a specimen washed into the lake. Marginally, in quiet bays, *Nymphoides indica* forms beautiful patches with large floating leaves and white flowers. Locally there is marginal swamp vegetation of *Cyperus* sp., *Limnocharis flava*, *Panicum repens*, and *Polygonum barbatum* growing in up to 40 cm and *Eleocharis dulcis* in up to 70 cm of water. *Ipomoea aquatica* sprawls over the water surface, and at the margin were found the large grasses *Themeda gigantea* and *Saccharum spontaneum.*

Danau di Atas, a small lake in the same general region, with quite dilute water though an alkaline pH, had as its main submersed plant *Potamogeton polygonifolius;* shoots of *Hydrilla* were found floating at the surface. Between 1.0 and 1.5 m there are beds of *Nitella.* Marginally there is a quaking bog of *Sphagnum* with tussocks of *Rhynchospora glauca* and *Eleocharis tetraquetra,* various ferns, and a variety of flowering plants of which many are not really aquatic.

A fourth Sumatran lake, Lake Ranau, had an association of *Potamogeton pectinatus* and *Hydrilla verticillata,* well developed in from 1 to 7 m of water, with *Ceratophyllum demersum* and *Najas falciculata* cast up on the beach. Along parts of the sandy shore of the lake isolated specimens of the trees *Gossampinus valetonii* (Bombacaceae) and *Hibiscus tiliaceus* (Malvaceae) grow in places where waves may break over the bases of the trunks and branches dip into the water.

Ranu Lamongan in East Java had *Hydrilla verticillata* and *Ceratophyllum demersum* to a depth of 5 m, with *Eichhornia crassipes, Spirodela polyrhiza,* and *Azolla pinnata,* with here and there *Colocasia esculenta. Ipomoea aquatica* grows out over the water twining among the most superficial plants of *Hydrilla.* The marginal vegetation also included *Phragmites karka,* the fern *Stenochlaena palustris,* and to a more limited extent *Typha domingensis,* the grass *Eriochloa subglabra, Polygonum barbatum,* and *Jussiaea repens.* The trees *Nauclea orientalis* of Rubiaceae and *Barringtonia racemosa* of the Lecythidaceae characteristically grow among the marginal *Eichhornia* rooted in sediment under water. In places a reduced more or less terrestrial form of *E. crassipes* rooted in marginal mud was found.

Ranu Klindungan had in a shallow bay a fine stand of *Nelumbo nucifera,* the only occurrence noted by Ruttner. The same lake had in other places marginal vegetation of *Eichhornia crassipes, Azolla pinnata, Spirodela polyrhiza, Limnocharis flava, Ipomoea aquatica, Colocasia esculenta,* and *Monochoria hastata.* The submersed flora was dominated by *Najas falciculata* with a little *Hydrilla verticillata.*

The slightly saline (NaCl 0.35%) Danau Batur in a large caldera in Bali had an entirely different flora from that of the other lakes. The dominant submersed flowering plant was *Najas marina* var. *zollingeri,* recorded some years before from the same lake and apparently an endemic variety. *Potamogeton pectinatus,* with much *Chara* sp. and *Enteromorpha* sp., also occurred. *Scirpus littoralis* grew locally at the margin.

Ruttner examined a few other lakes botanically, finding *Hydrilla verticillata* or *Nitella* as the main submersed plant when such were present. On the whole the rather restricted hyphydate flora compared with the diversified marginal bog vegetation is striking. Ruttner's Indonesian observations, together with those of Carter in Central Africa, suggest that rather complicated marginal quaking bogs, often without *Sphagnum*, are likely to be characteristic of many tropical lakes.

Doodhadhari Lake, a small eutrophic lake in India. Some observations have been made in India by Sankaran Unni (1971a, b, 1972), who studied Doodhadhari Lake, Raipur, Madhya Pradesh, a small partly artificial lake which varies in area from about 0.210 km^2 in July after the beginning of the seasonal rains to 0.207 km^2 in May before the rains begin. The maximum depth is given as just over 5.25 m, but the water level varies by 1.4 m during the annual seasonal cycle; a good deal of the bottom is exposed before rains begin in June. The water is quite hard with a bicarbonate alkalinity of 110–200 ppm, and a pH range from 7.5 to 9.6 or very occasionally as high as 10.0. The surface temperature varies from 16.0 to 35.0°C.

When the water level starts rising in June, *Cyperus alopecuroides* and *Echinochloa cruspavonis* develop along the very shallow eastern margin of the lake, with local patches of *Oryza rufipogon*, *Eleocharis plantaginea*, and the pleustonic *Eichhornia crassipes*. In water not more than 2 m deep *Nymphaea cyanea* comes up, and beyond it *Nelumbo nucifera* appears and may occupy the whole of the deeper part of the basin. Patches of *Trapa bispinosa* slowly develop in water 1–2.5 m deep. *Najas minor*, *Chara corallina*, and *Ceratophyllum demersum* are found wherever the emergent or floating-leaved plants are sparse enough to permit adequate light to penetrate into the water.

Late in the rainy season a number of species of shallow water and swamp plants appear in the very shallow water of the eastern side of the lake. *Oryza rufipogon* dies down and its place is taken by *Limnophyton obtusifolium;* a floating mat of *Azolla pinnata*, *Spirodela polyrhiza*, and *Pistia stratiotes* may form between the petioles of the emergent sagittate *Limnophyton* leaves.

Nymphaea cyanea plants degenerate after flowering and fruiting at the end of the rainy season and are partly replaced by *Nymphoides cristata*. In deeper water *Nymphoides indica* likewise appears as the leaves of *Nelumbo* and *Trapa* fall off, apparently as a result of decreasing temperature. The reduction in the emergent and floating vegetation also results in *Eichhornia* being wafted to the north side of the lake where it may form a sudd for 2 or 3 months. Where open water is present *Potamogeton crispus* may form almost unispecific meadows though in places it is associated with *Najas minor*.

These observations suggest that in at least small eutrophic lakes in the tropics there is more replacement of one species by another during the annual seasonal cycle than occurs in temperate latitudes. A greater proportion of the species may be annuals, but aspection is not dependent on this, as when *Nymphoides* occupies in winter the areas that had supported *Nymphaea* or *Nelumbo* after the summer rains.

The marked seasonal variation in water level produces another interesting feature in the cycle of vegetation, for as the water becomes increasingly shallow and dries up over the flat eastern side of the basin the newly exposed mud is colonized by a characteristic eulittoral flora in which the composites *Gnaphalium indicum* and *Sphaeranthus indicus* are important.

Lake Titicaca and other lakes in the High Andes. Lake Titicaca is a very large lake, of area 7600 km² and maximum depth 281 m, lying at a latitude of about 16°S and an altitude of 3815 m (Gilson 1939). On account of its tropical latitude and great altitude the surface temperature is always low and varies little throughout the year. Tutin gives extremes of 10.5–14.8°C with a mean of 12.9°C for the winter months from May to September and 11.7–15.0°C with a mean of 13.3°C during the summer from January to March. The winds are mainly local, blowing off the lake during the day and off the land by night; at least during the winter they average 14.4 km hr⁻¹. In summer the region is evidently windier, and at all times occasional storms from outside the basin of the lake may produce persistent strong winds of constant direction. It seems, however, that no one part of the shore line is regularly up- or downwind, and that such sheltered reaches of littoral that the lake affords are due entirely to physiographic features. Waves about 1 m high are commonly observed near the moderately exposed shores and higher waves must sometimes occur.

The open water of the lake is quite transparent; working in two bays, Tutin found that 2% of the surface illumination, which would be greater than at sea level, might reach from 8.5 to 14.5 m. In most cases at the stations where these observations were made, there is evidence of quite low transparency in the top 1 m. This may, at least in part, be attributed to the stirring up of the finest particles of the littoral silt by breaking waves with subsequent transfer of the suspended material causing turbidity, by wind-generated currents. When the wind is strong, transparency above the infralittoral zone, where the plants live, is greatly reduced.

The higher flora of Lake Titicaca is limited to eight species of flowering plants: *Myriophyllum elatinoides, Lilaeopsis* sp., *Elodea potamogeton, Potamogeton strictus, Ruppia filifolia, R. spiralis, Zannichellia palustris,* and *Scirpus tatora.* There are also three species of *Chara* of importance, namely, *Chara* cf. *nitelloides* (*Ch. vulgaris* cf. var. *nitelloides;* sub *denudata*), *Ch. globularis* (sub *fragilis*), and *Ch. andina* (*Ch. vulgaris* var. *vulgaris* f. *andina;* sub *papillosa*).[6] In the deeper water a moss, *Hygrohypnum* sp.

---

[6] I am much indebted to Dr. R. D. Wood for the probable correct names of the taxa of *Chara* recorded by Allen (1939) and discussed by Tutin.

(sub *Sciaromium* sp.), is important.[7] *Ruppia spiralis* has only once been recorded in the lake and the endemic *R. filifolia* is an ecologically insignificant plant.

It will be noted that only one species contributes to the emergent vegetation, the rush *Scirpus tatora*. It grows in quite shallow but well protected parts of the shoreline, at the heads of bays, or behind spits partially enclosing such bays. There is no floating-leaved vegetation.

In the shallowest water on a moderately exposed shore, *Zannichellia* forms a more or less open turf, with occasional patches of *Lilaeopsis*. The bottom here consisted of a clayey sand. Tutin found that in the winter this community was being eroded away as the lake level fell. *Zannichellia* was fruiting abundantly and Tutin notes that the seeds germinated readily. *Lilaeopsis*, of a possible new species near *L. andina*, flowered and formed fruits underwater, but also produced small tubers, which may remain buried if the plant is torn up by the waves. Redevelopment of the flora when the water level rises in the summer is doubtless from the seed of both species, from the tubers of *Lilaeopsis* and perhaps from broken fragments of the rhizomes of *Zannichellia*. At about 30 cm *Zannichellia* may give place abruptly to *Potamogeton strictus* which increases in abundance to a maximum on soft mud at 60 cm, but is present throughout the upper infralittoral to just over 11 m in some places. Both *Z. palustris* and *P. strictus* are narrow-leaved pliable rhizomatous plants well adapted to withstand water movements. Tutin regards the whole vegetation of the shallower water, whichever may be dominant, as part of a *Zannichellia–Potamogeton* association, in spite of the zonal arrangement of the two plants and of the fact that in the deeper *Myriophyllum–Elodea* association, *Potamogeton strictus* may be locally dominant.

Below 0.7 m in the quietest, or below 2.0 m in the more exposed places, *Zannichellia* becomes rare, and *Myriophyllum elatinoides* and *Elodea potamogeton* occur with *P. strictus*. The latter, as just indicated, reaches in some places to a depth a little over 11 m, which appears to be the greatest authentic depth for an angiosperm in fresh water. The probability that this depth range is determined by the low atmospheric pressure on the lake surface has already been mentioned (see p. 423). The Characeae in general occur from the lower part of the *Myriophyllum–Elodea* zone to about 14 m,

---

[7] Professor P. W. Richards tells me that he has reinvestigated the moss, which appears to be new; a description will appear shortly. Since the investigation by Tutin (1940), St. John (1964) has described as new and possibly endemic *Elodea titicacana* from the lake, in which he also records *E. potamogeton*. The ecological relationship of the two species remains unelucidated.

while the moss *Hygrohypnum* is found from 14 to 29 m. In the small basin joined to Titicaca, the Lago Pequeño, there is more *Chara* growing in shallow water than in the main lake. Tutin attributes this to the presence of a leached organic sediment, probably low in nutrients.

In the neighboring Lagunilla Lagunilla, the zonation is not unlike that in Titicaca but is vertically restricted, *P. strictus* reaching only to about 4 m and *Chara* to about 8.5 m. *Isoetes lechleri* occurs in shallow water, but *Hygrohypnum* is absent from the depths. In Lagunilla Saraconcha, the vegetation is like that of Lagunilla Lagunilla, but no angiosperms occur below 3.5 m. There seems to be an unvestigated zone from 3.5 to 6.5 m, below which *Chara* cf. *nitelloides* is found down to 16 m, and below it *Ch. andina* to 18 m, while *Hygrohypnum* grows from 18 to 29 m. The meaning of this zonation is far from clear, particularly as the two taxa of *Chara* occur mixed up together in shallow water in Lago Pequeño.

Growth forms and depth distribution. Spence (1964) in a study of the depth distributions of plants in the Scottish lochs, has examined the vertical frequency of different growth forms (Fig. 141), classified by him as *emergent* including both the graminid (B.I.a) and herbaceous (B.I.b) types, *rosette* roughly equivalent in Scotland to the isoetids (B.IV.b.3), *floating-leaved* (B.III), *broad-leaved submersed*, essentially magnopotamids (B.IV.a.1), and *narrow-leaved submersed* (B.IV.a.2 and 3) including both parvopotamids and myriophyllids. The emergent and floating-leaved forms naturally tend to occur in shallower waters than do the others. Both narrow- and broad-leaved vittate plants are commonest in the deeper waters; there is a slight tendency for this to be more accentuated in the broad-leaved species, but from the wide occurrence of *Ceratophyllum demersum*, *Potamogeton berchtoldii*, and *Nitella* spp. as the deepest recorded species elsewhere, this tendency may be purely local. The most interesting feature of the distribution is the rather uniform occurrence of the rosulate or isoetid form independent of depth. This suggests that the form is not primarily an adaptation to disturbance but rather to the oligotrophic nature of the waters in which such plants are commonest, with dependence on the sediments rather than the water as a source of nutrients.

Relationship of size of individuals to density of populations. In Lake Tałtowisko, Bernatowicz and Pieczyńska (1965) found a clear negative relationship between the weight of the stem of *Phragmites australis* and the density of the population (Fig. 142). The relationship seems closer to a simple inverse dependence than one in which the two-thirds power of the weight is inversely proportional to the density, as may occur in experimental populations of plants grown from seed (Yoda, Kira, Ogawa, and Hozumi 1963; White and Harper 1970).

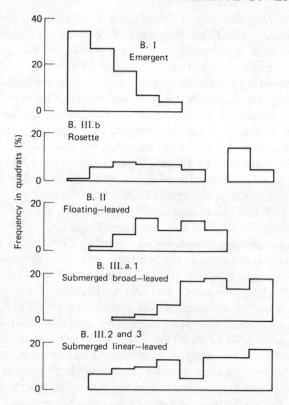

FIGURE 141. Distribution of growth forms with depth in Scottish Lochs (Spence). The categories are those of Spence, with an indication of the equivalent classes of Table 7.

In *Myriophyllum exalbescens* in University Bay, Lake Mendota, Lind and Cottam (1969) found that populations living between 2.0 and 2.5 m were about half as dense (73 stems m^{-2}) as one growing at around 1 m (143 stems m^{-2}), but the average weight of the plant at the time of its maximum development was about twice as great in the deeper water ($\sim$1.85 g compared with $\sim$0.85 g). The plants in the dense shallow-water stand may be limited in their growth by reaching the surface, beyond which the shoot extends but a short distance.

PHYTOSOCIOLOGY

The associations of plants in lakes, as elsewhere, have been classified according to the methods of the various schools of plant sociology. These classifications do permit the characterization of certain complex entities

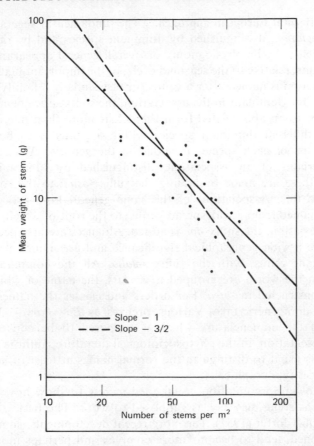

FIGURE 142.   Relationship of size and density of *Phragmites* plants.

that can be recognized as occurring over and over again in different localities or regions. This recognition is often useful, though if a scheme is
developed whereby what may be continuous variation in floristic composition is apparently broken down into discontinuous categories, the classification becomes not only artificial, but definitely deceptive. In the limnological literature two main classificatory and terminological procedures
have been adopted. The first is the European or more strictly the Zurich–
Montpellier approach associated with Braun-Blanquet, and used for
aquatic communities extensively by Koch (1926, 1928), Sauer (1937),
Oberdorfer (1957), and Krausch (1964). The second is the North American
approach associated with Clements (1916) and adopted by Pearsall (1918b)
in the English Lakes and, in a more modern form, in an important study of
the Scottish lochs by Spence (1964).

The continental European approach.   The fundamental vegetational unit is the *association*, distinguished by dominant species and by rarer species of high fidelity, by its physiognomy or overall general appearance, and by the life-forms, relative to the seasonal cycle, of the important plants present. The association is named after a genus (or occasionally a family), a species of which is the dominant in the association, the suffix -*etum* being added to the stem or to an abbreviated form thereof. If more than one association based on different dominant species within a genus is to be used, the specific name of each species is added in the genitive. Where there are several variants of an association, distinguished by subdominants, the names of these are made by adding the suffix -*osum* to the root; not all authors do this. Associations of the same general kind are grouped in *alliances*, named from a widespread-genus, to the root of which, sometimes after abbreviation, the suffix -*ion* is added. Alliances are grouped in *orders*, which have a wide geographical significance and are named usually from an important genus, with the suffix -*elalia*. All the comparable orders throughout the world are grouped in a *class*, the name of which is comparably constructed in -*etea*. For orders and classes the names are often based on suprageneric taxa. Various prefixes as *Eu-*, *Parvo-*, *Magno-* are allowed in the nomenclature which is supposed to be conservative; in formal presentation, in the phytosociological literature, authors' names are added. It is usual to distinguish the formal names at least of associations and alliances typographically.

The following presentation is intended merely to show how the system works or, as some may say, is supposed to work. The basic source used has been Oberdorfer (1957). The more recent developments, some of which are mentioned, tend to become more complex and perhaps more fluid; in this art clearly imitates nature. As Corillion (1957), thinking mainly of the Charophyceae, writes "L'association végétale est une de ces notions qui divisent encore les botanistes. Les uns en nient formellement l'existence, les autres lui donnent une caractère trop mathématique et trop doctinal qui ne parait guère conforme à la souplesse des phénomènes qui régissent le vivant." The reader is invited to pick some *via media* as he peruses the next few pages.

Algetea.   The associations of littoral algae have not often been included in the formal presentation of the vegetation of a lake. Sauer considers, in the single alliance *Algion*, the following formal associations of macroscopic filamentous algae in the lakes of north Germany, going from the deepest water (6–15 m) to the shallowest: *Aegagropiletum holsaticae*, *Cladophoretum fractae*, *C. glomeratae*, *Ulothricetum zonatae*. The dominant of the first association is referred by Kann (1940, 1958) to *Cladophora aegagropila*, but she does not recognize the distinctness of *C. fracta*, so we are left with two *Cladophoreta* and an *Ulothricetum*. The biology of these associations is discussed in the next chapter.

Charetea. The phytosociological classification of the fields of Charophyceae often encountered in lakes has undergone progressive elaboration. The *Characetum* of the older workers, such as Schröter and Kirschner (1902), is divided by Sauer (1937), working in northern Germany, into a *Magnocharacetum*, growing in the deeper waters, down to 9 m (formerly 30 m in some lakes), consisting of *Nitella flexilis, Chara intermedia*, and *Nitellopsis obtusa*, and a *Parvocharacetum* in 0–6 m of water consisting of *Chara aspera, Ch. vulgaris, Ch. globularis, Nitella opaca*, and other less important species.

Krausch (1964) recognizes a more complicated pattern. In the shallowest localities, usually under 1.3 m in depth, he found in the Stechlin See and other lakes near to it, a *Charetum asperae* consisting of pure associations of *Ch. aspera* on a sandy bottom, where reeds are absent. From 1.20 to about 5.0 m, there might be a *Charetum filiformis* with *Ch. filiformis, Ch. intermedia* (sub *Chara aculeolata* subsp. *papillosa*), often with *Ch. aspera* and other less important species. Subassociations with *Potamogeton pectinatus* or in deeper water *Nitellopsis obtusa* can be recognized. Usually in deep water and presumably corresponding to Sauer's *Magnocharacetum*, there is a *Nitellopsidetum obtusae*, usually rooted on fine calcareous sediment in 4–10 m of water. Below it on deep black mud there is a *Nitello–Vaucherietum dichotomae* in which *Nitella flexilis, Vaucheria dichotoma*, and specimens referred to *Ch. globularis* f. *hedwigii* may co-occur. Where the fine sediment is thin, owing to the slope of the bottom or to water movements, the Charophyceae tend to be replaced by the mosses, *Platyhypnidium rusciforme* or *Fontinalis antipyretica*. Though there is not much overlap in the occurrence of these two mosses, Krausch speaks of a subassociation of *P. rusciforme*. It is probable that the overall size difference between Sauer's *Parvocharacetum* and *Magnocharacetum* is due to the elongation of plants growing at low light intensity.

A still more elaborate treatment has been published by Krause (1969) partly following a less formal presentation by Corillion (1957), but also influenced by Krausch. Two orders are recognized, forming a Class Charetea and distinguished according to the dominance of Nitellaea or Charaea. There is obviously justification for this in the different chemical ecologies of the two tribes. Krause's categories within the Charetea are as follows:

Nitelletalia, characteristically in more dilute water
   Nitellion flexilis, in strongly acid waters, characterized by *N. flexilis, N. gracilis, N. translucens*, and *N. capitata*

Nitelletum flexilis, in soft-water mountain lakes with *Isoetes*

Nitelletum translucentis, in western European coastal regions, sometimes forming a *Magnonitelletum* in deep water (Corillion, 1957) often associated with *Hypericum elodes* (Krause, 1969)

Nitellion syncarpae-tenuissimae in less acidic waters with the following species being characteristic: *N. confervacea, N. tenuissima, N. opaca, N. hyalina, N. syncarpa, N. mucronata*, and *Chara fragifera*

Krause recognizes:

Nitelletum syncarpae-tenuissimae

Nitello–Vaucherietum dichotomae

but from Corillion's observations it is probable that several other associations might be recognized.

Charetalia, characteristic of hard waters

Charion asperae, with the following species characterizing various associations: *Ch. aspera, Ch. contraria, Ch. aculeolata, Ch. vulgaris, Ch. hispida, Ch. strigosa, Nitellopsis obtusa, Tolipella* spp. The associations are grouped under three variants of the alliance

Perennial and not reducing (*Eu–Charion asperae*)

Charetum asperae litorale; shallow disturbed water

Charetum hispidae, a *Magnocharetum* in deep water

Charetum tomentosae, as the last but in more eutrophic water

Nitellopsidetum obtusae, a *Magnocharetum* in deep water

Charetum filiformis, Baltic region

Charetum strigosae, oligotrophic mountain lakes in contact with *Potamogeton filiformis*

Perennial with strongly reducing mud (*Rhodo–Charion asperae*)

Rhodo–Charetum asperae, clear calcareous water over reducing muds; *Lamprocystis rosea* present

Rhodo–Charetum canescentis, in brackish water, *Vaucheria thuretii* present

Very temporary but not reducing (*Thero–Charion asperae*)

Several associations of no limnological significance

Charion canescentis, in brackish waters, with the following species characterizing the various associations: *Ch. canescens, Ch. connivens, Ch. horrida, Ch. galioides, Ch. baltica, Tolypella nidifica, Lamprothamnium* spp.

Charetum canescentis; shallow water over sandy sediments, grading into *Charetum asperae*

Charetum horridae-balticae, deeper and on mud

Chareto–Tolypelletum nidificae, deeper water with marine algae

Krause's classification takes more account of environmental factors than is usual in this kind of work; it also gets away from the distinction between the *Magnocharetum* and *Parvocharetum* which can be composed of identical species (see Fig. 11).

Potametea. The assemblage of submersed phanerogams, many with floating leaves. Two orders, the Potametalia in fresh water and the Zosteretalia in salt are recognized. The Potametalia is divided into two alliances, the *Eu–Potamion* of submersed and usually rooted plants, which in lakes occupy the lower infralittoral, and the *Nymphaeion* of floating-leaved species, which in lakes is best developed in the shallower water of the middle infralittoral (Oberdorfer 1957).

The *Eu–Potametum* appears to consist of at least the following associations.

The *Potametum lucentis* is an important association in fairly eutrophic European lakes, notable those north of Berlin described by Krausch (1964). In it *P. lucens* is ordinarily the most important species, though *P. perfoliatus* may be even more abundant, producing Koch's (1926) *Potametum perfoliati potametosum lucentis*. In Krausch's localities variants with Charophyceae may occur, usually in the more oligotrophic basins. In shallow water (0.8–1.5 m) *P. lucens* may be associated with *Chara virgata* and *Sagittaria sagittifolia* f. *vallisnerifolia*, while in deeper water *Ch. globularis* and *Nitellopsis obtusa* may accompany *P. lucens*. In such deep waters in north Germany *Stratiotes aloides* f. *submersa* may occur or a subassociation with *Myriophyllum alterniflorum* may develop.

The *Potametum perfoliati–Ranunculetum circinati* is recognized by Sauer as a lacustrine equivalent of Koch's *Potametum perfoliati–Ranunculetum fluitantis* in running water. He notes three subassociations, the *Potametum perfoliati potametosum lucentis*, which can have *P. lucens* as dominant and would be regarded as the *Potametum lucentis* by Oberdorfer, the *P. perfoliati potametosum praelongi*, and the *P. perfoliati potametosum mucronati* with *P. friesii* (sub *mucronatus*) dominant, apparently primarily in moderately deep (2.5 m in Kleiner Plöner See) and sheltered parts of the littoral. All these variant associations seem to occur in moderately deep (1.5–4.5 m) water.

The *Potametum crispi* var. *gemnifer-obtusifolii* is a deep -water association described by Sauer (1937) from some of the lakes of Baltic Germany, reaching to 6 m, or in a fragmentary form in the Krummensee, to 8 m. *P. crispus* var. *gemnifer* is ordinarily accompanied by *P. obtusifolius* var. *latifolius* and by *Fontinalis antipyretica* var. *latifolia*.

The *Potametum pusillo-graminei*[8] is a narrow-leaved association recorded by Koch (1926) and Oberdorfer (1957) from 0.4 to 0.7 m in Lake Constance

---

[8] Oberdorfer still uses *P. panormitanus* for what is now called *P. pusillus;* if the association name is to follow strict priority this would produce a most confusing situation, so that informally and without nomenclatural status, the above substitution has been made.

between Konstanz and Mainau, and undoubtedly widely distributed. It was found in a fragmentary form by Sauer (1937) in some north German lakes in shallow water on organic sediment. In Switzerland *P. pectinatus* and *Ch. aspera* are associated; if the bottom becomes sandy *Ch. aspera* tends to displace the species of *Potamogeton*, while with an increase in organic mud the association tends towards the *Parvopotamo–Zannichellietum*. In the north German localities *Sparganium minimum* and *Nymphaea alba* var. *minor* may be present.

The *Potametum filiformis*, in which *P. filiformis* is associated with *P. praelongus* and *P. alpinus*, with other less abundant species of the genus, is characteristic of alpine lakes in Switzerland. Krausch finds the same sort of association involving *P. filiformis* and *Chara rudis*. The occurrences are in line with the tendency of *P. filiformis* to grow in hard waters poor in phosphorus, as is suggested by the autecological data (see p. 397).

The *Potametum* × *nitentis* described by Koch (1926) and by Oberdorfer (1957) from sandy bottoms in moving water or near the shore in Lake Constance has as its dominant the hybrid *P. gramineus* × *P. perfoliatus*, usually associated with *G. densa* and *Zannichellia palustris*.

The *Parvopotameto–Zannichellietum* is an association of narrow-leaved *Potamogeton* spp., *Najas* spp., and *Zannichellia palustris*, with some Charophyceae. In the more eutrophic waters *Zanichellia* is important, but in mesotrophic localities it may be largely displaced by *Najas* giving a *Parvopotamogeto–Zannichellietum najadetosum*. The association as described by Koch, Sauer, and Oberdorfer appears to be characteristic of quite shallow water. It seems probable that these associations in the Eu-Potamion do not really do justice to the submersed phanerogamic vegetation of the lakes of central Europe.

The *Nymphaeion* consists of the associations in which at least some of the plants are floating-leaved, and includes the following:

The *Myriophyllo–Nupharetum* with *Nuphar lutea*, *Nymphaea alba*, *Potamogeton natans*, *Polygonum amphibium*, the temporarily neustonic *Stratiotes aloides* occurs in some localities, with the rooted *Myriophyllum verticillatum* and *M. spicatum*. No doubt this is the most widespread association of the upper infralittoral, but variable and perhaps not really a single entity.

A *Potamogo–Nupharetum* with *Nuphar lutea* and *Potamogeton natans* accompanied by *Utricularia vulgaris* is recognized by Krausch (1964) in the lake of northern Germany.

A *Sphagno–Nupharetum* with *Nuphar luteum*, *Sphagnum cuspidatum*, and various other mosses, liverworts, and algae is reported rarely in bog lakes in montane and northern Germany.

A *Nupharetum pumilae* with *N. pumila* and *N.* × *spennerana* (sub. *intermedium*) is noted by Oberdorfer from the margins of some of the lakes of the Black Forest, such as the Schluchsee and Titisee. The associated plants are angiosperms and not particularly acidophilic.

A *Nymphaeëtum minoris* in which *N. alba* var. *minor*[9] with *P. natans* locally are dominant, is known from upper Bavaria (Oberdorfer 1957). These less widespread associations characterized by water lilies are of some limnological importance in relation to Pearsall's observations, as will appear below (see p. 500).

The *Callitricho–Ranunculetum*, the *Sparganio–Ranunculetum*, and the *Potamogeto–Ranunculetum*, in which *Ranunculus fluitans* as a dominant or important subdominant is associated with *Callitriche hamulata*, *Sparganium simplex*, or *Potamogeton* spp., are considered by Oberdorfer (1957) but are mainly of significance in running water, though comparable associations with limnophile species of *Ranunculus* may well occur.

A *Hottonietum palustris* with *Callitriche platycarpa* is known in meso-trophic waters on very peaty sediments in Germany.

A *Trapo–Nymphoidetum* with *Trapa natans*, *Nymphoides*, *Ceratophyllum* spp., and various pleustonic plants, occurs in the Rhine Valley. It is com-parable to a *Nymphoido–Potametum pectinati* known from France, and similar associations certainly occur in the Mediterranean area and eastward into Asia.

A *Hydrocharitetum morsus-ranae* with *Stratiotes*, Lemnaceae, and in some cases *Potamogeton natans* and *Utricularia vulgaris*, is recorded by Krausch (1964) in very sheltered places in the Mehlitz See, Roofen See, and Kleiner Stechlin See. A comparable association is known in the Rhine Valley.

Lemnetea. The class contains a single order, the Lemnetalia, and alliance, the *Lemnion*, and consists of the pleustonic associations of fresh water.

Oberdorfer (1957) gives but two associations: the first is the *Wolffio–Lemnetum gibbae* or *Lemno–Spirodeletum* of somewhat varying composition, with a variant, the *Lemno–Spirodeletum salvinietosum* where *Salvinia* is significantly present; in somewhat more southern localities a corresponding *Lemno–Azolletum* may occur. The second is the *Lemnetum minoris* of wide distribution. Müller and Görs (1960) recognize eight associations, which include the larger pleuston of the *Hydrocharitetum morsus-ranae;* Krausch (1967) regards the *Lemnion minoris* as an alliance containing, in northern Germany, only Oberdorfer's two associations and the *Hydrocharitetum*.

---

[9] For the problematic taxonomic status of this plant see footnote p. 143.

More recently Hejny (1968) has grouped the associations of the *Lemnion* in the following way.

On oligotrophic and mesotrophic waters, as small patches among reeds
  Riccietum fluitantis
  Lemno–Utricularietum
  Spirodelo–Aldrovandetum
On mesotrophic and eutrophic waters, over large areas
  Lemnetum gibbae
  Salvinio–Spirodeletum polyrhizae
  Lemnetum minoris
On waters subject to human disturbance
  Wolffietum arrhizae
  Lemno–Azolletum
  Lemnetum paucicostatae

Insofar as this classification combines phytosociology with the nutrients of chemical ecology it is clearly the most satisfactory treatment of the alliance.

Phragmitetea.   This class of marginal emergent vegetation supposedly in most cases results from the successional replacement of the Potametea. A single order, the Phragmitalia and three alliances are recognized by Oberdorfer (1957); the first alliance, however, is very heterogeneous.

The *Phragmition* is regarded as consisting of four or five associations. The first of these, the *Scirpo–Phragmitetum*, is of great importance as the most characteristic vegetation of the upper infralittoral, forming the marginal reed beds of innumerable lakes. Along with *Phragmites australis*, *Schoenoplectus lacustris*, and *Typha* spp., some other reeds and a certain number of herbaceous plants are present. As has been indicated there are great differences in the proportion of the dominants, producing the *Scirpo–Phragmitetum scirposum, phragmitosum,* or *typhosum.*

The *Glycerietum maximae* is a rather feebly differentiated association characterized by the occurrence of *Glyceria maxima* as a codominant, usually in periodic shallow water over nutrient-rich calcareous mud.

The *Oenantho–Rorippetum* in still more astatic localities has *Rorippa nasturtium-aquaticum* and *Oenanthe aquatica* as dominants; *Phragmites australis* is normally present. Other associations of little limnological importance are the *Phalaridetum arundinis* and the seldom developed *Sparganio–Sagittarietum.*

The *Sparganio–Glycerion* contains mainly rheophile associations, namely, the *Glycerietum plicatae* (Oberdorfer 1957), with *Sparganium neglectum* and various herbaceous species, the *Sparganio–Glycerietum fluitantis* in less eutrophic and more acidic streams, and the *Helosciadetum* characterized by *Apium* (= *Helosciadium*) *nodiflorum*.

The third alliance, namely, the *Magnocaricion*, contains a number of associations of sedges, namely, the *Mariscetum*, often with *Phragmites australis* and *Scirpus tabernaemontani*, the *Caricetum elatae*, the *Caricetum appropinquatae*, the *Caricetum paniculatae*, the *Caricetum inflato-vesicariae*, the *Caricetum gracilis*, the *Caricetum vulpinae*, and the *Caricetum buxbaumii* or *Buxbaumietum*. In general these are not associations of permanent water, but may occur in the eulittoral of lakes.

Littorelletea. This is an alternative eulittoral and upper infralittoral class of vegetation, found usually in successional stages in less eutrophic waters. There is a single order, the Liltorellalia, and two alliances.

The *Litorellion* contains the following associations.

The *Littorello–Eleocharitetum* with *Eleocharis acicularis*, *Littorella uniflora*, and a moderate number of less frequent species. It is found on sandy sediment in the lower eulittoral of Lake Constance where it is submerged for a large part of the year.

The *Deschampsietum rhenanae*, in which *Deschampsia rhenana* is important, is a similar association found in the upper eulittoral of Lake Constance.

The *Isoetetum* or *Isoeto–Lobelietum* with *I. lacustris* as well as other species which have been regarded as characteristic in northern Europe usually contains *Lobelia dortmanna*, *Subularia aquatica*, and often some *Littorella uniflora*. It is normally infralittoral.

The *Ranunculo–Juncetum* with *Ranunculus flammula* and *Juncus bulbosus* may be a eulittoral association where, as in the larger lakes of the Black Forest, there is an upper infralittoral *Isoetetum*.

The *Sparganetum minimi* with *Sparganium minimum*, *Utricularia intermedia*, and *Juncus bulbosus* is found on mesotrophic basic or moderately acidic peaty sediments, mainly of ponds.

The *Callitro–Sparganetum* with several species of *Sparganium*, *Callitriche verna*, *Myriophyllum alterniflorum*, and a few other species occur on moderately acidic or neutral oligotrophic peaty sediments mostly in sheltered parts of lacustrine basins in the mountains of central Europe.

The *Sphagno–Utricularietum* with *Sphagnum cuspidatum* and other species of moss, *Utricularia ochroleuca* with *Rhynchospora alba*, and *Menyanthes trifolia* occur rarely in acidic temporary waters.

The second alliance, the *Helodo–Sparganion*, contains an important association, the *Eleocharitetum multicaulis*.

Extra-European associations. Few workers have attempted to use the system outside Europe. In an account of the vegetation of the Parc National

Albert in the former Belgian Congo, Lebrun (1947) has given some attention to water plants.

For the floating-leaved but not pleustonic plants he distinguishes two associations. The *Nymphaeëtum afro-orientale* is characterized by *Nymphaea calliantha* and *M. mildbraedii*, with *Ceratophyllum demersum* and *Potamogeton pectinatus*. It is recorded from protected inlets along the coasts of Lake Kirwa and also of Lake Kivu. The second floating-leaved association is the *Nymphaeëtum loti*, characterized by *N. lotus* found extensively in fluviatile backwaters in the forested region of the Congo Basin; it does not seem to be lacustrine.

Lebrun also distinguishes a pleustonic *Lemneto–Pistietum* in shallow and often astatic bodies of water in the northern part of the Rwindi-Rutshuru Plain, characterized by *Pistia stratiotes*, *Lemna paucicostata*, and at times *Jussiaea repens*.

The same author regards the emergent junciform vegetation of Africa as constituting a phytosociological order Papyretalia, with two alliances, the *Papyrion* corresponding to the *Phragmition* of Europe, and the *Magnocyperion africanum* the local representative of the *Magnocyperion* of Old World temperate latitudes. The associations of the *Magnocyperion africanum* are ordinarily found on land that is temporarily flooded during the wet season.

The *Papyrion* apparently contains the following associations.

The *Papyretum* not present in the area studied.

The *Phragmitetum afro-lacustre* with *Phragmites mauritianus*, *Aeschynomene elaphroxylon*, *Sporobolus* cf. *robustus*, and *Ipomoea lilacina* as characteristic species. It is well developed in quiet inlets of Lake Edward and, as a floristically less rich variant, in Lake Kivu.

The *Paniceto–Cyperetum flabelliformis*, with *Cyperus flabelliformis* and *Panicum trichocladum* or *Paspalidium geminatum* in water up to 120 cm deep but apparently not truly lacustrine.

The *Cypereto–Plucheëtum*, characterized by *Cyperus laevigatus* and *Pluchea bequaerti* in very shallow temporary waters at most a few centimeters deep, again mainly on the flood plains of rivers. *Typha angustifolia* subsp. *australis* may be present, becoming dominant where there is perennial water.

It is not clear whether all these associations belong to the *Papyrion* or whether some fall within the *Magnocyperion africanum*. The associations of the latter, such as the *Cyperto–Asteracanthetum* with *Cyperus articulatis*, *C. haspan*, *C. alopecuroides*, and *Asteracantha longifolia*, appear to characterize temporarily inundated localities. Some of the associations of both alliances, characteristic of fluviatile floodplains, may well occur in the eulittoral of lakes.

The Clements-Pearsall approach. The detailed use of the continental system has not appealed to English-speaking ecologists, and the most eminent student of the synecology of lacustrine plants, namely, Pearsall (1917, 1918a, 1918b, 1920) has based his approach and terminology on that of Clements (1916.).

All the plant communities of a lake are regarded as serial stages of a hydrarch succession, progressing landward from the vegetation of the deepest part of the euphotic zone through the various infralittoral, eulittoral, and fully terrestrial communities until the local climax is reached. Zonation, therefore, is taken to be the spatial equivalent of succession in time, even in the absence of any direct evidence of change.

Certain more recent studies have cast some doubt on this point of view. Tutin (1941) believes that erosion and deposition can be balanced in such a way that succession does not occur even when zonation is developed, as in Lake Titicaca. Spence (1964, 1967a) finds, in a number of Scottish lochs, that old photographs taken early in the present century at the time of the Bathymetric Survey of the Scottish Lochs, show the same vegetational features, in the same positions relative to conservative landmarks, as appear today (Fig. 143). Detectable changes occur only where streams, carrying sediment, enter the lake. Some discretion is therefore needed in any consideration of lacustrine succession. A few striking cases of vegetational change, notably a great extension of the *Phragmitetum* in the Neusiedlersee (Löffler 1974) in the past century, are indeed recorded.

However, if we merely consider zonation, it is obvious that vegetation, whatever it does in time, changes greatly with depth. For any given species it will often be found that there are fairly sharp boundaries to its distribution, probably as the result of environmentally controlled changes in competitive capacity along a gradient, as Gause and Witte (1936) pointed out more than a third of a century ago. If the species is a dominant, its appearance or disappearance may cause a complete change in the physiognomy of the vegetation, such as the incidence along a transect of a sharply defined zone of floating-leaved vegetation dominated by *Nuphar*, or of reed swamp dominated by *Schoenoplectus lacustris*. The whole sequence in space, whether or not it represents also a sequence in time, can reasonably be thought of as a unit, though not one of a particularly simple kind.

Clements was so impressed by the supposed successional significance of such a unit, that he employed different terms for the communities making up the seral stages from those making up the climax. Each of the former was an *associes*, each of the latter an *association*. Pearsall adopted this terminology, but since to him all aquatic communities were seral, only the associes occurred in limnology. Tansley (1949) in his later work regarded

FIGURE 143.   Loch Tarff, Inverness, Scotland. (A) About 1904 or 1905 (West); (B) in 1960 (Spence) to show negligible change in the nature of the littoral.

the main lacustrine communities as sufficiently stable to regard lake vegetation as made up of associations. The associes of Pearsall is moreover usually equivalent to the association of the continental limnological phytosociologists such as Koch (1926), Sauer (1937), Oberdorfer (1957), and Krausch (1964).

To Clements and to Pearsall, if within an associes more than one domi-nant is present, variants in which one or the other dominant takes over while the others are rare or absent are termed *consocies*. Thus the usual kind of reed swamp of a temperate mesotrophic or eutrophic lake, the *Scirpo–Phragmitetum*, to Pearsall could consist of consocies of *Typha latofolia*, *Schoenoplectus lacustris*, or *Phragmites australis*, corresponding to the *Scirpo–Phragmitetum typhosum*, *scirposum*, or *phragmitosum* of European workers.

Deep-water communities in the English Lakes. Pearsall's deepest community of flowering plants could be properly described, in the modern equivalent of the terminology that he adopts, as the *Potamogeton berchtoldii* subsp. *lacustris* associes; *Myriophyllum spicatum* and *Nitella opaca* are frequent, *Nitella flexilis*, *Isoetes lacustris*, *Potamogeton praelongus*, and *P. perfoliatus* are locally present, and *Elodea canadensis* is locally abundant. The associes grows in deep water on fine inorganic sediment.

In Estwaite Water there was a modification of this associes, producing what Pearsall calls the linear-leaved associes; it may intergrade with a *Najas flexilis* consocies. Characteristically the linear-leaved associes has *P. berchtoldii* var. *tenuissima* or subsp. *lacustris*, or *Najas flexilis* as dominant, with *Callitriche hermaphroditica*, *Elodea canadensis*, and *E. nuttallii* (sub *Hydrilla verticillata*) frequent or locally abundant. It occurs in very fine clayey bluish silt in 1.5–2.6 m water where the light penetration is reduced in this lake to 6–3 % of the surface flux. The organic content of the substrate under typical stands is 12–15%; where it falls below 10% *Najas flexilis* tends to displace the other common members of the associes. In slightly more illuminated waters on slightly more organic mud the linear-leaved associes is replaced in Esthwaite by that of *P. obtusifolius;* a comparable but fragmentary community is known from Windermere. The commoner associated plants are *Callitriche hermaphroditica*, *Sparganium minimum*, and *Elodea canadensis; P. pusillus* and *P. berchtoldii* subsp. *lacustris* are rare. The associes seemed to be spreading in Esthwaite. Though the various species making up these three communities are nearly all common in western Europe, the arrangement of these species in associations seems inconstant. Comparison of the linear-leaved or the *P. berchtoldii* subsp. *lacustris* associes with either the *Parvopotametum* or the *Potameton pusillo-graminei* does not suggest that Pearsall's deep-water communities can be assimilated to such continental associations, which occur in very shallow parts of a lake. Moreover Spence (1964) found in Scottish lochs that the deep-water species of *Potamogeton* were usually broad-leaved.

Pearsall also recognized in moderately deep water of the less oligotrophic or more evolved lakes, other than Esthwaite, several other consocies in which *Potamogeton* spp. are dominant. Of these presumably the *P. prae-longus* associes, following that of *P. berchtoldii* subsp. *lacustris* as shallower, more illuminated water over less fine silt is approached, corresponds in a general way with Sauer's *Potametum perfoliati–Ranunculetum circinalis* when it occurs in fairly deep water and lacks *Ranunculus circinatus*. The same sort of community appears to be typical of fairly deep water in Scotland (Spence 1964).

Pearsall also recognized a *P. alpinus* consocies, said to occur where silt is abundant but of high organic content. Since this sort of sediment is rare, the consocies is local and poorly developed, though recorded from Windermere, Esthwaite Water, and Derwentwater, on long-colonized sediments among abundant vegetation.

In all of Pearsall's consocies so far mentioned, each of the species dominant in one consocies, along with *Elodea canadensis* and *Nitella opaca*, can be present in any other.

Shallow-water and floating-leaved communities in the English Lakes. A *Myriophyllum* consocies, with *M. spicatum* the usual dominant, tends to displace the various *Potamogeton* associes when the organic content of the sediment rises much above 20%, though with very high organic contents *Juncus bulbosus* f. *fluitans* replaces *Myriophyllum*. All these communities are regarded by Pearsall as possible shallow-water successional stages following the occupation of eroded or at least unoccupied coastal bottom by the pioneer communities of *Littorella uniflora* or *Lobelia dortmanna*.

The floating-leaved communities studied by Pearsall were the *Potamogeton natans*, *Nuphar lutea*, *Nymphaea alba*, and *N. "minor"* consocies. The first three would be regarded as variants of the *Myriophyllo–Nupharetum* of Europe, the fourth perhaps the equivalent of the *Nymphaeëtum minoris* described by Oberdorfer (1957).

The other shallow-water associations described by Pearsall are clearly comparable to what have been described in Europe. His *Littorella–Lobelia* associes (Tansley 1939) is clearly the equivalent of the *Isoetetum* in at least some of its variants. The marginal reed swamps as have already been indicated are equivalent to variants of the *Scirpo–Phragmitetum* except in sheltered bays where there is little silting and organic sediment; here an obvious equivalent of the *Caricetum inflato-vesicariae* is found.

On the whole the marginal hyperhydate and ephydate communities are clearly equivalent in the English lakes and in continental Europe. The differences in the submersed vegetation are almost certainly far more apparent than real. Where the plants are plainly visible to the eye above water, vegetational studies have until recently obviously been much easier than underwater. The apparent differences probably mainly indicate that the phytosociological approach to the deeper-water communities, insofar as it is valid, is still not adequately developed.

The communities of the Scottish Lochs. Spence (1964) uses an approach comparable to that of Pearsall, but employing a slightly different nomenclature. His basic unit is the *sociation*, which corresponds loosely to the associes of Pearsall, and as a "plant community of definite floristic composition" to the association of Braun-Blanquet (1932). When a sociation is unspecific it becomes a society. Several sociations, distinguished by being composed of plants of comparable life-forms and growth forms and sharing some frequent species, may be grouped together to form an association. Apart from his use of different terminations in successional and climax stages, Clements used association essentially in this way; it is roughly the equivalent of *alliance* in the nomenclature of those more recent European workers who tend to split categories.

Spence found in the Scottish lochs distributions comparable to those of the English Lake District or some of the lakes of Scandinavia already discussed. The Scottish lochs, however, show greater variation than do the more limited array of English localities.

An *Eleocharis palustris–Littorella uniflora* sociation, in which *Juncus fluitans* occurs in the more oligotrophic waters, is characteristic of the more exposed sandy shores. In some localities *Eleocharis* is the only hyperhydate on such lake margins; in others it may be more or less completely replaced by *Equisetum fluviatile*, in extreme cases forming an *E. fluviatile* sociation. The last-named species may occur in deeper water than *Eleocharis*, where its occurrence is apparently negatively related to that of *Schoenoplectus lacustris*, which probably favors more organic sediments than *E. fluviatile*. A *Schoenoplectus lacustris* sociation in which *Juncus fluitans* is constantly present develops in shallow waters usually under 1 m and always over 30 cm deep. *Utricularia vulgaris* may cover sediment between the reeds.

On less exposed and less sandy shores, there may be sociations or societies of *Phragmites australis*, or of *Cladium mariscus* growing partly rooted below and partly above the mean water level. *Typha*, as elsewhere, occurs locally. A fairly complex eulittoral and supralittoral flora is developed landward of these hyperhydates.

Where a floating-leaved zone is developed, several sociations may occur. In oligotrophic water the *Nymphaea alba* var. *minor* (sub *occidentalis*) sociation occurs in quite shallow waters; 10 species, one of which is always *Juncus fluitans*, are recorded in this community. Elsewhere *N. alba* var. *alba* grows in deeper more mesotrophic or eutrophic water with fewer co-occurring species. *Nuphar lutea* may occur in deeper water than *N. alba*, but it is generally rarer in Scotland than the white species; *Nuphar pumila* occurs, but is rare. A *Potamogeton natans* sociation with *J. fluitans* and *Sparganium* spp. is found on sandier bottoms than those supporting the Nymphaeacea.

In the more exposed shores of the softer-water lakes (HCO_3^- 0–116 mg liter^{-1}) a *Juncus fluitans–Lobelia dortmanna* association composed of various sociations involving these two species and *Littorella uniflora*,

Utricularia vulgaris, and *Sphagnum subsecundum* var. *auriculatum*, occurs from the waterline to 170 cm. The *Juncus fluitans–Sphagnum subsecundum* sociation is found only at low alkalinities (<30.5 mg HCO_3^- liter^{-1}) and at pH values 6.6–6.8. In more alkaline water (43–192 mg HCO_3^- liter^{-1}) comparable shores are occupied by the *Potamogeton filiformis-Chara aspera* association, with three sociations, the *P. filiformis–Chara aspera* or *Littorella uniflora–P. filiformis* sociations in shallow water, less than 70–107 cm deep, and the *Chara aspera–Myriophyllum alterniflorum* sociation in deeper water to 250 cm or more. In deep water on mud various sociations of *Potamogeton* spp. occur. These are evidently comparable with those of Pearsall. *P. gramineus* may form localized pure stands or societies. All species appear to be found on mud. The local incidence of *Potamogeton* × *zizii* in any lake in which it occurs, seems to be in places not favored by *P. gramineus* or by *P. lucens;* all three taxa probably have their own definite niches (see pp. 243, 244).

In the deepest colonized water there is usually a unispecific society of either *Nitella* spp., *Fontinalis antipyretica*, *Isoetes lacustris*, or *Elodea canadensis;* West (1905, 1910) had earlier found that whereas *F. fontinalis* may go to 12.2 m in the Scottish lochs, no tracheophytes live below 6.1 m.

The difficulties of the phytosociological approach. There can be little doubt, as a number of plant ecologists now realize, that the difficulties with any phytosociological approach lie in attempting to define communities along a gradient on which individual species are distributed to a greater or lesser extent independently of each other (cf. Whittaker 1967). Swindale and Curtis (1957) have attempted to use a rather elaborate quantitative method originally put forward by Guinodet (1955) to examine the problem of continuity or discreteness in the structure of aquatic communities. Their primary data consist of quadrat studies in very shallow water in a large number of lakes in Wisconsin. Forty-one uniform community samples were selected for analysis.

The plants were ordered in the following way. Species that never occurred together were placed at either end of a list, species that most often co-occurred in the middle. The list was then divided into four sections of six to eight species of plants. All plants in section one were given a rating 1, in section two a rating 2, etc. In any given community the relative frequency of each species was multiplied by this rating and the results summed. This gives for communities mainly containing species in the first group, a *community index* of about 100, and for communities mainly containing species in the fourth group an index of about 400. The product of frequency and rating, for each species, as a fraction of the community index, is now plotted against the latter. If there were really associations having discrete and discontinuous limits, the resulting species graphs should be grouped

(Fig. 144). If the probability distributions form a continuum without discontinuous changes in occurrence of groups of species, then a more or less random distribution is to be expected and is indeed apparently obtained. Though the procedure seems somewhat inelegant, it is probably a fairly good way of achieving an ordination of the species; there can be little doubt from the final result that the communities that might be recognized are essentially artifacts. Moreover such work on physiological tolerances as exists strongly suggests that the rosulate community of *Lobelia* and *Isoetes*, which generally seems one of the most obvious limnetic associations, clearly consists of plants that co-occur in a particular set of habitats

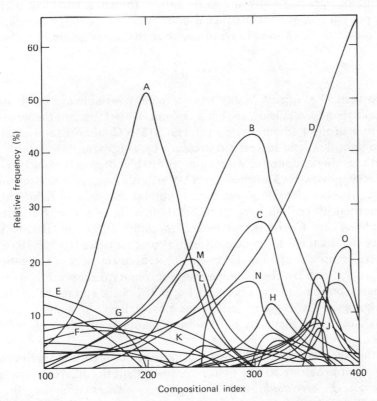

FIGURE 144. Relative frequency of taxa plotted against compositional index of shallow-water lacustrine floras in Wisconsin according to the procedure of Swindale and Curtis, suggesting a lack of rigorously defined associations. Taxa: 1. *Isoetes* spp., 2. *Najas flexilis*, 3. *Vallisneria americana*, 4. *Chara* spp., 5. *Elatina minima*, 6. *Potamogeton epihydrus*. 7. *Myriophyllum tenellum*, 8. *Heteranthera dubia*, 9. *P. illinoensis*, 10. *P. zosteriformis*, 11. *Juncus pelocarpus* f. *submersus*. 12. *Eleocharis acicularis*, 13. *P. gramineus*, 14. *Elodea* spp., 15. *M. exalbescens*.

for quite different reasons (p. 279) and which are therefore likely not to be as strictly associated as would at first sight seem likely. However, it must be realized that in the large series of lakes studied by Swindale and Curtis, the gradient, from oligotrophic *Isoetes–Lobelia* lakes to eutrophic *Potamogeton* lakes, is made up of a set of comparable vegetation stands in separate lakes. If the same method had been applied to the vegetational zonation from marginal hyperhydates to deep-water mosses of a single lake on a transect at right angles to the shore, from the top of the eulittoral to the bottom of the infralittoral, it is possible that more evidence of discontinuities and of real grouping might be obtained. The work, however, does strongly suggest that the phytosociological approach must be used in limnology pragmatically and with caution, though it is evident that such an approach can at least produce a convenient terminology, which, however, must not be allowed to tyrannize over the investigation of nature.

SUMMARY

The vertical gradients in any environmental variable are much steeper in a lake than on a hillside, so that a descent of 10–15 m into the water may lead to a drop of summer temperatures to 5–6°C, almost total extinction of the light flux, and increase in pressure by 1–1.5 atm.

With a single doubtful exception, probably due to technical errors, no tracheophytes are known below 11.5 m; only one species, *Potamogeton strictus*, reaches a depth of just over 11 m and that only in Lake Titicaca. The normal lower limit appears to be about 9 m, or possibly a little less. Bryophytes and Charophyceae extend in sufficiently clear lakes to much greater depths than do tracheophytes, in extreme cases to over 100 m.

There is no doubt that the lower limit of macroscopic vegetation of some sort is set by the illumination, the plants disappearing when the irradiance on the bottom is between 1 and 2% of the surface value. In very clear lakes the plants going deepest are mosses, liverworts, and Characeae; in less clear lakes they may be flowering plants or members of the genus *Isoetes*.

Within the range in which angiosperms may occur certain species clearly more often penetrate to low light intensities than do others. *Potamogeton praelongus*, *P. berchtoldii*, and *Ceratophyllum demersum*, among the very widely distributed species, are apt to extend to depths where the illumination is no more than 2% of its value at the surface, and *P. obtusifolius* may go almost as deep. This last species, which has been the subject of detailed experimental work, owes some of its efficiency in deep water to its low respiratory rate, so that net photosynthesis differs less from gross than would be the case in plants such as *P. polygonifolius* living habitually near the surface.

Aquatic angiosperms are apparently unable to grow normally when under pressures of 2 atm, corresponding to 1 atm of air at sea level and the pressure of 10 m of water. Some inhibition may occur at total pressures of 1.5 atm, corresponding to 5 m of water, in certain species. It is noteworthy that the deepest well-established occurrence of an angiosperm is in Lake Titicaca at an altitude of 3815 m. In this lake the pressure at 11.2 m where *P. strictus* is disappearing would correspond to that at 7.5 m at sea level.

In shallow water the occurrence of plants is obviously related to water movements and the possibility of buffeting by winds and waves. The herbid hyperhydates either occur in very sheltered places, such as protected covers and in the lee of tall rushes, or may be found at the heads of very wide and extremely shallow bays in which incoming waves are likely to break and become translatory, thus losing energy very quickly.

The margins of lakes have been classified in Poland as litholittoral or rocky, psammolittoral or sandy, and phytolittoral or with much vegetation. These terms may obviously be usefully employed in other regions.

The graminid hyperhydates, the various reeds, rushes, and sedges which may fringe a lake, are most likely to occur on the sheltered side of a lake upwind. This is very conspicuous in western Europe where the southwestern shores are conspicuously more vegetated than the northeastern. Characteristically in temperate regions *Phragmites australis* grows marginally, with *Schoenoplectus* or *Scirpus* in the water of the lakeward side of the reed bed. The terete leafless stems of these plants are no doubt adapted most perfectly to withstand wind and waves. *Typha* requires a more protected habitat and is usually present quite locally along the shore. The surface of the water in a reed bed, if it is not too dense, provides an optimal habitat for small pleustophytes or lemnids.

Lakeward of the reed bed or other marginal vegetation, the floating-leaved vegetation shows evidence of zonation depending on resistance to disturbance. *Nymphaea* often occurs landward of the stronger *Nuphar*, and there is a suggestion that the hybrid *Nuphar* × *spennerana* is more resistant than its parents. *Potamogeton natans*, with smaller more ovoid leaves than in the water lilies, seems still more able to withstand disturbance.

Along any exposed coast there is apt to be a zone of erosion, in mature lakes primarily determined by ice, then a neutral zone, and lakeward a zone of sedimentation. The plants of the erosional and neutral zones are usually small rosulate species such as *Isoetes setacea*, *Subularia aquatica*, *Ranunculus reptans*, and in some lakes *Lobelia dortmanna*. Such plants are particularly characteristic of oligotrophic waters in lakes with exposed shores. It is probable that they are primarily adapted to obtaining a large part of their nutrients from the sediments rather than the water, but they may also be somewhat more resistant to violent water movements than are trailing or vittate plants.

There is clear evidence that in some lakes the distribution of various species of plants depends on the nature of the sediment. This is most clearly seen around islands or off estuaries where the nature of the sediment is locally different from what it would be at the same depth elsewhere in the lake. In such cases the water plants tend to follow the pattern of sedimentation rather than the bathymetry. It does not, however, yet seem possible to categorize species accurately by the physicochemical parameters of the sediments on which they occur. Very organic sediments tend generally to be unfavorable, most of the vittate water plants usually occur in mud or fine silt, and many rosulate species grow on coarse silt or sand.

In the case of *Scirpus validus* there is evidence that the unfavorability of a sediment is due to its reductive capacity, oxygen falling to too low a value in the vicinity of the plants roots.

In many lake districts in the temperate Northern Hemisphere unproductive lakes containing a characteristic vegetation, composed largely of rosulate or isoetid plants, are known. If such lakes are transparent the euphotic zone extends well below the depth range of angiosperms so that the plants found deepest in the lake are usually mosses or species of *Nitella*. The distribution of plants in the shallower water is clearly partly determined by erosion and sedimentation though it is difficult to generalize from lake to lake exactly how any particular species behaves. *Subularia aquatica* appears characteristic of shallow water where some erosion can occur. *Lobelia dortmanna*, *Littorella uniflora*, and *Isoetes lacustris* seem to occur mainly in the neutral zone where erosion is balanced by sedimentation; *Nitella opaca* generally occupies bottom where at least a little fine sediment is deposited. There may be a zone between that occupied by tracheophytes and that occupied by mosses with practically no vegetation. This, in some cases at least, corresponds to the maximum slope of the basin. Where a considerable amount of humic color is present the vegetation may be confined to the top few meters, but mosses often penetrate further than other species, not because the latter are limited by pressure as in the transparent lakes, but because mosses seem to have lower light requirements than the other aquatic macroscopic plants.

In the more evolved basins ordinarily regarded as mesotrophic or eutrophic, vittate species, particularly members of *Potamogeton*, become more and more important. These are accompanied by *Ceratophyllum demersum*, and by species of *Myriophyllum*, *Najas*, and *Vallisneria*.

When marked eutrophication has resulted from pollution by sewage or from runoff from fertilized agricultural land, an increase in phytoplankton leads to a decrease in transparency and consequent compression of the zonation of macroscopic plants. Mosses and perhaps Charophyceae tend to disappear. At least in North America the most eutrophic waters seem often to be colonized by *Myriophyllum exalbescens* or the introduced *M. spicatum*. Other introduced pest species may well depend for their unwelcome abundance on artificial eutrophication.

Where a number of lakes lie on a river system there may be an interesting sequence in the vegetation, from the small lakes near the sources of the various streams that join to form the river, to the large lakes lying in the lower reaches. In Finland this sequence begins with darkly colored or chthoniotrophic waters with a typically rosulate flora and with *Equisetum* marginally, and ends with large lakes containing more vittate species and with reed beds of *Phragmites*. Part of the change is probably due to precipitation of humic matter on sedimenting particles and part to nutrient enrichment downstream.

Emergent vegetation in general shows a dichotomy similar to that exhibited by the hyphydate or submerged flora. The soft-water, unproductive lakes characterized by *Lobelia* and *Isoetes* usually have marginal vegetation with *Equisetum fluviatile*, *Carex* spp., and *Eleocharis palustris*, but in the more evolved and eutrophic lakes large reed beds of *Phragmites australis*, *Schoenoplectus*, *Scirpus*, and *Typha* are developed.

The vegetation of tropical lakes differs from that of temperate ones mainly in the species present, though in small lakes in which there may be considerable changes in water level during the year, it seems that any part of the basin may be occupied by two or more species with different times of maximum development and of flowering, in a way not possible in temperate lakes, the vegetation of which usually dies down in the winter.

In New Zealand, where the native aquatic flora is very restricted, it appears that certain species, notably *Potamogeton cheesemanii* and *Myriophyllum propinquum*, are very plastic and that their ecophenes occupy a number of niches which with a greater flora would probably be filled by different species.

Several systems of nomenclature have been invented to designate the qualitatively different communities of macroscopic plants living in fresh water. In these schemes it is assumed that the co-occurrence of species is not random but depends on the co-occurring species having the same general tolerances. Some degree of discontinuity is ordinarily assumed between the different unitary communities, variously termed associations, associes, or sociations; this is reasonable if one species is a dominant, not only numerically but also functionally, so that conditions are different for all other species if the dominant be present. It is also commonly believed that the spatial relations of plants in a lake can be translated into a temporal succession, because sediment, much of it formed by the plants themselves, piles up so the habitat finally emerges as dry land. The objective evidence for this view, except near inlets where inorganic silting contributes greatly to succession, is negligible.

No system of terminology for plant communities has been universally accepted. The Zurich–Montpellier school of Europe recognizes the association as the smallest unit with a definite floristic composition; this unit takes its name from the genus of the dominant species, as the *Phragmitetum* or association dominated by *Phragmites*. Such associations are arranged in alliances and orders, the latter usually geographically delimited, with all equivalent orders throughout the world forming a class. The American school, whose procedure has been used in aquatic habitats mainly in Britain, recognizes the basic unit variously as a sociation, socies, or society, several of which may form an associes or association. The latter is more inclusive than the continental European association, but rather less so than might first appear. These associations are grouped only as formations or primary vegetation types. Examples of these uses are given in the body of the chapter.

Recent thought, at least in North America, has cast some doubt on the validity of the discontinuity of associations. Studies of a great number of small samples of shallow-water lacustrine vegetation seem to show no association of species, but complete independence of the limits of tolerance. The association therefore is named only because it may be convenient to talk of *Phragmitetum* as a designation of a reed swamp in which *Phragmites* is dominant. Nothing is implied about the limits of distribution of the associated species. It is, however, possible that if sampling had been done with a comparable technique going from the eulittoral lakeward, much more real association of species would have been discovered.

CHAPTER 32

The Algal Benthos

The benthic algal communities, using the term benthic to refer to any organism resting on or moving along the bottom, or growing or burrowing through sediment, are of course in general confined to the euphotic zone. There may, however, be species present in the feebly illuminated transitional littoriprofundal zone that are at least partially heterotrophic. At somewhat greater depths, zooflagellates, not too far removed taxonomically from photosynthetic organisms, may with bacteria and fungi form part of the microbiota of the unilluminated bottom (Koppe 1924).

Though the maximum growth of benthic algae is always somewhere within the littoral zone, the exact position of greatest development will vary with the group considered and the physical nature of the lake shore. Important growth may occur on the surfaces of rocks in very shallow water, where there is too much disturbance and too little fine sediment to permit the establishment of macrophytes. When macrophytes are present, a large number of algae may be epiphytic. In many lakes considerable algal growth occurs at lower light intensities and at higher pressures than are tolerated by angiosperms.

The usual members of the deepest littoriprofundal algal taxocene are blue-green algae, with a few special members of other groups such as the red alga *Hildenbrandia*. There is often some chromatic adaptation, producing pink forms among the deep benthic species of blue-green algae. All the littoriprofundal algae are likely to be associated with large bacteria of little-known properties.

In the opposite direction, algal communities extend far up into the eulittoral, above mean water level, where they may be metabolically active only when temporarily wet. As a special case of a eulittoral plant community, primarily on bare rock, there is an interesting assemblage of eulittoral lichens. These lacustrine lichens seemingly cannot survive permanent immersion, though the rheobiont *Hydrothyria* apparently does so; many, however, spend much more than half their lives underwater, and they certainly must be considered in any comprehensive treatment of limnological botany.

THE NATURE OF THE ALGAL ASSOCIATIONS

It has long been recognized (Schröter and Kirchner 1896; Warming 1923; Hustedt 1922; Hurter 1928) that the nature of the substratum is of importance in determining the composition of the algal association living upon it, though it is probable that in some cases this influence has been exaggerated in the interests of neat classificatory schemes. In general two distinct types of association are logically reasonable. The *haptobenthos*[1] grows on a solid substratum, which is usually either rock or part of an aquatic plant, though sometimes wood, animal surfaces, or the remains of a man-made object, metallic, ceramic, plastic, or whatever. The *herpobenthos* grows in or on mud, which it can easily penetrate.

The rock-living algae of the haptobenthos, along with those found on hard artificial surfaces, are usually called *epilithic*, whereas those growing on plants are by a widely established usage *epiphytic*, though some authors as Godward (1937) use the latter term as practically synonymous with haptobenthic. It is useful to distinguish as *epizoic* algae living on animals, mainly Mollusca, Crustacea, and Chelonia; an *endolithic* category for algae penetrating into limestone and an *endophytic* category for those that grow more or less parasitically, into plants, though not always healthy or even living ones, together constitute the *endobenthos* (Warming 1923). There may be a characteristic epipsammic community living on water-covered sand, though this environment lacks the stability to accumulate fine sedi-

---

[1] The term periphyton, as now used in a wide sense (cf. Sládečková, 1962) is synonymous with haptobenthos. The latter term introduced by Warming (1923), though not mentioned by Roll (1939a) nor by Sládečková (1962), is preferred to periphyton because it emphasizes that the assemblages in question form a subclass of the organisms living at the water–sediment interface, coordinate with other subclasses such as the rhizobenthos and herpobenthos (Vol. II, p. 237). Periphyton was originally used for the growth of algae on artificial submerged bodies such as steamships on the Volga (Behning 1928).

ment. It is possible that the individual sand grains would be injurious when moved by currents that would permit an epilithic community on a solid rock surface. Dr. Robert G. Wetzel suggests that selection might act strongly in favor of very small forms that are capable of growing in crevices on the surfaces of the sand grains. The great development of the sand community is in the interstitial water of sand at a level below the water surface, but landward of the margin, in the eulittoral. This community, the *psammon*, will be considered in Vol. IV. The herpobenthos, living on or at times just below the mud surface, is *epipelic*.[2]

The epilithic environment is ordinarily washed clean of deposits of mud or silt by the water movements along an exposed beach. Higher vegetation, inevitably excluded from the most disturbed parts of the shore, nevertheless is likely to bear little mechanically sedimented material, so long as it is subject to some gentle movement of the ambient water. In contrast to these situations, the epipelic environment depends for its existence on the deposition of fine sediment.

If we consider a small lake, lying in glacial till or in some other easily eroded rock, 1 m per millenium would probably not be an unusual figure for the overall rate of deposition on the bottom where sedimentation is occurring. This corresponds to 1 mm yr^{-1}, or 2.7 μ day^{-1}. Even if this figure is rather too high for most littoral regions, it is clear that many small organisms, resting on fine sediment, would at geologically not extraordinary rates of deposition, find themselves covered by a new deposit, thicker than themselves, in the course of a few days. Such a problem would not face the members of either community of the haptobenthos. Motility is probably useful to the herpobenthos for several reasons (see p. 559); the inevitable progress of very fine-scale geological processes provides one fundamental reason for powers of movement in the members of the epipelic community.

Relative diversity and specificity of the three main categories of algal benthic communities. Very few detailed studies have been made on all the taxocenes present in the epilithic, epiphytic, and epipelic communities of a single lake. The best investigation on such a really comprehensive scale is probably that of Lund (1942) made in certain ponds in Richmond Park, Surrey, England. All the localities studied are very shallow. In them 139 taxa[3] of bottom-living and therefore largely epipelic algae, omitting the Euglenineae, were disclosed, and of these 119 were confined to this type of community; for the epiphytic communities the corresponding figures

---

[2] Dr. Ruth Patrick tells me that by very careful use of a spoon in shallow water over mud it is often possible to separate a characteristic group of planktobenthic organisms floating just above the mud surface, and specifically distinct from the true epipelic flora.

[3] These figures omit rare species for which the characteristic habitat could not be given.

were 77 and 53, while 51 taxa occurred in and 43 were confined to the plankton. The Euglenineae of the Richmond Park ponds consisted of no fewer than 57 species; of these one, *Colacium vesiculosum*, was as elsewhere evidently epizoic on copepods, while the others are all said to occur both in plankton and on the bottom. In deeper water they might all be regarded as benthic. The diatoms, included of course in the overall totals already given, had 64 taxa in the bottom community, 24 in the epiphytic, and only five in the plankton. The only striking overlap in the composition of the bottom-living and epiphytic communities occurred in the desmids, where 17 species occur in both communities, with five only on the bottom and none exclusively epiphytic. All nine species of Chaetophorales recorded are listed as epiphytes; of the other filamentous algae (Oedogoniales, Clado-phorales, Zygnemales), there were nine bottom-living, five epiphytic species, and two common to the bottom deposits and epiphytic situations, while three occurred in the plankton. In ponds in southern England no great development of an epilithic community is to be expected, and in the case of these localities was not observed.

Lund's observations suggest a fair amount of specificity in the separation between the epiphytic haptobenthos and the epipelic herpobenthos. It is possible that some of his bottom-living algae actually lived on dead leaves and the like and so were not fully epipelic.

In the only other investigation in which several hundred taxa were identi-fied, namely, Hustedt's (1922) study of the diatoms of the various com-munities of the Lunzer Untersee, the specificity appears to be less. He found 255 taxa in the epiphytic community compared to 192 in the epilithic, 190 in the epipelic, and only 49 in the plankton. Though it is obvious that many species were found only as epiphytes, these are quite rare, and it is not possible to exclude their occurrence sometimes in other situations. Almost all the common species, found in all but three or less of the stations in at least one category of community, also occur quite abundantly in one or both of the other categories (Table 75). There appears to be a fairly large quite eurytopic group and a somewhat smaller haptobenthic group, com-monest on rocks and stones, less so on plants, and usually missing from almost half the epipelic collections. A few species are predominantly epi-lithic and a rather greater number more epipelic and epiphytic than epi-lithic. Only two of the really common diatoms are characteristically epipelic. This type of treatment inevitably stresses the eurytopic nature of common species, but it is clear that it would be easy to exaggerate the specificity of the three communities.

Insofar as such specificity exists, in the diatoms it seems to lead (Lund 1942; Round 1953) to nearly all epipelic diatoms being biraphidean and freely motile, occurring primarily in the orders Naviculales and Nitzschiales,

TABLE 75. *Distribution of the commonest benthic diatoms of the Lunzer Untersee
according to the kinds of substratum occupied by their communities,
from the data of Hustedt*

Species	Epilithic (16 stations)		Epiphytic (22 stations)		Epipelic (15 stations)	
	No. of occur-rences	%	No. of occur-rences	%	No. of occur-rences	%
Eurytopic						
Amphora ovalis	16	100	21	95	15	100
Denticula tenuis	15	94	22	100	13	87
Navicula radiosa	15	94	18	82	15	100
Cocconeis placentula	14	88	21	95	12	80
Eunotia arcus	13	81	19	86	12	80
Navicula tuscula	13	81	19	86	11	73
Cyclotella bodanica	14	88	16	73	15	100
Cymbella ehrenbergii	12	69	17	77	14	93
Tabellaria flocculosa	14	88	19	86	11	73
Predominantly epilithic usually with better repre-sentation at epiphythic than epipelic stations						
Achnanthes minutissima	16	100	15	68	7	47
Achnanthes minutissima var. cryptocephala	13	81	13	59	0	0
Cymbella cymbiformis	13	81	13	59	4	27
Epithemia sorex	13	81	14	64	8	53
E. zebra	14	88	13	59	7	47
Cymbella cistula	15	94	14	64	10	67
Caloneis alpestris	13	81	13	59	7	47
Epipelic and epiphytic, less frequently epilithic						
Diploneis elliptica	6	38	19	86	15	100
Gyrosigma attenuata	10	63	19	86	15	100
Cyclotella comta	10	63	15	68	13	87
Cyclotella comta var. oligactis	1	6	14	64	13	87
Cyclotella comta var. radiosa	0	0	15	68	13	87
Neidium dubium	3	19	13	59	12	80
Predominantly epipelic						
Navicula placentula	1	6	3	14	12	80
Campylodiscus noricus	3	19	6	27	14	93

the genera *Diploneis, Caloneis, Anomoeoneis, Navicula, Pinnularia, Gompho-nema, Cymbella*, and *Nitzschia* being particularly important. Species of the monoraphidean genus *Achnanthes* may also be quite significant.

Among the haptobenthic diatoms, as may be expected from their large number of genera and species, the biraphidean orders are also very well represented, but there are also proportionately more members of the pseu-doraphidean Fragilariales, notably in the genera *Fragilaria, Diatoma*, and *Synedra*, of the Eunotiales, with a single short or rudimentary raphe, as in *Eunotia*, with numerous soft-water epiphytes, as well as in the monoraphi-dean Achnanthales. *Cocconeis*, in the Achnanthaceae, is flattened and highly modified for an appressed epiphytic or epilithic existence. As the name *C. pediculus* indicates, the early microscopists saw in these diatoms a vegetable analogue to the louse (Kolbe 1932). In *C. placentula* the minute details of the sculpture may be involved in attachment and the species seems to be able to move over the surfaces of leaves (Willer 1923). In most

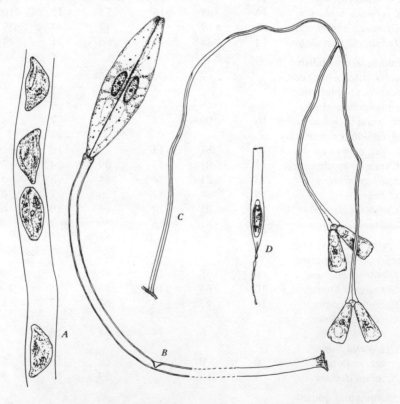

FIGURE 145.   Stalks and tubes of epiphytic diatoms. *A, Cymbella caespitosa*, four cells in a gelatinous tube; *B, C. cistula*, recently divided cell on basal stalk; *C, Gomphonema olivaceum*, stalked colony; *D, Navicula cyrptocephala* in stalked tube. All ×440 (Cholnoky, slightly modified).

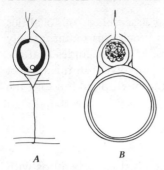

FIGURE 146. *Chrysopyxis stenostoma* with mucilage thread surrounding a filament of *Mougeotia* (internal details omitted). *A*, Filament in lateral view; *B*, (diagrammatic) filament in cross-section (Frisch, modified).

haptobenthic diatoms there are basal gelatinous stalks, or the cells live in gelatinous tubes. Unfortunately owing to the ordinary and inevitable methods of cleaning diatoms for taxonomic study, such structures are seldom examined by systematists. It is apparent, notably from Cholnoky's (1927) investigations, that within a large and diversified genus such as *Cymbella* both basal stalks and tubes may develop in different species (Fig. 145). A far more detailed study of the mechanism of attachment of diatoms to various kinds of natural and artificial surfaces would be rewarding. Dr. Ruth Patrick indicates verbally that a regular community structure dependent on attachment and orientation can develop on submersed glass slides that are receiving colonizing diatoms.

Outside the diatoms, mucilage attachment is evidently common among filamentous green algae. A very few epiphytes, such as the chrysophycean *Chrysopyxis*, have special types of attachment mechanism; in the case of the last-named genus, there are two curved basal projections that fit around a filamentous alga (Fig. 146).

Quantitative relationships of the various kinds of algal benthos. Moss (1968) has tabulated from his own unpublished work and from the literature the chlorophyll content per unit area of a number of epipelic, epilithic, epiphytic, and epipsammic communities, both from lakes and small bodies of standing water and rivers, together with some data for algal mats. The data for freshwaters are summarized in Table 76.

TABLE 76. *Range of biomass as chlorophyll* a *per square meter of algae in various benthic habitats (*Moss*)*

Habitat	Chlorophyll a content (mg m^{-2})
Epipelic	2.1–66.5
Epilithic	127–1200
Epiphytic	110–2350
Epipsammic (mean, one locality)	86
Algal mats	189–269

These figures from a limited but very varied assemblage of localities strongly suggest that the epipelic community is much less quantitatively rich than are attached haptobenthic communities. Moss concludes that the mechanical stability of the community is probably involved. In this respect the epipelic community probably lies between the phytoplankton and the haptobenthos.

THE HAPTOBENTHOS

It is convenient to begin a consideration of the algal haptobenthos with the epilithic forms which presumably compose the simplest possible associations. The subdivision of the littoral into a supralittoral, which is never submersed but may be influenced by spray, a eulittoral which lies between the lowest and highest water marks, and an infralittoral always underwater and embracing the whole zone of vegetation rooted below the surface, has been given in Vol. II (p. 240). Further subdivision of the eulittoral is desirable in a discussion of algal associations. At any moment the water level will lie somewhere within the eulittoral, rarely near its upper or lower boundaries, more usually not far from mean water level. The level at any given moment, however, may be variable over quite short periods of time owing to the existence of waves and of seiches. Waves may cause exposure and submergence of a given level every few seconds; seiches, in lakes large enough for their amplitude, which depends to a considerable extent on the fetch of the wind, to be significant, may cause such exposure or submergence after periods of some minutes (see Vol. I, Table 26). In either case there will be a wave (Hurter 1928) zone of comparatively rapid exposure and submergence. Above this whenever breaking waves meet a more or less vertical surface, either of a boulder or of a cliff, a spray zone will be developed. These zones, or formally subzones, will move up and down between the extreme water levels defining the eulittoral. When the water level is near the top of the latter, the spray zone defines the supralittoral. As the level changes there will be a newly wetted subzone if the water is rising, or newly dried subzone if it is falling. All these subzones may be expected to have some biological significance though few attempts have been made to relate their formal existence to the biological realities of a given shore.

The epilithic haptobenthos. The eulittoral zonation on the surface of almost vertical clifflike rocks probably provides the most easily analyzed set of haptobenthic communities. Such a zonation on the eastern exposed shore of the Traunsee in Upper Austria has been described by Kann (1958, 1959). The variation in water level here has a mean annual amplitude

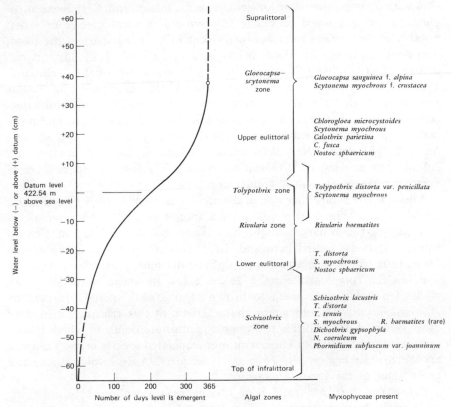

FIGURE 147.   Eulittoral zonation of Myxophyceae on rocky eastern shore of Traunsee (from the data of Kann).

of 1.36 m, with high levels in summer, usually in July and August, and low levels in late winter or spring. The mean annual exposure of rocks at given heights above or below the mean datum level of 422.54 m above sea level is shown in Fig. 147. The algal associations found on the steep rock faces that are an important feature of the eastern shore of the lake are also indicated in the same diagram. A dark band beginning 10–20 cm above mean water level and extending upward for 10–100 cm, at its highest point probably lies outside the eulittoral, being at the top watered only by spray at the time of highest lake levels, and so in part supralittoral. When dry, the band consists of a thin hard crust, but when wet it is easily scratched off the rock and has a brownish-violet glint. It is formed of two algae,

Gloeocapsa sanguinea[4] state or ecophene f. *alpina*[5], and *Scytonema myochrous* as its presumed ecophene f. *crustacea*. Several species of moss, notably of the genus *Crateroneurum*, occur in the lower part of the band, and continue down 20–30 cm below mean lake level. They support numerous algal epiphytes. There is also, in the lower part of the dark band, 5–20 cm above mean lake level, a characteristic development of *Nostoc sphaericum* both on rocks and on mosses. It is associated with both *Gloeocapsa sanguinea* f. *alpina* and *Scytonema myochrous* f. *crustacea* and more rarely with nominotypical examples of the latter, and also with *Calothrix fusca, C. parietina, Chlorogloea microcystoides, Schizothrix lacustris* and colonies, on mosses, of *Rivularia haematites*. The last two species are of great importance at slightly greater depths.

About 5–10 cm on either side of the mean water level *Tolypothrix distorta* var *penicillata* (Fig. 148) is common, a species evidently characteristic of this part of the zonation in the hard water subalpine lakes of Central Europe. It is associated here and there with *Scytonema myochrous* and forms tufts, often with abundant epiphytic diatoms, particularly *Synedra*.

Below the *Tolypothrix* zone, 5–25 cm below the mean water level, is a zone of nodular olive green to brown algal growth, mainly formed by *Rivularia haematites* and again characteristic in this relative position of other central European lakes, though the absolute depth to which it may extend is rather variable. The commoner associated species in the Traunsee are *Scytonema myochrous, Tolypothrix distorta, Nostoc sphaericum*, and green algae of the genus *Mougeotia*.

Below the *Rivularia* zone is a spongy gray-green crust forming the *Schizothrix* zone, and extending at least 1.5 m below mean water level and so well into the infralittoral. The principal species of *Schizothrix* present appears to be *S. lacustris* with some admixture of *S. fasciculata* in the upper part of the zone, though there are doubts about the valid separation of these and other species. The common associates of *Schizothrix*

---

[4] In view of the lack of agreement between the leading authorities on the Myxophyceae, no attempt has been made to modernize the nomenclature of the blue-green algae that appear in the present chapter. The characteristically lithophile filamentous forms usually fall into the categories recognized by Drouet (1959) and more recently by Golubić (1967). The coccoid forms present far more difficult problems. Drouet (1959; Drouet and Daily, 1955) fuses *Gloeocapsa, Microcystis, Chroococcus*, and *Aphanocapsa* to form the genus *Anacystis*, while few of the species recognized earlier remain. Since the various taxa living more or less sympatrically clearly imply to many workers recognizable populations, even if they are but transitory ecophenes, to disregard them nomenclatorially would involve loss of information, often potentially of an ecological sort. The names employed have therefore in general been those used by the investigators whose works are being considered.

[5] Golubić (1967) indicates that the violet or bluish color of this form is an indicator-like reaction to alkaline or neutral as opposed to acid water, in which the plant is reddish.

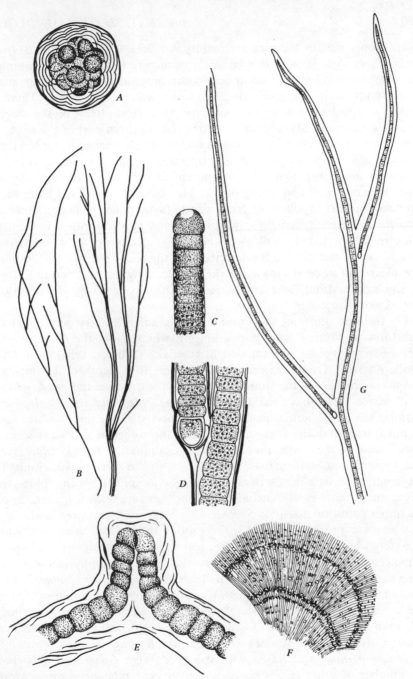

FIGURE 148. *A, Gloeocapsa sanguinea* (×∼1000); *B, Tolypothrix distorta* var. *penicillata*, whole plant (×∼3); *C*, the same, terminal part of filament (×∼1000); *D*. the same, base of branch (×∼1000); *E, Scytonema myochrous* st. *crustacea* (×∼1000); *F, Rivularia haematites* section through small colony (natural size); *G*, the same, filaments (×∼150).

in the upper part of the zone are mainly *Rivularia haematites* and *Tolypothrix tenuis* with *Dichothrix gypsophila* occurring lower down. A number of other blue-green algae occur less commonly, as do filamentous green algae, and rarely the green rhodophycean *Asterocytis ornata*. There is clearly a considerable population of epiphytic diatoms living on the sheaths of all the common Myxophyceae. Along the southern part of the shore of the Traunsee, between 15 cm above and 35 cm below mean water level, the red alga *Bangia atropurpurea* occurs on rocks. Kann suspects its presence is due to the rather high chloride content of the water, which in the top 20 m is between 30 and 40 mg liter^{-1}. This chloride is derived from water pumped into the hypolimnion from a soda factory. The evidence, however, that *B. atropurpurea* actually requires this amount of chloride is inadequate (Belcher 1960), and the ecology of the alga is clearly not fully understood. The zonation and flora so far described for the rocky parts of the Traunsee are clearly in general typical of the subalpine lakes of Central Europe. A similar situation, for example, is described in detail by Hurter (1928) for Lake Lucerne.

On the west shore of the Traunsee the gradient is very gentle and the eulittoral is covered with stones among which grow the forget-me-not *Myosotis scorpioides*, a plant that in this lake (Morton 1954) as in Lago Doberdo near Trieste, extends below water, to a depth of 1.5 m, as f. *submerse-florens*. On the stones below mean water level there is developed a *Rivularia haematites* zone and below it a *Schizothrix* zone. *Tolypothrix distorta* var. *penicillata*, which would be expected above the *Rivularia* zone, is not found, and above mean water level the stones at first sight seem to lack much algal growth, though careful examination reveals *Chlorogloea microcystoides*, *Calothrix fusca*, and *Chamaesiphon polymorphus* among the Myxophyceae, with the green alga *Pleurococcus* sp. A few other blue-green algae occur more rarely, including *Gloeocapsa sanguinea* f. *alpina*, though its upper eulittoral associate *Scytonema myochrous* f. *crustacea* is absent.

There are a number of cold springs along the western shore near which the stones bear a peculiar flora. The most important species on the exposed submersed surfaces of such stones are the green rhodophycean *Batrachospermum monoliforme* and the green alga *Chaetophora cornudamae*. Around the edges of the stones *Mougeotia* and *Spirogyra* are common. On the under surface there is a remarkable zonation. Externally there is the rhodophycean *B. monoliforme*, and within this is a brownish green zone characterized by *Pseudochantransia chalybea* which may be an ecophene of *Batrachospermum* sp., mixed with the green alga *Gongrosira debaryana*. A number of other less conspicuous green and blue-green algae are recorded. In the center of the underside of the stone, where it presumably is in contact with the bottom, is a pale blue-green zone with *Schizothrix*

perforans, Pleurocapsa minor, Chamaesiphon polymorphus, Phormidium au-
tumnale, Tolypothrix sp., and *Gongrosira debaryana.* At least this part of
the stone must be unilluminated and the plants therefore can live only
heterotrophically. The flora is in some ways like that of the deepest littoriprofundal of some lakes.

On the undersides of smaller stones on the eastern shore of the lake a
comparable, though rather different, assemblage of *Pleurocapsa minor,*
Chamaesiphon polymorphus, Phormidium corium, and *Homoeothrix varians*
was found.

Where a pipe conducting the effluent of the soda factory, supported by
massive wooden floats, moved up and down with the water surface and so
provided a solid substrate partly submersed to constant depth, a very clear
zonation developed, as is indicated in Fig. 149. The arrangement is interesting, for *Rivularia,* which on the natural fixed substrates grows below
mean water level, is here sharply confined to a region above the perennial
water level, though near enough to it for capillary water and some spray
to keep the *Rivularia* wet. Between and underneath the *Rivularia* colonies
there is a yellowish-pink to greenish layer of *Phormidium subfuscum.* In
the constantly submersed but well-illuminated region just below water
level there is a striking *Cladophora glomerata* zone, and below this *Schizo-*
thrix with green algae and diatoms. Elsewhere in the lake the local occurrence of *Cladophora glomerata* is associated with pollution.

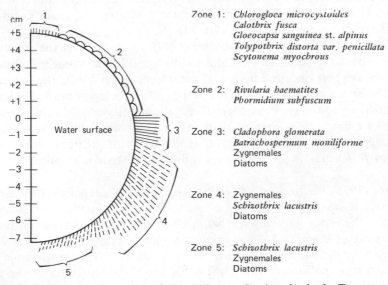

Zone 1: *Chlorogloea microcystoides*
Calothrix fusca
Gloeocapsa sanguinea st. *alpinus*
Tolypothrix distorta var. penicillata
Scytonema myochrous

Zone 2: *Rivularia haematites*
Phormidium subfuscum

Zone 3: *Cladophora glomerata*
Batrachospermum moniliforme
Zygnemales
Diatoms

Zone 4: Zygnemales
Schizothrix lacustris
Diatoms

Zone 5: *Schizothrix lacustris*
Zygnemales
Diatoms

FIGURE 149. Distribution of attached algae on floating pipe in the Traunsee.

Kann (1933) had earlier described the algal flora of the marginal stones of the Lunzer Untersee. The succession is not unlike that on the western side of the Traunsee. Below the highest water level there are stones bearing mosses and the lichen *Verrucaria*. Below this along the greater part of the south shore and the western part of the north shore the stones near the mean water level bear an algal incrustation. In the uppermost part the general coloration is blackish brown and the dominant alga, 10–20 cm above mean water level, is *Tolypothrix distorta* var. *penicillata*. It is to be noted that this species is here occurring a little higher up than on the rock faces on the east side of the Traunsee and that it does not occur on the stony shore of the west side of that lake. Below this, 10 cm above to 10 cm below mean water level, is a reddish-yellow zone with *Rivularia haematites*. The algae of both these zones have a considerable flora of epiphytic diatoms. From 10 cm below mean water level downward, there is a greenish-gray spongy growth of *Schizothrix lacustris* with *S. fasciculatus* and a good many other blue-green algae and bacteria. The difference in the nature and richness of the flora of the *Schizothrix* zone compared to the two other zones is probably due primarily to the greater exposure to the air of the *Tolypothrix* and *Rivularia* zones. The latter two zones are, moreover, liable to the greatest amount of disturbance from the breaking of waves; it is noteworthy, as Kann points out, that *Tolypothrix* and *Rivularia* are typically genera of streams (cf. p. 527, 529).

It is to be noted that although in general *Tolypothrix distorta* var. *penicillata* occurs as a dominant above the *Rivularia haematites* zone and the species of *Schizothrix* are dominant below the latter, the exact positions relative to the mean water level vary. On the floating pipe where the algal zones have a relatively invariant relationship to water level the *Rivularia* zone is above the latter. In the Lunzer Untersee it lies at about mean water level, though here of course the actual water level is variable. In the Traunsee the *Rivularia* zone lies for the most part 5–20 cm below mean water level, though *Rivularia* may perhaps grow less abundantly considerably deeper. In Lake Constance it certainly extends to 2 m below mean water level (Oberdorfer 1928). Kann suggests that the apparent greater depths occupied by *R. haematites* in larger lakes is due to the greater amplitude of the waves.

Kann (1958) describes an interesting zonation of large rocks in the Lunzer Mittesee, a small shallow body of water kept perennially cool by cold springs. There is a narrow dark band, 10–20 cm above mean water level, colonized by *Chlorogloea microcystoides*, *Scytonema myochrous* f. *crustacea*, *Calothrix parietina*, and *C. fusca*; below this is a red-brown zone of *Chamaesiphon polonicus*. Mixed with this are the uncommon blue-green algae *Homoeothrix varians*, *Phormidium autumnale*, and *Clastidium rivulare* with *Calothrix parietina*. These species tend to go further into the water as a brownish-green zone below the red-brown *C. polonicus*.

The epilithic algae of more eutrophic lakes. In north Germany Kann (1940, 1958) has made a study of the eutrophic hard-water lakes around Plön. Here the slope of the shore is very gentle and, at times of the lowest levels, wind or the artificial disturbance of boats will often cause water to move up over the greater part of the eulittoral zone. Zonation, therefore, is less sharp than in the localities already described. *Cladophora glomerata*, with other green algae, occurs from about 10 cm below the mean water level upward throughout most of the upper eulittoral. From about 10 cm below mean water level downward there is a more varied flora, including both *C. glomerata* and *C. aegagropila*, *Rivularia biasolettiana*, replacing *R. haematites* of the subalpine lakes, *R. dura*, *Gloeotrichia pisum*, *Nostoc pruniforme*, *Tolypothrix tenuis*, and the brown alga *Pleurocladia lacustris*.

Large projecting rocks present a steeper face to the water; such rocks in the Grosser Plöner See had a zone of *Cladophora glomerata* up to 10 cm on either side of mean water level. Above the *C. glomerata* there is a brownish-green zone, 10–15 cm wide, of *Phormidium* spp., *Dichotrix orsiniana*, and *Calothrix braunii*. Still higher at the top of the rock *Chlorogloea microcystoides*, *Tolypothrix byssoidea*, *Phormidium* spp., and *Haematococcus pluvialis* were found, the first named being one of the species occurring in this sort of situation in the Lunzer Mittesee.

Kann (1945) also made a study of six lakes surrounded by forest in east Holstein. These are often characterized by littoral growths of the brown alga *Heribaudiella fluviatilis* with the myxophycean *Dichothrix baueriana* and *Tolypothrix distorta* and the green alga *Gongosira debaryana*. In the Krummensee the rare alga *Cladophora basiramosa* occurred on stones along parts of the shore not shaded by trees. This alga is also known in Lake Tåkern in Sweden where it grew on the sides of stones, the tops of which were covered with the much commoner *C. glomerata* (Waern 1939). In the Krummensee *C. aegagropila* also occurs, extending well below the limit of higher vegetation (Sauer 1937, sub *Aegogropila holsatica*), where, as elsewhere in deep water, it is accompanied by *Hildenbrandia*.

In general in the north German lakes there are considerable differences between the hard- and soft-water localities. Among the Myxophyceae *Hapalosiphon* and *Plectonema* are mainly in waters low in calcium, *Tolypothrix* and *Rivularia* in those fairly rich in the element, and *Microcystis parasitica* and *Dichothrix baueriana* are transcursional. The last-named species and *Tolypothrix distorta* may occur in quiet, less calcareous woodland lakes; part of the difference between marked and moderately calcareous lakes seems to be the greater commonness of the same species of blue-green algae in the former as also occur in the latter. Among green algae the

Zygnemales, *Oedogonium* and *Gloeococcus* tend to be transcursional, and *Chaetophora*, *Cladophora*, *Stigeoclonium*, and *Drapanaldia* are absent in soft water. The brown alga *Heribaudiella* is primarily found in the less calcareous localities, though in the forest lakes it may occur at moderate (15.3–34.2 mg Ca liter⁻¹) calcium concentrations; *Pleurocladia* is a more characteristic hard-water genus.

In the flora epiphytic on these algae, diatoms are more abundant in the hard-water lakes, and desmids in the soft-water lakes, as would be expected.

Though it is difficult to describe the exact realized niches of any species, it is evident that the occurrences of the individual taxa of the epilithic flora are largely dependent on probability of exposure to the air, slope of the shore and consequent size and shape differences among rocks and stones, degree of waviness, and water chemistry. The examples given above suggest that these factors may interact in a fairly complex way.

The process of colonization. Hurter (1928) has made some interesting observations on the rate at which littoral algae can become established on a solid substratum as the water level rises in the late spring. He observed on May 31, 1919, after the level had risen about 65 cm and had then fallen 10 cm, five strikingly developed bands of the green alga *Ulothrix zonata*, on stones in the littoral of Lake Lucerne. The uppermost band was the best developed and lay with its upper margin at the mean water level recorded on May 31. The other bands below this were less striking, but were all well separated from each other. The lowest occupied a position that would have been dry prior to May 12. Except for the top very thick band, which corresponds to a mean water level more or less stationary over some days, Hurter concluded that each band represented a day's colonization by zoospores, at the then existing contact of the water surface and the substratum available for colonization. As the latter takes place only at a certain time of day, apparently in the morning, the rapidly rising water level ensures a discrete series of bands, each produced on a different day (Fig. 150). Observations on artificial surfaces placed in a position comparable to these stones suggest that enough colonization could occur at the surface in 1 hr to produce a visible band. Sauer (1937) finds that in Holstein a band of this alga develops on exposed stones at the lake surface in early spring when the temperatures lie between 1 and 6°C. Later when the water level falls, calcium carbonate precipitated by the photosynthesis of the alga, along with the frustules of dead diatoms, notably *Gomphonema olivaceum*, forms a white dry calcareo-siliceous girdle on the stones around the lake. In general in the Holstein lakes *Ulothrix* is replaced later in the year, at a rather lower level, by *Cladophora glomerata*, as already noted from Kann's description. Where some pollution occurs, as on the north–northeast side of the Grosser Plöner See, *U. zonata* may persist.

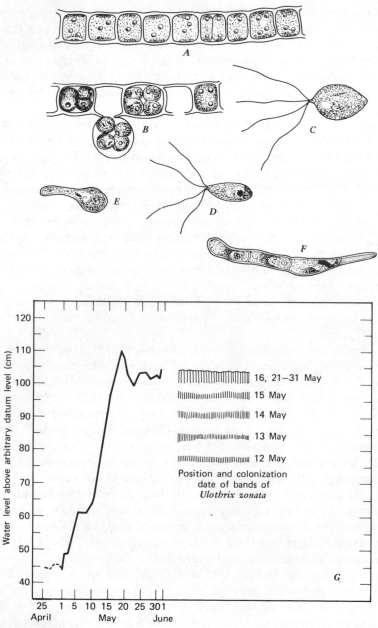

FIGURE 150. *Ulothrix zonata*. *A*, Part of filament in vegetative state (×200); *B*, formation of zoospores; *C*, macrozoospore; *D*, microzoospore; *E*, *F*, germination of zoospores to form a new filament (Klebs); *G*; *G* water levels in Lake Lucerne, Switzerland, in May 1919, with diagrammatic presentation of colonization of rock surfaces just below the boundary of the water and air.

Of the smaller species Hurter concluded that a taxon referred to as *Diatoma vulgaris* var. *ehrenbergii* (cf. Patrick and Reimer 1966) is the commonest colonist of a newly submersed surface, with *Cymbella affinis* one of the next best invaders. Hurter's work on the diatoms suggested that in some species, as *Navicula menisculus* and *Achnanthes microcephala*, specimens from permanently submersed surfaces are larger than are the representatives of the species in the eulittoral.

Evans (1958, 1959) has found that a number of algae can persist in a dormant condition in the surface layers of the bottom of bodies of water exposed at times of low water level. Though in some cases zygospores and other modified resting stages are certainly involved, in a number of filamentous algae, one desmid *Cosmarium cucurbitinum*, and in certain diatoms, notably *Stauroneis phoenicentrum* and *Pinnularia viridis*, vegetative cells can survive considerable drying. Oil droplets occur in such resting cells; in filamentous green algae the walls become thickened, and in *C. cucurbitum* and some of the other green algae mucilage sheaths apparently protect the cells. This mechanism may be of importance in providing continuity in the algal flora of the eulittoral.

Various studies made on the epilithic algae of other lakes in the North Temperate zone disclose similar patterns to those encountered in continental Europe.

Epilithic algae in the English lakes. Godward (1937) found in the spray zone of Windermere an association of *Tolypella distorta* var. *penicillata*, *Calothrix parietina*, *Homoeothrix fusca*, and species of *Phormidium*, *Pleurocapsa*, and *Schizothrix*. Below the waterline, in 0.0–0.5 m, *Ulothrix zonata* flourished, as elsewhere, in April and May, accompanied by *Cymbella ventricosa*; rather later in the season *Phormidium* spp. and *Pleurocapsa fusca* occurred. Diatoms other than *C. ventricusa* were more prominent in winter; they included *Achnanthes minutissima* as the commonest and most persistent form. *Hildenbrandia rivularis* occurred at one station only in this zone in shaded cracks in a rock face. In the zone extending down to 3.5 m. *Oedogonium* spp. forms a conspicuous belt in June and July, accompanied by various other filamentous green algae, and *Aphanocapsa* spp., which genus extends deeper on the bottom in winter. From 2.0 to 3.5 m *Nostoc verrucosum*, *Dichothrix baueriana* var. *crassa*, *Denticula tenuis*, *Plectonema tomasiniana* var. *cincinnatum*, and rare *Cladophora* sp. are recorded. Godward noted *Dichothrix orsiniana* and *Nostoc verrucosum* only on stones, and *Denticula tenuis* did not occur on plants. The other common species all occur as epiphytes, but there seems to be a group of epiphytes discussed later which do not occur on stones.

Godward suspected that part of the difference between the flora of inorganic shores and that of shores with vegetation and much organic matter might be due to a direct chemical influence of the latter.

Epilithic algae in the lakes of northwestern Ontario. Of the North American work in which both glass slides and direct observation was used, that of Stockner and Armstrong (1971) gives the most useful information about epilithic species. The work was done in four small lakes of the Experimental Lakes Area, northwestern Ontario, lake 240 being the most carefully studied. The shores of these lakes are typical litholittorals, largely formed of gravel or boulders. The epilithic flora consists of at least 43 species of diatoms, with eight or more genera of green and eight of blue-green algae. The diatoms form 60–70% of the total algal mass of the epilithic benthos. The total number of diatoms living or dead, constituting what Stockner and Armstrong call the *accumulated epilithic diatoms*, varies on natural surfaces from 300,000 to 1,300,000 cm^{-2}. Comparable figures are recorded from Lake Superior (Fox, Odlaugh, and Olson 1969), but much greater numbers are known from more eutrophic localities elsewhere, Evans and Stockner (1972) reporting up to 6,650,000 cm^{-2} on buoys in the shallow more productive waters of Lake Winnipeg.

The vernal epilithic phytobenthos is characterized by *Fragilaria pinnata*, *Anomoeoneis vitrea*, *A. serians*, and *Cymbella frigida*. Later *Achnanthes minutissima*, which is mainly an epiphyte on algae, becomes much the most abundant species and remains so at least until October. *Anomoeoneis serians* and *Fragilaria pinnata* show a most curious reciprocal variation in their depth ranges, as if *F. pinnata* excluded *A. serians* at intermediate values of light intensity or some other factor (Fig. 151).

Analyses of the epilithic algae taken on nine occasions from three un-fertilized lakes gave a mean value of 2.50% N and 0.05% P; a fertilized lake gave values of 3.14% N and 0.15% P. The higher nitrogen figure is due to a single determination without which the content would be 2.50%: the phosphorus content in the fertilized lake is almost always consistently higher than in the unfertilized. Stockner and Armstrong conclude that although the critical concentration of nitrogen in freshwater algae, above which luxury consumption may be presumed, is usually regarded as rather higher than their mean figures (Gerloff and Skoog 1954; Lund 1950), it is probable that phosphorus is limiting the mass of algal phytobenthos in these lakes under natural conditions.

Water movements and the ecology of epilithic algae. The ecology of *Cladophora glomerata* has been studied in the Great Lakes of the St. Lawrence by Herbst (1969) who concluded that the species does best in water rich in phosphate, at 20–25°C, while *Ulothrix zonata* had a lower temperature optimum. This is in line with what has been observed in Europe and also with the findings of Evans and Stockner (1972) who noted *C. glomerata* on the buoys of the southernmost eutrophic, but not in the northernmost oligotrophic, part of Lake Winnipeg. Herbst furthermore concludes that *C. glomerata* does best on surfaces exposed to turbulent

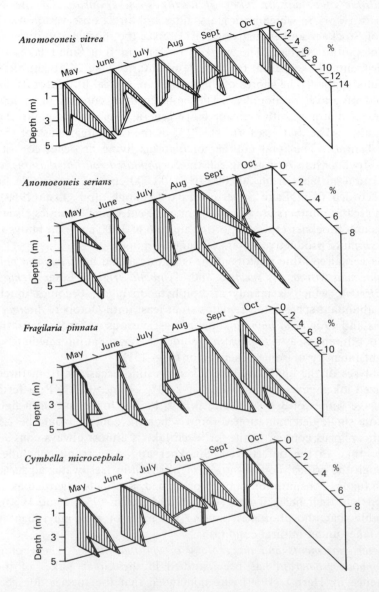

FIGURE 151. Depth distribution throughout the summer of four common diatoms on natural rock surfaces in Lake 240 (Stockner and Evans). Note the striking bimodality of the distribution of *Anomoeoneis serians* in late August with *Fragilaria pinnata* having a maximum at the *A. serians* minimum.

water. He points out that Whitford (1960) had found that 22 species of attached algae grew better in a current of 15–30 cm sec^{-1}. Moreover Whitford and Schumacher (1961) observed that *Oedogonium kurzii*, though its respiratory rate increased by 70% in a current of 18 cm sec^{-1}, actually showed a ten fold increase in the rate of phosphorus uptake over that from still water. These results are, as Whitford notes, a confirmation of an idea held by Ruttner (1926), who pointed out that flowing water is functionally richer than still, because in it turbulence accentuates the gradient across the laminar boundary layer of water over an organism respiring or taking up nutrients. This effect is likely to be very important to the epilithic algae of exposed rocks in oligotrophic lakes (cf. pp. 521, 522).

Glass slides as artificial surfaces for epilithic organisms. The immersion of glass slides in natural waters as a means of obtaining information about haptobenthic organisms seems to have been begun independently by Naumann (1915, 1919), studying iron bacteria in water supplies, and Hentschel (1916), who was interested in organisms, nearly all typically freshwater, that can attach themselves to surfaces in the harbor of Hamburg. Both authors are mentioned in a review of techniques available for the study of benthic microphytes by Thomasson (1925). In the same year, Duplakov (1925) reported the first results of studying various man-made surfaces in Lake Glubokoje. In the final posthumous report on this investigation, which appeared 8 yr later (Duplakov 1933) the results were based on the glass slide technique used in bacteriological work by his colleague Karsinkin. Butcher, Pentelow, and Woodley (1931) used the glass slide method in a study of the River Lark in England; Butcher (1932) noted that the slides in the spring were colonized mainly by common diatoms but that in the summer rare or even new green algae made their appearance. Godward (1934, 1937) adopted the method from these English studies in her work on ponds on the border of Epping Forest and in Windermere.

At about the same time both Karsinkin (1934) and Henrici (1933, 1936) were investigating the settling of bacteria on slides as a means of studying the bacteriology of the open waters of lakes. Gause (1936) published an important paper on the structure of biological communities, in which the work of Duplakov and Ivlev (1933) played a major part. Methods comparable to those of Hentschel seem to have been used at Woods Hole in the collection of ectoproct colonies (Bissonette 1930). Most of the marine work of this sort has been zoological, but that in freshwaters became increasingly more botanical. This is partly due to the marine epilithic biota being recruited by the settling of larvae of many different major groups, whereas in freshwaters there are few groups of sessile animals having such larvae. It is also due to the fact that diatoms are a major part of the epilithic algal flora of freshwaters. They can be easily prepared in situ, identified, and counted. Their populations are therefore amenable to statistical treatment. Patrick, Hohn, and Wallace (1954) not only introduced an improved collecting apparatus, the Catherwood diatometer, but also made a study of the fit of the observed populations of diatoms on slides to the Preston log-normal distribution. Since this paper, a great deal of the study of the haptobenthos or periphyton has been based on the assemblages of diatoms on glass slides. In a later paper Patrick (1967) considered not only Preston's estimates of species pools but also the index of diversity of Fisher, Corbet, and Williams (1943) and the now familiar Shannon-Weiner information-theoretic diversity (see Vol. II, pp. 360–368). The last-named quantity, as applied to diatoms on slides, has been the subject of an elaborate study by Brown (1973). Used along with the actual number of species observed it can probably be the most useful measure of diversity.

Patrick found that in any experiment the number of species present after a given length of exposure depended, as would be expected, on the area. Her data suggest that an asymptotic value would be approached when the area was somewhat over 625 mm^2. She also found that in running water the diversity of the final population depended on the rate of flow, which can be regarded as a measure of the rate of invasion.

Comparison of slides set out in two streams in the island of Dominica where the species pool is likely to be small, with results from a comparable stream at similar temperatures in Maryland gave 46–49 species in Dominica as against 79 in Maryland, which is a typical continental figure, but the information-theoretic diversities of 1.9–2.0 in Dominica were more than twice the Maryland value of 0.79.

Important technical aspects of the use of glass slides in estimating production in lakes are discussed by Wetzel (1964) and Dumont (1969), in natural streams by Kevern, Wilhm, and van Dyne (1966), and in artificial systems by Kevern and Ball (1965), and McIntire and Phinney (1965). Various historic aspects of this type of research can be retrieved from Cooke's (1956) review.

Succession on immersed slides. The early work of Henrici (1933) and of Karsinkin (1934)[6] established that bacteria are early settlers on submersed slides. Karsinkin found appreciable populations after 1 day's exposure. The bacteria ordinarily secrete mucilage, in which they become embedded, as a thin layer over the glass. It is probable that bacterial colonization is actually preceded by the sorption of dissolved organic matter from the water. Karsinkin concluded that as other organisms appeared the bacteria tended to decline in numbers. Ivlev found flagellates and sessile

---

[6] Karsinkin's work seems to have started before that of Henrici; the two investigations were clearly initiated quite independently.

protozoa to the first eucaryote colonists. Some of these disappeared as rotifers, motile ciliates, and diatoms replaced the earlier biota.

Brown (1973) found that as the population of algae on slides increased, the value of the Shannon–Weiner diversity declined. This is no doubt part of the process by which the initial rather haphazard unstable community of what Gause calls the *phase of accumulation* is converted into a more stable community during a *phase of reconstruction*. There are hints of these processes in Patrick's (1963) observations. When the slide is exposed for a long enough time various green and blue-green algae may appear. Godward (1937) found *Lyngbya perelegans*, of the various filamentous blue-green algae in Windermere, to be the only one commonly settling on slides. Castenholz (1960) noted rare occurrences of *Amphithrix*, *Calothrix*, and *Entophysalis* on slides in Falls Lake in the Grand Coulee where these algae are important epilithic species.

Comparison of the slide flora with natural epilithic and epiphytic communities. The clean surfaces of most rocks and of glass are chemically similar in that they are largely composed of ionically bonded oxygen atoms. This, however, is probably of little importance in nature. Spoon and Burbanck (1967) found that the same sessile ciliates as are known to settle on glass settled on plastic surfaces, which have quite a different composition. It is probable that in all cases in fresh water the surface that actually is settled is that of an organic layer, partly derived from sorbed material in the water and partly secreted by the initial bacterial colonists. It must be remembered, however, that some aquatic animals, notably Cladocera, have external surfaces that are unwettable and on which very little growth of microscopic plants or animals occurs. This will be considered at length in Vol. IV.

Several authors have discussed the nature of the biota of submersed plates, comparing it with that of natural surfaces. Godward (1934) working on the Golding's Hill Ponds, Laughton, Essex, England found the flora attached to slides like that growing epiphytically, though upright branched forms such as *Phaeothamnium*, *Microthamnion*, and *Gomphonema* were rather rare.

In Windermere Godward (1937) felt that the slide flora consisted mostly of species found among macrophytes in the more richly vegetated parts of the shore, and so probably epiphytic. Some species such as *Coleochaete soluta* and *Dicranochaete reniformis* may occur on slides and as epiphytes but not on stones.

Though the epilithic and epiphytic haptobenthos differ very little, the possible resemblance of the flora on glass slides to the latter rather than the former is not really unexpected. The slides are set out at a definite time and have not had many years to acquire and partially lose a flora. The leaves of plants also have unfolded at a definite time and have been settled over a period comparable to the exposure time of slides in most experiments. Moreover, for purely practical reasons in conducting experiments, slides are usually not put in an environment in which rocks would survive but plants would not.

Patrick, Hohn, and Wallace (1954) noted that on any slide 95% of those diatoms represented by at least eight specimens were also found in collections made from natural habitats near the slide. Castenholz (1960) likewise found that there were no epilithic or epiphytic diatoms in two freshwater lakes of the Grand Coulee that did not occur also on slides exposed for 2–4 weeks in these lakes. Among the larger green and blue-green algae *Cladophora glomerata* was not found attached to glass and encrusting blue-green algae did not occur commonly. The blue-green algae, however, did develop on slides exposed for much longer periods.

Ulothrix aequalis colonized such slides as crossed the air–water boundary; the species is localized in a like way on natural surfaces, probably as the result of the settling of positively phototactic zoospores. The absence of *Cladophora* is attributed to the infrequent production of motile stages, not coinciding with periods of exposure of the slides. However, Flint (1950) in one of the Metropolitan Water Board reservoirs at Barn Elms near London suspected that a selective effect of the glass was responsible for the restricted colonization of slides by *Cladophora*.

Position of slides and extent of colonization. Slides placed horizontally accumulate considerably more haptobenthos than do those set vertically (Newcombe 1950; Castenholz 1960). This difference seems greatest at times of maximum production. Castenholz found in Falls Lake in the Grand Coulee that the horizontal slides carried 12.4 times as much material as did the vertical at the time of the spring maximum, but only 6.2 times in the summer. Castenholz believed that the differences were not due primarily to sedimenting phytoplankton collecting on the slides.

Seasonal variation on slides. The time of maximum production varied considerably in the Grand Coulee Lakes. In Falls Lake, the most carefully studied of the freshwater lakes of the group, a striking maximum production, exceeding 500 mg m^{-2} day^{-1}, was observed, in the top 1 m, due largely to *Cymbella mexicana* with other species of the genus and *Synedra acus* and *S. ulna* occurred in April of 1955. This was followed by smaller productions due primarily to *Epithemia turgida* (Fig. 152). In 1956 the same type of qualitative sequence occurred but the large initial production of *C. mexicana* was not observed and the spring maximum in May was due largely to *E. turgida*. In both years the minimum production was in August and a feeble secondary maximum again due to *E. turgida* occurred in October. Striking spring maxima, late summer minima, and secondary autumnal maxima occurred in Alkali Lake (Fig. 153), in spite of its name the other

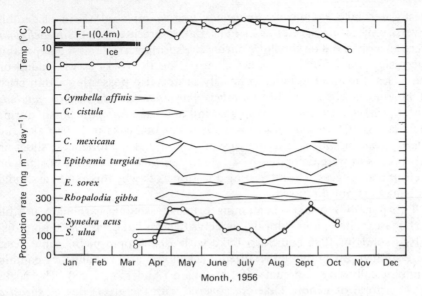

FIGURE 152. Production of diatoms on glass slides set at 0.4 m in Falls Lake, Garnd Coulee in 1956 (Castenholz). Note replacement of *Cymbella* spp. and *Synedra* spp. by *Epithemia turgida* during early sumemer.

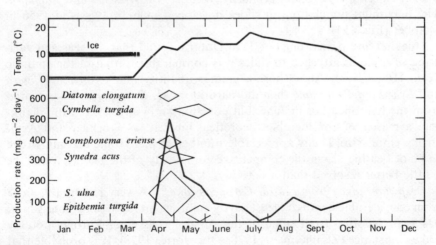

FIGURE 153. Production of diatoms on glass slides set at 0.4 m in Alkali Lake, Grand Coulee in 1956 (Castenholz). Strong spring bloom with some *Epithemia turgida* later.

freshwater lake examined; *Epithemia turgida* replaced the considerable diversity of spring species as in Falls Lake. Green tufts of *Stigeoclonium* were also observed on the slides during the spring maximum. A comparable succession among diatom species occurred on the rocks as was found on the slides, the latter differing primarily in not also possessing a thin crust of blue-green algae, notably *Calothrix parietina* and *Amphithrix janthina* with the green alga *Gongrosira* sp. and in Falls Lake *Entophysalis* sp. during the summer. *Cladophora fracta* was luxuriant on rocks in Falls Lake and *Gloeotrichia pisum* on macrophytes in Alkali Lake. Horizontal slides in this lake also were colonized by *G. pisum* on their undersides but not on their upper surfaces. The interesting question as to why this epiphyte should so behave is not discussed.

Two mineralized lakes, containing primarily sodium carbonate and bicarbonate, sulfate, and chloride, namely, Lenore Lake with 7500 ppm dissolved solids in 1956 and Soap Lake with 20,600 ppm in the same year, were studied. Like other mineralized lakes in semiarid regions they contain limnologically large amounts of phosphate (Anderson 1958). The rocks of the littoral of Lenore Lake are covered with the green alga *Gongrosira* sp., predominant where the rock surface was shaded, or with a tough crust of *Calothrix parietina*, *Amphithrix janthina*, and *Plectonema nostocorum*. Diatoms occurred in these algal communities and on supposedly bare rock, but few species were found, primarily members of *Nitzschia* and *Amphora*. The maximum population on slides developed in both 1955 and 1956 in October (Fig. 154).

Stockner and Armstrong (1971) in Ontario found that the seasonal variation of diatoms attached to slides was comparable to that of the epilithic flora. However, the slides bore a greater quantity of *Cyclotella stelligera* and *Synedra delicatissima* than did natural rocks. *C. stelligera* disappeared from the haptobenthos in June, but concomitantly appeared in the plankton, a matter of considerable theoretical interest, as Stockner and Armstrong emphasize. If any appreciable number of planktonic diatoms prove to be of benthic origin the competitive complexity of the plankton may be a little better resolved than it is today.

Deepwater algae from central European lakes. A very remarkable flora from considerable depths, at least partly epilithic, on loose calcareous sinter, has been reported from some of the subalpine lakes of Europe, notably Lake Constance (Zimmermann 1928; Oberdorfer 1928). It is probable that decreasing transparency of all the large lakes of this area has decimated this flora in the last few decades. When investigated it consisted of an *Hildenbrandia rivularis–Bodanella lauterborni* association (Fig. 155) some species of which (*B. lauterborni*, *Batrachospermum* sp. sub *Chantransia chalybea* var. *profunda*, and certain diatoms), penetrated to 40 m, with

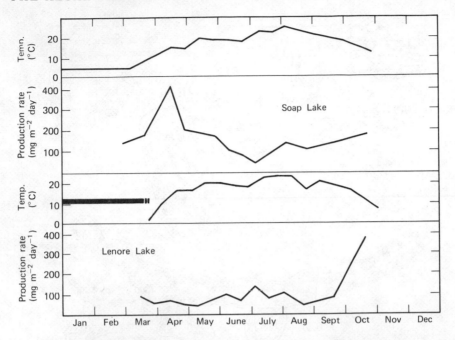

FIGURE 154.   Production of diatoms on glass slides set at 0.4 m in the mineralized Soap and Lenore Lakes, in the Grand Coulee (Castenholz).   Diatoms not determinable owing to solution in alkaline water. Note only autumnal bloom in Lake Lenore.

Gongrosira debaryana, Chamaesiphon incrustans on solid surfaces, and *Chroococcus* sp. to 30 m or a little less. At the latter depth the intensity of violet light was computed to be but 0.0064% of the surface irradiance and red light is reduced further by two orders of magnitude. Chromatic adaptation is most conspicuous.

The epiphytic haptobenthos.   We have already seen that there is great overlap between the floristic composition of the three main types of benthic community. It is therefore not surprising that within the epiphytic community there is little differentiation between the algae that occur on various flowering plants or on other algae.

Relation of epiphytes to their substrata.   Godward (1934) has studied some of the factors that determine the presence of epiphytes on a plant. In general on any water plant producing successive leaves the number of epiphytes is least on the youngest leaf, increases fairly rapidly to a maximum on an older living leaf, from which the number falls off slowly till dead leaves are reached. The proportion of young specimens of any multicellular thallose alga, in which growth stages can be recognized, is greatest

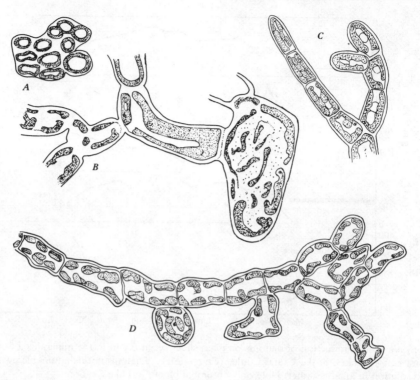

FIGURE 155. Variously colored algae from the deep water of Lake Constance. *A, Chroococcus* sp. (×300) Myxophyceae, pink; *B. Gongrosira debaryana* (1000) Chlorophyceae, dark green; *C, Batrachospermum* sp. sub *Chantransia chalybea* var. *profunda* (×600) very dark greenish gray; *D, Bodanella lauterborni* (×600) Phaeophyceae, brown (Zimmerman).

at the apex of the plant bearing the epiphytes. Presumably zoospores settle more readily on young leaves.

Usually there are more epiphytes on the upper surface of a leaf than on its lower surface, but if the leaf has unfolded at the water surface so that the upper side is initially dry, more epiphytes will naturally be found on its lower than its upper surface. Godward (1934) found that nearly all green algae tended to settle at the depressions demarcating the cell boundaries of a leaf. Some epiphytic algae such as *Coleochaete nitellarum* and *Aphanochaete repens* tend to follow the cell boundaries in their subsequent growth. This growth habit can be obtained on glass slides on which fine grooves have been made with a diamond. The same type of behavior doubtless leads to cases in which the epiphyte grows primarily between teeth on the margins of leaves, as with *Gongrosira* sp. on *Equisetum fluviatile* or *Stigeoclonium farctum* on *Elodea canadensis*.

In all cases, as Willer (1923) also often found, there is a tendency to settle at or near the midrib. Willer, however, noted considerable differences among the distributions of epiphytic algae of different species on a leaf of *Elodea canadensis* (*A* of Fig. 156), the pattern of settlement (*D* of Fig. 156) of *Cocconeis placentula* (*F* of Fig. 156) being quite different from that (*B* of Fig. 156) of *Protoderma viride* (*C* of Fig. 156). Both Willer and Godward found that on the lower dead leaves of a plant, the difference in distribution of epiphytes on the upper and lower surfaces, observed on living leaves, tended to disappear. Willer found evidence that *Cocconeis placentula* could move away from dying portions of an *Elodea* leaf and become concentrated on the still living parts (*E* of Fig. 156).

The field data suggest that there is little specificity in the choice of vegetable substrate. Epiphytes can also colonize inorganic solid surfaces or, under undisturbed laboratory conditions, even the surface film. In the case of the genus *Chrysopyxis*, as has already been mentioned, the lower end of the cell capsule is produced on either side into two curved structures that embrace a filamentous alga like a clip; *Chrysopyxis* is therefore presumably limited to substrate of the right shape. Other epiphytes show little or no specialization for attachment to plants of a particular form; however, Prowse (1959) found that if water plants are allowed to develop in a medium in which silver ions are maintained in solution, shoots entirely free from epiphytes but in a healthy condition can be obtained. Such shoots of *Utricularia* sp., *Najas graminea*, and *Enhydrias angustipetala* were exposed, for 2 weeks, in a fishpond in Malaya, protected by a screen that excluded large herbivores but permitted access by small organisms. A very remarkable specificity, indicated in Table 77, appeared in the epiphytic floras developed on the three kinds of plants. Only three epiphytes were common, but each plant bore a different florule; loose filaments of *Mougeotia capucina* were also present, but were evidently unimportant. Nothing in the botanical literature prepares one for such a clear-cut and convincing result. The preference of *Gomphonema* for *Utricularia* is, however, paralleled by certain sessile rotifers (Edmondson 1944), to be discussed in Vol. IV.

Most of the filamentous Conjugales, in which the growth pattern is intercalary, are usually devoid of an epiphytic flora, as Cholnoky (1927) pointed out, whereas the other filamentous green algae, with apical growth, ordinarily bear epiphytes distributed roughly as on flowering plants, the youngest apical cells bearing the fewest. Godward (1934), however, thinks that the difference in colonization between the Conjugales and the rest is not entirely due to the mode of division, but also to the nature of the sur-

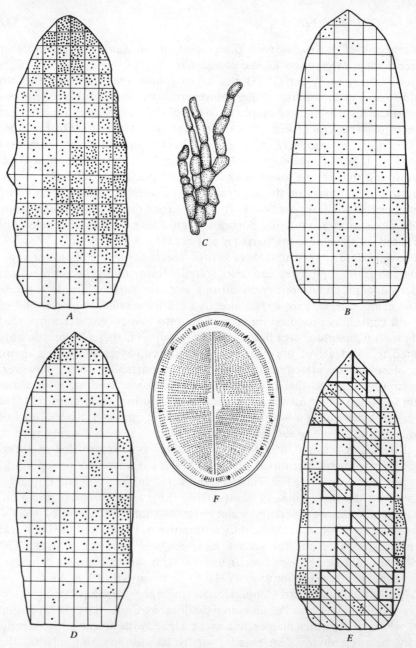

FIGURE 156. *A*, Total disposition of epiphytic flora on a leaf of *Elodea canadensis*; *B*, largely central distribution of the green alga *Protoderma viride* on a comparable leaf; *C*, a colony of *P. viride* (×520); *D*, apical and periphera distribution of *Cocconeis placentula* on a healthy leaf of *E. canadensis*; *E*, the same on a partly moribund leaf, the dead portions hatched showing apparent retreat of the diatom; *F*. *C. placentula* (×1000) (Willer, West, Hustedt).

TABLE 77.   *Mean number of various epiphytes on clean shoots of three species of angiosperm in a Malayan fishpond (Prowse)*

Species	Gomphonema cf. gracile (mean no. mm^{-2})	Eunotia cf. pectinalis (mean no. mm^{-2})	Oedogonium sp.
Utricularia sp.	14.05	0.00	0
Enhydrias angustepetala	1.83	0.07	Present
Najas graminea	2.05	4.77	Very rare

face of attachment. In most Conjugales there is a thick mucilage sheath over the cell wall; only when the cell is moribund and the mucilage is disappearing do epiphytes appear on the filaments of *Zygnema* and *Spirogyra*. It must of course be remembered that a moribund cell may not produce mucilage, but it has also ceased to divide. *Mougeotia*, which is exceptional among the filamentous Conjugales in bearing some epiphytes, is also exceptional in having a much more delicate mucilage sheath. Even in this case Godward concludes that only certain species, notably *Aphanochaete repens*, can be really successful on *Mougeotia*. More recently Pankov (1961) has suggested that the Conjugales inhibit epiphytes by the production of tannins. Chemical evidence for the existence of such materials in plants of this order is forthcoming; they seem to have a bacteriostatic action, but no information as to their effects on algae seems to have been reported.

Apart from the very limited specificity which has just been discussed and the geometrical influences of the shape of the plant, it is reasonable to suppose that the main factors involved in regulating colonization by epiphytes are hydrographic, notably water level and water movements, optical, and chemical. The observational data on the vertical distribution of epiphytes on reasonably uniform substrata such as reeds can be to some extent interpreted in terms of hydrographic and optical variables, but there is little information, either observational or experimental, that bears on the chemical factors that may be involved.

Vertical distribution of epiphytes on reeds.   Cholnoky (1929) made a very detailed study of the colonization by diatoms of the stems of *Phragmites australis* growing at seven stations along the shore of the Tihany peninsula projecting into Lake Balaton. He records 150 taxa of diatoms but of them only 50 are regarded as typically epiphytes. The mean vertical distribution of the commonest of these along the stem of the reed is shown in Fig. 157, together with an indication of relative light intensity and with drawings from Hustedt (1930) of the species involved. Unfortunately although Cholnoky (1927) has figured the two characteristic types of attachment in *Cymbella*, the basal stalk of *C. cistula* and the gelatinous tube in *C. caespi-*

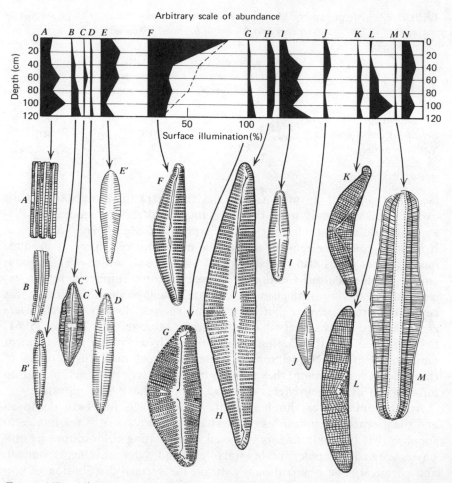

FIGURE 157. Above, mean distribution of various species of diatoms on seven stands of *Phragmites australis* in Lake Balaton, and below, the diatoms involved; *A, Fragilaria intermedia; B., B, Rhoicosphenia curvata; C, Mastogloia smithii* var. *lacustris; D, Navicula gracilis; E, Gomphonema olivacueum; F, Cymbella affinis; G, C. prostrata; H, C. helvetica; I, lacustris; J, C. ventricosa; K. Epithemia sorex; L, E. zebra* (mixed on reeds with some *E. turgida); M, Rhopalodia gibba; N*, other diatoms (Cholnoky, Hustedt).

tosa, these two species were not of major importance in his study of Lake Balaton, though *C. cistula* did occur. The reader may also be referred to the colored photographs of living *Cymbella prostrata* and *Gomphonema olivaceum*, opposite page 69 of Löffler's (1974) recent monograph of the Neusiedlersee, doubtless the most beautiful book on a limnological subject yet published. The most conspicuous feature of the distribution is the great abundance of *Cymbella affinis* at the surface. Since this species still forms quite respectable populations relative to its congeners deeper down on the reed, it clearly can live at light intensities lower than those prevalent at the surface and probably maintains the very high superficial population primarily on account of its efficient attachment by a strong stalk, comparable to that of *C. cistula*. The usually larger but structurally similar and similarly attached *C. helvetica*, however, is distributed quite differently and rather variably, the irregularities averaging out over all the seven stations. There is here always a clear minimum at or near the surface. Two other species of the genus, *C. prostrata* and *C. lacustris*, which live in gelatinous tubes rather than attached by stalks, tend to increase in numbers with depth, and a fifth species, *C. ventricosa*, has a highly irregular distribution with no consistency between the stations. These three species, particularly *C. prostrata* and *C. ventricosa*, are apt to produce auxospores, and Cholnoky thinks that the irregularity of their distribution may be dependent on this.

In the other genera, at most stations *Gomphonema olivaceum* has low populations at the surface and at depths of about 1 m, with larger ones between, being presumably limited by wave action on the one hand and low light intensities on the other. Most of the other species seem to increase in numbers with depth; this is particularly true of *Epithemia zebra* with which less numerous *E. turgida* are mixed. Apart from the species whose distribution was discussed in detail, the most important epiphytes appear to have been *Amphora* spp., *Cocconeis placentula*, *Achnanthes minutissima*, *Nitzscha* spp., and *Synedra* spp. In these genera there is clearly much overlap with the epilithic flora; *Diatoma tenue* is specifically mentioned as characteristic of eulittoral stones.

Considering diatoms which occur in July either as epiphytes or in the epilithic communities of the rockier shore of Windermere, Godward (1937) found consistent distribution of certain species that appeared to depend on exposure to light or shading. *Cocconeis placentula* was found to occur as a dominant on the upper sides of *Potamogeton* and *Elodea* leaves, and on the upper parts of stems. *Eunotia veneris* occurred on the lower side of leaves and low on the stems. *E. lunaris* was present only on the undersides of leaves. When these species occur epilithically on the stones of rocky shores, they are arranged in the same order, *C. placentula* being most abundant at 3 m, *E. veneris* at 4 m, and *E. lunaris* at 5–6 m. The two sets of habitats are clearly very different, but in both of them *C. placentula* appears to occur in the more and *E. lunaris* in the less illuminated situations, with *E. veneris* occupying an intermediate place.

Chemical factors influencing epiphytes.   The general distribution of the epiphytic flora from lake to lake is undoubtedly controlled by water chemistry in the same sort of way as are other types of algal flora in freshwaters. Very numerous, though evidently not necessarily specific, epiphytes, both among the desmids and in the diatoms of the genus *Eunotia*, are found primarily in soft water. Within a given locality seasonal changes in water chemistry are certain to be important, as for instance the variation of silicon content, so important to diatoms. The possibility that diatoms may obtain silicon directly from the plants on which they are growing (Jørgensen 1957) has already been discussed (Vol. II, p. 470).

Godward (1937), working in Windermere, believed that the overall nature of the littoral, whether primarily inorganic or largely vegetated, made a qualitative difference to the flora. She specified *Frustulia rhomboides*, *Mougeotia parvula*, and *Batrachospermum moniliforme* as particularly characteristic of the interior of evolved reed beds. The determining factors involved are likely to be chemical.

Of special significance to epiphytic algae are such changes brought about by the macroscopic vegetation on which the epiphytes grow. Stimulated by the observations of Hasler and Jones (1949) of an inhibitory effect of macrophytes on phytoplankton, Fitzgerald (1969) has studied the conditions under which various larger plants may become covered with epiphytes. He finds that in general epiphytic growth is negligible if the larger plant is, at the time, limited by nitrogen, either as nitrate or ammonia, but as soon as combined nitrogen is present in appreciable quantities in the water, in excess of the needs of the macrophytes, epiphytic growth becomes heavy. This was not only found in experiments with barley seedling roots in nutrient culture and pondweeds of various kinds in the laboratory, but was apparent on *Cladophora* in Lake Mendota. In the spring when the *Cladophora* was supplied with an excess of nitrogen in the water and took up only 1 μg N. $NH_3 \cdot mg^{-1}$ alga$\cdot hr^{-1}$, it was covered with *Rhoicosphenia*, *Melosira*, and *Nitzschia*. As the nitrogen demand rose to 1.4–2.7 μg N. $NH_3 \cdot mg^{-1}$ alga$\cdot hr^{-1}$, the epiphytic flora declined; later in August when the uptake fell again to ≤ 0.6 μg N. $NH_3 \cdot mg^{-1}$ alga$\cdot hr^{-1}$, epiphytic blue-green algae, mainly *Schizothrix*, appeared. The effect under Fitzgerald's broadly varied conditions seems to have involved only combined nitrogen and not phosphorus. It is, however, not clear whether nitrogen-fixing blue-green algae, which he found generally to be phosphorus limited, might not be affected by phosphorus uptake by macrophytes. Other factors were certainly involved in some of his observations. *Pithophora oedogonium*, which has a reputation for keeping down algae in fish tanks, did so only in the presence of low or moderate nitrogen contents. In this case there was also a suspicion of an associated *Cytophaga*-like organism being involved.

Interrelationships of epiphytes with macrophytes and the possibility of a coadaptive system. Two very important papers, by Wetzel and Allen

(1971) and Allen (1971), have investigated the dynamic aspects of the relationship of the epiphytes found growing in Lawrence Lake, Barry County, Michigan on submersed parts of the emergent rush *Scirpus acutus* and on the submersed flora of *Najas flexilis* and *Chara* spp. in the same lake. The water of the lake is very hard, containing 50–70 mg Ca liter^{-1}.

Owing to the greater surface provided by *Najas* and *Chara* than by *Scirpus* the epiphytic population was believed to be very much greater on the first two plants than on the third. On account of the difficulty of separating epiphytic material from the macrophytes that carried it, quantitative estimates were made from haptobenthos growing on unit area of plexiglass slides, multiplied by estimates of macrophyte area obtained by the use of surfactants (Harrod and Hall 1962).

The chlorophyll content, as a measure of biomass throughout the year in the two stations studied, and the primary productivity as measured by the ^{14}C technique, are given in Fig. 158. All productivities are corrected for deposition of Ca^{14}CO$_3$ as the result of photosynthesis; the correction is variable but can amount to as much as 71.7% of the photosynthetically fixed carbon. There seems to have been a slight tendency for slides in the *Scirpus* station to show a higher productivity per unit area of artificial surface than in the *Najas–Chara* station.

If we assume the validity of calculating natural productivity from the productivity on slides, the results presented in Table 78 are valid. These are compared with certain other data, all of which will again be considered in Vol. IV. It is evident that in relatively small lakes with abundant macrophytes the haptobenthic community may be of major importance in the dynamics of the lacustrine ecosystem.

Wetzel has found (see p. 390) that *Najas flexilis* loses considerable amounts of organic matter to the ambient water during photosynthesis. Even when conditions for retention are most favorable, with low potassium and high calcium concentrations in the medium, the loss is almost always over 10% of the carbon fixed; in less favorable circumstances it is more and

TABLE 78. *Productivity of different parts of the total mass of primary producers in two lakes (Allen 1971; Rich, Wetzel, and Thuy 1971; Wetzel 1964)*

	Productivity (mg cm^{-2} yr^{-1})	
Producer	Lawrence Lake	Borax Lake
Phytoplankton	5.07	9.11
Haptobenthic algae	3.79 (epiphytic)	26.70 (epilithic)
Macrophytes	8.79	2.79

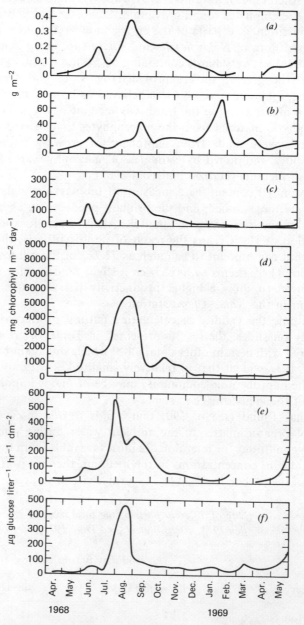

FIGURE 158. Seasonal variation in chlorophyll content association on slides. (*a*) At station I; (*b*) at station II, in Lawrence Lake, Michigan; (*c*) correlated primary productivity on slides set 5 cm above sediments at station I; (*d*) station II; (*e*) maximal bacterial uptake of glucose by same association, station I; (*f*) the same, station II (Allen).

sometimes very much more than this proportion. Allen's studies, in which $^{14}CO_2$ was supplied to the aerial tips of *Scirpus* plants and later appeared in organic matter in solution around the lower submersed parts of the plant, indicate that *Scirpus* also excretes organic matter. Allen showed experimentally that pure cultures of epiphytic bacteria (*Caulobacter*, *Pseudomonas*) and of algae (*Gomphonema*, *Chlorella*, and *Cyclotella*) took up labeled organic matter produced by *Najas flexilis*; the rate of uptake by the bacteria was considerably greater than that by algae, but mixtures of algae and bacteria were more efficient than bacteria alone. The epiphytic flora could be shown to metabolize glucose, fructose, galactose, acetate, glycolate, succinate, glycine, alanine, and serine. Acetate was most readily used. Experiments with glucose indicated first-order, Michaelis–Menten kinetics characterized active uptake by bacteria; algal uptake was slower and apparently passive. When the epiphytic populations from slides were examined the uptake was characteristically active and presumably nearly all bacterial. The uptake was greatest in summer when the standing crop and the temperature were both maximal. Though these experiments involve the addition of unnatural amounts of glucose or acetate to the water, there can be little doubt that at least some of the organic matter lost from the plant is contributed to its epiphytes. Even though the algae may use little or none directly, the respiration of the bacteria fed by such organic matter would contribute to the CO_2 concentration available to the algae within the mat. Moreover the precipitation of calcium carbonate causes the retention of some absorbed organic matter in the epiphyte layer which might become available if conditions for the solution of $CaCO_3$ intervene. The further role of the bacteria and their secretions in providing a substratum for diatoms is also made clear by Allanson (1973) in his very beautiful electron micrographs of the epiphytes of *Chara*, of which three are reproduced in Fig. 159.

Wetzel and Allen both stress the general importance of all these interactions in the biology of a shallow lake. It is, however, perhaps possible to go a little further.

The rates of loss of organic matter, at least from *Najas flexilis*, even in a water quite low in potassium and high in calcium, usually amount to a fifth to a quarter of the carbon fixed photosynthetically. This seems extraordinarily inefficient, unless it is adaptive. The fascinating work that has just been renewed would suggest that the excretion is advantageous to the haptobenthic organisms, both on the plants and also such as may be found on artificial surfaces in their neighborhood.

On earlier pages when the sodium content of water plants (p. 000) or the rather general lack of secondary compounds that might discourage herbivores (p. 000) was discussed, it was pointed out that the majority of

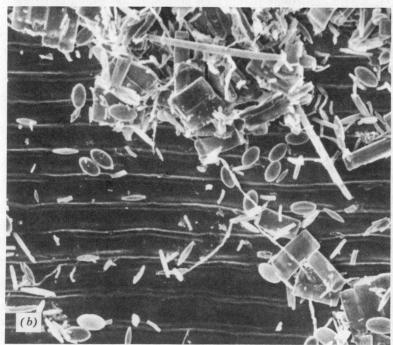

FIGURE 159.   (a) Early colonization by epiphytes on ventral surface of leaf of *Potamogeton natans* (×80); (b) mature association on stipule of same (×100); (c) decalcified association on *Chara* sp. showing diatoms, largely *Achnanthes minutissima*, attached to mucoid sheath (×1300) (Allanson).

the herbivorous invertebrates of freshwaters do not feed on higher plants but rather on the epiphytic and other benthic communities largely composed of algae, bacteria, and associated detritus. This was noted 70 years ago by Pond (1905) and a little later by Shelford (1913). Moore (1913) in the same year criticized the concept in detail, though in at least one of her counterexamples the chironomid larvae discussed were evidently primarily epiphyte feeders. The main exceptions to the generalization concern certain lepidopterous, and some leaf-mining dipterous, larvae. These will be discussed when the littoral benthic animals are considered in Vol. IV. For the present it is clear that in spite of these exceptions the generalization holds in a broad probabilistic way. Gajewskaia (1958), though she was to produce an impressive summary of existing knowledge on the role of higher aquatic plants as food for animals (Gaewskaia 1969), clearly felt that in many cases the haptobenthonic microphytes were, on account of their accessibility, of greater importance than the larger plants. Moreover the kind of microscopic epiphyte which plays such an immense role in freshwaters is developed only to a very slight extent on land, primarily as thin growths of green algae on tree trunks which, though important to the Psocoptera, play a very small quantitative role in terrestrial ecology. It is therefore not unreasonable to suggest that the epiphytic haptobenthos or periphyton constitutes a major protection for the plants that bear it, making existence easy for the species that feed by scraping off small plants and perhaps hard for those that live by biting off small pieces of large plants, or by sucking sap from the latter. If this is indeed the case it would seem likely that the excretion of dissolved organic matter discovered by Wetzel is not a nonsensical misadaptation as might first appear, but is in fact adaptive, leading to an increase in epiphytes that play the same sort of role in fresh water as do the chemical adaptations against excessive onslaughts of herbivores on land. Pond (1918) seems to have entertained such an idea, particularly with regard to gelatinous material secreted by the plant, as in *Brasenia*.

Endophytic algae.   A few algae, notably *Chlorochytrium* in the Chlorococcaes, are endoparasitic organisms invading the tissues of water plants; *C. lemnae* the best-known species is usually found in *Lemna* but has been recorded in *Ceratophyllum*, *Elodea*, and certain mosses. The older information about such plants is well reviewed by Fritsch (1935). Presumably the endophytic species evolved from epiphytes.

THE EPIPELIC ALGAE OF THE HERPOBENTHOS

The epipelic algae usually have a greater depth range than the other ecological groups of benthic algae, for although they do not ordinarily occur above mean water level, they extend to the littoriprofundal where they may be associated with colorless protists which extend downward on the mud into the profundal.

Nature of the epipelic flora and relation to the substratum.   A fair number of studies have been made of the composition of particular taxocenes, most notably the diatoms, but relatively few of the epipelic littoral flora as a whole. Of these few studies those of Round (1953, 1957a, b, c, d, 1960, 1961) on the lakes of the English Lake District are of particular importance and constitute a convenient entry into the subject. The mud examined was from shallow littoral stations, apparently at depths of 1–2 m. In all cases either diatoms or blue-green algae were the two most important classes of organisms encountered. The actual enumeration of individuals is not comparable for the two groups; it seems certain that in a good many collections the biomass of diatoms would have been greater than that of the blue-green algae, whereas in others it would have been less. The diatoms greatly exceeded the blue-green algae in number of taxa present, the former group being represented (Round 1957c) by at least 78 taxa, the latter by at least 20. In each case some groups of species could not be completely determined, but it is reasonable to conclude that the diatoms are represented by more than three times the number of species found among the Myxophyceae in Round's localities. A quantitatively very small but quite diverse flora of green algae occurs, and flagellates form a minor, but not entirely insignificant, part of the epipelic flora in a few localities.

Chemical ecology. In order to provide a chemical variable with which the biological data could be compared, Round considered all the analyses of the extracts of his mud samples made with dilute acetic acid. Each locality was scored for the rank order of each analyzed component, and these scores summed to give a nutrient index. Since there were 14 determinations made, the lowest value that a sediment could have would be 14, and since there are 23 stations, the highest value would be 322. Actually the various substances determined were only partially correlated, and the range was from 63 in littoral sediment from Crummock Water to 193 in that from Grasmere. The stations were divided into two groups: group I may be regarded as more or less oligotrophic; in no case did Round's nutrient index exceed 128. In the more mesotrophic localities of group II it never fell below 135.

The estimates of total standing crop were found to have a higher mean value for group II communities than for those of group I. Most of Round's actual estimates are not published, but fair approximations for the mean total, diatom, blue-green, and flagellate populations can be read off a histogram (Round 1957a, Fig. 1). When this is done, however, correlation of total epipelic population with nutrient index proves insignificant. The only significant simple correlation was with sodium and this is negative $(-0.630, P < 0.001)$. Comparable though rather less high negative correlations with sodium are given by the diatoms $(-0.563, 0.01 > P > 0.001)$ and blue-green algae $(-0.507, 0.02 > P > 0.01)$ separately. The meaning of this kind of correlation, which is the highest obtained for either of the most abundant algal groups with any chemical parameter, is far from obvious.

The diatom populations are moderately and positively correlated with both phosphorus $(0.450, 0.05 > P > 0.02)$ and calcium $(0.483, 0.05 > P > 0.02)$; the elements in question are themselves highly correlated $(0.729, P < 0.001)$. Comparable relationships are not shown by the Myxophyceae nor by the green algae, but are strikingly exhibited by the flagellates (with P $0.469, 0.05 > P > 0.02$; with Ca $0.567, 0.01 > P > 0.001$). Neither the green algae nor the flagellates are significantly negatively correlated with sodium, in fact the former group shows a significant positive correlation $(0.556, 0.01 > P > 0.001)$, presumably due to the desmid populations of the more dilute lakes. The flagellate populations are significantly correlated with those of diatoms (0.658, 0.01 > P > 0.001) and green algae (0.495, P ≃ 0.02), and are also the only group significantly correlated with Round's nutrient index (0.549, 0.01 > P > 0.001). All groups are clearly behaving somewhat differently but the blue-green algae differ more from the others than these do among themselves.

If a scatter diagram is made, relating occurrence of diatoms and of blue-green algae to extractable phosphorus or calcium (Fig. 160), it is apparent that as the amounts of these substances increase, so does the probability of obtaining a high diatom population, but that no such effect is obvious for the blue-green algae. This of course does not mean that blue-green algae are independent of calcium or phosphorus, but merely that these elements seem not to be limiting to epipelic Myxophyceae in the English Lake District. It is conceivable that their concentration may have a qualitative effect on the Myxophycean flora.

It is possible, even though the meaning of the negative correlation with sodium is obscure, to use the three variables which seem most significant, at least in determining the diatom populations, in constructing a new environmental index, following a procedure like that used by Round. The lakes are ordered from the lowest to highest for phosphorus and for calcium, and from highest to lowest for sodium. These ordinal numbers are then added up for each lake. The lowest possible value would be three, the highest 66. Actually, the range is from six (Wastwater) to 62 (Esthwaite). We may reasonably separate the lowest four lakes, Pearsall's rocky lakes (Wastwater 6, Buttermere 8, Crummock 21.5, and Ennerdale 21.5) as an oligotrophic group and the highest three (Elterwater 54, Loughrigg Tarn 58, and Esthwaite 62) as eutrophic, and regard the other lakes as mesotrophic. This arrangement has been occasionally employed as a supplement to the division into the two groups used by Round, in commenting on the distribution of species in the following sections.

Several taxa of diatoms are completely confined to Round's group I stations. Of these *Eucocconeis flexella* is found only in three of the four (Buttermere, Ennerdale, and Crummock) rocky oligotrophic lakes and at the north station in Brotherswater, while *Frustulia rhomboides* and its var. *saxonica* occur frequently at the stations in the four oligotrophic lakes and much less commonly in N. Brotherswater, Derwentwater, Rydal Water, and at the N. Windermere station. *Cymbella ventricosa* likewise occurred frequently in the four oligotrophic lakes and less so in four others also. *Gomphonema acuminata* var. *coronata* was also very frequent in all four rocky lakes and N. Brotherswater but rarer in the other four stations from which it is recorded. *Anomoeoneis* spp. including *A. serians* var. *brachystira* showed a similar distribution. These taxa may be regarded as character-

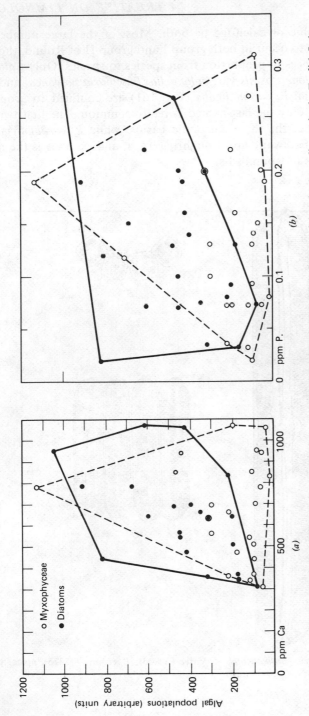

FIGURE 160. (a) Distribution of epipelic diatoms (solid) and blue-green algae (open) relative to calcium in the sediment in the English Lake District; (b) the same relative to phosphorus. Note that diatoms, unlike blue-green algae, become more abundant as these two elements are more concentrated. Concentrations in ppm in 0.5 N acetic acid extract.

istically oligotrophic or calcifuge or both. Most of the large number of
other species tend to occur in both group I and group II of Round, though
with slight differences in proportion from species to species. Only *Caloneis
amphisbaena, Diploneis ovalis* var. *oblongella, Pinnularia polyonca*, and the
remarkable colonial *P. cardinaliculis* (Fig. 161) are confined to group II
stations. Of these only the last-named is really common. The first two do
not occur in any of the three eutrophic basins, while *P. cardinaliculis* is
most frequent in Esthwaite and Loughrigg Tarn, and perhaps is the most
eutraphent species in Round's list.

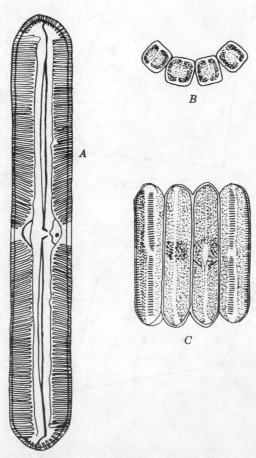

FIGURE 161.   *Pinnularia cardinaliculis. A*, Valve (×800); *B*, colony (×375), apical view;
C, colony (×575), surface view (Lund).

The most widespread and generally frequent species found at every station in the epipelic environment of the littoral of the English Lakes were *Caloneis silicula*, *Navicula cryptocephala*, *Pinnularia viridis*, and *Nitzschia palea* (sens. lat.). A good many more species, mostly in *Navicula*, *Pinnularia*, and *Nitzschia* are unrecorded only in one or two lakes.

When comparison of the autoecology of the taxa found in the Lake District is made with that of the same taxa found elsewhere, there is often agreement, but sometimes surprising differences. Of the taxa listed above as characteristic of group I stations and, in the English Lake District, reasonably regarded as oligotraphent, acidophilic, or calcifuge, Budde (1944) regards *Eucocconeis flexella* as having these ecological characteristics, but he considers *Cymbella ventricosa* to be transcursional and *G. acuminatum* var. *coronatum* as alkalophilic. Klotter (1953), however, agrees with Round's findings regarding the last two species. Such discrepancies could be due to the distributions not being dependent on the factors being studied, or if they are so, local races of varying tolerance may be involved, or the chemical properties of the environment may act indirectly regulating the direction in which competition may go, but this will also involve the identity of the competitor. For the present it is impossible to go further.

It should be noted that the littoral benthic diatom flora of the lakes of the English Lake District is likely to be characteristic of a rather moderate range of pH values and calcium concentrations, and the truly calcicole species are unlikely to occur there. Similarly the number of truly eutrophic localities is limited.

The blue-green algae tend to be more abundant and more diversified in the mesotrophic lakes of group II than in the oligotrophic lakes. This tendency seems to be more pronounced in the coccoid Chroococcales than in the filamentous forms. The most widespread species were *Oscillatoria splendida* and *Pseudanabaena catenata* which occurred in all the lakes studied. No species was clearly commoner in the oligotrophic than in the mesotrophic group. *Aphanothece stagnina*, *Holopedia geminata*, and *Oscillatoria agardhii* var. *isothrix* were obviously much commoner in the mesotrophic localities; the last-named is an important planker on occasion.

Undetermined species of *Cryptomonas* were present in all the lakes studied. The two fully identified members of the genus, *C. ovata* and *C. erosa*, were both much more widely distributed in the lakes of group II than those of group I. The Chrysomonads, of which no species occurred in all lakes, are widely represented by *Synura uvella* and *Mallomonas* spp., such taxa being most frequent in group II. Four of Round's group I lakes, but not any of the rocky oligotrophic members of the group, and one of the group II stations, lacked these flagellates entirely.

The Euglenineae show a comparable but more extreme distribution. At least eight species of *Euglena*, four of *Phacus*, nine of *Trachelomonas*, and *Lepocinclis ovum* were present in the area studied. Three lakes of group I, but only one of the truly oligotrophic ones (Ennerdale, with Bassenthwaite and Loweswater) and one station in group II (Ullswater N) lacked the group entirely. Of the fully determined species *Euglena mutabilis*, *Phacus pleuronectes*, *Trachelomonas volvocina*, and *T. hispida* are the most widespread; all occur in both groups of stations but more often in group II. No Euglenineae occurred in Ennerdale and none of the genera other than *Euglena*, represented only by *E. mutabilis* and *E.* sp., in any of the rocky oligotrophic lakes. It is not unlikely that here and perhaps in the Chrysomonadina the main limitation is due to lack of accessory nutrients such as cobalamin or thiamine. Dinoflagellates occur at all stations but like the other flagellates are more frequent at those of group II. *Gymnodinium aeruginosum* is the commonest species at stations of that group, while *Hemidinium nasutum* is fairly evenly distributed throughout the whole series of lakes. The two stations for *Ceratium cornutum* are both in Brotherswater, in which lake this species was the dominant epipelic dinoflagellate.

Among the green algae, the desmids are, as would be expected, commoner in group I than at the stations of group II, though the number of taxa, 31 for the former group and 27 for the latter, is not greatly different. The frequency is greatest in the four rocky oligotrophic lakes, in Derwentwater, and in the eutrophic Loughrigg Tarn.

The other green algae are far less numerous and are absent from the epipelic environment of the stations studied in Rydal Water, Loweswater, and three of the four oligotrophic lakes; the fourth of these, Buttermere, had only *Ankistrodesmus falcatus* var. *acicularis*. All other lakes have some Chlorococcales, usually the familiar *Pediastrum boryanum* and *Scenedesmus quadricauda*.

Round, in his investigation of the epipelic flora of Malham Tarn, Yorkshire, studied two quite different sediments on either side of the lake, overlain by essentially the same kind of fairly alkaline water, which contains about 73–159 mg HCO_3^- liter^{-1} (60–130 ppm alkalinity as $CaCO_3$), the higher values being from December to April, the lower in July, August, and, in one year, September. One sediment is a black flocculent peat, containing fibrous remains of flowering plants and mosses, washed into the lake. The other is calcareous with sand grains, also believed by Round to be largely allochthonous; it apparently has the texture of a silt or mud.

The epipelic flora of the two sediments is strikingly different. Diatoms are more numerous on the calcareous sediment, where twelve taxa contributed to the dominant flora, while on the peat only four were comparably common. Full floristic lists show a less striking difference, 19 on the calcareous and 14 on the peaty sediment. There is a fair amount of overlap, but *Amphipleura pellucida* common on the peat did not occur on the calcareous substratum, while *Diploneis ovalis*, *Navicula placentula*, *Cymbella ehrenbergii*, and *Cymatopleura solea* were common on the latter sediment but absent from the peat. The commonest species found in both environments were *Cymbella prostrata* and *Nitzschia palea* (sens. lat.), the latter being the only species common to both communities that was more abundant on the peat.

Pseudanabaena catenata was common on both types of sediment and *Holopedia geminata* was on the calcareous sediment, but when the scarcer forms were considered, there were many more, at least 14 taxa, of blue-green algae on the peat than on the calcareous sediment with only five taxa. This is rather surprising, in view of the distribution in the individual basins of the English Lake District. Chlorococcales are about equally well represented on both sediments. The nine desmids recorded are practically confined to the peat, though in comparison with peat under acidic water in the same part of England, the desmid flora is quite resticted. The comparison of the two stations strongly suggests that with a given water chemistry, a peaty substratum may be definitely unsuitable for some diatoms and suitable for some Myxophyceans and desmids, but that only when the water above the peat is dilute and acidic, as it ordinarily is, does the full characteristic flora of chthoniotrophic waters develop.

In interpreting these results it is important to note that though a rich desmid flora is ordinarily and rightly regarded (Vol. II, pp. 330–333) as characteristic of soft-water lakes, in regions where the influents have drained from igneous rocks of low solubility and low alkaline earth content, the most recent work (Tassigny 1971; Moss 1972, 1973a, b, c) provides no evidence of a generally applicable causal relationship. Tassigny did find that *Mictasterias crux-mellitensis* is indeed inhibited by 7 mg Ca liter^{-1} and *Closterium strigosum* by twice this amount. Moss concluded, however, that in culture most desmids of soft waters are not calcifuge nor affected significantly by the ($[Na^+] + [K^+])/([Mg^{2+}] + [Ca^{2+}])$ ratio. However, high pH proved inimical and it is probable that the main difficulty that any sort of soft-water alga in hard waters has to face is CO_2 deficiency; the eutrophic competitors either use HCO_3^- or are able to take up CO_2 in solution at very low concentrations (see also Shapiro 1973).

Moss's work greatly modifies some of the conclusions of Chapter 21 of this treatise. His papers must be studied by anyone seriously interested in the freshwater algae, whether benthic or planktonic.

Seasonal variation in the epipelic flora. The seasonal incidence of the diatoms of the epipelic community was studied at Malham Tarn (Round

1953) and at the three Windermere and three Blelham Tarn stations by Round (1960). Though there is some variation from year to year, and in Windermere from station to station, in the time of the heights of the maxima, it is evident that populations are minimal in midwinter and ordinarily start increasing in February. There are often considerable variations during the spring, which might be due to sampling error; if these are not considered, the most rapid rise in population is usually in March or April. There is usually a secondary minimum in July or August and a secondary autumnal maximum. When a number of depths are averaged both the diatoms and Myxophyceae of Windermere have maximal populations at the end of May, and in Blelham Tarn about 6 weeks later. At all the individual deeper stations there was much irregularity. The overall pattern is not unlike that of the concomitant variation in planktonic diatoms. Round points out that the decline after the main maximum is comparable to that which occurs in the plankton when silica deficiency begins to limit growth. However, in the plankton a population that has stopped growing can decline due to sedimentation of live cells, while in the benthos this cannot happen on a large scale and at least for a time a stationary population might be expected. The very rapid declines noted by Round might be largely due to predation, but need further study.

The factors regulating the seasonal variations are still not very clear. Presumably the initial spring rise, as in the phytoplankton, is due to the the increment in radiation flux at a time when the nutrient supply is good. The amplitude of the variation is evidently associated with the trophic potential of the mud, being least in those lakes, such as Ennerdale and Wastwater, with little extractable phosphorus, and greatest in some of the more eutrophic waters such as Elterwater. The relationship is irregular and there may well be at times some form of competition between the planktonic and epipelic floras of a eutrophic lake such as Esthwaite, that can have a quite low mean maximum in some years. Epipelic blue-green algae tend to have their maxima at about the same time as do the epipelic diatoms, whereas if there is a Myxophycean plankton maximum of any size it is usually in late summer well after the main diatom maximum (Round 1961a).

In Malham Tarn in which the blue-green algae increased rapidly to very high numbers on the peat bottom, and much less so on the calcareous bottom in April and early May, and then declined, there is a hint on the former substratum of a largely simultaneous decline in diatoms, which then somewhat increased again. It is, however, clear that in this locality in spite of the great differences in bottom chemistry between the two stations the broad effects of the march of the seasons are much the same.

Depth distribution of the epipelic flora. Round (1961b) later made observations on the epipelic flora at six depths (1–6) m) in both Windermere

and Blelham Tarn, over a whole annual cycle, and for the diatoms he
also gives some data on the sum of the number of cells observed with
standard procedure over half a year for 8, 10, and 12 m. In the histograms
of Fig. 162, which are based on those of Round for the sum of the numbers
at each station over a year, the figures for the three deepest stations have
been doubled. The summed and therefore the mean population at 2 m
seems always to be less than at 1 m, and also less than that at some depth
greater than 2 m. Below 6 m the flora clearly declines rapidly; in Windermere at least this decline corresponds to the lower limit of rooted vegetation
and so to the bottom of the infralittoral zone. The lower levels at which a
sparse algal flora occurs, evidently down to about 12 m in Windermere and
10 m in Blelham Tarn, may be regarded as littoriprofundal. Round thinks
that the minimum at 2 m and the maximum at some greater depth is due to

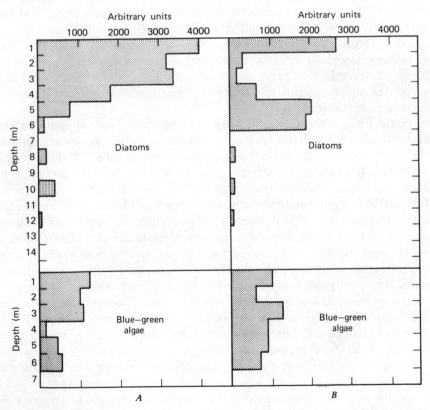

FIGURE 162.   Mean abundance of epipelic diatoms and blue-green algae at different depths.
(*A*) In Windermere; (*B*) in Blelham Tarn.   Note the minimum at 2 m in the latter locality.

an optimal light intensity at about 3 m in Windermere for most species present. The large diatom population at 1 m in Windermere is due to a few special species such as *Stauroneis phoenicenteron*, which in that lake is much more abundant at 1 m than deeper, and to *Pinnularia polyonca*, which occurs only at that depth. The other species of diatoms are either more or less invariant with depth, as *Amphora ovalis* and *Nitzschia palea*, or much more usually have maximal populations below the 1 m level. *Pinnularia* shows marked zonation with *P. polyoncha* maximal at 1 m, *P. cardinaliculis* and *P. viridis* at 4 m, and *P. mesolepta*, *P. divergens*, and *P. gibba* at 6 m. Though most of this type of variation with depth is likely to be dependent on illumination, other factors must be operating, for *Stauroneis phoenicenteron*, which increases with depth in Windermere, does the reverse in Blelham Tarn.

Temporal variation is most clearly shown at the 1 m stations and is rather better seen at the 3 m station than at the 2 m. When all stations are averaged, the maximum for both diatoms and blue-green algae is at the end of May in Windermere and rather later in Blelham Tarn.

Lund records that in the Richmond Park ponds, *Scenedesmus* and *Fragilaria construens*, both of which lack power of movement, are more likely to occur in the deeper part of the bottom, where mechanical disturbances and thus chance of burial are less probable than in shallower water (cf., however, p. 511).

Vertical migration of epipelic algae.   The epipelic biota of some marine and estuarine habitats has been observed on several occasions to exhibit a vertical movement, primarily photoperiodic, but usually also involving a secondary tidal effect. The rhythm persists in most cases for a number of circadian cycles under constant light (Fauré-Fremier 1951; Palmer and Round 1965; Round and Palmer 1966). Round and Eaton (1966) made the interesting discovery that the same kind of vertical movement can occur in freshwater mud. Using a method introduced by Eaton and Moss (1966) in which small squares of lens paper[7] are placed over a mud surface, from which the biota migrated up into the lens paper and then returned to the mud, statistically reputable samples of the organisms present at the mud surface were obtained, though there is no information available as to the depth to which organisms descended. Using mud from Abbot's Pond, Somerset, Round and Eaton found that diatoms in general and *Navicula cryptocephala*, *N. rhynchoceopala*, and *Nitzschia palea* in particular all move up by day and down by night. The rhythm persisted over at lease one

---

[7] Dr. Robert G. Wetzel tells me that the lens paper employed should be imported from Britain, as the American product is apparently cleaned in manufacture in such a way as to make it useless in the study of the migration of benthic algae.

cycle in constant light and more feebly in constant darkness. It seems to be less persistent under constant light than the comparable movement of *Euglena obtusa* recorded (Palmer and Round 1965) under estuarine conditions.

Oscillatoria and flagellates, apparently euglenoid, showed the same effects as diatoms but more feebly. There is some evidence that under natural illumination the upward movement begins before dawn; a biological clock set by the photoperiod seems to be involved. It is possible that at least part of the descent is a passive sinking of fairly dense cells into the flocculent mud. Round and Eaton suspect that the surface of the mud, on the one hand permits a maximal light flux for photosynthesis, but on the other hand presents hazards such as predation or removal by water movements. In darkness there is no advantage in remaining at the mud surface and presumably there are some disadvantages. The movement thus appears to be adaptive. Dr. Mary Gritten tells me that her extensive unpublished observations made in North Wales indicate that different species appear to come to the surface of the mud at different times of day, suggesting that they have different light requirements and so may achieve niche separation in this way.

THE EPIZOIC ALGAL FLORA

As well as growing on inanimate substrate and on plants, algae are recorded as occurring on various animals, notably mollusks, turtles, and in a very few cases on other reptiles and fishes. Such algae, though not really benthic, are conveniently treated in this chapter. The existence of certain unicellular forms living epizoically on planktonic Crustacea has already been mentioned (Vol. II, p. 335); it may be recalled that all kinds of epibionts appear to occur more frequently on the hydrophilic copepods than on the hydrofuge Cladocera (Vol. II, p. 275; Keiser 1921; Sebestyén 1951).

Epizoic algae on mollusks. Little work has been done. Campion (1956) studied 14 species of living Gastropoda and at least three of Bivalvia in English freshwaters. Algal growth on all the living shells consisted of rather reduced plants; when the animals were removed from the shells the algae grew extensively. In the case of *Oedogonium alternans* on *Coretus* (=*Planorbis*) *corneus*, the cells had a volume of 1.8 times that of the same species epiphytic on *Stratiotes* or *Lemna*. This is the only evidence given of the shell providing a better habitat than other substrata. When the reduced algae are allowed to grow in the absence of a living mollusk about 120 taxa of green algae appeared recognizable; there were 38 undeterminable but distinct taxa of Oedogoniales, 30 of *Stigeoclonium*, 24 of *Mougeotia* and 10 of the Ulotrichaceae. In view of these taxonomic uncertainties, which may have involved undescribed species, it is hard to draw any detailed conclusions about ecology. The number of supposed taxa involved does seem rather excessive. The commonest species were *Sphaerobotrys fluviatilis*, *Stigeoclonium tenue*, and an *Oedogonium* sp. (*Oedogonium* 71). Apart from the rarity of *S. tenue* and the absence of *Stigeoclonium farctum* on *Sphaerium* cf. *lacustre* while both species occur, the former abundantly, on the exposed parts of the shells of *Anodonta cygnea* and *Margaritana margaritifera*, there seemed to be no specificity in selection of a substratum. Both the species of *Stigeoclonium* that are rare or absent on *Sphaerium* are very sensitive to being covered by silt. Since more of a large bivalve shell projects above the mud than does the shell of *Sphaerium*, the danger of being covered by bottom sediments probably explains the observed distribution. It appeared that none of the shells studied by Campion produced a chemical attractant for the motile stages of green algae.

A very interesting case is provided by the algal growth on *Unio* and *Anodonta* in some Russian lakes in which a definite zonation develops (Fig. 163), the lowest zone being occupied by the peculiar green alga *Arnoldiella conchophila* (Miller 1928), of the order Cladophorales.

Vinyard (1955), working in Oklahoma, noted that algae were common on shells. He implied that a number of species were present that raised taxonomic problems, just as Campion had found. Unlike the latter worker, Vinyard apparently suspected that some of the problematic taxa were special stenotopic species limited to shells.

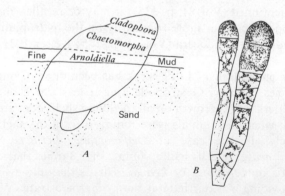

FIGURE 163.   *A*, Diagram of algal zonation on a unionid shell from Lake Pereslavl, Vladimir, U.S.S.R., with *Cladophora glomerata* on the most exposed part of the shell, *Chaetomorpha herbipolensis* below it, and still lower, on the part of the shell in contact with the most superficial deposit, *Arnoldiella conchophilia; B*, filaments (×90) of *A. conchophila* (Miller).

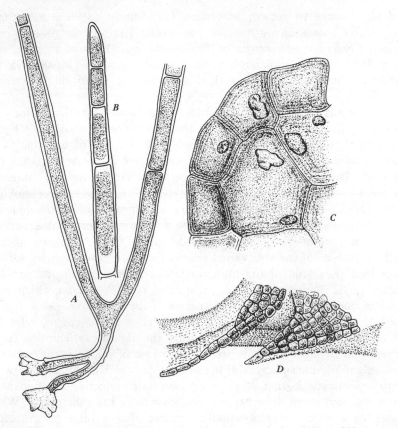

FIGURE 164. *A, Basicladia crassa*, basal region of mature plant with holdfast; *B*, apical region of a young plant (Hoffmann and Tilden); *C, Ulvella involvens* on carapace of *Clemmys caspica; D*, section of carapace showing invasion by the alga (Potter).

Algae epizoic on fish.   Vinyard (1955) found an undetermined member of the Chaetophorales on *Micropterus salmoides* from Lake Texoma, together with an apparently new and shade-tolerant species of *Cladophora*. The same species of *Cladophora* occurred on the operculum of *Ictiobus bubalus* from the same lake and again on *M. salmoides* in Grand Lake, Oklahoma. The holdfast of this *Cladophora* is said to have penetrated the bones of the fishes bearing the alga. Whitton (1970), in his recent review of the biology of *Cladophora*, mentions these cases but is able to add nothing to them.

Algae epizoic on reptiles, primarily turtles.   In contrast to the supposed lack of specificity in the commoner algae living on shells, there are two genera, *Ulvella* (= *Dermatophyton*, Ulotrichales, Chaetophoraceae) and *Basicladia* (Fig. 164) (Ulotrichales, Cladophoracea) that contain species practically limited to growth on turtles. In addition to these stenotopic algae, *Rhizoclonium hieroglyphicum* has been reported on *Sternotherus odoratus*, *Cladophora glomerata* on *Emys blandingi* (Edgren, Edgren, and Tiffany 1953), and *C. kützingiana* on *Clemmys guttata* (Moski 1957b). Doubtless other attached green algae occasionally occur on freshwater Chelonia.

Basicladia has presumably been observed in North America as long as snapping turtles have been captured, the expression "mossback"[8] being applied to these animals when bearing a rich growth of the alga. The taxonomy of the plants involved was, however, not adequately studied for some time. The genus *Basicladia* was erected by Hoffmann and Tilden in 1930 for two species, their own generotype *B. crassa* and *B. chelonium* previously described by Collins (1907) as a member of the genus *Cladophora*. Edgren, Edgren, and Tiffany (1953) made a large number of observations of the occurrence of *Basicladia*, mainly on turtles from Michigan, finding that the incidence of the alga varied greatly from species to species. Of the species that they studied the mud turtle *Sternotherus odoratus* and the snapping turtle *Chelydra serpentina* most often bore *Basicladia*, which grew much less frequently on the various species of the Emytidae.

Proctor (1958) greatly advanced our knowledge of the epizoic relationships of *Basicladia*. He was able to culture the alga away from the turtle carapace and to show that it is perfectly capable of independent existence on suitable inorganic substrata. If the surface on which the alga is growing is very smooth, as is that of glass or porcelain, effective attachment is not possible and slight disturbance detaches it from the substratum. When growing on turtles the plant usually consists of a holdfast or rhizoidal portion of 50–100 cells growing between or even below the horny layers of the lamellae covering the bony part of the turtle's carapace. From this 3 to 10 erect filaments develop, which ultimately produce zoospores. The alga can be grown successfully on rough surfaces and it is not infrequently found on stones in pools or tanks in which turtles have been kept. Proctor records an occurrence on a stone in Lake Texoma, and notes two cases of the alga growing on shells. The rarity of such occurrences in fully natural surroundings is probably explained by the capacity of other algae to compete successfully with *Basicladia;* the latter survives only because it is adapted to the conditions provided by the back of a turtle, which other algae usually cannot tolerate. *Basicladia* is able to stand some degree of desiccation when it is growing on the carapace of a turtle that habitually leaves the water. It can also tolerate considerable periods of low illumina-

---

[8] There is some doubt as to this being the primary meaning of the expression. See *Webster's International Dictionary* or the *Oxford English Dictionary*.

tion or darkness when the turtle bearing it is habitually submerged in shady places or actually burrows into the mud; this happens in the case of the snapping turtles. If *Chelydra* is kept in captivity in a brightly lighted aquarium, other algae tend to displace *Basicladia*. On *Pseudemys scripta* and *Chrysemys picta* the alga established itself less easily because of the relatively smooth carapace, but once establishment has occurred, the habit of these turtles of basking in shallow water will provide a warm and well-illuminated environment for the algae. In *Chrysemys picta* Moski (1957a) found the younger specimens supported a greater growth of the alga; apparently they are more likely to bask in open water than are the adults. This is the opposite of what happens in *Chelydra*, in which a rich growth only is found on old specimens. Here it appears that the lamellae over the bone of the carapace are shed very quickly in young specimens, carrying with them the holdfast rhizoidal parts of the *Basicladia* which have penetrated between the horny lamellar layers.

In *Chrysemys*, *Pseudoemys*, and *Dierochelys* the lamellar layers are shed more or less simultaneously over the entire turtle, so that often a well-developed growth of *Basicladia* may be decimated over a period of a week by molting.

In the genus *Clemmys* the hard and microscopically smooth lamellar layer, though never shed by adults, is an unsuitable substratum for *Basicladia*, which is very rare or absent on specimens of the genus (Proctor 1958). It also is not found on the soft-shelled *Amyda*.

The conditions for the good growth of *Basicladia* seem to differ among the species of turtle bearing the alga. Proctor points out that if *Chelydra* basked frequently in open water, its rough surface, favorable for the attachment of many other algae, would probably encourage establishment of numerous competitors in the warm illuminated water, comparable to that found in artificially illuminated aquariums. This may also be true of *Macrochelys*, *Kinosternon*, and *Sternotherus*. *Pseudemys*, which is much less rough, can support *Basicladia* in spite of basking in water, so favorable for other algae, because its surface is too smooth for easy algal attachment; once *Basicladia* is established, it suffers from little competition. The more frequent exposure of the carapace to air, when emytid turtles come out of water to bask in the sun, also favors *Basicladia* which is more resistant to desiccation than are most other filamentous green algae.

Edgren, Edgren, and Tiffany (1953) concluded that the larger *Basicladia crassa* was more likely to occur on *Chelydra serpentina* and *B. chelonium* on *Sternotherus odoratus*. They supposed that *Chelydra* was prone to expose itself to air, while *Sternotherus* was completely aquatic. They believed the smaller *B. chelonium* to be less resistant to drying. Proctor, however, points out that during most of its life *Chelydra* is decidedly photophobic and that the basking emytid turtles are more likely to bear the small *B. chelonium*. He suggests, in fact, that it is not impossible that *B. crassa* and *B. chelonium* are the shade and sun forms, respectively, of the same species of alga. Proctor concludes, from comparison of his data with that of his predecessors, particularly Edgren, Edgren, and Tiffany (1953), that *Basicladia* is less common in the northern parts of the United States than in the southern.

There is little direct evidence that the association has any functional significance for the turtle, though the mossback appearance may produce some degree of procrypsis, as Gadow (1901) suggested. Neill and Allen (1954) think that this is likely to be important to *Macrochelys temmincki*, the alligator snapper, which fishes by remaining quiet with its mouth open, while wiggling its tongue as a bait. It is suggested that a quite moderate algal growth can break the hard outline of the carapace and appreciably aid in deceiving the turtle's victims.

Ulvella involvens, better known as *Dermatophyton radicans*, was originally described from Europe and its occurrence on *Clemmys caspica* in Portugal has been described and figured by Potter (1888). The alga forms irregular patches up to 5 mm across on the carapace of the turtle. The thallus is somewhat platelike and grows into any cracks on the carapace proliferating between the layers of the lamellae. The same species is known from *Clemmys guttata* in North America (Moski 1957b), on which turtle *Basicladia* is very rare. *U. involvens* has also been recorded from the soft *Amyda ferox emoryi* in Oklahoma by Vinyard (1955), on which *Basicladia* is unknown, as well as from all the species on which he found the last-named alga.

Algae epizoic on other reptiles. Neill and Allen (1954) note algae occurring in captivity on sick water snakes, but never on healthy specimens or on individuals in nature. The same is, in general, true of *Alligator mississipiensis*, though Neill and Allen appear to imply the occasional occurrence of unspecified algae epizoic on wild alligators.

THE EPILITHIC LICHEN FLORA OF THE EULITTORAL OF LAKES

A very characteristic sequence of lichens is often observed on boulders or on the cliff faces of rocky shores above the low water level of the driest time of year, and extending upward throughout the eulittoral (Sernander 1912; Blomgren and Naumann 1925). This flora has been extensively studied in Sweden by Santesson (1939).

In the lakes studied by Santesson, namely, Lakes Stråken, Fiolen, Lammen, and Frejen in the neighborhood of Aneboda, the rock surface just above low water level may have a grayish-black lichen flora of *Verrucaria latebrosa*, *V. pachyderma*, and in unidentified *Jonaspis*-like species.

In some of the lakes, however, this zone, about 10 cm in vertical extent, lacked lichens, though it might bear blue-green algae such as *Gleocapsa magma* and *Calothrix parietina;* in such cases the rock surface bears a precipitate of ferric hydroxide or manganese dioxide derived from the water and apparently unsuitable as a substrate for lichens. The *Verrucaria* zone appears to be covered by water 80–90% of the year.

Above the *Verrucaria* zone is a blackish-brown zone in which *Staurothele fissa* is dominant, occupying a band 10–20 cm in vertical extent and reaching to 20–30 cm above the lowest summer water level. Such a zone is apparently submersed for 50–80% of the year, largely in the winter. Various species of *Dermatocarpon* accompany *S. fissa* as do *Lecanora lacustris*, *Ephebe lanata*, and *Lecidea* spp. from higher zones.

Above the *Staurothele* zone is the light-brown zone of *Lecanora lacustris*, developed best in lakes with humic waters and of variable vertical extent; the associated species are *Ephebe lanata* and *Lecitea* spp. Very roughly where this zone occurs it is covered by water for 25–50% of the year. Above it and largely replacing it in lakes with little organic color, is the grayish zone of *Lecanora caesiocinerea*. Where both *Lecanora* zones are developed the junction between them is sharp. A number of characteristically ter- restrial crustose lichens occur with *L. caesiocinerea*

Above the zone of *L. caesiocinerea*, at about the highest water level, there is a marked change in lichen flora, crustose species largely giving place to foliose members of *Parmelia* and to *Umbilicaria pustulata*, at least on normal rock surfaces. The transition between predominantly crustose and predominantly foliose associations is usually very abrupt, constituting the *Flechten linie* of Naumann (1931) and regarded by him of importance as indicating the highest water level in the immediate historic past. Where rocks are occupied by many birds as resting places, an ornithocoprophilous facies develops with *Lecanora muralis* or *Physcia caesia* dominant.

In most cases the various zones are visually quite distinct, even though there is considerable overlap of vertical distribuion among the species. The exact levels of the zonal boundaries depend to some extent on exposure, being higher where at any water level waves tend to break high on the face of the rock.

It is evident that the most aquatic of the eulittoral lichens, those of the *Verrucaria* zone, require a short period of exposure to aerial conditions and that this requirement becomes progressively greater in passing upward through the *Staurothele* zone and the *Lecanora* zones. The exact relationship of the lichen line to previous high water levels is of interest, but has not yet been fully investigated. In Lake Stråken the line lay 8 cm below the highest water level of the period 1927–1935, during which time the total amplitude of the variation of level was about 120 cm. Santesson concluded from experiments that immersion for about 2 weeks would probably kill *Parmelia saxatilis* and other foliose lichens found above the lichen line; such brief immersion no doubt explains the existence of the line. At any time, however, its exact position will depend on the very slow downward colonization of lichens and the historic incidence of particular years of very high water.

In addition to Santesson's excellent study, a few other observations have been recorded from northwestern Europe. McKnowles (in Smith 1921) reports a band of *Dermatocarpon miniatum* var. *complicatum* as growing between the winter and summer water levels on rocks around mountain lakes in Waterford, Ireland. Below this *D. aquaticum, Staurothele* sp., and *Polyblastia* sp. occurred with the moss *Fontinalis*. In Perthshire Wheldon and Wilson (1915) give a list of 14 taxa found on rocks submersed for long periods, including a number of species already mentioned. Watson's (1919) review of aquatic bryophytes and lichens in Britain relates almost entirely to rivers and streams.

In subarctic North America Raup (1930) has described the zonation on the vertical granite cliffs of Lake Athabasca in Canada, at an altitude of 212 m. From just below the observed water level of the summer of 1926 to about 25 cm above the water level, the rock was closely covered with the dark crustose *Verrucaria nigrescens*. Above this to a height of about 180 cm above the water level the same species occurred but mixed with an increasing quantity of *Dermatocarpon miniatum*. Above this there is a striking gray zone of about 60 cm of *Rhizocarpon disporum, Physcia caesia*, and *Lecanora cinerea*, with a number of less common associates including *Ephebe lanata, Lecanora* spp., *Parmelia olivacea, P. saxatilis, Buellia spuria*, and *Physcia* spp. This gives place to a zone bearing an association of *Parmelia saxatilis* and *Gyrophora muhlenbergii*. The lower boundary of this association, which is of considerable vertical extent, presumably marks the top of the eulittoral.

There are a few other less detailed records from less boreal North American lakes. MacMillan (1894) found on the rocky parts of the shore of Lake of the Woods, Minnesota, *Dermatocarpon* growing where waves might splash on the rock, and above it a zone of *Lecidea* of the section *Biatora*, and then *Cladonia*. Where the rock was very smooth *Umbilicaria* replaced the *Cladonia*. On the open faces of precipitous cliffs *Teloschistes* is important. The nature of the colonized rock seemed to be of some importance, but it is not clear from the account exactly what is involved.

Fink (1903), working in the northern part of Minnesota, recorded an *Umbilicaria* zone nearly to water level and on wet rocks an amphibious angiocarpic lichen association composed of *Dermatocarpon aquaticum, E. miniatum* var. *complicatum, Staurothele clopima*, and *Verrucaria viridula*.

Hale (1950) gives some information about the lichens on boulders in a Connecticut stream bed. The lowest zone lying from 5 to 10 cm above normal water level was characterized by *Staurothele umbrina, Arthropyrenia distans*, and increasing *Bacidia inundata* on going upward from the water. This hydrophilic zone is followed by a lower hygrophilous zone, characterized by *Dermatocarpon aquaticum* with *Placynthium nigrum, Staurotele diffractella, Leptogium cyanescens*, and *Bacidia inundata*. Above this in the upper hygrophilous zone *Lecanora laevata* occurs with *Lecidea* spp., *Buellia colludens, Parmelia stenophylla*, and *Rhizocarpon petraeum*. Presumably comparable associations may occur on rocks at the margins of New England lakes.

In addition to zonally arranged lichen associations on the eulittoral part of the lake margin, there are comparable but perhaps even more characteristic marine intertidal and supratidal associations, often containing special halophilic species of the same genera as occur on lacustrine rocks, notably *Verrucaria*.

SUMMARY

Characteristic benthic algal communities extend from the top of the eulittoral, well above mean water level, to the bottom of the euphotic zone well below the range of macrophytic vegetation. In general these communities may be classified as *haptobenthic*, living on solid substrata, and *herpobenthic*, living in or on mud. Most haptobenthic communities are *epilithic* on stones, rocks, and other dead solid substrata, or *epiphytic* on plants, with a rarer *epizoic* community on animals. The herpobenthos is described as *epipelic*. In general epilithic and epiphytic communities are denser than the epipelic; the available data suggest that about 100–1200 mg chlorophyll a m^{-2} would be usual in epilithic and 100–2350 mg chlorophyll a m^{-2} for epiphytic communities, while the epipelic communities are likely to have less than 100 mg chlorophyll a m^{-2}. Minor epizoic communities on mollusks, crustacea, and turtles and epipsammic algal communities on sand have been described. Algal mats lying on, but not attached to, the bottom may occur in deep or otherwise quiet water. A small category of *endobenthos* includes some boring *endolithic* and parasitic, comensal, or saprophytic *endophytic* organisms.

In any given locality the epipelic community, though of lower biomass per unit area than the other communities, may have an annual productivity greater than either that of the plankton or the macrophytes in shallow lakes. It is apt also to have a high diversity. Species lists including 100–300 taxa are probably normal for any of the benthic algal communities, while the phytoplankton is evidently ordinarily considerably poorer qualitatively. Diatoms and Myxophyceae usually predominate. There is a tendency for the members of the herpobenthos to be mobile, while the haptobenthic algae tend to be attached to the substrate in various ways. Among the diatoms mucilage stalks attach some species while others live in mucilage tubes. The commonest benthic species appear to show very little if any specificity, species such as *Amphora ovalis*, *Denticula tenuis*, and *Navicula radiosa* occurring indifferently on stones, plants, or mud. The haptobenthic communities, however, clearly contain more nonmotile or feebly motile diatoms such as members of the genera *Synedra*, *Fragilaria*, and *Diatoma*. Motility is clearly needed by small organisms living on bottoms where sedimentation is taking place, because at quite ordinary rates of accumulation of the order of 1 m per millenium, the daily deposit will be more than 1 μ thick.

The littoral zone in which the algal benthos occurs has been divided into a supralittoral wetted only by spray at the highest water levels, a eulittoral lying between the highest and lowest seasonal water levels, and an infralittoral, merging through the littoriprofundal into the dysphotic profundal zone. At any given time the water level of a large lake will be continuously disturbed by waves which will cause covering or exposure along the shore every few seconds, as well as by artificial mechanical disturbance, and often by seiches which cause exposure and submergence somewhat more slowly. Any alga growing at the level of the water surface is thus continually dried or wetted except in very small lakes in very quiet weather. Above this *wave zone* there will be a region, clearly defined on rocks, cliffs, walls, and other artificial structures, moistened by the spray from breaking waves and constituting a *spray zone*. These zones move up and down as the water level changes in the eulittoral.

The epilithic haptobenthos consists mainly of blue-green algae with diatoms which are often actually largely epiphytic. In the large hard-water lakes of central Europe, the upper part of the eulittoral along rocky shores bears a vegetation of forms of *Gloeocapsa* and *Scytonema* which withstand desiccation and are presumably metabolically active only when wet. These may be associated with mosses of the genus *Crateroneurum*, which like the blue-green algae extend downward well below mean water level. Various species of *Calothrix*, *Nostoc sphaericum*, *Chlorogloea microcystoides*, *Schizothrix lacustris*, and *Rivularia haematites* may also be found somewhat above mean water level, where the rock must be dry for more than half the year. On either side of the mean water level there is a characteristic band of *Tolypothirx distorta* var. *penicillata*, below which *Rivularia haematites* becomes conspicuous, and below it again a spongy gray-green crust of *Schizothrix* which extends into the infralittoral. Though this zonation is characteristic of the large lakes of the Swiss and Austrian Alps, the absolute widths and positions of the zones are variable, and may well depend largely on the height of the prevalent waves. Where the slope of the shore is very gentle *Tolypothrix distorta* var. *penicillata* may be absent on such stones as are found on the beach.

In the eutrophic Baltic Lakes of northern Germany *Cladophora glomerata* occurs throughout most of the very gently sloping eulittoral which is easily flooded temporarily by the wind-driven water movements or passing boats. Below mean water level there is a more varied flora with *C. glomerata*, *C. aegagropila*, *Rivularia biasolettiana* instead of *R. haematites*, a number of other blue-green algae, and the brown alga *Pluerocladia lacustris*. In the less calcareous forest lakes of the same general region the brown alga *Heribaudiella fluviatilis* replaces *Pleurocladia*, and occasionally the rare *Cladophora basiramosa* may occur on stones along unshaded parts of the shore, though elsewhere it is less of a sun plant than *G. glomerata*. *C. aegographila* may descend well below flowering plants, probably as an epipelic species and is here apparently accompanied by the red alga *Hildenbrandia*. Usually in the less calcareous lakes *Hapalosiphon* and *Plectonema* occur, whereas *Tolypothrix* and *Rivularia* characterize hard waters.

The rate of colonization of a newly wetted rock surface may be rapid. In Lake Lucerne five bands of *Ulothrix zonata* have been observed, the four lower ones apparently representing settling of zoospores during a short period of each day during a rapid rise in lake level. Among the diatoms *Diatoma vulgaris* var. *ehrenbergii* and *Cymbella affinis* are also very rapid colonists of rocks in the same lake. Several species of *Achnanthes* and *Epithemia*, with *Cymbella cymbiformis* and *Caloneis alpestris*, are characteristic of rocks in the Lunzer Untersee; all are common as epiphytes, but are much less so on mud and may be regarded as primarily haptobenthic.

Artificial associations of essentially epilithic algae can be grown on glass slides immersed in lakes. They have been extensively studied in investigations of productivity because they give clean communities uncontaminated with the tissue of macrophytes, as is often the case when epiphytes are studied. With some exceptions the artificial communities resemble epiphytic natural associations and tend to lack the slow-growing encrusting blue-green algae of the natural epilithon.

Epiphytic algae tend to settle on fairly young leaves so that on any stem there will be an increase in epiphytes from the tip downward to a maximum below which death and detachment without settling leads to a decline. Most species tend to settle at the depressions marking cell boundaries and some may grow along the latter. There are, however, often differences in behavior between different species. Usually a fully submersed leaf has more epiphytes on the upper illuminated surface, but on dead leaves the difference between the population on the two surfaces tends to disappear. Some epiphytes such as *Cocconeis* can move over the surface of the substratum and may avoid dead parts of a dying leaf. There is very little specificity in nature with regard to epiphytes and substrata. But in experiments with very clean shoots of water plants striking preferences may be found, *Gomphonema*, for example, settling differentially on *Utricularia*. The chrysomonad *Chrysopyxis* is provided with two curved projections that form a clip that goes round cylindrical algal filaments. The filamentous conjugates which show intercalary growth and are well covered with mucilage usually lack epiphytes, at least when healthy; *Mougeotia* with less mucilage is a partial exception. It has also been suggested that the presence of tannins may protect such algae from epiphytes.

When the epiphytic associations on reed are examined, it is found that striking patterns of vertical distribution may characterize individual species. These are probably due to interaction between light requirements and tolerance of disturbance by waves at or just below the water surface. Species which show marked vertical zonation when growing epilithically are apt to show characteristic distributions when growing as epiphytes, due apparently in both cases to variations in illumination. Thus *Eunotia lunaris* in Windermere was most abundant at a depth of 5–6 m on a rocky shore; in shallower water as an epiphyte on *Potamogeton* and *Elodea* it only occurred on the undersides of leaves.

There is considerable evidence of nutrient competition between epiphytes and their plant substrata. While the latter are limited by nitrogen no epiphytes appear, but when ammonia or nitrate accumulate in excess of the needs of the macrophytes, a rich growth of diatoms and blue-green algae may develop on the latter. It is, however, very probable that the epiphytic community composed of both algae and bacteria is dependent on organic matter lost from macrophytes for its full development. It is in fact conceivable that such loss is adaptive, the epiphytes diverting herbivores from the macrophytes.

The epipelic flora, like the epilithic and epiphytic, is largely composed of Myxophyceae and diatoms, the latter being represented by many more taxa than the former. There is evidently some determination of the flora by the chemical composition of the mud. In the English Lake District the diatoms and flagellates tend to be more abundant when extractable calcium and phosphorus are high, but the blue-green algae do not. *Eucocconeis flexella* appears to be the most characteristically oligotraphent member of the epipelic diatom flora in western Europe, while at least in England *Pinnularia cardinaliculis* is the most strikingly eutraphent. The very large numbers of other species are probably largely mesotraphent; some like *Cymbella ventricosa* that seem acidophilic and oligotraphent in the English

Lake District prefer harder water on the continent. Such preferences are clearly not properly understood. The epipelic flora both of blue-green algae and diatoms is maximal in the spring, at the time when the planktonic diatoms are most numerous but well before the development of typical summer Myxophycean blooms. In Malham Tarn where both calcareous and allochthonous peaty mud lie on either side of the lake under hard water, there is a great difference in the epipelic flora of the two substrata. *Cymbella prostrata*, *Nitzschia palea* (sens. lat.), and *Pseudanabaena catenata* were common on both sediments, but the diatom *Amphipleura pellucida* common on peat did not occur on the calcareous bottom, where a number of species absent from the peat appeared commonly. The blue-green *Holopedia geminata* occurred only on the calcareous mud, but most of the rarer blue-green algae were confined to the peat. Desmids were much commoner on the peat, which, however, did not develop the full desmid flora found in the region on peaty bottoms under soft water. Evidently some differences in flora are due to the chemistry of the mud, but a complete soft-water flora develops only under soft water. Recent work, however, has thrown great doubt on the supposed calcifuge nature of desmids, and it is possible that they occur in soft water mainly because they cannot compete with algae using HCO_3^- in hard water.

In very clear lakes a peculiar benthic flora has been found in deep water consisting of a mixture of a few species of green, red, brown, and blue-green algae constituting a group showing marked chromatic adaptation.

Diatoms, notably species of *Navicula* and *Nitzschia*, leave the surface of the mud by night and reascend just before daybreak. The rhythm persists over at least one cycle in constant light and more feebly in constant darkness; it must therefore involve a biological clock. *Oscillatoria* and flagellates exhibit comparable, if less striking, movement.

There is a small algal epizoic flora, best developed on the exoskeletons of Chelonia and exhibiting a fairly complicated ecology.

Lakes with rocky shores may have a rich eulittoral lichen flora. Though no lacustrine lichen appears able to live permanently submersed, some species, notably of the genus *Verrucaria*, may spend up to 95% of their lives underwater. There are often other lichen zones characterized by *Staurothele* and somewhat higher by *Lecanora*. At about the limit of the eulittoral there is a sudden increase in foliose lichens such as *Parmelia* and *Umbilicaria*. This change defines the "lichen line," which gives a good idea of the highest level that a lake has reached during the immediate historic past.

Bibliography

and

Index of Authors

So it is not simply the knowledge of many things, but a multifarious copulation of them in the mind, that becomes prolifick of further knowledge.
Nehemiah Drew,
An Idea of Phytological History Expounded, p. 17.

The journal titles are abbreviated according to the system of the National Clearinghouse for Periodical Title Word Abbreviations (NCPTWA), 1971.

The asterisks (*) indicate works of exceptional limnological importance, either on account of the discoveries reported or because of extensive lists of references.

Abelson, P. H., and Hoering, T. C., 1961. Carbon isotope fractionation of amino acids by photosynthetic organisms. *Proc. Natl. Acad. Sci. USA*, 47:623–632. **146**

Åberg, B., 1943. Physiologische und ökologische Studien über die pflanzliche Photomorphose. *Symb. Bot. Ups.*, 8, No. 1. 189 pp. **194, 195**

Achmatowicz, O., Banaszek, H., Spiteller, G., and Wróbel, J. T., 1964. Alkaloids from Nuphar luteum, Part IV. Mass spectroscopy of thiobinupharidine, neothiobinupharidine and their desulphuration products. *Tetrahedron Lett.*, 1964, no. 16, 927–934. **367**

Achmatowicz, O., and Bellen, Z., 1962. Isolation of alkaloids containing sulfur. *Tetrahedron Lett.*, 1962, 1121–1124. **365**

Achmatowicz, O., and Wróbel, J. T., 1964. Alkaloids from Nuphar luteum, Part III. A new alkaloid—neothiobinupharidine. Spectroscopic studies of the structure of thiobinupharidine and neothiobinupharidine. *Tetrahedron Lett.*, 1964, no. 2, 129–136. **365, 367**

Adams, F. S., Cole, H., and Massie, L. B., 1973. Element constitution of selected aquatic vascular plants from Pennsylvania: submerged and floating leaved species and rooted emergent species. *Environ. Pollut.*, 5:117–147. **286**

Adams, M. S., and McCracken, M. D., 1974. Seasonal production of the *Myriophyllum* component of the littoral of Lake Wingra, Wisconsin. *J. Ecol.*, 62:457–465. **353**

Ahl, T., and Jönsson, E., 1972. Boron in Swedish and Norwegian fresh waters. *Ambio*, 1:66–70. **309**

Allan, H. H., 1961. Flora of New Zealand, vol. 1. Wellington, N. Z. R. E. Owen, Government Printer. liv, 1085 pp. **474**

Allanson, B. R., 1973. The fine structure of the periphyton of *Chara* sp. and *Potamogeton natans* from Wytham Pond, Oxford, and its significance to the macrophyte–periphyton metabolic model of R. G. Wetzel and H. L. Allen. *Freshwater Biol.*, 3:535–542. **545–547**

Allen, G. O., 1940. The Percy Sladen Trust Expedition to Lake Titicaca in 1937 . . . ix. Charophyta. *Trans. Linn. Soc. Lond.*, 3rd ser. 1:155–160. **483 fn**

Allen H. L., 1969. Chemo-organotrophic utilization of dissolved organic compounds by planktic algae and bacteria in a pond. *Int. Rev. Gesamten Hydrobiol. Hydrogr.*, 54:1–33. **266**

*Allen, H. L., 1971. Primary productivity, chemo-organotrophy and nutritional interactions of epiphytic algae and bacteria on macrophytes in the littoral of a lake. *Ecol. Monogr.*, 41:97–127. **543–545**

Allen, H. L., 1972. Phytoplankton, photosynthesis, micronutrient interactions, and organic carbon availability in a soft-water Vermont lake. *Nutrients and Eutrophication*, ed. G. E. Likens, ASLO Special Symposia 1:63–80. **266**

Allen, J. F., 1854. *Victoria regia: or the Great Water Lily of America*. Boston . . . for the author by Dutton and Wentworth, 16 pp. **160**

Allenby, K. G., 1968. Some analyses of aquatic plants and waters. *Hydrobiologia*, 32:486–490. **333**

Allsopp, A., 1954a. Experimental and analytical studies of pteridophytes. XXIV. Investigations on *Marsilea*. 4. Anatomical effects of changes in sugar concentration. *Ann. Bot. (Lond.)*, n. s. 18:449–461. **166, 167**

Allsopp, A., 1954b. A comparison of the effects of 3-indolacetic acid and 3-indolyl acetonitride on the development of sporelings of *Marsilea* in aquatic environments. *J. Exp. Bot.*, 5:16–23. **167**

Allsopp, A., 1955. Cultural conditions and morphogenesis, with special reference to the origin of land and water forms. *Ann. Bot. (Lond.,)* n. s. 19:247–264. **167**

*Allsopp, A., 1953. Morphogenesis in *Marsilea*. *J. Linn. Soc. Lond. (Bot.)*, 58:417–427. **167**

*Allsopp, A., 1965a. Heteroblastic development in corinophytes. *Encyclopedia of Plant Physiology (Handbuch der Pflanzenphysiologie)*, ed. W. Ruhland and A. Lang. Berlin, Heidelberg, and New York, Springer Verlag XV, 1:1172–1221. **167**

*Allsopp, A., 1965b. Land and water forms: physiological aspects. *Encyclopedia of Plant Physiology (Handbuch der Pflanzenphysiologie)*, ed. W. Ruhland and A. Lang. Berlin, Heidelberg, and New York, Springer Verlag XV, 1:1236–1255. **137, 167**

Alluaud, C., 1923. Rapport à Monsieur le Directeur Général des Services de Santé du Maroc sur une mission antipaludique. *Bull. Soc. Sci. Natl. Maroc.*, 2:3–6. **30**

Almestrand, A., and Lundh, A., 1951. Studies on the vegetation and hydrochemistry of Scanian lakes. I–II. *Bot. Notiser Suppl.*, 2, no. 3, 174 pp. **243, 380, 381, 384, 386–388, 393**

Alston, A. H. G., 1959. Isoetaceae *Flora Malesiana* ser. II, 1.1 Pteridophyta; 1, 1:62–64. **73**

Amonkar, S. V., 1969. *Freshwater algae and their metabolites as a means of biological control of mosquitoes*. Thesis, University of California, Riverside, Calif. 119 pp. (*Diss. Abstr.*, 31 2037B). **29**

Amonkar, S. V., and Banerji, A., 1971. Isolation and characterization of the larvicidal principle of garlic. *Science*, 174:1343–1344. **29**

Amstutz, E., 1957. *Stylites*, a new genus of Isoetaceae. *Ann. Mo. Bot. Gard.*, 44:121–123. **72**

Anderson, G. C., 1958. Seasonal characteristics of two saline lakes in Washington. *Limnol. Oceanogr.*, 3:51–68. **534**

Anderson, R. G., 1958. *The growth and reproduction of Chara in a definable nutrient medium*. Thesis, Univ. Nebraska 127 pp. (*Diss. Abstr.*, 20:3034). **17, 20, 22, 23**

Andrews, J. D., 1943. See Andrews and Hasler, 1943.

Andrews, J. D., and Hasler, A. D., 1943. Fluctuations in the animal populations of the littoral zone in Lake Mendota. *Trans. Wis. Acad. Sci. Arts Lett.*, 35:175–185. **11, 466, 472**

Arber, A., 1912. *Herbals, their Origin and Evolution. A Chapter in the History of Botany*. Cambridge University Press, xviii, 253 pp. **176 fn, 177 fn**

Arber, A., 1918. The phyllode theory of the monocotyledenous leaf, with special reference to the anatomical evidence. *Ann. Bot. (Lond.)*, 32:465–501. **141**

*Arber, A., 1920. *Water Plants. A Study of Aquatic Angiosperms*. Cambridge University Press xvi, 436. **78, 83, 96, 134, 139, 140, 159, 162, 164, 165, 199, 208, 227, 232, 233**

Arens, K., 1930. Zur Kenntniss der Karbonatassimilation der Wasserpflanzen. *Planta* 10:-814–816. **148, 151**

Arens, K., 1933. Physiologisch polarisierter Massenaustauch und Photosynthese bei submersen Wasserpflanzer. I. *Planta* 20:621–658. **148, 151**

Arens, K., 1936a. Physiologisch polarisierter Massenaustauch und Photosynthese bei submersen Wasserpflanzen. II. Die Ca(HCO$_3$)$_2$ Assimilation. *Jahrb. Wiss Bot.*, 83:513–560. **148, 151**

Arens, K., 1936b. Photosynthese von Wasserpflanzen in Kalziumbikarbonatlosungen. *Jahrb. Wiss. Bot.*, 83:561–566. **148, 151**

Arens, K., 1939. Physiologische multipolarität der Zelle von Nitella während der Photosynthese. *Protoplasma*, 33:295–306. **19, 20**

Arima, J., and Takahashi, B., 1931. Alkaloid of *Nuphar japonicum*. *J. Chem. Soc., Japan*, 52:815–817. **365**

Armitage, K. B., and Fassett, N. C., 1971. Aquatic plants of El Salvador. *Arch. Hydrobiol.*, 69:234–255. **206**

Arms, K., Feeny, P., and Lederhouse, R. C., 1974. Sodium: stimulus for puddling behavior of tiger swallowtail butterflies, *Papilio glaucus*. *Science*, 185:372–374. **293**

Armstrong, W., 1964. Oxygen diffusion from the roots of some British bog plants. *Nature (Lond.)*, 204:801–802. **205**

Armstrong, W., 1967. The oxidizing activity of roots in water-logged soils. *Physiol. Plant*, 20:920–926. **205**

Arnell, S., 1963. *Hepaticae of South Africa*. Stockholm, Swedish Natural Science Research Council. 411 pp. **50, 52**

Arnold, C. A., and Dougherty, L. H., 1964. A fossil dennstaedtioid fern from the Eocene Clarno formation of Oregon. *Contrib. Mus. Paleontol. Univ. Mich.*, 19:65–68. **75, 202, 203**

Askenasy, E., 1870. Ueber den Einfluss des Wachsthumsmediums auf die Gestalt der Pflanzen. *Bot. Z.*, 28:193–201, 209–219, 225–236. **180, 181, 183**

Babington, C. C., 1848. On *Anacharis Alsinastrum* a supposed new British plant; with a synopsis of the species of *Anacharis* and *Apalanthe* by J. E. Planchon. *Ann. Mag. Nat. Hist.* (2nd ser.), 1:81–88. **248**

Bailey, C., 1884. Notes on the structure, the occurrence in Lancashire, and the source of origin, of *Najas graminea* Delile, var. *Dellilei* Magnus. *J. Bot.*, 22:305–333. **323**

Bailey, N. T. J., 1959. *Statistical methods in Biology*. New York, J. Wiley & Sons, Inc. ix, 200 pp. **395**

Ball, R. C., 1948, Relationship between available fish food, feeding habits of fish and total fish production in a Michigan lake. *Mich. Agr. Exp. Sta. Tech. Bull.*, 206, 59 pp. **301**

Bance, H. M., 1946. A comparative account of the structure of *Potamogeton filiformis*

Pers. and *P. pectinatus* L. in relation to the identity of a supposed hybrid of these species. *Trans. Proc. Bot. Soc. Edinburgh,* 34:361–367. **243**

Barber, M. A., 1924. The effect of Chara robbinsii on mosquito larvae. *U.S. Public Health Rep.,* 39:611–615. **30**

Barthélemy, A., 1874. De la respiration et de la circulation des gaz dans les végétaux. *Ann. Sci. Nat. Bot.,* 19:131–175. **202**

Batten, L., 1918. Observations on the ecology of *Epilobium hirsutum. J. Ecol.,* 6:161–177. **86**

Bauer, L., 1952. Studien zum Heterophyllie–problem. *Planta,* 40:515–528. **184**

Bauhin, C., 1596. ΦΥΤΟΠΙΝΑΞ *Seu Enumenatio Plantarum* . . . Basileae per Sebastianum Henricpetri (not seen ref Arber, 1912, Wood and Imahori, 1965). **29**

Bauhin, C., 1620. πρόδρομος *Theatri Botanici* . . . Francofurti ad Moenum, typis Pauli Jacobi, impensis Iohannis Treudelii, 160 pp., (not seen, ref Arber, 1912, Wood and Imahori, 1965). **29**

Bauhin, C., 1623. ΠΙΝΑΞ *Theatri Botanicae* . . . Basileae Helvet. Ludovici Regis [20] 522 [23] pp. **29**

Baumann, E., 1911. Die Vegetation des Untersees (Bodensee). Eine floristisch-kritische und biologische Studie. *Arch. Hydrobiol. Suppl.,* 1:1–554. **137**

Baumeister, W., 1960. *Das Natrium als Pflanzennährostoff.* Stuttgart, Gustav Fischer 165 pp. **288**

Bayly, I. A. E., Peterson, J. A., Tyler, R. A., and Williams, W. D., 1966. Preliminary limnological investigations of Lake Pedder, Tasmania, March 1–4, 1966. *Aust. Soc. Limnol. Newsl.,* 5:30–41. **118**

Beadle, L. C., and Lind, E. M., 1960. Research on the swamps of Uganda. *Uganda J.,* 24:84–87. **478**

Beal, E. O., 1956. Taxonomic revision of the genus *Nuphar* of North America and Europe. *J. Elisha Mitchell Sci. Soc.,* 72:317–346. **160 fn**

Beaver, E. G., 1962, ed. *Summary of 1962 Interagency research meeting on Eurasian Watermilfoil.* Natural Resources Institute, Univ. Maryland (mimeogr.) **251**

Behning, A., 1928. *Das Leben der Wolga: Zugleich eine Einführung in die Fluss-Biologie.* Die Binnengewasser. V. Stuttgart, E. Schweizerbart'sche Verlagsbuchhandlung vi, 162 pp. **510 fn**

Belcher, J. H., 1960. Culture studies of *Bangia atropurpurea* (Roth) Ag. *New Phytol.,* 59:367–373. **520**

Bennett, G. W., 1942. Management of small artificial lakes. *Bull. Illinois Natl. Hist. Surv.,* 22:357–376. **368**

Berg, A., 1961. Role écologique des eaux de la cuvette congolaise sur la croissance de la jacinthe d'eau [*Eichhornia crassipes* (Mart.) Solms.] *Mem. in 8°, Acad. R. Sci. d'Outre-Mer. Cl. Sci. Natl. Med.,* n. s. 12, fasc. 3, 120 pp. **389**

Berg, K., and Røen, U., 1958. Gennemsigtigheden i Furesø. Furesøundersøgelser 1950–54. *Folia Limnol. Scand.* 10:34. **465**

Bernatowicz, S., 1969. Macrophytes in the Lake Warniak and their chemical composition. *Ekol. Pol.,* Ser. A., 17:447–467. **286, 287, 288, 289, 299, 303, 356, 360, 361**

Bernatowicz, S., and Pieczyńska, E., 1965. Organic matter production of macrophytes in the Lake Tałtowisko (Mazurian Lakeland), *Ekol. Pol.,* Ser. A, 13:113–124. **485**

*Bernatowicz, S., and Zachwieja, J., 1966. Types of littoral found in lakes of the Mazurian and Suwałki Lakelands. *Ekol. Pol.,* Ser. A,, 14:519–545. **453–460**

Berrie, G. K., 1964. Experimental studies on polyploidy in liverworts. I. The *Riccia fluitans* complex. *Bryologist,* 67:146–152. **52**

Bierberg, W., 1908. Die Bedeutung der Protoplasmarotation für den Stofftransport in den Pflanzen. *Flora,* 99:52–80. **26, 200**

Birge, E. A., and Juday C., 1922. The Inland Lakes of Wisconsin, The Plankton I. Its quantity and chemical composition. *Bull. Wis. Geol. Natl. Hist. Surv.*, 64 (Sci. ser. 13), 222 pp. **286, 317**

Birge, E. A., and Juday C., 1929. Transmission of solar radiation by the waters of inland lakes. *Trans. Wis. Acad. Sci. Arts Lett.*, 24:509–580. **416**

Birge, E. A., and Juday, C., 1931. A third report on solar radiation and inland lakes. *Trans. Wis. Acad. Sci. Arts Lett.*, 20:383–425. **416**

Bissonette, T. H., 1930. A method of securing marine invertebrates. *Science*, 71:464–465. **529**

*Björk, S., 1967. Ecologic investigations of *Phragmites communis*. Studies in theoretic and applied limnology. *Folia Limnol. Scand.*, 14, 248 pp. **238, 240**

Blackman, E., 1971. Opaline silica bodies in the range grasses of southern Alberta. *Can. J. Bot.*, 49:769–781. **317**

Blomgren, N., and Naumann, E., 1925. Untersuchungen über die höhere Vegetation des Sees Stråken bei Aneboda. *Lunds Univ. Arsskr.*, Ard. 2 n. f. Bd. 21, no. 6, 55 pp. **439, 564**

Blow, T. B., 1924. Exhibition of a series of Charophyta collected in Madagascar. *Proc. Linn. Soc. Lond.*, 136:67–68. **30**

Blow, T. B., 1927. Observations on the alleged larvicidal properties of Charophyta. *Proc. Linn. Soc. Lond.*, 139:46–47. **30**

Bode, H. R., 1926. Untersuchungen über die Abhängigkeit der Atmungsgrösse von der H-Ionenkonzentration bei einigen *Spirogyra*-Arten. *Jahrb. Wiss. Bot.*, 65:352–387. **151**

Bodin, K., 1966. *Produktionsbiologiska Studier över Marsupella aquatica* (Schrader) Schiffner i Latnjajaure. Uppsala; Limnol. Instit. mimeogr. 43 pp. text, 20 pp. figs. **48, 49**

Bogin, C., 1955. Revision of the genus Sagittaria (Alismataceae) *Mem. N.Y. Bot. Gard.*, 9:179–233. **160, 162**

Bostrack, J. M., and Millington, W. F., 1962. On the determination of leaf form in an aquatic heterophyllous species of *Ranunculus*. *Bull. Torrey Bot. Club*, 89:1–20. **186, 188**

Botkin, D. B., Jordan, P. A., Dominski, A. S., Lowendorf, H. S., and Hutchinson, G. E., 1973. Sodium dynamics in a northern ecosystem. *Proc. Natl. Acad. Sci. USA.*, 70:2745–2748. **286, 288, 292, 293**

Bourne, W. S., 1932. Ecological and physiological studies on certain aquatic angiosperms. *Contrib. Boyce Thompson Inst.*, 4:425–496. **278, 416**

Bourdu, R., Cartier, D., and Gorenflot, R., 1963. Affinités biochimiques des genres *Littorella* et. *Plantago*. *Bull. Soc. Bot. (Fr.)*, 110:107–109. **361**

Bowen, H. J. M., 1966. *Trace Elements in Biochemistry*. London and New York, Academic Press, ix, 241 pp. **288, 289, 294, 295, 311, 312, 320, 326, 329, 339, 341, 342, 343, 345, 347**

Bowling, D. J. F., and Ansari, A. Q., 1972. Control of sodium transport in sunflower roots. *J. Exp. Bot.*, 23:241–246. **293**

Bowmaker, A. P. M., 1973. *A Hydrobiological Study of the Mwenda River and its Mouth, Lake Kariba*. Ph.D. Thesis, University of the Witwatersrand, Johannesburg, South Africa. **252**

Boyd, C. E., 1968. Freshwater plants: a potential source of protein. *Econ. Bot.*, 22:359–368. **357, 358, 360, 361**

Boyd, C. E., 1969a. The nutritive value of three species of water weeds. *Econ. Bot.*, 23: 123–127. **358, 359**

Boyd, C. E., 1969b. Production, mineral nutrition, absorbtion, and biochemical assimilation by *Justicia americana* and *Alternanthera philoxeroides*. *Arch. Hydrobiol.*, 66:139–160. **357, 358, 359**

*Boyd, C. E., 1970a. Chemical analyses of some vascular aquatic plants. *Arch. Hydrobiol.*, 67:78–85. **286, 288, 298-300, 303, 328, 330, 331, 335-337, 340, 342, 347, 358**

Boyd, C. E., 1970b. Amino acid, protein, and caloric content of vascular aquatic macrophytes. *Ecology*, 51:902–906. **358**

*Boyd, C. E., 1972. A bibliography of interest in the utilization of vascular aquatic plants. *Econ. Bot.*, 26:74–84. **286**

Boyd, C. E., and Walley, W. W., 1972. Studies of the biogeochemistry of boron. I. Concentrations in surface waters, rainfall, and aquatic plants. *Am. Midl. Natl.* 88:1–14. **309, 310**

Boye Petersen, J., 1917. In Wesenberg, Lund, Sand, M. J., Boye Petersen, J., Seidelin Raunkiaer, A., and Steenberg, C. M., 1917. Bemaerkninger til Plantekortene over Bastrup Sø, Farum Sø, Bagsvaerd Sø og Lyngby Sø. Furesøstudier, Chap. III, *K. Dan. Vidensk, Selsk. Skr. Nat. Mat. Afd.* **39–57, 411, 412, 464, 465**

Bradshaw, A. D., McNeilly, T. S., and Gregory, R. P. G., 1965. Industrialisation, evolution, and the development of heavy metal tolerance in plants. In G. J. Goodman (ed.) *Ecology and the Industrial Society,* 327–343. Oxford, Blackwell Scientific Publications; New York, John Wiley & Sons, Inc. **333**

Brand, F., 1896. Ueber die Vegetationsverhältnisse des Würmsees und seine Grundalgen. *Bot. Centralbl.,* 65:1–13. **140**

Braun-Blanquet, J., 1928. *Pflanzensoziologie: Grundzüge der Vegetationskunde.* Berlin, Springer, x, 330 pp. (for translation see next entry). **40, 487**

Braun-Blanquet, J., 1932. *Plant Sociology: The Study of Plant Communities.* Trans. G. D. Fuller and H. S. Conard. New York, McGraw Hill Book Co., xviii, 430 pp. (reprinted Hafner Publishing Co., 1965). **40, 487, 501**

Bristow, J. M., and Whitcombe, M., 1971. The role of roots in the nutrition of aquatic vascular plants. *Am. J. Bot.*, 58:8–13. **284, 285**

Brown, E., 1849. Occurrence of Anacharis Alsinastrum (Udora canadensis) in the Trent near Burton-on-Trent. *Phytologist,* 3:647. **248**

Brown, S. D., 1973. Site variation in littoral periphyton populations: correlation and regression with environmental factors. *Int. Rev. Gesamten Hydrobiol.,* 58:437–461. **530, 531**

Brown, W. H., 1913. The relation of the substratum to the growth of *Elodea. Philipp. J. Sci.,* Sect. C., 8:1–20. **278**

Brownell, P. F., and Crossland, C. J., 1972. The requirement for sodium as a micronutrient by species having the C_4 dicarboxylic photosynthetic pathway. *Plant Physiol.,* 49:794–797. **289**

Budde, H., 1942. Die benthale Algenflora, die Entwicklungsgeschichte der Gewässer und die Seentypen in Naturschutzgebiet "Heiliges Meer." *Arch. Hydrobiol.* 39:189–293. **553**

Buell, M. F., 1935. Acorus Calamus in America. *Rhodora* 37:367–369. **108, 137**

Buhôt, E. W. J., 1927. Effects on mosquito larvae of a Queensland *Nitella. Proc. R. Soc. Queensl.* n. s. 38:59–61. **31**

Buljan, M., 1949. Quelques investigations physiologiques sur la nutrition de *Chara.* Développement et functions des rhizoides de *Chara. Act. Bot. Univ. Zagreb,* 12–13:239–264 (not seen, ref. R. G. Anderson, 1958). **23**

Burgeff, H., 1943. *Genetische Studien an Marchantia.* Jena. **46, 47, 48**

Bures, E., and Hoffmann, M., 1934, Nympheine. *Časopi Českoslov. Lékárnictva.* 14:129–135 (not seen, ref. *Chem. Abstr.,* 28:5460). **365**

Burns, G. P., 1904. Heterophylly in Proserpinaca palustris. *Ann. Bot. (London)* 18:579–587. **147, 174, 175**

Butcher, R. W., 1932. Notes on new and little known algae from the beds of rivers. *New Phytol.,* 31:289–309. **529**

Butcher, R. W., Pentelow, F. T. K., and Woodley, J. W. A., 1931. An investigation of the River Lark and the effect of beet sugar polution. *Minist. Agric. Fish, Fish, Invest. (Gt. Brit.)* Ser. I, 3, no. 3, 112 pp. **529**

Buttery, B. R., Williams, W. T., and Lambert, J. M., 1965. Competition between *Glyceria maxima* and *Phragmites communis* in the region of Surlingham Broad. II. The fen gradient. *J. Ecol.*, 53:183-195. **429**

Buxton, P. A., 1924. Applied Entomology in Palestine. *Bull. Entomol. Res.*, 14:289-340. **30**

Caballero, A., 1919. La *"Chara foetida"* A. Br. y las larvas de *Stegomyia, Culex* y *Anopheles. Boll. R. Soc. Esp. Hist. Nat.*, 19:449-455. **29**

Caballero, A., 1922a. Acerca de los efectos de la *Chara* sobre las larvas de los mosquitos. *Boll. R. Soc. Esp. Hist. Nat.*, 22:337-338. **29**

Caballero, A., 1922b. Otras especies larvicidas del genero *Chara. Boll. R. Soc. Esp. Hist. Nat.*, 22:418-421. **29**

Campion, M., 1956. A survey of the green algae epiphytic on the shells of some freshwater molluscs. *Hydrobiologia*, 8:38-53. **559**

Carter, G. S., 1955. *The Papyrus Swamps of Uganda.* Cambridge: W. Heffer & Sons, 25 pp. **478, 479**

*Castenholz, R. W., 1960. Seasonal changes in the attached algae of freshwater and saline lakes in the lower Grand Coulee, Washington. *Limnol. Oceanogr.* 5:1-28. **531-535**

Cave, C. J. P., 1948. *Roof Bosses in Medieval Churches: an Aspect of Gothic Sculpture.* Cambridge University Press, viii, 235 pp. **176 fn**

Chadwick, M. J., and Obeid, M., 1966. A comparative study of the growth of *Eichhornia crassipes* Solms and *Pistia stratiotes* L. in water culture. *J. Ecol.*, 54:563-575. **388**

Chapman, V. J., 1970. A history of the lake-weed infestation of the Rotorua lakes and the lakes of the Waikato hydro-electric system. *N. Z. Dept. Sci. Res. Inf. Serv.*, 78, 52 pp. **249 fn, 250**

Chapman, V. J., Brown, J. M. A., Hill, C. F., and Carr, J. L., 1974. Biology of excessive weed growth in the hydro-electric lakes of the Waitako River, New Zealand. *Hydrobiologia* 44:349-367. **250**

Cheeseman, T. F., 1907. Notice of the occurrence of *Hydatella*, a genus new to the New Zealand flora. *Trans. N. Z. Inst.* 39 (for 1906):433-434. **118**

Cheeseman, T. F., 1925. *Manual of the New Zealand Flora,* 2nd ed., ed W. R. B. Oliver. Wellington, N. Z., W. A. G. Skinner, Govt. Printer, xliv, 1163 pp. **118**

Chiaudani, G., 1969. Contenuti normali ed accumuli di rame in *Phragmites communis* L. come risposta a quelli nei sedimenti di sei laghi italiani. *Mem. Ist. Ital. Idrobiol.* 25:81-95. **332-335**

Chodat, R., 1906. Observations sur le macroplancton des étangs du Paraguay. *Bull. Herb. Boissier,* (ser. 2) 6:143-147. **79, 83, 86**

Cholnoky, B. von, 1927. Untersuchungen über die Ökologie der Epiphyten. *Arch. Hydrobiol.,* 18:661-704. **514, 515, 537, 539**

Cholnoky, B. von, 1929. Epiphyten-Untersuchungen im Balatonsee. *Int. Rev. Gesamten Hydrobiol.* 22:313-345. **539, 540, 541**

Christensen, T., and Andersen, F., 1958. De større vandplanter i Furesø. Furesøundersøgelser, 1950-54. *Folia Limnol. Scand.* 10:114-128. **64, 464-466**

Chrysler, M. A., 1907. The structure and relationships in Potamogetonaceae and allied families. *Bot. Gaz.* 44:161-188. **225**

Clapham, A. R., Tutin, T. G., and Warburg, E. F., 1962. *Flora of the British Isles,* 2nd ed. Cambridge University Press, xlviii, 1269 pp. **72, 182, 241, 244**

Clayton, W. D., 1968. The correct name of the common reed. *Taxon* 17:168-169. **78 fn**

Clements, F. A., 1916. *Plant Succession: an Analysis of the Development of Vegetation.* Carnegie Inst., Washington, publ. 242, xiii, 512 pp. **478, 497, 498, 501**

Cockayne, L., 1928. *The vegetation of New Zealand.* 2nd ed. Weinheim, J. Cramer, xxvi, 456 pp. (reprinted 1958). **99**

Coleman, W. H., 1844. Observations on a new species of Oenanthe. *Ann. Mag. Nat. Hist.,* (1st ser.) 13:188–191. **226**

Collins, F. S., 1907. Some new green algae. *Rhodora,* 9:198–200. **562**

Conway, V. M., 1937. Studies in the autecology of *Cladium mariscus* R. Br. III. The aeration of the subterranean parts of the plants. *New Phytol.,* 36:64–96. **202, 205**

Conway, V. M., 1942. Biological flora of the British Isles: *Cladium mariscus* (L.) *R. Br. J. Ecol.,* 30:211–216. **202**

Cook, C. D. K., 1963. Studies in *Ranunculus* subgenus *Batrachium* (DC) A. Gray. II. General morphological considerations in the taxonomy of the genus. *Watsonia,* 5:294–303. **181, 182, 183**

Cook, C. D. K., 1966a. Studies in *Ranunculus* subgenus *Batrachium.* III. *Ranunculus hederaceus* L. and *R. omiophyllus* Ten. *Watsonia* 6:246–259. **182**

Cook, C. D. K., 1966b. A monographic study of *Ranunculus* subgenus *Batrachium. Mitt. Bot. Muenchen,* 6:47–237. **159, 181, 183–186, 247**

Cook, C. D. K., 1969. Review: C. D. Sculthorpe, The Biology of Aquatic Vascular Plants. *Watsonia* 7:51–53. **120, 202**

Cook, C. D. K., Gut, B. J., Rix, E. M., Schneller, J., and Seitz, M., 1974. *Water Plants of the World.* The Hague, W. Junk, viii, 561 pp. (not used; announced after this book was in page proof).

Cooke, W. B., 1956. Colonization of artificial bare areas by microorganisms. *Bot. Rev.,* 22:613–638. **530**

Core, E. L., 1967. Ethnobotany of the Southern Appalachian aborigines. *Econ. Bot.,* 21:199–214. **367**

*Corillion, R., 1957. Les Charophycées de France et d'Europe Occidentale. *Bull. Soc. Sci. Bretagne,* n. s., 32:1–499. **2, 8–14, 16, 19, 20, 32, 34–37, 39, 43, 45, 488–490**

Coult, D. A., 1964. Observations on gas movements in the rhizome of *Menyanthes trifoliata* L., with comments on the role of the endodermis. *J. Exp. Bot.,* 15:205–218. **202**

Coult, D., and Vallance, K. V., 1958. Observations on the gaseous exchanges which take place between *Menyanthes trifoliata* L. and its environment. Part II. *J. Exp. Bot.,* 9:384–402. **204**

Covich, A. P., 1970. *Stability of molluscan communities, a palaeolimnological study of environmental disturbance in the Yucatan Peninsula.* Thesis, Yale University, 202 pp. (*Diss. Abst.* 31 B 7112 B; microfilm No. 71–16, 141). **24**

Cowgill, U. M., 1970. The hydrogeochemistry of Linsley Pond, North Branford, Connecticut. I. Introduction, field work and chemistry by x-ray emission spectroscopy. *Arch. Hydrobiol.,* 68:1–95. **295, 306, 328, 333**

Cowgill, U. M., 1973a. Biogeochemistry of rare-earth elements in aquatic macrophytes of Linsley Pond, North Branford, Connecticut. *Geochim. Cosmochim. Acta,* 37:2329–2345. **264, 286, 311, 313–316**

Cowgill, U. M., 1973b. Biogeochemical cycles for the chemical elements in *Nymphaea odorata* Ait. and the aphid *Rhopalosiphum nymphaeae* (L.) living in Linsley Pond. *Sci. Total Environm.,* 2:259–303. **264, 286, 288, 291, 311–312, 326, 347**

*Cowgill, U. M., 1974a. The hydrogeochemistry of Linsley Pond. II. The chemical composition of the aquatic macrophytes. *Arch. Hydrobiol. Suppl.* 45:1–119. **264, 286, 288, 291, 293–300, 303–312, 317–323, 325–330, 332, 333, 335, 336, 338–350, 358**

Cowgill, U. M., 1974b. The hydrogeochemistry of Linsley Pond. III. The mineralogy of the aquatic macrophytes. *Arch. Hydrobiol.,* 74:350–374. **264, 286, 303**

Crawford, R. M. M., 1966. The control of anaerobic respiration as a determining factor in the distribution of the genus *Senecio. J. Ecol.,* 54:403–413. **207, 209, 210**

Crocker, W., 1907. Germination of seeds of water plants. *Bot. Gaz.* 44:375–380. **213, 215, 216, 233**

Crocker, W., 1948. *The growth of Plants: Twenty Years' Research at Boyce Thompson Institute.* New York, Reinhold Publishing Corp., v, 459 pp. **45**

Crocker, W., and Davis, W. E., 1914. Delayed germination in seed of *Alisma plantago. Bot. Gaz.,* 58:285–321. **217**

Dabbs, D. L., 1971. A study of *Scirpus acutus* and *Scirpus validus* in the Saskatchewan River delta. *Can. J. Bot.,* 49:143–153. **428, 429**

Dahm, P., 1926. Beziehungen der Sphagneen und einiger untergetauchter Wasserpflanzen zur Kalkkarbonat. *Jahrb. Wiss. Bot.* 65:314–351. **17, 148, 151**

Daily, F. K., 1967. *Lamprothamnium* in America. *J. Phycol.,* 3:201–207. **3**

Dainty, J., 1969. The ionic relations of plants. In *The Physiology of Plant Growth and Development,* ed. M. B. Wilkins. New York, McGraw-Hill Book Co., Inc. **453–485, 265**

Dale, H. M., 1957. Developmental studies of *Elodea canadensis* Michx. II. Experimental studies on the morphological effects of darkness. *Can. J. Bot.,* 35:51–64. **202**

Dandy, J. E., 1937. The genus *Potamogeton* in Tropical Africa. *J. Linn. Soc. Lond. Bot.,* 50:507–540. **479 fn**

Dandy, J. E., and Taylor, G., 1946. An account of *Potamogeton* × *suecicus* Richt. in Yorkshire and the Tweed. *Trans. Proc. Bot. Soc. Edinbu.,* 34:348–360. **243**

Dangeard, P., 1925. Limite de la végétation en profondeur de quelques plantes submergées du Lac d'Annecy. *Compr. Rend. Acad. Sci. Paris,* 180:304–306. **409**

Dansereau, P., 1945. Essai de corrélation sociologique entres les plants supérieurs et les poissons de la Beine du Lac Saint-Louis. *Rev. Can. Biol.,* 4:369–417. **118, 131**

Darwin, C. R., 1859. *On the Origin of Species by Means of Natural Selection, or, the Preservation of Favoured Races in the Struggle for Life.* London, John Murray, ix, 502 pp. (or any other edition). **78**

Daumann, E., 1963. Zur Frage nach dem Ursprung des Hydrogamie zugleich ein Beitrag zur Blutenökologie von *Potamogeton. Preslia,* 35:23–30. **230**

de Candolle, A. P., 1827. *Organographie végétale,* vol. 1, Paris (not seen, ref. Arber, 1920 to Bk. 2, Chap. III). **141**

Deevey, E. S., 1957. Limnological studies in Middle America with a chapter on Aztec limnology. *Trans. Conn. Acad. Arts Sci.,* 39:213–328. **51**

Deevey, E. S., Gross, M. S., Hutchinson, G. E., and Kraybill, H. L., 1954. The material C^{14} contents of materials from hard-water lakes. *Proc. Nat. Acad. Sci., USA.,* 40:285–288. **157**

De Marte, J. A., and Hartman, R. T., 1974. Studies on absorbtion of ^{32}P, ^{59}Fe, and ^{45}Ca by water-milfoil (*Myriophyllum exalbescens* Fernald). *Ecology,* 55:188–194. **285**

den Hartog, C., 1964. Over de oecologie van bloeiende *Lemna trisulca. Gorteria* (Leiden), 2:68–72 (not seen ref. Faegri and van der Pijl, 1971). **227**

*den Hartog, C., and Segal S., 1964. A new classification of water-plant communities. *Act. Botan. Neerl.,* 13:367–393. **52, 118, 119, 122, 124, 128, 139**

Denniston, R. H., 1921. A survey of the larger aquatic plants of Lake Mendota. *Trans. Wisc. Acad. Arts Sci. Lett.,* 20:495–500. **466–468, 471, 473**

Denny, P., 1972a. Lakes of south-western Uganda. I. Physical and chemical studies on Lake Bunyonyi. *Freshwater Biol.,* 2:143–158. **474**

*Denny, P., 1972b. Lakes of south-western Uganda. II. Vegetation studies on Lake Bunyonyi. *Freshwater Biol.,* 3:123–135. **474–478**

Denny, P., 1972c. Sites of nutrient absorbtion in aquatic macrophytes. *J. Ecol.,* 60:819–829. **279, 282, 283, 474**

Denny, P., and Lye, K. A., 1973. The *Potamogeton schweinfurthii* complex in Uganda. *Kew. Bull.*, 28:117–120. **221, 243**

Denny, P., and Weeks, D. S., 1968. Electrochemical potential gradients of ions in an aquatic angiosperm, *Potamogeton schweinfurthii* (Berm.), *New Phytol.*, 67:875–882. **293**

Denton, J., 1965. *Relationships between the chemical composition of plants and water quality.* Auburn University, Alabama, M. S. thesis (not seen; ref. from Gaudet, 1973). **286, 288, 299, 341**

Diels, L., 1906. Droseraceae in *Das Pflanzenreich* . . . herausgeg. A. Engler, Leipzig. W. Engelmann. Heft 26 (IV, 112), 136 pp. **100**

Dixon, H. H., 1898. Transpiration into a saturated atmosphere. *Proc. R. Ir. Acad.*, ser. 3, 4 (20 of whole):627–635. **199**

Dixon, H. H., 1938. Subaqueous transpiration. *Sci. Proc. R. Dublin Soc.*, 22:55–57. **199**

Dixon, H. H., and Barlee, J. S., 1940. Further experiments on transpiration into a saturated atmosphere. *Sci. Proc. R. Dublin Soc.*, 22:211–222. **199**

Dodoens, R., 1554. *Crüydeboeck* (not seen); colophon (Arber, 1912) reads Ghedruckt Tantwerpen by Jan vander Loe. **175, 176 fn**

Dodoens, R., 1557. *Histoire des Plantes, en laquelle est contenue la description entiere des herbes,* . . . nouvellements traduite de bas Aleman en François par Charles de l'Escluse. Antwerp . . . Jean Loe, 584 + 32 pp. **176, 177**

Dodoens, R., 1578. *A Nievve Herball or Historie of Plantes: wherin is contayned the whole discourse and perfect description of all sorts of Herbes and Plantes* . . . First set fourth in the Doutche or Almaigne tongue by that learned D. Rembert Dodoens . . . nowe first translated out of French into English, by Henry Lyte Esquyer. London . . . Gerard Dewes 779 + 24 pp. **176**

Dodoens, R., 1583. *Remberti Dodonaei Mechliniensis Medici Caesarei Stirpium Historiae Pemptades Sex.* Antwerp, C. Plantin 10 lf, 861 pp. **177 fn**

Downton, W. J. S., 1971. Adaptive and evolutionary aspects of C_4 photosynthesis. In *Photosynthesis and Photorespiration,* ed. M. D. Hatch, C. B. Osmond, and R. O. Slatyer. New York and London, Wiley-Interscience, x, 565 pp. **152**

Drouet, F., 1959. Myxophyceae. In H. B. Ward and G. C. Whipple, *Freshwater Biology,* 2nd ed., ed. W. T. Edmondson. New York, John Wiley & Sons, pp. 95–114. **518 fn**

Drouet, F., and Daily, W. A., 1956. Revision of the coccoid Myxophyceae. *Butler Univ. Bot. Stud.* 12:1–218. **518 fn**

Dumont, H., 1969. A quantitative method for the study of periphyton. *Limnol. Oceanogr.*, 14:303–307. **530**

Duplakov, S. N., 1925. Zur Kenntnis der Biocönosen untergetauchter Gegenstände. *Russ. Gydrobiol. Zh.*, 4:42–48 (Russian text); 48–49 (German summary). **529**

Duplakov, S. N., 1933. Materialien zur des Periphytons. *Arb. Limnol. Stat. Kossino,* 16: 9–136 (Russian text); 136–160 (German summary). **529**

Du Reitz, G. E., 1921. *Zur methodologischen Grundlage der modernen Pflanzensoziologie,* Uppsala, Thesis, 272 pp. (not seen, referenced in Hartog & Segal). **118, 122**

Du Reitz, G. E., 1931. Life-forms of terrestrial flowering plants. *Acta Phytogeogr. Suec.*, 3:1–95. **118, 122**

Duval-Jouve, J., 1864. Lettres de M. Duval-Jouve à M. de Schoenefeld. *Bull. Soc. Bot. Fr.*, 11:265–267. **245**

Eaton, J. W., and Moss, B., 1966. The estimation of numbers and pigment content in epipelic algal populations. *Limnol. Oceanogr.*, 11:584–595. **558**

Edgar, E., 1966. The male flowers of *Hydatella inconspicua* (Cheeseman) Cheeseman. *N. Z. J. Bot.*, 4:153–158. **117**

Edgren, R. A., Edgren, M. K., and Tiffany, L. H., 1953. Some North American turtles and their zooepiphytic algae. *Ecology*, 34:733–740. **562–564**

Edmondson, W. T., 1944. Ecological studies of sessile Rotatoria. Part 1. Factors affecting distribution. *Ecol. Monogr.*, 14:31–66. **380**

Edmondson, W. T., 1945. Ecological studies of sessile Rotatoria. Part 2. Dynamics of populations and social structures. *Ecol. Monogr.*, 15:141–172. **537**

Edwards, R. W., and Haywood, J., 1960. Effect of sewage effluent discharge on the deposition of calcium carbonate on the shells of the snail *Potamopyrgus jenksinsi* (Smith). *Nature (Lond.)*, 180:492–493. **301**

Edwards, T. J., 1933. The germination and growth of *Peltandra virginica* in the absence of oxygen. *Bull. Torrey Bot. Club*, 60:573–581. **217**

Eggerling, W. J., 1935. The vegetation of Namanve Swamp, Uganda. *J. Ecol.*, 23:422–435. **478**

Embody, G. C., 1928. Principles of pond fertilization. *Trans. Amer. Fisher Soc.*, 58:19–22. **368**

Epstein, E., 1972. *Mineral nutrition of plants: principles and perspectives*. New York and London, J. Wiley & Sons, ix, 412 pp. **265**

Epstein, E., and Hagen, C. E., 1952. A kinetic study of the absorbtion of alkali cations by barley roots. *Plant Physiol.*, 27:457–474. **266**

Ernst-Schwarzenbach, M., 1945. Zur Blütenbiologie einiger Hydrocharitaceen. *Ber. Schweiz. Bot. Ges.*, 55:33–69. **230**

Ernst-Schwarzenbach, M., 1956. Kleistogamie und Antherenbau in der Hydrocharitaceen-Gattung *Ottelia. Phytomorphologie*, 6:296–311. **233**

Eugster, C. H., Griot, R., and Karrer, P., 1953. Weiteres über die Sumpfschachtelhahnbasen. *Helv. Chem. Act.*, 36:1387–1400. **363**

Evans, D., and Stockner, J. G., 1972. Attached algae on artificial and natural substrates in Lake Winnepeg, Manitoba. *J. Fisher. Res. Board Can.*, 29:31–44. **527, 528**

Evans, J. H., 1958. The survival of freshwater algae during dry periods. Part 1. An investigation of five small ponds. *J. Ecol.*, 46:149–168. **526**

Evans, J. H., 1959. The survival of freshwater algae during dry periods. Part II. Drying experiments. Part III. Stratification of algae in pond margin litter and mud. *J. Ecol.*, 47:55–81. **526**

Ewer, D. W., 1966. Biological investigations on the Volta Lake, May, 1964 to May 1965. *Man-made Lakes* (ed. R. H. Lowe McConnell). Symp. Inst. Biol. 15:21–31. **252**

Eyster, C., 1958. Bioassay of water from a concretion-forming marl lake. *Limnol. Oceanogr.*, 3:455–458. **301**

Faegri, K., and van der Pijl, L., 1971. *The Principles of Pollination Ecology*. 2nd ed. Oxford and New York, Pergamon Press xii, 291 pp. **225, 228, 229, 233, 241**

Farner, D. S., 1942. The hydrogen ion concentration in avian digestive tracts. *Poult. Sci.*, 21:445–450. **223 fn**

Farnsworth, N. R., Blomster, R. N., Quimby, M. W., and Schermerhorn, J. W., 1974. *The Lynn Index. A Bibliography of Phytochemistry*. Monograph VIII. R. Farnsworth, Univ. Illinois Medical Center, vii, 10–412 pp. **361, 365**

Fassett, N. C., 1930. The plants of some northeastern Wisconsin lakes. *Trans. Wisc. Acad. Sci. Arts Lett.*, 25:157–168. **118, 130, 131, 137, 410, 430, 431**

Fassett, N. C., 1940. *A Manual of Aquatic Plants*. New York and London, McGraw Hill Book Co., Inc., vii, 382 pp. **79**

Fassett, N. C., 1957. *A Manual of Aquatic Plants*. 2nd ed. Madison, Univ. Wisconsin Press, 405 pp. **191**

Fauré-Fremiet, E., 1951. The tidal rhythm of the diatom Hantzschia amphioxys. *Biol. Bull.*, 100:173–177. **558**

Federici, E., 1927. L'azione tossica delle "Charae" sulle larve dei Culicidi. *Redia*, 16:17–28. **30**

Ferling, E., 1957. Die Wirkungen des Erhöhten hydrostatischen Druckes auf Wachstum und Differenzierung submerser Blütenpflanzen. *Planta*, 49:235–270. **420, 421**

Fernald, M. L., 1919. Two new Myriophyllums and a species new to the United States. *Rhodora*, 21:120–124. **250**

Fernald, M. L., 1932. The linear-leaved North American species of Potamogeton, section Axillares. *Mem. Amer. Acad. Arts Sci.*, 17:1–183. **193, 241**

Fernald, M. L., 1950. *Gray's Manual of Botany.* Eighth (Centennial) ed. New York, American Book Co., lxiv, 1632 pp. **193, 216 fn, 241**

Ferris, J. P., 1962. Lythraceae alkaloids. I. Isolation and structural studies of the alkaloids of *Decodon verticillatus* (L.) EIL. *J. Org. Chem.*, 27:2985–2990. **364**

Ferris, J. P., 1963. II. Lythraceae alkaloids. II. Structural studies on decodine and verticillatine. *J. Org. Chem.*, 28:817–822. **364**

Fink, B., 1903. Contributions to a knowledge of the lichens of Minnesota. VII. Lichens of the Northern Boundary. *Minn. Bot. Stud.*, 3:167–236. **566**

Fischer, A., 1907. Wasserstoff- und Hydroxylionen als Keimungsreize. *Ber. Dsch. Bot. Ges.*, 25:108–122. **213, 216, 217**

Fish, G. R., 1963. Observations on excessive weed growth in two lakes in New Zealand. *N. Z. J. Bot.*, 1:410–418. **322, 324**

Fisher, H. C., 1923. *Report of the Health Dept. of the Panama Canal Zone for 1922.* Mount Hope, C. Z. (not seen, ref. Matheson and Hinman, 1928). **30**

Fisher, R. A., Corbet, A. S., and Williams, C. B., 1943. The relation between the number of species and the number of individuals in a random sample of an animal population. *J. Anim. Ecol.*, 12:42–57. **530**

Fitzgerald, G. P., 1969. Some factors in the competition or antagonism among bacteria, algae, and aquatic weeds. *J. Phycol.*, 5:351–359. **542**

Flint, E. A., 1950. An investigation of the distribution in time and space of the algae of a British reservoir. *Hydrobiologia*, 2:217–239. **532**

Flössner, D., 1964. Zur Cladocerenfauna des Stechlinsee-Gebietes. II. Okologische Untersuchungen über die litoralen Arten. *Limnologica*, 2:35–103. **8**

Forsberg, C., 1963. Some remarks on Wood's Revision of Characeae. *Taxon*, 12:141–144. **3, 43**

Forsberg, C., 1964a. Phosphorus, a maximum factor in the growth of Characeae. *Nature (Lond.)* 201:517–518. **23**

Forsberg, C., 1964b. The vegetation changes in Lake Tåkern. *Sven. Bot. Tidskr.*, 58:44–54. **23–25**

Forsberg, C., 1965a. Environmental conditions of Swedish charophytes. *Symb. Bot. Ups.*, 18, no. 4, 67 pp. **43, 44**

Forsberg, C., 1965b. Sterile germination of oospores of *Chara* and seeds of *Najas marina*. *Physiol. Plant*, 18:128–137. **6, 217, 221**

Forsberg, C., 1965c. Nutritional studies of *Chara* in axenic cullures. *Physiol. Plant*, 18:275–290. **23**

Forsberg, C., 1966. Sterile germination requirements of seeds of some water plants. *Physiol. Plant.*, 19:1105–1109. **221**

Fox, J. L., Odlaugh, T. O., and Olson, T. A., 1968. The ecology of periphyton in western Lake Superior. I. Taxonomy and Distribution. *Univ. Minn. Water Resour. Res. Center, Bull. 14*, 99 pp. (not seen ref. Evans and Stockner, 1972). **527**

Franck, P. A., 1966. Dormancy in winter buds of American pondweed *Potamogeton nodosus* Poir. *J. Exp. Bot.*, 17:546–555. **223**

Frantz, T. C., and Cordone, A. J., 1967. Observations on deepwater plants in Lake Tahoe, California and Nevada. *Ecology*, 48:709–714. **38, 48, 61, 63, 152, 409**

Frederick, S. E., Gruber, P. J., and Tolbert, N. E., 1973. The occurrence of glycolate dehydrogenase and glycolate oxidate in green plants. *Plant Physiol.*, 52:318–323. **1 fn, 153**

Fritsch, F. E., 1935. *The Structure and Reproduction of Algae.* Cambridge at the University Press, I. xvii, 791 pp. **7, 8, 515, 548**

Frye, T. C., and Clark, L., 1937–1947. *Hepaticae of North America.* Univ. Washington Publ. in Biology, 1018 pp. **48, 52**

Fuchsig, H., 1924. Die im Wasser wachsenden Moose des Lunzer Seengebietes. *Int. Rev. Gesamten Hydrobiol.*, 12:175–208. **46, 56, 61, 63**

Fuhs, G. W., Demmerle, S. D., Canelli, E., and Min Chen, 1972. Characterization of phosphorus-limited plankton algae (with reflections on the limiting nutrient concept). In *Nutrients and Eutrophication*, ed. G. E. Likens. ASLO Special Symposia 1:113–132. **266**

Funderburk, H. H., and Laurence, J. M., 1963. Absorbtion and translocation of radioactive herbicides in submersed and emersed aquatic weeds. *Weed Res.*, 3:304–311. **201**

Funke, G. L., 1938. Observations on the growth of water plants. II. *Biol. Jaarb.*, 5:382–403. **230**

Gadow, H., 1901. *Amphibia and Reptiles.* The Cambridge Natural History, London, Macmillan & Co., xiii, 668 pp. (see p. 340). **564**

Gajevskaia, N. S., 1958. Le role des groupes principaux de la flore aquatique dans les cycles trophiques des differents bassins de l' eau douce. *Verh. Int. Ver. Limnol.*, 13:350–362. **249, 368, 547**

*Gaevskaya (= Gajevskaia) N. S., 1969. *The Role of Higher Aquatic Plants in the Nutrition of the Animals of Fresh-water Basins.* Trans. D. G. Maitland Muller, ed. K. H. Mann. Boston Spa, National Lending Library for Science and Technology, 629 pp. (in 3 vols. mimeogr.). **547**

Gams, H., 1918. Prinzipienfragen der Vegetationsforschung. *Vierteljahrssch. Natur. Ges., Zur.*, 63:293–493. **121**

Garcia-Novo, F., and Crawford, R. M. M., 1973. Soil aeration, nitrate-reduction, and flooding tolerance in higher plants. *New Phytol.*, 72:1031–1039. **210**

Gaudet, J. J., 1973. Growth of a floating aquatic weed, *Salvinia*, under standard conditions. *Hydrobiologia*, 41:77–106. **286**

Gause, G. F., 1936. The principles of biocoenology. *Q. Rev. Biol.*, 11:320–336. **529, 531**

Gause, G. F., and Witt, A. A., 1935. Behavior of mixed populations and the problem of natural selection. *Amer. Nat.*, 69:596–609. **118, 497**

Gay, P. A., 1958. *Eichhornia crassipes* in the Nile of the Sudan. *Nature (Lond.)*, 182:538–539. **388**

*Gertrude, M.-Th., 1937. Action du milieu extérieur sur le métabolisme végétal. VIII. Métabolisme et morphogénèse en milieu aquatique. *Rev. Gen. Bot.*, 49:161–181, 243–268, 328–352, 375–400, 449–467. **168**

Gerloff, G. C., and Krombholz, P. H., 1966. Tissue analysis as a measure of nutrient availability for the growth of aquatic plants. *Limnol. Oceanogr.*, 11:529–537. **351–357**

Gerloff, G. C., and Skoog, F., 1954. Cell content of nitrogen and phosphorus as a measure of their availability for growth of *Microcystis aeruginosa. Ecology*, 35:348–353. **527**

Gessner, F., 1933. Die Nahrstoffaufnahme der Submersen. *Ber. Dsch. Bot. Ges.*, 51:216–228. **274**

Gessner, F., 1937. Untersuchungen über Assimilation und Atmung submerser Wasserpflanzen. *Jahrb. Wiss. Bot.*, 85:267–328. **147, 151**

Gessner, F., 1938. Die Beziehung zwischen Lichtintensität und Assimilation bei submerser Wasserpflanzen. *Jahrb. Wiss. Bot.*, 86:491–526. **175**

Gessner, F., 1940. Beiträge zur Biologie amphibischer Pflanzen. *Ber. Dsch. Bot. Ges.*, 58:2–22. **183**

Gessner, F., 1945. Über die Wasseraufnahme emerser Wasserpflanzen. *Ber. Dsch. Bot. Ges.*, 67:340–343. **198**

*Gessner, F., 1952. Der Druck in seiner Bedeutung für das Wachstum submerser Wasserpflanzen. *Planta*, 40:391–397. **418, 419, 420**

*Gessner, F., 1955. *Hydrobotanik. I. Energiehaushalt* (Hochschulbücher für Biologie Band 3). Berlin, VEB Deutscher Verlag der Wissenschaften, 517 pp. **134, 144, 145, 159, 198, 418**

*Gessner, F., 1959. *Hydrobotanik. II. Stoffhaushalt.* (Hochschulbücher für Biologie Band 8.) Berlin, VEB Deutscher Verlag der Wissenschaflen 701 pp. **134, 148, 149, 159, 420**

Gessner, F., 1960. Die Blütenöffnung der *Victoria regia* in ihrer Beziehung zum Licht. *Planta*, 54:453–465. **81**

Gessner, F., 1961. Hydrostatischer Druck und Pflanzenwachstum. In *Encyclopedia of Plant Physiology*, ed. W. Ruhland. Berlin, Springer-Verlag 16:668–690. **420, 423**

Gessner, F., and Kaukal, A., 1952. Die Ionenaufnahme submerser Wasserpflanzen in ihrer Abhängigkeit von der Konzentration der Nährlösung. *Ber. Dsch. Bot. Ges.*, 65:155–163. **274**

Gibbs, R. D., 1974. *Chemotaxonomy of Flowering Plants.* Montreal and London, McGill and Queen's University Press 4 vols., 2370 pp. (paginated continuously). **361, 364, 367, 368**

Gifford, R. M., 1974. A comparison of potential photosynthesis, productivity, and yield of plant species with differing photosynthetic metabolism. *Aust. J. Plant Physiol.*, 1:107–117. **153**

Gilson, H. C., 1939. The Percy Sladen Trust Expedition to Lake Titicaca in 1937 under the Leadership of Mr. H. Cary Gilson. I. Description of the expedition. *Trans. Linn. Soc. Lond.*, ser. 3., 1:1–20. **483**

*Glück, H., 1905. *Biologische und morphologische Untersuchungen über Wasser und Sumpfgewächse. I. Die Lebensgeschichte der Europäischen Alismaceen.* Jena, G. Fischer, xxiv, 312 pp. **418**

*Glück, H., 1908. *Biologische und morphologische Untersuchungen über Wasser-und Sumpfgewächse. II. Untersuchungen über die mitteleuropäischen* Utricularia-*Arten, über die Turionenbildung bei Wasserpflanzen, sourie über* Ceratophyllum. Jena, G. Fischer, xvii, 256 pp. **236**

*Glück, H., 1911. *Biologische und morphologische Untersuchungen über Wasser-und Sumpfgewächse. III. Die Uferflora.* Jena, G. Fischer, xxxiv, 644 pp. **137, 139**

*Glück, H., 1936. *Pteridophyten und Phanerogamen. Süsswasser-Flora Mitteleuropas* (herausgeg. A. Pascher) Jena, G. Fischer, xx, 486 pp. **80, 86, 136, 137, 139, 159, 178, 179, 182, 183, 190, 191, 235**

Glück, H., 1940. Die Gattung *Trapella.*, *Bot. Jaarb.* 71:267–336. **93**

*Godward, M., 1934. An investigation of the causal distribution of algal epiphytes. *Beih. Bot. Zbl.*, 52 Abt. A., 506–539. **529, 531, 535, 536, 537, 539**

*Godward, M., 1937. An ecological and taxonomic investigation of the algal flora of Lake Windermere. *J. Ecol.*, 25:496–568. **510, 526, 529, 531, 542**

Godwin, H. 1923. Dispersal of pond floras. *J. Ecol.*, 11:160–164. **253–256**

Godwin, H., 1956. *The history of the British flora.* Cambridge University Press, viii, 385 pp. **243**

Godwin, H., and Willis, E. H., 1964. The viability of lotus seeds (*Nelumbium nucifera* Gaertn). *New Phytol.*, 63:410-412. **213**

Goebel, K., 1879. Ueber Sprossbildung auf Isoetesblättern. *Bot. Z.*, 37:1-6. **73**

Goebel, K., 1893. Wasserpflanzen. *Pflanzenbiologische Schilderungen* 2 Teil, 2 Lief.: 217-380. **207**

Goebel, K., 1895. Ueber die Einwirkung des Lichtes auf die Gestaltung der Kakteen und anderer Pflanzen. *Flora*, 80:96-116. **165**

Goldman, C. R., 1960. Molybdenum as a factor limiting primary production in Castle Lake, California. *Science*, 132:1016-1017. **344**

Golubić, S., 1961. Der Vrana-See an der Insel Cres-ein Chara-See. *Verh. Int. Ver. Limnol.* 14:846-849. **24, 39, 422**

Golubić, S., 1963. Hydrostatischer Druck, Licht, und submerse Vegetation im Vrana-See. *Int. Rev. Gesamten Hydrobiol.*, 48:1-7. **422**

Golubić, S., 1967. *Algenvegetation der Felsen. Eine Ökologische Algenstudie im dinarischen Karstgebiet.* Binnengewässer Bd. xxiii, Stuttgart Schweizenbart'sche Verlagstridihandlung, viii, 183 pp. **516 fn**

Gorham, E., 1964. Molybdenum, manganese, and iron in lake muds. *Verh. Int. Ver. Limnol.*, 15:330-332. **344**

Grainger, J., 1947. Nutrition and flowering of water plants. *J. Ecol.* 35:49-64. **159, 226**

Grant, V., 1950. The protection of the ovules in flowering plants. *Evolution*, 4:179-201. **227**

Grew, N., 1673. *An Idea of a Phytological History Propounded.* London . . . Richard Chiswell at the Rose and Crown in St. Paul's Churchyard [21] 144 [16] pp. **227**

Griffin, D. G., 1961. Reappearance of Riella americana in Texas. *Bryologist*, 64:57-58. **51**

Grigson, G., 1955. *The Englishman's Flora.* London, Phoenix House 478 pp. **248**

Grochowska, I. R., 1971. *Flora Słodkowodna Polski.* Tom 17. *Hepaticae Watrobowce.* Kracóv, Polska Akademia Nauk, Institut Botaniki, 335 pp. **46, 47, 52, 54**

Groves, J., and Bullock-Webster, G. R., 1920. *The British Charophyta.* I. *Nitelleae.* London, The Ray Society, xiv, 141 pp., xx pl. **5**

Groves, J., and Bullock-Webster, G. R., 1924. *The British Charophyta.* II. *Chareae.* London, The Ray Society, ix, 129 pp., xxi-xlv pl. **4, 13**

Guinochet, M., 1955. *Logique et dynamique du peuplement vegetale.* Paris (not seen, ref. Swindale and Curtis, 1957). **502**

Guppy, H. B., 1894. Water-Plants and Their Ways. Their dispersal and its observation. *Sci. Gossip*, n. s. 1894, 145-147. **223**

Guppy, H. B., 1897. On the postponement of the germination of seeds of aquatic plants. *Proc. R. Phys. Soc. Edinb.*, 13:344-359. **214, 218-221, 223**

Haberlandt, G. F. J., 1914. *Physiological Plant Anatomy.* Translated from the 4th German ed. by M. Drummond, London, Macmillan, xv, 777 pp. **317**

Hagström, J. O., 1916. Critical researches on the Potamogetons. *K. Sven. Vetenskapskad. Handl.*, 55, no. 5, 281 pp. **243**

Hale, M. E., 1950. The Lichens of Aton Forest, Connecticut. *Bryologist*, 53:181-213. **567**

Hamlyn-Harris, R., 1928. The relation of certain algae to breeding places of mosquitos in Queensland. *Bull. Entomol. Res.*, 18:377-389. **31**

Hamlyn-Harris, R., 1932. Some further observations on *Chara fragilis* in relation to mosquitos breeding in Queensland. *Ann. Trop. Med. Parasitol.*, 26:519-524. **31**

Harder, R., Döring, B., and Simonis, W., 1936. Über die Kohlensaureassimilation in verschiedenen Spektralbezirken durch grüne, in farbigen Licht kultivierte, Pflanzen. *Nachr. Ges. Wiss. Göttingen,* Math. Phys. Kl. n. f. Fachgr. VI, 2:129–133. **416**

Harder, R., 1963. Blütenbildung durch tierische Zusatznahrung und andere Faktoren bei *Utricularia exoleta,* R. Braun. *Planta,* 59:459–471. **226, 285**

Harper, H. J., and Daniel, H. A., 1934. Chemical composition of certain aquatic plants. *Bot. Gaz.,* 96:186–189. **286, 299**

Harris, B. B., and Silvey, J. K. G., 1940. Limnological investigations on Texas reservoir lakes. *Ecol. Monogr.,* 10:111–143. **256**

Harris, T. M., 1939. *British Purbeck Charophyta.* London, British Museum (N.H.), ix, 83 pp. **3**

Harrod, J. J., and Hall, R. E., 1962. A method for determining the surface areas of various aquatic plants. *Hydrobiologia,* 20:173–178. **543**

Hart, D. A., and Kindel, P. K., 1970. Novel reaction involved in the degradation of apiogalacturonans from *Lemna minor* and the isolation of apibiose as a product. *Biochemistry* (A. C. S.), 9:2190–2196. **361**

Hartman, R. T., and Brown, D. L., 1966. Methane as a constituent of the internal atmosphere of vascular hydrophytes. *Limnol. Oceanogr.,* 11:109–112. **204**

Hartman, R. T., and Brown, D. L., 1967. Changes in internal atmosphere of submerged vascular hydrophytes in relation to photosynthesis. *Ecology,* 48:252–258. **202**

Hasler, A. D., 1938. Fish biology and limnology of Crater Lake, Oregon. *J. Wildl. Manage.,* 2:94–103. **63**

Hasler, A. D., and Jones, E., 1949. Demonstration of the antagonistic action of large aquatic plants on algae and rotifers. *Ecology,* 30:359–364. **368, 542**

Hassack, C., 1888. Ueber das Verhältnis von Pflanzen zu Bicarbonaten und über Kalkinkrustation. *Tübingen Bot. Inst. Unters.,* 2:465–477. **148**

Hastings, A. B., Murray, C. D., and Sendroy, J., 1927. Studies on the solubility of calcium salts. I. The solubility of calcium carbonate in salt solutions and biological fluids. *J. Biol. Chem.,* 71:723–781. **301**

Hatch, M. D., Osmond, C. B., and Slatyer, R. O., 1971. *Photosynthesis and Photorespiration.* New York and London, Wiley Interscience, x, 565 pp. **152**

Hegnauer, R., 1962–1973. *Chemotaxonomie* der Pflanzen, Basel and Stuttgart, Birkhauser Verlag, 6 vols. published, **361**. vol 2 Monocotyledoneae, 1963, 540 pp. **364**. and vol. 5. Dicotyledoneae:Magnoliaceae to Quiinaceae, 1969, 506 pp. **363, 365, 367,** being specifically mentioned in text.

Heil, H., 1924. *Chamaegigas intrepidus* Dtr., Eine neue Auferstehungspflanze. *Beih. Bot. Centralbl.,* 41:41–50. **95**

*Hejny, S., 1960. *Oekologische Characteristik der Wasser- und Sumpfpflanzen in den Slowakische Tiefebenen (Donau und Theissgebiet).* Bratislawa, Verlag der Slowakischen Akademie der Wissenschaften. 478 pp. **118, 120, 121, 138, 139, 191, 234**

Hejny, S., 1968. Bemerkungen zu der Klassifikation einiger Makrophytengesellschaften der stehenden Gewässer. *Pflanzensoziologische Systematik.* Internationalen Vereinung für Vegetationskunde, Symposium Stolzenau/Weser, 1964. ed. R. Tüxen 230–238. **494**

Henrici, A. T., 1933. Studies of freshwater bacteria. I. A direct microscopic technique. *J. Bact.,* 24:277–286. **529, 530**

Henrici, A. T., 1936. Studies of freshwater bacteria. III. Quantitative aspects of the direct microscopic method. *J. Bact.,* 32:265–280. **529**

Hentschel, E., 1916. Biologische Untersuchungen über den tierischen und Pflanzlichen Bewuchs im Hamburger Hafen. *Mitt. Zool. Mus. Hamb.,* 33:1–176. **529**

Herbst, R. P., 1969. Ecological factors and the distribution of *Cladophora glomerata* in the Great Lakes. *Amer. Midl. Nat.,* 82:90–98. **527, 528**

Heslop-Harrison, Y., 1955a. Biological flora of the British Isles. *Nuphar* Sm. *J. Ecol.*, 43:342-364. **141, 143, 159, 227, 413**

Heslop-Harrison, Y., 1955b. Biological flora of the British Isles. *Nymphaea* L. *J. Ecol.*, 43:719-734. **139, 227**

Hickel, B., 1967. Zur Kenntnis einer xerophilen Wassenpflanze *Chamaegigas intrepidus* Dtz. aus Südwestafrika. *Int. Rev. Gesamten Hydrobiol.*, 52:361-400. **93**

Hiern, W. P., 1871. A theory of the floating leaves in certain plants. *Proc. Camb. Philos. Soc.*, 2:227-236. **143, 144**

Higinbotham, N., 1973. The mineral absorbtion process in plants. *Bot. Rev.*, 39:15-69. **265**

Hill, C. F., 1969. *Lake Ohakuri, its Limnology and Aquatic Vegetation.* Ph.D. Thesis, Auckland University, N. Z., 184 pp. **409**

*Hillman, W. S., 1961. The Lemnaceae or duck weeds. A review of the descriptive and experimental literature. *Bot. Rev.*, 27:221-287. **226, 229**

Hoagland, D. R., and Davis, A. R., 1923. Further experiments on the absorbtion of ions by plants, including observations on the effect of light. *J. Gen. Physiol.* 6:47-62. **270**

Hodgetts, W. J., 1921. A study of some of the factors controlling the periodicity of freshwater algae in nature, VII-XVI. *New Phytol.*, 20:195-227. **11, 37**

Hoffman, W. E., and Tilden, J. E., 1930. *Basicladia,* a new genus of Cladophoraceae. *Bot. Gaz.*, 89:374-384. **561, 562**

Hogeweg, P., and Brenkert, A. L., 1969. Structure of vegetation: a comparison of aquatic vegetation in India, the Netherlands, and Czechoslovakia. *Trop. Eco.*, 10:139-162. **118, 122-124, 131**

Höhn, K., and Ax, W., 1961. Untersuchungen über Wasserbewegung und Wachstum submerser Pflanzen. *Beiträge zur Biol. Pflanz.*, 36:274-298. **200**

Holm, L. G., Weldon, L. W., and Blackburn, R. D., 1969. Aquatic Weeds. *Science,* 166: 699-709. **247, 250, 251, 252**

Hooker, W. J., 1817. In Curtis, W. *Flora Londinensis,* London, 1:165, 170 (not seen, ref. Heslop-Harrison, 1955a). **227**

Hooker, J. D., 1847. *The Botany of the Antarctic Voyage of H. M. Discovery Ships Erebus and Terror.* I. *Flora Antarctica.* Part II. London, 364 pp. **232**

Hough, R. A., and Wetzel, R. G., 1972. A ^{14}C-assay for photorespiration in aquatic plants. *Plant Physiol.*, 49:987-990. **153**

Howe, M. A., and Underwood, L. M., 1903. The genus Riella, with descriptions of new species from North America and the Canary Islands. *Bull. Torrey Bot. Club,* 30:214-224. **51**

Hurter, E., 1928. Beobachtungen an den Litoralalgen des Vierwaldstättersees. *Mitt. Naturforsch. Ges. Luzern,* 10:142-400. **510, 516, 520, 524, 525, 526**

*Hustedt, F., 1922. Die Bacillariaceen-Vegetation des Lunzer Seengebietes. *Int. Rev. Geramten Hydrobiol.* 10:40-74, 233-270. **510, 512, 513**

Hustedt, F., 1930. *Bacillariophyta (Diatomeae) Süsswasser – Flora Mitteleuropas.* ed. A. Pascher. Hf. 10 (Zweite Auflage) Jena, G. Fischer, viii, 466 pp. **538, 540**

Hutchinson, G. E., 1943. The biogeochemistry of aluminum and certain related elements. *Quart. Rev. Biol.,* 18:1-29, 128-153, 242-262, 331-363. **311**

Hutchinson, G. E., 1948, 1953. In Memoriam D'Arcy Wentworth Thompson. Amer. Sci., 36:577-581, 600-606, reprinted in *The Itinerant Ivory Tower,* Yale University Press, 1953, pp. 169-185. **144 fn**

Hutchinson, G. E., 1970. The chemical ecology of three species of *Myriophyllum* (Angiospermae, Haloragacaea), *Limnol. Oceanogr.,* 15:1-5. **386**

Hutchinson, G. E., and Pickford, G. E., 1932. Limnological observations on Mountain Lake, Virginia. *Int. Rev. Gesamten Hydrobiol.,* 27:252-264. **431**

Hutchinson, G. E. and Wollack, A. C., 1943. Biological accumulators of aluminum. *Tr. Conn. Acad. Arts Sci.*, 35:73–128. **310**

Hutchinson, J. 1916. Aquatic Compositae. *Gardiner's Chron.*, 59:305–306. **99, 102, 386**

Hutchinson, J., 1959. *The Families of Flowering Plants*, 2nd ed. I. Dicotyledons, xi, 510 pp. II. Monocotyledons, viii, 511–792 pp. Oxford, Clarendon Press, **77, 81, 89**

Hutchinson, J., 1969. *Evolution and Phylogeny of Flowering Plants.* London and New York, Academic Press, xi, 717 pp. **79, 89**

*Hynes, H. B. N., 1972. *The Ecology of Running Waters.* University of Toronto Press, xxiv, 555 pp. **134**

*Imahori, K., 1954. *Ecology, Phytogeography, and Taxonomy of the Japanese Charophyta.* Kanazawa, 234 pp. **7, 8, 14, 15, 31, 38, 39**

Iskra, A. A., Kulikov, N. V., and Bakhurov, V. G., 1970. Role of freshwater vegetation in the process of migration and distribution of natural radioactive elements in the reservoir. *Ekologiya,* 2:83–87 (not seen, ref. Cowgill, 1974a). **322**

*Iversen, J., 1929. Studien über die pH-Verhältnisse dänischer Gewässer und ihren Einfluss auf die Hydrophyten-Vegetation. *Bot. Tidskr.,* 40:277–326. **50, 64, 370–372, 381**

Iversen, J., 1936. Biologische Pflanzentypen als Hiffsmittel in der Vegetationsforschung. Thesis Copenhagen, 224 pp. (not seen, ref. den Hartog and Segal, 1964). **118, 119**

*Iversen, J. and Olsen, S., 1946. Die Verbreitung den Wasserpflanzen in Relation zur Chemie der Wassers. *Botan. Tidsskr.,* 46:136–145. **392**

Ivlev, V. S., 1933. Ein Versuch zur experimentellen Erforschung der Ökologie der Wasserbiocönosen. *Arch. Hydrobiol.,* 25:177–191. **529**

Iyengar, M. O. P., 1958. *Nitella terrestris* sp. nov. a terrestrial charophyte from South India. *Bull. Bot. Soc. Bengal,* 12:85–90. **14**

Jacoby, B., 1965. Sodium retention in excised bean stems. *Physiol. Plant,* 18:730–739. **293**

Järnefelt, H., 1930. Ein kurzer Ueberblick über die Limnologie Finnlands. *Verh. Int. Ver. Limnol.,* 4:401–407. **452**

Järnefelt, H., 1938. Die Enstehungs-und Entwicklungsgeschichte der finnischen Seen. *Geol. Meere Binnengewässer,* 2:199–223. **449**

Jeanjean, R., Blasco, F., and Gaudin, C., 1970. Etude des méchanismes de l'absorbtion de l'ion phosphate par les chlorelles. *C. R. Acad. Sci. Paris Ser.,* D 270:2946–2949. **274**

Jeffreys, R. L., Laycock, D., Stewart, G. R., and Sims, A. P., 1969. The properties of mechanisms involved in the uptake and utilization of calcium and potassium by plants in relation to an understanding of plant distribution. *Ecological Aspects of the Mineral Nutritional Plants,* ed. I. H. Robson, Oxford and Edinburgh, Blackwell Scientific Publications, pp. 281–307. **389**

Jermy, A. C., 1964. *Isoetes,* in *Flora Europaea,* vol. 1. Tutin, T. G., Heywood, V. H., Burges, N. A., Valentine, D. H., Walters, S. M., and Webb, D. A. Cambridge, at the University Press, pp. 5–6. **72**

Jeschke, L., 1963. Die Wasser- und Sumpfvegetation im Naturschutzgebiet "Ostufer der Muntz," *Limnologia,* 1:475–545. **41**

Jeschke, W. D., 1970. Der Influx von Kaliumionen bei Blattern von *Elodea densa,* Abhängigkeit von Licht, von der Kaliumkonzentration und von der Temperature. *Planta,* 91: 111–128. **274**

Jeschke, W. D. and Simonis, W., 1965. Über die Aufnahme von Phosphat- und Sulfationen durch Blattern von *Elodea densa,* und ihre Beeinflussung durch Licht, Temperatur und Aussenkonzentration. *Planta,* 67:6–32. **274**

Johnson, D. S. and Chrysler, M. A., 1938. Structure and development of Regnellidium diphyllum. *Am. J. Bot.*, 25:141–156. 75

Jones, H., 1955a. Heterophylly in some species of *Callitriche*, with especial reference to *Callitriche intermedia. Ann. Bot.* (n. s.), 19:225–245. 171, 172

Jones, H., 1955b. Further studies on heterophylly in *Callitriche intermedia:* leaf development and experimental induction of ovate leaves. *Ann. Bot.* (n. s.), 19:369–388. 171, 173

Jørgensen, E. G., 1957. Diatom periodicity and silicon assimilation. *Dan. Bot. Ark.*, 18 (1), 54 pp. 542

Kalk, M., 1973. The Challenge of Lake Chilwa. *Afr. J. Trop. Hydrobiol. Fish.*, 1:141–146. 80, 413

Kann, E., 1933. Zur Ökologie der litoralen Algenaufwuchses in Lunzer Untersee. *Int. Rev. Hydrobiol.*, 28:172–227. 522

Kann, E., 1940. Ökologische Untersuchungen an Litoralalgen ostholsteinischer Seen. *Arch. Hydrobiol.*, 37:177–269. 488, 523

Kann, E., 1945. Zur Ökologie der Litoralalgen in ostholsteinischer Waldseen. *Arch. Hydrobiol.*, 41:14–42. 523

Kann, E., 1958. Der Algenaufwuchs in der eulitoralen Zone alpiner und norddeutscher Seen. *Verh. Int. Ver. Limnol.*, 13:311–319. 488, 516–523

*Kann, E., 1959. Die eulitorale Algenzone im Traunsee (Oberösterreich). *Arch. Hydrobiol.*, 55:129–192. 518–521

Kannen, S., 1971. Plasmalemma: the seat of dual mechanisms of ion absorbtion in *Chlorella pyrenoidosa. Science*, 173:927–929. 274

Karling, J. S., 1924. A preliminary account of the influence of light and temperature on growth and reproduction in *Chara fragilis. Bull. Torrey Bot. Club*, 51:469–488. 11

Karsinkin, G., 1934. Zur Studium des bakterialen Periphytons. *Arb. Limnol. Stat. Kossino*, 17:21–44 (Russian text); 45–48 (German summary). 529, 530

Kausik, S. B., 1939. Pollination and its influences on the behavior of the pistillate flower in *Vallisneria spiralis. Am. J. Bot.*, 26:207–211. 230, 231

Keiser, A., 1921. Die sessilen, peritrichen Infusorien und Suctorien von Basel und Ungebung. *Rev. Suisse Zool.*, 28:221–341. 559

Kerner von Marilaun, A., 1895. *The Natural History of Plants* (trans. F. W. Oliver). II. *The History of Plants.* London, Blacke & Son, xiv, 983 pp. 246

Kevern, N. R. and Ball, R. C., 1965. Primary productivity and energy relationships in artificial streams. *Limnol. Oceanogr.*, 10:74–87. 530

Kevern, N. R., Wilhm, J. L., and van Dyne, G. M., 1966. Use of artificial substrata to estimate the productivity of periphyton. *Limnol. Oceanogr.*, 11:499–502. 530

Keynes, R. D., 1969. From frogskin to sheep rumen: a survey of transport of salts and water across multicellular structures. *Quart. Rev. Biophys.*, 2:177–281. 271

Kilham, P. and Hecky, R. E., 1973. Fluoride: geochemical and ecological significance in East African waters and sediments. *Limnol. Oceanogr.*, 18:932–945. 348

Klapp, E., 1962. *Laki i pastwiska.* Warszawa (not seen, ref. Bernatowicz, 1969). 288, 289

Klinge, J., 1890. Über den Einfluss der mittleren Windrichtung auf das Verwachsen der Gewässer. *Engler's Bot. Jahrb.*, 11:264–313. 411

Klotter, H.-E., 1953. Die Algen in den Seen des südlichen Schwarzwaldes. *I. Arch. Hydrobiol. Suppl.*, 20:442–485. 553

Knoch, E., 1899. Untersuchungen über die Morphologie, Biologie und Physiologie der Blüte von *Victoria regia. Bibliotheca Bot.*, 9 (Heft 47):60 pp. 228, 229

Knuth, P., 1906–1909. Handbook of Flower Pollination. Trans. R. Ainsworth Davis, vol.

1, xix, 382 pp.; vol. 2, viii, 703 pp.; vol. 3, iv, 644 pp. Oxford, at the Clarendon Press. (German original 1895–1905 not seen.) **225**

Koch, W., 1926. Die Vegetationseinheiten der Linthebene unter Berücksichtigung der Verhältnisse in der Nordostschweiz. *Jahrb. St Gallischen Naturwiss. Ges.*, 61 (for 1925), Teil II:1–146. **243, 411, 487, 491, 492, 498**

Koch, W., 1928. Die höhere Vegetation der subalpinen Seen und Moorgebiete des Val Piora. *Rev. Hydrob.*, 4:131–175. **397, 487**

*Kolbe, R. W., 1932. Grundlinien einer allgemeinen Ökologie der Diatomeen. *Ergeb. Biol.*, 8:221–348. **514**

Koppe, F., 1924. Die Schlammflora der ostholsteinischen Seen und des Bodensees. *Arch. Hydrobiol.*, 14:619–672. **463, 509**

*Krause, W., 1969. Zur Characeenvegetation der Oberrheinebene. *Arch. Hydrobiol. Suppl.*, 35:202–253. **489, 490**

*Krausch, H. D., 1964. Die Pflanzengesellschaften der Stechlingsee-Gebietes. I. Die Gesellschaften der offenen Wassers. *Limnologica*, 2:145–203. **41, 397, 487, 489, 491–493, 498**

Królikowska, J., 1971. Transpiration of reed (*Phragmites communis* Trin.). *Pol. Arch. Hydrobiol.*, 18:347–358. **198**

Laing, H. E., 1940a. Respiration of the rhizomes of *Nuphar advena* and other waterplants. *Amer. J. Bot.*, 27:574–581. **205, 207**

Laing, H. E., 1940b. The composition of the internal atmosphere of *Nuphar advena* and other waterplants. *Amer. J. Bot.*, 27:861–868. **204, 205**

Laing, H. E., 1941. Effect of concentration of oxygen and pressure of water upon growth of rhizomes of semi-submerged waterplants. *Bot. Gaz.* 102:712–724. **205, 418, 429**

Lalonde, R., 1970. Aquatic plant chemistry. Its application to water pollution control. *Fed. Sci. Tech. Inf. P. B.* Rep. no. 192810, 40 pp. **365, 367**

Lalonde, R., Wong, C. F., and Cullen, W. P., 1970. Two new Nuphar alkaloids. 66′-dihydroxythio-nuphuline A. and B. *Tetrahedron Lett.*, 51:4477–4480. **365**

Lancaster, R. J., Coup, M. R., and Huges, J. W., 1971. Toxicity of arsenic present in lake weed. *N. Z. Vet. J.*, 19:141–145. **286, 288, 298, 299, 323, 324, 349**

Landergren, S., 1943. Geokemiska studier över Grängesbergsfältet järnmal mer. *Ing. Vetensk. Akad. Handl.*, no. 172 (not seen; ref. K. Rankama and T. G. Sahama, *Geochemistry*, Chicago Univ. Press, 1950). **338**

Laties, G. C., 1969. Dual mechanisms of salt uptake in relation to compartmentation and long-distance transport. *Ann. Rev. Plant. Physiol.* 20:89–116. **265**

Läuchli, A., and Epstein, E., 1970. Transport of potassium and rubidium in plant roots—the significance of calcium. *Plant. Physiol.*, 45:639–641. **295**

Lauterborn, R., 1934. Der Rhein, Naturgeschichte einer deutschen Stromes. *Ber. Naturf. Ges. Freiburg.*, 33 (not seen; ref. Gessner, 1952). **418**

Lawrence, J. M., 1968. *Dynamics of Chemical and Physical Characteristics of Water, Bottom Muds, and Aquatic Life in a large Impoundment on a River.* Final Report on OWRR Project 13-005-ALA. Auburn Univ. Agric. Exp. Stat., 216 pp. (mimeogr.). **286, 289, 304, 305, 306**

*Lawrence, J. M., 1971. *Dynamics of Chemical and Physical Characteristics of Water, Bottom Muds, and Aquatic Life in a Large Impoundment on a River. Phase II.* Final Report on OWRR Project B-010-ALA. Auburn Univ. Agric. Exp. Stat., 131 + 52 pp. (mimeogr.). **28, 286, 287, 288, 298, 299, 304, 305, 306, 328, 330, 331, 336, 337, 338, 340, 342, 343, 345, 346**

Lebrun, J., 1947. *Exploration du Parc National Albert, Mission J. Lehun (1937-1938)*. Bruxelles, 800 pp. **496**

Leentwaar, P., 1966. The Brokopondo Research Project. Surinam. *Man-made Lakes*, ed. R. H. Lowe-McConnell, Symposia of the Institute of Biology, 15. London and New York, Academic Press, pp. 33-42. (See also Hydrobiological observations in Surinam with special reference to the man-made Brokopondo Lake. Studies on the *Fauna of Suriname and other Guyanas*. Utrect 1975, received too late to use.) **75**

Leigh, E. C., 1972. The golden section and spiral leaf-arrangement. *Trans. Conn. Acad. Arts Sci.*, 44:163-176. **205**

Levins, R., 1968. *Evolution in Changing Environments; Some Theoretical Explorations*. Princeton Univ. Press, ix, 120 pp. **186**

Levy, G., 1931. La présence, la répartition et le rôle de l'aluminium ches les végétaux. Thése, Paris, 98 pp. **310**

Lind, C. T. and Cottam, G., 1969. The submerged aquatics of University Bay: a study in eutrophication. *Amer. Midl. Natur.*, 81:353-369. **11, 466, 468, 469, 472, 473**

Lineweaver, H. and Burk, D., 1934. The determination of enzyme dissociation constants. *J. Amer. Chem. Soc.*, 56:658-666. **266**

Linkola, K., 1933. Regionale Artenstatistik der Süsswasserflora Finnlands. *Suom. Eläinja Kasvitiet. Seuran Vanamon Kasvitiet. Julk. (Ann. Bot. Soc. Vanamo)*, 3, no. 5:3-13. **118**

Little, E. C. S., 1966. The invasion of man-made lakes by plants. In R. H. Lowe-McConnell ed. *Man-made Lakes. Symp. Inst. Biol.*, no. 15, pp. 75-86. **252**

Lloyd, F. E., 1942. *The Carnivorous Plants*. Waltham, Mass., Chronica Botanica, xv, 352 pp. **96**

Löffler, H., 1974. *Der Neusiedlersee: Naturgeschichte eines Steppensees*. Vienna, Munich, Zurich, Fritz Molden. 175 pp. **497, 540**

*Lohammar, G., 1938. Wasserchemie und höhere Vegetation schwedischer Seen. *Symb. Bot. Upsal.*, 3:1-252. **243, 380-387, 392-398**

Lohammar, G., 1954a. Matsmältningens inverkan på Potamogetonfrönas groning. The effect of digestion on the germination of Potamogeton seeds. *Fauna och Flora*, Häfter 1-2, 1954:17-32. **223, 224**

Lohammar, G., 1954b. The distribution and ecology of *Fissidens julianus* in Northern Europe. *Sven. Bot. Tid.*, 48:162-173. **62**

Lohammar, G., 1965. The vegetation of Swedish lakes. *Acta Phytogeogr. Suec.*, 50:28-48. **24, 241**

Lollar, A. Q., Coleman, D. C., and Boyd, C. E., 1971. Carnivorous pathway of phosphorus uptake by *Utricularia inflata*. *Arch. Hydrobiol.*, 69:400-404. **258**

Louanamaa, J., 1956. Trace elements in plants growing wild on different rocks in Finland. *Suom. Eläin-ja Kasvitiet. Seuran Vanamon Kasvitiet Julk. (Ann. Bot. Soc. Zool. Bot. Vanamo)*, 29, no. 4, 196 pp. **321**

Löve, A., 1961. Some notes on Myriophyllum spicatum. *Rhodora*, 63:139-145. **251**

Low, J., 1937. *Germination tests of some aquatic plants important as duck foods*. B. Sc. Thesis (unpublished). Utah State University, 27 pp. **224**

Lowenhaupt, B., 1956. The transport of calcium and other cations in submerged aquatic plants. *Biol. Rev.*, 31:371-395. **151**

Lowenhaupt, B., 1958a. Active cation transport in submerged aquatic plants. I. Effect of light upon the absorbtion and excretion of calcium by *Potamogeton crispus* (L.) leaves. *J. Cell. Comp. Physiol.*, 51:199-208. **151**

Lowenhaupt, B., 1958b. Active cation transport in submerged aquatic plants. II. Effect of aeration on the equilibrium content of calcium in *Potamogeton crispus* (L.) leaves. *J. Cell. Comp. Physiol.*, 51:209-219. **151**

Lucas, W. J., and Smith, F. A., 1973. The formation of alkaline and acid regions at the surface of *Chara corallina* cells. *J. Exp. Bot.,* 78:1–14. **19, 20**

Ludwig, F., 1886. Ueber durch Austrocknen bedingte Keimfähigkeit der Samen einiger Wasserpflanzen. *Biol. Zent.,* 6:299–300. **215**

Luerssen, C., 1889. *Die Farnpflanzen.* L. Rabenhorst's Kryptogramen-Flora von Deutschland, Oesterreich und der Schweiz. Zweiter Auflage, Bd. 3, Leipzig, E. Kummer, xii, 906 pp. (see pp. 855–856). **196**

*Lund, J. W. G., 1942. The marginal algae of certain ponds with special reference to bottom deposits. *J. Ecol.,* 30:245–340. **511, 512, 558**

Lund, J. W. G., 1950. Studies on *Asterionella formosa* Hass. II. Nutrient depletion and the spring maximum. *J. Ecol.,* 38:1–14. **527**

Lundh, A., 1951. See Almestrand and Lundh, 1951.

Luther, H., 1949. Vorschlag zu einer ökologischen Grundeinteilung der Hydrophyten. *Acta Bot. Fenn.,* 44:1–15. **118, 121**

MacArthur, R. H., 1972. *Geographical Ecology.* New York, Harper and Row, xviii, 269 pp. **246 fn**

MacArthur, R. H. and Wilson, E. O., 1967. *Theoretical Island Biogeography.* Princeton University Press, xi, 203 pp. **256**

MacAtee, W. L., 1915. Eleven important wild-duck foods. *Bull. US Dept. Agr.,* 205:32–35. **14**

McCallum, W. B., 1902. On the nature of the stimulus causing the change of form and structure in *Proserpina palustris. Bot. Gaz.,* 34:93–108. **175**

McCully, M. E. and Dale, H. M., 1961a. Variations in leaf number in *Hippuris.* A study of whorled phyllotaxis. *Can. J. Bot.,* 39:611–625. **172**

McCully, M. E. and Dale, H. M., 1961b. Heterophylly in *Hippuris,* a problem in identification. *Can. J. Bot.,* 39:1099–1116. **172, 174**

MacGregor, M. E., 1924. Tests with *Chara foetida* and *C. hispida* on the development of mosquito larvae. *Parasitology,* 16:382–387. **30**

McGregor, R. L., 1961. Vegetative propagation of Riccia rhenana. *Bryologist,* 64:75–76. **54**

MacIntire, C. D. and Phinney, H. K., 1965. Laboratory studies of periphyton production and community metabolism in lotic environments. *Ecol. Monogr.* 35:237–258. **530**

McMannon, M. and Crawford, R. M. M., 1971. A metabolic theory of flooding tolerance: the significance of enzyme distribution and behaviour. *New Phytol.,* 70:299–306. **210, 211**

MacMillan, C., 1894. Observations on the distribution of plants along shore at Lake of the Woods. *Minn. Bot. Stud.,* 1:949–1023. **566**

McNaughton, S. J., 1966. Ecotype function in the *Typha* community-type. *Ecol. Monogr.,* 66:297–325. **215, 413**

McNaughton, S. J. and Fullem, L. W., 1970. Photosynthesis and Photorespiration in *Typha latifolia. Plant Physiol.* 45:703–707. **153**

MacRobbie, E. A. C., 1962. Ionic relations of *Nitella translucens. J. Gen. Physiol.,* 45:861–878. **271**

MacRobbie, E. A. C., 1966. Metabolic effects on ion fluxes in *Nitella translucens.* I. Active influxes. *Austral. J. Biol. Sci.,* 19:363–370. **272**

*MacRobbie, E. A. C., 1970. The active transport of ions in plant cells. *Q. Rev. Biophys.,* 3:251–294. **29, 265–271**

MacRobbie, E. A. C., 1971. Vacuolar fluxes of chloride and bromide in *Nitella translucens. J. Exp. Bot.,* 22:487–502. **272**

*MacRobbie, E. A. C., 1974. Ion uptake *Algal Physiology and Biochemistry*, ed. W. D. P. Stewart, Berkeley and Los Angeles, Univ. California Press pp. 676–713. **265** (Received too late to use.)

MacRobbie, E. A. C. and Dainty, J., 1958. Ion transport in *Nitellopsis obtusa. J. Gen. Physiol.*, 42:335–353. **14**

McRoy, C. P. and Barsdate, R. J., 1970. Phosphate absorbtion in eelgrass. *Limnol. Oceanogr.*, 15:6–13. **285**

MacVicar, S. M., 1926. *The Student's Handbook of British Hepatics*, 2nd ed. Eastbourne & London, xxiv, 464, viii pp. **52**

Mangin, A., 1893. Recherches sur la végétation des lacs du Jura. *Rev. Gen. Bot.*, 5:241–257, 303–316. **234**

Manton, I., 1950. *Problems of Cytology and Evolution in the Pteridophyta*. Cambridge at the University Press, xi, 316 pp. **73, 196**

*Maristo, L., 1941. Die Seetypen Finnlands auf floristischer und vegetations-physiognomischer Grundlage. *Suom. Eläin-ja Kasvitiet. Seuran Vanamon Kasvitiet. Julk. (Ann. Bot. Soc. Zool. Bot. Vanamo)* 15, no. 5, 314 pp. **414, 420, 429, 439, 448–452**

Markham, V. R., 1935. *Paxton and the Bachelor Duke*. London, Hodder, and Stoughton, xii, 350. **81**

Marshall, W., 1852. Excessive and noxious increase of Udora canadensis. *Phytologist*, 4:705–715. **248**

Marshall, W., 1857. The American water-weed Anacharis alsinastrum. *Phytologist*, ser. 2, 2:194–197. **248**

Mason, H. L., 1957. *A Flora of the Marshes of California*. Berkeley and Los Angeles, Univ. California Press, viii, 878 pp. **165**

Mason, R., 1960. Three waterweeds of the family Hydrocharitaceae in New Zealand. *N. Z. J. Sci.*, 3:382–395. **260**

Mason, R., 1969. The vegetation of fresh waters. *The Natural History of Canterbury*, ed. R. A. Knox, Wellington, Auckland, Sydney, and Melbourne, A. H. and A. W. Reed, for the Canterbury branch of the Royal Society of New Zealand, pp. 452–457. **470, 474**

Massart, J., 1902. L'accomodation individuelle chez le Polygonium amphibium. *Bull. Jard. Bot. Etat Brux.*, 1:73–95. **169**

*Matheson, R., 1930. The utilization of aquatic plants as aids in mosquito control. *Amer. Nat.*, 64:56–86. **30**

Matheson, R. and Hinman, E. H., 1928. *Chara fragilis* and mosquito development. *Am. J. Hyg.* 8:279–292. **30, 31**

Matheson, R. and Hinman, E. H., 1929. Further studies on *Chara* spp. and other aquatic plants in relation to mosquito breeding. *Am. J. Trop. Med.* 9:249–266. **30**

Matheson, R. and Hinman, E. H., 1930. A seasonal study of the plancton of a spring fed Chara pool versus that of a temporary to semi-permanent woodland pool in relation to mosquito breeding. *Am. J. Hyg.* 11:174–188. **30**

Matheson, R., and Hinman, E. H., 1931. Further work on Chara spp. and other biological notes on Culicidae (Mosquitoes). *Am. J. Hyg.*, 14:99–108. **31**

Mathews, A. P., 1927. *Physiological Chemistry*, 4th ed. New York, W. Wood & Co., xv, 1233 pp. **348**

Mayer, A. M. and Gorham, C., 1951. The iron and manganese content of plants present in the natural vegetation of the English Lake District. *Ann. Bot.*, n. s. 15:247–263. **339, 341, 342**

Maynar, J., 1923. Contribución al studio de la acción larvicide de las *Characeas. Bull. R. Soc. Esp. Hist. Nat.* 23:389–392. **30**

Meeuse, A. B. J., 1961. Marsileales and Salviniales "living fossils?" *A. Bot. Neerl.*, 10:257–260. **75**

Metcalf, F. P., 1931. Wild-duck foods in North Dakota lakes. *US Dept. Agric. Tech. Bull.* 221, 72 pp. **372-376**

Meylan, C., 1924. *Les Hépatiques de la Suisse.* Zurich, Fretz Frères, 318 pp. **52**

Michener, C. D., 1951. Halictidae in Muesebeck, C. F. W., Krombein, K. V., and Townes, H. K. Hymenoptera of America north of Mexico—synoptic catalog. *US Dept. Agric. Agric. Monogr.* 2:1104-1134. **229**

Migula, W., 1900. Die Characeen. Rabenhorst ed. *Kryptogamen-Flora von Deutschland, Öesterreich und der Schweiz.* Zweite Auf. Fünfter, Bd. xv, 765 pp. **36**

Migula, W., 1909. *Kryptogamen-Flora von Deutschland Österreich und Schweiz. II. Algen,* 2. Teil *Rhodophyceae, Phaeophyceae, Characeae.* Gera, F. von Zezschwitz, 383 pp. **8**

Miki, S., 1959. Evolution of *Trapa* from ancestral *Lythrum* through *Hemitrapa. Proc. Jap. Acad.* 35:289-294. **86, 89**

Miki, S., 1960. Nymphaeaceae remains in Japan, with new fossil genus *Eoeuryale. J. Inst. Polytech. Osaka City Univ.,* ser. D, 11:63-78. **81**

Miki, S., 1961. Aquatic floral remains in Japan. *J. Biol. Osaka City Univ.,* 12:91-121. **86, 95**

Miller, V., 1928. Arnoldiella, eine neue Cladophoraceengattunc. *Planta,* 6:1-21. **560**

Minden, M. von, 1899. Beiträge zur anatomischen und physiologischen Kenntnis wassersecernirender Organe. *Bibl. Bot.* 9:Heft 46, 76 pp. **201**

*Misra, R. D., 1938. Edaphic factors in the distribution of aquatic plants in the English Lakes. *J. Ecol.,* 26:412-451. **427-428, 444**

Mitchell, D. S., 1969. The ecology of vascular hydrophytes on Lake Kariba. *Hydrobiologia,* 34:448-464. **252, 254**

Mitchell, D. S., 1972. The Kariba weed: *Salvinia molesta. Brit. Fern Gaz.,* 10:251-252. **253**

Mönkemeyer, W., 1931. Bryales. Pascher, ed. *Die Süsswasser-Flora Mitteleuropas* Heft 14 (Zweite Auflage) *Bryophyta,* 47-197. **57, 61, 62**

Morinaga, T., 1926. Effect of alternating temperatures upon the germination of seeds. *Amer. J. Bot.,* 13:141-166. **217**

Moore, E., 1915. The Potamogetons in relation to pond culture. *Bull. US Bur. Fish.,* 33:251-291. **547**

Morton, F., 1954. Das Vorkommen von *Myosotis palustris* L. forma *submerse-florens mihi* im Traunsee (Oberösterreich). *Arch. Hydrobiol.,* 49:335-348. **99, 520**

Morton, S. D., Sernau, R., and Derse, P. H., 1972. Natural carbon sources, rates of replenishment, and algal growth in G. E. Likens ed. *Nutrients and Eutrophication.* ASLO Special Symposia 1:197-202. **151**

Moski, H. C., 1957a. Further notes concerning algal growth on the painted turtles. *Herpetologia,* 13:46. **563**

Moski, H. C., 1957b. Algal occurrence on the turtle *Clemmys guttata. Copeia,* 1957:50-51. **562, 564**

Moss, B., 1968. The chlorophyll a content of some benthic algal communities. *Arch. Hydrobiol.,* 65:51-62. **515**

*Moss, B., 1972. The influence of environmental factors on the distribution of freshwater algae: an experimental study. I. Introduction and the influence of calcium concentration. *J. Ecol.,* 60:917-932. **555**

Moss, B., 1973a. The influence of environmental factors on the distribution of freshwater algae: an experimental study. II. The role of pH and the carbon dioxide-bicarbonate system. *J. Ecol.,* 61:157-177. **555**

Moss, B., 1973b. The influence of environmental factors on the distribution of freshwater algae: an experimental study. III. Effects of temperature, vitamin requirements, and inorganic nitrogen compounds on growth. *J. Ecol.*, 61:179-192. **555**

*Moss, B., 1973c. The influence of environmental factors on the distribution of freshwater algae: an experimental study. IV. Growth of test species in natural lake waters, and conclusion. *J. Ecol.*, 61:193-211. **555**

*Moyle, J. B., 1945. Some chemical factors influencing the distribution of aquatic plants in Minnesota. *Amer. Midl. Nat.*, 34:402-420. **279-281, 372-375, 444**

Mücke, M., 1908. Über den Bau und die Entwicklung der Früchte und über die Herkünft von *Acorus calamus* L., *Bot. Z.*, 66:1-23. **108, 248**

Muenscher, W. C., 1936a. Storage and germination of seeds of aquatic plants. *Bull. NY Agric. Exp. Stat., Cornell Univ.*, Ithaca, no. 652, 17 pp. **215, 218, 220**

Muenscher, W. C., 1936b. The germination of seeds of Potamogeton. *Ann. Bot.*, 50:805-821. **215, 218, 220**

Muenscher, W. C., 1944. Aquatic plants of the United States. Ithaca, N. Y. Comstock Publishing Co., Inc., x, 374 pp. **73, 76**

Mukerji, S. K., 1934. The Charophytes of the Dal Lake, Kashmir. *Proc. 21st Indian Sci. Congr.*, 295-296. **24**

Müller, G., 1971. Aragonite inorganic precipitation in a freshwater lake. *Nat., Phys. Sci.*, 229:18. **302**

Müller, K., 1941. Beiträge zur Systematik der Lébermoose. II. Riccia fluitans eine Sammelart. *Hedwigia*, 80:90-102. **52**

Müller, T. and Görs, S., 1960. Pflanzengesellschaften stehendes Gewässer in Baden-Württemberg. *Beitr. Naturk. Forsch. Südwestdeut.*, 19:60-100. **493**

Mulligan, H. F. and Baranowski, A., 1969. Nitrogen and phosphorus greenhouse studies on vascular aquatic plants and phytoplankton. *Verh. Int. Limnol. Ver.*, 17:802-810. **279**

Munk, W. H. and Riley, G. A., 1952. Absorbtion of nutrients by aquatic plants. *J. Mar. Res.*, 11:215-240. **148**

Muszynski, J., 1948. The alkaloids of clubmosses. *Q. J. Pharm. Pharmacol.*, 21:34-38 (not seen, ref. Hegnauer, 1962, *Chem. Abst.* 44:9122). **363**

Nathan, C. C., 1971. Vaterite in lake water. *Nat., Phys. Sci.* 231:158. **302**

Naumann, E., 1915. Skrifter utg. av S. Sveriges Fiskeriförening. Lund, 1915 (not seen, ref. Thomasson, 1925). **529**

Naumann, E., 1919. Eine einfache Methode zum Nachweis bezw. Einsammeln der Eisenbakterien. *Ber. Dtsch. Bot. Ges.*, 37:76-78. **529**

Naumann, E., 1931. Limnologische Terminologie. In E. Abderhalden ed. *Handbuch der Biologischen Arbeistsmethoden* Abt. ix, Teil 8, 2. Berlin & Wein, Urban & Schwarzenberg ii, 776 pp. **565**

Naumann, E., 1932. *Grundzüge der regionalen Limnologie.* Binnengewässer. XI. Stuttgart. E. Schweizerbart-sche Verlagsbuchhandlung, xiv, 176 pp. **26, 48**

Neill, W. T. and Allen, E. A., 1954. Algae on Turtles: some additional considerations. *Ecology*, 35:581-582. **564**

Nelson, J. W. and Palmer, L. S., 1938. Nutritive value and chemical composition of certain fresh-water plants of Minnesota. I. Nutritive value and general chemical composition of species of *Elodea, Myriophyllum, Vallisneria*, and other aquatic plants. *Univ. Minn. Agr. Exp. Stat. Tech. Bull.*, 136:4-34. **286, 292, 298, 341, 342**

Newcombe, C. L., 1950. A quantitative study of attachment materials in Sodon Lake, Michigan. *Ecol.*, 31:204-215. **532**

Nissen, P., 1972. Multiphasic uptake in plants. I. Phosphate and sulphate. *Physiol. Plant*, 28:304-316. **274**

Normann, H.-D., 1967. Versuche zur Aufnahme von Phosphat durch *Ranunculus fluitans* Lam. *Arch. Hydrobiol. Suppl.,* 33:243–254. **275**

Nygaard, G., 1955. On the productivity of five Danish waters. *Verh. Int. Ver. Limnol.,* 12:123–133. **432**

Nygaard, G., 1958. On the productivity of the bottom vegetation in Lake Grane Langsö. *Verh. Int. Ver. Limnol.,* 13:144–155. **202, 204, 420, 432, 433**

Oberdorfer, E., 1928. Lichtverhaltnisse und Algenbesiedlung im Bodensee. *Zeit. Bot.,* 20:465–568. **522, 534**

*Oberdorfer, E., 1957. Süddeutsche Pflanzengesellschaften. *Pflanzensociologie* 10, xiii, 1–564. **487, 488, 491–495, 498, 502**

Odum, S., 1965. Germination of ancient seeds. Floristic observations and experiments with archaeologically dates soils. *Dan. Bot. Ark.,* 24, no. 2:70 pp. **213**

Ohga, I., 1926. The germination of century-old and recently harvested Indian lotus fruits, with special reference to the effect of oxygen supply. *Am. J. Bot.,* 13:754–759. **217**

Okada, Y., 1930. Study of *Euryale ferox* (Salisb). V. On some features in the physiology of the seed, with special respect to the problem of delayed germination. *Sci. Rep. Tôhoku Imp. Univ. ser. 4. Biol.,* 5:41–116. **217**

Ohwi, J., 1965. *Flora of Japan* (in English). Washington, Smithsonian Institution, ix, 1067 pp. **73**

Oliver, F. W., 1888. On the structure, development, and affinities of Trapella, Oliv., a new genus of Pedalineae. *Ann. Bot.,* 2:75–114. **89**

Olsen, C., 1954. Hvilke betingelser må vaere opfyldte, for at *Helodea canadensis* kan opnå den optimale udvikling, der er årsag til dens massevise optraeden i naturen? (What are the conditions of optimum development enabling *Helodea canadensis* to grow profusely in nature.) *Bot. Tidsskrift,* 51:263–272 (Swedish text), 272–273 (English summary). **249**

*Olsen, S., 1944. Danish Charophyta, chorological, ecological, and biological investigations. *K. Danske Vidensk. Selsk., Biol. Skr.,* 3. **15–17, 39–41**

Ophel, I. L., 1950. Some ecological effects of substances produced by the *Characeae. Proc. Okla. Acad. Sci.,* 29:15–17. **31**

Ophel, I. L., 1963. The fate of radiostrontium in a freshwater community. V. Schultz and A. W. Klement ed. *Radioecology.* New York, Reinhold, pp. 213–216. **304, 306**

Ophel, I. L. and Fraser, C. D., 1970. Calcium and strontium discrimination by aquatic plants. *Ecology,* 51:324–327. **299, 303–307**

Orloci, L., 1966. Geometric models in ecology. I. The theory and application of some ordination methods. *J. Ecol.,* 54:193–215. **376**

Otis, C. H., 1914. The transpiration of emersed water plants: its measurement and its relationships. *Bot. Gaz.* 58:457–497. **196, 197**

Pal, B. P., 1932. Burmese Charophyta. *J. Linn. Soc. Lond. (Bot.)* 49:47–92. **11, 30**

Pal, B. P., Kundu, B. C., Sundaralimgan, V. S., and Venkataraman, O. S., 1962. *Charophyta.* I. C. A. R. Monograph on Algae, New Delhi, x, 130 pp. **37**

Palmer, J. D. and Round, F. E., 1965. Persistent, vertical-migration rhythms in benthic microflora. I. The effect of light and temperature on the rhythmic behaviour of *Euglena obtusa. J. Mar. Biol. Ass. UK* 45:567–582. **558, 559**

Pankow, H., 1961. Über die Ursachen der Fehlens von Epiphyten auf Zygnemales. *Arch. Protistenk.* 105:417–444. **539**

Pardo, L., 1923. Observaciones acerca de la acción de la Chara sobre las larvas de los mosquitos. *Bol. Soc. Esp. Hist. Nat.* 23:154–157. **30**

Parija, P., 1934. Physiological investigations on water hyacinth (E. crassipes) in Orissa, with notes on some aquatic weeds. *Indian J. Agric. Sci.* 4:399–429. **388**

Park, R., and Epstein, E., 1960. Carbon isotope fractionation during photosynthesis. *Geochem. Cosmochim. Acta,* 21:110–126. **146**

Park, R., and Epstein, E., 1961. Metabolic fractionation of C^{13} and C^{14} in plants. *Plant Physiol.,* 30:133–138. **146**

Parker, D., 1943. Comparison of aquatic and terrestrial plants of *Isoetes engelmanni* in the Mountain Lake, Virginia area. *Am. Midl. Nat.,* 30:452–455. **140, 431**

Parry, D. W., and Smithson, F., 1958. Silicification of bulliform cells in grasses. *Nature,* 181:1549. **317**

Parry, D. W., and Smithson, F., 1964. Types of opaline silica depositions in the leaves of British grasses. *Ann. Bot.* (n. s.), 28:170–185. **317**

Paton, J. A., 1973. *Riccia fluitans* L., with sporophytes. *J. Bryol.,* 7:253–259. **52**

Patrick, R., 1963. The structure of diatom communities under varying ecological conditions. *Ann. NY Acad. Sci.,* 108:353–358. **531**

*Patrick, R., 1967. The effect of invasion rate, species pool, and size of area on the structure of the diatom community. *Proc. Nat. Acad. Sci., USA* 58:1335–1342. **530**

*Patrick, R., Hohn, M. H., and Wallace, J. H., 1954. A new method for determining the pattern of the diatom flora. *Notul. Nat.* (Acad. Nat. Sci., Philadelphia), no. 259, 12 pp. **530, 532**

Patrick, R., and Reimer, C. W., 1966. *The Diatoms of the United States* exclusive of Alaska and Hawaii. Vol. I. Philadelphia, Academy of Natural Sciences, Monograph 13, xi, 688 pp. **526**

Patten, B. C., 1954. The status of some American species of Myriophyllum as revealed by the discovery of intergrade material between M. exalbescens Fern. and M. spicatum L. in New Jersey. *Rhodora,* 56:213–225. **250, 251**

Paul, H., 1931. Sphagnales in Pascher ed. *Die Susswasser-Flora Mitteleuropas,* Heft 14 (Zweite Auflage). *Bryophyta,* Jena, G. Fischer pp. 1–46. **55, 56, 57**

Paynter, R. A., 1953. Autumnal migrants on the Campeche Bank. *Auk* 70:339–349. **246 fn**

Pearsall, W. H., 1917. The aquatic and marsh vegetation of Esthwaite Water. *J. Ecol.,* 5:108–202. **37, 38, 63, 423, 442–444, 497, 499, 500**

Pearsall, W. H., 1918a. The aquatic and marsh vegetation of Esthwaite Water. *J. Ecol.,* 6:53–74. **38, 423, 442–444, 497, 499, 500**

Pearsall, W. H., 1918b. On the classification of aquatic plant communities. *J. Ecol.,* 6: 75–83. **487, 497, 498**

Pearsall, W. H., 1920. The aquatic vegetation of the English Lakes. *J. Ecol.,* 8:163–199. **37, 38, 62, 141, 243, 397, 410, 415, 423–426, 439–442, 497, 499, 500**

Pearsall, W. H., 1921. The development of vegetation in the English Lakes, considered in relation to the general evolution of glacial lakes and rock basins. *Proc. R. Soc. Lond.,* 92B: 259–282. **37, 38, 423–426, 429, 439–442, 497**

Pearsall, W. H., 1930. Phytoplankton in the English Lakes. I. The proportions in the water of some dissolved substances of biological importance. *J. Ecol.,* 18:306–320. **429**

Pearsall, W. H., and Hanby, A. M., 1925. The variation in leaf form in *Potamogeton perfoliatus. New Phytol.,* 24:112–120. **193**

Pearsall, W. H., and Pearsall, W. H., 1921. Potamogeton in the English Lakes. *J. Bot.,* 59:160–164. **193, 241**

Pearsall, W. H., and Pearsall, W. H., 1923. Potamogeton in the English Lakes. *J. Bot.,* 61:1–7. **191**

Peck, R. E., 1953. Fossil Charophytes. *Bot. Rev.,* 19:209–227. **2**

Penfound, W. T., and Earle, T. T., 1948. The biology of the water hyacinth. *Ecol. Monogr.,* 18:447–472. **227**

Pennack, R. W., 1973. Some evidence for aquatic macrophytes as repellents for a limnetic species of *Daphnia*. *Int. Rev. Gesamten Hydrobiol.*, 58:569–576. **369**

Pennington, W., 1962. Late-glacial moss records from the English Lake District: Data for the study of post-glacial history. *New Phytol.*, 61:28–31. **63**

Percival, M. S., 1965. *Floral Biology*. Oxford, New York, Pergamon Press, xv, 243 pp. **225, 229**

Petkova, L. M. and Lubyanov, I. P., 1969. Konsentratsiia deiakykh mikroelementiv u makrofitiv vodoim stepvoi zony Ukrainy. *Ukr. Bot. Zh.*, 26:90–96. **286, 318, 325, 326, 329, 330, 331, 341–346**

Pia, J., 1933. *Kohlensäure und Kalk*. Kie Binnengewässer xiii. Stuttgart. Schweizerbart'sche Veilagsbuchhandlung, vii, 183 pp. **301, 303**

Pickett-Heaps, J. D. and Marchant, H. J., 1972. The phylogeny of the green algae: a new proposal. *Cytobios*, 6:255–264. **1 fn**

Polunin, N., 1959. *Circumpolar Arctic Flora*. Oxford University Press, xxviii, 514 pp. **73**

*Pond, R. H., 1905. The relation of aquatic plants to the substratum (contributions to the biology of the Great Lakes). *Rep. US Fish. Comm.*, 21:483–526. **276–278, 547**

Pond, R. H., 1918. The larger aquatic vegetation. *Fresh-water Biology*, ed. H. B. Ward and G. C. Whipple, 1st ed. New York, John Wiley & Sons pp. 178–209. **548**

Popoff, K. J., 1941. Über die Assimilation von Landpflanzen-Blättern unter Wasser. *Jahrb. Wiss. Bot.*, 89:754–831. **145**

Potter, A. W., and Milburn, J. A., 1970. Subaqueous transpiration in new perspective. *New Phytol.*, 69:961–969. **199**

Potter, M. C., 1888. Notes on an alga (*Dermatophyton radicans* Peter) growing on the European Tortoise. *J. Linn. Soc. Bot.*, 24:251–254. **561, 564**

Potzger, J. E., and Van Engel, W. A., 1942. Study of the rooted aquatic vegetation of Weber Lake, Vilas County, Wisconsin. *Trans. Wisc. Acad. Sci. Arts Lett.*, 34:149–161. **431**

Prankerd, T. L., 1911. On the structure and biology of the genus *Hottonia*. *Ann. Bot.*, 25:253–267. **137**

Pringsheim, E. G., and Pringsheim, O., 1962. Axenic culture of *Utricularia*. *Amer. J. Bot.*, 49:898–901. **285**

Proctor, M. and Yeo, P., 1973. The pollination of flowers. London. The New Naturalist, Collins, 418 pp. **225, 231**

Proctor, V. W., 1958. The growth of Basicladia on Turtles. *Ecology*, 39:634–645. **562–564**

Proctor, V. W., 1960. Dormancy and germination of *Chara* oospores. *Phycol. News Bull.*, 40:64. **6**

Proctor, V. W., 1961. Dispersal of Riella spores by waterfowl. *Bryologist*, 64:58–61. **51**

Proctor, V. W., 1962. Viability of *Chara* oospores taken from migratory water birds. *Ecology*, 45:656–658. **7**

Proctor, V. W., 1972. *Chara globularis* Thuillier (= *C. fragilis* Desvaux) breeding patterns within a cosmopolitan complex. *Limnol. Oceanogr.*, 16:422–436. **6**

Proctor, V. W., Carl de Donlerberg, C., Hotchkiss, A. T., and Imahori, K., 1967. Conspecificity of some Charophytes. *J. Phycol.*, 3:208–211. **3, 5, 15**

Prowse, G. A., 1959. Relationship between epiphytic algal species and their macrophytic hosts. *Nature*, 183:1204–1205. **537, 539**

Ramsbottam, J., 1942a. In recent work on germination. *Nature*, 149:658–659. **213**

Ramsbottam, J., 1942b. In recent work on germination. *Proc. Linn. Soc. Lond.*, 154:183–184. **213**

Rauh, W. and Falk, H., 1959. *Stylites* E. Amstutz, eine neue Isoëtacee aus den Hochanden Perus. *Stizungsber. Heidelb. Akad. Wiss.*, 1959:1-160. **72**

Raunkiaer, C., 1896. *De Danske Blomsterplanters Naturhistorie. I. Helobieae.* Copenhagen. **236, 238**

Raunkiaer, C., 1904. Om biologiske Typer, med Hensyn til Planternes Tilpasning til at over leve ugunstige Aarstider. *Bot. Tidsskrift.*, 26, xiv-xv (English translation in Raunkiaer, 1934). **122**

Raunkiaer, C., 1934. *The life forms of plants and statistical plant geography.* Oxford, Clarendon Press. **119, 122**

Raup, L. C., 1930. The lichen flora of the Shelter Point Region, Athabasca Lake. *Bryologist*, 33:57-66. **566**

Raven, J. A., 1967. Ion transport in *Hydrodictyon africanum. J. Gen. Physiol.*, 50:1607-1625. **266, 271**

Raven, J. A., 1968. The mechanism of photosynthetic use of bicarbonate by *Hydrodictyon africanum. J. Gen. Physiol.*, 50:1627-1640. **151**

Raven, J. A., 1969. Action spectra for photosynthesis and light-stimulated ion transport processes in *Hydrodictyon africanum. New Phytol.*, 68:45-62. **271, 272**

*Raven, J. A., 1970. Exogenous inorganic carbon sources in plant photosynthesis. *Biol. Rev.*, 45:167-221. **135, 145, 151**

Reay, P. F., 1972. The accumulation of arsenic from arsenic-rich natural waters by aquatic plants. *J. Appl. Ecol.*, 9:557-565. **323, 324**

Regnard, P., 1891. Recherches expérimentales sur les conditions physiques de la vie dans les eaux. Paris, vii, 500 pp. **135**

Rich, P. H., Wetzel, R. G., and Thuy, N. van, 1971. Distribution, production, and role of aquatic macrophytes in a southern Michigan marl lake. *Freshwater Biol.*, 1:3-21. **26, 42, 43, 543**

Richmond, D. V., 1973. Sulfur compounds. *Phytochemistry*, 3:41-73. **29**

Rickett, H. W., 1922. A quantitative study of the larger aquatic plants of Lake Mendota. *Trans. Wisc. Acad. Arts Sci. Lett.*, 20:501-527. **466-468, 471, 473**

Rickett, H. W., 1924. A quantitative study of the larger aquatic plants of Green Lake, Wisconsin. *Trans. Wisc. Acad. Arts Sci. Lett.*, 21:381-414. **469, 470**

Ridley, H. N., 1930. *The Dispersal of Plants Throughout the World.* Ashford, Kent. L. Reeve & Co., xx, 744 pp. **245-247**

*Riemer, D. N., and Toth, S. J., 1968. A survey of the chemical composition of aquatic plants in New Jersey. *NJ Agr. Exp. Stat., Coll. Agric. Environ. Sci. Rutgers Univ., Bull. 820*, 14 pp. **26, 27, 28, 286, 287, 288, 289, 291, 292, 298, 299, 300, 303, 328-333, 335-337, 339, 340, 342, 347, 349, 353, 355, 356**

Riemer, D. N., and Toth, S. J., 1969. A survey of the chemical composition of *Potamogeton* and *Myriophyllum* in New Jersey. *Weed Sci.*, 17:219-223. **286**

Riemer, D. N., and Toth, S. J., 1970. Chemical composition of five species of *Nymphaeaceae. Weed Sci.*, 18:4-6. **287**

Robinson, J. B., 1969a. Sulphate influx in characean cells. I. General considerations. *J. Exp. Bot.*, 20:201-211. **272**

Robinson, J. B., 1969b. Sulphate influx in characean cells. II. Links with light and metabolism in *Chara australis. J. Exp. Bot.*, 20:212-220. **272**

Robinson, W. O., Steinkoenig, L. A., and Miller, G. F., 1917. The relationship of some of the rare elements in soils and plants. *Bull. US Dept. Agric.* 600, 27 pp. **288, 289, 292, 339, 349**

Robison, C. R., and Person, C. P., 1973. A silicified semiaquatic dicotyledon from the Eocene Allenby Formation of British Columbia. *Can. J. Bot.*, 51:1373-1377. **75, 202**

*Rodewald-Rudescu, L., 1974. Das Schilfrohr *Phragmites communis* Trinius. *Die Binnengewässer*, xxvii. Stuttgart. E. Schweizerbart'sche Verlagsbuchhandlung, ix, 302 pp. **198, 413**

Roll, H., 1939a. Zur Terminologie des Periphytons. *Arch. Hydrobiol.*, 35:59–69. **510 fn**

Roll, H., 1939b. Isoetes, Lobelia und Litorella in kalkarmem und kalkreichem Wasser. *Beih. Bot. Centralbl.*, 59, Abt. B:345–358. **278, 444**

*Round, F. E., 1953. An investigation of two benthic algal communities in Malham Town, Yorkshire. *J. Ecol.*, 41:174–197. **512, 548, 555, 556**

*Round, F. E., 1957a. Studies on bottom-living algae in some lakes of the English Lake District. Part I. Some chemical features of the sediments related to algal productivities. *J. Ecol.*, 45:133–148. **548–554**

*Round, F. E., 1957b. Studies on bottom living algae in some lakes of the English Lake District. Part II. The distribution of Bacillariophyceae on the sediments. *J. Ecol.*, 45:343–360. **548–554**

*Round, F. E., 1957c. Studies on bottom living algae in some lakes of the English Lake District. Part III. The distribution of algal groups other than the Bacillariophyceae. *J. Ecol.*, 45:649–664. **548–554**

Round, F. E., 1960. Studies on bottom-living algae in some lakes of the English Lake District. Part IV. The seasonal cycles of the Bacillariophyceae. *J. Ecol.*, 48:529–547. **556**

Round, F. E., 1961a. Studies on bottom-living algae in some lakes of the English Lake District. Part V. The seasonal cycles of the Cyanophyceae. *J. Ecol.*, 49:31–38. **556**

Round, F. E., 1961b. Studies on bottom-living algae in some lakes of the English Lake District. Part VI. The effect of depth on the epipetic algal community. *J. Ecol.*, 49:245–254. **556–558**

Round, F. E., and Eaton, J. W., 1966. Persistent, vertical-migration rhythms in benthic microflora. III. The rhythm of epipelic algae in a freshwater pond. *J. Ecol.*, 54:609–615. **558**

Round, F. E. and Palmer, J. D., 1966. Persistent, vertical-migration rhythms in benthic micro-flora. II. Field and laboratory studies on diatoms from the banks of the River Avon. *J. Mar. Biol. Ass. UK*, 46:191–214. **558**

Roux, M. le, 1908. Recherches biologiques sur le lac d'Annecy. *Ann. Biol. Lacustre*, 2:220–387. **409**

Rowlands, D. L. G. and Webster, R. K., 1971. Precipitation of vaterite in lake water. *Nat. Phys. Sci.*, 229:158. **302**

Roze, E., 1887. Le mode le fécondition du *Zannichellia palustris* L. *J. Bot. Paris*, 1:296–299. **232**

Roze, E., 1892. Sur le mode de fécondation du *Najas major* Roth et du *Ceratophyllum demersum* L. *Bull. Soc. Bot. Fr.*, 39:361–364. **232**

Ruttner, F., 1921. Das electrolytische Leitvermögen verdünnter Lösungen unter den Einfluss submerser Gewachse. *Sitzungsber. Akad. Wiss. Wien Math-nat.* Kl. Abt. 1, 130:71–78. **148, 150**

Ruttner, F., 1926. Bemerkungen über den Sauerstoffgehalt der Gewässer und dessen respiratorischen Wert. *Naturwissenschaflen*, 14:1237–1239. **529**

Ruttner, F., 1933. See van Steenis and Ruttner, 1933.

Ruttner, F., 1940, 1962. *Grundriss der Limnologie*. W. de Gruyler, Berlin, 1st ed., 167 pp., 3rd ed., 332 pp., also in translation by D. G. Frey and F. E. J. Fry, as *Fundamentals of Limnology*, University of Toronto Press. **80**

*Ruttner, F., 1947. Zur Frage der Karbonatassimilation der Wasserpflanzen. I. Teil. Die beiden Haupt typen der Kohlenstoffaufnahme. *Österreichische Bot. Z.*, 94:265–294. **148–150**

Ruttner, F., 1948. Zur Frage der Karbonatassimilation der Wasserpflanzen. II. Teil. Das Verhalten von *Elodea canadensis* and *Fontinalis antipyretica* in Losungen von Natrium-bzw. Kalciumbikarbonal. *Österreichische Bot. Z.*, 95:208-238. **148**

Ruttner, F., 1955. Zur Ökologie tropischer Wassermoose. *Arch. Hydrobiol. Suppl.*, 21: 343-381. **46**

St. John, H., 1964. Monograph of the genus *Elodea* (Hydrocharitaceae). II. The species found in the Andes and western South America. *Caldesia*, 9:95-113. **484 fn**

Salisbury, E. J., 1961. *Weeds and Aliens*. London, Collins, New Naturalist, 384 pp. **249**

Samuelsson, G., 1925. Untersuchungen über die höhere Wasserflora von Dalarne. *Sven. Växtsociol. Sällskapets Handl.* 9 (not seen, ref. Neumann, 1932). **463**

Sangster, A. G., 1970. Intracellular silica deposition in immature leaves in three species of Gramineae. *Ann. Bot.*, 34:245-257. **317**

Sankaran Unni, K., 1971a. An ecological study of the macrophytic vegetation of the Doodhadhari Lake, Raipur M. P. India. 1. Distribution and seasonal change in aquatic plants. *Hydrobiologia*, 37:139-155. **482**

Sankaran Unni, K., 1971b. An ecological study of the macrophytic vegetation of the Doodhadhari Lake, Raipur M. P. India. 2. Physical factors. *Hydrobiologia*, 37:139-155. **482**

Sankaran Unni, K., 1972. An ecological study of the macrophytic vegetation of the Doodhadhari Lake, Raipur M. P. India. 3. Chemical factors. *Hydrobiologia*, 38:25-36. **482**

Santesson, R., 1939. Über die Zonationsverhältnisse der lakustrinen Flechten einiger Seen im Anebodagebiet. *Medd. från Lund. Univ. Limnol. Instit.*, 1, 70 pp. **564-566**

*Sauer, F., 1937. Die Makrophytenvegetation ostholsteinischer Seen und Teiche. *Arch. Hydrobiol. Suppl.*, 6:431-592. **40, 411, 460-464, 487, 489, 491, 492, 523, 524**

Sauvageau, C., 1894. Notes biologiques sur les *Potamogetons*. *J. Bot. Paris*, 8:1-9, 21-43, 45-58, 98-106, 122-123, 140-148, 165-172. **220, 236, 237**

Sayre, G., 1945. The distribution of *Fontinalis* in a series of moraine ponds. *Bryologist.*, 48:34-36. **64**

Scannel, M. J. P., 1974. '*Elodea nuttallii*,' Renvyle, in flower at Glasnevin. *Irish Nat. J.*, 18:126. **241**

Schaumann, K., 1926. Über die Keimungsbedingungen von *Alisma Plantago* und anderen Wasserpflanzen. *Jahrb. Wiss. Bot.*, 65:851-934. **217, 221**

Schenck, H., 1889. Ueber das Aërenchyma, ein dem Kork homologes Gewebe bei Sumpfpflanzen. *Jahrb. Wiss. Bot.*, 20:526-574. **207**

Schiffner, V., 1931. Hepaticae in Paecher, ed. *Die Susswasser-Flora Mitteleuropas*, Heft 14 (Zweite Auflage), *Bryophyta*, Jena, G. Fischer 169-214. **46**

Schiffner, V., 1955. Die Lebermoose der Deutschen Limnologischen Sunda-Expedition. *Arch. Hydrobiol. Suppl.*, 24:382-407. **46, 52**

Schmucker, T., 1932. Physiologische und ökologische Untersuchungen an Bluten tropischer *Nymphaea*-Arten. *Planta*, 16:376-412. **228, 229**

Schreiter, T., 1928. Untersuchunger über die Einfluss einer Helodeawucherung auf das Netzplankton des Hirschberger-Grossteiches in Böhmen in den Jahren 1921 has 1925 incl. *Sb. Vyzk. Ustavh Zemed. Res. Vysk. Praze*, 98 pp. (not seen, ref. Hasler and Jones, 1949). **368**

*Schröter, C. and Kirchner, O., 1896. Die Vegetation der Bodensees. *Lindau, Bodensee Forsch.*, 9, Tl I:1-222. **76, 121, 510**

Schröter, C., and Kirchner, O., 1902. Die Vegetation der Bodensees. *Lindau Bodensee Forsch*, 9, Tl II:1-86. **489**

Schuette, H. A., and Hoffmann, A. E., 1921. Notes on the chemical composition of some of the larger aquatic plants of Lake Mendota. I. *Cladophora* and *Myriophyllum*. *Trans. Wisc. Acad. Sci. Arts Lett.*, 20:529–532. **285, 286, 310**

Schuette, H. A., and Alder, H., 1927. Notes on the chemical composition of some of the larger aquatic plants of Lake Mendota. II. *Vallisneria* and *Potamogeton*. *Trans. Wisc. Acad. Sci. Arts Lett.*, 23:249–254. **286, 310, 317**

Schuette, H. A., and Alder, H., 1929a. Notes on the chemical composition of some of the larger aquatic plants of Lake Mendota. III. *Castalia odorata* and *Najas flexilis*. *Trans. Wisc. Acad. Sci. Arts Lett.*, 24:135–139. **286, 298**

Schuette, H. A., and Alder, H., 1929b. A note on the chemical composition of *Chara* from Green Lake, Wisconsin. *Trans. Wisc. Acad. Sci. Arts Lett.*, 24:141–145. **26, 27, 28**

Schultz, O. E., and Gmelin, R., 1952. Papierchromatographie der Senfölglucosid-Drogen. *Z. Naturforsch.*, 7b:500–506. **364**

Schuster, R. M., 1953. Boreal Hepaticae. A manual of the liverworts of Minnesota and adjacent regions. *Amer. Midl. Nat.*, 49:257–684. **46**

Schwarz, K., Milne, D. B., and Vinyard, E., 1970. Growth effects of tin compounds in rats maintained in a trace element controlled environment. *Biochem. Biophys. Res. Commun.*, 40:22–29. **338**

Schwoerbel, J., 1968. Untersuchung über die Rolle der submersen Wasserpflanzen bei der Eliminierung von Phosphaten. *Münchner Beiträge* 5:361–374. **275**

Scott, D. H., and Wager, H., 1888. On the floating-roots of *Sesbania aculeata* Pers. *Ann. Bot.*, 1:307–314. **80**

*Sculthorpe, C. D., 1967. *The Biology of Aquatic Vascular Plants*. London, Edward Arnold, xviii, 610 pp. **72, 75, 76, 77, 81, 134, 135, 141, 148, 202, 210, 225, 228, 229, 230, 232, 233, 243, 247, 248, 286**

Sebestyén, O., 1951. Epibiontok Balatoni Diaphanosomán. *Ann. Inst. Biol. (Tihany) Hung. Acad. Sci.*, 20:161–165 (Magyar text), 165–166 (Russian and English summaries). **559**

Seddon, B., 1965. Occurrence of *Isoetes echinospora* in eutrophic lakes in Wales. *Ecology*, 46:747–748. **72, 279, 428**

Seddon, B., 1967. The lacustrine environment in relation to macrophytic vegetation. *Quaternary Paleoecology*, ed. E. J. Cushing and H. E. Wright. New Haven and London, Yale Univ. Press, 205–215. **377**

*Seddon, B., 1972. Aquatic macrophytes as limnological indicators. *Freshwater Biol.*, 2:107–130. **376–379**

Seidel, K., 1955. *Die Flechtbinse* Scirpus lacustris L. Binnengewässer 21, Stuttgart, Schweizerbart'sche Verlagsluchhandlung, xv, 216 pp. **413**

Seidel, K., 1957. Zweiter Fund von *Myosotis palustris* L. forma *submerse-florens*. *Arch. Hydrobiol.*, 53:438–439. **99**

Seidelin Raunkiaer, A., and Boye Petersen, J., 1917. In Wesenberg Lund, C., Sand, M. J., Boye Petersen, J., Weidilin Raunkiaer, A., and Steenberg, C. M., Furesøstudier. *K. Dan Vidensk. Selsk. Skr. Nat. Mat. Afd.*, Rackke 8, 3, no. 1:58–77. **465–466**

Senior-White, R., 1925. Physical factors in mosquito ecology. *Bull. Entomol. Res.* 16: 187–248. **30**

Sernander, R., 1912. Studier öfver lafvarnes biologi. I. Nitrophila lafvar. *Sven. Bot. Tid.* 6:803–880. **564**

Shapiro, J., 1973. Blue-green algae: why they become dominant. *Science* 179:382–384. **555**

Shelford, V. E., 1913. *Animal Communities in Temperate America*. Chicago Univ. Press, xiii, 362 pp. (see pp. 66–67). **547**

Shepherd, R. H. and Bowling, D. J. F., 1973. Active accumulation of sodium by roots of five aquatic species. *New Phytol.*, 72:1075–1080. **293, 303**

Siddall, J. D., 1888. The American water weed *Anacharis Asinastrum*, Bab.: its structure and habit; with some notes on its introduction into Great Britain. *Proc. Chester Soc. Nat. Sci.,* 3:125–134. **248**

Sifton, H. B., 1945. Air space tissues in plants. *Bot. Rev.,* 11:108–143. **201, 202**

Sifton, H. B., 1957. Air space tissues in plants. II. *Bot. Rev.,* 23:303–312. **201**

Sifton, H. B., 1959. The germination of light-sensitive seeds of *Typha latifolia. Can. J. Bot.,* 37:719–739. **217, 223**

Singh, V., 1965. Morphological and anatomical studies in Helobiae. II. Vascular anatomy of the flower of Potamogetonaceae. *Bot. Gaz.,* 126:137–144. **225**

Sládečková, A., 1962. Limnological investigation methods for the periphyton ("Aufwuchs") community. *Bot. Rev.,* 28:286–349. **510 fn**

Smith, A. L., 1921. *Lichens.* Cambridge at the University Press, xxviii, 464 pp. **566**

Smith, B. N., and Epstein, S., 1969. C^{13}/C^{12} ratio as evidence for two pathways of carbon fixation in photosynthesis. XI. *Int. Cong. Bot. Abstr.,* 203. **146**

Smith, E. V., and Swingle, H. S., 1942. The use of fertilizer for controlling several submerged aquatic plants in ponds. *Tr. Am. Fish. Soc.,* 71:94–101. **368**

Smith, G. E., Hall, T. F., and Stanley, R. A., 1967. Eurasian watermilfoil in the Tennessee Valley. *Weeds,* 15:95–98. **250, 251**

Smith, F. A., 1966. Active phosphate uptake by *Nitella translucens. Biochem Biophys. Acta.,* 126:94–99. **272**

Smith, F. A., 1968. Rates of photosynthesis in characean cells. II. Photosynthetic $^{14}CO_2$ fixation and ^{14}C bicarbonate uptake by characean cells. *J. Exp. Bot.,* 19:207–217. **17, 18**

Smith, F. A., 1970. The mechanism of chloride transport in characean cells. *New Phytol.,* 69:903–917. **272**

Snell, K., 1907. Untersuchungen über die Nahrungsaufnahme der Wasserpflanzen. *Flora,* 98:213–249. **277, 278**

Sobotka, D., 1967. Roślinność strefy zarastania bezodpływowych jezior Suwalszczyzny. (Vegetation of the zone subject to overgrowth in endorheic lakes of Suwałki Region.) *Monogr. Bot.,* 23:175–258. **56**

*Sørenson, H., 1948. Studies on the ecology of Danish water- and bog-mosses. *Dan. Bot. Ark.,* 12, no. 10, 47 pp. **55 fn, 56, 64**

Spear, D. G., Barr, J. K., and Barr, C. E., 1969. Localization of hydrogen ion and chloride ion fluxes in *Nitella. J. Gen. Physiol.,* 54:397–414. **20, 271**

*Spence, D. H. N., 1964. The macroscopic vegetation of freshwater lochs, swamps and associated fens. J. H. Burnett, ed., *The Vegetation of Scotland,* Edinburgh, and London. Oliver & Boyd, pp. 306–345. **215, 397, 418, 451, 485, 486, 487, 497–502**

Spence, D. H. N., 1967a. Factors controlling the distribution of freshwater macrophytes with particular reference to the lochs of Scotland. *J. Ecol.* 55:147–170. **148, 149, 151, 376, 385, 411, 444, 497**

Spence, D. H. N., 1967b. Factors controlling the distribution of *Potamogeton schweinfurthii* in Uganda. *J. Ecol.,* 55:54 p. **221, 223, 479**

*Spence, D. H. N., and Chrystal, J., 1970a. Photosynthesis and zonation of freshwater macrophytes. I. Depth distribution and shade tolerance. *New Phytol.,* 69:205–215. **154–156, 416**

*Spence, D. H. N., and Chrystall, J., 1970b. Photosynthesis and zonation of freshwater macrophytes. II. Adaptability of species of deep and shallow waters. *New Phytol.,* 69:217–227. **154–156, 416**

*Spence, D. H. N., Milburn, T. R., Ndawula-Senyimba, M., and Roberts, E., 1971. Fruit biology and germination of two tropical *Potamogeton* species. *New Phytol.,* 70:197–212. **221, 418**

Spencer, N. R., and Lekić, M., 1974. Prospects for biological control of Eurasian water-milfoil. *Weed Sci.,* 22:401–404. **233**

Spoon, D. M., and Burbanck, W. D., 1967. A new method for collecting sessile ciliates in plastic petri dishes with tight-fitting lids. *J. Protozool.* 14:735–739. **531**

Spruce, R., 1908. *Notes of a botanist on the Amazon & Andes . . . during the years 1849-1864.* Edited and condensed by A. R. Wallace. London, Macmillan, vol. 1, lii, 518 pp., vol. 2, xii, 542 pp. **78, 79, 80**

Stahl, E., 1888. Pflanzen und Schnecken. Biologische studie über die Schutzmittel der Pflanzen gegen Schneckenfrass. *Jena. Z. Naturwiss.,* 22:557–684. **317**

Stolberg, N., 1939. Lake Vättern, outlines of its natural history, especially its vegetation. *Act. Phytogeogr. Suec.,* 11:1–52. **37**

Stangenberg, M., 1968. Bacteriostatic effects of some algae- and *Lemna minor* extracts. *Hydrobiologia,* 32:88–96. **369**

Stanley, R. A., 1970. *Studies on Nutrition, Photosynthesis, and Respiration in* Myriophyllum spicatum *L.* Ph.D. Thesis, Duke University. **250**

Stanley, R. A., and Naylor, A. W., 1972. Photosynthesis in Eurasian watermilfoil (*Myriophyllum spicatum* L.). *Plant Physiol.,* 50:149–151. **152**

Stanley, R. A. and Naylor, A. W., 1973. Glycolate metabolism in Eurasian watermilfoil (*Myriophyllum spicatum* L.). *Physiol. Plant,* 29:60–63. **152**

Stant, M. Y., 1964. Anatomy of the Alismataceae. *J. Linn. Soc. Lond. (Bot.),* 59:1–42. **101**

Starmach, K., 1966. *Cyanophyta-Sinice Glaucophyta-Glaukofity.* Flora Słodkovodna Polski 2. Warsawa Państwowe wydwnietwo Naukowe. 807 pp. **519**

Starling, M. B., Chapman, V. J., and Brown, J. M. A., 1974a. A contribution to the biology of *Nitella hookeri* A. Br. I. Inorganic nutritional requirements. *Hydrobiologia,* 45:91–113. **24**

Starling, M. B., Chapman, V. J., and Brown, J. M. A., 1974b. A contribution to the biology of *Nitella hookeri* A. Br. II. Organic nutrients and physical factors. *Hydrobiologia,* 45:157–168. **11, 38**

Steemann-Nielsen, E., 1944. Dependence of freshwater plants on quantity of carbon dioxide and hydrogen ion concentration. Illustrated through experimental investigations. *Dan. Bot. Ark.,* 11, no. 8, 25 pp. **151**

Steemann-Nielsen, E., 1946. Carbon Sources in the photosynthesis of aquatic plants. *Nat. Lond.,* 158:594–596. **148, 149, 151**

*Steemann-Nielsen, E., 1947. Photosynthesis of aquatic plants with special reference to the carbon sources. *Dan. Bot. Ark.,* 12, no. 8, 71 pp. **148, 149, 151**

Steenis, J. H., 1932. Lakes of Sawyer County. *Bull. Wis. Dept. Agric.,* no. 138, 58 pp. **118, 130**

Stockner, J. G., and Armstrong, F. A. J., 1971. Periphyton of the Experimental Lakes Area, Northwestern Ontario. *J. Fish. Res. Board Can.,* 28:215–229. **527, 534**

Stoklasa, J., 1922. *Über der Verbreitung der Aluminiums in der Natur und seine Bedeutung beim Bau- und Betriebstoffwechsel der Pflanzen.* Jena, G. Fischer. **310**

Stoll, A. and Seebeck, E., 1951. Chemical investigations on alliin, the specific principle of garlic. *Adv. Enzymol.,* 11:377–400. **29**

Straškraba, M., 1968. Der Anteil der höheren Pflanzen an der Produktion der stehen den Gewässer. *Mitt. Int. Ver. Limnol.,* 14:212–230. **286, 360, 361**

Stroede, W., 1931. *Ökologie der Characean.* Thesis, Berlin 119 pp. **14, 43, 45**

Stroede, W., 1933. Über die Beziehungen der Characeen zu den chemischen Faktoren der Wohngewässer und der Schlammes. *Arch. Hydrobiol.,* 25:192–229. **14, 15, 17, 26**

Studhalter, R. A., 1933. *Riella americana:* disappearance due to floods; two new stations. *Bryologist,* 36:78–82. **51**

Su, K. L., Staba, E. J., and Abul Hajj, Y., 1973. Preliminary chemical studies of aquatic plants from Minnesota. *Lloydia,* 36:72–79. **363**

Su, K. L., Abul-Hajj, Y., and Staba, E. J., 1973. Antimicrobial effects of aquatic plants from Minnesota. *Lloydia,* 36:80–87. **369**

Subramanyan, K., 1962. *Aquatic Angiosperms.* Bot. Monogr. 3, CSIR, New Delhi, viii, 190 pp. **80, 89, 93, 107**

Sutton, D. L., and Bingham, S. W., 1970. Uptake and translocation of 2-4-d-1 ^{14}C in parrot-feather. *Weed Sci.,* 18:193–196. **201**

Swindale, D. N., and Curtis, J. T., 1957. Phytosociology of the larger submerged aquatic plants in Wisconsin. *Ecology,* 38:397–407. **502–504**

Swingle, H. S., 1945. Improvement of fishing in old ponds. *Trans. 10th Northeam. Wildl. Conf.* 299–308. **368**

Tansley, A. G. (1939, 1949). *The British Islands and their Vegetation.* originally in one volume (1939), reprinted with corrections (1949), in two volumes. Cambridge University Press xxxviii, 930 pp. **497, 500**

Tassigny, M., 1971. Action du calcium sur la croissance des Desmidiées axeniques. *Mitt. Int. Ver. Limnol.,* 19:292–313. **555**

Tate, M. W., and Clelland, R. C., 1957. *Non-parametric and Shortcut Statistics.* Danville, Illinois: Interstate Printers and Publishers, Inc., ix, 171 pp. **381**

Taylor, S. R., 1964. Abundance of chemical elements in the continental crust. *Geochim. Cosmochim. Acta.,* 28:1273–1287. **312, 314, 318, 325, 326, 328, 340**

Teresawa, Y., 1927. Experimentelle Studien über die Keimung von *Trapa natans* L. *Bot. Mag. Tokyo,* 41:581–587. **217**

Thomasson, H., 1925. Methoden zu Untersuchung der Mikrophyten der limnischen Litoral-und Profundalzone. In E. Abderhalden ed., *Hanbuch der Biologischen Arbeitsmethoden,* Berlin & Wien, Urban & Schwartzenberg. Abt., ix, Teil 2, 1:681–712. **529**

Thomasson, K., 1959. Nahuel Huapi. *Acta. Phytogeogr. Suec.,* 42, 83 pp. **73**

Thompson, D'A. W., 1917, 1942. *On Growth and Form.* Cambridge, University Press, xv, 793 pp., 2nd ed., 1116 pp. **144 fn**

Thompson, R. H., 1940. A second species of Riella in North America. *Bryologist,* 43: 110–111. **51**

*Thunmark, S., 1931. Dee See Fiolen und seine Vegetation. *Acta. Phytogeogr. Suec.,* 2; v, 198 pp. **74, 233, 411, 434–439, 444**

Thunmark, S., 1952. Karaktärsdrag i sormlandsk sjövegetation. *Nat. Södermanland* (not seen, summary in Bjork, 1967). **118, 119, 122, 124, 128**

Thut, H. F., 1932. The movement of water through some submerged water plants. *Am. J. Bot.,* 19:693–709. **199**

Timperley, M. H., Brooks, R. R., and Peterson, P. J., 1970. The significance of essential and non-essential trace elements in plants in relation to geochemical prospecting. *J. Appl. Ecol.,* 7:429–439. **314, 317**

Tralau, H., 1965. New facts and new finds of fossil *Trapella* Oliver in Europe. *Bot. Notisl.* 118:21–24. **95**

Turekian, K. K., Katz, A., and Chan, L., 1973. Trace element trapping in pteropod tests. *Limnol. Oceanogr.,* 18:240–249. **314**

Turesson, G., 1961. Habitat modifications in some widespread plant species. *Bot. Not.,* 114:435–452. **168, 170**

Turner, N. C., and Bell, M. A. M., 1972. The Ethnobotany of the Coast Salish Indians of Vancouver Island. *Econ. Bot.,* 25:63–104. **367**

Tutin, T. G., 1940. The Percy Sladen Trust Expedition to Lake Titicaca in 1937 under the leadership of Mr. H. Cary Gilson, M.A. X. The macrophytic vegetation of the lake. *Trans. Linn. Soc. Lond.,* 3rd ser., 1:161–189. **73, 409, 423, 483–485**

Tutin, T. G., 1941. The hydrosere and current concepts of the climax. *J. Ecol.,* 29:268–279. **497**

Tutin, T. G., Heywood, V. H., Burges, N. A., Valentine, D. H., Walters, S. M., and Webb, D. A., eds., 1964. *Flora Europaea.* Cambridge University Press, vol. 1, xxxii, 464 pp. **72**

Twinn, C. R., Observations on some aquatic animal and plant enemies of mosquitoes. *Can. Entomol.,* 63:51–61. **30**

Unger, F., 1862. Beiträge zur Anatomie und Physiologie der Pflanzen. XII. Neue Untersuchungen über die Transpiration der Gewächse. *Sitzungsb. Akad. Wiss. Wien.,* 44, Abt. II: 327–368. **199**

Vaidya, B. S., 1966. Study of some environmental factors affecting the occurrence of charophytes in Western India. *Hydrobiologia,* 29:256–262. **20–22**

Valenta, Z., and Khalique, A., 1959. The structure of castoramine. *Tetrahedron Lett.,* 12:1–5. **365**

Vallance, K. V., and Coult, D., 1951. Observations on the gaseous exchanges which take place between *Menyanthes trifoliata* and its environment. Part I. The composition of the internal gas of the plant. *J. Exp. Bot.,* 2:212–222. **204**

van Beusekom, C. F., 1967. Uber einige Apiose-vorkommnisse bei den Helobiae. *Phytochemistry,* 6:573–576. **361**

van Meel, L., 1952. Le milieu végétal. *Exploration Hydrobiologique du Lac Tanganika (1946-1947).* Bruxelles, Institute Royal des Sciences Naturelles de Belgique, 1:51–68. **479**

van Steenis, C. G. G. J., 1957. Specific and infraspecific delimitation. *Flora Malesiana,* ser. 1, 5:clxvii–ccxxxiv. **103**

*van Steenis, C. G. G. J., and Ruttner, F., 1933. Die Pteridophyten und Phanerogamen den Deutschen Limnologischen Sunda-Expedition, von Vegetationsskizzen nach Tagebuch aufgezeichungen von F. Ruttner. *Arch. Hydrobiol. Suppl.,* 11:231–387. **76, 409, 480–482**

van Wazer, J. R., and Callis, C. F., 1958. Metal complexing by phosphates. *Chem. Rev.,* 58:1011–1046. **301**

Varenko, N. I., and Chuiko, V. T., 1971. Role of higher aquatic plants in the migration of manganese, zinc, copper, and cobalt in the Dneprodzerzhinsk Reservoir. *Hydrobiol. J. (Gydrobiol. Zh.* trans), 7:45–48. **286, 329, 331, 333, 335, 336, 337, 341, 345, 346**

Vasconcelos, A. R., 1923. The algae of the genus Chara and mosquito larvae. *Am. J. Publ. Health,* 13:543–546. **30**

Verdcourt, B., 1973. A new combination in *Myriophyllum* (Haloragaceae). *Kew Bull.,* 28:36. **201 fn**

Vernadsky, W. I., Brunowsky, B. K., and Kunasheva, C. G., 1937. Concentration of mesothorium-I by duckweed (Lemna). *Nat., Lond.,* 140:317–318. **322**

Viereck, H. L., 1904. A bee visitor to Pontederia (Pickerel-weed). *Entomol. News,* 15: 244–246. **229**

Vinyard, W. C., 1955. Epizoophytic algae from mollusks, turtles, and fish in Oklahoma. *Proc. Okla. Acad. Sci.,* 34:63–65. **560, 561, 564**

*Vitt, D. H., and Slack, N. G., 1975. An analysis of the vegetation of Sphagnum dominated kettle-hole bogs in relation to environmental gradients. *Can. J. Bot.,* 53:332–359. **50, 55 fn, 58–61**

Vouk, V., 1929. Zur Biologie der Charophyten. *Verh. Int. Limnol. Ver.,* 4:634–639. **26**

Waern, M., 1939. Epilithische Algenvegetation in zur Kenntnis der Vegetation der Sees Tåkern. *Acta. Phytogeogr. Suec.,* 12:43–50. **523**

Walker, A. O., 1912. The distribution of *Elodea canadensis* Michaux in the British Isles in 1909. *Proc. Linn. Soc. Lond.,* 124:71–77. **248, 249**

Warming, E., 1895. *Plantesamfund, Grundträk at den ökologiske Plantegeografi.* Kjöbenhavn (not seen, issued as German translations in 1896 and 1902, and in English in a very revised form as *Oecology of Plants: An Introduction to the Study of Plant Communities,* assisted by M. Vahl, prepared for publication by P. Groom and I. B. Balfour, Oxford at the Clarendon Press, 1909; xi, 422 pp.). **118**

Warming, E., 1923. Økologiens Grundformer udkas til en systematisk Ordning. *K. Dan. Vidensk.-Selsk. Skr. Naturw. Mat. Afd.* 8 Raekke IV:119–187. **118, 510**

Watson, E. V., 1955. *British Mosses and Liverworts.* Cambridge, University Press, xiii, 419 pp. **52, 54**

Watson, E. V., 1968. *British Mosses and Liverworts,* 2nd ed. Cambridge University Press, xiv, 495 pp. **52–54**

Watson, S., 1888. Contributions to American Botany. *Proc. Amer. Acad. Arts Sci.,* 23: 249–287. **99**

Watson, W., 1919. The Bryophytes and Lichens of fresh water. *J. Ecol.,* 7:71–83. **566**

Watson, W., 1920. The liverworts of Somerset. *Somerset Archaeol. Nat. Hist. Soc.,* 66: 134–159. **46**

*Weber, C. A., 1907. Aufbau und Vegetation der Moore Norddentschlands. *Beibl. Bot. Jahrb.,* 90:19–34. **391, 392**

Weddell, H. A., 1849. Observations sur une espeċe nouvelle du genie *Wolffia* (Lemnacées). *An. Sci. Nat. (Bot.),* sér. 3, 12:155–173. **245**

Weinrowsky, P., 1899. Untersuchungen über die Scheiteloffnungen bei Wasserpflanzen. *Beitr. Wiss. Bot.,* 3:205–247. **201**

Weir, C. E., and Dale, H. M., 1960. A developmental study of wild rice *Zizania aquatica* L. *Can. J. Bot.,* 38:719–739. **135**

Welch, W. H., 1943. The systematic position of the genera *Wardia, Hydropogon,* and *Hydropogonella. Bryologist,* 46:25–46. **64**

Welch, W. H., 1960. *A monograph of the Fontinalaceae.* The Hague, Martinus Nijhoff, 357 pp. **62–64**

West, G., 1905. A comparative study of the dominant phaneroganic and higher cryptogamic vegetation flora of aquatic habit in three lake areas of Scotland. *Proc. R. Soc. Edinb.,* 25:967–1023. **498, 502**

*West, G., 1910. An epitome of a comparative study of the dominant phanerogamic and higher cryptogamic flora of aquatic habit, in seven lake areas of Scotland. *Bathymetric Survey of the Scottish Fresh-water Lochs. Report on Scientific Results,* vol. 1, Edinburgh, Challenger Office, pp. 156–260. **48, 56, 62, 369, 391, 502**

West, G. S., 1927. *A Treatise on the British Freshwater Algae.* 2nd ed. revised by F. E. Fritsch, Cambridge, University Press, xvii, 534 pp. **538**

Wetzel, R. G., 1960. Marl encrustation on hydrophytes in several Michigan lakes. *Oikos,* 11:223–228. **301**

*Wetzel, R. G., 1964. A comparative study of the primary productivity of higher aquatic plants, periphyton, and phytoplankton in a large shallow lake. *Int. Rev. Gesamten. Hydrobiol.,* 49:1–64. **543**

*Wetzel, R. G., 1969a. Factors influencing photosynthesis and excretion of dissolved organic matter by aquatic macrophytes in hard-water lakes. *Verh. Int. Ver. Limnol.,* 17:72–85. **289, 390, 543**

Wetzel, R. G., 1969b. Excretion of dissolved organic compounds by aquatic macrophytes. *BioScience,* 19:539–540. **543**

Wetzel, R. G., and Allen, H. L., 1971. Functions and interactions of dissolved organic matter and the littoral zone in lake metabolism and eutrophication. *Productivity Problems of Freshwaters,* ed., Kajak, Z. and Hillbricht-Ikowska, A., Warsaw, Polish Academy of Sciences. **543**

Wetzel, R. G., and McGregor, D. L., 1968. Axemic culture and nutritional studies of aquatic macrophytes. *Am. Midl. Nat.,* 80:52–64. **221, 223, 224**

Wheldon, J. A., and Wilson, A., 1915. The Lichens of Perthshire. *J. Bot. Suppl.,* 53, 73 pp. **566**

White, J., and Harper, J. L., 1970. Correlated changes in plant size and number in plant populations. *J. Ecol.,* 58:467–485. **485**

White, R. A., 1966. The morphological effects of protein synthesis inhibition in *Marsilea. Am. J. Bot.,* 53:158–165. **167**

White, J., and Harper, J. L., 1970. Correlated changes in plant size and number in plant populations. *J. Ecol.,* 58:467–485. **485**

Whitford, L. A., 1960. The current effect and growth of freshwater algae. *Trans. Am. Microsc. Soc.,* 79:302–309. **529**

Whitford, L. A., and Schumacher, G. J., 1961. Effect of current on mineral uptake and respiration by a fresh-water alga. *Limnol. Oceanogr.,* 6:423–425. **529**

Whittaker, R. H., 1967. Gradient analysis of vegetation. *Biol. Rev.,* 42:207–264. **502**

Whitton, B. A., 1970. Biology of *Cladophora* in fresh waters. *Water Res.,* 4:457–476. **561**

Wick, A. N., and Sandstrom, W. M., 1938. Nutrient value and chemical composition of certain fresh-water plants of Minnesota. II. The nitrogen distribution of Elodea canadensis. *Univ. Minn. Agr. Exp. Stat. Tech. Bull.,* 136:35–42. **358**

Wigglesworth, G., 1937. South African species of *Riella,* including an account of the developmental stages of three of the species. *J. Linn. Soc. Bot.,* 51:309–332. **50, 51**

Wild, H., 1961. *Harmful aquatic plants in Africa and Madagascar.* Conseil scientifique pour l'Afrique du sud du Sahara, Publ. 73 (Joint CCTA/CSA Project No. 14, reprinted from *Kirkia* vol. 2) iv, 68 pp. **75, 76, 108**

Wilken, G. C., 1970. The ecology of gathering in a Mexican farming region. *Econ. Bot.,* 24:286–295. **367**

*Willer, A., 1923. Der Aufwuchs der Unterwasserpflanzen. *Verh. Int. Ver. Limnol.,* 1: 37–57. **514, 537, 538**

Williams, W. T., and Barber, D. A., 1961. The functional significance of aerenchyma in plants. *Symp. Soc. Exp. Biol.,* 15:132–144. **205**

Willis, J. C., and Airy Shaw, H. K., 1966. *A Dictionary of the Flowering Plants and Ferns.* 7th ed. Cambridge, at the University Press, xxii, 1214, liii, pp. **76 fn, 93, 95**

Wilson, K., 1947. Water movement in submerged plants, with special reference to cut shoots of *Ranunculus* fluitans. *Ann. Bot.,* n. s. 11:91–122. **199**

Wilson, L. R., 1935. Lake development and plant succession in Vilas County, Wisconsin. Part I. The medium hard water lakes. *Ecol. Monogr.,* 5:207–247. **118, 130, 131, 137, 411, 430, 444–448**

Wilson, L. R., 1939. Rooted aquatic plants and their relation to the limnology of freshwater lakes. *Problems of Lake Biology. Pub. Amer. Assoc. Adv. Sci.,* 10:107–122. **118, 130, 131**

Wilson, L. R., 1941. The larger aquatic vegetation of Trout Lake, Vilas County, Wisconsin. *Trans. Wisc. Acad. Arts Sci. Lett.,* 33:135–146. **416, 417**

Włodek, S., Brysiek, M., and Grzybowska, D., 1970. Autochthonous caesium and behaviour of allochthonous caesium in a fish pond. *Ekol. Pol.,* 18:613–623. **295**

Wood, R. D., 1950. Stability and zonation of Characeae. *Ecology,* 31:641–647. **32, 45**

Wood, R. D., 1952. An analysis of ecological factors in the occurrence of Characeae of the Woods Hole region, Massachusetts. *Ecology,* 33:104–109. **15, 33–36**

Wood, R. D., 1955. Characeae. *Exploration Hydrobiologique du Lac Tanganika (1946-1947)*. Bruxelles, Institute Royal des Sciences Naturelles de Belgique 4(2):5-13. **479**

Wood, R. D., and Imahori, K., 1965. *A Revision of the Characeae. First Part Monograph of the Characeae* [by R. D. Wood] xxiv, 904 pp. *Second Part Iconograph* [by K. Imahori]. xv, 395 pl. 7 pp. Weinheim, J. Cramer **2, 3, 6, 7, 9 fn, 10, 12, 13, 14, 15, 16 fn, 19**

Woodruffe-Peacock, E. A., 1917. The means of plant dispersal. Wild duck carriage. *Selborne Mag., 28*:97-101. **244**

Woodruffe-Peacock, E. A., 1918. Means of plant dispersal. Water-hen carriage. *Selborne Mag., 29*:9-12. **245**

Wooten, J. W., 1970. Experimental investigations of the *Sagittaria graminea* complex: transplant studies and genecology. *J. Ecol., 58*:232-241. **162**

Wróbel, J. T., 1967. *Nuphar* alkaloids. *The Alkaloids: Chemistry and Physiology*. IX. ed. R. H. F. Manske, New York and London. Academic Press pp. 441-465. **366, 367**

Wulff, H. D. and Stahl, E., 1960. Chemische Rassen Bei Acorus calamus. *Naturwiss., 47*: 114. **364**

Wynne, F. E., 1944. Studies on Drepanocladus. IV. Taxonomy. *Bryologist, 47*:147-189. **64**

Yeo, R. R., 1964. Life History of the Common Cattail. *Weeds, 12*:284-288. **239**

Yoda, K., Kira, T., Ogawa, H., and Hozumi, H., 1963. Self-thinning in overcrowded pure stands under cultivated and natural conditions. *J. Biol. Osada City Univ., 14*:107-120. **485**

Zaneveld, J. S., 1940. The Charophyta of Malaysia and adjacent countries. *Blumea, 4*: 1-224. **15**

Zastrow, T., 1934. Experimentelle Studien über die Anpassung von Wasser- und Sumpfmoosen. *Pflanzenforschung, 17*:1-70. **62**

Zimmermann, W., 1928. Über Algenbestände aus der Tiefenzone des Bodensees. Zur Ökologie und Soziologie der Tiefseepflanzen. *Z. Bot., 20*:1-35. **534**

Index of Lakes

In the case of a large lake the bearings refer to the approximate center. When no bearings are given, the exact position of the lake is not available.

Only those lakes mentioned in the text are listed; this index does not include a few lakes that appear only as localities of plants illustrated in the figures.

Italic page numbers refer to figures.

Index of Genera and Species of Organisms

The authors of species are given according to botanical conventions for plants and according to zoological conventions for animals. In the very few cases in which a name has been cited without an author, prolonged search has failed to disclose the latter. Much effort has been expended in trying to determine the correct names of the organisms discussed, but it is certain that in some cases the attempt was not fully successful. Synonyms are listed only where there is a reasonable possibility of confusion. In general the use of infraspecific taxa has followed that of the author whose work is being discussed, but some attempt at uniformity has been made whenever there are obvious inconsistencies. Extinct species are marked with the symbol †.

Italic page numbers refer to figures.

Achnanthes, Bacillariophyceae, 569
  A. microcephala Kützing, 526
  A. *minutissima* Kützing, 513, 526, 527, *547*
      var. *cryptocephala* Grunow, 513
Acorus calamus Linnaeus, Araceae, 108, 137, 197, 220, 247, *362,* 364, 374
      var. *americanus* (Rafinesque) Wulff, *362,* 364
      var. *spurius* (Schott) Engler, *362,* 364
Aedes, Diptera, 29
  A. *albopictus* (Skuse), 31
  A. *togoi* (Theobald), 32
Aeschynomene, Fabaceae (Leguminosae),
80, 127, 207
  A. *aspera* Linnaeus, 80
  A. *elaphroxylon* (Guillemin & Perrottet) Taubert in Engler, 80, 496
  A. *hispidula* Humboldt, Bonpland & Kunth, 80
  A. *pfundii* Taubert, 80
Agrostis tenuis Sibthorpe, Gramineae (Poaceae), 333
Aldrovanda, Droseraceae, 96, 233, 285
  A. *vesiculosa* Linnaeus, *100,* 124
Alisma, Alismataceae, 103, 127, 245, 451
  A. *plantago-aquatica* Linnaeus, *106,* 162, 198, 213, 214, 216, 218, 221, 254,

General Index

Acanthaceae, aquatic, 96, 126
Acetaldehyde, 209, 210, 211
Achene, 212
Acropetal translocation, of herbicides, 201
  of phosphate, 284, 285
Acropleustophytes, 121, 123
Active transport into cells, 266-276, 399
  light dependence, 270, 271
  multiple mechanisms, 273-275
    in angiosperms, 274-276
  temperature dependence, 271, 273-275
Adaptation to aquatic life, 135-140
  structural basis of, 139, 140
Adventive water plants, 247-253, 263
  decline, 249
  explosive spread, 248, 250, 252, 253
  in Europe, 247-249
  in New Zealand, 250
  in North America, 250, 251
  tropical pleustophytes, 251-253
Aegagropiletum holsaticae, 488
Aerenchyma, 206-207, 259
  buoyancy, 207
  in Lythraceae and Onagraceae, 207
  respiratory function, 207

Aeschynomids, 122, 127, 131
Africa, Tropical, higher lacustrine vegetation
  of, 474-479
Air film on submerged plants, 135, 149
Air spaces, 139, 201-207, 259
Alanine in water plants, 359
Alcohol, *see* Ethanol
Alcohol dehydrogenase, 209, 211
Algal communities, main categories of, 510,
  511, 567
  biomass of, 515, 516, 567
  diversity of, 511-515, 567, 568
  specificity of, 511-515, 568
Algetea, 488
Algion, 488
Alismataceae, generic diversity, 77
  possible relation to dicotyledons, 100-101,
    103, 127, 129, 130
  pseudolamina in, 141
Alkaloids, 361-367
  Decodon, 364, 406
  Equisetum, 363
  Lepidotis, 363
  Nelumbo, 364, 366, 367
  Nuphar, 364, 365, 366, 367, 406